More Praise for *The Skilled Facilitator Fieldbook*

"This book provides the tools, techniques, and actual experience to truly practice shared leadership. Roger Schwarz and his colleagues provide not only the theory but the practical, hands-on experience required to develop high-performance teams."

—Jay Hennig, vice president, Moog, Inc.

"Although I consider myself already familiar with Roger's Skilled Facilitator approach, I was amazed at the breadth and depth this *Fieldbook* provides. It is a compelling resource for anyone interested in building his or her facilitative capabilities."

—Sandy Schuman, University at Albany, SUNY; editor, *The IAF Handbook of Group Facilitation*; and moderator, the Electronic Discussion on Group Facilitation

"*The Skilled Facilitator Fieldbook* is a must-have for anyone serving as a third-party intervener, coach, consultant, or a manager with a desire to develop people and groups."

—Thomas P. Zgambo, corporate ombudsman, Coca-Cola Enterprises Inc.

"*The Skilled Facilitator Fieldbook* truly provides the reader with an understandable 'root cause' perspective on why people interact the way they do and the means to create change. It goes way beyond the 'memorize these rules' approach advocated by many practitioners."

—Sid Terry, director of organization development, NA Manufacturing, Kraft Foods

Also by Roger Schwarz

The Skilled Facilitator: A Comprehensive Resource for Consultants, Facilitators, Managers, Trainers, and Coaches (New and Revised)

The Skilled Facilitator Fieldbook

The Skilled Facilitator Fieldbook

Tips, Tools, and Tested Methods for Consultants, Facilitators, Managers, Trainers, and Coaches

Roger Schwarz, Anne Davidson,
Peg Carlson, Sue McKinney, and Contributors

Published by Jossey-Bass
A Wiley Imprint
989 Market Street, San Francisco, CA 94103-1741 www.josseybass.com

Jossey-Bass books and products are available through most bookstores. To contact Jossey-Bass directly call our Customer Care Department within the U.S. at 800-956-7739, outside the U.S. at 317-572-3986 or fax 317-572-4002.

Jossey-Bass also publishes its books in a variety of electronic formats. Some content that appears in print may not be available in electronic books.

Library of Congress Cataloging-in-Publication Data

The skilled facilitator fieldbook : tips, tools, and tested methods for consultants, facilitators, managers, trainers, and coaches / Roger Schwarz ... [et al.].—1st ed.

p. cm.- (The Jossey-Bass business & management series)

Includes bibliographical references and index.

ISBN-13 978-0-7879-6494-8 (alk. paper)

ISBN-10 0-7879-6494-8 (alk. paper)

1. Communication in management. 2. Communication in personnel management. 3. Group facilitation. 4. Group relations training. I. Schwarz, Roger M., 1956— II. Series.

HD30.3.S373 2005

658.4'5—dc22

2004025821

Printed in the United States of America

FIRST EDITION

PB Printing 10 9 8

The Jossey-Bass
Business & Management Series

To my parents, Richard and Jeanne Schwarz, for all their love and encouragement

R.S.

To my family, friends, and clients for their love and support, and especially to my nieces and grandnieces, Carson, Alex, Emily, and Allison—the young women who will create the world I dream about

A.D.

To Andrew, Jacob, and Lena, with love and thanks for their unfailing wisdom, humor, and support

P.C.

To my family, who encouraged me to be curious and open-minded about all things; to Reba, Oz, and Rain, who keep me grounded; and to my new husband, Matthias Ender, for his unconditional support

S.M.

Contents

Part Five: Seeking Your Path

Part Six: Leading and Changing Organizations

Part Seven: Integrating the Skilled Facilitator Approach in Your Worklife (and Non-Worklife)

Editors, Authors, and Contributors

Roger Schwarz is founder and president of Roger Schwarz & Associates, a consulting firm that is dedicated to helping people change how they think and act so they can improve their business results and relationships—often in ways they didn't think possible. For more than twenty-five years, he has been helping groups and organizations by facilitating as well as consulting, coaching, and teaching and speaking on the subjects of facilitation, teams, and leadership. His clients include Fortune 500 corporations; federal, state, and local government; educational institutions; and nonprofit organizations. His book *The Skilled Facilitator* (Jossey-Bass, 2002) is a standard reference in the field. An organizational psychologist, Roger was formerly associate professor of public management and government at The University of North Carolina at Chapel Hill. He earned his Ph.D. and A.M. in organizational psychology from The University of Michigan, his M.Ed. from Harvard University, and his B.S. degree in psychology from Tufts University.

Anne Davidson is a consultant with Roger Schwarz & Associates. She specializes in leadership development, facilitator training, and long-term organizational and community change projects. She works internationally with management groups, work teams, and nonprofit and local government boards. She increasingly coaches individuals who want to embrace learning and creative development in their jobs and personal lives. Her journey toward organization development and training started almost thirty years ago when she began teaching eleventh-grade English in South Carolina. Since that time, she has served as a media center director; a marketing and management instructor in the School of Business at Western Carolina University; the training and organization development director for the City of Asheville, North Carolina; and a lecturer in public management and government at The University of North Carolina at Chapel Hill. Anne learned the Skilled Facilitator approach in 1988 during the early phases of its development when the City of Asheville became a client of Roger Schwarz & Associates. She earned her B.A. in English and secondary education from Presbyterian College. She holds an M.L.S. from The University of North Carolina at Chapel Hill and an M.B.A. from Western Carolina University.

Peg Carlson is an organizational psychologist who earned her Ph.D. from The University of Michigan. She is a consultant with Roger Schwarz & Associates and adjunct associate professor of public management and government at The University of North Carolina at Chapel Hill. She teaches, consults, and writes in the area of organizational change and development. She leads workshops on facilitation and facilitative leadership and frequently facilitates meetings for governing boards, management teams, and community groups. She has published articles on developing effective groups, assessing the chief executive's performance, and multirater feedback. Peg started using the Skilled Facilitator approach with Roger Schwarz and colleagues Dick McMahon and Kurt Jenne when she joined the UNC faculty in 1992. She resigned her tenured position in 2000 to better balance work and family life.

Sue McKinney is a consultant with Roger Schwarz & Associates and independently. Formerly, she was director of organizational development for an international nongovernmental organization based in Chapel Hill, North Carolina. Sue developed her facilitation skills in the early 1980s while working for an international nonprofit grounded in the consensus decision-making process. She first worked with Roger Schwarz in 1990–1991 while serving as an intern to a county social services management team working with him. In 1997, she attended the two-week Skilled Facilitator class offered by The University of North Carolina Institute of Government and within one year began working with Schwarz to teach classes around the country. McKinney has practical expertise in leadership development, board development, mediation, facilitation, and training of trainers. She believes in the value of humor and play to stimulate creativity and productivity and is known for her energetic and humorous approach to working with groups. She leads workshops on a variety of topics, including facilitative leadership, and facilitates public and nonprofit board and staff retreats. Sue earned her A.B. in history from Duke University and her M.S.W. from The University of North Carolina at Chapel Hill, with a specialization in human services administration.

Matt Beane is an organization development, coaching, and training professional who helps individuals, groups, and organizations exceed performance expectations while increasing both the quality of their relationships and their ability to learn from adversity. His specialty and passion lie in helping people assess gaps between their behavior and their espoused values, allowing them to make more informed choices about their behavior and values in the future. He is an associate with Roger Schwarz & Associates and has worked with a number of Fortune 1000 companies in the financial, professional services, pharmaceuticals, manufacturing, hi-tech, travel, consumer goods, and hospitality sectors, with a variety of nonprofit and governmental organizations, and in the public workshop format. Before becoming an independent in 2002, he was independent workforce director at the Forum Corporation, a consultancy specializing in workplace learning solutions. Matt holds a B.A. in philosophy from Bowdoin College and has done graduate work at Harvard's School of Education in Adult Learning.

Guillermo Cuéllar is an international organization development consultant, facilitator, psychotherapist, and artist who brings a unique multicultural and multidisciplinary perspective to engage others in the change processes. He is the cofounding president of the Center for Creative Consciousness. For over thirty years, he has guided individuals and groups in processes to develop creative intelligence and discover and use their talents and gifts. He has taught cross-cultural management at the School of International Training in the Program of International Management, in Brattleboro, Vermont, and at NTL Institute in Bethel, Maine. He has worked since 1990 for two consulting firms in the field of managing diversity: Elsie Y. Cross and Associates and Alignment Strategies. He provides professional services in both English and Spanish. Guillermo earned his B.F.A. and M.A. in counseling at the University of South Florida in Tampa Florida. He then earned an Ed.D. from the University of Massachusetts.

Diane Florio is the manager of human resources development for SpectraSite Communications, a wireless infrastructure company based in Cary, North Carolina. She is responsible for leading and implementing development initiatives in a fast-paced organization. She works with individuals, groups, and departments to improve services, teamwork, and leadership. Diane has worked in both the private and public sectors and has fifteen years of experience in the work of human behavior and professional development. She was trained in the Skilled Facilitator approach in 2000. She received a B.S. in health education from SUNY, Cortland in New York and her M.S. in human resources education from Fordham University, New York. She holds a business coaching certification from The University of North Carolina.

Harry Furukawa is an organization architect and a consultant with Roger Schwarz & Associates. He helps people design and transform the organizations in which they work in order to achieve better financial, environmental, and social results. He consults in strategic planning, values and culture identification and development, organizational change, and quality and productivity improvement. He has served as the associate director of the University of Maryland Center for Quality and Productivity and as the senior director for strategic planning at the American Red Cross. He also has served as examiner on the board of examiners for the Malcolm Baldrige National Quality Award for five years (four as a senior examiner). He earned a B.A. from the Johns Hopkins University, a master of architecture from Harvard University, and an executive M.B.A. from Loyola College.

Peter Hille has been director of Brushy Fork Institute of Berea College, which since 1988 has carried out a unique leadership development program in Kentucky, Tennessee, Virginia, and West Virginia. Peter has worked extensively in Brushy Fork's leadership development program, recruiting participants, organizing workshops, and working with teams of community leaders as they carry out local projects. He has created custom workshops, designed and led retreats, and facilitated strategic planning processes for regional nonprofits, foundations, government agencies, and development organizations. He has also conducted community development workshops nationally and internationally, in Russia and Slovakia. In recent years, Peter has focused on building collaborative networks of diverse organizations serving the Appalachian region. A graduate of Swarthmore College, his background includes experience in grassroots environmental organizing and small business management.

Greg Hohn is the director of Transactors Improv Co., the South's oldest improvisational theater, based in Chapel Hill, North Carolina. He joined the company in 1989 and became director in 1996. Since 1998 he has been teaching Applied Improv in a wide variety of venues. He is adjunct lecturer in business communication at The University of North Carolina's Kenan-Flagler Business School and a visiting faculty member at Baruch College, City University of New York. In addition to work in academia, Greg teaches Applied Improv, improvisational theater, acting, and presentation skills for businesses, organizations, and educational institutions across the country. As an actor, he works in film, television, radio, scripted theater, and industrial media. He has written for stage, radio, and periodicals and has written two books. He received a degree in English from The University of North Carolina at Chapel Hill.

Joe Huffman has served as a local government manager in North Carolina since 1990 in Elkin, Havelock, and Laurinburg. His exposure to learning organization concepts began with his employment in Laurinburg and has been augmented by his completion of The University of North Carolina Institute of

Government course of instruction in group facilitation and consultation. Joe has served as a North Carolina Eastern Municipal Power Agency commissioner since 1999. His current local nonprofit involvement includes serving as a member of the board of directors of the Scotland County Chapter of the American Red Cross. He received a B.S. in criminal justice and an M.P.A. from Appalachian State University. His professional training includes completion of The University of North Carolina Institute of Government Municipal Administration program in 1991.

Verla Insko was elected to the North Carolina General Assembly in 1997; she represents the Fifty-Sixth House District in Orange County. She serves as chair of the Health Committee. Her other committee assignments are Appropriations (Health and Human Services), Education (Universities), Environment and Natural Resources, and Judiciary I. In 1998, House Speaker Jim Black appointed her as House chair of the Legislative Oversight Committee on Mental Health, Developmental Disabilities and Substance Abuse. In the 2001 session she was the primary sponsor of HB381, Mental Health Reform, which began a five-year process of modernizing the state's system of services for these three disability groups. She has received numerous awards for her leadership, including in 2003 the Award for Leadership in Mental Health Reform presented jointly by six agencies. She has sponsored the Repeal Involuntary Sterilization Act, the Matthew Shepard Memorial Act, the State Earned Income Tax bill, and the Health Care for All bill.

She earned an M.P.A. from The University of North Carolina at Chapel Hill, did graduate work at Golden Gate Theological Seminary, received a secondary teaching certificate from the University of California at Berkeley, and received an A.B. from California State University at Fresno.

Steve Kay is a founding partner of Roberts & Kay, a firm established in Lexington, Kentucky, in 1983 to provide interrelated services for clients that include facilitation, training, organizational development, and public policy research. His work at the local, state, and national levels includes serving as facilitator for multiparty groups with divergent perspectives or constituencies; training beginning and intermediate facilitators and coaches to guide sound public and organizational processes; building internal capacity to increase work group and organizational effectiveness; and providing analysis and technical assistance for complex, long-term change efforts within organizations and communities. He holds a B.A. from Bowdoin College, an M.A. from Yale University, and an Ed.D. from the University of Kentucky.

Jeff Koeze is president and chief executive officer of Koeze Company in Grand Rapids, Michigan. He represents the fourth generation of the family to have served as the company's general manager. Before joining Koeze Company in September 1996, he was associate professor of public law and government at The University of North Carolina at Chapel Hill. In that capacity he provided consulting services and professional education on issues of health care law, finance, and policy. His work focused on issues of concern to public hospitals and public health providers in North Carolina. He is the author of several articles and other publications in that field. He has also served as law clerk to the Honorable Morey L. Sear, U.S. district judge for the Eastern District of Louisiana in New Orleans. He received a B.A. in English from The University of North Carolina at Chapel Hill and a J.D. from the University of Virginia School of Law.

Dick McMahon is a retired lecturer in public management from the Institute of Government, The University of North Carolina at Chapel Hill. During his tenure as a lecturer, he had extensive experience working with both state and local government organizations. He has conducted supervisory and leadership training for literally thousands of public supervisors and managers. He also worked with Roger Schwarz at the university in developing training programs in skilled facilitation. He is currently an associate with Roger Schwarz & Associates and has worked on a long-term organization development project with Laurinburg, North Carolina. He has worked as well with a number of other organizations on developmental projects using the Skilled Facilitator approach in his work. Since his retirement, he has continued to work as a consultant, facilitator, and trainer for public agencies. He received his master's degree at Ohio University and did doctoral work at UNC Chapel Hill.

Betsy Monier-Williams is a process improvement leader for a worldwide aerospace and industrial supplier. She has over fifteen years of manufacturing experience, including twelve years of corporate training and over three years facilitating work groups. She has also coordinated large-scale change in proprietary information technology systems, lean manufacturing, and cultural transformations focusing on teams and facilitative leadership. Monier-Williams leads a variety of workshops including facilitative leadership, Ground Rules for Effective Groups, team training, and competency management. She is certified in lean manufacturing from The University of Michigan and in structured teamwork through Performance Resources. She earned her B.S. and M.B.A. from Medaille College with a specialization in operations management and strategic training and human resource development. She is currently pursuing her doctorate in human and organization development.

Tom Moore is director of the Wake County Public Library. He became interested in learning organization issues in 1993 and has studied them since. He has received extensive training in facilitative leadership and systems thinking as well as learning organizations. The Wake County Public Library is becoming a learning organization through training of its staff and reflective thinking about its actions and policies. Tom is a consultant with Roger Schwarz & Associates and has worked with the Institute of Government at The University of North Carolina at Chapel Hill, as well as several local governments, on training about facilitative leadership and becoming a learning organization. His bachelor's degree is in philosophy. He has a master's degree in library science and completed two years of postgraduate study in theology.

Dale Schwarz is the cofounding vice president of the Center for Creative Consciousness and executive director of the New England Art Therapy Institute, which she cofounded in 1981. As a registered art therapist and licensed mental health counselor, she has a private practice working with individuals of all ages. Her work has evolved to include personal and professional coaching and facilitating groups in developing their creative behavior, based on a method she designed. She also works with organizations as a management consultant to develop creative behavior in the leadership ranks. A key aspect of her work is helping people use metaphor and images to enhance communication and bring forth their unique talents. Interwoven in her work is the foundation of mutual learning and the core values of the Skilled Facilitator approach. She earned her B.S. at New York University and her M.Ed. in expressive therapies at Lesley College (now Lesley University) in Cambridge, Massachusetts.

Bron D. Skinner is an educator in the family practice residency program at The University of North Carolina at Chapel Hill Department of Family Medicine. In his role as the assistant residency director, he has lent his educational expertise to the development of its evaluation system and its curriculum. The department has been developing an approach to faculty performance reviews that emphasizes career development. As part of the new approach to faculty evaluation, the department implemented a 360-degree feedback system. Bron has conducted training for staff and faculty to teach principles of assessment as a learning process based on Roger Schwarz's ground rules for effective groups. He has designed forms that emphasize this approach and been a member of the team that has converted the system to Web-based data forms. He has a Ph.D. in education from The University of North Carolina at Chapel Hill and an M.A. in music education from the University of California at Los Angeles.

Chris Soderquist is the founder and president of Pontifex Consulting, an organization committed to helping individuals, teams, and organizations in building their capacity to develop strategic solutions to complex issues. He uses his experience in systems thinking and system dynamics, group facilitation, communication skill development, and statistical and process analysis to facilitate the development of solutions that are effective and actionable. For over fifteen years, he has worked with Fortune 1000 companies, international development organizations, national and state government organizations, and communities to help them better achieve the future they desire. Chris is a contributing author to *The Change Handbook* (Berrett-Koehler, 1999) and has published several features in *Systems Thinker.* He has also been an invited speaker at conferences. He earned a B.A. in mathematical methods in the social sciences and a B.A. in political science from Northwestern University.

Susan R. Williams is executive editor at Jossey-Bass, an imprint of John Wiley & Sons. She attended a week-long Skilled Facilitator workshop with Roger Schwarz and edited the revised edition of his best-selling book *The Skilled Facilitator* (2002).

Introduction

People in organizations and communities around the world are using the Skilled Facilitator approach to develop effective teams and organizations and generate open, honest, and productive working relationships. Since the publication of the first edition of *The Skilled Facilitator* in 1994 (and the second edition in 2002), we have been privileged to work with a number of them. Some attended our public workshops, others we coached, and still others invited us to help them improve their organizations. Our clients learned from us, we learned from them, and we have learned together. *The Skilled Facilitator Fieldbook* reflects these lessons.

THE PURPOSE OF THE *FIELDBOOK*

Our purpose in this *Fieldbook* is to share what our colleagues, clients, and we have learned so far on our journey with the Skilled Facilitator principles and methods. If you are new to the Skilled Facilitator approach, you will find a summary of it in Part One. We hope that you will benefit from our experiences and integrate them with your own. We also hope that this *Fieldbook* will be a catalyst for you to expand the approach in new ways and settings, so that it can realize the possibilities we believe it offers for individuals, groups, organizations, and communities.

The book reflects how our work has evolved and expanded over the years. When we began, facilitative skills were considered the domain of professional helpers. A group or manager who needed a meeting facilitated called on a facilitator or organization development consultant. From the 1980s to the mid-1990s, we spent much of our time working with facilitators and organization development professionals who were serving communities, boards, and work groups.

During the 1990s, managers and leaders began to see facilitative skills as a core competency to create responsive, successful organizations. As a result, we began to expand our work with managers and leaders (both formal and informal leaders) with large corporations and pioneering organizations, helping them develop a facilitative leader approach. At the same time, we engaged in long-term work with small and midsized public and private sector organizations in applying the principles to guide organizational transformation. This book includes the stories of our efforts and synthesizes our learning from all of these experiences.

WHAT TO EXPECT

The *Fieldbook* spans the full scope of the Skilled Facilitator approach, from how to get started to how to integrate the approach with existing organizational structures and processes. It provides tips on introducing the ground rules as well as guidelines for engaging in deep-level interventions. Many tips, exercises, and sample agendas come from highly successful facilitations of board retreats, strategic planning meetings, community visioning and conflict resolution, and management team problem-solving sessions. We offer them as useful models to adapt. Many other examples and stories are about work in progress; we do not know the final outcome or whether the promise of the efforts will be fully realized. They are often about creating deep, long-term personal or organizational learning. We honestly share the questions, dilemmas, and frustrations that arise, along with the successes and rewards. Often our goal is to explore the challenges involved in true transformation rather than highlight a simple quick fix. We believe this long-term and fundamental orientation to growth embedded in the Skilled Facilitator approach is much of what gives it strength, staying power, and a committed following.

Over the years, we have been fortunate to work with a wide variety of colleagues and clients who have integrated their area of focus with the Skilled Facilitator approach. So the *Fieldbook* also explores a wide variety of applications, ranging from teaching to parenting to running for and serving in political office. Across these settings, individuals have adopted the core values of the approach to guide profound personal growth and development. The voices throughout this book are varied. Each contributor shares his or her unique learning journey, but all of them speak from their experience of using the Skilled Facilitator approach in the field.

This book is an invitation to explore, reflect on, and find connections for your own growth and practice, wherever that might be. We hope the tools and suggestions add to the conceptual strength of the Skilled Facilitator approach. We hope you use whatever resonates for you and your organizations. And we hope you will share your learning with the expanding number of Skilled Facilitator practitioners. In doing so, you will join a growing community engaged in a challenging and rich exploration of new possibilities for how we work and live together.

WHO THE *FIELDBOOK* IS FOR

This book is for anyone who wants to work with others to develop more powerful results and more productive working relationships. This includes facilitators, consultants, leaders and managers, team members, coaches, and teachers. People use facilitative skills in various roles, and we address each of them in the book. We use the following terms and definitions:

- *Facilitator:* a substantively neutral third party who helps a group improve its effectiveness by improving its process and structure.
- *Facilitative consultant:* a third party who uses the Skilled Facilitator approach while providing substantive expertise to a group or organization.
- *Facilitative trainer:* a teacher or trainer who uses the principles and skills of the Skilled Facilitator approach to help students learn a particular content area.
- *Facilitative coach:* a person who coaches individuals using the principles and skills of the Skilled Facilitator approach.
- *Facilitative leader:* a formal or informal leader in a group or organization who uses the Skilled Facilitator principles and skills as the basis of his or her leadership approach. We refer to this as the Facilitative Leader (TFL) approach.

Depending on the context, we use the term *Skilled Facilitator approach* (which we abbreviate as TSF) to refer specifically to the facilitator role or to using the principles of the approach in any other role.

HOW THE *FIELDBOOK* IS ORGANIZED

The *Fieldbook* is organized into seven parts.

Part One, "Understanding the Skilled Facilitator Approach," summarizes the Skilled Facilitator approach and describes its major principles, features, and outcomes. If you are new to this approach, Part One will give you a foundation for appreciating the rest of the book. If you have read the first edition of *The Skilled Facilitator* (1994) but not the revised edition (2002), you will find new ideas in Chapter Three, "Using Facilitative Skills in Different Roles"; Chapter Four, "Understanding What Guides Your Behavior"; Chapter Five, "Ground Rules for Effective Groups," which contains a shorter, revised set of ground rules; and Chapter Seven, "Thinking and Acting Systemically." If you're already familiar with the revised edition, you will find new ideas in Chapters Four and Seven. Throughout the *Fieldbook,* when we cite *The Skilled Facilitator,* we mean the 2002 revised edition unless we specify otherwise.

Part Two, "Starting Out," gives guidance on using TSF with one-on-one conversations, basic facilitations, and typical work team tasks. It includes guidelines for specific types of interventions like agreeing on a work group's purpose and vision, chartering a team, or clarifying organizational roles and expectations. These are the kinds of issues that many facilitators, human resource professionals, organization development consultants, and leaders frequently are called on to help groups address.

Part Three, "Deepening Your Practice," focuses on refining your skills. As you use the Skilled Facilitator approach, you may want to hone your diagnosis and intervention abilities so that you can work more effectively with groups. The chapters in Part Three provide ways to practice using the ground rules to quickly diagnose what is happening in a group and ways to begin your interventions with it. This part also helps you increase your personal awareness, which contributes to making your interventions more precise and powerful.

Part Four, "Facing Challenges," offers help for dealing with some of the most challenging situations: giving negative feedback, disagreeing with the boss, and holding other difficult conversations. It explains why it makes sense to engage in difficult conversations and offers specific steps and examples for how to do so. It also continues the theme of expanding self-awareness so you can see how you contribute to the very problems that frustrate you.

Part Five, "Seeking Your Path," describes the personal learning journey involved in integrating this approach into your own life and practice. It offers the experiences of others in taking TSF back to their organizations and guidelines for doing so yourself.

Part Six, "Leading and Changing Organizations," focuses on applying the Skilled Facilitator approach to create significant change in how people lead and manage their organizations and how organizational systems function. We refer to this as the Facilitative Leader approach. The chapters in Part Six offer methods and stories from formal and informal leaders seeking to transform all or part of their organization as well as chapters from consultants working with these leaders. It also describes dilemmas that arise when engaging in fundamental organizational change and how to address them.

Part Seven, "Integrating the Skilled Facilitator Approach in Your Worklife (and Non-Worklife)," shows how you can integrate the Skilled Facilitator approach with other approaches and with other facilitative roles. It includes chapters that describe how to use the approach with the Myers-Briggs

Type Indicator and systems analysis. It explains how to use the principles as a teacher or trainer, coach, consultant, and parent. Part Seven ends with two examples of using the approach in the world of elected politics.

HOW TO USE THE *FIELDBOOK* TO ENHANCE YOUR LEARNING

We realize that people reading this book learn in different ways and are likely to want to learn different things. We have designed the *Fieldbook* so you can create your own learning journey. There are several features that will help you easily find what you need.

Icons

Throughout the book, we have used seven different icons to help you quickly identify items that may be useful to your learning. These icons appear in two places: in the margins next to an item and at the beginning of chapters when the chapter contains primarily a particular type of material indicated by one of the icons, such as a model conversation that you might want to use as a template. The icons and the items they indicate are:

Key points: a key concept, principle, or other point that is central to the Skilled Facilitator approach.

Stories: real examples of applying (or not applying) the approach.

Tools and techniques: specific tools, techniques, or methods and samples of the outcomes they produce.

Reflections: an invitation to reflect on the reading and apply it to yourself or your own situation.

Model conversations: verbatim examples of what to say using the Skilled Facilitator approach. Short examples such as opening lines or questions are highlighted with boldface type in the text.

Resources: materials such as books, articles, and Web sites that we recommend.

Definitions: the meaning of certain key words. Other definitions appear in boldface in the text.

Cross-References

The Skilled Facilitator approach is a system; every element of the approach is related in some way to every other element. So throughout the book we cross-reference other chapters that build on or support the chapter you are currently reading.

Choosing the Chapters That Meet Your Interests

The *Fieldbook* is designed so you can start anywhere and go anywhere. Depending on your interests there are different places to start. Here are a few:

- If you are new to the Skilled Facilitator approach, consider beginning with Chapter One, "The Skilled Facilitator Approach," for an overview of its key components.
- If you want to understand the core of the Skilled Facilitator approach, see Chapter Four, "Understanding What Guides Your Behavior."
- If you are planning a facilitation, start with Chapter Five, "Ground Rules for Effective Groups"; Chapter Eight, "Contracting with Groups"; Chapter Eleven, "Basic Facilitation"; and Chapter Twelve, "Do the Math."
- If you are looking for specific tools and techniques to improve working with groups or teams, consider starting with Chapter Ten, "Process Designs"; Chapter Fifteen, "Using the Group Effectiveness Model"; and Chapter Nineteen, "Using the Skilled Facilitator Approach to Strengthen Work Groups and Teams."
- If you are looking for ways to address difficult conversations, consider starting with Chapter Twenty-Eight, "Holding Risky Conversations"; Chapter Thirty, "Moving Toward Difficulty"; and Chapter Forty-One, "'I Can't Use This Approach Unless My Boss Does.'"
- If you are looking for ways to introduce the approach in your organization, considering beginning with Chapter Thirty-Five, "Introducing the Skilled Facilitator Approach at Work," or Chapter Thirty-Six, "Bringing It All Back Home.
- If you're interested in helping groups make significant change, consider reading Chapter Forty, "Helping a Team Understand the System They Created"; Chapter Forty-Three, "Developmental Facilitation"; and Chapter Forty-Four, "Guidelines for Theory-in-Use Interventions."
- If you are a formal organizational leader interested in the challenges and rewards of applying the approach in your organization, consider starting with Chapter Forty-Seven, "Reflections of a Sometimes Facilitative Leader," or Chapter Thirty-Eight, "Daily Challenges of a Facilitative Leader."
- If you are a coach, consider starting with Chapter Fifty-Seven, "The Facilitative Coach."
- If you are a teacher or trainer see Chapter Fifty-Eight, "Becoming a Facilitative Trainer."
- If you are involved in human resources or organization development efforts, consider starting with Chapter Forty-Eight, "Integrating the Skilled Facilitator Approach with Organizational Policies and Procedures"; Chapter Forty-Nine, "360-Degree Feedback and the Skilled Facilitator Approach"; Chapter Fifty, "Implementing a 360-Degree Feedback System"; and Chapter Fifty-One, "Do Surveys Provide Valid Information for Organizational Change?"
- If you want to learn about how you may be contributing to problems around you, start with Chapter Twenty-Nine, "Exploring Your Contributions to Problems"; Chapter Forty-Two, "How to Stop Contributing to Your Boss's and Your Own Ineffectiveness"; and Chapter Fifty-Three, "The Drama Triangle. "

No matter what path you choose, you will discover that the Skilled Facilitator approach is based on a model of mutual learning, which rests on the assumption that all of us see some things and miss others. In other words, we are all both teachers and learners. We hope that the lessons offered in the *Fieldbook* enrich your learning journey and that you will make us part of your extended learning community. Information on how to reach us is included at the end of the book.

Wherever you begin, we hope you find the journey fruitful.

January 2005
Chapel Hill, North Carolina
Charlotte, North Carolina
Durham, North Carolina
Durham

ROGER SCHWARZ
ANNE DAVIDSON
PEG CARLSON
SUE MCKINNEY

The Skilled Facilitator Fieldbook

PART ONE

Understanding the Skilled Facilitator Approach

In Part One, we introduce the Skilled Facilitator approach and describe the major concepts, principles, and key features of the approach. If you are new to this approach, Part One will give you a foundation for appreciating the rest of the book. If you are already familiar with the approach, you will find some of our new thinking in Chapters Four, Five, and Seven.

In Chapter One, "The Skilled Facilitator Approach," Roger Schwarz provides an overview of the approach. Each of the following chapters explains a section of the overview in more detail.

To understand how to improve groups, we think it is necessary to have a model of what makes effective groups. Chapter Two, "The Group Effectiveness Model," presents a model that describes the elements necessary for an effective group. You can use the model to identify and address problems groups are facing and to establish new groups. In a sidebar to Chapter Two, Anne Davidson responds to questions that our clients frequently ask about the Group Effectiveness Model, such as where trust and leadership fit in.

Many people who use the Skilled Facilitator approach are not substantively neutral third-party facilitators; they are consultants, leaders and managers, trainers, and coaches. Roger explains in Chapter Three, "Using Facilitative Skills in Different Roles," how these roles are similar and different. He describes how applying the skill set and mind-set of the Skilled Facilitator approach increases your value in each of these roles.

At the heart of the Skilled Facilitator approach is the idea that the way we act and the consequences we create begin with the way we think. Unfortunately, in difficult situations, most of us think in ways that lead us to take actions that create unintended negative consequences—and we are unaware that we are doing so. In Chapter Four, "Understanding What Guides Your Behavior," Roger describes the unilateral control model: the values and assumptions we use in difficult situations and how they undermine our own and groups' effectiveness. Then he contrasts it with the mutual learning model, the foundation for the Skilled Facilitator approach. He shows how to create high-quality results and productive relationships by beginning to change the way you think.

In Chapter Five, "Ground Rules for Effective Groups," Roger describes a specific set of behaviors that you and group members can use to increase the quality of decision making, increase commitment, reduce implementation time, and improve working relationships. The ground rules are the strategies for implementing the mutual learning model described in Chapter Four. These ground rules are not the kind that you agree on at the beginning of a meeting, post on a flip chart, and then maybe occasionally refer to. They guide your behavior, help you identify effective and ineffective behaviors in the group, and guide you in intervening to help the group become more effective. Examples include testing assumptions and inferences, explaining your reasoning and intent, and combining advocacy with inquiry. Roger explains how each ground rule works and how to use them.

Facilitators often ask, "What do I say when I see behavior in the group that I think is ineffective?" In Chapter Six, "The Diagnosis-Intervention Cycle," Peg Carlson addresses this question. The diagnosis-intervention cycle is a tool that provides a simple structured way to think about what is going on in a conversation and intervene to make it more productive. Together with the mutual learning model and the ground rules for effective groups, it enables you to help others without creating defensiveness.

The Skilled Facilitator approach is a systemic approach. We see groups as systems in which each element needs to interact effectively with all the other elements. In the same way, each element of the approach is integrated with all the other elements so that they form an internally consistent powerful approach. In Chapter Seven, "Thinking and Acting Systemically," Anne Davidson provides a brief summary of the basics of systems thinking and shows how the Skilled Facilitator approach uses systems thinking principles to create sustainable change and reduce unintended consequences.

We conclude Part One by exploring how to develop an effective working agreement with a group. In Chapter Eight, "Contracting with Groups," Roger describes the principles and specific steps that you can use to establish an agreement with groups about whether and how you will work together.

def·i·ni·tion **Chapter 1**

The Skilled Facilitator Approach

Roger Schwarz

The Skilled Facilitator approach is a values-based, systemic approach to group facilitation. It is designed to help groups (1) increase the quality of decisions, (2) increase commitment to decisions, (3) reduce effective implementation time, (4) improve working relationships, (5) improve personal satisfaction in groups, and (6) increase organizational learning. This chapter provides an overview of the approach.

WHAT IS GROUP FACILITATION?

Group facilitation is a process in which a person whose selection is acceptable to all members of the group, who is substantively neutral, and who has no substantive decision-making authority diagnoses and intervenes to help a group improve how it identifies and solves problems and makes decisions, to increase the group's effectiveness.

Group facilitation is a process in which a person whose selection is acceptable to all members of the group, who is substantively neutral, and who has no substantive decision-making authority diagnoses and intervenes to help a group improve how it identifies and solves problems and makes decisions, to increase the group's effectiveness.

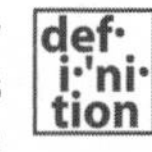

The facilitator's main task is to help the group increase its effectiveness by improving its process and structure. *Process* refers to how a group works together. It includes how members talk to each other, identify and solve problems, make decisions, and handle conflict. *Structure* refers to stable recurring group processes, such as group membership or group roles. In contrast, *content* refers to what a group is working on—for example, whether to enter a new market, how to provide high-quality service to customers, or what each group member's responsibilities should be. Whenever a group meets, it is possible to observe both its content and process. For example, in a discussion about how to provide high-quality service, suggestions about installing a customer hotline or giving more authority to those with customer contact reflect content. However, members responding to only certain members' ideas or failing to identify their assumptions are facets of the group's process.

This chapter is adapted from Chapter One, "The Skilled Facilitator Approach," in *The Skilled Facilitator: A Comprehensive Resource for Consultants, Facilitators, Managers, Trainers, and Coaches, New and Revised Edition* by Roger Schwarz (San Francisco: Jossey-Bass, 2002). All references to *The Skilled Facilitator* in this *Fieldbook* are to the 2002 edition unless otherwise noted.

Underlying the facilitator's main task is the premise that ineffective group process and structure reduces a group's ability to solve problems and make decisions. By increasing the effectiveness of the group's process and structure, the facilitator helps the group improve its performance and overall effectiveness. The facilitator does not intervene directly in the content of the group's discussions; to do so would require the facilitator to abandon neutrality and would reduce the group's responsibility for solving its problems.

To ensure that the facilitator is trusted by all group members and that the group's autonomy is maintained, the facilitator needs to meet three criteria: (1) be acceptable to all members of the group, (2) be substantively neutral—that is, display no preference for any of the solutions the group considers—and (3) not have substantive decision-making authority. In practice, the facilitator can meet these three criteria only if the facilitator is not a group member. Although a group member may be acceptable to other members and may not have substantive decision-making authority, the group member has a substantive interest in the group's issues.

By definition, a group member cannot formally fill the role of facilitator.

By definition, a group member cannot formally fill the role of facilitator. Nevertheless, a group leader or member can use the Skilled Facilitator principles and techniques to help a group. Effective leaders regularly use facilitation skills as part of their leadership role.

KEY FEATURES OF THE SKILLED FACILITATOR APPROACH

The Skilled Facilitator approach is one approach to facilitation. Often facilitation approaches represent a compilation of techniques and methods without an underlying integrated theoretical framework. The Skilled Facilitator approach is based on a theory of group facilitation that contains a set of core values and principles and a number of techniques and methods derived from the core values and principles. It integrates the theory into practice to create a values-based, systemic approach to group facilitation. In doing so, it answers two key questions: "What do I say and do in this situation?" and "What are concepts and principles that lead me to say and do this?" Exhibit 1.1 identifies the key features of the Skilled Facilitator approach and their purpose.

The Group Effectiveness Model

To help groups become more effective, you need a model of group effectiveness to guide your work. The model needs to be more than descriptive—that is, it needs to do more than explain how groups typically function or develop because many groups develop in a way that is dysfunctional. To be useful, the model needs to be normative: it should tell you what an effective group looks like.

Exhibit 1.1 Key Features of the Skilled Facilitator Approach

- The Group Effectiveness Model
- A clearly defined facilitative role
- Useful in a wide range of roles
- Explicit core values
- Ground rules for effective groups
- The diagnosis-intervention cycle
- Low-level inferences
- Exploring and changing how we think
- A process for agreeing on how to work together
- A systems approach

The *Group Effectiveness Model* (GEM) identifies the criteria for effective groups, identifies the elements that contribute to effectiveness and the relationships among them, and describes what these elements look like in practice. The model enables you to determine when groups are having problems, identify the causes that generate the problems, and begin to identify where to intervene to address the problems. When you are creating new groups, the model helps you identify the elements and relationships among the elements that need to be in place to ensure an effective group.

The *Group Effectiveness Model* (GEM) identifies the criteria for effective groups, identifies the elements that contribute to effectiveness and the relationships among them, and describes what these elements look like in practice.

See Chapter Two, "The Group Effectiveness Model," page 15, and Chapter Fifteen, "Using the Group Effectiveness Model," page 135.

A Clearly Defined Facilitative Role

To help groups, you need a clear definition of your facilitative role so that you and the groups you are helping have a common understanding about and agree on the kinds of behaviors that are consistent and inconsistent with your role. This has become more difficult as organizations have used the word *facilitator* to define many different roles. Human resource experts, organization development consultants, trainers, coaches, and even managers have sometimes been referred to as facilitators. The Skilled Facilitator approach clearly defines the facilitator role as a substantively neutral person who is not a group member and who works for the entire group. Still, as I describe in the next section, even if you are not a facilitator, you can use facilitative skills.

The Skilled Facilitator approach distinguishes between two types of facilitation: basic and developmental. In ***basic facilitation,*** you help a group solve a substantive problem by essentially lending the group your process skills. When your work is complete, the group has solved its substantive problem, but by design, it has not learned how to improve its process. In ***developmental facilitation,*** you help a group improve its process by learning to reflect on and change its thinking and behavior so it can solve substantive problems more effectively.

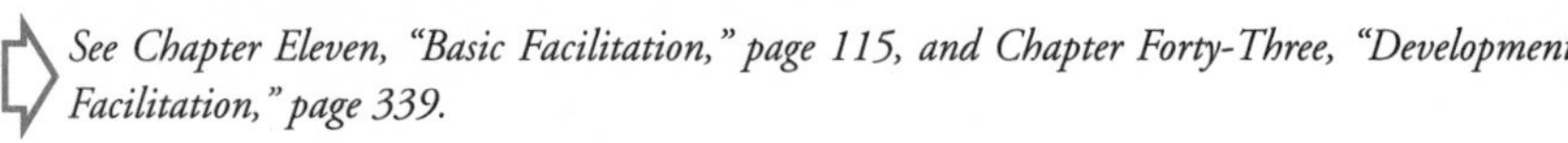
See Chapter Eleven, "Basic Facilitation," page 115, and Chapter Forty-Three, "Developmental Facilitation," page 339.

In ***basic facilitation,*** you help a group solve a substantive problem by essentially lending the group your process skills. When your work is complete, the group has solved its substantive problem, but by design, it has not learned how to improve its process. In ***developmental facilitation,*** you help a group improve its process by learning to reflect on and change its thinking and behavior so it can solve substantive problems more effectively.

Useful in a Wide Range of Roles

Although I have described the Skilled Facilitator approach in terms of a substantively neutral third-party facilitator, the approach also recognizes that everyone needs facilitative skills. So the approach encompasses additional facilitative roles: facilitative consultant, facilitative coach, facilitative trainer, and facilitative leader. All are based on the same underlying core values and principles as the role of neutral, third-party facilitator.

Chapter Three, "Using Facilitative Skills in Different Roles," page 27, has basic information on the different facilitative roles. Many of the chapters in Parts Six and Seven explore how the different roles work in practice.

A Note on Terms

The Skilled Facilitator Fieldbook focuses on all five of the facilitative roles. When we are writing about a specific role—and only that role—we use the appropriate term, such as *facilitative leader* or *facilitative trainer.* We use the term ***Skilled Facilitator approach*** to refer specifically to the facilitator role and to using the principles of the approach in any other role.

Explicit Core Values

All approaches to facilitation are based on some core values, explicit or implicit. Whatever the approach, core values provide its foundation and serve as a guide. They enable you to craft consistent new methods and techniques and to reflect continually on how well you do in acting congruently with them. But if you are to benefit most from a set of core values, they need to be explicit. The Skilled Facilitator approach is based on four explicit core values, and the principles that follow from them: (1) valid information, (2) free and informed choice, (3) internal commitment, and (4) compassion. (The first three core values come from the work of Chris Argyris and Donald Schön, 1974.) *Valid information* means sharing all the relevant information that you have about an issue in a way that others can understand the reasoning. *Free and informed choice* means members make decisions based on valid information, not on pressure from inside or outside the group. *Internal commitment* means each member feels personally responsible for the decision and is willing to support the decision, given his or her role. *Compassion* means adopting a stance toward others and yourself in which you temporarily suspend judgment.

As a facilitator, you need not only a set of methods and techniques but also an understanding of how and why they work. By using an explicit set of core values and the principles that follow from them, you can improvise and design new methods and techniques consistent with the core values. Without this understanding, you are like a novice baker who must either follow the recipe as given or make changes without knowing what will happen.

Making the core values explicit also helps you work with groups. You can discuss your approach with potential clients so that they can make more informed choices about whether they want to use you as their facilitator. When clients know the core values underlying your approach, they can help you improve your practice, identifying when they believe you are acting inconsistently with the values you espoused. Because the core values for facilitation are also the core values for effective group behavior, when you act consistently with the core values, not only do you act effectively as a facilitator, but you also model effective behavior for the group you are working with.

See Chapter Four, page 33, "Understanding What Guides Your Behavior," for an introduction to how assumptions and values guide behavior. For some applications, try Chapter Thirty-Four, "Being a Mutual Learner in a Unilaterally Controlling World," page 287, and Chapter Forty-Four, "Guidelines for Theory-in-Use Interventions," page 349.

Valid information means sharing all the relevant information that you have about an issue in a way that others can understand the reasoning. *Free and informed choice* means members make decisions based on valid information, not on pressure from inside or outside the group. *Internal commitment* means each member feels personally responsible for the decision and is willing to support the decision, given his or her role. *Compassion* means adopting a stance toward others and yourself in which you temporarily suspend judgment.

Ground Rules for Effective Groups

As you watch a group in action, you may intuitively know whether the members' conversation is productive even if you cannot identify exactly how they either contribute to or hinder the group's process. Yet a facilitator needs to understand the specific kinds of behaviors that improve a group's process. The Skilled Facilitator approach describes these behaviors in a set of ground rules for effective groups. The ground rules make specific the abstract core values of facilitation and group effectiveness (Figure 1.1).

See Chapter Five, "Ground Rules for Effective Groups," page 61, for an introduction to the ground rules. For practical detail on using them, try Chapter Fourteen, "Introducing the Ground Rules and Principles in Your Own Words," page 131; Chapter Twenty-One, "Ways to Practice the Ground Rules, page 189; Chapter Twenty-Six, "Ground Rules Without the Mutual Learning Model Are Like Houses Without Foundations," page 217; and Chapter Thirty-Five, "Introducing the Skilled Facilitator Approach at Work," page 293.

The behavioral ground rules in the Skilled Facilitator approach differ from the more procedural ground rules that many groups use ("start on time, end on time"; "turn off your pagers and cell phones"). Procedural ground rules can be helpful, but they do not describe the specific behaviors that lead to effective group process.

Figure 1.1 Ground Rules for Effective Groups

1. Test assumptions and inferences.
2. Share all relevant information.
3. Use specific examples and agree on what important words mean.
4. Explain your reasoning and intent.
5. Focus on interests, not positions.
6. Combine advocacy and inquiry.
7. Jointly design next steps and ways to test disagreements.
8. Discuss undiscussable issues.
9. Use a decision-making rule that generates the level of commitment needed.

The Diagnosis-Intervention Cycle

The group effectiveness model, the core values, and the ground rules for effective groups are all tools for diagnosing behavior in groups. But you still need a way to put these tools to work. Specifically you need to know when to intervene, what kind of intervention to make, how to say it, when to say it, and to whom. To help put these tools into practice, the Skilled Facilitator approach includes a six-step process called the *diagnosis-intervention cycle.* The cycle is a structured and simple way to think about what is happening in the group and then to intervene consistent with the core values. It serves to guide you into effective action.

Chapter Six, "The Diagnosis-Intervention Cycle," page 69, is an introduction to the diagnosis-intervention cycle. For more on applications, see Chapter Eleven, "Basic Facilitation," page 115.

Low-Level Inferences

To help groups become more effective requires that you constantly try to make sense of what is happening in the group. You watch members say and do things and then make inferences about what their behavior means (an ***inference*** is a conclusion you reach about something that is unknown to you based on things that you have observed) and how it is either helping or hindering the group's process. For example, in a meeting, if you see someone silently folding his arms across his chest, you may infer that he disagrees with what has been said but is not saying so.

An ***inference*** is a conclusion you reach about something that is unknown to you based on things that you have observed.

The kinds of inferences you make are critical because they guide what you will say and they affect how group members will react to you. To be effective, you need to make these inferences in a way that increases the chance that you will be accurate, enables you to share your inferences with the group to see if they disagree, and does not create defensive reactions in group members when you share your inferences.

The Skilled Facilitator approach accomplishes this by focusing on what I refer to as *low-level inferences.* Essentially, this means that you diagnose and intervene in groups by making the fewest and the smallest inferential leaps necessary.

By learning to think and intervene using low-level inferences, you can increase the accuracy of your diagnosis and your ability to share your thinking with others, and reduce the chance that you will create defensive reactions when you do so. This ensures that your actions increase rather than decrease the group's effectiveness.

See the Ladder of Inference sidebar in Chapter Five, "Ground Rules for Effective Groups," page 61, for an explanation of how we make inferences.

Exploring and Changing How We Think

Facilitation is difficult work because it is cognitively and emotionally demanding. It is especially difficult when you find yourself in situations you consider potentially embarrassing or psychologically threatening. Research shows that in these situations, most people tend to think and act in a way that seeks to unilaterally control the conversation, win the discussion, and minimize the expression of negative feelings (Argyris and Schön, 1974). The same problem that reduces your effectiveness as a facilitator reduces the effectiveness of the groups you are seeking to help. Like the facilitator, the group members are also unaware of how they create these problems for themselves.

The Skilled Facilitator approach helps you understand the conditions under which you act less effectively and understand how your own thinking leads you to act ineffectively in ways that you are normally unaware of. It provides tools for increasing your effectiveness, particularly in situations you find emotionally difficult. This involves changing not only your techniques, but also how you think about or frame situations, including the core values and assumptions that underlie your approach.

The Skilled Facilitator approach is grounded in a way of thinking and acting calling the *mutual learning model.* In the *mutual learning model,* you think that you have some information and that others have other information; you think that others may see things that you don't just as you may see things that they don't; you consider differences as opportunities for learning rather than opportunities to show the others that they are wrong; and you assume that people are trying to act with integrity given their situations.

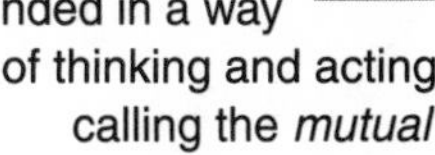

The Skilled Facilitator approach is grounded in a way of thinking and acting calling the *mutual learning model.*

The Skilled Facilitator approach also rests on several key principles: curiosity, transparency, and joint accountability. ***Curiosity*** about others' views enables you to continue a productive conversation and learn how your ideas and those of others can be integrated. ***Transparency*** means sharing your reasoning and intent underlying your statements, questions, and actions. It includes sharing with others your strategy for how you are having the conversation with them. ***Joint accountability*** means that you share responsibility for the current situation, including the consequences it creates. Rather than seek to blame others, you recognize that because you are part of a system, your actions contribute to either maintaining the system or changing it.

Changing your way of thinking is difficult but rewarding work. By doing this work for yourself, you increase your effectiveness. Then you can help groups learn to reflect on and change the ways they think in difficult situations so that they can work more effectively together.

See Chapter Four, "Understanding What Guides Your Behavior," page 33; Chapter Seventeen, "Developing Shared Vision and Values," page 149; Chapter Twenty-Six, "Ground Rules Without the Mutual Learning Model Are Like Houses Without Foundations," page 217; Chapter Forty-Four, "Guidelines for Theory-in-Use Interventions," page 349; Chapter Forty-Five, "Introducing the Core Values and Ground Rules," page 361; Chapter Forty-Six, "From Learning to Lead to Leading to Learn," page 367; Chapter Forty-Seven, "Reflections of a Somewhat Facilitative Leader," page 377; Chapter Fifty-Four, "Using Creative and Survival Cycles to See and Shift Mental Models, page 433; and Chapter Sixty-Two, "Using the Facilitative Leader Approach in Public Office," page 515.

A Process for Agreeing on How to Work Together

Facilitation involves developing a relationship with a group—a psychological contract in which the group gives you permission to help them because they consider you an expert and trustworthy facilitator. Building this relationship is critical because it is the foundation on which you use your facilitator knowledge and skills; without the foundation, you lose the essential connection with the group that makes your facilitation possible and powerful. To build this relationship, you need a clear understanding and agreement with the group about your role as facilitator and how you will work with the group to help it accomplish its objectives. I have found that many of the facilitation problems my colleagues and I have faced stemmed from a lack of agreement with the group about how the group and facilitator will work together.

The Skilled Facilitator approach includes an explicit process for developing this agreement that enables the facilitator and the group to make an informed free choice about working together. By using this process, you act consistently with your facilitator role and increase the likelihood that you will help a group achieve its goals.

See Chapter Eight, "Contracting with Groups, page 89; Chapter Fifty-Seven, "The Facilitative Coach," page 457; and Chapter Fifty-Eight, "Becoming a Facilitative Trainer," page 479.

A Systems Approach

Facilitators often tell me stories of how, despite their best efforts to help a group in a difficult situation, the situation gets worse. Each time the facilitator does something designed to improve things, the situation either deteriorates immediately or temporarily improves before getting even worse. One reason this occurs is that the facilitator is not thinking and acting systemically. The Skilled Facilitator approach recognizes that a group is a ***social system***—a collection of parts that interact with each other to function as a whole—and that groups generate their own system dynamics, such as deteriorating trust or continued dependence on the leader. You enter into this system when you help a group. The challenge is to enter the system, complete with its functional and dysfunctional dynamics, and help the group become more effective without becoming influenced by the system to act ineffectively yourself.

The Skilled Facilitator approach recognizes that any action you take affects the group in multiple ways and has short-term and long-term consequences, some of which may not be obvious. The approach helps you understand how your behavior as facilitator interacts with the group's dynamics to increase or decrease the group's effectiveness. For example, a facilitator who privately pulls aside a team member she believes is dominating the group may seem to improve the team's discussion in the short run. But this action may also have several unintended negative consequences. This person may feel that the facilitator is not representing the team's opinion and may see the facilitator as biased against him, thereby reducing the facilitator's credibility with that member. Even if the facilitator is reflecting the other team members' opinions, the team may come increasingly to depend on her to deal with its issues, thereby reducing rather than increasing the team's ability to function.

> The Skilled Facilitator approach recognizes that any action you take affects the group in multiple ways and has short-term and long-term consequences, some of which may not be obvious.

Using a systems approach to facilitation has many implications, a number of which are central to understanding the Skilled Facilitator approach. One key implication is treating the entire group as the client rather than only the formal group leader or the member who contacted you. This increases the chance of having the trust and credibility of the entire group, which is essential in serving as an effective facilitator.

A second implication is that effective facilitator behavior and effective group member and leader behavior are the same thing. Taking into account that the facilitator is substantively neutral and not a group member, the Skilled Facilitator approach does not have different sets of rules for the facilitator and group members. A third key implication is that to be effective, your system of facilitation needs to be internally consistent. This means that the way you diagnose and intervene in a group and the way you develop agreements with the group all need to be based on a congruent set of principles. Many facilitators develop their approach by borrowing methods and techniques from a variety of sources. There is nothing inherently wrong with this, but if the methods and techniques are based on conflicting values or principles, they can undermine the facilitator's effectiveness as well as that of the groups they work with.

See Chapter Seven, "Thinking and Acting Systemically," page 75; Chapter Twenty-Nine, "Exploring Your Contributions to Problems," page 255; Chapter Forty, "Helping a Team Understand the System They Created," page 323; Chapter Forty-One, "'I Can't Use This Approach Unless My Boss Does,'" page 331; Chapter Forty-Two, "How to Stop Contributing to Your Boss's and Your Own Ineffectiveness," page 335; and Chapter Fifty-Six: "Applying the Skilled Facilitator Approach to a Systems Thinking Analysis," page 447.

INTEGRATING THE SKILLED FACILITATOR APPROACH WITH OTHER PROCESSES

Facilitators, consultants, and leaders can use the Skilled Facilitator approach with other processes and tools to make the processes and tools more effective. For example, people often use the approach with problem-solving methods, strategic planning processes, and quality improvement tools.

Because the Skilled Facilitator approach is a values-based systems approach, it works well with other approaches that have a compatible value set. For example, using a performance feedback process that prevents the person receiving the feedback from talking with the people who provided it is inconsistent with the Skilled Facilitator core values. It creates a situation in which people can neither assess whether the information is valid nor learn specifically how they might change their behavior. This prevents them from making a free and informed choice about whether to change their behavior and reduces their internal commitment to change. In many cases, it is possible to modify the tool or process to be compatible with the Skilled Facilitator approach.

See, for example, Chapter Forty-Nine, "360-Degree Feedback and the Skilled Facilitator Approach," page 391; Chapter Fifty, "Implementing a 360-Degree Feedback System," page 403; and Chapter Fifty-One, "Do Surveys Provide Valid Information for Organizational Change?" page 409.

THE EXPERIENCE OF FACILITATION

Facilitation is challenging work that calls forth a wide range of emotions. Part of this work involves helping group members deal productively with their emotions while they are addressing difficult issues. It is equally important to deal with your own emotions as facilitator. Because your emotions and how you deal with them profoundly determine your effectiveness, the Skilled Facilitator approach involves understanding how you as a facilitator feel during facilitation and using these feelings productively. For example, you may feel satisfied having helped a group work through a particularly difficult problem or proud to see the group using some of the skills they have learned from you. When the group is feeling confused and uncertain how to proceed in their task, you may be feeling the same way about the facilitation. You may be frustrated by a group's inability to manage conflict even if you have been asked to help the group because they are having problems managing conflict. You may feel sad watching a group act in ways that create the very consequences they are trying to avoid, feel happy that you can identify this dynamic in the group, and feel hopeful seeing that the group's pain is creating motivation for change.

At one time or another I have experienced each of these feelings as a facilitator; they are part of the internal work of facilitation. The Skilled Facilitator approach enables you to become more aware of these feelings and increases your ability to manage them productively—what some refer to as emotional intelligence (Goleman, 1995; Salovey and Mayer, 1990). I have found that my ability to develop these emotional skills is both distinct from and related to my larger set of knowledge, skills, and experience as a facilitator. While there are many ways to improve my facilitation skills that do not focus on dealing with my emotions, my use of any of these skills becomes more powerful if I am attuned to my own feelings and others' feelings and deal with them productively.

Through facilitating groups, you can also come to know yourself by reflecting on how you react to certain situations, understanding the sources of your feelings, and learning how to work with your feelings productively. In doing so, you not only help yourself but in turn increase your ability to help the groups with which you work—the people who face the same issues.

Resource

Argyris, C., and Schön, D. A. *Theory in Practice: Increasing Professional Effectiveness.* San Francisco: Jossey-Bass, 1974.

References

Argyris, C. *Intervention Theory and Method: A Behavioral Science View.* Reading, Mass.: Addison-Wesley, 1970.

Argyris, C., and Schön, D. A. *Theory in Practice: Increasing Professional Effectiveness.* San Francisco: Jossey-Bass, 1974.

Goleman, D. *Emotional Intelligence.* New York: Bantam Books, 1995.

Salovey, P., and Mayer, J. D. "Emotional Intelligence." *Imagination, Cognition, and Personality,* 1990, *9,* 185–211.

Chapter 2

The Group Effectiveness Model

Roger Schwarz

YOU HAVE PROBABLY had a variety of experiences working in groups. For most people, the experience is mixed. In some groups, the members work well together, accomplish the task, and meet some of one another's needs. In others, the task is done poorly (if at all), the members do not work well together, and people feel frustrated. What factors might each group say contributed to its success or ineffectiveness? For example, do the members agree on how they should work together? Do they have clear goals? Is there undiscussed conflict? Are some members of the group not motivated by the task? Are they missing certain expertise?

The answers to these questions begin to describe a model of group effectiveness. Each of us has a mental model about what makes a group effective, even if it includes only a few elements. Whether or not you are conscious of your mental model, you use it to guide your diagnosis and intervention, decide where to look when things go wrong, and know what to change.

Because a model is a simplified way to describe how something works, it does not need to capture all the complexities of what it attempts to represent. But if your model of a group is underdeveloped, it limits your ability to help groups become more effective. If you have a model that shows you what an effective group looks like, the elements that contribute to its effectiveness, and how the elements should interact, you have a foundation from which to help members of a group diagnose problems they are having and help them make changes to improve their effectiveness. Figure 2.1 is the Group Effectiveness Model (GEM) of the Skilled Facilitator approach.

We think of a model as a particular way to see and think about something. The Group Effectiveness Model is like a special pair of lenses that enable you to see and understand what is determining a group's effectiveness.

WHAT IS A WORK GROUP?

To discuss what makes an effective work group, we first need to define what we mean by *work group*. A *work group* is a set of people with specific interdependent roles who are collectively responsible for producing some output (service, product,

This chapter is an adaptation of *The Skilled Facilitator,* Chapter Two, "What Makes Work Groups Effective?" In general, the Group Effectiveness Model is adapted from Hackman (1987) and Sundstrom, De Meuse, and Futtrell (1990).

Figure 2.1 The Group Effectiveness Model

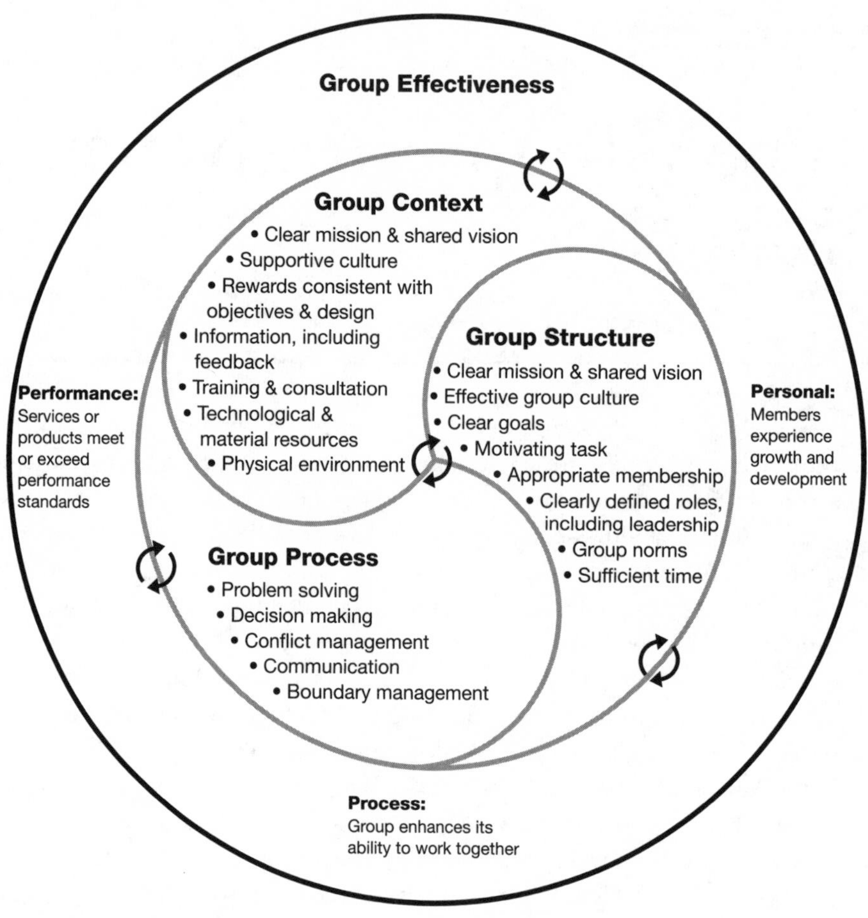

Source: Adapted from Hackman (1987) and Sundstrom, De Meuse, and Futtrell (1990).

def·i·'ni·tion A *work group* is a set of people with specific interdependent roles who are collectively responsible for producing some output (service, product, or decision) that can be assessed and who manage their relationships with those outside the group. Examples of groups that have these characteristics are a board of directors, a task force or committee, and a work team.

or decision) that can be assessed and who manage their relationships with those outside the group. Examples of groups that have these characteristics are a board of directors, a task force or committee, and a work team.

In this definition, what makes a group is the presence of key ***structural elements*** rather than the level of motivation or effectiveness of its members. Some people use *team* to describe what we define as an effective group (Katzenbach and Smith, 1993). Throughout this *Fieldbook,* we use the terms *group* and *team* interchangeably, recognizing that either can be more or less effective.

GROUP EFFECTIVENESS CRITERIA: PERFORMANCE, PROCESS, AND PERSONAL

What does it mean for a group to be *effective*? In the Skilled Facilitator approach, an effective work group meets three criteria (displayed in the outer rings in Figure 2.1): performance, process, and personal.

Performance

Rather than simply measure the quality and quantity of the service or product against some objective or internal group standard, *performance* uses the expectations and satisfaction of the group's internal and external customers to determine whether its work is acceptable. The group's own standards are still important, but they do not replace the assessments of others. To be effective, a group must meet all three criteria, which are interrelated. If in the long run, if one criterion is not met, it affects the other two.

Process

The second criterion takes into account that most groups work together over an extended period on a series of tasks. Consequently, the processes and structures they use must enable them to work together in a way that enhances their ability to do so in the future. For example, processes that burn group members out reduce their capability to work together on subsequent tasks.

Personal

The *personal* criterion of group effectiveness is that the group experience contributes to the growth and well-being of its members. Group members reasonably expect that through their work group, they can meet some of their personal needs—for example, doing work that makes a difference in others' lives or satisfies their need to learn. In the long run, a group that does not meet its members needs is less effective than one that does.

FACTORS CONTRIBUTING TO GROUP EFFECTIVENESS

Groups are not either effective or ineffective; group effectiveness is measured on a continuum and in our model is a function of three factors: group process, group structure, and group context. Each factor has a number of elements, and the interrelationship among them is complex, with each element influencing the others (as symbolized by the arrows in Figure 2.1).

> Facilitators intervene primarily through a group's process and structure, enabling the group to examine and perhaps change its process, structure, and context.

Process refers to how things are done rather than what is done. To be effective, a group must manage a number of processes, from problem solving to boundary management (see Figure 2.1).

Group Process

Process refers to how things are done rather than what is done. To be effective, a group must manage a number of processes, from problem solving to boundary management (see Figure 2.1).

Problem Solving

A group with an effective problem-solving process meets two conditions:

1. It uses a *systematic process* for solving problems that is appropriate for the problem the group is trying to solve. For example, when a group does not consider the effect of its solution over time and throughout the system, it can solve one problem in a way that creates more difficult ones.
2. All members *focus on the same step* of the problem-solving process at the same time. A group gets off track when some members are trying to identify the cause of the problem and others are already proposing solutions.

Decision Making

Decision making means reaching a conclusion or making a choice. The process includes determining who should be involved when, in what decisions, and how those involved will decide. In an effective decision-making process, a number of people are involved: those responsible for planning or implementing the decision, those directly or indirectly affected by the decision, and those who can influence whether or how it is implemented. The core values of the Skilled Facilitator approach state that the group includes people who have the relevant information about the problem, its causes, its solutions, and their potential effects.

There are various ways for groups to make decisions, from the leader deciding alone, with or without consulting other members, to delegation, majority vote, and consensus. If more than one person is to make the decision, the group needs to decide what method they will use. The core values of the Skilled Facilitator approach state that a group is more effective when it is internally committed to its choices.

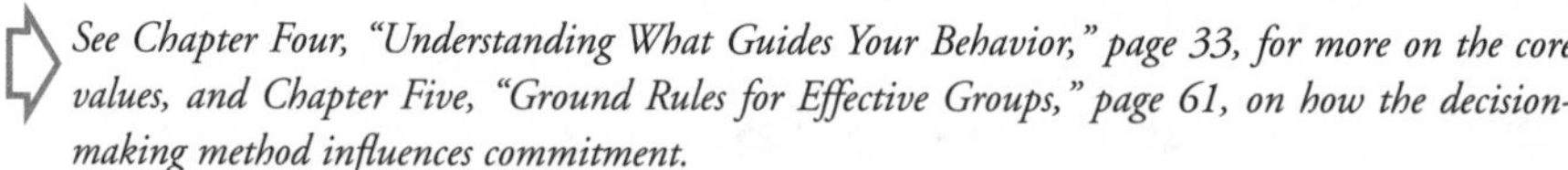
See Chapter Four, "Understanding What Guides Your Behavior," page 33, for more on the core values, and Chapter Five, "Ground Rules for Effective Groups," page 61, on how the decision-making method influences commitment.

Conflict Management

An effective group considers conflict a natural part of group life; when managed well, conflict improves members' ability to work together to accomplish their task and contributes to personal growth. They use conflict to learn more about the problem and how others see it rather than simply persuading people that they are right and others are wrong. To do this, they share previously hidden thoughts and feelings and openly test any difference of opinion. Ultimately, they resolve conflict so that it stays resolved and in a way that members understand how the conflict arose, how they contributed to it, and how they can act differently to prevent unnecessary conflict.

Some of the chapters that explore how the Skilled Facilitator approach enables groups to do this are Chapter Fifteen, "Using the Group Effectiveness Model," page 135; Chapter Twenty-Nine, "Exploring Your Contributions to Problems," page 255; Chapter Thirty, "Moving Toward Difficulty," page 261; and Chapter Thirty-Two, "Raising Issues In or Out of Group," page 273.

Communication

The communication process is embedded in all other group processes. Essentially, ***communication*** means exchanging information such that the sender and receiver understand the meaning in the same way. The ground rules and core values of the Skilled Facilitator approach describe elements of effective communication.

For an introduction, see Chapter Four, "Understanding What Guides Your Behavior," page 33, and Chapter Five, "Ground Rules for Effective Groups," page 61. For an introduction to using the ground rules in e-mail, see Chapter Twenty, "Using the Ground Rules in E-Mail," page 181.

For discussions about creating a performance feedback system, see Chapter Forty-Nine, "360-Degree Feedback and the Skilled Facilitator Approach," page 391, and Chapter Fifty, "Implementing a 360-Degree Feedback System," page 403.

Boundary Management

In an effective group, members can articulate the group's task and what they are responsible for accomplishing, so that they do not take on tasks unrelated to their purpose and outside the group's expertise. Similarly, they know what kind of authority and autonomy the group has.

At the same time, a group must coordinate its work with other parts of the organization, including deciding what information to share and how, what tasks are performed by whom, and how decisions are made. Effective groups also manage boundaries to ensure that the larger organization provides the materials, technology, people, and information needed to accomplish their tasks. Some groups have to manage boundaries directly with the organization's external customers.

Group Structure

Group structure is the second factor contributing to group effectiveness (Figure 2.1). The term ***group structure*** refers to the relatively stable characteristics of a group, including mission and vision, tasks, membership, roles, time available, shared values def·i·'ni·tion Group structure is the second factor contributing to group effectiveness (Figure 2.1). The term ***group structure*** refers to the relatively stable characteristics of a group, including mission and vision, tasks, membership, roles, time available, shared values and beliefs, and norms.

and beliefs, and norms. Understanding the dynamic relationships that create the structure is important because changing the relationships in the activity changes the structure.

Clear Mission and Shared Vision

A group's ***mission*** answers the question, "Why do we exist?" A ***vision*** is a mental picture of the future that a group seeks to create. It identifies what the group should look like and how it should act as it seeks to accomplish its mission. In an effective group, members can articulate their mission and vision, find it engaging, and use it to guide their work.

See Chapter Seventeen, "Developing Shared Vision and Values," page 149.

Effective Group Culture

Group culture means the set of fundamental values and beliefs shared by the members of a group that guide their behavior. A ***belief*** is an assumption about what is true—for example, "People are naturally motivated to do a good job." A ***value*** is an assumption about what is worthwhile or desirable—for example, "maintaining honesty at all times." An ***artifact*** is a product of the culture—for example, a policy, a procedure, or a structure that members create.

In an effective group, members can articulate its core values and beliefs, and they take actions and make decisions that are congruent with them. Inferring values and beliefs from a group's cultural artifacts, including how members act, is a primary method of ***developmental facilitation*** used to help groups examine their process and structure.

See, for example, Chapter Four, "Understanding What Guides Your Behavior," page 33, and Chapter Forty-Three, "Developmental Facilitation," page 339.

Goals, Task, and Membership

An effective group has ***clear goals*** that are consistent with the organization's mission and vision and allows members to select the means by which they achieve their goals. Clear goals enable a group to measure its progress toward achieving them. Without clear goals, a group has difficulty solving problems and making decisions, and this often leads to conflict.

A ***group task*** is the work the group performs to accomplish its goal. In the Group Effectiveness Model, this includes the idea that group members must be interdependent with each other in accomplishing the task and share collective responsibility for the group's output.

A ***motivating group task*** meets certain conditions (Hackman, 1987):

- It enables members to use a variety of their skills.
- It is a whole and meaningful piece of work with a visible outcome.
- Its outcomes have significant consequences, for either customers or for others in the organization.
- It gives members significant autonomy over how they accomplish it so that they feel ownership of their work.
- Working on the task generates regular and trustworthy feedback to members about how well the group is performing.

An effective group also has an appropriate membership, meaning that its members are carefully selected according to several criteria:

- The members bring an appropriate mix of knowledge and skills to complete the task successfully.
- The group is just large enough to handle the task. A group with more members than it needs to complete the task spends time on coordination that could be spent working directly on the task. In addition, as the group grows, members can lose interest in the work and reduce their effort.
- The composition of the group should be stable enough to maintain continuity of effort yet fluid enough to ensure that members do not all think the same way and discourage new or differing ideas.

Clearly Defined Roles, Including Leadership

In an effective group, members understand clearly what role each plays and what behavior people expect in each role. With clear, agreed-on roles, members can coordinate their actions to complete the task. Without these roles, they are likely to experience unnecessary conflict and stress. Effective groups clarify the roles of their members as the task changes or as members change.

Defining the leader role means defining the relationship between the leader and other group members regarding how the group handles its processes, structures, and functions. As a group becomes more self-directed, more elements of the leadership role are integrated into the roles of the members.

For more on the facilitative leader role, see Chapter Three, "Using Facilitative Skills in Different Roles," page 27; Chapter Eighteen, "Helping Groups Clarify Roles and Expectations," page 159; Chapter Thirty-Eight, "Daily Challenges of a Facilitative Leader," page 309; and Chapter Forty-Seven, "Reflections of a Somewhat Facilitative Leader," page 377. The Skilled Facilitator core values are introduced in Chapter Four, "Understanding What Guides Your Behavior," page 33, and the ground rules in Chapter Five, "Ground Rules for Effective Groups," page 61.

Group Norms

A ***norm*** is an expectation about how people should or should not behave that all or many of the group members share. Norms stem from the values and beliefs that constitute the group's culture. In an effective group, members explicitly discuss and agree on the norms that they want to guide their group. They also agree to hold one another accountable for following the norms by raising the issue if someone acts in some way inconsistent with them. The ground rules for effective groups are a set of group norms that are based on the core values and beliefs of the Skilled Facilitator approach.

Sufficient Time

Finally, a group needs two kinds of time to complete its tasks and achieve its goals: performance time and capacity-building time.

During ***performance time,*** the group produces its product or service. During ***capacity-building time,*** the group engages in activities that help build capacity to improve performance—for example, redesigning the flow of work to increase efficiency or reflecting on how the group managed a conflict so as to improve its skills. Typically, groups spend too little time on building capacity.

See Chapter Seven, "Thinking and Acting Systemically," page 75, and Chapter Twelve, "Do the Math: Creating a Realistic Agenda," page 119.

Group Context

The third factor in the GEM is ***group context,*** which includes aspects of the larger organization that influence the group's effectiveness but that the group usually does not control (Figure 2.1).

The third factor in the GEM is ***group context,*** which includes aspects of the larger organization that influence the group's effectiveness but that the group usually does not control (Figure 2.1). The elements of group context include clear mission and shared values, a supportive organizational culture, rewards consistent with group objectives and design, information (including feedback about performance), training and consultation, technology and material resources, and a physical environment that fits the group's needs. An effective group recognizes that although it may not control the group context, it might influence the larger organization to create a more supportive one. Understanding the group context helps a facilitator identify how the larger organization is likely to help or hinder a group's efforts to improve effectiveness. It also helps identify the extent to which facilitation alone can help a group.

See Chapter Two in The Skilled Facilitator for more detail on the elements of group context. For discussions about performance feedback systems, training, and consultation that are congruent with the Skilled Facilitator approach, see Chapter Forty-Nine, "360-Degree Feedback and the Skilled Facilitator Approach," page 391; Chapter Fifty, "Implementing a 360-Degree Feedback System," page 403; Chapter Fifty-Seven, "The Facilitative Coach," page 457; Chapter Fifty-Eight, "Becoming a Facilitative Trainer," page 479; and Chapter Fifty-Nine, "Being a Facilitative Consultant," page 495.

PUTTING THE PIECES TOGETHER

The Group Effectiveness Model proposes three criteria for an effective group: performance, process, and personal. Three factors—process, structure, and context—contribute to making a group effective. And each factor comprises its own elements (Figure 2.1). You can think of these elements—for example, conflict management, a motivating task, and technology and material resources—as pieces of a puzzle that must fit together for the group to be effective. The elements themselves have to be effective, and the relationships among the elements need to be congruent.

You can use the model to help groups explore how well they are meeting the effectiveness criteria and what elements and relationships among elements may need to change to improve effectiveness. You can also use the model to help new groups get off to a good start.

See Chapter Fifteen, "Using the Group Effectiveness Model," page 135.

Frequent Questions About the Group Effectiveness Model

Anne Davidson

When people are introduced to the Group Effectiveness Model, they often ask about elements they believe may be missing. They also wonder about the limits of applying the model. Below are some of the thoughts I share when responding.

Trust

Groups often ask why *trust* is not in the Group Effectiveness Model or if one can introduce and discuss the model in low-trust environments. Trust is an aspect of group culture. People become vulnerable when they take actions they perceive as risky within their culture. Whether they feel others have taken advantage of their vulnerability builds or erodes trust. Trust, then, is an outcome of effective behavior.

The Group Effectiveness Model identifies elements that you can intervene on directly, and you cannot intervene directly on trust. Instead, using the Skilled Facilitator approach, you would intervene on the specific behaviors, norms, values, and assumptions that create or destroy trust. For example, if coworkers say they support a decision in a meeting but afterward talk about all the problems with it and how they will avoid implementing it, you are unlikely to trust their support of future decisions. Using the Group Effectiveness Model and the Skilled Facilitator approach principles, we would intervene on the group norms and underlying values and assumptions that led people not to openly disagree in the meeting, not to feel they could share all relevant information (their feelings and concerns), and/or the processes used that contributed to false consensus.

The Group Effectiveness Model identifies elements that you can intervene on directly, and you cannot intervene directly on trust.

In discussing group culture, I might ask group members about their level of trust and whether and how that affects their ability to work together, but I quickly follow up their assessment with a request for examples of the specific behaviors that contributed to or reduced trust. In a low-trust culture, we may need to come back to this issue several times because it may initially feel too risky to raise certain examples. But I do not assume that if trust is low, I cannot use the model. That would be self-fulfilling and self-sealing. That is, if I were to need a trusting environment to use the Group Effectiveness Model, then the only place I would be able to use it to build trust is where I already have trust—in which case I don't much need it anyway. The value of the tool is using it to help overcome obstacles. If I assume I cannot use it, I seal off the possibility of helping individuals develop the skills to overcome their lack of trust. I may need to change norms and develop skills by degrees, but if I assume I cannot work toward raising increasingly difficult issues, then I see no way to build the very trust a group lacks. By helping group members identify and consistently engage in trustworthy behavior, groups build relationships to the point that increasingly difficult issues can be addressed. Like many other broad descriptors of group interaction, such as respect, fairness, and support, trust needs to be defined and discussed at the level of behavior consistent with desired group values, assumptions, and norms.

Leadership

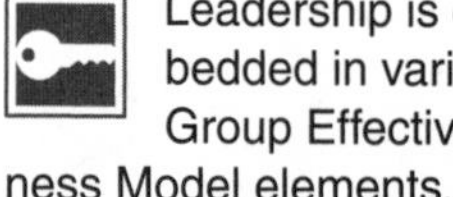

Leadership is embedded in various Group Effectiveness Model elements. A more useful conversation than discussing leadership generally is to clarify the behaviors expected in formal and informal leader roles.

Similar to trust, people often wonder why leadership is not included in the Group Effectiveness Model. *Leadership* is a broad term that is often interpreted differently by each individual in a group. Some define leadership in terms of unilateral behaviors, like telling the group to get back on track or dictating a choice. Others see leadership as influencing quietly behind the scenes. Beliefs about leadership are embedded in the group culture and norms, and they influence expectations about how individuals should help groups set goals, solve problems, and communicate. To complicate this issue, *leader* can also be a formal role people fill. And as facilitative leaders, every group member can engage in leadership behaviors to support group effectiveness. So leadership is embedded in various Group Effectiveness Model elements. A more useful conversation than discussing leadership generally is to clarify the behaviors expected in formal and informal leader roles.

No Control over Context

The elements of group context can contribute to group problems or support increased effectiveness. Yet by definition, group context contains elements that "influence the group's effectiveness but that the group usually does not control."[1]

Groups sometimes feel it is hopeless to engage in process or structure interventions since, they believe, "we are helpless unless upper management changes." Subordinates argue that change must start from the top, because otherwise they will be punished for acting differently. They may believe they cannot gain access to information they need to make effective decisions. In a few cases, they may be right. More frequently, I find that groups *can* influence context elements even if they do not control them. Chapter Forty-One, about not being able to use the Skilled Facilitator approach unless the boss knows it, and Chapter Forty-Two, about how we contribute to our boss's ineffectiveness, speak to this issue. The learned helplessness born of working in traditional patriarchal organizations is pervasive.[2] It is a recurring excuse for not attempting improvement. It is harder and perhaps riskier to try to change the elements of context but entirely possible. Many organizations have changed slowly from the bottom up or the middle out. For an example, see Tom Moore's story in Chapter Thirty-Eight about how his department slowly became a model for an entire organization.

See Chapter Thirty-Eight, "Daily Challenges of a Facilitative Leader," page 309; Chapter Forty-One, "'I Can't Use This Approach Unless My Boss Does,'" page 331; and Chapter Forty-Two, "How to Stop Contributing to Your Boss's and Your Own Ineffectiveness," page 335.

Groups seldom consider how they themselves contribute to the very conditions they complain about. Frequently I work with groups whose members tell me they cannot raise issues with those above them in the organization. Yet when I talk with the senior executives, I find that those executives are completely unaware of the issues, say they would be more than willing to make changes, and say they are frustrated because no one will tell them "what is really going on around here." In diagnosing Group Effectiveness Model issues, I challenge groups to think about how they contribute to ineffectiveness in context elements.[3] In designing interventions, we discuss how a group might influence improvements in those elements even if they do not control them. Examining carefully how organizational ineffectiveness is cocreated by all levels significantly increases the likelihood that groups can positively influence organizational context. And if groups discover their efforts unwelcome and their worst suspicions correct, they have valuable data to help them wisely invest their time and energy.

Limits of the Model

When thinking about influencing the culture of an entire organization, clients and facilitators frequently ask about the limits of the model. Can it be used as a model of an entire organization or just for a group within an organization? What about using the model with community and nonprofit groups? Does it apply only to work groups? What are the reasonable limits to applying the effectiveness criteria and key factors?

The research on which the Group Effectiveness Model is based was conducted with work teams—groups in organizations with fairly clear goals, membership, and interdependent tasks (Hackman, 1987; Sundstrom, De Meuse, and Futtrell, 1990). There are probably conditions to which the assumptions behind the model will not extend. Yet I have used the model for years to successfully analyze whole organizations, community groups with loose structure and weak interdependence, local governments with ever-changing and poorly defined membership and boundaries, and work groups at all levels of large and small organizations.

The primary factor that changes across situations is context. When thinking about an organization, the context is usually an entire industry or industry group. When mapping a community, the context comprises a broad array of groups and individuals. The definitions of the elements within context need to shift, change, or expand. For example, an entire community is unlikely to have a clear mission or shared vision, but there may be pervasive values or sets of values that can be clearly defined. Or there may be one clear goal, like downtown renewal or economic development, that most of the community share. In the community example, the remaining elements within context may all be relevant—for example, physical environment, training and consultation available, material resources (regional economy), rewards for local businesses that beautify their storefronts, and broad community support. In other situations, some or all of the elements may be less relevant. The key to successfully using the model in non–work group contexts is to share it with clients, discuss which elements are relevant, and adapt the definitions and examples to fit the situation. When adapted, the Group Effectiveness Model proves useful to help a wide variety of groups and organizations think systemically about their problems and design lasting improvements.

---

1. See *The Skilled Facilitator,* p. 31.
2. For a compelling discussion of the ways in which our organizational experiences have contributed to our feelings of powerlessness, lack of accountability, and conflicting belief systems, see Peter Block's *Stewardship* (1993).
3. For an example and additional thoughts about this topic, see Chris Argryis's "Good Communication That Blocks Learning" (1994).

Resources

Argryis, C. "Good Communication That Blocks Learning." *Harvard Business Review,* July-Aug. 1994, pp. 77–85.

Block, P. *Stewardship: Choosing Service over Self Interest.* San Francisco: Berrett-Koehler, 1993.

References

Argryis, C. "Good Communication That Blocks Learning." *Harvard Business Review,* July-Aug. 1994, pp. 77–85.

Block, P. *Stewardship: Choosing Service over Self Interest.* San Francisco: Berrett-Koehler, 1993.

Hackman, J. R. "The Design of Work Teams." In J. Lorsch (ed.), *Handbook of Organizational Behavior.* Upper Saddle River, N.J.: Prentice Hall, 1987.

Katzenbach, J. R., and Smith, D. K. *The Wisdom of Teams.* Boston: Harvard Business School Press, 1993.

Sundstrom, E., De Meuse, K. P., and Futtrell, D. "Work Teams: Applications and Effectiveness." *American Psychologist,* 1990, *45,* 120–133.

Chapter 3

Using Facilitative Skills in Different Roles

Roger Schwarz

MANY OF YOU READING this book need to use facilitative skills but are not (or at least sometimes are not) a substantively neutral third-party facilitator. Instead, you are involved in the group's discussions and decisions as an expert consultant, a team leader or member, a coach, or a trainer. Increasingly, people who serve in these roles are recognizing that facilitative skills are essential for working effectively with groups. If you serve in any of these roles, you can apply the same core values, principles, and ground rules discussed throughout the book in working with groups.

It is important to understand how the facilitative roles are similar and different and to select the appropriate facilitative role—the one that accurately represents your relationship with the group. If group members see your facilitative role as appropriate, they are likely to be legitimately influenced by you. If members think you are filling an inappropriate facilitative role, they may not be open to being influenced by you, even if your observations and suggestions make sense within that role. For example, a group sometimes rejects the help of an expert consultant who, by inappropriately serving as a neutral facilitator, leads the members to wonder whether the consultant is trying to subtly steer them in a certain direction without saying so. Table 3.1 shows the five facilitative roles and how they are similar and different.

You do not have to give up your leadership role or your expertise to use facilitative skills. On the contrary, using facilitative skills enhances your leadership or consulting role and expertise.

THE FACILITATOR ROLE

A ***facilitator*** is a substantively neutral third party, acceptable to all members of the group, who has no substantive decision-making authority. The facilitator's purpose is to help a group increase its effectiveness by diagnosing and intervening largely on group process and structure.

This chapter is an adaptation of *The Skilled Facilitator,* Chapter Three, "The Facilitator and Other Facilitative Roles."

Table 3.1 Facilitative Roles

Facilitator	Facilitative Consultant	Facilitative Coach	Facilitative Trainer	Facilitative Leader
Helps a group increase its effectiveness by diagnosing and intervening on group process and structure	Helps a client make informed decisions by bringing content expertise to the client's particular situation	Helps individuals achieve their goals by helping them learn to rigorously reflect on their behavior and thinking	Helps clients develop knowledge and skills they can apply to real problems or opportunities	Helps groups of which they are the formal leader or a member increase their effectiveness by diagnosing and intervening on group process and structure while contributing their content expertise
Process expert	Process expert	Process expert	Process expert	Skilled in process
Content neutral	Content expert	Involved in content	Content expert	Involved in content

Substantively Neutral

By *substantively neutral,* I don't mean that you have no opinions on the issues that the group is discussing. That would be unrealistic. Rather, I mean that you facilitate the discussion without sharing your opinions, with the result that group members cannot discern what you think about the group's issues; consequently, you don't influence the group's decisions. Group members are easily and justifiably annoyed by a facilitator who claims to be neutral and then acts in a way that is not.

To remain neutral requires listening to members' views, and remaining curious about how their reasoning differs from others (and from your private views), so that you can help the group engage in productive conversation. If you trade your curiosity for a belief that some members are right and others are wrong, or that the group as a whole is going in the wrong direction, you give up your ability to help group members explore their own views and differences and replace it with your desire to influence the content of discussion. If you find yourself invested in an issue or in having the group reach a particular outcome, or if you have expertise on the subject that makes it difficult for you to remain neutral, then consider serving in one of the other facilitative roles.

Third Party

A facilitator needs to be a third party because it is difficult to act neutrally in your own group. If you are a group member or leader, people would reasonably expect you to be involved in the content of discussion and to have a role in decision making.

The term *third party* is open to interpretation. Even if you are not a member of the immediate group that requests facilitation, members may not consider you a third party. This may happen, for example, if the group is seeking facilitation to address concerns with the division it is part of and you are an internal facilitator working in the larger division. To serve as a facilitator, the group requesting help needs to consider you a third party.

Process Expert

A facilitator is content neutral but a process expert and advocate. As a process expert, you know what kinds of behavior, process, and underlying structure are likely to contribute to high-quality problem solving and decision making, and you know which elements contribute to making an effective group. If you ask a group to use certain ground rules or identify certain ineffective behavior in the group, it is on the basis of this process expertise.

As a process expert, you advocate for processes, structures, and behaviors necessary for effective facilitation, such as appropriate membership, useful problem-solving methods, sufficient time, and ground rules. You inquire whether the group you are working with sees any problems with your design for the facilitation. For all of these decisions about the facilitation process, you are a partner with the group.

It is being skilled in group process that makes each of the five roles a facilitative role.

THE FACILITATIVE CONSULTANT ROLE

Unlike the facilitator, a facilitative consultant is used for expertise in a particular content area. The facilitative consultant is a third-party expert whose purpose is to help the client make informed decisions. The facilitative consultant does this by applying the area of expertise (marketing, management information systems, organizational change, service quality, and so forth) to the client's particular situation, recommending a course of action, and in some cases implementing it for the client. Any substantive decision-making authority the consultant has results not from the role but from its being delegated by the client. A facilitative consultant uses facilitative skills while serving as an expert in a particular content area. Like the facilitator, the facilitative consultant may be external or internal to the organization. Internal human resources or organization development consultants often serve as facilitative consultants in an organization.

Facilitative skills are essential for expert consulting, which typically requires developing effective relationships, working with groups, and dealing with difficult conversations. The issues on which the expert consultant is called in are often ones on which members have strong and differing views. Consequently, the ability to help the group address the issues depends partly on the consultant's ability to effectively manage the process of exploring the issues. To paraphrase one of my clients, an expert consultant, "What do I do when I am talking to the client about what I found

The Internal Role

Some of you reading this book are internal consultants, coaches, trainers, and coaches. The concepts, principles, and tools and techniques of the Skilled Facilitator approach apply equally whether you are working internally or externally to the organization. There is essentially no difference between what constitutes effective behavior for internal and external facilitative roles. You may be thinking, "The Skilled Facilitator approach could really improve my organization, but how do I apply it as an internal person? I don't have the freedom or power of an external person, and I can't say what an external person can say. The risks are greater than I can take."

There are a variety of actions you can take to reduce the potential risks you face as an internal person and increase your effectiveness with your clients. I describe these in detail in *The Skilled Facilitator* in Chapter Fifteen, "Serving as a Facilitator in Your Own Organization," and Resource H, "Guidelines for Contracting with Your Manager."

and what I recommend, and people start disagreeing with each other in front of me?" When this occurs, the facilitative consultant can help in the conversation while still being a participant in the content of the discussion. By integrating facilitative skills with expertise, the facilitative consultant increases the value provided to the clients.

See, for example, Chapter Fifty-Nine, "Being a Facilitative Consultant," page 495.

THE FACILITATIVE COACH ROLE

In recent years, organizations have made coaches available for many of their executives and managers. A coach usually works individually with people, helping them improve their effectiveness. Depending on her background, a coach may bring subject area expertise in certain areas. At the heart of the facilitative coaching role is the ability to help people improve their effectiveness by helping them learn to rigorously reflect on their behavior and thinking.

A facilitative coach jointly designs the learning process with the client instead of assuming that she knows how the client can best learn. She also models mutual learning by exploring with the client how her coaching methods are helping or hindering the client's ability to learn. Facilitative coaches and clients explore the coaching relationship itself as a source of learning for both the client and the coach.

For more on this approach, see Chapter Fifty-Seven, "The Facilitative Coach," page 457.

THE FACILITATIVE TRAINER ROLE

Like the expert consultant, a trainer also has knowledge to share with participants; like the facilitative consultant, the facilitative trainer models the Skilled Facilitator core values and ground rules and uses facilitative skills to enhance the participants' learning experience. But although both facilitative consultants and facilitative trainers use their substantive expertise to help clients learn, they differ in their primary goal and focus. For consultants, the primary goal is to help the client solve a real problem or create a specific opportunity. For trainers, the primary goal is to help the client develop knowledge and skills that they can apply to real problems or specific opportunities. Consequently, for consultants, the client's situation takes center stage; for trainers, the substantive topic is the focus. Still, facilitative trainers design workshops so that participants use the training sessions to test out and get feedback on their new knowledge and skills on real issues that face them.

When feasible, a facilitative trainer works with the participants to design the training so that it meets their interests. During the training, the facilitative trainer regularly inquires whether the training is meeting the participants' needs and is flexible enough to modify the design if not. The facilitative trainer also considers the training setting an opportunity for his own learning, not just for participant learning. This means he is open to changing his views and inviting participants to challenge his assumptions, just as the trainer himself challenges participants.

In recent years, some trainers have changed their title to facilitator. To the degree that this signals a shift in trainers' recognizing the value of facilitative skills and integrating them into their work, it makes me hopeful. Yet calling a trainer a facilitator obscures the fact that the individual is expert in and has responsibility for teaching some particular topic. I use the term *facilitative trainer* to recognize both sets of responsibilities and skills.

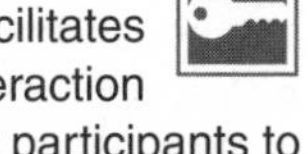

The facilitative trainer facilitates the interaction among participants to enhance learning.

To learn more about the facilitative training role, see Chapter Fifty-Eight, "Becoming a Facilitative Trainer," page 479.

THE FACILITATIVE LEADER ROLE

The facilitative leader may be the formal leader of the group or just a group member. In either case, the facilitative leader role is the most difficult to fill because this person needs to use his facilitative skills at the same time that he has views—sometimes strong views—about the issue being discussed.

The facilitative leader uses the Skilled Facilitator core values and principles to help groups and organizations increase their effectiveness. This includes helping to create the conditions in which group members can also learn to use the core values and principles.

The facilitative leader may be the formal leader of the group or just a group member. In either case, the facilitative leader role is the most difficult to fill because this person needs to use his facilitative skills at the same time that he has views—sometimes strong views—about the issue being discussed. For example, this requires that the facilitative leader openly state his views on a subject, explain the reasoning underlying those views, and then encourage others to identify any gaps or problems in his reasoning. Underlying the facilitative leader role is the premise that a group increases its effectiveness as members take on more responsibility for the group and increase their ability to learn from their experiences.

See, for example, Chapter Thirty-Eight, "Daily Challenges of a Facilitative Leader," page 309; Chapter Forty-Six, "From Learning to Lead to Leading to Learn," page 367; and Chapter Forty-Seven, "Reflections of a Somewhat Facilitative Leader," page 377.

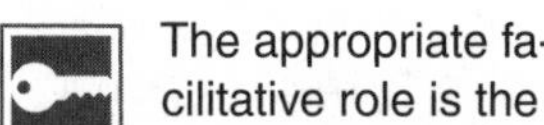

The appropriate facilitative role is the one that accurately represents your relationship with the group. If you select an inappropriate role, you create problems for yourself and the group.

The facilitator role is appropriate for a situation in which you are not a member of the group, have no stake in the issues, and have no role in the group's decision making given your roles in the organization.

A Note on Terms

The Skilled Facilitator Fieldbook focuses on all five of the facilitative roles. When we are writing about a specific role (and only that role), we use the appropriate term, such as *facilitative leader* or *facilitative trainer.* We use the term *Skilled Facilitator approach* to refer specifically to the facilitator role and to using the principles of the approach in any other role.

CHOOSING THE APPROPRIATE ROLE

The appropriate facilitative role is the one that accurately represents your relationship with the group. If you select an inappropriate role, you create problems for yourself and the group. One common problem occurs when an internal or external consultant or leader tries to serve as a facilitator rather than as a facilitative consultant or facilitative leader. Consider, for example, an internal human resources (HR) manager who works with groups across the organization to develop and implement HR policy. The manager begins the group meeting by describing her role as a facilitator and asking for each group's thoughts about a particular policy. But the manager is an expert in the area of HR and has her own thoughts about what makes effective HR policy. When she realizes that the groups have ideas differing from those of HR, the "facilitator" begins asking leading questions in order to influence the group members' views without saying so explicitly, or she simply identifies some problems with others' proposals. Some group members begin to feel set up, believing that the HR person misled them about her role. At the same time, the manager is frustrated because she feels she cannot openly influence the group's ideas in the facilitator role. In this case, serving as a facilitative consultant or facilitative leader enables the manager to share subject matter expertise, be involved in the decisions, and still use facilitative skills to improve the quality of the group's interaction.

SERVING IN MULTIPLE FACILITATIVE ROLES

At times, you may serve in two or more of these facilitative roles. You may be a facilitative leader in your own group, a facilitator or facilitative consultant to other parts of the organization, and a facilitative trainer as well. Because all five facilitative roles are based on the same core values and principles, you can move among the roles as necessary with integrity. Whether serving in one facilitative role or more than one, the underlying principle is the same: select the appropriate role given the situation, accurately and explicitly describe to the group the facilitative role you plan to fill, seek agreement with the group, and then fill the role according to that agreement. If you plan to use facilitative skills in a nonfacilitator role, say so, being clear to distinguish between using facilitative skills and serving as a substantively neutral third-party facilitator.

Chapter 4

Understanding What Guides Your Behavior

Roger Schwarz

INCREASING ONE'S EFFECTIVENESS in a facilitative role is not simply a matter of learning new strategies and tools or techniques. The challenging internal work for those in facilitative roles is to identify and explore the core values and assumptions that guide our actions, rigorously reflect on how they increase or decrease our effectiveness, and develop a new set of values and assumptions that we can use to increase our effectiveness and that of the groups we work with.

YOUR THEORIES OF ACTION

As described by Argyris and Schön, you have in your head theories of action about how to act effectively and respond quickly to situations; without them, you would have to invent a new response to every situation you face, and you would never be able to act in time.[1] You have two types of theories of action in your head—your *espoused theory* and your *theory-in-use*—or to oversimplify, what we say we do and what guides how we actually act.

Espoused Theory

Your ***espoused theory*** is what you say you do and why you do it. You describe your espoused theory when you tell others how you would act in a given situation, including the values and beliefs that lead you to act that way. One way to recognize your espoused theory is to say, "In this situation, I would . . . because I believe that . . ." and fill in the blanks.

Your ***espoused theory*** is what you say you do and why you do it. def·i·'ni·tion

This chapter is an adaptation of *The Skilled Facilitator,* Chapter Four, "Understanding the Theories That Guide Our Actions." I derived the models from the work of Chris Argyris and Don Schön (1974) who originally labeled them as Model I, Opposite Model I, and Model II, and from adaptations by Robert Putnam, Diana McLain Smith, and Phil MacArthur at Action Design (1997), who refer to them as the Unilateral Control, Give-Up-Control, and Mutual Learning Models. Action Design is an organization and management development firm that has built on the work of Argyris and Schön. Putnam and McLain Smith are coauthors with Argyris of *Action Science* (1985).

The challenging internal work for those in facilitative roles is to identify and explore the core values and assumptions that guide our actions, rigorously reflect on how they increase or decrease our effectiveness, and develop a new set of values and assumptions that we can use to increase our effectiveness and that of the groups we work with.

Mental Models, Theory-in-Use, and Espoused Theory

Throughout the book, we use the terms *mental models, theory-in-use,* and *espoused theory.* The terms are related but different.

Mental Models

Like some other psychological terms, the term *mental models* has migrated into the popular management literature and become part of managers' vocabulary. *The Fifth Discipline* (1990) by Peter Senge at MIT helped introduce many leaders and managers to the concept of mental models and the impact it can have on organizations.

According to cognitive psychologist Philip N. Johnson-Laird (1989), cognitive psychologist Kenneth Craik developed the modern concept of mental models. In *The Nature of Explanation* (1943), Craik reasoned that individuals translate external events into internal models and use their models to reason through situations. They also use the models they create to guide their actions.

The Fifth Discipline Fieldbook states that *mental model* "refers to both the semipermanent tacit 'maps' of the world which people hold in their long-term memory, and the short-term perceptions which people build up as part of their everyday reasoning processes" (Kleiner, 1994, p. 237).

As we understand it, people can have mental models that represent any part of the world. They can have mental models about how our solar system works (we used to think the sun revolved around the earth), how car engines work, or how people work effectively in groups. Mental models include but are not limited to that part of the world that involves our behavior.

Theory-in-Use and Espoused Theory

Theory-in-use and *espoused theory* are terms that Argyris and Schön (1974) coined to describe two kinds of theories of action. Theories of action involve assumptions about ourselves, others, and the situation, and the causal connections between them and the consequences that result. A theory of action takes this form: "If I'm in situation *S* and I want to create consequences *C,* given assumptions $a_1, \ldots, a_n$, I should do A."

Argyris and Schön distinguished espoused theory from theory-in-use because they found that people tended to be unaware of the assumptions that guided their behavior and the unintended consequences they created. They thought that the problem people would encounter learning a new theory of action would have less to do with learning the new theory and more to do with unlearning their current theories-in-use.

How We Use the Terms

We use ***mental models*** as a general term to refer to the tacit models that people hold in their memory about how some part of the world works. Mental models can include models that do not involve the model holder's behavior (for example, how an engine works) and models that do involve the model holder's behavior (for example, how to get a group to support your decision).

We think of ***theories-in-use*** and ***espoused theories*** as particular forms of mental models. We use these terms to refer specifically to the unilateral control model or mutual learning model described in this chapter. We use *theory-in-use* to refer to the theory we infer that actually guides a person's behavior, and *espoused theory* to refer to the theory they say guides their behavior, recognizing that their espoused theory and theory-in-use may or may not be the same.

Theory-in-Use

Your ***theory-in-use*** is reflected by what you actually do. It is called theory-in-use because if we examined your actions, it is the theory we would infer that you used, whether conscious or not, as having guided those actions.

Theory-in-use can only be inferred from watching your actual behavior. It includes a set of (1) core values and assumptions, (2) strategies that follow from the core values and assumptions and specify how you should act, and (3) the consequences of your interactions with others. For example, if I watched you in the situation in which people were disagreeing with your point of view, I might observe that you do not ask people why they have a different view than you do, and I might see you respond with comments like, "Trust me, this plan will work" or "What you don't understand is . . ." Without practice, most people are unaware of their theory-in-use and how it differs from their espoused theory.

Theory-in-use can only be inferred from watching your actual behavior. It includes a set of (1) core values and assumptions, (2) strategies that follow from the core values and assumptions and specify how you should act, and (3) the consequences of your interactions with others.

The theory-in-use I might infer from your behavior is likely to be very different from, and less effective than, the theory you espouse.

Part of what makes your theory-in-use so powerful is that it operates very quickly, skillfully, and effortlessly. You act and react using core values and assumptions, yet you are typically unaware of what your theory-in-use is or how you are using it to design your behavior. While people have different espoused theories, when we find ourselves in embarrassing or psychologically threatening situations, almost all of us use the same theory-in-use to guide our behavior—the *unilateral control model,* which is what Argyris and Schön (1996) called Model I. This theory-in-use leads us to act in ways that create misunderstanding, conflict, and defensiveness and reduce our ability to help groups. Unfortunately, our unawareness of our theory-in-use, and the speed and effortlessness with which we apply it, becomes a liability and compounds our problem. Not only are we acting ineffectively, but also our theory-in-use leads us to do it quickly, skillfully, and effortlessly and without even being aware that we are doing so. Consequently we are usually blind to the inconsistencies between our espoused theory and theory-in-use and to how our theory-in-use is reducing our effectiveness. We are not walking our talk, so to speak.

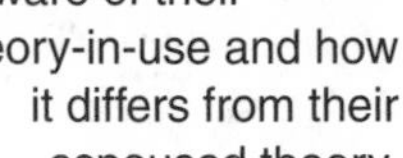

Without practice, most people are unaware of their theory-in-use and how it differs from their espoused theory.

This blindness makes it difficult to discover your inconsistencies for yourself and then to reduce the negative consequences that stem from your theory-in-use. Fortunately, others can often see your inconsistencies and help you become more aware of what is going on.

UNILATERAL CONTROL MODEL

def·i·'ni·tion The terms ***unilateral control*** and ***unilateral control model*** refer to the theory-in-use that almost all of us use to design our behavior in situations that are psychologically threatening or potentially embarrassing.

The terms ***unilateral control*** and ***unilateral control model*** refer to the theory-in-use that almost all of us use to design our behavior in situations that are psychologically threatening or potentially embarrassing.

Core Values of the Unilateral Control Model

When you use a unilateral control theory-in-use, you design your behavior using the set of core values listed in the far left-hand column of Figure 4.1. People use a mix of these core values and to different degrees. Together these core values provide a basis for shaping the way you think:

Figure 4.1 Unilateral Control Model

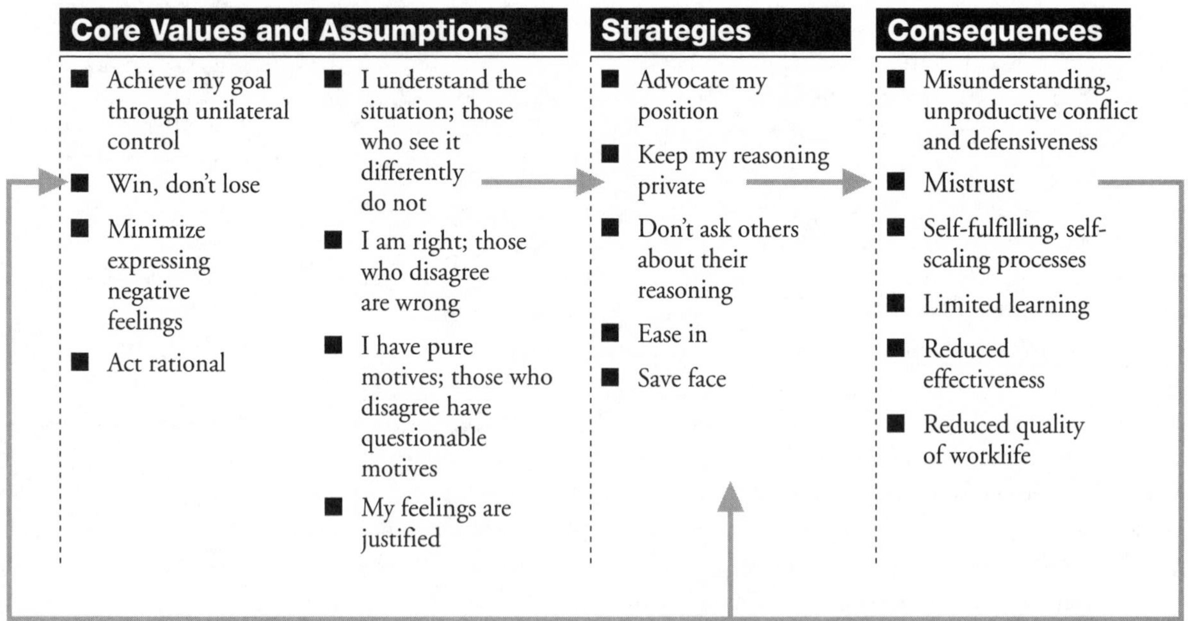

Source: Argyris and Schön (1974); Action Design (1997).

- *Achieve my goal through unilateral control.* This essentially means to get others to do what you want them to do. It includes conceiving of the purpose of the meeting, task, or activity by yourself rather than jointly deciding the purpose with others. Once you have defined your goal, you try to achieve it by acting unilaterally to control the conversation.
- *Win, don't lose.* You define winning as achieving your intended purposes. Anything that happens that leads to either changing the purposes or not achieving them is considered losing and a sign of weakness.
- *Minimize expressing negative feelings.* You keep your own and others' unpleasant feelings out of the conversation, believing that expressing negative feelings like anger or frustration is acting incompetently or undiplomatically because it can hurt people and make it difficult to accomplish goals. Raising negative feelings can lead things to get out of your control.
- *Act rational.* This means being objective and logical, not becoming emotional, and thinking of any discussions of the issues as being purely objective, regardless of the emotions that might underlie them. It means acting as if your behavior is internally consistent even if it is not.

Core Assumptions

In conjunction with the core values you use to design your behavior, there is a set of assumptions embedded in unilateral behavior (Figure 4.1).

- *I understand the situation; those who see it differently don't understand.* You assume that whatever information you bring to understanding the situation is valid and complete, as are the conclusions you draw about it. In other words, the way you see it is the way it really is. Those who disagree with you are misinformed and do not understand. If they understood what you understand, they would agree with you.
- *I am right; those who disagree are wrong.* You assume that there is a right and wrong perspective and that if you are right, others who disagree or see it differently must be wrong.
- *I have pure motives; those who disagree have questionable motives.* You assume you are acting in the best interests of the group or organization and that those who disagree with you are motivated by self-interest or other motives that are inappropriate.
- *My feelings are justified.* Because others do not understand the situation as it is (that is, as you see it) and because their lack of understanding results in part from their questionable motives, you are justified in being angry or feeling whatever you are feeling toward them. In the unilateral control model, you consider your feelings as the natural inevitable result of others' actions toward you. You do not consider the possibility that your feelings result from your own thoughts and that to the extent that your thinking may not be reflecting the full situation, neither do your feelings.

Strategies

You use the combination of the core values and assumptions to develop unilateral control strategies for dealing with your conversations. These are strategies that you use to guide your actions whether or not others use them.

- *Advocate my position.* You tell people what decision should be made or course of action should be taken.
- *Keep my reasoning private.* As you advocate your positions, you are careful to keep your reasoning private. For example, part of your strategy might be to ask other people leading questions so they will "see the light" and think that they have come up with the ideas that you want them to implement. Given that this strategy is designed based on unilaterally controlling the situation, you would need to keep it private. Sharing it with group members would reduce your ability to implement the strategy. The ability to implement a unilateral control strategy often depends on the ability to withhold the strategy from those on whom you are using it.

To determine whether your strategy is unilateral, try this transparency thought experiment: imagine saying your strategy out loud to your intended audience; if it seems embarrassing or absurd to reveal your strategy or doing so would hinder your ability to implement your strategy, the strategy is probably unilateral.

- *Do not inquire into others' reasoning.* When others' advocate their points of view, you may respond by telling them why they are wrong, but you typically do not ask them to explain how they reached their conclusions. If you do inquire into others' reasoning, you do so in a way that does not fully answer your private questions.
- *Ease in.* ***Easing in*** is an indirect approach designed to get others to see things your way for themselves. It can involve asking others' questions or making statements that are designed to get them to figure out and state what you are privately thinking without your having to say it. For example, when you say, "Don't you think it would be a good idea if we outsourced the work?" you are easing in because you are indirectly stating your point of view.
- *Protect yourself and others.* Together, these strategies enable you to unilaterally control the situation and protect yourself and others. If you fully explain your reasoning, you become vulnerable by enabling others to question your reasoning and identify places where your reasoning has gaps or inconsistencies.

By inquiring into others' reasoning, you fear that you might make public what you have privately thought—that there are gaps and flaws in the other person's reasoning. You assume this would embarrass or threaten the other person and possibly yourself and that this would lead to raising negative feelings, which you are trying to suppress. Also, if you inquire into others' reasoning, it becomes more likely that they will feel free to inquire into yours.

Rather than inquiring into others' reasoning or behavior, you simply assume that you know what they are saying and why they are saying it. Rather than test with others whether your inference is accurate, you privately conclude it is accurate and then use your untested inference to respond to them. Your untested inferences form the faulty foundation for all sorts of other conclusions you might make and actions you take. In short, you have built a compelling but potentially flawed data base about others.

Consequences

All of these strategies are designed to unilaterally control the situation and suppress negative feelings and defensiveness. Ironically, by attempting to control the situation, you also create the very results that you say you are trying to avoid.

> Ironically, by attempting to control the situation, you also create the very results that you say you are trying to avoid.

Your core values and assumptions and strategies interact in complex ways to create these consequences (see Figure 4.1):

- *Misunderstanding, unproductive conflict, and defensiveness.* You create misunderstanding because you assume that the situation is as you see it, and you base your actions on untested inferences about others rather than test them out. To the extent that you make negative attributions about other's motives and do not test them, you generate your own mistrust of others, and vice versa. Acting on untested inaccurate inferences contributes to others' getting defensive and generates unproductive conflict.
- *Self-fulfilling and self-sealing processes.* Believing that openly sharing your reasoning with others will make them defensive, you ease in by asking others questions without explaining why you are asking them. This leads them to be wary and cautious in their responses, which you see as defensive. In this way, you create a self-fulfilling process, generating the very consequence you set out to avoid.

When others recognize that you are withholding information but acting as if you are not, they mistrust you. Of course, they are unlikely to point this out to you because that would be potentially embarrassing, so they play along but withhold their concerns. If you sense that they have concerns about you but are not raising them and you do not raise this issue with them, you create a self-sealing process, sealing off the opportunity for learning how your own behavior may be contributing to the group's reduced effectiveness.

Getting results we do not intend leads us to be even more controlling and focused on winning. We try to suppress negative feelings, thus reinforcing our unilaterally controlling approach. By attempting to control the conversation and simply pushing our point of view and by not being open to influence from others, we are seen as being defensive ourselves.

See Chapter Twenty-Nine, "Exploring Your Contributions to Problems," page 255, and Chapter Forty-Two, "How to Stop Contributing to Your Boss's and Your Own Ineffectiveness," page 335.

- *Reduced learning and effectiveness.* By focusing on unilaterally controlling the conversation and having your point of view prevail, you reduce the opportunity to learn how others see the issues differently and to learn about flaws or gaps in your own reasoning. In addition, you reduce the opportunity to learn how your own behavior may be contributing to the group's reduced effectiveness. This reduces your effectiveness in working with groups on both process and content issues.

• *Reduced quality of worklife.* It can be stressful when you cannot say what you are thinking without creating negative consequences. A great deal of mental energy gets tied up in trying to withhold what you are thinking or carefully craft what you are saying to dress up your intentions. Conflict can be created when you make untested inferences about others that lead them to get defensive. Relationships can also be difficult when others use the unilateral control approach with you.

Creating a Dilemma

Using a unilaterally controlling approach creates a dilemma in which there is no good answer to the question, "What should I do with my thoughts and feelings during a conversation?" If you say exactly what you are thinking and feeling in the form you are thinking and feeling it, you will likely create defensive reactions in others. If you self-censor, not sharing at all what you are thinking and feeling, others will not hear your views. If you are indirect and ease in, you still create defensiveness and others don't fully understand your views.

Learning and Unlearning Unilateral Control

You probably began to learn the unilateral control model as a child. My clients often say that their parents taught them this approach. They continued to learn it and have it reinforced in school, by friends, and in organizations they joined. In short, they began to learn the approach when they were young enough that they could not easily understand the implications or question them. And because the unilateral approach hinders testing assumptions, seeking negative feedback, and learning, it makes it difficult to become aware of the fact that you are using the unilateral control approach. Given this, it's fair to say that you are not responsible for having become unilaterally controlling. However, once you are aware of this, you have a choice about whether to change.

GIVE-UP-CONTROL MODEL

When people recognize that they use the unilateral control model, they often want to change. Unfortunately, they often shift from one form of control to another: the give-up-control model, which I think of as a subset or variation of the basic unilateral control model.

The core values of the give-up-control model are (1) everyone participates in defining the purpose, (2) everyone wins and no one loses, (3) express your feelings, and (4) suppress using your intellectual reasoning (Argyris, Putnam and McLain Smith, 1985). A key assumption is that in order for people to learn and be involved and committed, they must come to the right answer by themselves. Of course, the right answer is the one you have already come up with. When others don't see the answer that you see, a common strategy is to ask easing-in or leading questions to help the others get the answer by themselves. The results of the give-up control model are the same as those of the unilateral control model: increased misunderstanding, unproductive conflict and defensiveness, as well as reduced learning, effectiveness, and quality of worklife.

People often move from the unilateral control model to the give-up-control variation and back. A common occurrence is with a manager who seeks to empower his employees. After recognizing that he has been micromanaging and unilaterally controlling the group, the manager shifts to letting his group make decisions. He delegates an important decision to the group and, in an effort not to influence them, does not share relevant information he has, including criteria that need to be met in the solution. When the group proudly returns with a solution, the manager rejects it because it does not meet the criteria (which he did not share) or take into account the information he withheld. As a result, the group infers that the manager doesn't want to give up control and that the manager thinks the group is not ready to be empowered. The manager responds by shifting back to a unilaterally controlling approach.

In the unilateral control model, you take control; in the opposite model, you give up control. But because you take control and give up control unilaterally, fundamentally both models are unilaterally controlling.

MUTUAL LEARNING MODEL

The mutual learning model is the theory-in-use that enables you and the groups you work with to become more effective, particularly under difficult conditions. The Skilled Facilitator approach is based on the mutual learning model. Like the unilateral control model, it has three components: (1) core values and assumptions, (2) strategies, and (3) consequences (Figure 4.2).

Core Values

The core values that guide the mutual learning model are the core values of the Skilled Facilitator approach.

Valid Information

Valid information means that we share all information relevant to an issue, including our assumptions and our feelings about how the issue is being addressed. It means using specific examples so that others can understand clearly what we mean and can ideally determine independently whether the information is accurate. Valid information also means that others understand the information that we share with them. This means that we share not only our conclusions but also the reasoning by which we reach our conclusions. Valid information is the core value on which the next two core values are built.

Figure 4.2 Mutual Learning Model

Core Values and Assumptions		Strategies	Consequences
■ Valid information ■ Free and informed choice ■ Internal commitment ■ Compassion	■ I have some information; others have other information ■ Each of us may see things the others do not ■ Differences are opportunities for learning ■ People are trying to act with integrity given their situations	■ Test assumptions and inferences ■ Share all relevant information ■ Use specific examples and agree on important words ■ Explain reasoning and intent ■ Focus on interests, not positions ■ Combine advocacy and inquiry ■ Jointly design the approach ■ Discuss undiscussables ■ Use a decision-making rule that generates the commitment needed	■ Increased understanding, reduced unproductive conflict and defensiveness ■ Increased trust ■ Reduced self-fulfilling, self-sealing processes ■ Increased learning ■ Increased effectiveness ■ Increased quality of worklife

Source: Argyris and Schön (1974); Action Design (1997).

Free and Informed Choice

When you make an ***informed choice***, it is based on valid information. You make ***free choices*** to the extent that you can define your own objectives and the methods for achieving them. When you make free choices, you do so not because you are being coerced, manipulated, or acting out of defensiveness, but because the choice is related to fulfilling some important personal need.

Internal Commitment to the Choice

You are ***internally committed*** when you feel personally responsible for the choices you make. You are committed to the decision because it is intrinsically compelling or satisfying, not because you will be rewarded or penalized for making that choice. When you are internally committed to a decision, you take ownership for implementing it. As a result, there is little need for traditional over-the-shoulder monitoring to make sure you are really doing what you said you would do. You monitor the consequences of your decisions and implement or consider changes if results differ from those intended.

Compassion

Compassion involves adapting a stance toward others and yourself in which you temporarily suspend judgment. When you act with compassion, you infuse the other core values with your intent to understand, empathize with, and help others. *Compassion* literally means "to suffer with" and is sometimes mistakenly thought of as having pity for others. The kind of compassion I have in mind enables you to have empathy for others and for yourself in a way that still holds you and others accountable for your actions. This kind of compassion does not involve unilateral protection and enhances the other core values rather than diminishing them.

Compassion comes from the heart. If you act out of compassion rather than out of fear and guilt, you are able to move beyond defensiveness and be open and vulnerable. This enables you to create conversations in which you can mutually learn with others how to increase your effectiveness.

Core Assumptions

There are three core assumptions in the mutual learning model and the Skilled Facilitator approach (see Figure 4.2).

I Have Some Relevant Information; Other People Also Have Relevant Information

You assume that you may have only part of the information necessary to understand and address the issue. You assume that others have relevant information that may affect how you think about the subject. In other words, you know that you don't know all that you need to know. Information includes many things, including what you believe to be facts, your point of view and the reasoning by which you came to that point of view, and your feelings.

Each of Us May See Things Others Do Not

You assume that just as you may know or see things that others do not, others may see things that you miss. You see conversations partly as puzzles in which each person brings different pieces; the task is to jointly figure out what pieces each person is bringing and how the pieces fit together. You recognize that whether you are working with another person, a group, or an organization, you are part of a system. The information and perspective you bring are limited; you can only see certain things from your vantage point in the system. You recognize that you may be contributing to the problem and not seeing it.

> You recognize that you may be contributing to the problem and not seeing it.

In the mutual learning approach, by starting with the assumption that you may be contributing to the problem and may be unaware of it, you are recognizing your own limits. This leads you to be curious and to ask about the ways in which others see you as contributing to the problem.

Another part of this assumption is that your feelings may be one of the ways you are contributing to the problem and not seeing it. In mutual learning, you consider the possibility that your feelings have resulted from your own conclusions based on untested inferences, assumptions, and attributions. You recognize that to the extent you act on these feelings, you are contributing to the problem. Using the mutual learning model does not preclude your feeling angry or disappointed; rather, it asks you to reflect on the thinking you used that generated these feelings.

Differences Are Opportunities for Learning

You are curious about others' perspectives because you consider differences in points of view as opportunities for learning. By exploring how people see things differently, you can help the group create a common understanding that enables them to move forward in a way that everyone can support. You are eager to explore differences because you see them as possibilities for developing greater understanding and creating solutions that integrate multiple perspectives.

People Are Trying to Act with Integrity Given Their Situations

You begin with the assumption that people's motives are pure rather than that they are suspect. If people are acting in ways that do not make sense to you or that you think you understand but disapprove of, you do not assume that they are acting that way because of a dubious motive. Instead, you begin with the assumption that people are striving to act with integrity; part of your task becomes understanding the reasons for their actions rather than assuming you know, and evaluating them accordingly.

Key Principles

Several key principles are associated with the mutual learning core values and assumptions. One principle is ***curiosity,*** the desire to learn more about something. Being curious enables you to find out whether the data you and others have are valid. It motivates you to find out what information others have that you might be missing. When others see things differently, it helps you explore how they came to a different conclusion rather than simply trying to persuade others their conclusions are wrong. When others do things that don't make sense to you, curiosity leads you to learn about how it makes sense to them. Combined with compassion, curiosity enables you to learn about yourself and others without generating defensiveness.

Another principle is ***transparency,*** the quality of sharing all relevant information, including your strategies, in a way that is timely and valid. Being transparent means sharing your reasoning and intent underlying your statements, questions, and actions. It includes sharing with others your strategy for how you want to have the conversation with them, so together you can jointly design the strategy and make a free and informed choice about how they want to work with you.

Combined with compassion, curiosity enables you to learn about yourself and others without generating defensiveness.

It is difficult to be transparent when you are acting unilaterally; to do so, you would have to tell others that you were trying to unilaterally control the conversation, and that would undermine your strategy. But being transparent when using a mutual learning approach actually increases the effectiveness of your strategy because your strategy is to learn jointly rather than control the situation.

It is difficult to be transparent when you are acting unilaterally; to do so, you would have to tell others that you were trying to unilaterally control the conversation, and that would undermine your strategy. But being transparent when using a mutual learning approach actually increases the effectiveness of your strategy because your strategy is to learn jointly rather than control the situation.

Transparency is the other half of curiosity. Curiosity leads you to ask questions so you can learn; transparency leads you to share information so others can learn.

A third principle is ***joint accountability,*** which means that you share responsibility for the current situation, including the consequences it creates. Rather than seek to blame others, you recognize that because you are part of a system, your actions contribute to either maintaining the system or changing it.

Rather than seek to blame others, you recognize that because you are part of a system, your actions contribute to either maintaining the system or changing it.

Being accountable means you are responsible for addressing your problems with others directly with them rather than avoiding them or asking others to intercede for you. It means offering feedback directly to others—even those who have more power and authority—so they can ask about your thinking and can make an informed choice about whether to change their behavior. And it means seeking the same kind of feedback so you can become more effective. This accountability is a joint accountability recognizing that you are interdependent with others in the system.[2]

These three principles are interwoven with the core values and assumptions of the mutual learning model. Together they are put into action in the strategies that follow.

Strategies

You use the combination of the core values and assumptions to develop strategies for dealing with a conversation. These are strategies that you use whether or not others use them. The strategies for mutual learning are the ground rules for effective groups of the Skilled Facilitator approach (Figure 4.2).

See Chapter 5, "Ground Rules for Effective Groups," page 61, for a basic introduction. The use of the ground rules in various settings is explored in Chapter Fourteen, "Introducing the Ground Rules and Principles in Your Own Words," page 131; Chapter Twenty-One, "Ways to Practice the Ground Rules," page 189; and Chapter Twenty-Six, "Ground Rules Without the Mutual Learning Model Are Like Houses Without Foundations," page 217.

Consequences

All of the mutual learning strategies are designed to create valid information, free and informed choice, and internal commitment, and to do so with compassion. Together, the mutual learning core values and assumptions and the strategies create results that are very different from unilateral control.

Increased Understanding, Reduced Unproductive Conflict, and Defensiveness

With the mutual learning approach, you increase understanding because you test assumptions and create valid information. You also assume that others have information you do not have and that they may see things you are missing. By assuming that people are striving to act with integrity, you reduce the negative attributions you make about others. When you do make attributions, you test with the people about whom you are making them. In this way, you reduce the unproductive conflicts that arise from acting on untested inaccurate assumptions, and you reduce the defensive behavior associated with it. Similarly, you increase trust. Using a mutual learning approach does not ensure that others will respond nondefensively; however, it does reduce the chance that you will create or contribute to others' defensive reactions.

Reduced Self-Fulfilling, Self-Sealing Processes

Acting on untested, inaccurate assumptions is the first step in self-fulfilling and self-sealing processes. By testing out your assumptions, you reduce the likelihood of self-fulfilling and self-sealing processes. Even if you do create a self-fulfilling process, your openness to learning how you created the problem will reduce the chance that it becomes self-sealing.

Increased Learning

All of this information enables you and others to create shared meaning that increases learning for you and the group. This includes learning how you and group members each contribute to the group's effectiveness and ineffectiveness.

Increased Effectiveness

Together these results increase the group's effectiveness: its performance, process, and meeting group members' personal needs.

Increased Quality of Worklife

The mutual learning values and assumptions enable you to increase understanding and trust and reduce defensive behavior. This reduces feelings of anxiety, fear, and anger that create stress.

(Continued on p. 58)

The Unilateral Control and Mutual Learning Models in Action

One way to begin to identify a person's theory-in-use is with a left-hand column case. In a left-hand column case, you write about a challenging conversation you had in which you wanted to be more effective. In the right column, you write the verbatim dialogue as best as you can remember it. In the left column, you write your thoughts and feelings during the conversation.

For more on this method, see Chapter Twenty-Seven, "Writing and Analyzing a Left-Hand Column Case," page 235.

By seeing what the case writer was thinking and saying, you can begin to infer the case writer's theory-in-use. By talking with the case writer about it, you can also test your inferences about the case writer's theory-in-use.

The data feedback case below is a left-hand column case that Barbara (a pseudonym) wrote to use during one of our public workshops. I have analyzed her case, placing my notes in italic type in brackets, indicating the ways in which Barbara's thoughts and feelings and what she says reflect elements of the unilateral control approach, with boldface type highlighting some of the core values, assumptions, and strategies at work here.

In the data feedback case revised that follows, I have rewritten the conversation to highlight some of the values, assumptions, and strategies in Barbara's left-hand column that are representative of the mutual learning model that guides the Skilled Facilitator approach.

The Data Feedback Case

The new chief information officer (CIO) of an organization had heard of long-standing management and performance problems in his office and had asked a consulting group to conduct interviews and focus groups to generate data on the issue. In the meeting described below, the consulting group was presenting its findings. One of the group's main findings was that employees were waiting to see if the new CIO's team would release the results of the interviews and focus groups. Because of conflict within the CIO's team, the consulting group expected that this would be a difficult conversation for the team.

Barbara, a member of the consulting group, facilitated the meeting of the CIO and his team. The consulting group saw their challenge as allowing the group to discuss whether to share the findings and, in Barbara's words, "without the discussion degenerating into out-and-out warfare, and to guide the group to what we saw as the right decisions without appearing to take sides ourselves."

Unilateral Control Model

Barbara's Thoughts and Feelings	The Conversations
Uh-oh, this wasn't supposed to happen until this afternoon. I never thought they'd bring it up themselves! There goes the whole agenda.	Mike: My God, we can't possibly let this stuff out of this room. It's dynamite. We'll look like idiots. I for one don't want to have anything to do with it!

Barbara's Thoughts and Feelings	The Conversations
*[**Achieve my goal through unilateral control**. Although Barbara believes the group needed to bring up this issue, she assumes that unless it occurs in the order she desired, the agenda will not be completed.]*	
Looks like it's going to get ugly real fast. This guy Joe just doesn't get it! *[**I understand the situation; others don't.** Barbara infers that Joe doesn't get it but doesn't share her reasoning and test it with Joe. Nor does she explore what Joe might know that she or others do not.]*	Joe: This just goes to show why we can never get the work done around here. The people are more interested in sitting on their butts and blaming their managers than in actually doing their jobs.
	Sandy: Well, wait a minute, these results are so striking I don't see how we can ignore them . . .
He's gonna be real trouble. If he doesn't have a stroke first, with those veins popping out . . . Time to do something so Sandy can get some support if there is any. Why isn't Frank saying something? *[**Save face.** Barbara believes that Joe's comments create trouble for Sandy and that Barbara needs to provide support for Sandy because she may not be able to do it herself.]*	Joe: We don't have to let them make our decisions for us though! [Continues with a lengthy diatribe about why people today don't have the same values and work ethic they used to.]
	Barbara: Okay, let's do a process check here. I think this an important conversation for you all to have, but it might take some time. You can do it now or wait until we work on the action plan this afternoon. What's the sense of the group? *[Barbara does not check with the group whether they think it's an important conversation to have, but only when to have it.]*

Barbara's Thoughts and Feelings	The Conversations
	Susan: Let's get it out there now! [Some expressions of agreement around the table.]
Finally! Why'd he wait until now to speak up? Some leadership style! *[Barbara attributes to Frank that his leadership style is ineffective but does not test her attribution about why he waited to speak.]*	Frank: I think we need to take the time to do this now. It's pretty important.
This ought to flush everyone out up front so I know what we're dealing with here. I need to get this thing back under control. *[**Achieve my goal through unilateral control.** Barbara thinks of her strategy as being in the service of her continuing to control the conversation.]*	Barbara: Okay. Here's what I propose: let's go around the table and ask everyone for their views before we get into the discussion. [Barbara **keeps private her reasoning** for getting out everyone's views.]
I wonder if I should have set a time limit for each person. This is turning into a debate and no one is really listening to each other. *[Barbara infers that people are not listening to each other but does not test this out with team members.]*	[The group does that, but it takes a lot longer than expected, and some people, on both sides, hog the floor.]
This ought to get some structure into the conversation and maybe tone down some of the emotional content. *[**Minimize expressing negative feelings.** Barbara considers team members' expression of negative feelings as unproductive.]*	Barbara: Now that we have a sense of where you are as a group on this issue, and you're about one-third for release and two-thirds against, it's a good time to step back and look together at pros and cons. I'll divide a flip chart into two columns, and you can brainstorm on that. Here goes. . . .
No one is listening to anyone else; they're just hardening their positions. The clock is ticking and the group really hasn't started its work yet. I wonder how much	[The group charts the pros and cons, and although the discussion becomes more orderly, it is no less heated and no closer to a conclusion.]

Barbara's Thoughts and Feelings	The Conversations
longer I should let them go. But if they can't even deal with this issue, how are they going to do any of the hard work down the road? *[Barbara's suggestion for listing pros and cons unknowingly causes team members to harden their positions rather than focusing on interests.]*	*[Barbara advocates a process without checking to see whether team members have any concerns with it.]*
Oh no, now they're going to move in for the kill against her. I don't want to break my neutral stance, but she's going to need some help here soon. *[Barbara assumes she needs to unilaterally protect Sandy. In doing so, she also realizes that she will be leaving her substantively neutral facilitator role.]*	Sandy [near tears]: I just can't believe we're even having this discussion! Who are we kidding? The employees already know what they think. Who would we be hiding it from? If this group can't face up to the truth, what right do we have to be in our jobs? [eye-rolling from Joe] Frank, don't you agree?
This guy is absolutely hopeless! *[**I am right; those who disagree are wrong.** Barbara makes a high-level inference about Frank.]*	Frank: Well, I think you have a real point there, but . . .
Well, I guess this is my opening. Should I tell them what I really think? I might lose them all if I do.	Mike: I'd like to hear from the consultants what they think. After all, they work with a lot of other organizations. What do other people do about things like this?
	Barbara: Thanks, Mike. I have to say that you all are not the first to face this issue, and it's always tough. But Sandy is on to something: your people know what they think, but they don't think you do. They want to know that they've been heard, and because there's so little trust here, they want more than just your assurances on that. By responding to their request to release the results, you'd be sending them

Barbara's Thoughts and Feelings	The Conversations
	a big signal that you really mean business about changing the culture. They're handing you a big opportunity. And in our experience with other groups, you need to make a clear gesture up front to get people's attention if you want to move ahead with change.
	[Barbara leaves her substantively neutral facilitator role and enters the facilitative consultant role without asking whether this is acceptable to the rest of the group. She ***advocates her position*** *without asking for others' reactions to what she said.]*
Oh, that's great. He obviously thinks I'm an idiot and doesn't want to release the stuff. *[Barbara makes an* ***untested inference*** *about how Frank has reacted to her point of view.]*	Frank: How about a break now? I'd like us to mull this question over and revisit it this afternoon.

There are several key aspects to Barbara's thinking and behavior. First, Barbara defines her role as a substantively neutral facilitator, but acts inconsistently with the role when she seeks to guide the group to the right substantive decisions without appearing to take sides. This requires that she keep her reasoning and strategy private so that the group does not learn that she is guiding them to what she considers the right decision. Second, Barbara views Mike and Joe as "not getting it" and being wrong. This leads her to make negative inferences about Mike and Joe's views when they differed from Barbara's. This makes it difficult for Barbara to be curious about their views and ask about them, which could lead the group and Barbara to learn some new information.

Barbara also believes that she needs to protect Sandy from others in the group, perhaps because Sandy shares Barbara's view and Barbara does not believe that Sandy can persuade others to accept her point of view. This compromises her role as a neutral facilitator. Finally, when asked by Mike to provide the consultants' view, Barbara responds without giving the full group a free and informed choice about whether she should enter the content of the conversation.

The Feedback Case Revised: The Mutual Learning Model

The feedback case revised illustrates how Barbara's left-hand column case might have looked if her theory-in-use had been the mutual learning model. This changes not only the conversation but what Barbara is thinking and feeling during it. I have placed my notes in italic type in brackets, indicating the ways in which Barbara's thoughts and feelings and what she says reflect elements of the mutual learning approach. As before, boldface type signals some of the mutual learning values, assumptions, and strategies at work here.

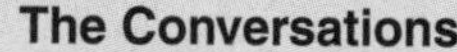

Barbara's Thoughts and Feelings	The Conversations
Uh oh, I didn't expect this to happen until this afternoon. I never thought they'd bring it up themselves! This will change the agenda. I need to see if they want to discuss this now or later when it's scheduled. *[Barbara assumes that it is ultimately the group's* ***free and informed choice,*** *with her process input—* ***valid information****—to decide when to discuss the topic.]* Mike is taking a position on this and assuming that they'll look like idiots if they release the data. *[Barbara identifies the elements of Mike's behavior that makes the conversation less effective.]* I wonder what his underlying concerns and interests are. I wonder how he thinks it will blow up if they share it. ***[I have some information; others have other information.*** *Barbara remains curious about Mike's reasoning, suspending judgment about it.]*	Mike: My God, we can't possibly let this stuff out of this room. It's dynamite. We'll look like idiots. I for one don't want to have anything to do with it!
Joe's also taking a position. He's also attributing some negative motives to employees. Does he think the data aren't valid? This conversation is not going to get any more productive if Joe and	Joe: This just goes to show why we can never get the work done around here. The people are more interested in sitting on their butts and blaming their managers than in actually doing their jobs.

Barbara's Thoughts and Feelings	**The Conversations**
Mike are hunkered down in their positions and making untested assumptions. *[Barbara identifies the elements of Joe's behavior that make the conversation less effective. She remains curious about Joe's reasoning, suspending judgment about it.]*	
Should I intervene now or first see what Sandy and Frank think? Good—Sandy's speaking.	Sandy: Well, wait a minute. These results are so striking I don't see how we can ignore them.
Joe's started to interrupt her midsentence, and she's just pulled back from the table. If she wasn't finished, she doesn't look as if she's going to finish talking. I want to get out her views, whatever they are; otherwise the conversation is going to be even less productive.	Joe: We don't have to let them make our decisions for us though!
	Barbara: Sandy, it looked as if you weren't finished talking when Joe started to talk, yes?
	Sandy: Yeah, he just cut me off.
	Barbara: Joe, would you be willing to let Sandy finish?
	Joe: Go ahead.
Sandy has also taken a position. She sees it differently from Joe and Mike. She's asking some questions, but they sound rhetorical. *[Barbara identifies Sandy's behavior that contributes to making the conversation less productive.]*	Sandy: The employees already know what they think. Who would we be hiding it from? We have to share the results. If this group can't face up to the truth, what right do we have to be in our jobs?
Let me see if the group is ready to have this conversation now. If they do, I'm going to suggest they focus on interests and identify their underlying assumptions so they can explore each other's reasoning.	Barbara: Okay, let's do a process check here. I think the conversation you're having about whether to share the data is an important one. Before you go further, I want to see if everyone is ready to have this conversation now. I think it's

Barbara's Thoughts and Feelings	The Conversations
[Barbara plans to give the group a ***free and informed choice*** *about how to proceed and will also advocate a process, which is part of her facilitator role.]*	important that everyone be clear on what the feedback data say so you can have a more informed conversation about whether to share the data. Anyone see that differently? *[Barbara checks for different views.]* [People nod in agreement.] Okay, so are there any questions about the results? [People say no.] Then what does each of you think: Do you want to continue the conversation now? *[Barbara gives the group a free and informed choice about how to proceed.]* Susan: Let's get it out there now! [Some expressions of agreement around the table.]
Okay, everyone wants to talk about it. Now I can suggest the process.	Frank: I think we need to take the time to do this now. It's pretty important.
I think Mike has assumed that they won't look like idiots if they withhold the information. But I think it's premature to ask him about this. It's more relevant to discuss when they are exploring their interests. *[Barbara identifies an assumption that she thinks Mike has made but decides not to test it out at this point.]*	Barbara: Okay. Right now those of you who have spoken on the issue—Joe, Mike, and Sandy—have taken a position to either not share the data with employees or share the data. Am I off? [People agree she is correct.] Right now I think you're about to get stuck because you are starting to go back and forth arguing your position—either sharing or withholding the data. But your positions may be in conflict even when your underlying interests or needs are compatible. So by exploring your interests, together you have a better chance of crafting a solution that meets all the interests. *[Barbara* ***explains her reasoning*** *for advocating a different process.]*

Barbara's Thoughts and Feelings	The Conversations
	Given that, let me propose a different process and get your reactions. I suggest that as a group, you develop a list of interests or needs underlying your positions. In other words, each of you identifies the needs you are trying to address in dealing with the data. For example, Mike, when you said earlier that you thought by sharing the information, you would look like idiots, it sounded as if one of your interests is that whether you end up sharing the data or not, you want to do it in a way that the team looks competent rather than incompetent. Did I get your interest correct?
	Mike: Absolutely, I don't want us to look like fools.
	Barbara: So we would list all of your interests on the board. Then you would clarify what each of your interests meant so everyone understands them the same way. You'll get a chance to ask each other why your interests are important. Next, I'll ask each of you if there are any interests on the list that you think should not be considered in coming up with a solution. Assuming everyone considers all of the interests legitimate, I'll ask you to brainstorm some ways to meet all the interests. What questions do you have about what I'm proposing?
Good question, even if it's rhetorical.	Joe: Why don't we just list the pros and cons?
	Barbara: In my experience, listing pros and cons encourages people to come up with as many reasons as possible to support their initial positions. Each side tries to build the longest list, and both sides try to convince the others they are

Barbara's Thoughts and Feelings	The Conversations
I wonder what Joe thinks of this *[Barbara assumes that* ***differences are opportunities for learning****.]*	wrong. I'm asking you to do something different. By focusing on your interests, I'm asking you to temporarily suspend focusing on whether to share the data and instead identify what needs you are trying to meet in the data feedback process. Then you can figure out how to meet those needs whether or not you share the data. What's your reaction, Joe? *[Barbara* ***combines advocacy and inquiry*** *by advocating for a process, explaining her reasoning, and then asking Joe for his reactions.]*
So, they've been in this situation before.	Joe: Sounds like you've seen some of our other meetings. I'm willing to try it, but I'm not sure how we'll close the gap between us.
	Barbara: I agree, Joe. I think it's too early to know how you'll close the gap. By identifying all of your interests, we can find out what's causing the gap. Then you will have a better idea of whether and how you can close it.
I want to make sure I address any questions before I ask for their commitment. *[****Internal commitment.*** *Barbara assumes that people need to make an informed choice in order to be committed to the process she's suggesting.]*	Barbara: Any other questions or concerns? [Everyone shakes their heads no.] Let me check with each of you to see if you are willing to use this process: Joe, Sandy, Mike, Frank, Susan? [Each nods agreement.]
Well, this raises questions about my role. I was supposed to be the neutral facilitator in this meeting. If I answer his question, I'm leaving my role. But Mike's question is a fair one, and it deserves an answer. Let me lay out the options and my concerns and see what they want to do.	Mike: I'd like to hear from the consultants about what they think we should do. After all, they work with a lot of other organizations. What do other people do about things like this?

Barbara's Thoughts and Feelings	The Conversations
*[Barbara assumes that **sharing all relevant information** will enable the group to make a better decision.]*	
	Barbara: Your question's a fair one and deserves an answer. Before the consultants answer it, let me describe our situation and then as a group we can figure out how to answer your question. *[Barbara identifies that they will **jointly design the decision**.]* The group and I agreed that I would be a neutral facilitator in this meeting today, which means I wouldn't get into the content of your discussion. If I answer your question, I think I'm getting into the content. Does anyone see that differently? *[**Each of us may see things that others do not.** Barbara describes the situation as she sees it and checks for differing views.]*
I agree.	Mike: It is content, but it's also what we hired your consulting group to help us with.
	Barbara: I agree. So I have two options. Fred and Elise can answer your questions, and I can still serve as the substantively neutral facilitator. Or I can step out of my facilitator role and become a facilitative consultant, sharing my views on the issue while still facilitating. I'm okay moving to a facilitative consultant role as long as the group recognizes that I'll be involved in the content of the conversation at the same time I'm facilitating your conversation. *[Barbara **shares relevant information** so the group can make an **informed choice**.]*

Barbara's Thoughts and Feelings	The Conversations
	The other point I want to make is that the core values and ground rules you have been using today provide some guidance to answering the questions whether and/or how to share the feedback data. Again, if the group is interested, I'm happy to explain how you could use the core values to guide your decisions.
	So, given this, would you rather I continue to serve as a neutral facilitator or move to the facilitative consultant role?

There are several key differences in the way Barbara thinks and acts in this left-hand column case and her original case. In this case, Barbara sees herself as helping the group generate valid information so that they can make a free and informed choice they will be committed to rather than implicitly steering the group to a decision she thinks is correct. Second, she is curious about the reasoning underlying Mike's and Joe's comments. This curiosity and a sense of compassion enable her to suspend judgment about their views rather than assume that she is right and they are wrong. With the mutual learning model as her theory-in-use, Barbara is able to more fully share her views about the process, explain her reasoning, and genuinely inquire about the team members' concerns. If we were able to play out her left-hand case to its conclusion, we would see some of the expected consequences of Barbara and the group operating with the mutual learning model as their theory-in-use: increased understanding and trust, reduced unproductive conflict and defensiveness, and increased learning and effectiveness.

Results Reinforce the Model

The mutual learning consequences you create feed back to the mutual learning core values and assumptions, reinforcing the approach. For example, when you are in a difficult conversation and temporarily withhold judgment to test inferences and inquire into others' reasoning, you are able to learn more about yourself and others while minimizing defensive behavior, and you are more likely to continue using the approach.

A key point for anyone trying to use the Skilled Facilitator approach is this: simply changing what you say and how you say it (using the ground rules, for instance) is not sufficient to significantly change the unintended consequences you get. If you try only to learn new mutual learning phrases, your theory-in-use values and assumptions will sometimes override them, and your conversation will take a unilateral control form. When I hear my clients wondering why the ground rules have stopped working for them, we often discover that they were using them in a unilaterally controlling way.

One of the kinds of learning that the Skilled Facilitator approach requires is learning to reflect rigorously on and redesign your core values and assumptions in order to think differently and use the new strategies and tools effectively. To engage in this level of learning, you need to explore the question, "What is it about the values and assumptions that I hold that leads me to design the kinds of strategies that create unintended consequences for me and others?" This is the difficult but rewarding work of facilitation.

Resources

Block, P. *Stewardship: Choosing Service over Self-Interest.* San Francisco: Berrett-Koehler, 1993.

Argyris, C., and Schön, D. *Theory in Practice: Increasing Professional Effectiveness.* San Francisco: Jossey-Bass, 1974.

Argyris, C., and Schön, D. *Organizational Learning II: Theory, Method, and Practice.* Reading, Mass.: Addison-Wesley, 1996.

Notes

1. Argyris and Schön have written extensively and compellingly about how our theory-in-use creates many unintended negative consequences and how groups and organizations can create a powerful alternative (1974, 1996). Their seminal research, writing, and practice is reflected in management writings about mental models. Schön died in 1997.
2. For a compelling view of joint accountability, read *Stewardship* (1993) by Peter Block.

References

Action Design. Workshop Materials. Newton, Mass.: Action Design, 1997.

Argyris, C., Putnam, R., and McLain Smith, D. *Action Science.* San Francisco: Jossey-Bass, 1985.

Argyris, C., and Schön, D. *Theory in Practice: Increasing Professional Effectiveness.* San Francisco: Jossey-Bass, 1974.

Argyris, C., and Schön, D. *Organizational Learning II: Theory, Method, and Practice.* Reading, Mass.: Addison-Wesley, 1996.

Craik, K. *The Nature of Explanation.* Cambridge: Cambridge University Press, 1943.

Johnson-Laird, P. N. "Mental Models." In M. I. Posner (ed.) *Foundations of Cognitive Science.* Cambridge, Mass.: MIT Press, 1989.

Kleiner, A. "Mental Models." In P. M. Senge and others, *The Fifth Discipline Fieldbook.* New York: Currency, 1994.

Senge, P. M. *The Fifth Discipline: The Art and Practice of the Learning Organization.* New York: Doubleday, 1990.

Chapter 5

Ground Rules for Effective Groups

Roger Schwarz

WHAT ARE THE SPECIFIC kinds of behavior that contribute to or hinder a group's effectiveness? Experienced facilitators may intuitively know some of the answers to this question. The Skilled Facilitator approach makes them explicit by describing these behaviors in a set of nine ground rules for effective groups.

DEFINITIONS AND APPLICATIONS

The nine ground rules of the Skilled Facilitator approach are not the same as the procedural ground rules that many groups and facilitators use ("start on time, end on time"; "turn off your cell phones and pagers"). They are also different from the desired behaviors that some groups and facilitators may express at a relatively abstract level ("treat everyone with respect," "be constructive"). The ground rules for effective groups describe specific behaviors that improve group process. In fact, they are the strategies for bringing to life the core values and assumptions of the mutual learning model.

The ground rules can be used in several ways:

- *For diagnosis.* They enable you to quickly identify ineffective group behavior so that you can intervene on it.
- *As a teaching tool.* They serve as a teaching tool for developing effective group norms. When groups commit to using the ground rules, they set new expectations for how members will interact with one another.
- *To guide your behavior.* They are used to guide your work and increase your own effectiveness in whatever role you serve. Also, by modeling the ground rules in your facilitative roles, you demonstrate how others can do the same.

This chapter is an adaptation of *The Skilled Facilitator,* pp. 9, 96–135. In general, the ground rules are derived from Argyris (1982) and Argyris and Schön (1974). Ground Rule Five is from Fisher, Ury, and Patton (1991), which was based on the work of Mary Parker Follett in the early twentieth century (Graham, 1995). See Chapter Five, p. 96, and Resource A, p. 345, in *The Skilled Facilitator* for more depth and an illustration of the evolution of the ground rules.

Keep in mind that the ground rules for effective groups are not a group's ground rules until they commit to using them in this way.

Keep in mind that the ground rules for effective groups are not a group's ground rules until they commit to using them in this way.

Chapter Four, "Understanding What Guides Your Behavior," page 33, discusses how the ground rules link to the core values, assumptions, and strategies of the mutual learning model. To explore the introduction and use of the ground rules in more depth in various settings, see also Chapter Fourteen, "Introducing the Ground Rules and Principles in Your Own Words," page 131; Chapter Twenty, "Using the Ground Rules in E-Mail," page 181; Chapter Twenty-One, "Ways to Practice the Ground Rules," page 189; Chapter Twenty-Four, "Reducing the Skilled Facilitator Jargon," page 207; Chapter Twenty-Six, "Ground Rules Without the Mutual Learning Model Are Like Houses Without Foundations," page 217; and Chapter Forty-Five, "Introducing the Core Values and Ground Rules," page 361.

Ground Rule One: Test Assumptions and Inferences

When you *assume* something, you take for granted that it is true without verifying it. When you *infer* something, you draw a conclusion about what you do not know on the basis of things you do know. When you *attribute* something, you make an inference about someone's motives.

When you *assume* something, you take for granted that it is true without verifying it. When you *infer* something, you draw a conclusion about what you do not know on the basis of things you do know. When you *attribute* something, you make an inference about someone's motives. Assumption, inference, or attribution, the effect is the same: an untested supposition.

How we make inferences is described in "The Ladder of Inference" sidebar in this chapter, page 63.

The problem is not that we make assumptions and inferences; we must do that to make sense out of what people are saying. The problem is that if we are unaware of the inferences we are making, our only choice is to consider them as facts rather than as hypotheses and to act on them as if they are true.

When you test assumptions and inferences, you ask others whether the meaning you are making of their behavior or of the situation is the meaning they make of it.

Ground Rule One links to two Skilled Facilitator core values directly: it generates ***valid information*** that you and others can use to make ***free and informed choices.***

Testing an assumption or inference: **"A few minutes ago I think you said, 'The plans are incomplete.' Did I get that right?"** [If the person says yes, continue.] **"It sounded to me as if you thought we can't meet the original deadline. Is that what you're thinking?"**

See Chapter Six, "The Diagnosis-Intervention Cycle," page 69, for guidance on when and how to test assumptions and inferences in a group.

Ground Rule Two: Share All Relevant Information

This rule means that each group member shares all the relevant information she or he has that affects how the group solves a problem or makes a decision. *Relevant information* includes not only data that bear directly on the problem, decision, or other content the group is working on; it also includes information that does not support one's preferred position and information about group members' feelings about one another and the work they are doing.

The Ladder of Inference

How you make inferences is illustrated in the ladder of inference in Figure 5.1. You begin at the bottom of the ladder with directly observable data. In a conversation, you are faced with a lot of directly observable data, including what people are saying and their nonverbal behavior. I think of directly observable data as whatever a video camcorder can record.

You cannot attend to everything, so at the first rung of the ladder of inference, you observe and select certain data to pay attention to while ignoring other data. Some of what you choose to pay attention to is selected consciously, but much of it happens out of your awareness. In the case of Hank (see the figure), he pays attention to the part of Jim's comment that says, "But the analyses have been slowing your group down. I'm going to give Donna's group the weekly sales figures to analyze." He ignores entirely Jim's comment that "your group's been working really hard and doing good work."

At the second rung, you begin to infer meaning from the data by translating into your own words and labeling. Essentially, you say to yourself, *What does it really mean when this person says or does this?* Hank thinks to himself, *Jim is saying that I haven't managed the job well and that we're not going to be responsible for the sales analysis anymore. He is taking away part of my job.*

Figure 5.1 The Ladder of Inference

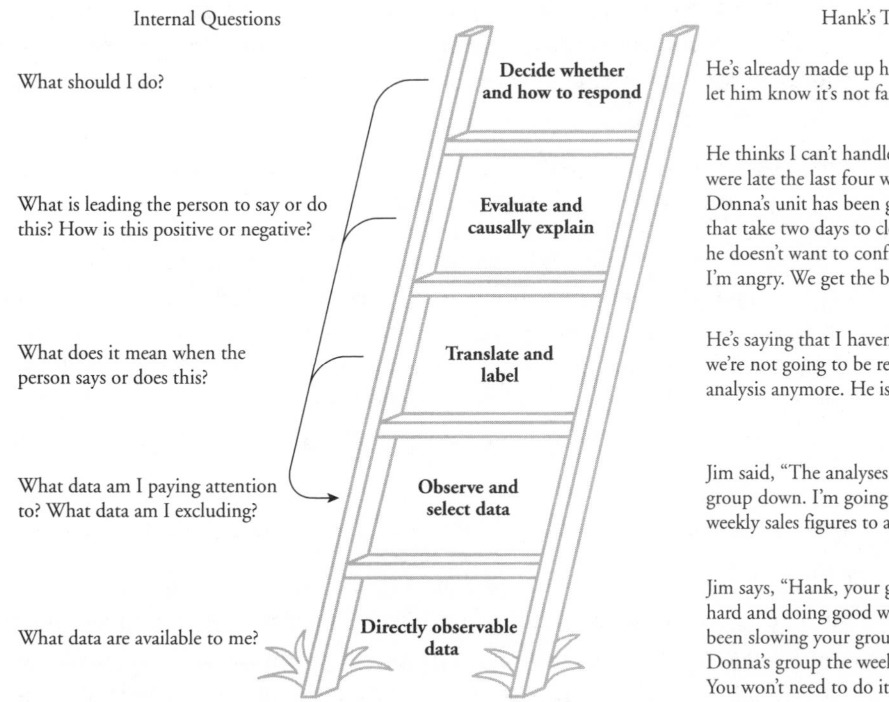

Sources: Argyris (1985); Action Design (1997).

Notice that in translating and labeling Jim's comment, Hank infers that Jim thinks he has not done the work well and also that the change is permanent.

At the third rung, you evaluate and explain what you have translated and labeled at the second rung. Whereas on the second rung, you describe what is occurring, on this rung you judge it and create a causal explanation. You ask yourself, *In what way is this positive or negative?* You also ask yourself, *What is leading the person to say or do this?* Hank thinks, *He thinks I can't handle the sales analyses because we were late the last four weeks. It's not my fault that Donna's unit has been giving us data sets full of errors that take two days to clean up. Jim is doing this because he doesn't want to confront Donna with the problem. I'm angry. We get the blame for her group's mistakes.*

Notice that the causal explanation that Hank creates includes an attribution about Jim (that he is doing this because he doesn't want to confront Donna with the problem)—that is, an inference about what is motivating Jim to do this.

At the top of the ladder, you decide whether and how to respond. Hank decides, *He's already made up his mind, but I still need to let him know it's not fair.* Like Hank, we go up the ladder of inference in milliseconds, without even being aware that we are doing so.

You turn the inferences you make into facts that influence what you observe, and this becomes the basis for further inference. This is illustrated in the loop that starts at the top of the ladder and returns to lower rungs.

Using a specific example: **"Amy and Rollie, an example of your not taking initiative on the project is when you didn't schedule the team meeting until this week after I reminded you that you said you would schedule it last week."**

Using words to mean the same thing: **"George, when you say you propose to finish your report by the end of the year, I'm taking that to mean by December 15 so people will see it before we close for the holidays. Is that what you were thinking, or did you mean something different?"**

This rule implements the core values by sharing information in a way that can be validated, which ensures that members have a common basis for making an ***informed choice*** and ***generating commitment.*** Ground Rules Three, Four, Five, and Eight identify specific ways of sharing all relevant information.

Ground Rule Three: Use Specific Examples and Agree on What Important Words Mean

Ground Rule Three encourages a particular way of sharing relevant information that generates ***valid data.*** Using specific examples means sharing detailed relevant information, including who said what and when and where it happened. Unlike general statements, specific examples enable others to determine independently whether the information in them is valid. By agreeing on what important words mean, you make sure that you are using words to mean the same thing that others mean.

Ground Rule Four: Explain Your Reasoning and Intent

Ground Rule Four means explaining to others what leads you to make a comment, ask a question, or take an action. Your *intent* is your purpose for doing something. Your *reasoning* represents the logical process that you use to draw conclusions on the basis of data, values, and assumptions. Ground Rule Four includes making your private reasoning public, so that others can see how you reached your conclusion and ask you about places where they might reason differently. A key part of explaining your reasoning is to make transparent the strategy you are using to hold the conversation. Explaining your reasoning and making your strategy transparent are opportunities to learn where others have differing views or approaches and where you may have missed something that others see.

Explaining your reasoning and intent: **"I'm thinking that starting the project next month makes more sense because we will have everyone back from vacation and will have finished the current project."**

For a discussion of transparency, see the core assumptions of the mutual learning model in Chapter Four, "Understanding What Guides Your Behavior," page 33.

Ground Rule Five: Focus on Interests, Not Positions

Focusing on interests is another way of sharing relevant information (see Ground Rule Two). *Interests* are the needs, desires, and concerns that people have in regard to a given situation (Fisher, Ury, and Patton, 1991; Graham, 1995). *Positions* or solutions are how people meet their interests. In other words, people's interests lead them to advocate a particular solution or position. An effective way for groups to solve problems is to begin by sharing their individual interests. Once they agree to a set of interests for the group, which may or may not include all the individual interests identified, they can begin to generate solutions or positions that take that set of interests into account.

Focusing on interests, not positions: **"However we decide to announce the layoffs, I want to do it in a way that enables people to plan for the transition and still maintain productivity."**

Ground Rule Six: Combine Advocacy and Inquiry

When you combine advocacy with inquiry, you (1) explain your point of view including the interests and reasoning you used to get there, (2) ask others about their point of view, and/or (3) invite others to ask you questions about your point of view (Argyris and Schön, 1974).

Combining advocacy and inquiry accomplishes several goals. First, it can shift a series of monologues into a focused conversation. For example, in some meetings, one person speaks after the other but no one's comments seem to directly address the previous person's. Without an explicit invitation to inquire about or comment on the previous person's remarks, the meeting switches focus with each person who speaks. The second goal that Ground Rule Six accomplishes is to create conditions for learning. By identifying where people's reasoning differs, you can help a group explore what has led them to reason differently: Are they using other data, making other assumptions, or assigning different priorities to certain issues?

Combining advocacy and inquiry: **"I think it would help to give division heads their own budgets so that their accountability will be commensurate with their responsibility. Here's the reasoning that led me to suggest this."** [Explains reasoning.] **"I'd like to hear what each of you thinks about this idea. What are your thoughts? What, if anything, do you see differently?"**

Ground Rule Seven: Jointly Design Next Steps and Ways to Test Disagreements

Ground Rule Seven means deciding with others what topics to discuss, when to discuss them, how to discuss them, and when to switch topics rather than making such decisions privately and unilaterally. In general, jointly designing next steps means

Jointly designing next steps and ways to test disagreements: **"You and I disagree about whether the current product is being produced within specifications. How can we figure out together what the situation is?"**

(1) advocating your point of view about how you want to proceed, including your interests, relevant information, reasoning, and intent; (2) inquiring about how others may see it differently; and (3) jointly crafting a way to proceed that takes into account group members' interests, relevant information, reasoning, and intent. Jointly designing ways to test disagreements is one specific type of next step.

Chapter Thirteen, "Beginning Meetings," page 125 describes how to jointly design the beginning of a conversation.

Jointly designing ways to test disagreements means considering such important questions as, "How might it be that we are both correct?" and "How could we each be seeing different parts of the same problem?" A useful analogy for testing disagreements this way is two scientists who must design a joint experiment to test their competing hypotheses; the research design needs to be rigorous enough to meet the standards of both.

Ground Rule Eight: Discuss Undiscussable Issues

You begin to raise an undiscussable issue when you say something like: **"This may be a difficult issue, but I want to talk about how I think we, as your direct reports, withhold information from you because of how you react when we share bad news. I'm raising this not because I want to put anyone on the spot, but because I want us to make the best strategic decisions possible. I'd like to share what I've seen that leads me to say this and test out whether others see it the same or differently."**

An *undiscussable issue* is one that is relevant to the group, that is reducing or may reduce the group's effectiveness, and that people believe they cannot discuss without creating defensiveness or other negative consequences. By using this ground rule together with the previous ground rules, you can discuss these issues fruitfully and reduce the level of defensiveness.

Groups often choose not to discuss undiscussables, reasoning that raising them might make someone embarrassed or defensive and that avoiding them will save face for the group's members (and themselves). In other words, they see discussing undiscussable issues as not being compassionate. Yet people often overlook the negative systemic—and uncompassionate—consequences they create by not raising an undiscussable issue. Examples of undiscussables are members who are not performing adequately, or are not trusting one another, or are reluctant to disagree with their manager who is also a member of the group.

Although Ground Rule Eight is emotionally difficult to use, the process for discussing undiscussables is contained in all the previous ground rules.

See Chapter Twenty-Nine, "Exploring Your Contributions to Problems," page 255.

Ground Rule Nine: Use a Decision-Making Rule That Generates the Level of Commitment Needed

Ground Rule Nine makes specific the core value of *internal commitment.* Its premise is that group members' commitment to a decision is in part a function of the degree to which they make an informed free choice to support it. The more they are able to make an informed free choice, the more likely they are to be internally committed to the decision.

Practicing Ground Rule Nine means understanding that there are different types of group decision-making processes that generate different degrees of acceptance of a decision. The Skilled Facilitator approach recognizes four such types: *delegative, consensus, democratic,* and *consultative.*[1] The degrees of acceptance of a decision range from *resistance,* to *noncompliance,* to *compliance,* to *enrollment,* to *internal commitment.*[2] *Internal commitment* means that each member of the group believes in the decision, sees it as his or her own, and will do whatever is necessary to implement it effectively.

Ground Rule Nine does not state that all decisions should or need to be made by consensus, however. It recognizes that some decisions do not require the internal commitment generated through the consensus process.

When implementation of a decision requires the support and cooperation of the group members and there are differing perspectives within the group, the decision-making process needs to help members (including the leader) explore their differences and create a shared understanding. Consensus decision making accomplishes this by ensuring that a decision is not reached until each group member can commit to the decision as his or her own. Ground Rule Nine does not state that all decisions should or need to be made by consensus, however. It recognizes that some decisions do not require the internal commitment generated through the consensus process.

LEARNING TO USE THE GROUND RULES

The ground rules are like dance steps: each is part of the foundation of the Skilled Facilitator approach, but their power usually results from combining the steps to create movement with a purpose. Also, the ground rules are necessary but not sufficient for effective group process; they can create effective group behavior in the moment, but a group also needs larger processes to impart direction—for example, problem-solving and systems thinking models for understanding complex systems.

It is natural to feel unnatural when beginning to use the ground rules—for example, when trying to translate your left-hand column into sentences that use the grammatical structure of the ground rules, trying to integrate them with your own natural speech pattern and word choice, and trying to put it all together so you can talk at the speed of normal conversation. With regular practice, you will probably find that you can use the ground rules in a way that sounds like you and doesn't require you to talk at an unnaturally slow pace to find the words you are looking for.

For learning how to use the ground rules, see Chapter Twenty-One, "Ways to Practice the Ground Rules," page 189, and Chapter Twenty-Two, "Some Tips for Diagnosing at the Speed of Conversation," page 195. For different examples of using the ground rules, see Chapter Twenty-Three, "Opening Lines," page 201, and the ground rules example in Chapter Twenty-Four, "Reducing the Skilled Facilitator Jargon," page 207.

Notes

1. The four types of decision making are distilled from the work of Victor Vroom and his colleagues (Vroom and Jago, 1988; Vroom and Yetton, 1973).
2. Adapted from Senge (1990) and Vroom and Jago (1988).

References

Action Design. Workshop materials. Newton, Mass.: Action Design, 1997.

Argyris, C. *Reasoning, Learning, and Action.* San Francisco: Jossey-Bass, 1982.

Argyris, C. *Strategy, Change, and Defensive Routines.* Boston: Pitman, 1985.

Argyris, C., and Schön, D. A. *Theory in Practice: Increasing Professional Effectiveness.* San Francisco: Jossey-Bass, 1974.

Fisher, R., Ury, W., and Patton, B. *Getting to Yes: Negotiating Without Giving In.* (2nd ed.) New York: Penguin, 1991.

Graham, P. (ed.). *Mary Parker Follett: Prophet of Management.* Cambridge, Mass.: Harvard Business School Press, 1995.

Senge, P. *The Fifth Discipline: The Art and Practice of the Learning Organization.* New York: Doubleday, 1990.

Vroom, V. H., and Jago, A. G. *The New Leadership: Managing Participation in Organizations.* Upper Saddle River, N.J.: Prentice Hall, 1988.

Vroom, V. H., and Yetton, P. W. *Leadership and Decision Making.* Pittsburgh: University of Pittsburgh Press, 1973.

Chapter 6

The Diagnosis-Intervention Cycle

Peg Carlson

As Roger Schwarz describes in the overview of the Skilled Facilitator approach, the Group Effectiveness Model, the core values, and the ground rules all create the foundation for diagnosing behavior in groups, but they don't tell you exactly what to say when, and to whom. The diagnosis-intervention cycle provides this guidance. It is a straightforward and structured six-step process that enables you to think about what is happening in a group and then to intervene consistent with the core values.

For an overview, see Chapter One, "The Skilled Facilitator Approach," page 3.

STEPS IN THE CYCLE

Figure 6.1 illustrates the six steps of the diagnosis-intervention cycle. The first three steps reflect your private diagnosis as you observe behavior (step 1), infer meaning (step 2), and decide whether and how to intervene in order to help an individual or group be more effective (step 3). The second three steps reflect what you actually say as you describe the behavior (step 4), share the meaning you have inferred (step 5), and help a group member decide whether and how to change his or her behavior to be more effective (step 6). The two sides of the cycle are parallel: steps 1 through 3 track your unspoken diagnosis, and steps 4 through 6 enable you to share your observations and inferences, see if others agree, and if appropriate, give them the choice to redesign their behavior. That is, in step 4, you publicly share what you observed in step 1; in step 5, you share the inference you made in step 2; and in step 6, you help group members decide whether and how to change their behavior, as consistent with your choice in step 3. This parallel structure gives you a way to intervene that is *transparent*; by publicly sharing your private reasoning, you allow others to understand what you're thinking and what led you to make your intervention.

This parallel structure gives you a way to intervene that is *transparent*; by publicly sharing your private reasoning, you allow others to understand what you're thinking and what led you to make your intervention.

Figure 6.1 The Diagnosis-Intervention Cycle with Diagnostic Frames

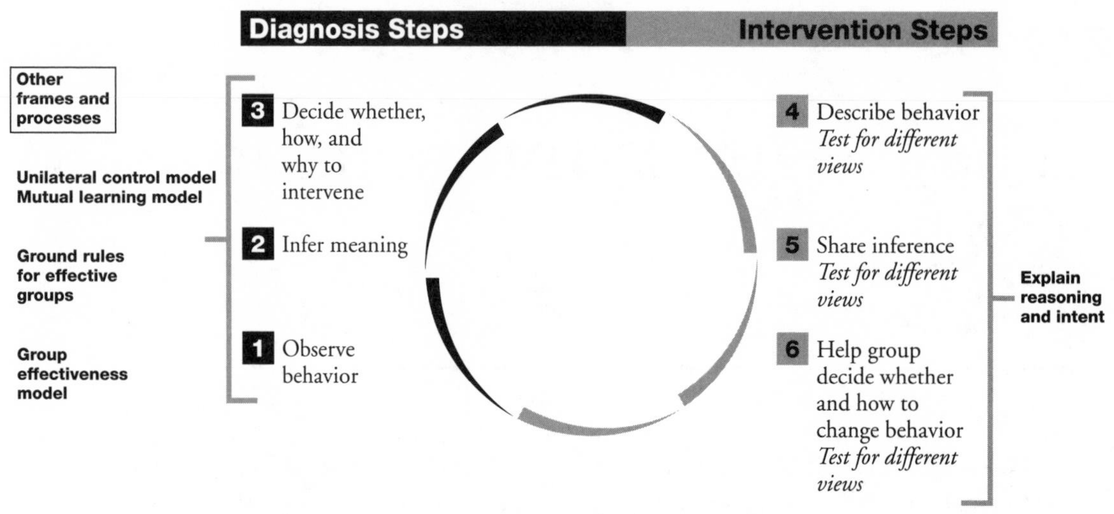

Intervention Steps

Each intervention step (steps 4 through 6) has two parts. The first part of each step is described above: sharing your observation, the inference you've made, and helping others decide whether and how to change behavior. The second part of each step is a test for different views in which you check to see whether the group member agrees or disagrees with your observation (step 4), inference (step 5), and recommendation (step 6). This explicit test reinforces the importance of checking to make sure that others agree with your assessment before moving on to the next step. If the person or people who are the focus of the intervention disagree with your observations or interpretation at any step, you cannot unilaterally proceed with the rest of the intervention. The test for different views ensures that group members make a free choice to accept—or reject—the facilitator's interventions.

To help the group understand why you have chosen to intervene at a certain point and why you're asking them to change their behavior, you may share your reasoning and intent at steps 4, 5, or 6.

For example, to begin step 4, you might say, **"I'd like to share some observations about a term, *benchmark,* you've been using in the conversation because it sounds as if it may mean different things to different people."** Or, at step 6 you might say, **"Can you say what you mean by *benchmark*? The reason I'm asking is that I think it will help the group figure out whether everyone is using this term to mean the same thing."** By helping group members understand your own reasoning and intent, you are also enabling them to make an informed choice about whether to change their behavior to increase the effectiveness of the discussion.

A Step-by-Step Example

To illustrate how it looks to go around the diagnosis-intervention cycle, here is an example of how to use it to intervene on a common issue in meetings: keeping a conversation focused. Picture a meeting where you are facilitating a discussion of ideas for how to absorb the latest round of budget cuts. The group is brainstorming possible strategies and has suggested several ideas. Paul, a group member, states, "I don't see how we can ask people to take on any more responsibilities than they currently have." Maria, another member, says, "I agree. Everyone is completely overloaded and stressed out." Using the cycle to diagnose and intervene may look like the following:

Step 1: Observe behavior. Paul said, "I don't see how we can ask people to take on any more responsibilities than they currently have," and Maria said, "I agree. Everyone is completely overloaded and stressed out."

Step 2: Infer meaning. It sounds as if Paul and Maria are evaluating the feasibility of some of the budget-cutting suggestions. If so, they are unilaterally moving the group forward instead of jointly designing next steps (Ground Rule Seven).

Step 3: Decide whether, how, and why to intervene. Since the group agreed to brainstorm possible strategies before evaluating them, it's important to check my inference that Paul and Maria's comments are evaluative. If I don't, some members may continue generating suggestions while others are moving on to the next step of evaluation.

Step 4: Describe behavior and test for different views. **"Paul, a minute ago you said that you didn't think people could be asked to take on more responsibilities than they have now. Is that right?"** (Paul: "Right.") **And Maria, you agreed and said that people are overloaded?"** (Maria, "Yes, they're really stressed.")

Step 5: Share inference and test for different views. **"It sounds as if you're both evaluating the feasibility of some of the suggestions we've got up on the flip chart. Am I correct?"** (Paul: "Yeah, it's hard for me to see how some of these things are going to work." Maria: "Me too.")

Step 6: Help group decide whether and how to change behavior and test for different views. **"Since the group agreed to brainstorm ideas before evaluating any of them, would you be willing to hold your thoughts for now and share them during the next step, or check with the group to see if others are ready to move on to evaluating ideas?"** My intent at this step is to help the group jointly design next steps in their discussion, so continuing to brainstorm is one option, but the group may also choose to move on to evaluation.

Although I am focusing on Ground Rule Seven (jointly designing next steps) in this intervention, there are other ground rules embedded in steps 4 through 6. For example, step 4 uses specific examples of Paul and Maria's conversation (Ground

Rule Three), step 5 tests an inference (Ground Rule One), step 6 shares my reason for intervening at this point (Ground Rule Four), and the second part of each step uses inquiry to confirm or disconfirm my interpretation (Ground Rule Six).

For more examples of language for steps 4 through 6 of the cycle, see the Diagnosis-Intervention Cycle in Chapter Twenty-Three, "Opening Lines," page 201, and Chapter Twenty-Four, "Reducing the Skilled Facilitator Jargon," page 207.

SKIPPING STEPS OF THE CYCLE

It's not always necessary to include each step of the cycle in your intervention. In fact, it can sometimes sound overly methodical and artificial to do so. For example, you can skip the "test for different views" part of step 4 and go on to step 5 if you're intervening on a comment the person just made: **"Laurie, a minute ago when you said, 'All staff agreed with the decision,' I assume that means the department heads. Is that right?"**

You can skip step 5 (sharing inferences) if you are making a low-level inference, and there is little chance that others would misunderstand or disagree with your inference.

For example, if a group member, Bridget, says, "I think our quality control system does a poor job of identifying persistent problems in our manufacturing process," I'm likely to infer that Bridget has some specific examples in mind and ask her, **"Would you be willing to give an example of a problem that the system failed to identify in the past?"**

Avoid skipping steps in the cycle when (1) it is a high-conflict situation or group members have a history of misunderstanding each other, (2) the group is beginning developmental facilitation and members are learning to use the diagnosis-intervention cycle in their own discussions, and (3) you are doing a complex intervention and sharing multiple observations that you have gathered over time (for example, discussing an undiscussable issue).[1]

USING THE DIAGNOSIS-INTERVENTION CYCLE WITH OTHER FRAMES

In the Skilled Facilitator approach, we frequently use the ground rules, the Group Effectiveness Model, and the unilateral control and mutual learning models to diagnose and intervene on behavior. However, you can use other diagnostic frames and processes with the cycle as long as you can identify directly observable behavior to support your inferences. For instance, in the example with Paul and Maria earlier in this chapter, I used a problem-solving frame to make and test my inference that group members were on different steps of the process, with some members brainstorming alternatives and others evaluating them.

CONCLUSION

The diagnosis-intervention cycle is the primary tool that individuals trained in the Skilled Facilitator approach learn to help others use the ground rules. Its six steps operationalize the core values, since they emphasize the importance of using valid information, testing inferences, explaining reasoning, and giving people a free and informed choice to change their behavior.

This chapter is intended as a summary of the diagnosis-intervention cycle. Additional guidance on using the cycle for intervening may be found in many of the chapters in Parts Two, Three, and Four of this Fieldbook.

Note

1. For more on when to skip—and not skip—intervention steps, as well as other guidelines for how to intervene, see Chapter Eight in *The Skilled Facilitator.*

Chapter 7

Thinking and Acting Systemically

Anne Davidson

THINKING AND ACTING systemically is one of the key elements of the Skilled Facilitator approach. When Roger Schwarz points out in Chapter One that the Skilled Facilitator approach "recognizes that any action you take affects the group in multiple ways and has short-term and long-term consequences, some of which may not be obvious" (p. 11), he highlights three of the fundamental principles of the discipline of systems thinking. He is speaking about the principles of interrelatedness, delay and separation between cause and effect, and the difficulty of seeing systemic structure. When later in that same chapter he discusses the need to treat an entire group as the client, he is, in essence, speaking about the principle of systems integrity.

Understanding how systems thinking is embedded in the Skilled Facilitator approach strengthens your ability to use the approach effectively across a wide variety of situations. This chapter discusses how this approach incorporates many of the basic principles or laws of systems thinking.

BASIC PRINCIPLES OF SYSTEMS THINKING

The field of systems thinking is relatively young. The published theory dates from the 1940s, and the primary concepts of system dynamics that we apply to groups and organizations were articulated in the 1960s.[1] The principles, tools, and applications of systems thinking are still being discovered and developed. The principles presented here are fundamental concepts that appear in one form or another in most approaches to applying systems thinking to groups and organizations. They are based on eleven "laws" of systems thinking summarized by Peter Senge in *The Fifth Discipline* (1994). (See the sidebar, "The Laws of Systems," page 76.)

There is a great deal more to know about systems thinking and the analytical systems tools that are increasingly being applied to the fields of organization and human development.[2] But as you begin to learn and practice using the Skilled Facilitator approach, understanding these basic principles is a good foundation for designing your conversations and interventions.

The Laws of Systems (Learning to Think Systemically)

1. **Today's problems come from yesterday's "solutions."** Solutions that merely shift problems from one part of a system to another often go undetected because those who solved the initial problem are different from those who inherit the new problem.

2. **The harder you push, the harder the system pushes back.** Well-intentioned interventions often call forth responses from the system that offset the benefits of the intervention. Systems thinking calls this phenomenon *compensating feedback.* Nearly everyone knows what it feels like to be facing compensating feedback: the harder we push, the harder the system pushes back; the more effort you expend trying to improve matters, the more effort seems to be required.

3. **Behavior grows better before it gets worse.** In complex human systems, there are always many ways to make things look better in the short run. A typical solution feels wonderful when it cures symptoms. Now there's improvement, or maybe the problem has even gone away. It may be two, three, or four years before the problem returns or some new, worse problem arrives. By that time, given how rapidly most people move from job to job, someone new is often sitting in the chair.

4. **The easy way out usually leads back in.** Most people find comfort in applying familiar solutions to problems, sticking to what we know best. Pushing harder and harder on familiar solutions while fundamental problems persist or worsen is a reliable indicator of nonsystemic thinking. This is often called the "what we need is a bigger hammer" syndrome.

5. **The cure can be worse than the disease.** The long-term, most insidious consequence of applying nonsystemic solutions is the increased need for more and more of the solution. The phenomenon of short-term improvements leading to long-term dependency is so common that it has its own name: "Shifting the Burden to the Intervenor." The intervenor may be federal assistance to cities, food relief agencies, welfare programs, or supervisors who take responsibility for doing their employees' work. All "help" in such a way that they leave the system fundamentally weaker than before and more in need of further help.

6. **Faster is slower.** It is not often that you can just jump in and fix something and expect it to work in the long term. Each situation has its optimum rate of change.

7. **Cause and effect are not closely related in time and space.** There is a fundamental mismatch between the nature of reality in complex systems and our predominant ways of thinking about reality. The first step in correcting that mismatch is to let go of the notion that cause and effect are close in time and space. Some of the most important effects of changes may not be noted until years later.

8. **Small changes can produce big results, but the areas of highest leverage are often the least obvious.** Systems thinking is often called the new dismal science because it teaches that most obvious solutions don't work. At best, they improve matters in the short run, only to make things worse in the long run. Systems thinking also shows that small, well-focused actions

can sometimes produce significant, enduring improvements if they're in the right place. When actions are taken in the right place, this is called leverage. The problem is that many high-leverage changes are usually not obvious to most participants in the system.

9. **You can have your cake and eat it too, but not all at once.** The best example of this is played out in the search for high-quality service and products. It was once thought in the business world that high cost and high quality were always linked and that you could not have high quality and lower costs. As it turns out, this is true in the short term, but in the long term, it is not true. Many apparent dilemmas, such as central versus local control, happy and committed employees versus competitive labor costs, and rewarding individual achievement versus having everyone feel valued, are by-products of static thinking. They only appear as rigid either-or choices because we only think of what is possible at a fixed point in time.

10. **Dividing an elephant in half does not produce two elephants.** Systems have integrity. Their character depends on the whole. To understand the most challenging issues requires seeing the whole system that generates the issues. This does not mean that every organizational issue can be understood only by looking at the entire organization. Some issues can be understood only by looking at how major functions interact, but there are other issues where critical systemic forces arise within a given functional area or subsystem. The key principle, called *the principle of the system boundary,* is that the interactions that must be examined are those most important to the issue at hand, regardless of the traditional organizational boundaries.

11. **There is no blame.** We tend to blame outside circumstances for our problems. Systems thinking shows us that there is no outside, that you and the cause of your problems are part of a single system. The cure lies in your relationship with your "enemy."

Source: Condensed from "The Laws of the Fifth Discipline" in Senge (1990), pp. 57–67. Used by permission.

Interrelatedness: Everything Affects Everything Else

First, systems thinking is about the principle of interrelatedness. My working definition of a system is "a perceived whole whose elements 'hang together' because they continually affect each other over time and operate toward a common purpose" (Senge and others, 1994, p. 90).

My working definition of a system is "a perceived whole whose elements 'hang together' because they continually affect each other over time and operate toward a common purpose" (Senge and others, 1994, p. 90). def·i·'ni·tion

Organizations can be thought of as systems, as can families, teams, habitats, and even our planet. The discipline of systems thinking moves us away from linear interpretations of events (A causes B, which results in C) and toward an appreciation of more complex patterns of interaction. Elements of systems are linked in a web of relationships so that every element can affect every other element. Here is a simple example. When you drive a car, you and your car form a simple system. Your actions influence what the car does; the responses you get from the car (speed, direction) influence your subsequent actions (pressing the accelerator harder, applying the brakes, turning the steering wheel to the right or left). The car responds again, and you further adjust. In this way, the outcome of one action is fed back to influence the next. We call this cycle of information a *feedback loop.* Simple feedback loops are linked together to form complex systems.

These feedback loops are at work in individual conversations, group dynamics, and the interactions between facilitators and groups as well. Let's look at an example from a typical situation. If I ease in to a difficult topic by asking leading questions, I actually contribute to getting a defensive reaction from you in return.

See Chapter Four, "Understanding What Guides Your Behavior," page 33.

Your defensive reaction shapes my next response. I can either inquire into what created the defensiveness, in which case I might learn how to improve my own behavior, or I can decide that your defensiveness proves your inability to receive feedback, in which case I withhold information and future feedback. In either case, your response provides feedback that influences my next choice. My mental model—unilateral control or mutual learning—determines which choice I make and begins to create the background structure of the cycle.

The first choice contributes to creating a virtuous cycle: the more we understand how we both contributed to an ineffective conversation, the more productive this and future conversations become. The second choice, withholding feedback, contributes to creating a vicious cycle: the capacity to improve conversations will be diminished and our relationship is more likely to deteriorate over time. Either way, we co-evolve our responses, each affecting the other. Whatever approach I take will change your behavior but will also loop back and influence my own behavior. The process will cycle back on itself again and again.

See Chapter Two, "The Group Effectiveness Model," page 15.

The Group Effectiveness Model is a clear example of the concept of everything affecting everything else: any element can cause changes in any other element. Unclear roles might generate conflict that leads to a group's missing deadlines and not accomplishing its goals, which will likely contribute to further conflict. Trust may erode because of unclear communications, and unclear communications may further erode trust. In reality, the patterns are quite complex and emerge and evolve over time, but they are always following this process of interrelatedness. Systems thinking is basically a worldview (mental model) and a language for communicating about these complex interdependencies. As Daniel Kim (1995a) points out, many of the most vexing problems confronting managers and corporations today are caused by a similar web of tightly interconnected circular relationships.

There Is No Blame

In trying to understand problems, we usually look outside, that is, to other people's actions rather than our own and to other work groups or organizations rather than those to which we belong. But if we are affected by a system, we must accept that at some level we are part of that system. Based on the principle of interrelatedness, any action we take has the potential of improving or degrading the behavior of the system, even if in seemingly minute ways.

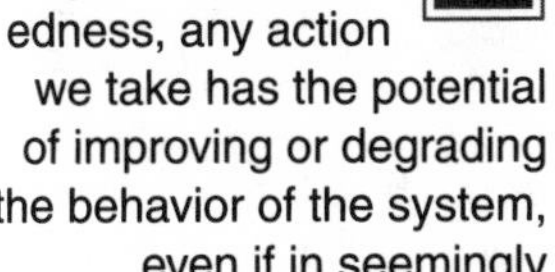

Based on the principle of interrelatedness, any action we take has the potential of improving or degrading the behavior of the system, even if in seemingly minute ways.

"An inherent assumption of the systems thinking worldview is that problems are internally generated—that we often create our own 'worst nightmares'" (Kim, 1995a, p. 7). "Us" and "them" are part of the same system and share responsibility for both its problems and their solutions. Chris Argyris points this out clearly in his article "Good Communication That Blocks Learning" (1994).

> Argyris tells the story of a company celebrating a highly successful Total Quality Management initiative. He reveals that the employees knew about critical problems for three to five years before Total Quality Management and blamed them on management's blindness and timidity, as well as a culture of unilaterally protecting people by not raising difficult issues. They were blind to the fact that they were colluding to keep problems in place by not raising them and by making undiscussable the fact that they felt they could not raise them without repercussions.

See Chapter Forty-Two, "How to Stop Contributing to Your Boss's and Your Own Ineffectiveness," page 335, for a further discussion of this dynamic.

What becomes clear when studying systems principles is that we cocreate our own problems. Every issue, every difficult conversation, every ineffective employee is in part a result of our own actions within a complex system.

Cause and Effect Are Not Closely Related in Time and Space

Feedback loops are often hard to see because they influence behavior over time, and there may be long delays between cause and effect. There may also be significant differences between the result we get in the short run and how things play out in the long run. We typically think of problems and challenges from the perspective of an isolated event: the crash of the space shuttle, the collapse of the stock market, a disagreement with the boss. But systems are structured by complex networks of relationships that evolve among elements over time. The genesis of the *Challenger* disaster occurred in decisions, discussions, and misinterpretations of data that happened years before the tragedy. The difficult relationship with the boss started in small ways, often with the initial work agreement, and deteriorated over time as each party built actions on higher and higher levels of untested assumptions.

> The Skilled Facilitator approach is built on the structure of helping people examine how their core values and assumptions led them to adopt a particular strategy and then helping them appreciate the unintended long-term consequences that their strategy created.

Of course, it is not always easy or even possible to predict the consequences of a decision. Every decision has both intended and unintended (positive and negative) consequences. But learning to play out possible implications in plausible scenarios is an important systems thinking skill. The Skilled Facilitator approach is built on the structure of helping people examine how their core values and assumptions led them to adopt a particular strategy and then helping them appreciate the unintended long-term consequences that their strategy created. Where human behavior is concerned, it is often quite possible to accurately predict the consequences of the short-term strategies we use to get out of difficult situations. With fairly short delays, we often see misunderstanding, conflict, decreased trust, increased dependence, and reduced overall effectiveness.

Once we appreciate the nature of delay and unintended consequences, we can see the value of slowing down decision-making processes to consider the possible feedback loops and potential unintended consequences. This kind of thinking is fundamental to many Skilled Facilitator interventions, which often focus on helping groups apply the principle, **Faster is slower.** One of the most frequent objections to following the ground rules is that they will take more time, slowing the group down. In the short run, this is true. In the long run, slowing down planning or data-gathering steps pays huge dividends in most cases. We frequently use the diagram in Figure 7.1 to help groups think through how planning and building commitment to a decision everyone can support actually speeds implementation and helps avoid unintended consequences.

I often tell the story of one team I worked with that rushed to change its funeral leave policy:

> The group felt employees were abusing the leave by taking unnecessary days, so they sought to tighten the guidelines. They also did not believe the issue was worth a lot of time to investigate. They wanted to get it done quickly and move on to what they viewed as "more substantive" matters, so they revised the policy in a couple of hours. Because they had not considered a number of contingencies, like shift differentials, union requirements, record-keeping requirements, or employee opinion, a series of problems arose when the policy was implemented.

Figure 7.1 Speeding Implementation

Planning	Implementation	
Planning	Implementation	Time Saved

It turned out that the group had done a poor job of reaching consensus on the policy changes. Several of the team members responsible for implementing the policy did not like it, so they did not enforce it consistently. At last count, the team had dealt with problems resulting from the new policy on twenty-two separate occasions! Each discussion lasted an hour or more. In hindsight, the group estimated that had they taken more time up front to have a productive discussion, gather valid information, and reach genuine consensus, they could probably have revised the policy in two meetings of two hours each. Instead, each of seven team members spent up to eighteen unnecessary hours.

Similar examples abound in most organizations. Talking through them can help groups see that rushing through decisions actually costs them time in the long run. Pointing out this outcome can build support for using Skilled Facilitator skills to have a different kind of conversation.

Quick Fixes Can Backfire

Whether or not time is the issue, it is productive to discuss unintended negative consequences of past well-intended decisions. Most groups and organizations have examples of situations in which the easy way out led back in or the cure was worse than the disease. Once groups begin to talk through the notion of unintended consequences and how they usually result from short-term thinking, the advantages of "going slow to go fast" become clear. After seeing a few organizational examples, it is easier for people to realize how the same dynamic is at work in individual conversations. They begin to see how strong advocacy without genuine inquiry may create resistance or noncompliance in the long run, even if it looks as if they are winning the argument in the moment.

See Chris Soderquist's example in Chapter Fifty-Six, "Applying the Skilled Facilitator Approach to a Systems Thinking Analysis," page 447, about the impact on customer satisfaction that could result from a special investment program implemented without carefully analyzing the potential systemic consequences.

Often one must look elsewhere in the system (in a different space) to see where problems are created. The source of a problem may be separated by several levels of hierarchy or located in a related but not directly involved function.

In trying to fix one problem easily (repair parts were being pilfered from trucks), an organization I worked with implemented a complex inventory control process that included having purchasing department staff deliver parts to job sites. In the short run, fewer parts disappeared from trucks. Yet job productivity declined gradually and steadily over a period of several years. No one really knew why. The organization blamed the repair crews, citing turnover, poor training, mistakes, and laziness. When a more systemic analysis was completed after repair backups had reached critical levels, it became apparent that the cause of the problem was located in a different place in the system from where the symptoms appeared. Solutions required working with the purchasing and inventory control systems. Even though it was not obvious, the system of delivering parts to job sites caused crews to wait up to two hours when an unanticipated part was needed. And the system they were repairing had never been properly documented, so there were a lot of surprises when the crews began working. The solution included intervening in the inventory control system and generating documentation from engineering, not just in how repair crews handled parts.

It is not uncommon to find that well-intended attempts to resolve a problem quickly create unintended, negative consequences that show up in other parts of a system and worsen over time. This repair parts case also illustrates the systems principles of **behavior grows better before it gets worse** and **today's problems come from yesterday's solutions.**

Applying these principles of delay, separation, and unintended long-term consequences to interpersonal and group interactions helps explain why groups become dependent on leaders who solve their problems for them. In the short run, it looks like an effective strategy to meet a deadline when the leader jumps in to fix a mistake or complete a task. But in the long run, this does nothing to develop capacity. Employees don't learn to do the task themselves or to plan their time and prioritize their work appropriately. In time, the leader is overwhelmed doing things for others they can and should do for themselves, and her performance deteriorates. In the Skilled Facilitator approach, we are always trying to expand the capacity of the system so that problems do not just move elsewhere—to a future time or a different person or department.

See Chapter Fifty-Three, "The Drama Triangle," p. 421, for more about this dynamic.

In the Skilled Facilitator approach, we are always trying to expand the capacity of the system so that problems do not just move elsewhere—to a future time or a different person or department.

We know that **the harder we push, the harder the system will push back.** The harder we try to solve a problem, the more likely it is that it will move elsewhere. Changing the inventory system for repair parts just moved the problem to crews, but the system capacity stayed the same in the short run and got worse in the long run. These principles of delay and separation between cause and effect explain why we would use the Skilled Facilitator approach to discuss more difficult issues rather than avoid or gloss over them. We resolve relevant issues in groups rather than privately so that we are not at risk of revisiting the issues again and again. These principles are behind our reasons for advocating decision rules likely to generate commitment to decisions rather than short-term compliance, since without commitment, there is usually a lack of follow-through or adequate monitoring of decision results. And the principles help explain why we may advocate for a theory-in-use or more developmental intervention that is more likely to get at fundamental or root causes of difficulties rather than simply to manage a conflict to help relieve discomfort in the short run.

Small Changes Can Produce Big Results, But the Areas of Highest Leverage Are Often the Least Obvious

One of the problematic aspects of working with systems is that the systemic structure driving a problem is frequently difficult to see—not just because of time delays but because of the nature of the structure itself. By *structure,* I am referring to the network of relationships that build up over time as key system components interact. Richard Karash (1997) distinguishes between *internal* structure and *external* structure. Internal structure is made up of the way we think about things, that is, the assumptions and mental models of the individuals involved in a system. External structure is made up of such elements as hierarchy and information and process flows. Karash likens systems structure to the submerged portion of an iceberg: "As opposed to events and patterns, which are usually more observable, much of what we think of as structure is often hidden. We can witness traffic accidents, for example, but it's harder to observe the underlying structure that causes them" (p. 6). Yet resolving problems and making systems more productive frequently requires intervening at the structural level.

One of the problematic aspects of working with systems is that the systemic structure driving a problem is frequently difficult to see—not just because of time delays but because of the nature of the structure itself.

Seeing systems structure requires thinking and observing at multiple levels. Daniel Kim articulates five levels or perspectives from which we can study a system (1996, pp. 6–7). (See Figure 7.2.) He points out that the further one moves from specific events toward mental models or vision, the more leverage one has to resolve a problem. By "leverage" we mean small, well-focused actions that can produce significant, lasting changes (Senge, 1990). For example, for decades the health care system in the United States has been structured around a mental model of treating disease. Had the mental model started out as "creating wellness," it is likely the system would have been structured very differently. Leverage to alter a system might come from intervening at any level, but a key principle of systems thinking is that intervening at the higher levels (external structure, mental models or vision) is more likely to increase influence over future outcomes.

Structure in systems, then, is built up from the choices people make consciously or unconsciously over time. Problems may be created by the system (for example, from the way a job is designed and the internal reporting structure), but that fact is often not apparent. The feedback loops that occur within a system are often hard to see or predict. For example, many groups make the mistake of thinking that they must make either-or choices, like providing the insurance package employees want at greater expense or choosing less coverage at lower cost to keep the budget in line. If, however, they reframe their thinking, they may find that other options exist. One group I worked with used the "focus on interests" ground rule and testing assumptions to reframe their thinking about their health insurance plan. They created a plan for the organization to become self-insured after they realized that part of the systems structure was based on their mental models of how insurance could be provided. They were able to meet both cost and coverage interests more fully once they changed the system structure by altering their mental model. The principle **you can**

Figure 7.2 Levels of Perspective

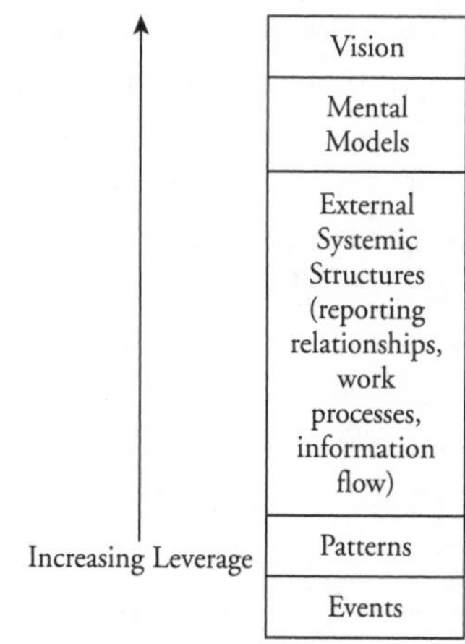

Source: Adapted from Kim (1996).

have your cake and eat it too, but not all at once also applies here. If time delays are factored in, assumptions about either-or trade-offs often fall away, and when this happens, the structure of the system changes. The organization could not become self-insured in the short run, but looking at how the system could be restructured over a year's time showed how the organization could have its cake and eat it too.

Understanding this concept of levels of perspective helps one choose higher-leverage interventions. This principle explains why I might recontract with a group to engage in a theory-in-use intervention (for example, address mental models) rather than continue to intervene on missed ground rules (events or patterns). Just as a good systems thinker is looking at all five levels simultaneously, a good facilitator is analyzing each level as well and selecting the most productive places to intervene accordingly. We understand that group process may be part of the structure running behind a team's effectiveness.

Intervening on process or the theory-in-use of individuals or organizational defensive routines may take time in the short run, but it is likely to alter the structure of the system and leverage significant improvement in the longer run.

Intervening on process or the theory-in-use of individuals or organizational defensive routines may take time in the short run, but it is likely to alter the structure of the system and leverage significant improvement in the longer run.

Dividing an Elephant in Half Does Not Produce Two Elephants

Each system has its own integrity. You cannot pull out pieces separately without creating a fragmented mess. Understanding most challenging issues requires seeing the whole system that generates the issues. We constantly see the results of people trying to solve problems without seeing the whole system at work. We address symptoms without getting at root causes. We try to treat wounds without understanding why they recur. We try to correct isolated errors by blaming individuals without seeing how the system produced the likelihood of mistakes, as in the initial response to parts missing from repair trucks in the previous story.

A powerful example of this principle comes from Mohrman, Cohen, and Mohrman's (1995) research on knowledge-work teams. They found that what prevented most teams from good, integrated performance was a set of factors external to the team, such as lack of consistent direction, inconsistent goals, or shifting resource commitments. Organizations usually invest enormous resources on internal team development and internal team processes, yet Mohrman, Cohen, and Mohrman became convinced that they needed to look at the whole organizational system to understand team effectiveness. Understanding systems integrity also helps explain why trying to split off and apply selected Skilled Facilitator tools, like the ground rules or the diagnosis-intervention cycle, without understanding and using mental models and core values creates defensiveness and limits effectiveness. The higher-leverage aspects of systemic structure are being ignored.

See, for example, Chapter Twenty-Six, "Ground Rules Without the Mutual Learning Model Are Like Houses Without Foundations," page 217.

Systems integrity is also one of the principles behind the Skilled Facilitator contracting process. We emphasize the importance of getting the whole system (or representatives of the whole system) involved early in the planning process for a facilitation or consultation. Since systems are hard to see and are cocreated, it requires multiple perspectives to gather enough valid information to see feedback loops and predict intended and unintended consequences.

See Chapter Eight, "Contracting with Groups," page 89.

I believe that at the outset of any engagement, it is critical to help people understand and define the relevant system boundaries for the issue at hand. Only in this way can we have the various systems perspectives and components represented in the room. It is not necessary to have the entire system represented for every issue, but it is critical to understand the integrity of the whole and consider what elements must be present. Otherwise, the easy way out will just lead back in: problems and unintended negative consequences will result, the problem or a worse one will recur, and the situation will have to be addressed all over again.

THE LAWS ARE INTERRELATED

The laws or principles of systems thinking are themselves interrelated. It is hard to talk about the easy way out leading back in or faster is slower without also discussing the fact that systems have integrity. Part of what one needs to slow down to do is analyze the whole system. And one cannot talk about analyzing the whole system without considering systems structure, leverage, and interrelated feedback loops. This is exactly the way the Skilled Facilitator approach works: you cannot use the diagnosis-intervention cycle without understanding the ground rules of combining advocacy and inquiry, explaining reasoning and intent, sharing specific examples, and testing assumptions. And you cannot recognize the need to test assumptions if you are not seeking to learn from valid information and seeking processes that generate commitment to decisions. In essence, the principles of systems thinking are at work any time we use the Skilled Facilitator approach to design a conversation, intervene with a group, contract to facilitate, consult, or engage in a long-term organizational change effort.

Notes

1. General systems theory began in the 1940s with the work of theoretical biologist Ludwig von Bertalanffy and others, founded on principles from biology, physics, and engineering. Jay Forrester originated the primary concepts of system dynamics that we apply to groups and organizations in his 1961 book, *Industrial Dynamics.* Peter Senge, who synthesized and popularized the current thinking on systems dynamics in 1990 with the publication of *The Fifth Discipline,* based his initial work on Forrester's. In 1964, Daniel Katz and Robert Kahn drew on Bertalanffy's work to present a systems view of groups and organizations in *The Social Psychology of Organizations.* And Margaret Wheatley's 1992 *Leadership and the New Science* linked the principles of quantum physics, self-organizing systems, and chaos theory to the forces that shape organizations.
2. For an excellent summary of five of the primary forms or schools of systems thinking, see Charlotte Roberts's and Art Kleiner's discussion in *The Dance of Change* (Senge and others, 1999).

References

Argyris, C. "Good Communication That Blocks Learning." *Harvard Business Review,* July-Aug. 1994, pp. 77–85.

Forrester, J. *Industrial Dynamics.* Cambridge, Mass.: MIT Press, 1961; Cambridge, Mass.: Productivity Press, 1992.

Karash, R. "How to See Structure." *Systems Thinker,* 1997, *8*(4), 6–8.

Katz, D., and Kahn, R. *The Social Psychology of Organizations.* (2nd ed.) New York: Wiley, 1978.

Kim, D. H. *Systems Thinking Tools: A User's Reference Guide.* Cambridge, Mass.: Pegasus Communications, 1995a.

Kim, D. H. "Vision Deployment Matrix: A Framework for Large-Scale Change." *Systems Thinker,* 1995b, *6*(1), 1–5.

Kim, D. H. "From Event Thinking to Systems Thinking." *Systems Thinker,* 1996, *7*(5), 6–7.

Mohrman, S. A., Cohen, S. G., and Mohrman, A. M., Jr. *Designing Team-Based Organizations: New Forms for Knowledge Work.* San Francisco: Jossey-Bass, 1995.

Senge, P. M. *The Fifth Discipline: The Art and Practice of the Learning Organization.* New York: Doubleday, 1990.

Senge, P., and others. *The Fifth Discipline Fieldbook: Strategies and Tools for Building a Learning Organization.* New York: Doubleday, 1994.

Senge, P., and others. *The Dance of Change: The Challenges to Sustaining Momentum in Learning Organizations.* New York: Doubleday, 1999.

Wheatley, M. J. *Leadership and the New Science: Learning About Organization from an Orderly Universe.* San Francisco: Berrett-Koehler, 1992.

Chapter 8

Contracting with Groups

Roger Schwarz

ONE OF THE MOST POWERFUL interventions you can make is to contract effectively with the group you are working with. I define contracting as the process of developing a shared understanding and agreement about what outcomes the group seeks and how the group and you will work together to achieve the outcomes.

I define contracting as the process of developing a shared understanding and agreement about what outcomes the group seeks and how the group and you will work together to achieve the outcomes. def·i·'ni·tion

Many facilitators, even those with excellent diagnostic and intervention skills, reduce their effectiveness and their ability to help their clients because they have not contracted well. Effective contracting creates the foundation for a successful working relationship. The Skilled Facilitator approach includes a set of principles and stages for developing this relationship.

WHY CONTRACT?

There are several reasons for contracting. First, contracting increases the chance that the group and I understand and agree on the goal of the facilitation and how we will work together, including time constraints, our roles, ground rules, and how decisions will be made. Second, the contracting process serves as a microcosm of the facilitation itself. It gives me an opportunity to watch how group members interact, to demonstrate how I would intervene during the facilitation, and it enables the group to make a more informed choice about whether they want me to facilitate. Third, contracting begins to develop the trust between the group and me that is essential for facilitation.

CONTRACTING PRINCIPLES

The principles for contracting are based on the mutual learning model of the Skilled Facilitator approach and reflect a systems approach to working with groups.

See Chapter Four, "Understanding What Guides your Behavior," page 33, and Chapter Seven, "Thinking and Acting Systemically," page 75.

This chapter is an adaptation of *The Skilled Facilitator,* Chapter Thirteen. A different version of this piece appeared as "How to Contract for Effective Facilitation" in M. Silberman, *The 2004 Team and Organization Development Sourcebook* (2004).

First, the entire group is the client.

First, the entire group is the client. To be seen as a credible, effective facilitator, the client must be the entire group (what I call the *primary client*) that I am facilitating. Consequently, only the full group can commit to hiring me as a facilitator, not the sponsor, group leader, the person who signs my check, or the person who initially contacts me (what I call the *contact client*). Third, the group commitment to the facilitation and to hire me needs to be based on valid information and a free and informed choice. Finally, my actions in the contracting process must be transparent to all client group members, and I cannot collude with one or more group members against the other members.

CONTRACTING STAGES

Finally, my actions in the contracting process must be transparent to all client group members, and I cannot collude with one or more group members against the other members.

To put the principles in action, there are four contracting stages with a set of tasks to accomplish at each stage (Figure 8.1).

Stage 1: Initial Conversation with a Primary Client Group Member

In stage 1, I identify whether the person contacting me is a member of the primary client group—someone who is a member of the group and will be present in the group I am being asked to facilitate. If the person is not, I explain why I need to talk with a member of the group. If the person is a member of the group, I begin my initial diagnosis of the situation by asking a series of questions and discuss my approach to facilitation.

Questions for the Initial Contact

Before asking the questions, I explain that I am asking the questions to better understand the situation and decide whether I can help. Without explaining my reasoning and seeking agreement to proceed, the person may wonder what purpose the questions serve:

1. Who is seeking the services?
2. Are you are member of the group?
3. Has the group already set a date for the facilitation, or it is flexible?
4. What does the group want to accomplish with the help of a facilitator?
5. What problems, if any, is the group experiencing?

Figure 8.1 Contracting Stages

Stage	Major Tasks
1 Initial contact with a primary client group member	1. Identify member of primary client group. 2. Conduct initial diagnosis. 3. Discuss approach to facilitation. 4. Agree on whether to proceed. If so . . . 5. Set up meeting for stage 2.
2 Planning the facilitation	1. Send letter to planning group about purpose and agenda for planning meeting. Conduct diagnosis with full group or representative of primary client group. 2. Agree on facilitation objective, agenda, ground rules, and other elements. 3. Send tentative agreement to full client group. 4. Check for any changes in conditions before actual facilitation occurs.
3 Reaching agreement with the full primary client group	1. Agree on objective, identify expectations, and address any concerns. 2. Agree on the agenda and time allocation. 3. Agree on the process, including ground rules. 4. Define roles.
4 Completing and evaluating the facilitation	1. Evaluate facilitation using self-critiques. 2. Evaluate contract.

Questions When the Initial Contact Is a Member of the Primary Client Group

If the contact is also a member of the group that I will be facilitating, I ask additional questions to learn more about the group's situation as the person sees it. Some key questions include:

For Opportunity-Oriented Issues

1. What is the group trying to create that doesn't currently exist?
2. What is leading to the need or desire now?
3. What barriers do you or others anticipate facing as you seek to create this change?

For Problem-Focused Issues

4. Tell me more about the problems the group is facing. What are some specific examples?
5. How widespread are the problems, and when did they begin?
6. How do members contribute to the problems?
7. What are the consequences of these problems for the group and the larger organization?
8. What are the potential causes of the problems?

Motivation and Resources for Change

9. What, if anything, has the group done to work on this issue already? What were the results?
10. What strengths can the group draw on as it works on these issues?

Experience with Facilitators and Current Request for Help

11. Have you used other facilitators in the past? If so, what did the facilitator do that you found helpful and not helpful?
12. What has led you to call me in particular?
13. How do you see me helping the group accomplish its goals?

Describe Your Interest and Ability to Help

After learning about the client's situation, I describe whether I have the ability to help and whether I am interested in the work. These are two different factors. I sometimes get requests for facilitation that I am able to meet but are not that interesting to me. If you have the flexibility, consider focusing on the types of facilitation that most interest you. Even if I am interested and able to meet the need as the person has presented it, it is important to tell the person that I need to meet with the full group or representatives (stage 2) before either the group or I can make an informed choice about working together.

Describe Your Approach to Facilitation

Describing my approach to facilitation gives the person relevant information about how I will work with the group. It enables him or her to make a more informed choice about how well my approach will meet the group's needs.

I share several elements of my approach: (1) how I define my facilitator role and the consequences for the group; (2) the core values and beliefs that guide my approach; (3) the Ground Rules for Effective Groups that I use to both diagnose and intervene to help the group function more effectively; and (4) examples of how I would intervene with the group. I give specific examples of what I would say and do in a variety of situations so that the person has a clear picture of my approach. I also state my fee and expenses for the facilitation. I ask for the person's reactions to my approach and invite the person to ask questions about how I would work with the group and to raise any concerns.

Summarize and Agree on Next Steps

If both the individual and I are interested in pursuing the facilitation, I summarize my initial understanding of the client's situation and check to see that I have understood it correctly. I describe the rest of the contracting process, explaining the purpose of each step, and address any questions or concerns.

The next step will be for the person to discuss our conversation with the primary client group. If the group is interested, we will arrange a conference call or meeting in which the group and I will plan the facilitation and decide if we want to work together. This will be stage 2.

Address Concerns About Time

When I tell the primary client group member that the stage 2 planning meeting takes about two hours, sometimes the person is concerned that the contracting process will take too much time. I offer two responses. First, I note that a major goal of the contracting process is to ensure that all group members are committed to facilitation. Without this commitment, the facilitation is likely to be unsuccessful and the group will have wasted valuable time. Second, sometimes the person suggests that the planning meeting is not necessary because all group members agree on the purpose and approach for the facilitation. I respond that if this is the case, the planning meeting will take very little time. I do not shorten the contracting process simply because the client is concerned about time. To do so would be to abandon my responsibilities as a process expert and to knowingly create potential problems for the group later on.

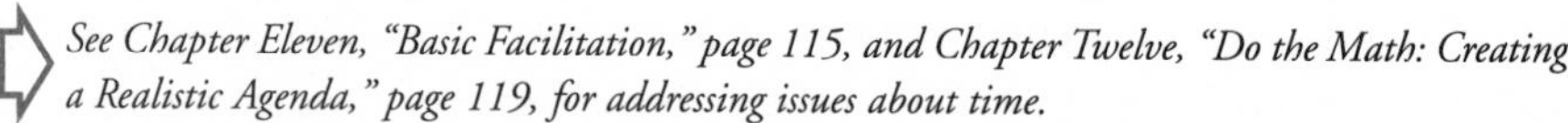
See Chapter Eleven, "Basic Facilitation," page 115, and Chapter Twelve, "Do the Math: Creating a Realistic Agenda," page 119, for addressing issues about time.

Stage 2: Planning the Facilitation

"Ground Rules for Effective Groups" and "A Consumer's Guide to Hiring and Working with a Group Facilitator" are available from Roger Schwarz and Associates at www.schwarzassociates.com.

The purpose of stage 2 is to reach agreement with the primary client group about whether and how we will work together. We also tentatively agree on the agenda and logistics for the facilitation. In this stage, I try to meet with the entire group I will be facilitating. If it is not logistically possible to do that, I meet with a representative sample of the group, so that the diversity of views on the issues is represented. Before the meeting, I send a proposed agenda for meeting and copies of two articles that describe my approach: "Ground Rules for Effective Groups" and "A Consumer's Guide to Hiring and Working with a Group Facilitator." This enables group members to come to the meeting prepared to ask me about my approach to helping them.

See Chapter Five, "Ground Rules for Effective Groups," page 61; Chapter Eleven, "Basic Facilitation," page 115; and Chapter Forty-Three, "Developmental Facilitation," page 339.

Ask Questions and Describe Your Approach

During the meeting, I ask the same general set of questions and share the same kind of information I shared in stage 1. The significant difference is that I am now meeting with the group and facilitating the conversation. This enables me to observe how the group members interact and to demonstrate the kinds of interventions I would make if we worked together. In addition to the questions I described in stage 1, the group and I address a set of more specific questions, which form the basis of our working agreement.

Questions for an Effective Contract

1. Who is the primary client (that is, who will attend the meetings)?
2. What are the objectives of the facilitation?
3. What are the agendas for the meetings?
4. Where, when, and how long will the group meet?
5. What are the roles of the facilitator, leader, and team members?
6. What ground rules will the group follow?
7. How will the group assess its performance?

Deciding What Ground Rules to Use and How

A central part of the Skilled Facilitator approach is the core values and ground rules. I use them as the basis for diagnosing and intervening in the group, and I ask group members if they are willing to commit to using them as well. On the belief that group members will support what they have developed, some facilitators ask the group to develop a set of ground rules. Because some of these facilitators also have their own ground rules, they privately hope that group members will identify ground rules that coincide with their own. If this does not happen, sometimes these facilitators may even put their ground rules in place by rephrasing group members' suggestions for ground rules or suggesting some of their own.

I believe that group members do not have to develop their ground rules to be committed to them; rather, they need to make a free and informed choice to use them. As group process experts, we should have a clear idea what kinds of ground rules lead to effective group behavior. Sharing this expertise is consistent with our facilitator role. By discussing the ground rules, I make explicit the kind of group behavior that I consider effective and will be helping group members use. Because the ground rules are so central to my approach to facilitation, in the planning meeting I advocate for the set of ground rules that I have developed, explain the reasoning underlying them, and encourage members to raise questions and concerns they have about using these ground rules.

The group has several choices to make regarding the ground rules. First, the members need to decide whether they are willing to have me use the ground rules to intervene with the group. Because the ground rules are central to my approach, if the group chooses not to have me use them, then they are also choosing not to use me as their facilitator. If this occurs (and it has not yet), I would find out what the group's concerns were, and if I could not meet the concerns, then I would help the group find another facilitator. The second choice the group has to make is whether to commit to practicing the ground rules during the facilitation. The group can revisit this choice if, after practicing the ground rules and understanding them better, members have new concerns about using them. The ground rules for effective groups are not the group's ground rules until the group has explicitly committed to using them.

In the course of making the first two decisions, the group and I make a third decision: whether to add, delete, or modify any ground rules. A group might add a ground rule about whether the information discussed in the meeting is confidential (this is fairly common). Here, my interests are that any change in the ground rules be consistent with the underlying core values; if ground rules are eliminated, it does not entirely limit me as the facilitator from intervening on behavior that is decreasing the group's effectiveness.

See Chapter Fourteen, "Introducing the Ground Rules and Principles in Your Own Words," page 131.

8. How will the facilitator's performance be assessed?
9. What are the facilitator's fees and other charges?
10. When and how can the agreement be changed?
11. How will the contract be conveyed to all the primary group members?

Summarize and Agree on Next Steps

Here I explicitly state whether I am willing and able to facilitate and explicitly ask the group whether it wants to hire me to facilitate. If we have agreed to work together, I send a memo to all group members (including those not in attendance) reflecting the agreements reached in the meeting.

Stage 3: Reaching Agreement with the Entire Primary Client Group

This stage occurs at the beginning of the actual facilitation. The purpose is to ensure that all members attending the facilitation are committed to agreements reached in stage 2. If all group members were present at the planning meeting in stage 2, stage 3 becomes a simple review of the agreement: (1) the purpose, agenda, and time allocation; (2) the process, including ground rules; and (3) the role of the facilitator, leader, and other group members.

If the group members who attended the planning meeting represented the diversity of views on the issues, including the views of those who were absent, then this stage will be easy; those who did not attend the planning meeting will likely support the agreements made at the meeting, and the content of the facilitation begins. However, if the views of those who were absent were not incorporated in the agreement, this stage becomes difficult. Because the entire group is the client, I now need to facilitate a discussion between those who attended the meeting and those who did not and whose needs are not met by the current agreement. This discussion is essential but frustrating for group members who thought the contracting process was completed.

Stage 4: Completing and Evaluating the Facilitation

In this stage, the client group and I evaluate and complete the facilitation. The evaluation process and the term of the facilitation are both agreed on in stage 2. Depending on the length and nature of the facilitation, conditions may change during the facilitation that may lead either the group or me, or both of us, to want to reconsider elements of the agreement. This is a natural part of contracting, and the process for recontracting is agreed on in stage 2.

The Dilemma of Group versus Individual Interviews

Facilitators face a dilemma when deciding whether to meet with group members individually before the full group facilitation. When I used to conduct these individual interviews, group members would tell me their concerns about other group members, especially if I agreed to keep their comments confidential. They often wanted me to address their concerns in the facilitation without mentioning that they had the concern or about whom they had it. In short, the interviews provided me with diagnostic information, but I could not act on it without violating confidentiality, leaving the role of facilitator by raising group members' issues for them or colluding with one team member against others. If I did act on the information I could not explain that I was doing so, and therefore would violate the principle of transparency.

If I did not meet with individuals or subgroups, I avoided these problems but may have created others. If members were reluctant to share information in the full group, I may have designed the facilitation without knowing about important group issues or dynamics until I began the actual facilitation, and some issues may not have been raised at all.

Unlike many other facilitators, I usually deal with the dilemma by not conducting individual interviews with group members or the group leader (apart from the initial telephone calls), recognizing that although issues may not get raised as quickly in the facilitation, group members will always maintain accountability for raising their issues. I have shared this reasoning with the client. When clients request to meet individually before meeting as a group, I typically ask to talk first with the members as a group. This gives me an opportunity to discuss the dilemma that the group and I face, talk with the group about the concerns they have about sharing information in the planning session or facilitation, and inquire about what leads to these concerns. If members are willing to share some of their concerns, I then ask, "What would need to happen for you to be willing to raise and address these concerns?" If group members agree to these conditions (for example, no retribution for raising an issue), they can then discuss issues that they previously chose not to discuss.

Whenever members' concerns about sharing information in the full planning group were discussed, I have never had a group state they were unwilling to continue planning in the full group. If it were to happen, however, I might agree to talk to individuals or a subgroup if the planning group (1) agreed on how the information discussed in the private meeting would be shared in the full group and (2) agreed that the responsibility for raising issues remained with group members. Underlying all of my choices to meet as a full group whenever possible is the principle that the facilitator seeks to create the conditions in which members can publicly share as much information as possible in a way that permits each member to make a free and informed choice about the risk of sharing the information.

Some of you reading this book who are internal consultants, coaches, trainers, and coaches may be thinking, *The Skilled Facilitator approach could really improve my organization, but how do I apply it as an internal person? I don't have the freedom or power of an external person, and I can't say what an external person can say. The risks are greater than I can take.*

The concepts, principles, and tools and techniques of the Skilled Facilitator approach apply equally whether you are working internally or externally to the organization. There is essentially no difference between what constitutes effective behavior for internal and external facilitative roles. There are a variety of actions you can take to reduce potential risks you face as an internal person and increase your effectiveness with your clients. I describe these in detail in *The Skilled Facilitator* in Chapter Fifteen, "Serving as a Facilitator in Your Own Organization," and Resource H, "Guidelines for Contracting with Your Manager."

Contracting with Your Manager

As an internal facilitator (or an external facilitator who works for someone else), the first agreement to reach is with your manager. You thereby reduce potential misunderstandings between the group, the manager, and you, all of which better serves the group. Here are some key questions to discuss with your manager:

- How will groups request my facilitation services?
- Under what conditions may I decline or accept a facilitation request?
- What information will I need to share with you about the facilitation?
- How will my facilitator performance be evaluated?
- What special arrangements will we make if you are part of the group I am asked to facilitate?

FACILITATING IN YOUR OWN ORGANIZATION

See Chapter Forty-Five, "Introducing the Core Values and Ground Rules," page 361.

USING CONTRACTING IN OTHER FACILITATIVE ROLES

Because contracting is essentially about developing a clear agreement about whether and how you will work together, the principles underlying it are equally relevant for facilitative consultants, facilitative coaches, facilitative trainers, and facilitative leaders, even if the stages and tasks within them differ. For example, if a facilitative consultant is consulting to a group whose members have various needs, it is important for the consultant and group to agree whether and how those needs will be met. Applying the principles to the facilitative trainer role means that the trainer identifies the learning needs of the participants even if the training was initially brought in by others in the organization. Although coaches typically work one-on-one, seeking agreement about the way in which you will work with the person, including what information, if any, will be shared with the person's boss, is essential. Even facilitative leaders engage in contracting, although they don't call it that. The "contracting process" begins when people join an existing group or when the group is newly formed. Agreeing on how team members and the leader will work together is part of setting clear goals, agreeing on roles, developing an effective group culture and norms, and agreeing on how problems will be solved, decisions will be made, and conflicts will addressed. All of these are elements of the Group Effectiveness Model—elements that need to be in place for a group to function well.

See Chapter Three, " Using Facilitative Skills in Different Roles," page 27. For some examples, see also Chapter Eleven, "Basic Facilitation," page 115; Chapter Eighteen, "Helping Groups Clarify Roles and Expectations," page 159; Chapter Thirty-Five, "Introducing the Skilled Facilitator Approach at Work," page 293; and Chapter Fifty-Seven, "The Facilitative Coach," 457.

The process for contracting is essentially the same whether you are an internal or external facilitator. In fact, the contracting process is especially important if you are facilitating in your own organization. If groups have worked with you before, they are likely to have implicit expectations of your role that may be different from your expectations. This contracting process enables you to discuss and agree on them.

Whatever your role, effective contracting takes time so that the group and you can work effectively and efficiently together. In systems thinking terms, it's a matter of going slow to go fast.

Resource

Schwarz, R. "Ground Rules for Effective Groups" and "A Consumer's Guide to Hiring and Working with a Group Facilitator." [www.schwarzassociates.com/sfp.htm].

Reference

Silberman, M. (ed.). *The 2004 Team and Organization Development Sourcebook.* Princeton, N.J.: Active Training, 2004.

PART TWO

Starting Out

WITH AN UNDERSTANDING of the Skilled Facilitator foundation principles, you can begin applying this approach to improve conversations and group meetings. Every conversation is an opportunity to practice your skills. In every meeting, you can use the principles to improve the validity of information shared and the quality of decisions reached. Part Two offers guidance on using the Skilled Facilitator approach with one-on-one conversations, basic facilitations, and typical work team tasks. It includes guidelines for specific types of interventions, such as agreeing on a work group's purpose and vision, chartering a team, or clarifying organizational roles and expectations. These are the kinds of issues that many facilitators, human resource professionals, organization development consultants, and leaders frequently are called on to help groups address. Many just learning the Skilled Facilitator approach struggle to integrate what they already know about basic facilitation with their new skills. The chapters in Part Two aim to help you get started.

We begin by helping you use the Skilled Facilitator approach to build a foundation for any conversation, whether one-on-one or with a group. Chapter Nine, "Jointly Designing the Purpose and Process for a Conversation," shows you how to jointly design the purpose and process for any discussion before you start working on content. Once you know how to set up this basic structure, you will be ready to design group processes and use them to conduct basic facilitations.

Chapters Ten through Fourteen focus on planning a basic facilitation and opening your first group meeting. Chapter Ten, "Process Designs," discusses the three levels of group process (designs, methods, and tools). It offers criteria for selecting appropriate processes with examples of agendas the authors have used successfully. Chapter Eleven, "Basic Facilitation," and Chapter Twelve, "Do the Math," help you apply your theoretical understanding of group process to determining what can (and cannot) be accomplished in a basic facilitation. This chapter offers practical guidance and sample agendas to help you jointly design a process with a group and determine how much time is needed and how to allocate it, as well as what to do when you and the group disagree about or need to reallocate time.

Chapter Thirteen, "Beginning Meetings," and Chapter Fourteen, "Introducing the Ground Rules and Principles in Your Own Words," help you set up the first part of a group session. Chapter Thirteen discusses the sorts of working agreements we set up with groups for issues as broad as confidentiality and as specific as managing breaks. It offers suggestions for handling group introductions and provides a typical set of guidelines for workshops and basic facilitations. Chapter Fourteen shares suggestions for how to condense the principles for a short, basic facilitation. It offers a way to quickly introduce a group to five basic principles that can guide a focused work session when a group is not familiar with the ground rules or core values.

Chapters Fifteen to Nineteen address fundamental work group issues. Chapter Fifteen, "Using the Group Effectiveness Model," suggests steps for introducing the model, conducting a diagnosis of group strengths and weaknesses, and jointly designing with a group which effectiveness elements to address. It then covers how to intervene on a specific aspect of group effectiveness. Chapter Sixteen, "Helping Group Members Focus on Interests Rather Than Positions," adds another decision-making skill. Chapter Seventeen, "Developing Shared Vision and Values," and Chapter Eighteen, "Helping Groups Clarify Roles and Expectations," discuss ways to establish these critical components of a group's structure. Chapter Nineteen, "Using the Skilled Facilitator Approach to Strengthen Work Groups and Teams," points out how the Skilled Facilitator approach supports the factors that recent research shows create successful teams and collaborative organizations. It focuses on creating a strong team charter and adapting the chartering process for executive-level management teams. Together, these chapters should help you get any work group or team off to sound start.

E-mail is increasingly a primary method of communication in many organizations. The concluding chapter in this part suggests ways to apply key ground rules that can overcome the additional challenges of communicating when you cannot see or hear those you are "conversing" with. Chapter Twenty, "Using the Ground Rules in E-Mail," provides a sample e-mail, shows how to analyze it to see whether ground rules are being used, and then offers a rewritten version modeling Skilled Facilitator principles.

Chapter 9

Jointly Designing the Purpose and Process for a Conversation

Roger Schwarz
Anne Davidson

Beginning a conversation well can make the rest of a conversation more productive. For us, this includes agreeing on the purpose and process of a discussion before engaging in the content of the conversation. Anne Davidson calls this the ***PPC approach***, and it represents one of the applications of Ground Rule Seven: jointly design next steps. It is equally important for one-on-one conversations and group meetings.

Beginning a conversation well can make the rest of a conversation more productive. For us, this includes agreeing on the purpose and process of a discussion before engaging in the content of the conversation.

See Chapter Five, "Ground Rules for Effective Groups," page 61.

Unfortunately, people often begin conversations by immediately discussing the content without first agreeing about the purpose of the conversation or the process they will use to have it. Consequently, each person may have a different understanding of the purpose and uses his or her own process to guide the conversation. This can create misunderstanding and unnecessary conflict.

Jointly designing the purpose and process of a conversation provides the valid information for people to make an informed choice about committing to having the conversation. By agreeing first on the purpose, you begin to create a shared understanding about what kinds of comments will be relevant. This enables people to focus their comments and monitor the conversation to see if it is on track.

Similarly, agreeing on the process of the discussion gives everyone the same road map. In conversations that involve conflict, people are sometimes concerned that the process will be used to push a particular point of view and exclude their point of view. You can reduce this concern if all group members agree to the process. In formal meetings, people are more likely to have an agenda and sometimes even an agreed-on process. But in our experience, as a conversation becomes less formal and more spontaneous, an agreed-on purpose and process disappear.

By sharing your purpose and process, you are making your reasoning transparent. By advocating and then checking for any concerns, you are combining advocacy with inquiry.

If you initiate a conversation or meeting, it's reasonable to have not only a purpose in mind but also a suggested process. By sharing your purpose and process, you are making your reasoning transparent. By advocating and then checking for any concerns, you are combining advocacy with inquiry.

For a simple, informal conversation, using PPC might look like this: **"Jeff, I have some additions I'd like to make to your grant proposal to cover small town projects. Would you be willing to take about thirty minutes to talk through them with me and then agree about whether you are willing to add them?"** [If yes] **"When would be a good time to do that?"**

Below is an example of beginning a more formal meeting by agreeing on purpose and process:

Step	***Opening Line***
1. Agree on Purpose	
Explain your purpose	"Today I'd like for us to reach a decision about how we will handle allocation of costs for the internal consultants."
Inquire about different views Reach agreement about the purpose	"Does anyone have a different understanding of the purpose of the meeting? Is there any other issue we need to address in order to make this decision?"
2. Jointly design a process	"Now that we've got agreement on the purpose, I want to suggest a process for the meeting and get your reactions."
Advocate a process and share reasoning	"I suggest we start by clarifying our interests or needs in terms of allocating costs for the internal consultants. In other words, I want us to answer the question, 'However we end up allocating internal consultant costs, we need to do it in a way that . . .'" "Next, I suggest we reach agreement about the set of interests. Then we can jointly craft a solution that meets as many of the interests as possible—hopefully, all of them."

	"I think if we start by identifying our interests, we'll better understand the needs that each of us has, so we'll be better able to come up with a solution that works for everyone.
	"I want to see if we can reach a consensus decision on this because the decision affects each of your budgets. But we need a decision to Finance by the end of the day, so if we aren't able to reach agreement by then, I'll make the decision based on all of your input."
Inquire about different views	"What problems if any do you see with the process I'm proposing?"
Reach agreement about the process	"Do we have agreement to use the process?"
3. Begin discussing the content of the conversation	"Okay, now that we've agreed on the process, let's begin with the first step: identifying interests."

Chapter 10

Process Designs

Anne Davidson

In the same way you lay the foundation for a productive conversation by jointly designing its purpose and process, every time you facilitate, you will need a clear purpose and a process or blueprint for completing the project. There are literally hundreds of tools and methods skilled facilitators use to help groups accomplish their goals, and these can be combined to create thousands of process designs. The Skilled Facilitator approach can be used productively with numerous approaches to improve the quality of dialogue and decision making within those designs.

In the same way you lay the foundation for a productive conversation by jointly designing its purpose and process, every time you facilitate, you will need a clear purpose and a process or blueprint for completing the project.

See Chapter Nine, "Jointly Designing the Purpose and Process for a Conversation," page 103.

THREE LEVELS OF GROUP PROCESS

We distinguish three levels of process. By ***process*** I mean any set of steps or activities that participants follow to perform a task. First, process ***designs*** structure the whole facilitation or a major portion of it. This level represents the more macro processes that address the group's purpose for meeting, such as developing a vision and mission statement, creating a strategic plan, or chartering a new team. ***Methods*** are more specific processes used to move the group through a series of steps. Problem-solving models and process mapping are examples of group process methods.[1] At the most micro level, ***tools*** represent discrete activities used within a method, such as brainstorming or Pareto analysis or mind mapping. Tools structure the group's experience for a relatively shorter period of time.

In working with groups, we first determine the purpose and overall design for a session. The design then guides the methods chosen. The tools appropriate to that method are the ones from which we select to complete our plan for a facilitation. Table 10.1 lists some of the designs, methods, and tools that I find useful to combine with the Skillful Facilitator approach. Skilled Facilitator principles and tools can strengthen each level. For example, the Group Effectiveness Model can guide the discussion during a team chartering process. The ground rules may help the group stay focused on one step at a time during problem solving or test assumptions behind a cause-and-effect diagram.

Table 10.1 **Some Useful Process Designs, Methods and Tools**

Design (Purpose)	Recommended Group Size	Method	Sample Tools
Group Formation	Small (3–12)	Group Effectiveness Model review	Pairs introductions Ground rules development GEM diagram Posted introduction sheets
	Large	Purpose and goals review Chartering authority presentation	Group biographies Roles and responsibilities
Vision/values/mission	Large	Future Search Open Space	Stakeholder selection Timelines and milestones Trend analysis
	Large or small	Future scenario development	Common theme identification Public commitments
	Small	Search conference Dialogue Focused conversation	Four principles and one law Visioning exercises
Strategic planning	Large	Open Space Balanced Scorecard	Four principles and one law Force-field analysis Trend analysis
	Medium to small	ICA Strategic Planning Process SWOT analysis Scenario planning	Visioning exercises
Problem solving	Medium to small	9-, 7-, or 5-step problem-solving model	Problem definition Gap analysis Pareto charting Checksheets Root cause diagrams Multivoting Brainstorming Decision grids
		Interest charting	"Strawman" development Priority setting
Project planning	Medium to small	Goals/Objective/Action Item Development Interest charting Project timeline Asset mapping	Stakeholder identification Mind-mapping Goal wishing (Synectics) Control charts Critical Path analysis Force-field analysis Storyboarding

Design (Purpose)	Recommended Group Size	Method	Sample Tools
Conflict resolution	Small to large (in subgroups)	Interest charting Ground rules–based dialogue Mediation Focused conversation	Left-hand column dialogues Assumption and intention testing Prouds and sorrys Hopes and fears Project piloting
Process improvement	Medium to small	Process mapping	Checksheets Histograms Flowcharting
Group development	Medium to small (include all group members)	Group Effectiveness Model review Appreciative Inquiry Roles and expectations review Focused conversation	Ground rules Mental models Biases and defensive triggers exercise Group critique Experiential activities

Note: This list is not intended to be comprehensive. It is merely a sample list of processes that my colleagues and I find work well with the Skillful Facilitator approach for the purposes indicated.

The sample process designs (agendas) in Exhibits 10.1 and 10.2 at the end of this chapter demonstrate how once a group sets a purpose or intent and number of participants, you can then select methods and tools well matched to the task. In the town visioning exercise (Exhibit 10.1) we had a large group that needed an opportunity to create and share possible future scenarios. Town leaders needed some sense of the ideas people most supported, but no final agreement would be reached until ideas had been further developed and researched. For this purpose, creating a process for citizens to brainstorm future scenarios was an ideal method, and brainstorming and multivoting were sufficient and productive tools.

I suggest that you develop a basic set of tools in each of several categories that you can explain and facilitate well. Choose categories that represent the types of facilitation and consultation you do or want to do. However, be aware that every group and every session is different. With experience, you will develop templates that often work for you and the groups you typically facilitate, but you will always be testing new designs and tools. Keep several basic references on process design at hand. For suggestions, see the resource list at the end of this chapter. Constantly seek, develop, and test new processes.

Always carefully match designs to the specific needs and goals of your clients. Clarify the criteria you are using to select designs, methods, or tools. The next section contains the basic set of criteria that I use to guide my choices.

Always carefully match designs to the specific needs and goals of your clients. Clarify the criteria you are using to select designs, methods, or tools.

DESIGN SELECTION CRITERIA

The most important guideline is to be certain that any design, method, or tool can be used in a manner consistent with the Skilled Facilitator core values.

In general, as long as the intent of a design can be shared and mutually agreed on between the facilitator and participants, it can be successfully used or adapted. In other words, the primary principle for combining the Skilled Facilitator and other processes is to make the process design transparent.

The most important guideline is to be certain that any design, method, or tool can be used in a manner consistent with the Skilled Facilitator core values. This means that manipulative designs that withhold information and trick participants for the sake of making a point are not a wise choice. It is difficult to ask groups to share valid information as they work through a process if you have modeled withholding it in an earlier exercise. Following this guideline means that many tools may need adaptation for successful combination with the Skilled Facilitator approach (see Table 10.1).

In general, as long as the intent of a design can be shared and mutually agreed on between the facilitator and participants, it can be successfully used or adapted. In other words, the primary principle for combining the Skilled Facilitator and other processes is to make the process design transparent.

See Chapter Fifty-Eight, "Becoming a Facilitative Trainer," page 479, for some specific examples of consistent and inconsistent group activities.

Here are the basic design selection criteria:

- *Purpose.* What is the group trying to accomplish? What problems, if any, have you and the group diagnosed? What designs will address these problems and allow the group to accomplish its purpose?
- *Time/length.* What is the duration of the project? How much time has the group allotted? Is it sufficient to accomplish the goals, or can the time or goals be renegotiated? (Most groups plan to accomplish too much in too little time.)

See Chapter Twelve, "Do the Math," page 119, for suggestions about determining the time needed for a process design.

- *Group size.* Some tools and processes are specifically designed to work with very large or very small groups. Often large groups need to spend some time in subgroups to accomplish their tasks. Determining which processes are appropriate for the size of the group is very important, as is determining how to manage transitions between small group work and larger group work. Be certain there is sufficient time or a specific process for each small group or individual to report out and have their work shared with the full group.

- *Facilitator skill.* Match process designs to your skill level. If you have never facilitated a process you feel would be effective for a group, tell them so. Agree about whether it is okay to try this together to see how it works, whether to cofacilitate with someone experienced in this process, or whether to use a different design.
- *Consistency with the core values.* Does the process allow for being transparent about how it is designed and the intentions for using it? Can you share all valid information about a process and still use it effectively? (For example, one option is to share with a group that an exercise withholds key information that they must discover to succeed, and then mutually agree about whether the group members still want to engage in it.) Can an activity be used in a way that provides every individual free and informed choice (including whether or not to participate) and is compassionate?
- *Internal consistency of processes.* Is the method or tool consistent with the purpose the group is trying to achieve? Watch out for selecting tools that work at cross-purposes to one another. For example, don't choose icebreakers that establish competing subgroups if you are trying to help the group develop boundary spanning or collaboration skills in subsequent activities. Watch out for setting up subgroups in ways that reinforce existing group barriers. Avoid using tools that seem repetitious. Consider different learning or information processing styles as well.

SAMPLE DESIGN A: TOWN VISIONING EXERCISE

Sample Design A (Exhibit 10.1) was a design for a half-day town meeting to brainstorm a set of special community projects that would be completed in honor of the millennium and the town's two-hundredth birthday celebration. The town had previously engaged in similar, longer sessions to develop a vision and Year 2020 Plan. This was an update to that plan.

SAMPLE DESIGN B: BOARD OF COMMISSIONERS RETREAT

This design (Exhibit 10.2) was for an annual planning retreat for a town board of commissioners. One unique feature was inclusion of the manager's evaluation. The facilitator helped board members reach agreement about each item on the manager's evaluation form and then facilitated a feedback conversation between the Board and the manager.

Exhibit 10.1 "New Century, New Carrboro" Town Meeting Agenda

9:45–10:15	**Registration**, Coffee, Informal Greeting, Introductions at Tables
10:15–10:25	**Welcome and Explanation of the Project**
10:25–10:30	**Overview of Process for the Meeting**
	Invitation to Imagine Carrboro in 2011
10:30–10:50	**Background Information** on Major Projects, Recreation Master Plan, etc.
10:50–11:00	**Instructions to Small Groups** (brainstorming, posting, combining, prioritizing)
11:00–11:40	**Brainstorming Ideas**
	Posting, Clarifying, and Combining Ideas
11:40–12:10	**Reviewing and Multivoting on ideas**
12:10–1:00	**Review of Priorities from each group**
	Next Steps
	Questions from Participants

Charge to Groups

What projects (large or small), if completed by 2011, would make Carrboro a better place to live?

Guidelines for Brainstorming Projects

- Everybody in the group contributes something, if only one idea.
- One person speaks at a time.
- Nothing is challenged or criticized during brainstorming.
- It is okay to add to ideas others contribute.
- It is okay to pass when you have nothing more to offer.
- Add brief, clarifying points to ideas after brainstorming but before posting.

Guidelines for Prioritizing Projects

- Scribes will post ideas on the wall, one idea per page.
- Scribes will combine duplicate ideas as they post.
- You have seven colored "sticky dots"; place *one dot each* on the seven projects you believe will most contribute to enhanced quality of life in Carrboro.
- If you have questions about the meaning or content of a project, locate a member of the group that originated the project and ask for clarification before you select your priority projects. (The number of the group that originated the idea is on the idea sheet and on the name tags of group members.)

YOUR BREAKOUT GROUP NUMBER IS 5

Exhibit 10.2 **Board of Commissioners Retreat: Proposed Agenda**

Day 1

5:00 P.M.	**Agenda Review, Revision, and Agreement**
	Review Role of Facilitator
5:15–5:45	**Dinner and Networking**
5:45–8:30	**Discussions with Department Heads**
5:45–6:15	Police
6:15–6:45	Public Works
6:45–7:15	Water/Sewer
7:15–7:30	*Break*
7:30–8:00	Recreation
8:00–8:30	Finance
8:30–9:00	Brief **Review of Previous Year's Accomplishments**
	Adjourn

Day 2

8:00–10:00 A.M.	Closed session: **Manager's Evaluation and Feedback to Manager** (board reaches consensus rating of each item on evaluation form and then discusses each rating, reasons for the rating, and specific examples with the manager)
10:00–10:15	*Break*
10:15–11:00	**Review and Update of Commissioner and Mayor Roles and Expectations**
11:00–12:30	**Discussion of Special Topics** (with working lunch)
12:30–2:00	**Brainstorm Coming Year Commission Goals and Projects**
2:00–3:00	**Agree on Top Priorities**
	Multivote
	Develop consensus on top priorities
3:00–3:30	**Wrap-Up and Evaluation**

Resources

For some excellent proven process designs, methods, and tools, review these resources. Note that some of the uses described are not consistent with the Skilled Facilitator approach. Use the design criteria set out in this chapter before combining with the Skilled Facilitator approach.

Bens, I. *Facilitating with Ease.* San Francisco: Jossey-Bass, 2000.

Bunker, B. B., and Alban, B. T. *Large Group Interventions.* San Francisco: Jossey-Bass, 1997.

Justice, T., and Jamieson, D. W. *The Facilitator's Fieldbook.* New York: AMACOM, 1999.

Kaner, S. *Facilitator's Guide to Participatory Decision-Making.* Gabriola Island, B.C.: New Society Publishers/Canada, 1996.

Stanfield, B. *The Art of Focused Conversation.* Toronto: ICA Canada, 1997.

Note

1. See *The Skilled Facilitator,* Chapter Ten, pp. 215–232, for further discussion of using the Skilled Facilitator approach with other processes and for a detailed example of using the approach with a problem-solving model.

Chapter 11

Basic Facilitation

What Can Be Accomplished? What Cannot?

Peg Carlson

WHEN I DO ***basic facilitation,*** I help a group use effective process to discuss a particular substantive topic. Because the facilitator assumes the primary responsibility for attending to the group's process, basic facilitation does not result in reduced dependence on the facilitator over time. I have little expectation that the group will learn and transfer these skills to future discussions, as occurs with developmental facilitation. Based on my experience, I have developed both an appreciation for what a group can accomplish using basic facilitation and an understanding of where limitations often arise.

WHAT CAN BE ACCOMPLISHED WITH BASIC FACILITATION?

As I use the term, *basic* does *not* mean that the substantive topic being discussed is easy or simple; a group may use basic facilitation to discuss some very difficult topics. For example, a management team may ask a facilitator to help them use effective process skills as they decide who will be laid off during lean budget times, or a group may ask a facilitator for assistance in identifying and discussing past events where group members ended up extremely angry at one another over perceived violations of trust. Here are some examples of the issues groups have addressed when I worked with them:

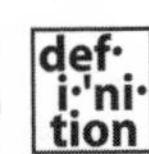

Basic facilitation is helping a group use effective process to discuss a particular substantive topic. *Basic* does not mean that the substantive topic being discussed is easy or simple; a group may use basic facilitation to discuss some very difficult topics.

- Clarified roles and expectations
- Agreed on a vision and core values for the organization
- Set long- and short-term goals
- Developed a new performance management system
- Agreed on criteria to select a new chief executive officer

In my experience, there's no limit to the substantive content a group can tackle in basic facilitation.

Although the facilitator is not explicitly teaching process skills to a group in a basic facilitation context, group members frequently develop an awareness of and appreciation for the importance of group process as they work with a facilitator. When I work with a group in basic facilitation, members have seen the "Ground Rules for Effective Groups" article and heard me briefly describe the core values and ground rules at the beginning of the meeting (and sometimes in the planning meeting as well).[1] I explain to the group that these are the tools I use to help group members have more effective conversations and ask if they are interested in trying to use them during the time we are working together. I assure them that there is no expectation that they will be able to use the ground rules consistently. My role is to help the group use the core values and ground rules during the discussion. Typically, groups readily agree to try to use the ground rules during the meeting.

LIMITATIONS

Although I am the primary person monitoring and intervening on the group's process in basic facilitation, group members often pick up on what I am doing and begin to use the ground rules themselves. For example, after seeing me intervene several times in a conversation, group members may begin to say to each other, "I think we're making an assumption in this conversation," "You've told us your position, but I still don't understand your interests," or "Let me explain why I asked that question." This recognition of the value of the ground rules and how they can help the group have a more effective discussion can help group members monitor their own behavior and use more effective process to discuss their issues even when a facilitator is not present.

Difficulties can arise, however, because without a full understanding of the ground rules, individuals run the risk of intervening in a way that is unilateral and increases defensiveness among other members.

Difficulties can arise, however, because without a full understanding of the ground rules, individuals run the risk of intervening in a way that is unilateral and increases defensiveness among other members. For example, it often creates tension when an individual tells another person, "You're making an inference," without recognizing the need to test out his or her own inference that the other person is making an inference. This type of unilateral intervention, or "ground rules police," can create bad feelings and a disincentive toward using ground rules in future meetings.

There are two roots to this problem. First, at the operational level, people lack the knowledge of how to intervene using the diagnosis-intervention cycle. Second, at a deeper level, groups that have not been trained in the Skilled Facilitator approach often lack the understanding of the mutual learning model underlying the core values and ground rules. This results in using the ground rules in a unilaterally controlling way. In these situations, I intervene, applauding the effort to use the ground rules but then adding the steps needed to, for example, add inquiry to what might otherwise be a unilateral declaration.

For an introduction to these foundational principles, see Chapter Four, "Understanding What Guides Your Behavior," page 33; Chapter Five, "Ground Rules for Effective Groups," page 61; and Chapter Six, "The Diagnosis-Intervention Cycle," page 69.

Basic facilitation is not likely to result in group members' reflecting deeply on the consequences of their own behavior and recognizing when they may be contributing to the very group outcome that they believe to be ineffective. Groups frequently express frustration at finding themselves in the same boat again and again, whether the topic is failing to meet overly ambitious sales targets or developing a compensation system that is perceived as equitable and effective. In my experience, the questions that are valuable for a facilitator or group member to raise at this point are "double-loop learning" questions intended to help a group examine their values and strategies.[2] For example, to help a group reflect on its underlying values and strategies, I may ask, "What is it that leads this group to create long lists of projects year after year, even when you say you want to scale back and set key priorities?" Although it is possible to have these conversations in a basic facilitation context, group members are often better equipped, and more willing, to have a discussion of how they have contributed to the problem the group is facing as part of a developmental facilitation when they have committed to learning and using the core values and ground rules in their work.

Basic facilitation is not likely to result in group members' reflecting deeply on the consequences of their own behavior and recognizing when they may be contributing to the very group outcome that they believe to be ineffective.

AN EXAMPLE

The following example illustrates the tremendous progress groups can make using basic facilitation and the difficulty they have in maintaining a more effective group process once the facilitator departs.

> I worked with a governing board that was divided into two camps, according to their beliefs about what their constituents wanted. Each side had made accusations about the other, and they were nursing hurt feelings that went back several years. There were also different ideas about how to work effectively with the executive director, and board members had accused other members of not doing their job correctly (as each side defined it). I worked with them over a period of several months as they agreed on roles and expectations for other board members and the executive director

See Chapter Eighteen, "Helping Groups Clarify Roles and Expectations," page 159.

> As they explored what they expected of other members and the director, they uncovered assumptions they had made about others' actions and motives. The group members learned that these assumptions were frequently incorrect, and they changed their interpretation of the meaning of past events after hearing the explanations and perspectives of other members. After three sessions, the group expressed great satisfaction with the

progress they had made and felt that they were now in a very different place in terms of their ability to work together effectively. Several members described the experience as a real breakthrough that permanently changed the way they viewed their role as a board member.

However, when I checked on the group's progress six months later, there appeared to be little change in individuals' behavior regarding the assumptions they made about other board members' actions, motives, and intent. Even though they saw the value of testing assumptions in the earlier basic facilitation context, they did not move to the next step of monitoring their own behavior: recognizing when they were starting to make untested assumptions that might bring them down the same (ineffective) road they had been down before. They continued to view the work they had done clarifying roles and expectations as extremely valuable, but felt that they had lapsed back into old patterns fairly quickly.

For groups that use basic facilitation and see the value of having a more effective group process when tackling a specific problem, the experience may ultimately help them make an informed choice about committing to improve their process more permanently through developmental work.

For groups that use basic facilitation and see the value of having a more effective group process when tackling a specific problem, the experience may ultimately help them make an informed choice about committing to improve their process more permanently through developmental work.

Notes

1. "Ground Rules for Effective Groups," available at www.schwarzassociates.com.
2. For a description of single- and double-loop learning, see the writings of Chris Argyris, for example, "Good Communication That Blocks Learning" (1994).

Reference

Argyris, A. "Good Communication That Blocks Learning," *Harvard Business Review,* July-Aug. 1994, pp. 77–85.

Chapter 12

Do the Math

Creating a Realistic Agenda

Peg Carlson

ONE AREA IN WHICH a facilitator can add value is in helping a group craft a realistic agenda to help it accomplish its stated goals. In my experience, doing the math is a major part of determining what a group can reasonably expect to accomplish in a meeting. By calculating specific time estimates for the various portions of the discussion, a facilitator and group can jointly decide how much material the group is likely to cover in a given period.

It's common for groups to be overly ambitious in their estimates of what can be done in a full day, a half-day, or an hour. Here are some examples of time estimates given by groups during the initial phases of planning a meeting or retreat:

It's common for groups to be overly ambitious in their estimates of what can be done in a full day, a half-day, or an hour.

> "We would like to agree on a vision for our community and set annual goals for the staff's work. We can meet from 9:30 a.m. to noon."
>
> "We want to agree on roles and expectations of each other as board members and set a strategic plan to guide the organization's priorities for the next five years. The board has agreed to set aside four hours—most members aren't willing to meet for longer than that."

My job is not to convince group members that their time allotments are incorrect and mine are correct; rather, my goal is to have each of us share our assessment and our reasons for what leads us to that assessment, and jointly design an agenda that represents our best estimate.

When I sit down with group members in a planning meeting, it often feels as if participants are trying to put twenty pounds of flour in a ten-pound sack. This tendency is completely understandable. Having an entire management team, department, or governing board come together for a half-day or more represents a big commitment of time and money, and it's tempting to try to fit in as many important issues as possible.

SOME RULES OF THUMB FOR GENERATING TIME ESTIMATES

Here are the general principles that I use to estimate the amount of time a group needs to accomplish its agenda goals.

Factor in the Number of People in the Group

Generally, the larger the group, the more time is needed to allow participation by members. This seems self-evident, but it's easy to overlook when trying to construct the agenda. For example, I was recently working with group representatives to plan a meeting for a fifteen-member board. One portion of the agenda involved discussion and adoption of an employee compensation plan. The group had originally allocated fifteen minutes for a staff member's presentation, followed by thirty minutes of board discussion. I pointed out that this translated to two minutes per person of discussion time and asked if this was a topic that people saw as important and was likely to generate differing views. The answer was yes to both, and the group decided that setting aside ninety minutes for the board discussion was more realistic.

In a large group, some portions of the discussion may occur in subgroups. This is a useful technique for allowing more people to participate in a discussion. However, if the group ultimately needs to reach agreement on a topic, it's still important to allow additional large group time to fully process the different perspectives and suggestions that may emerge from the small group discussions.

Incorporate Some Slack into the Agenda

An estimate on how long each agenda item will take is just that: an estimate. Sometimes an agenda item may be addressed more quickly than anticipated, but in my experience, it has been more common for a portion of the discussion to need more time than originally allocated. By proposing that a group create a cushion of time in the event that some agenda items take longer than expected, a facilitator can help a group avoid the frustration associated with not accomplishing everything on the list or limiting the contribution of individual group members because of time constraints.

Consider the Group's History and Your Knowledge of the Group

Is this the first meeting of a newly formed group? If so, the members are likely to need some extra time at the outset to get to know each other and understand their place in the group. If the group has a history of working together, ask group members whether they normally complete discussion of agenda items within the allotted time or whether their conversations tend to run long. While a facilitator may certainly help frame and focus the discussion, it is useful to consider the group's established working style (if it has one) when creating the agenda. Using the Skilled Facilitator approach, it is not your role to determine this unilaterally or make untested inferences about the way the group works together. As part of a contracting session, you can ask the group about this, as well as make your own observations of the group's interactions.

WHEN THE FACILITATOR AND GROUP DISAGREE ABOUT TIME

A group (or group representatives in a contracting session) may disagree with your assessment of how much time is needed for each of the agenda items. This may be because the group thinks your estimates are probably accurate, but the group just can't afford to take that much time, or your estimates are unnecessarily generous, and the group is likely to progress more quickly than you think. It can be difficult to jointly design a way to test this disagreement ahead of time, as the test is likely to be the meeting itself.

I have two recommendations for how to handle this situation. First, if the group is concerned because it looks as if they won't be able to get through all they had planned, I may say something like this:

"Part of my job as a facilitator is to help you move effectively and efficiently through your agenda. I think I can help you do that in two ways. One way is to intervene in your group's discussion as needed to help people stay focused, identify their interests, and make decisions that have the necessary support.

"The other—and perhaps more important—way is to help you create an agenda that reflects a realistic estimate of how long the discussion is likely to take. If we have a realistic agenda, it reduces the chance that group members will become frustrated because they didn't accomplish everything on the list, or because some members didn't get a chance to contribute to the discussion because of time constraints.

"Does this help address your concern? What problems do you see with this approach?"

Second, if the group disagrees with my time estimates, I say something like this:

"If you believe that the discussion will not take as long as my estimate, I think we should use your recommended time allotment. However, if it turns out to be less time than the group needs, I want you to know that I cannot compress the work to fit the time allotted. So I propose that if the group is not finished at the end of the allotted time, I will work with the group to jointly design how to move forward. How does that sound to you?"

WHAT TO DO WHEN THINGS TAKE LONGER THAN ANTICIPATED

Despite the best estimates of the facilitator and group, sometimes the meeting time turns out to be inadequate for what the group wants to accomplish. If it looks as if there will not be sufficient time to complete the discussion, Ground Rule Seven (jointly design next steps) will help determine how to move forward. A group may decide to add extra time, drop an item, plan another meeting, or come up with another idea.

The important point to remember is that jointly designing next steps will take some time; as a facilitator, you don't want to have this conversation with the group when only five minutes remain. To prevent this, I do frequent process checks throughout the meeting—for example,

"We are nearing the end of the time allotted for this topic. Would you like to continue this discussion, or move on to the next agenda item?" I frequently add something like, "If you choose to continue this discussion, I think it may reduce the time you have available to discuss X later in the meeting. Do others agree, or do you see it differently?" [If group agrees] "Given that, how would you like to spend your remaining time?"

A key part of the facilitator's role is to help the group make informed choices about how it is spending its time. Frequent process checks will help a group do that and avoid the frustration associated with being unaware that time is running out.

A key part of the facilitator's role is to help the group make informed choices about how it is spending its time. Frequent process checks will help a group do that and avoid the frustration associated with being unaware that time is running out.

No two groups will use exactly the same amount of time to move through an agenda. However, by using the right questions and careful planning, a facilitator can work with a group to create an estimate that has an increased likelihood of being accurate. Exhibits 12.1 and 12.2 are two sample retreat agendas. The first can be used for a one-day retreat to clarify roles and expectations of board members and chief executive officer and the second works for a two-day retreat to agree on vision, mission, and goals for an organization or department.

Exhibit 12.1 Sample One-Day Retreat Agenda: Roles and Expectations for the Board and Chief Executive Officer

Introduction

- Introduce participants
- Review and agree on agenda
- Review role of facilitator
- Agree on ground rules
- Identify expectations for retreat (for example, "What needs to happen to make this retreat a success?")

Board members' expectations of each other

Each board member completes the statement, "I expect other board members to . . ."

Board members' expectations of chair and vice chair (and vice versa)

Each board member completes the statement, "I expect the chair and vice chair to . . ."

Chair and vice chair complete the statement, "I expect board members to . . ."

Board members' expectations of CEO (and vice versa)

Each board member completes the statement, "I expect the manager to . . ."

CEO completes the statement, "I expect board members to . . ."

Clarification of/agreement on expectations

Group reaches agreement on a set of expectations for each role [This may be done after each set.]

Next steps

Group agrees on next steps for implementing ideas suggested/commitments made during the retreat, including what they will do if people fail to meet expectations.

Self-critique

Group members identify what went well during the retreat and what they would do differently next time.

Exhibit 12.2 Sample Two-Day Retreat Agenda: Vision, Mission, Goals

Introduction

- Introduce participants
- Review and agree on agenda
- Review role of facilitator
- Agree on ground rules
- Identify expectations for retreat (for example, "What needs to happen to make this retreat a success?")

Vision for Stevens County

- Participants share their desired future for Stevens County
- Group identifies common themes and interests
- Group drafts vision statement for Stevens County

Mission Statement for Stevens County

Using the new vision statement, group drafts/updates a mission statement for Stevens County.

Goal Setting

Group sets goals for the next three to five years, given their mission and vision for Stevens County.

Prioritizing Goals

Group agrees on most important goals for Stevens County.

Action Planning

Group identifies strategies to help them reach goals, including discussion of possible barriers they will need to overcome.

Next Steps

Group agrees on next steps for implementing ideas suggested/commitments made during the retreat.

Self-Critique

Group members identify what went well during the retreat and what they would do differently next time.

Chapter 13

Beginning Meetings

Introductions and Guidelines for Working Together

Anne Davidson

The opening of any meeting, retreat, or workshop sets the tone for the entire gathering. Just like beginning a conversation, this is the time to build a structure to support the session. We rely on the steps in Stage Three of our contracting process (reaching agreement with the entire group) and Ground Rule Seven (Jointly design next steps and ways to test disagreements) to create a firm foundation. This is the time to reach clear and mutual agreement about the purpose of any session and the process that will be used for doing our work together before we begin on content.

> The opening of any meeting, retreat, or workshop sets the tone for the entire gathering. Just like beginning a conversation, this is the time to build a structure to support the session.

The opening of a session is also an opportunity to begin to model the Skilled Facilitator principles by, at a minimum, sharing valid information, explaining reasoning and intent, and combining inquiry with advocacy (testing for agreement). I often see problems later in a workshop or meeting that could have been resolved by spending a bit more time understanding who will be in the room and their expectations. Confusion and frustration are also avoided by agreeing about some procedural guidelines for working together. Yet I frequently see trainers, facilitators, and leaders dive right in without investing time on introductions or guidelines.

This chapter outlines some thoughts about the value of going slow to go fast as you open a session and some examples of what I share with groups.

See Chapter Eight, "Contracting with Groups," page 89, and Chapter Nine, "Jointly Designing the Purpose and Process for a Conversation," page 103.

INTRODUCTIONS

Introductions are a good way for people to begin to get their voices in the room. Taking more time here can pay dividends by setting group norms of people speaking up, of sharing responsibility for the success of the session, and for taking at least mild risks in revealing something of themselves. This is the time to check and clarify expectations so that the session content can be adapted, if necessary, or so that you can identify expectations that you believe cannot be met. This allows participants to make a free and informed choice about whether they need or want to remain at a session or to decide whether and how to align their goals for the session with those of others. I have seen more than one facilitation or training disrupted when participants began leaving because their expectations were not met and because no one clarified what they could or should expect at the outset.

The length of time I take with introductions depends on the length of the session. Exhibits 13.1 and 13.2 are two examples. The first is for a workshop where I am in the role of facilitative trainer. The group will be together for several days and will be asked to engage in activities together that reveal a fair amount about their thinking, strategy, and past struggles. This can feel risky, so I take more time at the start to allow people to get to know one another, help them gain information to decide with whom they would like to work most closely, and clarify what all of us want from the session.

In sessions like this one, people usually work together in small groups. Unless they already know one another well or have agreed to remain together as an intact work group during the session, I generally do not have them sit in small groups or select their small group partners until after the introductions. At Skilled Facilitator trainings and most of the other sessions I conduct, we start out in a circle, in rows, in a horseshoe, or in some other seating design that will have to be reconfigured to form working groups. We want to provide participants as free and informed a choice as possible about the partners they will spend time with during a lengthy session. If people come in and sit in the same-size groups they will work in, it is often harder to reconfigure the group after introductions. (Of course, to be transparent, we share this reasoning with the group when we explain why the group is sitting in a circle.)

Exhibit 13.2 is an abbreviated set of introductory questions for use in a shorter session (one day or less). Although these introductions cannot be as lengthy, I still want to take time for others to know who is in the room and for all of us to check the alignment of our objectives and expectations.

GUIDELINES FOR WORKING TOGETHER

We separate procedural guidelines from ground rules. Although many groups use the term *ground rules* for the sorts of things we cover in guidelines, we do not want to confuse the mutual learning behavioral strategies we call Ground Rules in the Skilled Facilitator approach with other group agreements.

Exhibit 13.1 Example 1: Introductions for Multiday Sessions

Listed below are some suggestions to guide you in introducing yourself to the group. We believe this introduction is important because it helps each of you get to know one another better and may make it easier for you to take risks and ask questions in order to learn most productively. You may share information related to some of the suggested points or information that is different from the suggestions, or you may choose not to share anything about yourself.

Information we suggest sharing and the reasons for sharing this information:

1. **Your name—what you like to be called.** Reason: So that each person will know how you like to be addressed when they speak to you.
2. **Your job and how long you have been with your organization.** Reason: So that each of us knows the jobs of the people in the room, your level of experience, and how your jobs relate to one another. This will help you create effective learning partnerships.
3. **Something important about yourself that others may not know.** Reason: A fun way to get to know and appreciate the talents of other people. Also helps you identify some of the group's commonalties and differences.
4. **The concerns, if any, you have about this training.** Reason: Allows instructors and group members an opportunity to help you address your concerns and clarify assumptions about the workshop.
5. **What needs to happen for this to be a good learning experience for you.** Reason: Allows instructors and others an opportunity to make adjustments to meet your expectations, identify expectations that cannot be met in this workshop, and make adjustments for your unique learning style.

Note: Dick McMahon and Anne Davidson created this example for a three-day workshop. With twenty-four people, this can take up to fifty minutes, which allows one and a half to two minutes per person.

I use the term ***guidelines*** in two ways. First, this is the term I use for our specific working agreements as a group, such as how we will handle breaks and absences. Second, I include principles that are much broader than behavioral guidelines, such as keeping a sense of humor, sharing responsibility for the success of a session, or adopting an open, curious stance toward discussions. We may include a guideline about confidentiality if this is a consideration for the type of session in question. So my guidelines statement (see the sidebar) is a catchall for those important foundational agreements that do not fit within the ground rules.

In addition to proposing these guidelines, I invite the group to add others, and I check to see if there is anyone who cannot fully support one of the guidelines. If

Exhibit 13.2 Example 2: Introductions for Sessions of One Day or Less

You will have several opportunities to network and participate with others in the room today. So that we may work together more productively and comfortably, please share the items listed below (or similar information of your choosing) with the other participants at your table. Ask one person at the table to serve as the spokesperson for the group. This person will be asked to briefly summarize the expectations in attending this session of those at your table. We will check quickly to see whether and how your expectations can be met.

Please share (about 45 seconds per person):

Your name:

The group you represent:

One thing that needs to happen for you to consider this meeting time well spent (or what you expect to gain from attending this meeting today):

Note: This was created for a half-day facilitation.

someone has a concern about a guideline, we try to change it to address the concern. The extent to which we discuss and edit the guidelines is in part a function of time and group size, but if we cannot reach general agreement to follow a guideline, the default is to drop it from the list. So far in my hundreds of trainings and facilitations, I have never needed to drop a guideline from the basic set I propose.

The "Workshop Guidelines" sidebar is an example of what I use for workshops and consultations. I edit the set to reflect the role or roles of facilitator or consultant, and I change the language to be consistent with the meeting at hand. For example, I may drop the statement about "here-and-now learning," change *workshop* to *session,* shift from a focus on *learning* to *meeting needs,* or add a specific guideline a group has requested, like how to proceed if there is a fire alarm. I hand out a copy of the guidelines so group members can refer to them during the session. If the guidelines change and the session runs more than one day, I hand out a revised copy at our second meeting.

Workshop Guidelines

1. Joint responsibility. The success of this workshop is the joint responsibility of the instructors and the participants. Please help us meet your needs by asking questions and giving us feedback. Let us know, for example, about the pace of the workshop and whether discussions and activities are meeting your learning needs. Request breaks if you need them. Challenge our thinking, and share your own.

2. Breaks. We will announce starting and ending times for breaks and activities. We will resume the session promptly at the end of a break. It is your responsibility to be where you need to be when the group reconvenes. We recognize that there may be times when you need to return a telephone call or take care of other matters that don't precisely fit our break time. We encourage you to be mentally and physically present with the group at all times during the workshop, because group members often learn as much from each other as from the instructors. However, we will assume you are taking responsibility for balancing your needs with those of the group. We will not round you up when it is time to reconvene or make assumptions about your interest or commitment to the workshop if you are not present at some point. If you need to be absent for an extended time, please let us know so that we won't worry about your health or safety.

3. Modeling. The workshop itself is a valuable here-and-now learning lab about group behavior and effective leadership. The instructors will make every attempt to model the skills we are teaching and encourage you to use every opportunity to practice your own skills. Because we are all human, each of us at times will behave inconsistently with the very principles we are trying to model. When you see a behavior that you believe is inconsistent, please raise your concern in the group. When you see a behavior that you think is particularly effective, point this out so all of us may note it. By observing and discussing instructor and participant behaviors, all of us can learn.

4. Confidentiality. We encourage you to share your experience and wisdom through your specific examples and stories. In this way, we can all learn from one another, you can receive suggestions about how to handle difficult situations, and we can follow your reasoning clearly. At the same time, we ask that you keep others' stories and examples confidential. If you wish to share someone else's story outside the session, we ask that you (1) get permission from the person who shared the example in the workshop and/or (2) strip away all information that could identify the organization or people involved in the example. The second condition is often difficult to meet unless you discuss exactly what you plan to share with the person who told the story. If you cannot do this and you have any doubt about the story being identified without permission, refrain from sharing it.

5. Humor. We believe that keeping a sense of humor about human behavior is critical to working together effectively. While the work we do is very important, we should not take ourselves too seriously or judge others harshly. It helps to laugh together about our foibles and struggles. As instructors, we will often point out the lighter side of the principles we teach. We invite you to join in the fun with your own stories, examples, and humorous thoughts!

Chapter 14

Introducing the Ground Rules and Principles in Your Own Words

Sue McKinney

I OFTEN WORK with groups that ask me to attend one or two meetings to help them get off on the right foot or to help with a particularly difficult conversation. In these situations, the group is not asking me to help them learn a new method of communicating with each other. They simply want my help for a few hours. In these cases, I share my approach to facilitation at the first meeting. I explain the core values and then share a simple list of guidelines through a series of stories and examples. I write the list on a flip chart so participants can refer to it during the meeting. Here is what I often say:

I want to share my thoughts about what makes groups more or less effective and suggest some guidelines that in my experience will likely enhance the quality of conversation that takes place today. It is my experience that groups often communicate in ways that make a group less effective than it can be.

In many meetings, I hear someone say something that makes me immediately want to respond. I start thinking about my response and exactly what I want to say. While I'm thinking, I'm waiting for the person to stop talking so I can speak. Sometimes I get so excited to speak that I take even the briefest pause as an invitation to jump in with my important thought! Can some of you identify with this? [I wait for responses.]

I think the danger in this example is that when I am thinking about how to respond, I am no longer listening. I may be hearing what the person is saying, but I'm not listening with an intention of trying to understand where the person is coming from and what leads him or her to say what he or she is saying. If I were listening, I would probably respond with questions so I could better understand, rather than the statement I've been rehearsing while they were talking.

So ***the first guideline I recommend is that you listen to understand and avoid interrupting*** because you cannot be listening when you are talking at the same time someone else is talking. Does that guideline work for the group?

The second guideline is to remain curious and open to the perspective of others. Often I am in a series of meetings with the same people, and over time, I come to develop opinions about these people. I guess you could say I begin to figure them out. I look for predictability in their behavior and responses. Soon I have them in a box and keep them there since it makes it easier for me to understand them. I think things like, "John always has it in for the employees. He doesn't even want to understand them. He just doesn't get it." Or, "Clearly Sally has a hidden agenda. She is never totally open in these meetings, and she is always whispering to Dan afterward. I don't trust her." Of course, at the same time, I'm thinking, "I have the best interests of this organization at heart. And Tom agrees with me, so he must too."

If I take a step back from these thoughts, I have to consider how many people actually get up out of bed and think, "I cannot wait to get to that meeting and mess up the group again!" or better yet, "I am excited to go to the team meeting and make Sue angry again. That is so much fun!" I have to admit to myself that it is not very likely. I think most group members think, as I do, that they have the best interests of the group at heart. So the key is to stay curious and open to their perspective so I can better understand why they think differently than I do. Rather than being judgmental without a good understanding of their thoughts and perspective, I can stay open to learning. What do all of you think about following this guideline?

The third guideline is sharing the reasons behind your questions and statements. One of the things that people naturally do is to try to understand what motivates a person to think or say a certain thing. If listeners don't understand the motivation, they begin to make up stories that make sense to *them,* given their own perspective. We are, in fact, making up stories about each other.

For example, if I walk down the hall and pass a person higher than me in the hierarchy and say, "Hello!" and the person does not respond, I begin to make up stories. They could go like this: "He never speaks to me. He thinks I'm a nobody. He doesn't give credence to anything I say." Or like this: "He must be hard of hearing. I noticed he didn't speak to so-and-so the other day either. He needs to go to a doctor, but he is too vain to get a hearing aid." Or: "He is so busy and important. I shouldn't bother him when he is clearly thinking hard." Have you ever noticed yourself doing something like this? Making up stories to explain the behaviors, actions, or comments of others? To reduce the likelihood of someone making up stories about you, it is important to share the reasons behind your statements, questions, and comments. Doing so makes your motivation and intentions clear, and no one has to make up a story to understand where you are coming from. Is this a guideline you are willing to follow during this meeting?

The fourth guideline is to focus on needs and interests instead of solutions. This will help the group out when you are trying to arrive at decisions or solutions that everyone can support. In many groups, I have had the experience of members' arguing back and forth for a certain solution or decision. The group can go around and around making little progress and increasing member frustration as time passes without forward movement. Have any of you had that experience? [Usually many heads nod.] I have found that talking about what it is about the solution or decision that you feel is important helps move the conversation in a more productive direction. Group members talk about what their needs are. This discussion opens up the possibility of many more solutions than may be originally proposed. Is this a guideline that you can support following?

My final guideline is to relax and enjoy ourselves today. I find that groups that have fun together are more creative. Plus, since we are spending a day together, we might as well enjoy ourselves. Does anyone have a concern with following this guideline?

Does anyone want to add to this list of guidelines or modify my suggested guidelines?

Once the group agrees to use these guidelines, we discuss how using them will affect communications for the day. I share some quick examples with the group. I explain that when I see people speaking at the same time, I will stop them and ask them to check with each other about who speaks first and so on. Or if the group starts getting stuck when seeking solutions to a problem, I will ask some questions about the underlying interests or needs they are trying to meet.

I also explain that I don't expect all of the participants to act consistently with these guidelines, but that I will do so and will try to help them do so when it seems to be causing a problem for the group. I then ask if anyone has a concern with how I am suggesting the group and I use the guidelines. This often leads to a brief discussion about how everyone will use or try to use the guidelines and how I will specifically use them. Once we reach agreement, we begin the meeting.

Meeting Guidelines

- Listen to hear (avoid interruptions).
- Stay curious and open to the perspective of others.
- Share reasons behind questions and statements.
- Focus on underlying interests or needs rather than solutions.
- Relax and enjoy ourselves.

Chapter 15

Using the Group Effectiveness Model

Anne Davidson

YOU ARE WORKING at your desk when the phone rings. Dragging yourself from the task at hand, you answer. After the briefest of greetings, you are invited into the world of an anxious caller: "Glad I got you," he says. "We need some help with team building. The department heads need to work together better. Are you available?"

Where do you start? I have found one of the most useful places for me to start is with the Group Effectiveness Model (GEM). For years I kept the model posted near my telephone and used it to guide my questions for potential clients and as a starting point for working with groups.

DIAGNOSING GROUP ISSUES

As soon as I establish that the person calling is a member of the group requesting my services (or start my first conversation with someone who is a group member), I ask questions based on the three group effectiveness criteria. For example, I might ask:

> As soon as I establish that the person calling is a member of the group requesting my services (or start my first conversation with someone who is a group member), I ask questions based on the three group effectiveness criteria.

"What is happening that leads you to feel you need team building?" Or **"What is not happening in the group that you want to happen?"** Or more specifically, **"How well is the group meeting its work goals?"** [*Performance*]

"How well are group members making decisions together and handling conflict?" [*Process*]

"How are the needs of group members being met or not met?" [*Personal*]

Usually, I do not go into great depth with just one group member, but questions based on the group effectiveness criteria help me gauge whether the client will benefit from my services and whether my skills seem a good match. If working together holds promise, I set up a planning meeting or conference call with the group or with representative group members.

For details of this process see Chapter Eight, "Contracting with Groups," page 89.

INTRODUCING THE GROUP EFFECTIVENESS MODEL TO GROUPS

Early in my career, I kept my diagnostic process more private than I do now. My customary approach was to set up a planning meeting and ask a series of questions based on the elements of the GEM.[1] I still use this approach occasionally, especially when the client makes a free (and somewhat informed) choice not to spend time discussing the model. I might ask questions like, **"How would you describe the group's purpose and goals?"** or **"How do group members behave when you disagree with one another?"** Responses, particularly specific examples, provide data for an initial diagnosis of critical group effectiveness issues and indicate possible interventions.

Now I customarily share the GEM itself with a group in the planning or diagnostic meeting. I see several advantages to this approach. First, it ensures that I ask about each important element of group effectiveness and elicit examples. I get more specific and comprehensive data this way. Second, I make my diagnostic frame transparent to the group. Participants can see if the model fits their own experience and raise areas they think may be missing from the model. They can more clearly confirm or disconfirm the diagnosis I make from their descriptions of group behavior.

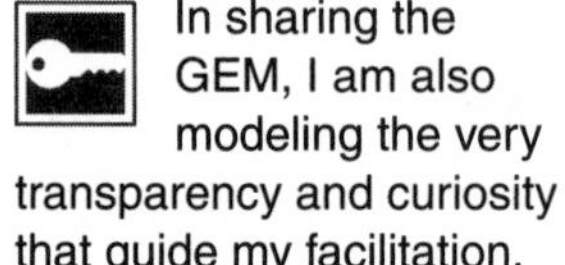

In sharing the GEM, I am also modeling the very transparency and curiosity that guide my facilitation.

In sharing the GEM, I am also modeling the very transparency and curiosity that guide my facilitation. The group experiences what it will be like to work with me, how I model my values, and whether and how my approach fits for them. Another advantage is that the group begins to learn the GEM so they can use it themselves as a tool to assess their future progress or set up new groups on their own.

STEPS FOR INTRODUCING THE GEM

To introduce the model, I spend about fifteen minutes briefly explaining the group effectiveness criteria, setting out the three major factors (group process, structure, and context), and defining a few of the less common terms, like *boundary spanning.* Then the group and I use stories and examples of past group situations to map their issues and develop a shared diagnosis and intervention plan. Here are the specific steps I follow.

Step 1: Explain the Model

First, explain the purpose of the model and why you are introducing it. I say something like this:

"To help us identify what is working and what is not working for this group, I would like to introduce a model of group effectiveness. The model shows the elements that need to be in place for groups to work well together and how these things are interrelated. It will also point to places where you can begin to make changes. By examining the model together, I think we will have much better information about how I might help you and how you can continue improving after my consultations. Does anyone have questions about why I am proposing we spend time working through the model?"

Then I briefly define the effectiveness criteria, the three factors, and the terms describing the elements. I show how criteria and elements are interrelated and point out that this is a model of a group as an open system: everything affects everything else.

Step 2: Ask the Group Members to Describe a Time When the Group Was Effective

This should be a specific incident or decision process, supported by examples of group behavior and discussion, recreated in as much detail as possible. Identify which of the three group effectiveness criteria were met. Then identify the elements of the group's process, structure, and context that might be supporting its effectiveness. List these or map them and how they are interrelated as in Figure 15.1 later in the chapter. These will be strengths you and the group can build on to address less effective elements.

Step 3: Ask the Group to Describe a Specific Time or Incident When the Group Was Ineffective

Identify which of the three group effectiveness criteria were not met. Then identify the elements of the group's process, structure, and context that might be hindering its effectiveness. Using lines and arrows to connect the elements, illustrate how ineffectiveness in one element contributes to ineffectiveness in other elements in the model. (See the sample map in Figure 15.1 later in the chapter.) Repeatedly ask two questions: **"What elements contribute to causing this effect?"** and (2) **"What other elements are affected by problems with this element?"**

Step 4: Share Observations and Reach Consensus About the Highest-Leverage Elements to Address

A high-leverage element addresses root causes, builds a foundation for other elements, or has significant impact on a number of other elements. For example, if a group is unclear whether it has the right members and is also unclear about its purpose and goals, it is a higher-leverage intervention to first clarify mission, vision, and goals because goals will determine membership needs and roles.

Introducing the Group Effectiveness Model

The director of a human services agency for a large, metropolitan county requested help improving the effectiveness of a ten-member team she led.

She shared that about six months earlier, one of the members, whom we'll call Sarah, confronted her during a team meeting. Sarah accused the director of a series of biased or unfair decisions. She implied that the director's racial prejudice contributed to poor decisions. Other team members were silent during the meeting, but afterward several of them wrote a memo defending the director and counterattacking Sarah. The director felt that team morale had been poor since the incident, meetings frequently got off track, and the group had difficulty reaching agreement on any course of action. The group managed critical county services that often were scrutinized by the local press. In the past, they had worked together fairly well, but lately they seemed to be working at odds with one another in ways the director saw as risky, wasteful, or inconsistent with the stated interests of county commissioners. She wanted to turn the situation around as quickly as possible.

I suggested that we introduce the group to the GEM and start with their assessment of effective and less effective elements. We e-mailed all group members, asking if they would spend up to one hour reading a description of the GEM and preparing responses to three questions.[1] Everyone agreed to prepare and to come to a three-hour diagnostic meeting. We stated clearly that at the end of the meeting, the group would decide whether and how to continue working with the facilitator.

At the meeting, the group first asked questions to clarify their understanding of the GEM. Then they shared responses to the following questions:

1. What are three specific, concrete wishes you have for this work group?
2. Looking at the elements of the Group Effectiveness Model, which elements work together to help you perform well? Tell a story or share an example that supports your view.
3. Which elements of the model are missing or need strengthening? What specifically has happened that leads you to say these elements need strengthening?

In a little over two hours, the group heard each person's vision of how the group would be functioning when more effective, where each member saw strengths, and where each person thought the group needed to improve. Members listed eighteen specific wishes for the group representing eight of the elements of the Group Effectiveness Model. We did not try to reach consensus about each item on every list; rather, we asked which items on each list everyone fully agreed about. In this case, there was consensus that six elements of the GEM represented clear strengths, including shared vision, clear mission and goals, and motivating task. The discussion appeared to refocus the group on their commitment to and clarity about the important services they provide. Using the lists of wishes and elements that needed strengthening, the group reached consensus to work to improve five elements of the model: communication, conflict management, group culture, group norms, and decision making.

Since group values and beliefs (culture) and norms (ground rules) significantly influence how individuals communicate, manage conflict, and make decisions, I recommended that the group begin by addressing values, beliefs, and norms. The group quickly designed a process and schedule to do this work. Over subsequent weeks, they were able to raise difficult issues and process past incidents (including the memo) in ways that were productive and modeled their desired norms. Group members said that starting with the GEM helped them focus on their overall task, helped them acknowledge and use their strengths, and made the task seem less overwhelming. Although they knew at the outset that the work would be hard and personally challenging, seeing the model helped them fit the pieces together in a way that made sense to them. They could see how effectiveness or ineffectiveness can build on one another and affect the larger system. This group plans to revisit the model periodically to assess progress and keep things in balance.

1. I used my colleague Peg Carlson's article, "A Model for Improving a Group's Effectiveness," in *Popular Government,* 1998, *63,* 37–45. Chapter Two, "The Group Effectiveness Model," page 15, contains an updated version of the model that will work well with most groups. See also *The Skilled Facilitator,* pp. 17–39.

Example: Mapping the System

Several years ago, a client who worked for a large national bank called to ask me to help her with a team-building effort for her work group. After agreeing to meet with the group, I guided them through the four steps for introducing the GEM:

The group described how effectively it had designed training materials and promotional literature for the bank. They had won several awards and had earned an excellent reputation throughout the banking community. The group performed effectively, and they felt proud of their results. Their mission, goals, and tasks were clear and motivating. The team was staffed with experienced and talented individuals who could work well under pressure. We listed mission, vision, goals, task, and membership as group strengths, as well as their ability to solve work problems collaboratively.

When we got to the third step, describing when the group was ineffective, they told me that they had related well and had collaborated fully on every project until the organization adopted a new ranking and rating system. In implementing the new system, the corporate office insisted that each team member have his or her own separate score and ranking for merit pay purposes. Although the team requested a shared rating for the whole group, they were instructed to discriminate the top to bottom persons on the team with individual rankings for each. Trying to develop the ratings led to arguments, accusations, and mistrust among team members. They had worked together so closely that no one clearly remembered who contributed what. People started feeling others were taking credit for their work. Morale deteriorated. The group was not meeting the personal or process criteria for effectiveness.

We mapped the problem and the causal connections on a diagram of the Group Effectiveness Model (see Figure 15.1). The most obvious issues were communication problems and conflict within the group. There was a mismatch between established group norms of team production with shared recognition and individual evaluation. But as the diagram clearly shows, the problem was generated by an element in group context: rewards were not consistent with the objectives of working as a self-managed, creative team. Using the data generated by the group, we agreed that team building would not help. The highest-leverage intervention was to help the group craft a productive conversation with those implementing the reward system rather than working on group process issues.

Figure 15.1 Using the Group Effectiveness Model to Map the Problem and Causal Connections

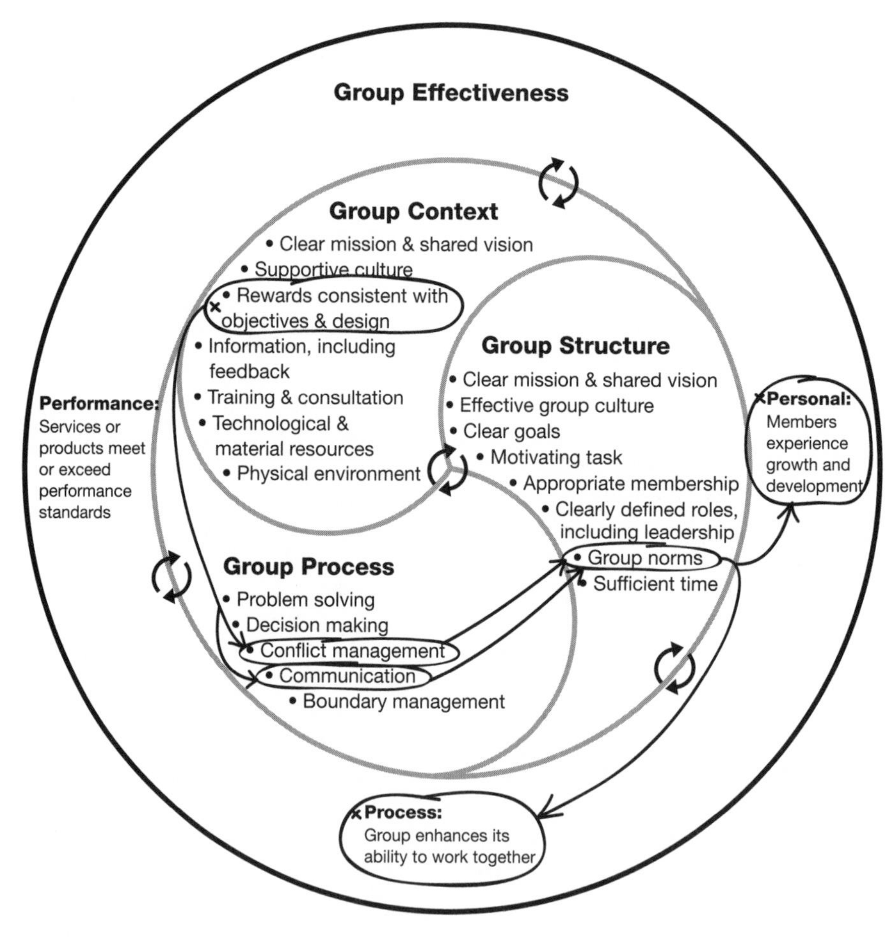

DESIGNING INTERVENTIONS

After you and the group map an issue using the GEM, the next step is to agree about where and how to create change. There is no right or perfect place to begin. Having said this, there are more or less productive places. As I described in step 4 for introducing the GEM, my approach is to look for the highest-leverage intervention. With the bank team, that was to address the reward system that was generating the conflict. Often one of the first places I look is among the elements of group structure. Once a group sets its fundamental structure, it is easier to clarify communication needs, decision processes, and work flow. Conflict frequently lessens or disappears after there is agreement about elements like group mission, roles, and boundaries. Later, it may be productive to discuss how the group handles differences, but to me this does not seem as efficient as resolving the root causes of many of those differences.

Honor the principle of starting where the group is. I am guided by the choices of group members and the reasons they seek my assistance. If the facilitation is fairly basic (for example, putting together an annual plan), I may not go deeper than discussing the group's mission, goals, roles, and membership. But if the group tells me they have put together plans in the past that they never implemented, I delve into the group norms and culture that create such a situation. I may raise subjects like mental models and defensive routines. We talk about the challenges of reshaping one's thinking, the length of time it might take, and the consequences of not doing deeper-level work. My responsibility as the consultant or facilitator is to advocate going deep enough to address the root causes of problems so that they do not return again and again. But ultimately the group makes a choice about how to spend its time and how deep to go. Often our starting place is not at the deepest level possible. Rather, we start with the elements all the group members fully support addressing.

My approach is to look for the highest-leverage intervention. Often one of the first places to look is among the elements of group structure.

Honor the principle of starting where the group is. 

See Chapter Four, "Understanding What Guides Your Behavior," page 33, and Chapter Forty-Three, "Developmental Facilitation," page 339, for discussions of mental models and defensive routines.

WHAT IF YOU MAKE THE WRONG DIAGNOSIS OR START IN THE WRONG PLACE?

The good news is this: since groups are systems and since, in systems, everything is related to everything else, no matter where you start, the fundamental issues will arise. Your initial approach may not be the most efficient, and the group may become frustrated, so there is merit in getting to the core issues as quickly and clearly

Avoiding a Misguided Effort

Sharing the GEM early in my work with a new client has saved me from making bad contracts. On one memorable occasion, I met with a CEO and his top management team to discuss the CEO's request for team building.

The CEO had seen references to top management teams and heard this approach discussed at a recent conference. The assistants and department heads who worked most closely with him were enthusiastic about the idea of a team. The group customarily held lengthy monthly planning meetings. Everyone thought team building might improve the efficiency and productivity of these sessions.

I scheduled an initial session with the CEO and four of the prospective team members to discuss whether and how we might work together. To get us started, I briefly explained the GEM and its usefulness as a template for building an effective team. I asked what role the team might play, which aspects of the model were already in place, and which would need to be added or strengthened.

The CEO stared at the model in silence for several minutes following my questions. After what seemed an eternity, he looked up and said, "I just realized sitting here that my strength is creating organizational [group] context. I have always worked in that area, and perhaps a little in helping structure other groups in the organization. But for the most part, the department heads have teams, and they should work with them. I do not want to work on group process. I do not think working on the things in this model will change how I work or will be the most productive use of my skills. Department heads advise me, but I really do not want to spend time working with them on making decisions, managing boundaries, conflict, even goals or roles, because I believe those are clear."

I asked the others present if they saw the situation similarly or differently. Basically, they agreed with the CEO's assessment: "He's a strong leader, and he is effective. He does allow us to advise him, but unless he wants to change his style and focus, I think we don't need a team. We are not that interdependent. We know our mission. It's clear. The CEO delegates broad areas for us to manage. Then we need teams and collaborative processes to guide those areas."

The CEO was quite clear that he could support team-building efforts for departments, but that he was just not interested in investing his energy to do so with his own department heads. We all agreed that the discussion had been extremely useful. The department heads present requested help sharing the GEM with their subordinates but agreed it would be better not to start a team-building effort with the CEO. I concurred that this would not be a good use of my time. Using the GEM had improved effectiveness for many top management teams, but this was not the right time or place. Had we forged ahead without this clear assessment, I think the effort would have failed in the long run while expending organizational resources and goodwill unproductively.

as possible. Nevertheless, groups need to learn for themselves the effects of addressing or not addressing difficult issues. Since they make free choices not to talk about certain subjects, the facilitator using a mutual learning approach cannot rescue the group by saving them from errors. The facilitator can advocate for addressing an issue and explain his or her reasoning (for example, the consequences of not addressing a difficult issue) but cannot direct the group to deal with a challenging element. Pushing groups too hard to take risks they feel unready or unwilling to face can generate resistance. Unaddressed issues almost always return. In my experience, if you jointly design your work with the group and gain their full support for addressing the issues you do process, you will usually be invited back when a concern reemerges and the group is prepared to go deeper.

Since groups are systems and since, in systems, everything is related to everything else, no matter where you start, the fundamental issues will arise.

If you are using a mutual learning approach, you cannot rescue the group by saving them from errors.

Note

1. See *The Skilled Facilitator,* pp. 278–279, for a list of diagnostic questions based on the Group Effectiveness Model.

Chapter 16

Helping Group Members Focus on Interests Rather Than Positions

Peg Carlson

In the classic story that illustrates the difference between positions and interests, two children, holding one orange, bring it to an adult and state that they both want it. The adult asks each of them to describe why they need the orange. One child is hungry and wants to eat it; the other needs the grated rind for a cake recipe. Problem solved: by focusing on the interests rather than the position, both children get 100 percent of what they want.

Although not all organizational problems are as easily solved as this one, Ground Rule Five, "Focus on interests, not positions," is an extremely useful way to approach many of the issues we face daily at work. A ***position*** is a single answer or solution to a problem; an ***interest*** is a need, hope, or concern that frequently can be met by more than one solution (Fisher, Ury, and Patton, 1991).

A ***position*** is a single answer or solution to a problem; an ***interest*** is a need, hope, or concern that frequently can be met by more than one solution (Fisher, Ury, and Patton, 1991).

Because people tend to move quickly from thinking about their own interests to advocating a position that meets their interests, it is easy for parties in conflict to argue and bargain over different solutions instead of generating a solution that meets the underlying interests.

Whether formulating a policy, making choices about allocating scarce resources, or mediating a dispute between coworkers, focusing on identifying and meeting shared interests is a key technique for resolving a problem in a way that stays resolved.

Here are ways to help people focus on interests rather than positions.

START WITH A SENTENCE PROMPT

A useful technique for getting the discussion started on the right foot is to give people an opportunity to identify interests before any positions have been stated. For example, if a group has the task of designing a new pay-for-performance plan for the organization, you can write, "The pay-for-performance plan needs to be designed in a way that . . ." at the top of a flip chart pad. Group members then complete this sentence with as many statements as they can, each stated in the form of an interest. Typical interests may include "rewards high performers," "retains good employees," and "allows good budget projections." The group can then look at the entire list and share ideas for pay-for-performance plans that meet the set (or a portion of the set) of interests.

This approach helps frame a discussion around interests from the very beginning, avoiding the common scenario where group members offer proposals for various plans, based on their own interests, and other group members point out flaws in the plan, based on their interests not being met.

GENERATE ONE COMMON LIST OF INTERESTS RATHER THAN A TWO-COLUMN PRO-CON FORMAT

In the example, the group will create one list of interests and can then use this list to identify which interests are shared by most members, which ones are considered highest priority to meet, and other parameters. Avoid a two-column format at this stage of generating interests—sometimes referred to as pro-con or cost-benefit analysis. The usual process for a two-column format involves naming a solution and then listing the pros and cons of this solution. Although the intent is to help groups reach a decision based on a rational weighing of the merits of a particular solution, this format frequently results in group members' fixating on a position and then using the two columns to justify it (the pro) or object to it (the con). The tool doesn't appear to help groups identify all their interests when solving a problem and then search creatively for a position that meets all, or most of, the interests.

ARRANGE THE ROOM SO PEOPLE CAN SEE EACH OTHER AND THE LIST OF INTERESTS

This is related to Fisher, Ury, and Patton's idea (1991) of separating the people from the problem. If group members can see and contribute to a growing list of shared interests, it helps counter the tendency to see other members of the group as opposition, or people who are standing in the way of achieving a preferred solution.

USE QUESTIONS THROUGHOUT THE DISCUSSION TO HELP PEOPLE UNCOVER INTERESTS

Identifying the interests underlying positions is often like peeling an onion: you get through the initial position only to find another position under it. This is seldom due to intentional resistance from the group member; instead, it reflects how deeply ingrained is our tendency to think in terms of positions.

For example, picture a group discussion in a company's training and organization development department about when to offer a series of leadership workshops. One group member, Sarah, may propose the third Tuesday of each month (a *position*). If I were facilitating this discussion and using the ground rule of focusing on interests rather than positions, I may ask, **"What is it about the third Tuesday of the month that works well, in your view?"** If Sarah responds, "If we follow that schedule, it won't conflict with Tony's time management classes," then the group has learned something about her interests. However, "not conflicting with Tony's time management classes" is still a position, although Sarah's interests are beginning to emerge. So I may ask a follow-up question: **"And can you say some more about why it would be good to avoid scheduling at the same time as Tony's time management classes?"** It may turn out that Tony is needed to teach in both workshops or that Sarah believes there is a similar audience for both types of classes.

This process of peeling the onion with questions that help group members focus on their interests is similar to the Total Quality concept of asking "Why?" five times in order to get to the root cause of a problem. The key is asking the questions in a way that reflects compassion and curiosity, not cross-examination. It is rare, in my experience, to have people hold tightly to their interests as a hidden agenda, revealing them only under duress. It is much more common to see multiple interests emerge throughout the conversation because people are so accustomed to talking—and thinking—in terms of positions that it takes some time to recognize and articulate their interests.

Interest-Eliciting Questions

- "What is it about X [the position] that makes it a good solution, in your view?"
- "Can you say some more about why X is important to you?"
- "I heard you propose that the group do X, but I didn't hear you say how this would meet the needs the group has identified. Can you say more about the needs X would address?"

Note that none of these questions requires the use of the word *position* or *interest.* It's fine to use these terms if the group is familiar with them; in fact, in a developmental facilitation context, where group members are learning to use the ground rules themselves, it can be helpful to draw their attention to the distinction by using the words. However, if you are working in or with a group that views the words *position* and *interest* as jargon, it's quite possible to use your facilitative skills to help people focus on the interests underlying their positions without ever using these words.

Whether I'm facilitating a half-day retreat for a city council or teaching facilitation skills to an organization over a period of months, I continue to be struck by the power of Ground Rule Five. Helping group members focus on interests can change the entire tone and direction of the conversation from its outset. Exploring interests before moving on to positions frequently shifts the focus from what divides us to what unites us, enabling people to build on commonalities and create innovative solutions.

Exploring interests before moving on to positions frequently shifts the focus from what divides us to what unites us, enabling people to build on commonalities and create innovative solutions.

Reference

Fisher, R., Ury, W., and Patton, B. *Getting to Yes.* (2nd ed.) New York: Penguin Books, 1991.

Chapter 17

Developing Shared Vision and Values

Anne Davidson

The Group Effectiveness Model highlights clear mission and shared vision in two factors: group context and group structure. Clients and colleagues often ask us why the element is repeated. One reason is that the meaning shifts depending on its scope. Organizational mission, for example, is different from the purpose of an operating division. I believe a second reason for listing this element twice is the importance of defining vision, mission, and the values underpinning them.

Unclear or misaligned direction is a frequent cause of team failure. Unfortunately, this problem often does not show up in the short run. Teams and groups may work for months before they recognize that their mission and purpose are at odds with the organizational direction. I have worked with groups that got as far as trying to create an implementation plan before discovering that individual members had vastly different interpretations of the vision, the mission, or the values. The team became stuck and had to go all the way back to the beginning of their process, wasting valuable time and resources.

Unclear or misaligned direction is a frequent cause of team failure.

A DIFFERENT VIEW OF VISION

In discussing vision here, I am not talking about a lofty vision statement with carefully crafted wording that goes up on plaques and is seldom referenced. Consistent with the terminology in *The Skilled Facilitator* (pp. 27–31), I work with the notion of vision as a specific, richly detailed picture of a desired future that a group seeks to create. The focus is more on the dream than the words, on creating a compelling picture of the way things could be that engages people's imagination and invites others to join in a quest to "reach the far-away lights." Mission then defines what the group or organization exists to do, its fundamental purpose. And values describe what is worthwhile or desirable—what it is most important to do and stand for in the group or organization.

Visioning has earned a bad name in many quarters as faddish and ineffective. I believe there are several reasons for this. One is that too much emphasis is placed

In ineffective visioning, too much emphasis is placed on lofty, poorly defined language and not enough on how the vision will be realized: the behaviors and goals that will guide daily movement toward a specific dream.

on lofty, poorly defined language and not enough on how the vision will be realized: the behaviors and goals that will guide daily movement toward a specific dream. A second reason is that many managers are less comfortable with imagination than with analysis of concrete data, so making up a future seems too "touchy feely." In other words, they are less accustomed to using their feeling-based or imaginative brain functions and have little regard for or trust in dreams, metaphors, and feelings as sources of information. More fundamental, I believe there is underlying ambivalence about how a vision functions in complex organizations.

According to widely accepted theory, a compelling vision generates what Robert Fritz (1989) defines as "structural tension," more popularly known by the term used in Peter Senge's *The Fifth Discipline* (1990): creative tension. Creative tension is generated by the gap between a vision and current reality. The desire to close that gap is said to be the source of the creative energy needed to fully engage purposeful action. The more specific and visual the vision is, the better defined the gap is. And the better defined the gap is, the easier it is for individuals and groups to design specific actions to move toward their ideal future. I have seen individuals and groups progress or completely change direction as the result of clarifying their vision through dialogue, art experiences, reflective writing, or some combination of these approaches. I believe a powerful vision can make a difference. But I do not start my work with groups there.

Many organizations stumble when trying to develop shared vision as a foundation for organizational alignment or change. I have had the privilege of working long term with a number of organizations, either intermittently or continually. Some of these relationships span a decade or more. Most of these organizations developed visions or vision statements (or both). I facilitated many of the efforts to generate these. And yet most did not really stick. The vision statements may be shared by a few leaders or by those who generated them, but not by others in the organization. People seldom reference the elements of the vision when making day-to-day decisions or when developing goals or work plans. Vision statements sound great but do not perform a useful function that makes a performance difference.

I am beginning to deeply challenge the assumptions about how vision works in large organizations and other complex systems. As I study the fields of complexity theory and systems thinking, I think of organizations and collections of work or community groups as more closely following the laws of complex adaptive systems.

Success in complex adaptive systems means "fit with the environment" or continuous adaptation to an ever-changing set of circumstances rather than trying to close a gap with a specific ideal that may become irrelevant during the journey toward it.

Success in complex adaptive systems means "fit with the environment" or continuous adaptation to an ever-changing set of circumstances rather than trying to close a gap with a specific ideal that may become irrelevant during the journey toward it. By focusing on fit, change emerges one interaction at a time. It is not dependent on a predetermined detailed design of a future state. Each decision changes the landscape, and the future is generated through a complex process of coevolution among the individual participants. The result is organizations that are sustainable over time under adverse conditions, concentrated on growth and agility rather than any particular end state. They place a premium on attending to relevant information and improvising to respond rapidly to changing conditions (Olson and Eoyang, 2001).

Mary Catherine Bateson makes much the same argument in *Composing a Life,* her inspirational treatment of the lives of five outstanding women. She writes that jazz improvisation is an appropriate metaphor for creating success in each of these lives: "Each of us has worked by improvisation, discovering the shape of our creation along the way, rather than pursuing a vision already defined" (1989, p. 1). The biographies make a convincing case that in our rapidly changing world, more is achieved by evolving a life decision by decision, opportunity by opportunity, challenge by challenge, based on a few clear principles. To the extent that there is vision, it is emergent and highly unstable. So at both the personal and organizational levels, the role of vision is less clear and more complex than much of the literature suggests.

EMPHASIZING VALUES AND PURPOSE

Most resources on developing shared missions and visions recommend starting with the personal vision of individuals, next discovering shared vision, and then agreeing on goals or milestones to close the gap between vision and reality. Many correctly assess the importance of attending to values as part of a shared vision effort. The values become "like a figurehead on a ship: a guiding symbol of the behavior that will help people move toward the vision" (Senge and others, 1994, p. 302). But most of these resources, which I cherish and use, still underestimate the importance of values or guiding principles. (See the list of visioning resources at the end of the chapter.)

The organizations and work groups that I see maximizing the criteria for effective groups spent significant time discovering or generating a short list of shared core values. So now I start my shared mission and vision interventions by working first on core purpose and values.

Jim Collins and Jerry Porras (1994) come closest to articulating the importance of core values in their examination of enduring, visionary organizations. They point out that companies enjoying enduring success have a vision comprising both a core ideology and an envisioned future. The two distinct elements of core ideology are core values (a system of guiding principles and tenets) and core purpose (the organization's most fundamental reason for existence). Their work emphasizes helping organizations discover their authentic values, the ones they would stick to whether or not they were popular or offered competitive advantage. Success comes from preserving this core and being open to changing everything else, including the actual products or services on which the organization was founded.

In many ways values supplant vision for organizations that aspire to become transformational, generative, or learning organizations.

Although Collins and Porras's points relate to organizations as a whole, I have found the same emphasis to catalyze the passion of work groups at all levels and of all sizes. In fact, for organizations that aspire to become transformational, generative, or learning organizations, the values in many ways supplant the vision. That is, the shared vision becomes to live and learn and change in ways wholly consistent with the core values. The primary vision is about creating a workplace that is values driven and fully open to change around those values.

THE PURPOSE OR VALUES (AND MAYBE VISION) INTERVENTION

My interventions to clarify mission and vision are more productive when I start by reviewing the purpose and clarifying the values of a group or organization. I follow essentially the steps below (although often iteratively rather than just sequentially).

1. Review Purpose

I ask a group to review its mission or purpose, asking questions like, **"Why does this group [organization] exist? What are or will be your most important contributions to society? What is the fundamental reason for your existence?"** If mission or purpose statements already exist, this is the time to review and question these. I encourage deep reevaluation, not just a little editing. Often I encourage revisiting purpose after values are clarified to check for consistency.

2. Agree About a Basic Set of Authentic Core Values

I spend more time helping groups discover and reach consensus on their core values than on any other step. There is no "right" set of core values. What is crucial is how committed the group is to the values and how consistent their collective and individual behavior is with the values they espouse. Often the real values are rooted in a group's history, so at this stage, we may create a group time line, talking about significant past events that shape or illustrate what is important to this organization.

Agreeing about core values should be a deeply reflective dialogue, examining exactly what each value means to the group. It is tempting to use lofty words like *honesty* or *integrity*, but these terms can imply vastly different behaviors to each individual in the room. One executive team spent five hours discussing the meaning of *honesty* before coming to consensus about exactly what they would do or not do to live out this value. Frequently I help a group develop a list of beliefs that lays out the assumptions or actions that support the core values. Whether or not a list of beliefs is added to the list of values, it is critical at this stage to examine in detail the thinking and behavior that will support each value.

To have a productive dialogue about deeply held values, it is necessary for groups to understand and practice ground rules consistent with those of the Skilled Facilitator approach. Group members need to share interests, understand the meaning of consensus and internal commitment, explain their reasoning in detail, and agree on what important words mean. They also need to grasp the notion of distinguishing espoused theory from theory-in-use. A statement of core values is a statement of ideals. Actual behavior will always fall short of realizing aspirations. Publicly recognizing this fundamental distinction is essential in addressing the cynicism that can breed when inconsistencies between values and behavior are not openly discussed.

See Chapter Four, "Understanding What Guides Your Behavior," page 33, for a further discussion of the distinction between espoused values and theory-in-use, and Chapter Five, "Ground Rules for Effective Groups," page 61, for an introduction to the ground rules.

To create genuine dialogue that generates living values, groups need some awareness of mental models and ground rules before the values discussion is meaningful. I usually ask group members to complete some reading and then conduct a half- or full-day training session on mental models and ground rules. With this background, groups can deeply examine and commit to values that will inform daily actions.

3. Create a Vision

Some individuals and groups are motivated by a more specific picture of their ideal future. I present this as an option. Several groups have chosen to work on living out their values for some period of time and then have created a vision after grasping more fully what image would be consistent with their values. If a group wishes to develop a shared vision or vision statement, I recommend starting with individual vision statements. I often use visual exercises, scenarios, or a set of questions for reflective writing to help individuals clarify their desires. A wonderful side benefit is that people often tell very personal stories to illustrate why they are passionate about elements of their personal vision. Sharing these stories, in my experience, engenders levels of respect, understanding, and appreciation among the individuals on a team that build trust and lasting support. Because groups often develop vision scenarios or statements at some stage, Exhibits 17.1 and 17.2 offer some sample exercises and questions that have worked well for me.

Exhibit 17.1 Sample Exercise and Questions for Discovering Personal Vision

Lifeline Exercise

1. On a blank piece of paper, draw your lifeline. Here we are thinking of your lifeline as similar to a history time line. Start as far back as you can remember, and stop at the present time.
2. Draw your lifeline as a graph, with the peaks representing the highs in your life and the valleys representing the lows.
3. Next to each peak, write a word or two identifying the peak experience. Do the same for the valleys.
4. Now go back over each peak. For each peak, make a few notes on why this was a peak experience for you.

Analyze your notes. What themes and patterns are revealed by the peaks in your life? What important personal strengths are revealed? What do these themes and patterns tell you about what you are likely to find personally compelling or important in the future?

Questions for Clarifying Vision

The following questions may help you in clarifying your vision:

1. How would you like to change the world for yourself and your organization?
2. If you could invent the future, what future would you invent for yourself and your organization?
3. What mission in life absolutely obsesses you? (Don't be too quick to judge that nothing obsesses you.)
4. What is your dream about your work?
5. What is the distinctive role or skill of your organization (or department)?
6. About what do you have a burning passion?
7. What work do you find absorbing, involving, enthralling? What will happen in ten years if you remain absorbed, involved, and enthralled in that work?
8. What does your ideal organization look like?
9. What is your personal agenda? What do you want to prove?

Exhibit 17.2 Group Visioning Scenarios

To help a group create a concrete picture of its shared, desired future, I find it useful to ask each individual to reflect on an imaginary scenario. Here are a couple of examples that work well.

Scenario One

Imagine fifteen years into the future. Mount Holly Products [your organization, group, or community] has just been featured in *Fortune Magazine* as one of the best employers [or communities under fifty thousand people, for example] in the country. A news team is on its way to town to do a story for *Sixty Minutes*: "What's So Great About Mount Holly Products (MHP)?" Each group member will have a brief interview with the news team and an opportunity to show off one or two of their favorite things about [living or working] here. In preparation for your interview, describe:

1. What you think Mount Holly Products has accomplished in the past ten years that makes it special.
2. The key contributions you believe you made to MHP's progress.
3. What you are personally most passionate about for MHP.
4. What you want the news team to photograph to demonstrate MHP's progress.

Scenario Two

It is five years from now. You are taking a hot air balloon ride over your facility [or town]. You are thinking back over the past five years and about how many of your dreams you have achieved. Draw a picture of what you see that represents progress toward your ideals. Use stick figures, shapes, symbols, words—whatever quickly expresses your image. Next, write a brief description of what you see in your picture and what it means to you.

After sharing individual visions, it is easier to establish common ground and reach consensus about a desired future to work toward. Sometimes the agreement looks more like one or two broad goals than a fleshed-out vision statement. The important thing is for the group to have a very specific, challenging, and shared aspiration that will inform their daily actions and that they can clearly communicate to those who must support its achievement.

RESULTS

The values and beliefs statement from the City of Laurinburg management team in Exhibit 17.3 illustrates the final product of an intervention like the one I am describing:

> The team has successfully used the statement in Exhibit 17.3 to guide its decisions since 1996. Has it created an organization wholly consistent with

Exhibit 17.3 Values and Beliefs for the Laurinburg Management Team

The values and beliefs listed below were developed by the Laurinburg Management Team. They serve as our guiding principles for managing the City of Laurinburg. They describe our future and will be the basis for decisions and actions taken by the management staff of the organization. These common values will make us more effective. They are the foundation for building a sense of teamwork, clarifying why things are done, and promoting general understanding among employees and the public of what is important to us. We believe the following statements should serve as a guide for our actions:

We value:

- Honesty; our actions and communications are free of fraud and deception.
- Collaboration and teamwork.
- People's contributions to our organization and our community.
- Government; the things we do are important.
- People making informed choices, without threat.

We believe:

- All citizens have equal access to and delivery of the services for which they qualify.
- We are responsible stewards of the public trust, including money, property, and the environment.
- The council-manager form of government increases the efficiency and effectiveness of the delivery of services.
- We relate to people in a helpful, courteous manner.
- We gather valid information and share all relevant information.
- People work better when they are committed to what they do.
- We employ people based on qualifications and abilities and employ the best possible people.
- Individuals are accountable and responsible for their actions.
- People are rewarded for their work based on its quality, quantity, and complexity.
- We have a responsibility to assure that the city has competent employees and to provide opportunities for them to develop to the best of their ability.
- We improve service delivery through innovation, and each of us is responsible for taking the risks associated with innovation.
- A sense of humor is an important part of our behavior.
- In taking individuals' circumstances into consideration in our actions toward them.

its values? No. Is making decisions based on these values quick and easy? Not usually. Dealing with the complexities of governing a community (or any other organization) often requires careful consideration of multiple facets of each issue and a delicate balancing act among various interests. For example, in trying to create a new water and sewer system extension policy, the group members found themselves wrestling with the trade-offs between being stewards of citizens' tax dollars and being good stewards of the environment. The most environmentally friendly approaches are often the most expensive. Trade-offs and best fits with the existing situation are required. Yet the team reaches few significant decisions without considering their values and beliefs and how to help the organization move toward consistency with them. Decisions are revisited less often, their rationale is clearly understood by every department head, and issues of people not supporting an agreement during implementation seldom arise.

The use of the values, not one specific vision or the wall poster statement, is the significant touchstone for Laurinburg. The values have been the lasting guide for each individual's decisions and actions.

Since 1996, the Laurinburg team has realized several visions: becoming an All-America city, revitalizing its downtown, and planning for a major brownfields reclamation among them. To accomplish results, the management team had to collaborate broadly with the city's governing board and an array of citizen groups. Throughout, the values have been the lasting guide for each individual in his or her decisions and actions. The use of the values, not one specific vision or the wall poster statement, is the significant touchstone. For this group and others, aligning core values makes all the difference.

See Chapter Forty-Six, "From Learning to Lead to Leading to Learn," page 367, for the Laurinburg city manager's account of his personal journey.

Resources

A number of resources offer visioning processes and questions to guide individual and group thinking. Some of my favorites are:

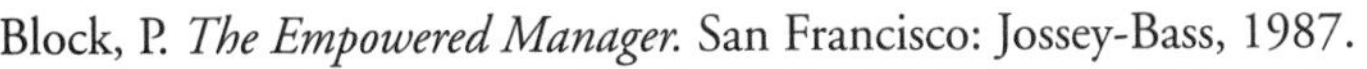

Block, P. *The Empowered Manager.* San Francisco: Jossey-Bass, 1987.

Collins, J., and Porras, J. *Built to Last.* New York: HarperCollins, 1994.

Justice, T., and Jamieson, D. W. *The Facilitator's Fieldbook.* New York: AMACOM, 1999.

Senge, P., and others. *The Fifth Discipline Fieldbook.* New York: Doubleday, 1994.

References

Bateson, M. C. *Composing a Life.* New York: Atlantic Monthly Press, 1989.

Collins, J., and Porras, J. *Built to Last.* New York: HarperCollins, 1994.

Fritz, R. *The Path of Least Resistance.* New York: Fawcett-Columbine, 1989.

Olson, E. E., and Eoyang, G. H. *Facilitating Organization Change: Lessons from Complexity Science.* San Francisco: Jossey-Bass/Pfeiffer, 2001.

Senge, P. M. *The Fifth Discipline.* New York: Doubleday, 1990.

Senge, P., and others. *The Fifth Discipline Fieldbook.* New York: Doubleday, 1994.

Chapter 18

Helping Groups Clarify Roles and Expectations

Anne Davidson

UNCLEAR ROLES AND unstated expectations are a frequent source of unnecessary and unproductive group conflict. Conflicts that appear to arise at the group process level often have at their core misaligned role definitions or implicit and inconsistent expectations. Consequently, helping groups clarify roles and expectations is one of the most basic and useful group structure interventions. The roles and expectations intervention answers the questions, "What roles [formal duties] are needed?" and "How do we expect people to behave while carrying out their duties?"

> The roles and expectations intervention answers the questions, "What roles [formal duties] are needed?" and "How do we expect people to behave while carrying out their duties?"

> Our colleague Dick McMahon tells the story of two individuals serving on an elected board who spent years at odds. Their disagreements affected the productivity and personal satisfaction of all the other board members.
>
> When asked to facilitate a board retreat and help to deal with these "difficult" individuals, Dick began by guiding a discussion of what the board members expected of each other. One of the "difficult" individuals stated that he wanted the mayor and the other board members to stop having "secret meetings." He cited the member with whom he was at odds as frequently instigating such meetings. Everyone else denied such sessions were occurring. When asked for specifics, the accuser said that he "knew" everyone else talked by telephone and exchanged information before attending board meetings, and he gave some specific examples of times this had occurred. His "partner in crime" immediately asked if this was what the other board member had been upset about "all this time." After a yes, the response that followed was, "Oh, my gosh! Don't you remember five years ago when I called you at home about the State Street incident? You told me then to never again bother you at home with issues like that. So I haven't. We never call you because we know you don't want to be bothered."
>
> "But I did not mean for you to leave me out of all the information," the accuser replied. "I just meant that the State Street issue seemed trivial and that it could have waited until a later meeting."

While at one level straightening out this misunderstanding was just a matter of agreeing on what important words mean ("secret meetings"), at another level the issue probably would not have surfaced without structuring a roles and expectations conversation. In this instance, the board members were able to clarify that no decisions were being made in private. They specified what information to share before meetings and when and how to share it. The two individuals at odds significantly improved their relationship and worked together effectively for a number of years following this discussion.

I have had similar experiences working with top management teams who, for example, wait for the boss to speak or strategically plan what to present to the boss without ever clarifying the boss's desires. In one memorable instance, group members shared during a roles and expectations conversation that they never worked on anything until they had heard support from the director and the assistant director. If there was any hint that both individuals did not agree, they assumed a project would not be implemented. "We just hunker down until we are sure both people named John see things the same way. And we don't usually say what we think until we are pretty sure both of them are on the same page." For their part, the director and assistant director were extremely frustrated with the team members for not showing more initiative and not implementing decisions quickly. Working from implicit assumptions about expectations created misalignments for this group that had gone on for years and significantly degraded the performance of the entire organization.

Time and again, roles and expectations clarification is one of the most systemic and lasting interventions in facilitation with work groups, appointed and elected boards, and community project committees

THE POWER OF THE INTERVENTION

One of the reasons the roles and expectations intervention is so powerful is that it elicits clarification of multiple elements of the group effectiveness model.

One of the reasons the roles and expectations intervention is so powerful is that it elicits clarification of multiple elements of the group effectiveness model.

Expectations are essentially group norms that grow out of group values and beliefs (culture), so each of these elements is discussed. ***Roles*** address the more formal job duties and tasks to be performed. In clarifying roles, it is generally necessary to revisit group membership and issues of boundary management, asking, for example, "What other roles have a deep impact on this group's effectiveness? Do the individuals in those roles need to be added to this group?" It is difficult to discuss roles and expectations productively without asking, "Roles in service of what? How do our roles link to our purpose? What results are we trying to achieve here? How are our expectations helping or hindering us in accomplishing our purpose?" Sometimes the group realizes that it must back up a step and revisit its mission and vision. In these cases, starting with roles and expectations may lead to addressing an even more fundamental structural problem.

See Chapter Seventeen, "Developing Shared Vision and Values," page 149.

Often I find that group members agree about their purpose even if their visions for the future differ. But unfortunately, each assumes his or her own personal expectations are shared (or should be shared) by everyone else. When individuals behave inconsistently with others' expectations, they are usually judged harshly, but the inconsistency is never raised. Over time, an escalating cycle occurs: each person assumes that those not meeting his or her private expectations are not fully committed to the group or just "don't get it." When this is the case, information certainly cannot be shared openly and differences candidly discussed. Relationships become increasingly strained and communication gaps more serious. The inability to discuss differences about how roles should be performed is viewed as confirmation that the group cannot address other difficult issues. And avoiding difficult issues compromises the group's creativity and performance. The roles and expectations intervention can halt this downward spiral. Dealing with ineffective group member behavior is much less difficult when the group has previously agreed about what constitutes appropriate behavior.

Dealing with ineffective group member behavior is much less difficult when the group has previously agreed about what constitutes appropriate behavior.

STEPS OF THE INTERVENTION

If a group has never developed role descriptions or agreed on expectations, allow some time for preparation in advance of the discussion. Figure 18.1 is an overview of the roles and expectations intervention. The group will need to agree ahead of time about which roles to include so members can decide who needs to participate. A ten- to twelve-member group can generally work through the steps in three to four hours. More time will be needed if the group needs to revisit its purpose or develop descriptions of new or changing roles. Make sure each group member can be present for this discussion. If one person is absent, it can make a considerable difference in the level of commitment the group gains for following expectations and for future decisions.

If a group has never developed role descriptions or agreed on expectations, allow some time for preparation in advance of the discussion.

Step 1: Identify Critical Roles and Participants

Although usually obvious in hindsight, key roles are rather frequently overlooked when planning a discussion. Each party must be fully committed to performing his or her role according to expectations, and full participation in the conversation is necessary to gain that commitment and shared understanding. When working with teams and boards, the group usually thinks of including the various roles that currently exist in the intact group (for example, mayor, manager, board members, director, department heads). Roles frequently overlooked but crucial to a group's performance may be facilitator, consultant, sponsoring manager for a work team, clerk for an elected board, or town or chamber of commerce staff for a community group.

Figure 18.1 Steps in the Roles and Expectations Intervention

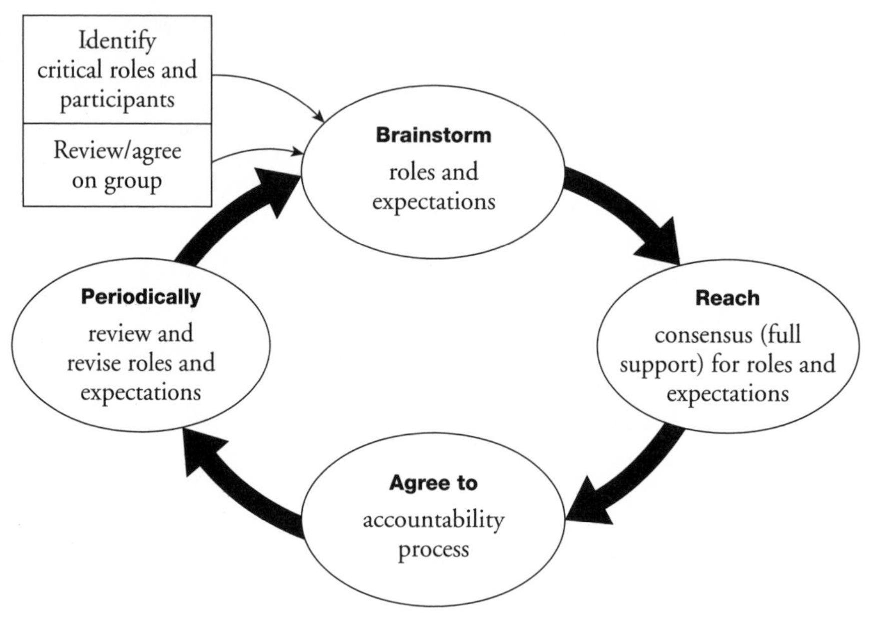

Even if those holding key liaison roles will not meet with a group as regular members, it is important to work with them to agree about how they will support the group. When working with a new group, it is helpful to have the group imagine roles that will be crucial to accomplishing the defined purpose. A recurring source of role conflict is to find that certain individuals hold critical information but do not see themselves as having a role to support a particular group. The group then finds those individuals unresponsive to important requests, and relationships and work product suffer. There are limits to how many people and roles can be productively included in the discussion, but it is important to ensure that the most critical ones are all in the same room at the same time participating in one conversation. Then expectations for ancillary roles can be addressed and communicated separately.

Step 2: Review/Agree on Group

Review or ask the group to review before the discussion any vision, purpose, or goal statements. Check for agreement about the purpose of the group, and jointly decide if this needs clarification before roles and expectations can be developed. For example, if a work group realizes it will not need a facilitator or a consulting engineer for a particular project, it is inefficient to spend time clarifying an unnecessary role just because such a role has existed in the past or is useful on other projects. It is often necessary to review step 1 after the purpose is clarified or changed, because the purpose may now indicate new individuals who should participate in the conversation.

Step 3: Brainstorm Roles and Expectations

Group members generate a list of expectations for how members will perform in each of the roles. It is helpful to move from general to specific. If a mayor or manager is also a full member of the group, define general expectations that group members have of one another first (for example, come to a meeting fully prepared). Then add any expectations that relate to special or added responsibilities (for example, represent the board on a regional task force or keep other departments informed about project status). We use a prompt like, "I expect other group members to . . ." and ask each individual to complete the sentence with statements reflecting his or her own expectations.

When a group already knows or wishes to learn the ground rules for effective groups, it is helpful to include some of the key principles in the expectations. Many of the groups we work with create expectations lists that include such items as "clarify the decision-making rule for all important issues" or "be sure all members have the same valid, relevant information before meetings." Frequently we recommend that groups read a short article describing the ground rules (Schwarz, 2002). Some groups adopt the ground rules as part of their expectations. However, expectations are often more general in nature and ground rules are adopted or developed separately as group norms.

Step 4: Reach Consensus (Full Support) for Roles and Expectations

Groups seldom agree with all of the items on a brainstormed list of roles and expectations. The purpose of this step is to identify common ground and adopt only roles and expectations that are fully supported by every member of the group. To this end, we clarify and answer questions about each item on the list and then check with each individual to see if he or she supports each item. This may seem laborious, but it often brings to light hesitations that indicate unresolved concerns. To prevent future conflicts, it is critical to check into these and to be certain of unrestrained support for each expectation. The final result is a fully supported and fairly short list of key expectations for each role that can meaningfully guide the group's work together.

Step 5: Agree to Accountability Process

Role descriptions and shared expectations will not improve group dynamics unless the members agree to hold one another accountable for behaving consistently with them. This is the Achilles heel of many groups. Most people say that they want honest, direct feedback. Yet at the same time they say that they are reluctant to "embarrass" others or "put them on the spot" by telling them when they fall short of expectations. Most individuals seem especially fearful of raising the group leader's inconsistencies with him or her.

It is critical at this stage to discuss the dilemma created when people want and need feedback to improve performance but no one is willing to offer it. Reframe with a group the importance of feedback for mutual learning. Point out that withholding feedback discounts another's ability to learn and grow. Help the group explore the risk of not raising an issue—for example, deteriorating performance, impaired product quality, the high cost of firing and hiring new people, or hampered competitive position. This discussion may elicit an even deeper examination of the group's norms, values, and theories-in-use. At a minimum, this is an opportunity to reinforce skills for raising potentially undiscussable issues. The group should have a clear understanding of when and how to give each other feedback on meeting expectations.

Step 6: Periodically Review and Revise Roles and Expectations

Roles and expectations change as group responsibilities evolve and as members' skills develop. Part of accountability is to regularly review the expectations and assess whether and how the group is meeting them. Many groups we work with annually review their roles and expectations statements, deciding what to keep and what to change or drop. If even one member of the group changes, the group should review roles and expectations and invite additions and changes from the new members. This is an important part of integrating new members into a group and of building and continuing shared commitment to expectations. Periodic reviews may take only a few minutes; annual review and revision may take an hour or so.

CHANGES AND ADAPTATIONS TO THE INTERVENTION

In practice, the basic steps of the roles and expectations intervention may be expanded or adapted. Two particularly useful adaptations are responsibility charting and use of scenarios.

Responsibility Charting

Developing a chart of critical functions for each important role is particularly useful when creating a new team or restructuring a work team that is expected to remain intact permanently or for a long project. Responsibility charts also become

Useful Questions for Each Step of the Intervention

1. Identify critical roles and decide who needs to participate:
   - What are the most important roles in this group at this time?
   - Who is in charge in each situation we regularly face?
   - What formal role or job descriptions already exist? Do these need to be reviewed at this time?
   - From whom will we need critical information and support in the near future? Do these individuals need to be group members? What are the consequences of not creating explicit expectations with those individuals whether or not they are group members?
2. Review group purpose:
   - What is your understanding of this group's central purpose?
   - What key contributions do you think this group can make?
   - What are your hopes and dreams for this group? What are you personally most passionate about for this group?
   - What are the group's statutory responsibilities?
   - For what critical outcomes is this group responsible?
3. Brainstorm roles and expectations:
   - What are your expectations of yourself as a member of this group?
   - What do you expect of other group members? Of the individuals who fill each of the important roles identified in step 1?
   - What are examples of times you have been effective as a group? Why were you effective? What behaviors do you want to continue?
   - What are examples of times you were ineffective as a group? Why do you think this occurred? What are examples of behaviors you want to improve?
   - What understandings do you have for communicating issues, concerns, or complaints to one another?
4. Reach consensus on roles and expectations:
   - Is there any expectation listed that does not seem fair or legitimate for this group?
   - Are there any similar expectations listed that can be combined?
   - Have you listed any expectations that even one member cannot commit to working to fulfill?
5. Agree about how to hold one another accountable:
   - If you think another party is not fulfilling an expectation or responsibility, how will you raise this with him or her?
   - How will you decide if the group or individual members are or are not meeting expectations?
6. Periodically review and revise roles and expectations:
   - When will you review these expectations to determine how well you are meeting them?
   - What process will you use to integrate the expectations of new members when membership changes?

increasingly useful as a team becomes more self-managing because they can indicate which responsibilities or roles members will fill now, in six months, or in a year.[1] A brief example is shown in Table 18.1.

Creating a role analysis this detailed takes teams several sessions and often involves assistance from human resource specialists or outside consultants. However, it can form the basis of very productive conversations about what is expected, how a team will develop, and how members will be evaluated.

Table 18.1 Sample Responsibility Chart

Roles	Team Members Now	Team Members in Six Months	Leader Now	Leader in Six to Twelve Months	Sponsoring Manager
System management					
Approve applications designs	X	X		X	
Set conversion schedule		X	X		
Performance management					
Perform quarterly reviews	X				
Perform annual reviews		X	X		
Team development					
Train new team members		X	X		
Grant module training certification				X	X

Source: Adapted from the Technology Work Group Charter, Town of Carrboro, North Carolina (2000).

Sample Roles and Expectations from Real Work Groups

Real groups often develop expectations that reflect their current concerns. Although the examples here are not all precisely worded, they were developed and used by groups I facilitated. The emphasis in my facilitation was not on elegant wording. Rather, the written expectation is an artifact or reminder of a significant group conversation. Meanings sometimes shift, so regular review and clarification are needed for statements like these to serve their purpose over time.

Management Team Members [Expectations] of One Another

- Help monitor the consistency with which we fulfill our mission and goals across the organization.
- Communicate shared accountability for success throughout the organization—"upward" and "downward."
- Before deciding important issues, clarify who decides and how we decide.
- Agree about exactly what supporting a decision means.
- Balance informality with task accomplishment.
- Do not list an item as a priority unless it is genuinely important and we are all committing to get it done.
- Support each other outside meetings. Don't talk negatively to employees about each other.
- It is acceptable to use each other as a sounding board to define difficult issues and to plan for future conversations.
- We accept our responsibility to fully understand important issues by doing our homework, asking questions, and insisting on full discussion of each important issue.

Management Team Members of the CEO

- Help us coordinate our work but do not run our departments for us.
- Keep us informed of key board issues and concerns.
- Communicate with all group members on important issues, not just with one or two.
- Explain your reasoning and intent when you make a request.
- Be open to hearing things from us that you may not like; don't "kill the messenger."

CEO of Management Team Members

- Take responsibility for getting the information you need; read the agenda ahead of meetings and ask for additional information if you need it.
- Monitor your own behavior for consistency with group expectations and ground rules.
- Let me know if you think I have failed to behave consistently with expectations.
- Share responsibility for keeping meetings on track and group process well managed.
- Monitor performance of all key programs, and keep me informed of results.
- Consult me on professional resources available to assist with your decisions.

Work Team Members of One Another

- Develop a process for setting priorities and check with all team members before changing priorities.
- Come to meetings prepared.
- Take turns scribing and preparing minutes and agendas.
- Commit to meet the timetables we set for ourselves and to assist others when unforeseen events create slippage.
- Make decisions based on verifiable facts or best available sources.
- We respect our differences, separating differences in communication style and preferred ways of participating from fundamental values differences.

Scenario Development

Sometimes groups find it difficult to develop expectations in the abstract. A useful adaptation of the roles and expectations intervention is to create three to five short scenarios of one to two paragraphs each that reflect recent experiences. It is helpful if groups can think of one or two times when they worked well together and one or two times when problems occurred. Then, by considering questions like the following, the group can clarify their expectations:

- Think about the situations in which the group worked well together. What did each person do that contributed to this effectiveness? What do you expect one another to continue to do to support the group's effectiveness?
- Think about the situations in which the group was not as effective as it might have been. What did not happen that you would expect to see happen in the future?

- What other commitments would you make or ask others to make in situations like the ones described in the sidebar "Sample Roles and Expectations from Real Work Groups"?

Note

1. For more a more detailed discussion of responsibility charting and additional examples, see Mohrman, Cohen, and Mohrman (1995).

References

Mohrman, S. A., Cohen, S. G., and Mohrman, A. M., Jr. *Designing Team-Based Organizations: New Forms for Knowledge Work.* San Francisco: Jossey-Bass, 1995.

Schwarz, R. "The Ground Rules for Effective Groups." Chapel Hill, N.C.: Roger Schwarz & Associates, 2002. [www. schwarzassociates.com].

Town of Carrboro, North Carolina. "Technology Work Group Charter." Carrboro, N.C.: Town of Carrboro, 2000.

Chapter 19

Using the Skilled Facilitator Approach to Strengthen Work Groups and Teams

Anne Davidson

MUCH OF WHAT WE have said so far about the Skilled Facilitator approach implies that we are interacting with teams and similar work groups. My own early work focused almost exclusively on work teams, and I continue to facilitate and consult extensively with organizations trying to improve or establish team-based structures. TSF is a powerful addition to the practice of creating work teams or any collaborative work system.

WHAT ARE WORK GROUPS AND TEAMS?

Individuals and organizations frequently disagree about what a work team is and is not. Some use *team* to define formally chartered groups that share a specific purpose or outcome and use the term *group* for all other collections of individuals. In *The Wisdom of Teams,* for example, Katzenbach and Smith (1993) state that "a team is a small number of people with complementary skills who are committed to a common purpose, performance goals, and an approach for which they hold themselves mutually accountable" (p. 45). Katzenbach (1997) also writes specifically about "The Myth of the Top Management Team," pointing out that "a so-called top team seldom functions as a *real* team" (p. 83) because of the absence of many of the factors such as specific performance goals and mutual accountability for tasks.

In the Skilled Facilitator approach, we use the terms ***work group*** and ***team*** interchangeably. In either case, we are referring to "a set of people with specific interdependent roles who are collectively responsible for producing some output (service, product or decision) that can be assessed, and who manage their relationships with those outside the group" (*The Skilled Facilitator,* p. 20).

def·i·ni·tion In the Skilled Facilitator approach, we use the terms **work group** and **team** interchangeably. In either case, we are referring to "a set of people with specific interdependent roles who are collectively responsible for producing some output (service, product or decision) that can be assessed, and who manage their relationships with those outside the group" (*The Skilled Facilitator,* p. 20).

The first steps in using the Skilled Facilitator approach with work groups are to clearly specify interests and develop a solid contract to address the interests.

The factors or principles that create successful teams and collaborative organizations are precisely those addressed by the Skilled Facilitator.

The level of interdependency and types of responsibility shift with the role of the team, but the key factors of interdependency, shared responsibility, and boundary management are present in some form whenever we use the terms *team* or *work group.*

It often helps during initial contracting to clearly define such important terms as *group, team,* and *teamwork.* More important is to discover the interests behind a request. Many people request teams or team-building activities when what they seek are collaborative behaviors like listening, joint problem solving, or effective conflict management. Or they want to create teams or a team-based organization as a means of reducing hierarchy and improving responsiveness to customers. Debating whether a group is or is not a "real team" is not often a productive discussion. There is a range, from a specific work group with a narrowly defined charge through a top team with strategic responsibilities, to an organization based on teamwork and mutual accountability. Beyerlein, Freedman, McGee, and Moran (2003) at the Center for Collaborative Organizations (formerly the Center for the Study of Work Teams) define the range most clearly when they describe three levels of collaborative work systems: traditional teams, team-based organizations, and collaborative organizations. TSF skills are powerful in addressing the full range of interests, but the players, the interventions, and the time and resource commitment differ significantly. The first steps in using the Skilled Facilitator approach with work groups are to clearly specify interests and develop a solid contract to address the interests.

WHY IS TSF SO POWERFUL?

Over the past decade or so, a large body of new research has identified critical factors for work group success in a wide range of contexts. There is a good deal of consistency among the studies. They emphasize the importance of team structure (purpose, roles, norms, accountability), supportive organizational context, and group process skills like conflict resolution and decision making. The factors or principles that create successful teams and collaborative organizations are precisely those addressed by the Skilled Facilitator.

The Group Effectiveness Model (GEM) specifically addresses issues of group context such as rewards, material resources, and information. Each of the critical group structure criteria is also addressed in the GEM: clear mission and goals, motivating task, clearly defined roles, membership, and group norms. And the group process elements of the model are essentially the same ones identified by the researchers as important for effective teams: ability to solve problems and make decisions, manage conflict, communicate, and manage organizational boundaries.

See Chapter Two, "The Group Effectiveness Model," page 15, and Chapter Fifteen, "Using the Group Effectiveness Model," page 135, on the model and its applications.

In addition, TSF adds two components that are missing from much of the team and group development literature. First, the approach is internally consistent and integrated. Using the tools of the approach, one can address all of the critical success factors. You do not have to teach a new vocabulary for each skill set or ask groups to develop fundamentally different skills. Second, the approach offers behaviorally specific methods for addressing the components of effectiveness. Many programs identify success factors, and some offer specific examples of items like meeting guidelines. But few provide tools like the Ground Rules for Effective Groups that cut across multiple success factors. Rather than having to learn lots and lots of different models for boundary spanning, team chartering, decision making, and so forth, work groups that master the ground rules can move fluidly from task to task in a consistent and skilled manner. TSF provides both the fundamental underpinnings for each team success factor and, in most cases, the specific behaviors that support them.

TSF provides both the fundamental underpinnings for each team success factor and, in most cases, the specific behaviors that support them.

HOW DID TSF HELP A TEAM-BASED ORGANIZATION?

At one point in my career, I helped a large utility set up self-directed work teams:

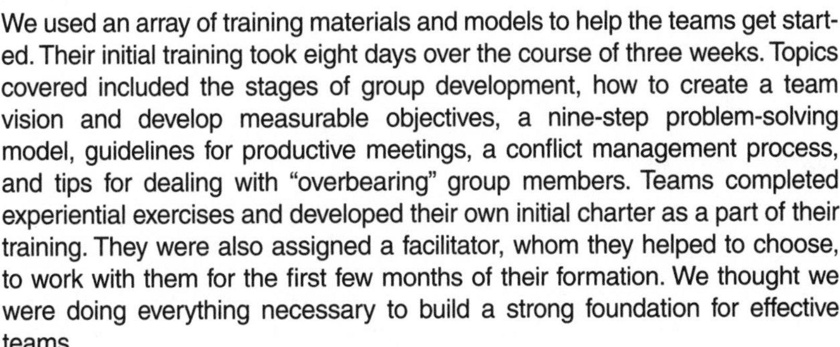

> We used an array of training materials and models to help the teams get started. Their initial training took eight days over the course of three weeks. Topics covered included the stages of group development, how to create a team vision and develop measurable objectives, a nine-step problem-solving model, guidelines for productive meetings, a conflict management process, and tips for dealing with "overbearing" group members. Teams completed experiential exercises and developed their own initial charter as a part of their training. They were also assigned a facilitator, whom they helped to choose, to work with them for the first few months of their formation. We thought we were doing everything necessary to build a strong foundation for effective teams.
>
> But the results were disappointing. A few teams produced one or two finished projects, but most floundered. None was able to meet consistently on their own without feeling they needed guidance from their facilitator. Facilitators were quickly overwhelmed trying to support seven or eight teams each. In refresher sessions, we found that all the teams had significant gaps in their skill set.
>
> About this time, I began using the TSF approach in my practice. This led me to introduce the Group Effectiveness Model to a meeting of team leaders at the utility and to ask them to diagnose which elements were working well and which contributed to less-than-stellar results. The leaders did not all agree, but each could pick out three or four key elements in the GEM that were problematic (or altogether missing) for their team. Most did agree on one thing: there were too many different tools and techniques in our team training program. They could not figure out when to use what. And they still got stuck in disagreements and felt as if they made decisions without good information. Most had problems getting managers who had formerly controlled data and processes to release reports the teams needed to make improvements or to manage their own processes. In general, the leaders advised abandoning the team process.

Instead, we went through a series of meetings in which we introduced an early version of the GEM and discussed it across all levels of the organization. We also revised the training, reduced it to four days, and replaced a number of the tools with an introduction to what were then the sixteen ground rules of the Skilled Facilitator approach. We began to use the GEM as the basis for chartering teams rather than having a separate chartering system. It took about six months to introduce the revisions to the teams, and the results were by no means perfect. We still did not address the issue of mental models effectively, and over time this created additional problems. But the improvement was dramatic. Teams began to get results because they were more focused and could develop valid information more easily. A smaller, more targeted set of tools allowed them to concentrate their efforts on a manageable set of skills. The successes achieved generated energy to continue with and improve the team processes. And the trainers responsible for developing new teams reduced the manual from two thick volumes to just over one hundred pages in one notebook. The team journey became an important stage in the organization's becoming more collaborative, more profitable, and more focused on serving customers.

See the section on chartering teams below. See also Chapter Twenty-Six, "Ground Rules Without the Mutual Learning Model Are Like Houses Without Foundations," page 217.

HOW DOES TSF STRENGTHEN TEAM CHARTERING?

A team chartering process is similar to, and as important as, the contracting process that supports effective facilitation or consultation.

A team chartering process is similar to, and as important as, the contracting process that supports effective facilitation or consultation. Developing a clear working agreement lays the foundation for an effective work group. The initial inclusion of the critical success factors happens during chartering. Early in my work with teams, I thought charters useful but perhaps not critical, especially not for internal teams working within a broad team process shared across an organization. A few experiences with teams and their sponsoring managers taught me to value the chartering process and to treat it as sacred.

In one memorable experience, I helped establish a team of employees charged with revising the policy for after-hours callback:

> During the initial meeting, the sponsoring manager told the team, "I will agree to try whatever you recommend, even if I disagree with it. I will give anything you come up with a shot, as long as it does not increase our overtime pay budget more than 5 percent. I would like to see you reduce that budget. Anything else goes that is legal."
>
> Months later (and following several unsuccessful attempts to get the manager to go over preliminary recommendations), the team presented their recommendations to a council that included the CEO and other top managers in the organization. The sponsoring manager became visibly upset during the presentation. At the conclusion, he jumped up and said, "That is a terrible policy; I did not agree to it. You have to go back to the drawing board."

> Luckily, the manager's initial agreement was written into a team charter. One of the team members took what he deemed a significant risk (in front of the top executives) and reminded the sponsoring manager of what was in the charter. The manager immediately apologized, shared his concerns, and promised to give the recommendation his support despite his reservations. Without the charter, the team member may not have spoken up, the recommendations would have been shelved, and the team would likely have given up and become cynical about the team process. Instead, the experience added to the team's sense of accountability and authority and gave other teams more faith in the process and management's support of it.

What I learned from the experience was not only the importance of getting agreements about purpose and process into a written charter. I also recognized that we had missed an important element of the charter: clarifying the sponsoring manager's role and responsibilities during the development of the team's recommendation so that we had his commitment to review the team's work regularly and offer his feedback. By overlooking this agreement with the manager up front, we had contributed to placing him in the dilemma of either having to accept a decision he had reservations about or turning it down and alienating employees. Without owning and addressing our part in creating the problem, we risked alienating other sponsoring managers. This experience led me to advise groups to develop more complete charters that considered the whole system in which they operated.

I began taking two steps: first, I introduce groups briefly to the ground rules and invite them to use the ground rules during our discussions for developing a charter; second, I spend ten to twenty minutes introducing the GEM to a group, and we decide which elements are most important for their team charter. I advocate for the basic elements that I find important to almost all teams: clear purpose, clearly defined roles, agreement about group norms, a boundary management or escalation process, and a clear understanding of how to get and share information and resources. Within these elements, many others can be discussed and agreed on, such as the role and expectations of the sponsoring manager, the rewards available to the team, and how the team purpose fits into the organizational mission. Even if the group does not practice the ground rules during these discussions, part of my agreement with them is that I will use them to intervene and help the group have a productive discussion. My use of the rules results in good modeling for the group, so that they often decide to use the Skilled Facilitator ground rules or principles as part of their process, and we develop a sound charter that supports groups over time.

Charters are living documents. Just having a written charter does not guarantee a successful group. While it is important to have a document to reference agreements, the key value is the process that people go through to develop a charter and the shared meaning and commitment they generate. During the process, a good charter is also adapted for the particular circumstance, so that no two look alike. Exhibit 19.1 is an excerpt from a charter developed using the process I have described.

While it is important to have a document to reference agreements, the key value is the process that people go through to develop a charter and the shared meaning and commitment they generate.

Exhibit 19.1 Excerpts from the Town of Carrboro Technology Work Group Charter, March 2000

Name: Technology Work Group

Work Group Purpose

The purpose of the Technology Work Group is to provide recommendations to the management team on matters relating to Town information systems.

Work Group Tasks

Typical tasks may include:

1. Assessing technology needs and updating the strategic plan.
2. Working toward a centralized, computerized information system for the Town.
3. Recommending technology policies to the Management Team (department heads, assistant manager and manager). A top priority in this area is public records law compliance.
4. Recommending systems standards and service priorities.
5. Helping to span boundaries between "common" and departmental projects and sharing information about technology related to day-to-day activities in departments. For example, helping individual departments decide the role of technology for them and providing a forum to discuss and to make recommendations about variances from the technology plan. . . .

8. Being a catalyst for ideas and pilot projects. Recommending projects. Projects will be the responsibility of the department implementing them.
9. Helping identify training needs, work with Network Administrator and Management Team to set up training.

Expectations of the Work Group and Work Group Members

The Management Team expects the Work Group to:

- Create a work plan that supports the group's purpose and implement the plan.
- Provide information regularly to the management team for purposes of accountability and information sharing. The Work Group will report two times a year to the Management Team and informally to the sponsoring manager (Assistant Town Manager) as needed. The Management Team expects the work group to make decisions at the lowest level possible and to avoid unnecessary reporting.
- Commit to getting valid, relevant information from all departments before making recommendations and decisions.
- Provide decision options supported by valid information.

Escalation Path

The escalation path for questions, recommendations and decisions that cannot be decided within the Work Group will be from the Work Group to the Network Administrator. The Network Administrator will work with project leaders and report to the sponsoring manager. If necessary or desired, the project leader may meet with the sponsoring manager or invite the sponsoring manager to meet with the Work Group. The Work Group may escalate issues to the Management Team, if necessary, and from the Town Manager to the Town Council. The final level of escalation will depend upon the issue being addressed.

Management Team's Commitment to the Technology Work Group

The Management Team makes the following commitments to the Work Group:

- Members will be given reasonable time to attend Work Group meetings and perform Work Group tasks.
- The management team will respond to recommendations from the Technology Work Group within a reasonable, mutually agreed-upon time frame. The management team will share with the Work Group actions to be taken based upon the Group's recommendations or provide explanations for not taking action.
- The management team will work with the Work Group to design ways to recognize the Group's contributions to the organization.

Key Roles

Sponsoring manager for the Work Group (liaison to management team)—Assistant Town Manager

Facilitator—Anne Davidson will assist the Work Group initially and be available on an as-needed basis

Work Group Coordinator—Will schedule meetings, book meeting rooms, open meetings and assist the project leader(s), who will lead meetings

Project Chairs—Individual Work Group members will take the lead on specific projects and chair meetings related to those projects.

Liaison to Sponsoring Manager—The Network Administrator will fill this role by meeting with the Work Group, working with the Project Chairs, and reporting regularly to Assistant Town Manager

Other Advisors—as needed

Membership Criteria

The revised list of criteria to use when selecting Work Group Members is that candidates should be:

1. Knowledgeable about technology or willing to learn.
2. Willing to respect the opinions of others.

3. Broadly representative of the organization (good mix of department and job level representation).
4. Willing to spend reasonable time to attend Work Group meetings and perform Work Group Tasks.
5. Willing to accept the fact that the group will function by charter.
6. Willing to work for the good of the group and to fully support the decisions of the group.
7. Interested in serving as a Work Group member.

Group Norms

[Included were the TSF ground rules and a short set of meeting guidelines.]

WILL THE SAME PROCESS WORK WITH TOP MANAGEMENT TEAMS?

The principles and tools of the Skilled Facilitator approach are just as valuable for top management teams as for teams responsible for specific work products or processes.

Management groups at the top of organizations (at least traditional, hierarchical organizations) often do not have tangible performance goals for which they are mutually accountable, and their purpose is much broader than that of most organizational teams. But I have found principles and tools of the Skilled Facilitator approach just as valuable for top management teams as for teams responsible for specific work products or processes. I believe the elements of the GEM may need to be more broadly defined. For example, the top team's mission and vision may be indistinguishable from the organization's mission and vision. The elements of group context may take on more significance for a management team because they are often the one group that can change elements like the reward structure, the performance feedback process, and the physical environment. They can even change the organization's entire mission.

Although the elements in an executive team charter may be different from those in other team charters, I find it just as valuable for top teams to develop written charters. Part of the reason can be seen by examining the Carrboro Technology Work Group Charter example in Exhibit 19.1. For the work group to manage its boundaries and command the necessary resources to function, it needed certain commitments from the organization's management team, its top executives. The list of management team commitments runs longer than the sample here, and those commitments created the framework in which the team could begin to operate in a context that was traditionally hierarchical. In other words, unless and until the culture of the larger organization changed, the Technology Work Group needed the top team to create space for the work group to operate. And for the executive team to carry out its commitments, each member needed to share responsibility and accountability with all others, even if they were not interdependent around their other tasks.

In organizations that strive to become more team-based or collaborative, such as learning organizations, a written executive team charter takes on even greater significance. The executive management team provides overall strategic direction for the organization and fosters the kinds of values and behaviors that must support a move to more collaborative processes. "The importance of leadership from this team cannot be overestimated. Unless the macrocontext is brought into alignment with the team approach, organizational members will be caught in the tension between the new and old ways of operating" (Mohrman, Cohen, and Mohrman, 1995, p. 263). Mohrman, Cohen and Mohrman outline four large clusters of responsibilities for executive teams in team-based organizations: (1) setting and communicating corporate strategy and goals, (2) designing the organization's structure and systems, (3) orchestrating performance management of business units, and (4) modeling team-oriented norms. They found that what separated effective from ineffective management teams were "the ability . . . to develop a shared understanding of where and how they are leading the organization, the extent to which the team plans and sets goals collaboratively, and the extent to which the team is managed (and manages itself) as a team" (pp. 266–267). Having a written charter that addresses these elements is particularly helpful in communicating direction to other employees (and customers) and to modeling the desired values and norms.

The components of the Skilled Facilitator approach address specifically the behaviors required of the top team and help its members develop the skills necessary to set goals collaboratively. Here is a list of the elements in the management team charter of one executive group that has made significant progress in its journey toward becoming a more collaborative organization:

The components of the Skilled Facilitator approach address specifically the behaviors required of the top team and help its members develop the skills necessary to set goals collaboratively.

- Purpose of the management team (strategic direction)
- Membership criteria (who is included, the rationale for inclusion, and the conditions under which new members may be added permanently or temporarily)
- Values and beliefs of the management team (a statement of the importance of values and beliefs in guiding management team decisions and a list of the specific values and beliefs the group seeks to embody)

See Chapter Seventeen, "Developing Shared Vision and Values," page 149, for an example of a set of management team values and beliefs.

- Meeting guidelines (under what conditions the team will and will not meet)
- Decision criteria (which types of decisions require consensus and how this will be reached)
- Group norms (Skilled Facilitator ground rules)

The process for developing the written charter is no different from that of any other team. However, I do find it even more important to address mental models early on with an executive team. Team members at the top have frequently reached their position by and been rewarded for using unilateral control strategies, and it is important for them to understand this.

If they do not make a clear choice about the values the team seeks to live by, then the executive team charter is likely to be internally inconsistent and inconsistent with the very principles the top managers are asking others in the organization to follow.

If they do not make a clear choice about the values the team seeks to live by, then the executive team charter is likely to be internally inconsistent and inconsistent with the very principles the top managers are asking others in the organization to follow. Obviously, this is a recipe for disaster. The result will not be a collaborative organization but increased distancing, avoidance, and cynicism. So I tend to take more time initially with executive teams to help them understand unilateral control and mutual learning, as well as ground rules, before we undertake developing a charter.

References

Beyerlein, M. M., Freedman, S., McGee, C., and Moran, L. *Beyond Teams.* San Francisco: Jossey-Bass, 2003.

Katzenbach, J. R. "The Myth of the Top Management Team." *Harvard Business Review,* 1997, *75*(6), 82–91.

Katzenbach, J. R., and Smith, D. K. *The Wisdom of Teams.* Boston: Harvard Business School Press, 1993.

Mohrman, S. A., Cohen, S. G., and Mohrman, A. M., Jr. *Designing Team-Based Organizations.* San Francisco: Jossey-Bass, 1995.

Chapter 20

Using the Ground Rules in E-Mail

Roger Schwarz

For many organizations, e-mail has become a primary method for communicating. Compared with face-to-face conversation, e-mail presents additional challenges to communicating effectively. E-mail doesn't convey your nonverbal behavior and doesn't allow you to observe others' nonverbal reactions to your behavior. And it doesn't allow you to immediately check others' reactions and respond accordingly. However, unlike real-time conversation, e-mail allows you to review and edit what you "say" before the recipients "hear it."

I use several steps for writing e-mail: (1) I think about what I want to say before I start writing (or sometimes, by writing I figure out what I want to say), (2) write my e-mail with the mutual learning approach and the ground rules in mind, (3) review my message for congruency, and (4) hit the Send button when I'm satisfied that my e-mail is congruent.

Keep in mind that you do not need to use this process for all your e-mail. Many e-mails are short comments or questions about simple logistical matters. The process I describe in this chapter becomes more valuable as your e-mail messages involve matters that may be ambiguous, involve people with differing points of view, or are challenging in some other way.

Some ground rules need to be approached differently because e-mail does not allow for the same degree of interaction as face-to-face conversation. The process here becomes more valuable as e-mail messages involve matters that may be ambiguous, involve people with differing points of view, or are challenging in some other way.

APPLYING THE GROUND RULES

Many of the ground rules are used in the same way in e-mail as in face-to-face conversation. Examples include explaining your reasoning and intent and focusing on interests, not positions. However, some ground rules need to be approached differently because e-mail does not allow the same degree of interaction as face-to-face conversation.

For a review of the ground rules, see Chapter Five, "Ground Rules for Effective Groups," page 61.

Test Assumptions and Inferences

In face-to-face conversation, you can immediately test an inference or assumption you are making. And if your inference or assumption turns out to be inaccurate, you can immediately change what you had planned to say. In e-mail, testing inferences and assumptions takes more time.

There are at least two approaches to this. First, you can state your assumption or inference, test it with others, and wait for a response before continuing your thoughts. The advantage of this approach is that you avoid spending time writing on a subject that may be based on invalid information. In addition, to the extent that your assumptions and inferences about other team members are inaccurate, you avoid contributing to defensive reactions on the part of others by continuing to discuss your concerns about an issue that are based on invalid information. For example, if you have assumed that a teammate had not followed through on her work, you might write, **"Susan, I have some concerns about not receiving your outlines last week. My concerns are based on my inference that you were going to get them to me by last Friday at close of business, because you said you would get them to me by the end of the week. Before I continue, I want to check to see: Was my inference accurate?"**

In the second approach, you also state your assumption and inference. However, you then continue your thoughts, stating that you are continuing assuming that your assumption or inference is accurate but recognizing that it may not be. The advantage of this approach is that if your assumption or inference is accurate, you reduce the number of e-mails needed to convey your thoughts. For example, you might write, **"I think that we should use the Internet exclusively to publicize the database because I'm assuming that most of our target population has Internet access. Does anyone have any information about my assumption? If my assumption is valid (and it may not be), then we could use the Internet in several ways. First, we could . . . Second, . . . "**

Combine Advocacy and Inquiry

One purpose of this ground rule is to find out how others see things differently and to use these differences to make better decisions. For example, in face-to-face conversation you might say, **"I think we should begin the project by spending time agreeing on our roles and how we will work together. I am suggesting this because I think if we spend a few hours in the beginning clarifying how we will work, we can avoid getting bogged down a number of times later. Does anyone see this differently?"**

In e-mail, you would write the same message. Then you would be faced with the same choice discussed in testing assumptions and inferences: whether to wait for a response or continue your thoughts. The same advantages and disadvantages apply here.

Share Relevant Nonverbal Information

Although it is less ambiguous when you express your feelings using words, in face-to-face conversation, you can use tone of voice, facial expressions, and body language to convey feelings. In e-mail you are limited essentially to words. To convey this nonverbal information in e-mail, it's necessary to convert the feelings in your tone of voice, facial expressions, and body language into words. To do this, pay attention to what you are feeling as you are writing an e-mail. Then describe the specific things that others have said or done (explain your reasoning and intent) that lead you to feel this way. Check whether others see it differently. Also consider the possibility that your feelings may result partly from your own behavior (for example, you are frustrated because you did not raise an issue that needed to be raised) or with something unrelated to the situation.

For example, you might say, **"My understanding was you would personally provide me the data by last Friday or find someone who could. Is that correct? If so, I'm frustrated because by not receiving the data by last Friday, we missed the November cutoff for submitting the proposal. I'm wondering, was there anything I did that contributed to your not being able to submit the data?**

Jointly Design Next Steps

Because e-mail is less interactive than face-to-face conversation, it is easier to act unilaterally. I jointly design next steps by suggesting a process and then asking others whether that process meets their needs. For example, I might write, **"I think that before we discuss solutions for the downsizing, we should identify our interests, and then craft a solution based on them. Anyone see any problems with that approach?"**

Save Undiscussable Issues for Face-to-Face or Telephone Conversations

Even with using the ground rules, e-mail still has limits, so I use the telephone or, if feasible, face-to-face conversation for what have been undiscussable issues or issues that I think may be difficult for me or for others to discuss. The other person's voice or, better yet, presence provides nonverbal data that we can use to test inferences. Being in the same room (or at least on the telephone) also allows more personal interaction.

ANALYZING AND EDITING YOUR E-MAIL

Your ability to communicate effectively, either face-to-face or in e-mail, increases as you become more aware of what you are thinking and feeling (your left-hand column) and are able to share your thoughts and feelings in a way that is consistent with the core values and ground rules. Generally, the larger the gap is between your e-mail message and your left-hand column, the less productive it will be.

See Chapter Four, "Understanding What Guides Your Behavior," page 33, and Chapter Twenty-Seven, "Writing and Analyzing a Left-Hand Column Case," page 235.

To narrow the gap, as you review your e-mail, compare it with your left-hand column. Look for things that you are thinking and feeling but have not put into the e-mail. Is your e-mail based on assumptions that you haven't tested? Are you withholding relevant information?

Again, as in face-to-face conversation, simply sharing your left-hand column in ways that are consistent with the ground rules is often not enough. In difficult conversations, we often use a unilateral control approach that makes it difficult to share what is in our left-hand column. Consider, for example, if you are thinking, "This person hasn't done her assignment in two weeks, and I have had to do extra work as a result. She is simply lazy. I know she is trying to get out of doing her share." If you were reluctant to share these thoughts in their current form, you would have good reason. Doing so would likely contribute to making the other person defensive and make the conversation unproductive. A more fundamental step you can take to make it easier to share what is in your left-hand column is to begin to think differently, that is, to use the mutual learning approach.

By beginning to change your frame of mind, you can change your feelings about the situation and what you might say. For example, instead of believing that you are right and others are wrong, consider that others have information that you do not have and ask yourself and others, "What am I missing that others see?" If the effect of others' actions is to create a problem for you, assume that they meant to act effectively and did not intend to create this problem. This can lead you to point out the problem that was created for you and then ask with genuine curiosity, **"What were you wanting to accomplish when you took this action?"** In the long run, changing the way you think about difficult situations will make it much easier to share what you are thinking.

WHY BOTHER?

At this point you may be thinking that the process for writing and analyzing I described is tedious and not worth the time. After all, the advantage of e-mail is its speed, and, in fact, many e-mails often involve one or two comments on simple topics like logistics (for example, where to meet). Although it's always useful to use the ground rules in e-mail (such as agreeing on what important words mean), simple e-mails don't require much analysis before sending them. The process of following the ground rules becomes more valuable as e-mail addresses more complex topics or topics on which people have differing or strong views or is challenging in some other way.

E-mail is fast. But speed that generates misunderstanding ultimately slows things down as it creates new problems to solve. Using the ground rules and reviewing your e-mail before hitting Send is an example of going slow to go fast.

See Chapter Seven, "Thinking and Acting Systemically," page 75.

PART THREE

Deepening Your Practice

THE CHAPTERS IN Part Three are about refining your skills. They show many ways to hone your diagnosis and intervention abilities so that you can effectively move into a discussion, make a powerful process intervention, and then move back out. You may find, as we have, that as you begin to use the Skilled Facilitator approach, much of the work you need to do is in your own head: practicing until you can, during the conversation, think of what to say, how to say it, and explain why. Refining your skills requires deepening your personal awareness as well as increasing the precision of your interventions.

For example, using the ground rules becomes much easier when you know them and have lots of examples of times when they were or could have been used. For the ground rules to become a useful template for diagnosing and intervening, you must learn to diagnose quickly and accurately, learn to change your own conversation, and then learn to invite others to use the ground rules. Chapters Twenty-One and Twenty-Two address this process.

Chapter Twenty-One, "Ways to Practice the Ground Rules," summarizes tips for enjoyable and productive ways to learn the ground rules by heart. Chapter Twenty-Two, "Some Tips for Diagnosing at the Speed of Conversation," expands on those learning tips to address ways to develop real-time diagnostic skills. This chapter discusses opportunities to practice your diagnostic skills and then goes into the deeper issue of managing your own internal conversation. It points out that a critical component of being able to diagnose at the speed of conversation is being able to clear your own mind so you can fully attend to what others are saying. The chapter also offers suggestions for quieting your "inner critic" and becoming fully present with a group, as well as a list of key words and phrases to listen for when you are diagnosing group behavior.

The chapters on opening lines and dealing with jargon will help you think about exactly what to say when you complete a diagnosis and are ready to intervene. Chapter Twenty-Three, "Opening Lines," focuses on ways to start each of the intervention steps of the diagnosis-intervention cycle (steps 4 through 6). It also provides one or more opening lines for each of the nine ground rules. Chapter Twenty-Four, "Reducing the Skilled Facilitator Jargon," points out that many Skilled Facilitator phrases have a specific meaning to those familiar with the approach. However, the terms may not convey that meaning to others, who may feel that we are speaking a foreign language if we ask them to, for example, "combine advocacy with inquiry." This chapter provides useful suggestions for reducing jargon and a chart of jargon-free alternatives for key Skilled Facilitator terminology.

Chapter Twenty-Five, "Now What Do I Do? Using Improv to Improve Your Facilitation," builds on the themes of deepening your practice through fully attending to others and being able to quickly and effectively respond at the speed of conversation. Roger converses with improv instructor Greg Hohn as both draw parallels between what makes good improvisation and what makes good facilitation. As they draw out principles such as "treat surprises as gifts" and "good lines come from good listening," you can see how methods that strengthen your ability to be fully present in one situation expand your ability to intervene effectively in another.

Part Three concludes with two chapters about addressing mental models, the deepest level of self and group awareness. Chapter Twenty-Six, "Ground Rules Without the Mutual Learning Model Are Like Houses Without Foundations," addresses the inadequacy of the ground rules alone to effect fundamental change. It clearly explains why it is important for those of us practicing the Skilled Facilitator approach to be aware of our own unilateral control tendencies while we help others understand how the ground rules can be misused if the intent behind their application is clouded by unilateral thinking. Chapter Twenty-Seven, "Writing and Analyzing a Left-Hand Column Case," closes out the theme of deepening your practice by offering a practice methodology for helping yourself and others expand your awareness of your mental models: the left-hand column case exercise. This is an exercise we use with clients in workshops and on our own to learn from past difficult conversations and prepare for upcoming difficult situations. It helps us see and change the thinking behind our behavior and then change our actions. Using a sample case, the chapter demonstrates how to use this exercise and how to redesign a conversation once you have spotted opportunities to incorporate the Skilled Facilitator core values and principles.

Chapter 21

Ways to Practice the Ground Rules

Anne Davidson

WHENEVER PEOPLE ASK us about how to learn to use the ground rules and core values consistently, we usually answer, "Practice, practice, practice." To fully use the ground rules, you must work on how you think going into a conversation.

The issue of working on how you think is addressed in Chapter Four, "Understanding What Guides Your Behavior," page 33, and Chapter Twenty-Six, "Ground Rules Without the Mutual Learning Model Are Like Houses Without Foundations," page 217.

But using the ground rules gets much easier once you know them by heart. They then become your template for diagnosing and designing conversations. Actually, they become a lens through which you view the entire world. But just memorizing the list of nine ground rules is not much fun or particularly meaningful. You need lots of examples in your head in order to use them yourself and identify opportunities to use them with others at the speed of conversation. Here is a compilation of suggestions from the *Fieldbook* authors, our colleagues, and our clients.

DIAGNOSIS

As Peg points out in Chapter Twenty-Two, "Some Tips for Diagnosing at the Speed of Conversation," page 195, just listening to any conversation, radio, or television program while attending to the use or nonuse of the ground rules is excellent practice. Here are some other specific suggestions:

- ***Make or purchase a pocket-sized card listing the ground rules.***[1] Keep it handy. People are horrified to know that I kept one taped to my steering wheel when I was first learning the ground rules. No, I did not read it while driving. I had a long commute in stop-and-roll traffic each day. Listening to talk radio and glancing down at the card during stops helped me learn the ground rules quickly.

• ***Pick one ground rule to listen for at a time.*** I often did this while listening to the radio or watching television. For example, I would say to myself, "I am going to see how many untested assumptions and inferences I can pick out in the next thirty minutes," or "I am going to look for all the places people advocate without inquiring." I made a game of this with some teenaged friends, and we kept little scorecards during sit-coms. It helped me endure the shows they enjoyed, and we all learned.

• ***For more intense practice, watch a movie that is particularly rich in dialogue, and diagnose the use and nonuse of ground rules.*** Two of my favorites are *Mindwalk* (1991) and *My Dinner with André* (1981). In our training workshops, we use segments of *Twelve Angry Men* (1957), which contains hundreds of examples of use and nonuse of principles similar to the ground rules. But the practice does not have to be that serious. The opening scenes of *Jerry McGuire* (1996), for example, demonstrate a lot of untested assumptions, including Jerry's attempt to "share relevant information" with his colleagues in the form of his new vision. There are also a lot of missed opportunities to engage in joint design. And *Good Will Hunting* (1997) has a hilarious scene in which Will, played by Matt Damon, shares why he is not taking a job with the National Security Agency. It is a masterpiece of explaining reasoning and systems thinking. Looking playfully at missed opportunities to use the ground rules and core values helps the principles stick. And it's fun to think about how using them might have changed the story.

• ***During meetings, look for instances when people use and do not use the rules.*** Keep your ground rules card handy as you do this. Think about whether people are more effective when the conversation more closely matches using the ground rules.

• ***Display a ground rules poster.*** If one or more of your work groups is willing to learn the ground rules with you, it helps tremendously.

• ***Tape actual meetings*** (with permission). Then go back and practice coding use and nonuse of the ground rules. *Coding* means identifying which ground rule was used (you can jot down a plus symbol and the ground rule number) or not used (a minus symbol and the ground rule number). This is a useful practice for facilitators and leaders because it most closely mirrors the actual situations in which they will find themselves and speeds transfer of learning and comfort in trying interventions.

• ***Find examples of cartoons that illustrate nonuse of the ground rules.*** The humor of many cartoons hinges on not using ground rules principles. For example, a client brought in a cartoon for his group about executives not agreeing on what an important word meant. In the first panel, an executive directed an employee to "file these." In the next panel, the employee was seen jabbing a nail file through the center of each document. It was silly but memorable. One of my creative peers found at least one cartoon to illustrate every ground rule. We were just completing our first Skilled Facilitator workshop together, and she gave a set of the cartoons grouped by ground rule to each member of the class. I still see those cartoons flash through my head sometimes when I am about to intervene or teach a ground rule.

CHANGING YOUR OWN CONVERSATION

Making what you say consistent with the ground rules can be particularly challenging since we are all often blind to our own unilateral routines. Here are some productive ways to practice redesigning your own part of the conversation:

- ***Pick one ground rule and look for opportunities to use it during a conversation.*** This kind of focused practice can help you master using the ground rules over time rather than trying to think about them all at once.
- ***Tape-record meetings or conversations in which you know you will be speaking or sharing your ideas*** (with the permission of other participants). Afterward, review the tape and pick out instances where you think you could have productively used one or more ground rules but did not. Write out what you could have said differently to be more consistent with the ground rule. After doing this a few times, you will find that the appropriate words will come to you more easily during the actual conversation.
- ***Reread and redesign your e-mails, voice mails, and memos.*** Before sending out written communications or before releasing a voice mail message you record, review it for consistency so that you can rewrite or rerecord it.

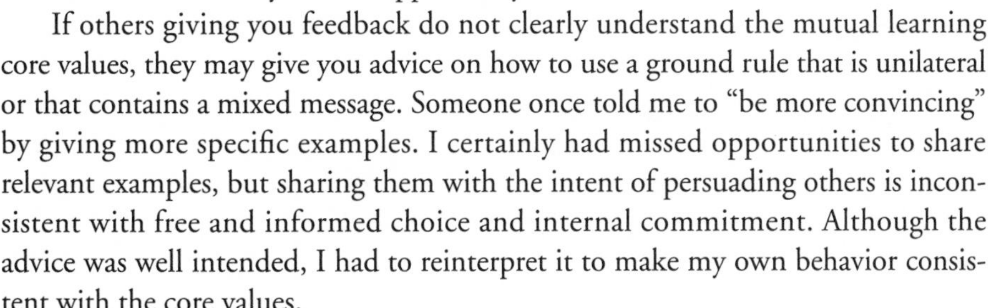

For more guidance on using the ground rules in e-mails, see Chapter Twenty, "Using the Ground Rules in E-Mail," page 181.

- ***Invite others to give you feedback.*** Ask them whether and how you are using the ground rules. Of course, to do this, you will need to explain the ground rules to them. An easy way to do this is to ask them to read a copy of the short article "Ground Rules for Effective Groups."[2] Even if others are not interested in using the ground rules themselves, they can often help you spot where you are or are not consistent in your own use. I found the feedback from a few close friends and colleagues invaluable in helping me catch myself when I failed to inquire or explain my reasoning. One of my colleagues got to the point that he would say to me at least once a day after I made a statement, "And your reason is . . . ?" We would just both smile, and I would correct my missed opportunity.

If others giving you feedback do not clearly understand the mutual learning core values, they may give you advice on how to use a ground rule that is unilateral or that contains a mixed message. Someone once told me to "be more convincing" by giving more specific examples. I certainly had missed opportunities to share relevant examples, but sharing them with the intent of persuading others is inconsistent with free and informed choice and internal commitment. Although the advice was well intended, I had to reinterpret it to make my own behavior consistent with the core values.

INTERVENING

Once you have practiced using the ground rules to diagnose conversations, it is not as difficult to begin using the diagnosis-intervention cycle to invite others to use the rules. Obviously, whenever you do this, you are practicing using the ground rules yourself, because advocacy and inquiry, using specific examples, explaining your reasoning, and so forth are built into the cycle. But the additional, intentional practice of saying the words to intervene on each ground rule is also helpful. People often find it useful to:

- ***Practice and role-play with others.*** Create a learning group with the intention of practicing the ground rules together. Many clients form "lunch and learn" groups that meet weekly or monthly. Others who live and work near one another gather regionally on a periodic basis to practice. It does not help to just describe how you would use the ground rules. More productive is to code left-hand column cases that people prepare and bring to the group or to role-play scenarios suggested by group members. Then participants can give one another feedback on how you did or did not use the ground rules. This approach has the advantage of helping you practice diagnosis, changing your own conversation, and intervening all at once.

See Chapter Twenty-Seven, "Writing and Analyzing a Left-Hand Column Case," page 235.

- ***Put one or two ground rules to practice on the bottom of printed meeting agendas.*** Many of our clients work with groups that are committed to practicing and using the ground rules. They have found it useful to practice one or two rules at a time until the group masters them, and they have agreed to print the ground rules to practice at the bottom of agendas they send out for regular meetings. Then group members can review the ground rules before attending. At the end of each meeting, the group critiques their use of the rule or rules they are trying to practice and then agrees whether they need to continue practicing these rules at the next meeting or whether they are ready to move on to others. As a group improves its skills, it is helpful to identify patterns common to the group and to practice ground rules that address those. One group I worked with had a pattern of advocacy without inquiry, and it took a lot of practice to improve on it. Another had a habit of not agreeing on decision rules and assuming that silence meant support, so we practiced Ground Rule Nine for about six months.
- ***Tape-record meetings and review them as a group.*** This is similar to the practice suggested in diagnosis, but here the groups can go back to instances where they thought their discussion did not go as well as they wanted and then redesign the conversation together. This helps everyone learn both diagnosis and intervention. It often helps the group pick up on nonuse of multiple ground rules and on patterns that lead discussions to spiral into unilateral designs.

• ***Link ground rules to a problem-solving or decision-making model.*** Many groups adopt (or could adopt) a systematic problem-solving model that helps them consistently define their goals, generate valid information, and consider multiple perspectives before generating actions plans. Each step of a typical problem-solving model can be linked to two or three ground rules that are particularly useful at that step. The example in Exhibit 21.1 is a chart one of my clients produced that helped him concentrate on practicing a few ground rules when working on each step. Of course, all of the rules are always useful; groups should not limit themselves just to one or two, but concentrating practice on a few at a time does seem to help in the beginning.

Exhibit 21.1 Linking the Ground Rules to a Problem-Solving Model

Five Problem-Solving Steps	Be Sure to Practice Ground Rules . . .
1. **Identify the problem or goal.**	
	Explain reasoning and intent.
	Share all relevant information.
	Test assumptions and inferences.
2. **Analyze.**	
	Focus on interests.
	[Gather] and share all relevant information.
	Combine advocacy with inquiry.
3. **Evaluate alternatives.**	
	Test assumptions and inferences.
	Explain reasoning and intent.
	Discuss undiscussables.
4. **Test-implement.**	
	Jointly design next steps and ways to test disagreements.
	Use a decision-making rule that generates the level of commitment needed.
5. **Standardize.**	
	Share all relevant information.
	Test assumptions and inferences.
	Jointly design next steps and ways to test disagreements.
	Use a decision-making rule that generates the level of commitment needed.

Source: Adapted from Kelly (1992).

Resources

Good Will Hunting. Miramax, 1997.
"Ground Rules for Effective Groups" article, pocket cards, and posters available at www.schwarzassociates.com.
Jerry McGuire. Columbia/TriStar, 1996.
Mindwalk. Atlas Productions, 1991.
My Dinner with André. Fox, 1981.
Twelve Angry Men. MGM, 1957.

Notes

1. Ground rules pocket cards and posters are available from Roger Schwarz and Associates, www.schwarzassociates.com.
2. The "Ground Rules for Effective Groups" article is available at www.schwarzassociates.com.

Reference

Kelly, M. *Everyone's Problem Solving Handbook.* White Plains, N.Y.: Quality Resources, 1992.

Chapter 22

Some Tips for Diagnosing at the Speed of Conversation

Peg Carlson

WHEN PEOPLE FIRST LEARN the Skilled Facilitator approach, they frequently express a sense of being overwhelmed by the speed of real-life conversations. After reading (or hearing) about the diagnosis-intervention cycle and trying to put it into practice, they often ask, "How do you attend to all of the interactions in a meeting, check them against the ground rules and core values to make diagnoses, and decide whether and how to intervene, all without falling way behind the flow of the discussion?"

In this chapter, I share tips for real-time diagnosis. These fall into two categories: opportunities to practice listening to conversation with the core values and ground rules in mind and the internal work you can do as a facilitator to increase your readiness to hear the group's conversation.

See Chapter Six, "The Diagnosis-Intervention Cycle," page 69, for an introduction to the process.

OPPORTUNITIES TO PRACTICE

Your initial focus is on attending to a conversation in a new way, using the core values and ground rules to interpret how people are communicating with each other. Remove any expectation that you will (or should) be intervening in the conversation at this point. This will help to free your mind to consider only the data at hand—the words and nonverbal cues present in the interaction—without concern for next steps.

Your initial focus is on attending to a conversation in a new way, using the core values and ground rules to interpret how people are communicating with each other.

Through practice, I have learned to "see" conversations in terms of the core values and ground rules. I liken this to the difference between how chess players and nonchess players look at the same chessboard. I don't play chess, so if someone asked me to remember where the pieces were on a board, I'd have difficulty. I would have to memorize the layout in some way, but without an understanding of the pieces and the moves, it would just be rote memorization, and it would be hard to remember more than a few. By contrast, expert chess players have a perceptual set that allows them to see the board in terms of patterns and potential moves.

Everyday Practice Ideas

As you go about your daily activities, there are many opportunities to practice diagnosing conversations. Here are a few suggestions:

- Practice the first two steps of the diagnosis-intervention cycle (observe behavior, verbal or nonverbal, and infer meaning) by keeping a copy of the ground rules and diagnosis-intervention cycle in front of you as you watch a television show or listen to the radio. The plots of situation comedies, for example, are often based on untested inferences. The dynamic of talk radio in many cases illustrates people focusing on positions rather than interests, together with untested inferences. Since intervening in the dialogue is not an option, this venue can help you concentrate on diagnosis.
- You can listen to casual conversations almost anywhere: on an airplane, train, or bus; standing in line at the grocery store; or driving a carload of kids to soccer practice. I'm not talking about situations where you need to strain to hear what is being said; for most of us, there are times during the day when we are exposed to others' conversations without being given a choice. Think of it not as eavesdropping but as an opportunity to practice your diagnosis skills. As with the television and radio practice opportunity, this forum gives you a place to focus on diagnosis more than intervention, given that it's generally not considered socially acceptable to intervene in strangers' conversations (and violates the core value of free and informed choice as well)!
- Another opportunity to practice listening for core values and ground rules is during meetings where you do not need to be an active participant or facilitator. Jot down a participant's exact words when you infer that he or she has used, or not used, one of the ground rules. You can also imagine whether, how, and why you might intervene, but don't be too concerned about what you would say to intervene at this point.

In my experience, people often discount the importance of these first three steps, the "interior" side of the cycle, in their haste to figure out what to say to help the group improve its effectiveness.

In my experience, people often discount the importance of these first three steps, the "interior" side of the cycle, in their haste to figure out what to say to help the group improve its effectiveness.

Remember that the intervention side of the cycle (steps 4, 5, and 6) simply shares and tests openly the private diagnosis you have made. By training yourself to listen for the core values and ground rules in regular conversation, you will be well on your way to crafting an effective intervention.

Listen for Key Words or Phrases

Certain words or phrases are red flags that the speaker is about to say something inconsistent with one or more of the ground rules. When I hear these or similar words, I pay particular attention to the statement or question that follows. (For examples, see Table 22.1.)

One Last Tip: An Opportunity Once Missed Will Present Itself Again

One thing that allayed my fear of missing critical diagnoses in an ongoing discussion was a growing appreciation of the principle of repeating opportunities. In concrete terms, this means that interactions tend toward fairly stable patterns.

Even if you see the relationship between a part of the conversation and the ground rules too slowly to be able to decide on or plan an intervention the first time something comes around in a discussion, chances are it will come around again. For example, you may have observed group members making statements without inquiring into others' views. Or you may have noticed some members asking questions of others without explaining why they are asking the question, and those being questioned appear to be getting defensive as a result. There is a good chance that these interactions illustrate a pattern of how group members communicate with one another, and if you weren't confident of your initial diagnosis, you will get another opportunity. It's not always necessary or desirable to intervene immediately. In fact, sharing several examples of what you've observed can make your diagnosis more understandable when you are ready to share and test it with the group.

Even if you see the relationship between a part of the conversation and the ground rules too slowly to be able to decide on or plan an intervention the first time something comes around in a discussion, chances are it will come around again.

CLEARING YOUR MIND: THE INTERNAL WORK NEEDED TO DIAGNOSE AT THE SPEED OF CONVERSATION

The theme of the tips is practice. Getting to the point where you can diagnose at the speed of conversation is not difficult if you see everyday conversations—at work or home, on radio or television—as your potential practice field. This frequent practice is necessary, but not sufficient.

Getting over the hump to truly feel comfortable diagnosing conversations in real time may involve some significant internal work as well. For some, the hump is making high-level inferences about group members. In my case, the problem was more often the internal conversation I was having regarding my own (perceived lack of) competence as a facilitator.

Getting over the hump to truly feel comfortable diagnosing conversations in real time may involve some significant internal work as well.

Here is an example. When I started to learn the Skilled Facilitator approach, I was excited to have a new way to diagnose and help improve groups' effectiveness

Table 22.1 Listen for These Phrases

When I Hear Someone Say . . .	I Am Likely to Infer and Test That He or She . . .
"Everyone thinks there is a problem with X."	Has one or more specific examples to share (Ground Rule Three)
"When you implied that . . . "	Has made an inference about the other person's statement or motive (Ground Rule One)
"Don't you think that . . . "	Is using rhetorical inquiry; has a statement to make but is asking a leading question (Ground Rule Six) instead of sharing his or her own reasoning (Ground Rule Four)
"I believe the way to address this is [proposes a solution]."	Has stated a position, but not shared the interests behind it (Ground Rule Five) or has advocated but not inquired into others' views (Ground Rule Six)
"The manager is never going to go along with that idea."	Has made an untested inference about the manager (Ground Rule One) or has relevant information to share about the manager's interests (Ground Rule Two)
"Let's get back on track."	Has heard group members say something that he or she thinks is off the topic but has not shared what it is (Ground Rule Four) or checked to see if others agree that the topic has shifted (Ground Rule Seven)
"What Frank is saying is . . ."	Is paraphrasing another group member's comments but is not likely to check with that person to see if the paraphrasing is correct (Ground Rule Six)

as well as my own effectiveness as a facilitator. I liked the idea of using one set of core values to guide effective behavior for me as a facilitator as well as for the group. The problem was that once I learned that this was the standard I was striving for, I began evaluating myself against this standard on a minute-by-minute basis throughout a meeting. I would make an intervention and then the internal chatter would start: "Did I just ask Bob to give an example when I didn't ask Justine for a example of what she was talking about? Maybe the group will now see me as biased in some way, not treating all members equally." Or, "I asked Molly if she was willing to check out her assumption that Ted couldn't meet for longer than one hour, but I don't think I tested *my* assumption that she was making an assumption! Was I being unilateral?"

My overly enthusiastic internal monitor of my facilitation skills was getting in the way of attending to the group. Each time I went "off-line" to reflect on something that had happened earlier, I risked missing something important that was currently occurring in the group.

My overly enthusiastic internal monitor of my facilitation skills was getting in the way of attending to the group. Each time I went "off-line" to reflect on something that had happened earlier, I risked missing something important that was currently occurring in the group.

While I was busy reflecting, I might have been missing a new statement or question by a group member or data that would lead me to propose a new process or way to frame the discussion. I was having trouble staying in the moment with the group. My mind frequently seemed to be racing ahead or reflecting back instead of focusing on what was going on right now. This pattern made it more difficult for me to diagnose at the speed of conversation, which then increased my anxiety that I was not being as effective as I could be. I seemed to be stuck in a self-fulfilling loop. My effectiveness as a facilitator was reduced, but it wasn't because I couldn't figure out what was going on in the group; it was because my focus on my own performance was taking me away from what was happening in the group, and I was missing important cues. The solution was not a new tool or technique; it was learning to be fully present with the group.

The concept that has been most helpful to me in turning off the internal conversation and remaining present with the group is the Zen notion of beginner's mind.[1] Beginner's mind holds many possibilities; it comes without preconceptions, judgments, and prejudices. For the Skilled Facilitator using the diagnosis-intervention cycle, this takes the form of low-level inference, an appreciation for the data of a conversation without the complex, and sometimes inaccurate, structures added by unchecked assumptions that result in higher-level inferences. Without these more elaborate ladders of inference, the mind is more fully present to explore, observe, and see something as it is, more full of curiosity, not answers. The notion of beginner's mind is consistent with the mutual learning model: both emphasize the importance of remaining open to new information, remaining curious rather than judgmental, and closely observing what is actually there instead of our own feelings and beliefs about what is there.

Another fundamental aspect of beginner's mind is to remain in the moment, neither tarrying behind nor moving ahead of what is happening right now. As I described in my example, early in my facilitation work I frequently found my thoughts straying back to an earlier intervention or jumping ahead to anticipate what might occur later in the meeting.

To remain in the moment, it helps to remember that any diagnosis is preliminary and subject to the confirmation (or disconfirmation) of the group. This frees you from internal self-talk about your performance, because the data about whether your diagnosis is appropriate and adequate are available only from the group itself.

Paradoxically, this willingness to share my assessment of my performance as a facilitator has helped me let go of my concerns about it, which frees me to remain fully attentive to the group and pay careful attention to what is happening.

Note

1. For a more complete explanation of this concept, see Shunryu Suzuki's *Zen Mind, Beginner's Mind.*

Reference

Suzuki, S. *Zen Mind, Beginner's Mind.* New York: Weatherhill, 1970.

Chapter 23

Opening Lines

Roger Schwarz

WHEN YOU BEGIN TO practice the ground rules and the diagnosis-intervention cycle, one challenge is figuring out what words to say. If you have read other parts of this book or *The Skilled Facilitator,* you have probably noticed that we begin our interventions in similar ways, using similar phrases. In short, we have a set of opening lines. Each of us uses somewhat different language, but we all derive it from the same core values and assumptions. Opening lines are useful because they get you started. They answer the question, "What do I say when someone says or does X?"

Good opening lines can create a structure to make the rest of the conversation more productive. But opening lines are not designed to get you through an entire conversation. You can't predict how someone will respond to you. So after you share your opening line, you need to listen to how people respond and then decide how to craft your next line in a way that moves the conversation forward effectively.

Opening lines are useful because they get you started. They answer the question, "What do I say when someone says or does X?"

To make this approach work for you (and those you work with), you need to feel comfortable with the words you are using. This means using the Skilled Facilitator approach in a way that still sounds like you speaking rather than like someone else who has inhabited your body (for example, me). Some people use a two-step process to find their voice: they learn the opening lines and then begin to incorporate them with their own style. Other people work on both tasks at the same time; from the beginning they integrate opening lines with their own language and style.

To make this approach work for you (and those you work with), you need to feel comfortable with the words you are using.

See Chapter Twenty-Four, "Reducing the Skilled Facilitator Jargon," page 207, and Chapter Thirty-Three, "Finding Your Voice," page 279.

Many of the opening lines I use are related to the diagnosis-intervention cycle and the ground rules. Let's look at some examples.

THE DIAGNOSIS-INTERVENTION CYCLE

The diagnosis-intervention cycle has opening lines for each intervention step.

Step 4: Describing Behavior and Testing for Different Views

My opening line for this step has three parts. I address by name the person or people I am intervening with, repeat what I thought they said or did, and check if my understanding is accurate:

Example A1: **"Dennis, a minute ago you said, 'The project can't start until next quarter.' Did I get that right?"**

Example B1: **"Louise, I think you said, 'Would it be better to let people know sooner rather than later.' Is that what you said?"**

Sometimes I begin by explaining my reasoning and intent for the intervention:

Example C1: **"Alain, I want to check out an inference I made. A minute ago you said, 'The problem is that the data are missing.' Did I misstate it?"**

I don't begin by saying, "Excuse me" or "Let me interrupt." If I have contracted effectively with the group, the group has agreed that they want me to intervene, so I don't need to excuse myself for doing the job they asked me to do. And as long as I wait until a person has finished speaking, I'm not interrupting.

See Chapter Six, "The Diagnosis-Intervention Cycle," page 69, on the diagnosis-intervention cycle and Chapter Nine, "Jointly Designing the Purpose and Process for a Conversation," page 103.

Step 5: Sharing Inferences and Testing for Different Views

My opening line for this step has two parts: I share my inference about which ground rule the person or people did not use but could have and test for different views. Continuing from examples A, B, and C:

Example A2: **"I heard you say next quarter won't work, but I didn't hear you say which of your interests it didn't meet. Did I miss anything?"** (Ground Rule Five)

Example B2: **"I'm thinking you're not simply asking a question, but that you have your own view on your question. Yes?"** (Ground Rule Six)

Example C2: **"It sounds as if you're thinking that Carmela isn't going to correct the data set. Is that what you're thinking or something else?"** (Ground Rule One)

Step 6: Helping the Group Decide Whether and How to Change Behavior and Testing for Different Views

This step has two parts. First, I explain my reasoning for asking the person to change his behavior (that is, use either a ground rule or another part of the Skilled Facilitator approach), and then I ask if he is willing. In many cases, when the person is familiar with the ground rules, I skip the first part:

Example A3: **"I think it would be helpful to explain which of your interests the next quarter solution doesn't meet so that the group can try to incorporate them. Can you say what they are?"**

Example B3: **"Would you be willing to share your view and then ask others if they have a different view?"**

Example C3: **"Do you want to check with Carmela to see if you're right?"**

GROUND RULES

Many of the opening lines I use stem directly from the ground rules. Following are examples of opening lines without using the entire diagnosis-intervention cycle.

> Many of the opening lines I use stem directly from the ground rules.

Ground Rule One: Test Assumptions and Inferences

When you're making an inference about someone or when you think someone is making an inference about you:

"I'm thinking you're concerned we won't make the deadline if we add the additional sections. Am I off?"

"My intent was not to create more work for you, but to ensure that the readers have all the information they need. Still, I may have done something I'm not aware of. Can you tell me what I've said or done that's led you to think I'm trying to create more work for you?"

See Chapter Five, "Ground Rules for Effective Groups," page 61, for an introduction to the ground rules.

Ground Rule Two: Share All Relevant Information

When you think someone has more information than he or she has shared:

"When you say, 'Not everyone will support it,' it sounds to me as if you have other information about this issue. If so, can you share it?"

Ground Rule Three: Use Specific Examples and Agree on What Important Words Mean

When someone is talking in general terms:

> **"Can you tell me about a time when that happened so I can better understand?"**

Ground Rule Four: Explain Your Reasoning and Intent

When you don't understand someone's reasoning:

> **"Can you walk me through how you came to that conclusion? I'm not following your reasoning."**
>
> **"When you said X, it didn't make sense to me because . . .**
>
> **"I see a potential problem with that process. Let me describe it and get your reaction."**

Ground Rule Five: Focus on Interests, Not Positions

When you don't understand why someone is proposing or rejecting a possible solution:

> **"What needs of yours does the solution meet?"**
>
> **"What needs do you have that the solution doesn't address?"**

Ground Rule Six: Combine Advocacy and Inquiry

When you think someone is asking questions without sharing his or her views:

> **"I'm thinking you're not simply asking a question, but that you have your own view on your question. If so, can you say what you're thinking about the issue?"**

Ground Rule Seven: Jointly Design Next Steps and Ways to Test Disagreements

When you have a process you want to suggest:

> **"Let me suggest a way to proceed and get your reactions. I suggest we do X because . . . What problems does anyone see with this?**

"I came to a different conclusion than you did. How about if we figure out together how we came to different conclusions?"

"I'm not seeing how your comment is related to the topic we were discussing. Can you help me see how it's related?"

Ground Rule Eight: Discuss Undiscussable Issues

When you want to raise an undiscussable issue:

"I want to raise what might be a difficult issue and get your reactions. I'm not trying to put anyone on the spot, but instead trying for us to work better as a team. Here is what I've seen and what I think the issue is . . . How do others see this?"

Ground Rule Nine: Use a Decision-Making Rule That Generates the Level of Commitment Needed

When you want to clarify the decision rule:

"This is a decision I want us to make by consensus, because I believe it is important that each of us is fully committed to the final solution. We will each have important and different responsibilities for getting the whole project to fit together. Does anyone think it's unnecessary to reach consensus?" [If no one thinks it's unnecessary, continue.] **"If we can't reach consensus, then I think Brian and I will have to make a decision by tomorrow since we must report to the vice president. We would take into account each of your interests and the information shared during our discussions today. Any concerns about doing it this way?"**

Chapter 24

Reducing the Skilled Facilitator Jargon

Roger Schwarz

The American Heritage Dictionary defines jargon as "the specialized or technical language of a special trade, profession, or group" and "speech or writing having unusual or pretentious vocabulary, convoluted phrasing, or vague meaning." The Skilled Facilitator approach contains jargon (such as "combine advocacy and inquiry") that has a specific meaning among those who know the approach and is not clear to those unfamiliar with the approach. In the meaning of *jargon,* I don't include examples like "share all relevant information"; people may have different views about what is relevant information, but the concept of relevant information is widely understood and the words are familiar.

You might reasonably wonder why the Skilled Facilitator approach includes jargon, given that it can create misunderstanding. My answer is that jargon can be valuable for the same reason that it creates a problem: within the group using it, it has a specific agreed-on meaning. Consequently, it serves as a shorthand way to express a more complex set of meanings. For example, in the ground rule "combine advocacy and inquiry," the meaning of ***advocacy*** includes sharing your point of view, explaining your reasoning, expressing your interests, and identifying your assumptions. The meaning of ***inquiry*** includes asking a question that is designed to learn how others see the situation (including what they may see that you miss), without embedding your own point of view in the question and without trying to suggest what the correct answer should be.

Jargon can actually help those outside the group become aware that they may not understand an important concept. If you used everyday phrases like, "share your view and ask others what they think," someone who was not exposed to ground rules might reasonably think she knows what those words mean, but she will likely have a different understanding of the phrase than what you meant to convey.

Unfortunately, using jargon without explaining it may cause others to feel that they are excluded from some special in-group. They may infer you are using it to show your expertise, cover up your lack of expertise, control the conversation in some way, or act superior. People who have learned the ground rules in a workshop recognize this problem. They sometimes tell me, "We just don't talk like that where I work. No one uses the words *inquiry* or *inferences.* If I did, people would look at me like I was strange." This is the very issue that people comment on when they come to a workshop that others in their organization have already attended. They say things like, "I'm coming to the workshop partly so I can understand what my teammates are really saying."

Still, some people feel comfortable using the language of the core values and ground rules and find that the people they introduce it to in their organizations are also comfortable using the terms once they are defined. But don't assume that others' comfort will necessarily be related to his or her level of education or nature of his or her work. I facilitated a long-term change process for a city fire department in which the employees quickly began using the language of the ground rules and incorporated it into their work, yet many of them had no more than a high school education.

If your group knows the language of the Skilled Facilitator approach, then you can use the terminology if you choose. However, if some people in the group or meeting do not know the language, either explain what the terms mean or use other language. Table 24.1 shows some alternative language for describing and using terms that are often considered jargon.

See also Chapter Fourteen, "Introducing the Ground Rules and Principles in Your Own Words," page 131, and Chapter Twenty-One, "Ways to Practice the Ground Rules," page 189.

Table 24.1 **Reducing the Jargon**

The Skilled Facilitator Terminology	Alternative Language
CORE VALUES	
Valid information	Relevant information
Internal commitment	Commitment
Compassion	Empathy
GROUND RULES	
Test assumptions and inferences	*Check your assumptions*
"I'm inferring . . ." or "I'm assuming . . ."	"I'm thinking . . ."
	"It sounds to me as if . . ."
	"I'm getting the feeling . . ."
	"It looks to me . . ."
"I think you climbed the ladder [of inference]!"	"I'm thinking that you added some meaning to what was said."
Share all relevant information	
"Let me share my left-hand column . . ."	"Here's what I'm thinking . . ."
"What's in your left-hand column?"	"What are you thinking or feeling right now?"
	"What's running through your head?"
Explain your reasoning and intent	"Would you share with us why you feel [or why you want] . . .?"
	"Can you say more about why . . .?"
"Would you explain your reasoning and intent?"	"Would you say what leads you to feel that way?"
	"Can you say more about why. . .?"
Focus on interests, not positions	*Focus on needs, not solutions*
"What are your interests?"	"What is it about this solution that doesn't work for you?"
	"Putting aside for now what the solution should be, what needs have to be met for the solution to be effective?"
	"I heard you describe your solution, but I didn't hear what about it is important to you. Can you share that?"

(continued)

Table 24.1 ***(continued)***

The Skilled Facilitator Terminology	Alternative Language
Combine advocacy and inquiry	*Share your view, and ask what they think* *State your view, and ask for reactions*
"I'd like to advocate my point of view, then inquire as to what you think about it."	"I'd like to share with you what I'm thinking, then get your thoughts."
"I heard you advocate, but not inquire."	"I heard you share your view, but I didn't hear you ask for others' reactions."
"I heard you inquire but not advocate. Am I correct?"	"When you asked your question, I'm thinking you have your own view on the issue. Am I correct?"
"That sounds like a rhetorical question." Or "That's a leading question."	"When you ask that, I'm thinking you have a thought on that. Is that right?"
Jointly design next steps and ways to test disagreements	*Agree on next steps* *Jointly develop next steps*
"I'd like to jointly design our next steps."	"I'd like to figure out a way together to move forward. Would that work for you?"
The diagnosis-intervention cycle	
"I'd like to intervene on that."	"I want to check something out with you."

Chapter 25

Now What Do I Do?

Using Improv to Improve Your Facilitation

Roger Schwarz
Greg Hohn

A few years ago I took a couple of courses in improvisation from Greg Hohn. Greg is the director of Transactors Improv Co., the South's oldest improvisational theater, based in Chapel Hill, North Carolina. I had always liked watching improv and had even tried it a few times. I loved the thrill of spontaneously creating something with others and of trying to make something out of the lines others gave me. So when I signed up for my first improv course, I expected to learn a lot about improvisation techniques—and I did. But I also learned a lot about myself and how I interact with others when we are working together to create something.

After each improv exercise, Greg would ask us what we thought of our performance. As I listened to others' comments and reflected on my own comments, I realized that what it takes to create good improv is similar in many ways to what it takes to create a good facilitated conversation.

Recently, Greg and I talked about how improv and facilitation principles are similar.

TREAT SURPRISES AS GIFTS

Roger: In improv, the only line you have to work with is the one that others have given you. If your improv partner looks at the imaginary plate of food you are eating and says, "When did you become a vegetarian?" that is the only line you have to respond to. You can build on the line and play with it, but it is the only line you have to work with.

I found that sometimes I didn't like the line I was given, usually because I had another line in my head that I wanted my partner to give me. The more I focused on what lines I wanted others to give me, the less I was able to focus on what was possible. However, when I began to see the line I was given as a gift, I began to look for the possibilities and make a connection with both the content of the scene and the people I was creating improv with.

It's similar with facilitative skills. The only lines I have to work with are the ones my clients give me. By looking for the gift in each line, I focus more on what they think is important and how I can work with them to explore that.

Greg: Expectation will hang you up. A pianist friend told me about going into the studio to record one day and emerging distraught because he didn't do what he intended to do. Months later he listened to the tape of the session and realized that what he did was better than what he set out to do.

There's a fine line between accident and inspiration. Indeed you can treat them as the same thing. Most people tend to be afraid of the unknown. In improv, you treat it as an opportunity.

In my improv work, we focus on exploration rather than invention. Instead of one person having an idea and manipulating others to follow him or her, there is a give-and-take among the players so that they can discover something that not one person alone could have come up with. Invention is about the ego, whereas discovery and exploration are about the group.

An improviser who isn't open to surprises isn't open to true exploration and discovery. Instead he or she is concerned with advancing a personal agenda. This is equally true, I would imagine, for facilitators. Sometimes my students are frustrated by a lack of syllabus and stated goals in my course, but I counter that I want us to focus on the process rather than the outcome or product. And what if what they need is different from the goal?

GOOD LINES COME FROM GOOD LISTENING

Roger: To generate a good line, you need to see the gift in others' lines to you. To see the gift, you need to listen carefully. The more carefully I listened to the lines that my improv partners gave me, the better I was able to play off them rather than simply create my own. For example, if my about-to-be-first-time-partner-in-crime says to me, "I'm just not sure whether robbing the First National Bank will look good on my résumé," I can respond by playing off the absurdity of putting bank robbery on a résumé, playing off her concerns about her noncriminal career, or explaining how bank robbing requires a set of skills that many organizations value. All of these responses make explicit some implicit message in my partner's statement. If my response relates to her concern, I build the relationship between us by focusing on her concern, and we advance the scene at the same time.

In facilitative work, as I listen to people in the group discuss an issue, I ask myself, "What seems to be under the surface of what they are saying?" "What question can I ask or observation can I make to help people constructively share the stories that lie within their seemingly meaning-packed comments?" When I listen well, I get the gift that group members are giving me, and I return the gift by helping them tell the real stories they want to tell.

Greg: Listening is crucial in improv because it is part of the give-and-take process and it gets the players out of their heads. Usually people are formulating responses instead of truly listening. When we listen, we learn. We explore and discover. When we talk, it is often about ourselves and what we think we know or about the past instead of the present. Therefore, if good improvisation relies on exploration, discovery, and the group, listening cannot but help us, although it's also important that we carry our own weight and are assertive so that others can learn from and respond to us.

IT'S A SYSTEM: THE LINE YOU GET IS RELATED TO THE LINE YOU GIVE

Roger: In improv, there is a relationship between the line you give and the line you receive. If you give your partners a good line to work with, you have a better chance of getting a good line back that you can work with. What makes a good line in improv does not necessarily make a good line in facilitation. For example, a good improv line can have one person telling the other in great detail what is wrong with that person as if it is truth. While a good facilitation line can involve specifics, it does not represent them as truth, but rather as a hypothesis to be explored.

With facilitative skills, if you're thinking that people aren't being forthcoming, consider the lines you're giving them. Are you genuinely inquiring, or are you trying to get them to say what you're thinking? Are you focusing on positions or exploring interests?

Greg: This is one way that facilitation and improv may differ. Good improv is often about bad psychology. For example, "you" statements are much more effective than "I" statements because we're giving our partners valuable information. They also tend to make the emotional stakes higher. A better gift than wiggle room in improv is to give someone indisputable proof that he or she did something or is insufferable or what-have-you and that allows him or her to react to that truth. The value here is as a negative example: you don't want to do that while you're facilitating.

BE SPECIFIC

Roger: As in facilitation, in improv, specifics give the actors and the audience material to work with and move the conversation forward. If I begin by saying to my improv partner, "Listen, Laurie, this just isn't working out between us," at some point soon, one of us will need to get more specific. Laurie might say, "What do you mean? Here we are strolling on the beach, laughing. I think we're fine." Without specifics and details, the improv partners don't know exactly what they are talking about, and so neither does the audience.

With facilitative skills, specific examples help the group understand exactly what each member is talking about and create shared understanding. Shared understanding enables the group to move the conversation forward.

Greg: Yes, in improv you need to get to the specific heart of the matter.

DON'T BE AFRAID TO TAKE THE OBVIOUS ROUTE

Greg: When it comes to the obvious in improv, it is often simply the thing that fits best. In improv and comedy, we often work with patterns, usually in groups of three. The first two incidences of a thing set a pattern, and the third either confirms or confounds the pattern. Either conclusion works. For example, two women are at a dance, talking about how much they want men to ask them to dance. A man approaches and asks one to dance. They decline and continue to talk about wanting to dance. A second man approaches and asks to dance. He too is rebuffed. The pattern continues, and the third time the women can either dance or not dance or dance at the same time with one man. If the third man enters and asks if they want to buy a house, well, that's not going to fit. Even if that man says something "funny" like asking them to watch his pet lobster, it's still not going to be as effective as doing the predictable thing. The audience and players are deprived of the resolution of the dancing issue.

When we improvise songs, one of the most important things to do is create a structure, and the structure involves patterns. Catchy tunes have a certain predictability, and when the familiar refrain returns, we tend to like that. It is obvious, recognizable. A certain resolution of a measure may not be very original, but if it is obvious, it is often what the ear wants to hear.

Roger: With facilitation or facilitative leadership, group members also expect you to follow through on the obvious. When someone says, "Trust me, I just don't think the reorganization will happen," an obvious question is, "What leads you to say you don't think it will happen?" When you or the group chooses not to follow up on the obvious, the learning stops, and the group doesn't reach closure on the issue.

RAISE THE STAKES: NAME THE ISSUE AND ENGAGE IT

Roger: Facilitators and facilitative leaders show leadership by helping the group name and engage important issues that the group may be tiptoeing around. In doing so, they take important risks to help the team address the issues that really affect it. For example, a facilitator might point out that each time the team leader shares a view that is different from one that team members have expressed, team members change their views to that of the leader. The facilitator would then ask others if they saw the same thing and, if so, what led to that behavior. Is there a similar principle in improv?

Greg: In one improv scene, I came onstage and got down on one knee, ready to propose. The audience knew right away that the issue was high stakes. In improv, leadership means raising important issues and engaging them rather than playing it safe, no matter what the topic of the skit.

INCORPORATE MISTAKES INTO THE GROUP'S EXPERIENCE AND LEARNING

Roger: One principle of the Skilled Facilitator approach is transparency, which means that you explain to the group why you are doing what you are doing. So when you make a mistake, you publicly acknowledge it and may even use it as an opportunity for the group's learning. So, when you make a mistake and you're aware of it (or someone points it out to you), you also acknowledge it and can use it to move the group's learning and your own forward. For example, if you realize that you've been asking certain group members and not others their opinions, you can point that out to the group and ask group members whether they noticed and, if so, what their reaction was. By talking about the mistake you made, getting others' reactions, and agreeing on what you and others will do differently next time, you and the group model that mistakes can be opportunities for learning. Is there a similar principle in improv?

Greg: If you start to enter the stage and suddenly realize two characters are having an intimate moment, you can either stop, look embarrassed, and return to the wings with your "mistake," or you can burst in and be the nosey coworker or the father-in-law who can't bear to be alone for a moment or whatever. If you get all mush-mouthed while trying to speak, you are now playing a character who is awkward or drunk or has a speech defect. Again, there's a fine line between accident and inspiration. In improv, everything is happening now; it's not written or supposed to be anything, and therefore your mistakes aren't mistakes but rather opportunities or curves in the road.

TRUST THE PROCESS; DON'T CONTROL IT

Roger: I discovered that in good improv, just as in good facilitation, it's important to trust the process rather than control it. Facilitative work involves jointly establishing a process and using it. I trust the process when I honor the core values and assumptions. This means staying in a mutual learning approach and jointly designing the process with the group. Rather than control the conversation to go where I want it to go, I let the conversation emerge from the interaction among the group members and me. When I do this, both the group and I learn more and are more satisfied with the process itself.

Sometimes I got anxious in an improv scene. I worried about coming up with a line that was useful and maybe even funny. Of course, the more I spent my energy worrying about this and trying to push the conversation in a way that would give me a "good line," the less I attended to what my partners were saying and the less likely I was to come up with a line that was funny or even moved the scene along. Paradoxically, I remember that my line that got the biggest laugh from my classmates and you was one that I hadn't even planned or remembered after the scene. What does improv have to say about trusting the process?

Greg: Improv is about process, not product. It's not about the ego's invention but the group's exploration and discovery. Improv at its highest level produces that which is so much greater than the sum of its parts.

Actors simply must believe in the process. If there were a simple way to do that, then there'd be better improv in the world. Experience teaches this belief better than anything else. When you do something and have no idea what it is or how it's going to turn out and then have it turn out better than things you've actually intended, that teaches you to trust the process. Or sometimes you learn the hard way by falling flat on your face while trying to hammer your square agenda through a round opportunity.

The first step in gaining this experience and thus trust is to practice simple exercises when the stakes are low. Once you become familiar with how wonderful you (and others!) can be in the moment, you'll want greater challenges and you'll develop that trust.

Resources

www.appliedimprovisation.com. This Web site offers articles, books, and research about improvisation, as well as links to events, discussion groups, and improv trainers and consultants.

www.transactors.org. Transactors Improv Company director Greg Hohn writes a "Mouthing Off" column on the company's Web site, in which he shares his thoughts about fundamental principles of improvisation. He makes his points eloquently, concisely, and humorously. His writings about improv are equally relevant for facilitative work. In his pieces about Applied Improv, Greg shows how improv principles and techniques can help people become more effective in their organizations.

www.yesand.com. This Web site is a source for many things improv. It includes improv events, improv readings, games, other Web sites, and a bulletin board for finding out anything about improv.

Chapter 26

Ground Rules Without the Mutual Learning Model Are Like Houses Without Foundations

Sue McKinney

The Skilled Facilitator approach is known for its development of a set of ground rules for improving group effectiveness. While the ground rules have great value, on their own they are inadequate to bring about the kind of change needed to fundamentally improve a group's effectiveness.

While the ground rules have great value, on their own they are inadequate to bring about the kind of change needed to fundamentally improve a group's effectiveness.

See Chapter Five, "Ground Rules for Effective Groups," page 61.

The ground rules are simply strategies for putting the mutual learning model values and assumptions into practice. Without understanding and embracing the mutual learning model values and assumptions that guide them, the ground rules are little more than techniques.

See Chapter Four, "Understanding What Guides Your Behavior," page 33, and Chapter Five, "Ground Rules for Effective Groups," page 61.

THE LIMITS OF USING ONLY THE GROUND RULES

Learning the ground rules without a thorough understanding of the foundation on which they stand is like learning the vocabulary of a foreign language without a thorough understanding of its grammar or trying to install new application software without a supporting operating system. In other words, the ground rules help describe a new set of behaviors, but do not provide the deeper understanding of why developing new behaviors is worthwhile.

In other words, the ground rules help describe a new set of behaviors, but do not provide the deeper understanding of why developing new behaviors is worthwhile.

The ground rules help us decide how to change our behavior. They are useful in a specific moment as we decide what to say and how to say it. However, they will not shift a person out of the win-lose mentality or away from the desire to achieve a very specific outcome at any cost. This kind of shift occurs when we understand that how we think directly affects how we behave. Understanding this means understanding our theory-in-use.

Two examples from my own life illustrate this point more clearly:

After I participated in a two-week Skilled Facilitator course, I was eager to introduce these ideas to my workplace. As a trainer within a local municipality, I had ample opportunity to teach these concepts to others. As it happened, I completed the class two weeks before my organization began the intensive roll-out of a continuous improvement campaign. The hope was to improve customer service through an emphasis on teamwork and empowerment. Phase 1 of the roll-out involved training all of the employees on the basic concepts of continuous improvement. Phase 2 involved training for the supervisors, and phase 3 was training the teams.

I quickly adapted the curriculum for the team training to incorporate an emphasis on the Skilled Facilitator ground rules and the core values. Sixteen teams were taught about team problem solving, team processes, and team developmental stages. We did not incorporate any discussion about theory-in-use or the basics of the mutual learning approach. I expected that each team would use the ground rules and core values to discuss specific issues, including conflicts within the team, and improve their ability to work together effectively. Unfortunately, that didn't happen.

Most teams never used most of the ground rules. The team I was facilitating did use them on occasion, but usually in a unilateral strategy to win. I remember trying to reach consensus about whether to continue the meeting past the scheduled end time, and one team member said, "I don't agree, so we don't have consensus. Meeting over." And he stood up and walked out of the room. I inferred from his actions that the individual was using unilateral control to meet his needs while ignoring the needs of other team members. It was not exactly what I had in mind when I introduced the ground rules.

Another time, I asked a team leader to identify his interests underlying an assignment he had delegated to his team. He refused to, stating simply, "I'll let them know if I like their solution or not." In the end, he told the team what to do, since their solution, he said, was "unrealistic." Had he understood that using the ground rules effectively was rooted in his use of the mutual learning model, I think he would have realized that he had interests the team needed to meet, the organization had interests the team needed to meet, and the individual team members had interests that needed to be met in order for a lasting solution to be identified. This understanding would have led to a different type of interaction with the team and probably a more successful conclusion.

The biggest shift that I see when people understand that the mutual learning approach is the willingness to temporarily suspend judgment of another person or group of people and work to fully understand one another.

This awareness does not come easily. People come to the approach with years of history with other individuals whom they label "difficult." "If you only knew Joe," they emphatically tell me, "you would understand why we have to be unilateral. He is hopeless!" As long as they hold on to that label and the belief they must manipulate Joe, it is unlikely they will be able to use the ground rules effectively. Mutual learning occurs because of a deep belief that people are attempting to act with integrity given their particular situation. Following this belief, it becomes easier to share one's own reasoning, inquire into the reasoning of others, and probe for full understanding. Differences become moments for learning rather than judgment of the other person. Still, it takes a conscious awareness to stay in this frame of mind and use the ground rules to increase individual and group effectiveness.

The biggest shift that I see occurs when people understand that the mutual learning approach is the willingness to temporarily suspend judgment of another person or group of people and work to fully understand one another.

DEEPENING YOUR UNDERSTANDING OF THE GROUND RULES

The ground rules can be understood and appreciated on several levels. Moving toward mutual learning requires developing a deeper awareness of how to use each ground rule as a strategy to support the mutual learning core values.

Ground Rule One: Test Assumptions and Inferences

This ground rule is fundamental to the Skilled Facilitator Approach. It supports remaining curious and acting consistent with the core value of valid information. The first—and often the most difficult—step in using the ground rule well is to become aware of the inferences we are making. Then we learn to test inferences in increasingly challenging situations.

Becoming Aware of My Inferences

One of my early challenges was to recognize when I was making an inference. I could always tell that I had made a negative inference when I felt my body getting hot and my hands getting sweaty. This also usually indicated one of my "hot buttons" had been pressed. In less dramatic situations, I simply got angry or frustrated with a person. Over time, I learned that this was another warning sign that I was making untested inferences. Another indicator was when I became judgmental and began to think I knew what was best for someone else or, at the least, what this person needed to be doing.

Frequently I had the feelings before I recognized that I was making untested inferences. For example, I would hear one of my superiors stating that the employee team's recommendation simply didn't make sense and had to be overturned since it didn't take into account the political realities of the situation, and I would become angry. My thinking can best be captured in the left-hand column format (Table 26.1).

Table 26.1 The Original Conversation: Not Testing Inferences

My Thoughts and Feelings	Conversation
I'm proud of Team A. This was a difficult problem to solve and they did a great job.	**Me:** Having read Team A's recommendation regarding underground cable improvements, what are your reactions?
What do you mean it won't work?!! They put a lot of time and effort into this project. If you kill their recommendation straight out, they'll never want to work on another team problem again. [***Untested inference.***] And I don't blame them!	**Superior:** They obviously put a lot of work into the recommendation, but it simply won't work.
	Me: Why won't it work?
Did you tell them about these "political realities" ahead of time? How do you know what the citizens are going to put up with?	**Superior:** It doesn't take into account any of the political realities of the situation. Citizens are never going to put up with this kind of digging in their yard even if it is legal.
	Me: Did you share these parameters with the team while they were working on solutions?
Of course, not! You withheld vital information and let them go on a wild goose chase. [***Untested inference.***] You don't care about this team process and whether it succeeds. [***Untested inference.***] Why do we even bother?!	**Superior:** No, I never thought about it. Well, it is too bad they put all that work into a solution that we cannot use.

It took me a while to realize that my angry feelings were often generated by untested assumptions and inferences that I needed to verify. Many times, when I have tested my inferences carefully, I discover that I misinterpreted the situation and no longer had angry feelings.

A nonwork example of this came when I was expecting an important e-mail that wasn't forthcoming:

> I am an equestrian rider and had the opportunity to ride with a well-respected clinician in an upcoming dressage clinic. Dressage is a classical form of horseback riding. These particular clinics are very popular, and it can be difficult to get a riding time slot. I was anxiously waiting to hear if I would be accepted into the clinic.

Unfortunately for me, the clinic organizer was waiting until the last minute to put a schedule together with the confirmed riders. It was a problem for me because I was going on vacation the week before the clinic was to be held. Normally, I would not choose to participate under such conditions, but I was determined to ride with this particular clinician.

Because I had not heard from the clinic organizer by the day before my vacation, I loaded up my new laptop so I could get e-mail during my vacation. The clinic organizer promised to e-mail everyone with the schedule as soon as she had it. Every day of my vacation, I checked my e-mail. I was getting totally frustrated that no e-mails were arriving. I had written the clinic organizer once or twice, and she never responded. I began to feel as if I were being blackballed. I must have done something wrong to anger the clinic organizer, and now she wouldn't let me in the clinic. Or someone had told her something about me, and she wouldn't let me in. None of these thoughts made any logical sense whatsoever—I didn't know the clinic organizer or any of her friends—but the dressage world has a reputation among some as being a bit cliquish, so I made up the only story that made any sense to me. Of course, there was one story I hadn't considered.

I finally e-mailed friends who were riding in the clinic and found out it had been postponed and that it looked as if I had been accepted to ride when it did take place two weeks later. A week or so after returning from my vacation, I was talking to a friend and bemoaning the lack of e-mail communication with the organizer and wondering if I had done something to make the organizer angry. My friend, who is a computer professional, said, "Something like that happened to me once, and I had inadvertently blocked the sender's e-mail. Do you have a block on your system?" "I'm not sure," I responded. "My computer is new, and I have new e-mail software." "Check it," she suggested. "It would certainly explain the problem."

So I went home and opened up a folder on my e-mail software I had never noticed before. It was labeled "Junk." I opened it up, and there was every e-mail ever sent to me by the clinic organizer. I was embarrassed. For every test e-mail I had asked her to respond to, there was an answer. She had been a faithful correspondent, and I had closed the door to an obvious solution by wearing blinders created by untested inferences. Humbly, I returned to the clinic organizer and begged her forgiveness for bugging her over and over about not responding to my e-mails.

Theory-in-use makes a difference in how you test inferences. Used with a unilateral controlling approach, testing inferences is simply a way of finding out who is right and who is wrong. It's part of keeping score in the win-lose mentality. Used with a mutual learning approach, it changes how you experience others and yourself.

Becoming aware of my own inferences has been a liberating experience. As my awareness increased, I began to see how many times I was actually making up stories about people's intent so that I could explain their behavior to myself. Often my stories were rather judgmental and viewed the other person's motivation and intent harshly. In short, making untested inferences about others led me to act in ways that did not treat others with compassion.

My frustrations were often self-generated. As I learned to test my inferences as soon as I noticed them, I gained energy by not having to make up a story to help me explain other people's motivations.

My frustrations were often self-generated. As I learned to test my inferences as soon as I noticed them, I gained energy by not having to make up a story to help me explain other people's motivations.

By testing my inferences, I learned that there was often a plausible explanation for things I didn't understand. Over time I began to adopt the mutual learning assumption that people are trying to act with integrity given their situation. As a result, I found myself making fewer kinds of these negative inferences. I was beginning to treat others with more compassion.

Working My Way Down the Ladder of Inference

It wasn't until I was working with a local learning group that I began to recognize my own strategy for processing inferences.

As a member of a six-person learning group dedicated to working on the Skilled Facilitator approach, I would sometimes notice that I was becoming irritated by one or two members. At this point in my own learning process, I was aware that I had some data that were moving me up the ladder of inference to a feeling of irritation and judgment. What I wasn't sure of was what those data were. I began watching what these particular members were saying and doing that seemed to bother me. I vowed not to say anything until I could make an effective intervention using the diagnosis-intervention cycle, which requires I can state the data on which I'm making my inference.

See Chapter Six, "The Diagnosis-Intervention Cycle," page 69.

I began to take notes of what each group member was saying. And slowly, awareness began to form. One member in particular bothered me because he seemed to be taking a "superior" role within the group. He had much more experience with the concepts in the Skilled Facilitator approach, having worked for several years with a group in a different state that practiced the mutual learning skills. This was a definite benefit to the learning group—to have someone with advanced knowledge—so I wasn't sure what exactly was bothering me about his interactions with the group. I worked hard to suspend my judgment and to watch his behavior, what he was actually saying and doing, to see what triggered my inferences.

Over time, I began to realize that this group member made unilateral statements, did not inquire to see what the rest of us thought, and then continued to talk, building on his unilateral statements as if they were factual and we were in agreement. This made it difficult to follow his conversation because I was internally arguing with one of his earlier statements. The problem was exacerbated by the fact that he talked in large chunks of time (three to six minutes). It took me two or three meetings to identify this pattern of behavior, and then I was willing to take the risk to intervene (it felt risky to me at that time as I respected this group member and didn't want to anger him). It was through my intervention, set out in Table 26.2, that I learned the power of using the ladder of inference.

Table 26.2 **The Revised Conversation: Using The Ground Rules Effectively**

Thoughts and Feelings	Conversation	Skill Used
Ugh. This feels risky. I hate bringing up things like this. But, he did ask, so I'm assuming he will be open to the input.	**Me:** Burt, in one of our first meetings, you asked all of us in the group to give you feedback when we felt that you were acting inconsistently with the mutual learning approach. Is that correct?	Combine advocacy and inquiry.
Whew.	**Burt:** Yes. I need the feedback in order to improve in these skills.	Explain your reasoning and intent.
Go to the data. This is easier than I thought it would be.	**Me:** Okay. I am seeing something in your behavior that is bothering me, and I would like to share what I'm seeing and how it makes me feel and get your reaction. Are you okay with that?	Share all relevant information. Combine advocacy and inquiry.
Wow. You impress me.	**Burt:** Sure, please do.	
	Me: A minute ago, you were explaining your understanding of the principles of mutual learning and how to best apply them. I cannot repeat you exactly, because you talked for several minutes. Do you recall what I'm referring to?	Share all relevant information. Explain your reasoning and intent. Combine advocacy and inquiry. Step 4 of the diagnosis-intervention cycle.
Yes, you did, and I still don't agree with you.	**Burt:** Yes, I think I was explaining that you can argue vehemently for your position and still act consistently with the Skilled Facilitator approach.	Share all relevant information. Use specific examples and agree on what important words mean.
Identify the assumption. He just goes on and on, and I won't follow him blindly!	**Me:** Yes, I think that was the subject. What I noticed was that you started by stating that everyone takes a win-lose approach to conversations initially. Is that your recollection too?	Share all relevant information. Step 4 of the diagnosis-intervention cycle.
Hmm. I think he is correct. That sounds more accurate.	**Burt:** I think I actually said that many of us take a win-lose approach to our conversations, but that doesn't make us unilateral.	Share all relevant information.

(continued)

Table 26.2 ***(continued)***

Thoughts and Feelings	Conversation	Skill Used
	Me: Yes, that does seem more accurate. What bothered me is that you didn't check that assumption. I see that as an assumption, do you?	Explain your reasoning and intent. Combine advocacy and inquiry.
No, don't you get it? Wait, Sue, stay curious.	**Burt:** That being win-lose doesn't mean you are unilateral?	Combine advocacy and inquiry.
	Me: No, that many of us take a win-lose approach to conversations.	Share all relevant information.
	Burt: Oh, yes, I guess that is an assumption.	
	Me: Well, I didn't agree with your assumption, and then you continued talking for a few minutes building an argument hinged on our agreement with that initial assumption. Since you didn't have my agreement, I quit listening and just felt annoyed. Can you understand how I could feel that way?	Share all relevant information. Explain your reasoning and intent. Combine advocacy and inquiry.
That is what I thought. Good to check with others. I wonder if I'm the only one that is bothered by this.	**Burt:** Of course. I hadn't stopped to consider that first statement as an assumption—it just seemed factual. But you are correct: I should have checked. What do the rest of you think? Did this bother you too?	Explain your reasoning and intent. Combine advocacy and inquiry.

See The Ladder of Inference sidebar in Chapter Five, "Ground Rules for Effective Groups," page 61.

Rather than simply telling this person that he talked too much or that I couldn't follow his train of thought, I was able to map out what I heard, check to see if he saw it similarly or differently, and then tell him why I thought it made it difficult for me to respond to his ideas. Presented in this clear way, Burt was able to understand his own behavior and the impact it had on me. He was also able to check with other group members to see if this was unique to me or whether others also had this experience of him. His openness to the feedback was commendable, and I felt it was a turning point for the learning group. We had finally come to the place where we could begin intervening on our behaviors within the group rather than simply talking about interventions we had made or should have made on behaviors outside of the group.

Some people see their inferences first and then have to backtrack to find the data that triggered the inference. Over time, with practice watching the behavior of others, I began to notice my inferences as I was making them, thus making an intervention more quickly and on the spot.

As noted above, I have physical cues that I have shot up the ladder of inference. In meetings, whenever I feel myself getting hot and my face feeling flushed, I know that I have run up the ladder of inference. Instead of responding in anger, I am able to use that cue to ask myself what has caused my inferences. I then use the ground rules to explore my concerns and to have a conversation that strives toward mutual understanding rather than simply letting off steam or strategizing to show I'm right and the other person is wrong.

Ground Rule Two: Share All Relevant Information, and Ground Rule Three: Use Specific Examples and Agree on What Important Words Mean

The second and third ground rules are easy to understand, but it can be challenging to apply them. Together these ground rules suggest that specific names be shared—something that I was not comfortable doing initially. Most of my life, I hid behind generalities as I argued my points. I would point out dramatically that "the employees" did not support the latest organizational initiative or that "management" was making a bad decision. When asked, "Which employees?" or "Which managers?" I thought to myself, "I don't know!" or "I can't say!" Many times, if I had been specific, I would have named only two or three individuals, much less compelling, in my mind, than "the employees" named as a unit.

Agreeing on what important words mean can be very powerful. I have noticed that a lot of groups use the word *respect* in their ground rules. The ground rules state something like, "Show respect for one another." Interestingly enough, when I ask individuals to tell me what "respect" looks like to them, in behavioral terms, they come up with very different definitions:

Once, in a discussion about self-perception and how others in the organization were seeing her, an employee and I discussed our different interpretations of the word *respect* as demonstrated through her behavior at a meeting. I described a meeting that we had both been in early that year. In that meeting, I had noticed that she and her two colleagues were passing slips of paper back and forth. Often they would smile upon reading the note or as they passed it. I felt that this action looked rather juvenile; it reminded me of high school girls passing notes in class. I felt it was disruptive and wondered if some people saw it as disrespectful of the ongoing presentation.

I made the assumption that this employee didn't mean to show disrespect, so I was curious what motivated her to pass the notes. I did not mention this to her at the time, because I wasn't her supervisor and had few interactions with her; I didn't feel it was my place to say anything. But as I

> look back, I think that was a mistake on my part. Sharing this kind of information and checking to see what her thoughts were about it would have given me information, and her feedback could have provided valuable learning for both of us.
>
> During our discussion in my office, I asked if she remembered the meeting and the actions I was describing, and she agreed that my memory was accurate. I told her the meaning I made of the action and asked her what she was thinking at the time, because I assumed that she was not trying to be disrespectful during the meeting. She told me that she had actually thought that she was being more respectful by passing notes to her colleague than talking in whispers. Her colleague was from out of the country and needed additional information periodically throughout the meeting. I shared my belief that there is no one definition of *respect* and that the group has to define what respect means to them. Therefore, it wasn't that she should or should not pass notes; my suggestion was that in those kinds of situations, it would be most helpful to share the dilemma with the group and ask what people were most comfortable with her doing (this would be using Ground Rule Seven: jointly design next steps and ways to test disagreements). I explained that had she done this, I would not have made any inferences about her behavior at all or, if I had, I would have been comfortable bringing them up in the meeting, since the subject had been discussed by the group.

With the mutual learning model as my foundation, I was able to be curious about how she saw her own behavior. And my curiosity led me to raise the issue in a way that I was less concerned about generating negative feelings.

This example illustrates the difference between using these two ground rules with or without the mutual learning model. Without the mutual learning model, I would have been sharing relevant information and using specific examples in an effort to show the employee that she was treating people with disrespect. Agreeing on what important words mean would mean having her agree with my definition. With the mutual learning model as my foundation, I was able to be curious about how she saw her own behavior. And my curiosity led me to raise the issue in a way that I was less concerned about generating negative feelings.

Ground Rule Four: Explain Your Reasoning and Intent

In order to reduce the chances that someone will make untested inferences and assumptions about me, I have learned the value of explaining my reasoning when I ask questions, make suggestions, or state my opinion. When asking, "Have you placed my memo in the mail yet?" I've learned that adding the statement, "And the reason I'm asking is that I found some mistakes in the memo, and I'd like to correct them before you put it in the mail," allows the person to answer me directly and clearly without trying to read between the lines or guess what it is I'm really asking.

In addition, providing my reasoning allows individuals to respond to my specific concerns or thoughts and helps prevent them from making untested inferences. For example, when I ask my assistant about earlier assignments, it is important to give her my reasons so she can respond to each specifically. Let's say that I asked my assistant to get a letter out by the end of the day. After lunch, I come to her with a follow-up question. Without sharing my reason for asking, my question might sound like this: "Mona, have you gotten that letter out yet?"

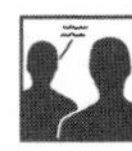

When I share my reasoning, it goes like this, **"Mona, have you gotten that letter out yet? The reason I'm asking is that I found some typos in it that I want to correct if you haven't sent it already."** The second example provides Mona with background information so that she isn't left guessing why I'm asking about this assignment. By sharing my reasoning, I reduce the chance that she will travel up her own ladder of inference.

If I am using this ground rule in the service of mutual learning, I want to explain my reasoning and intent so that others can help me see what I may be missing. I assume that I might not have all the information and that there may be flaws in my reasoning; I want others to help me see them. In turn, I want them to share their reasoning and intent. Where we identify differences in our thinking, we can genuinely explore the differences to jointly develop an approach that both of us can commit to. But if I am using this ground rule without the mutual learning model, my purpose in explaining my reasoning and intent is to get you to understand and accept my point of view.

Ground Rule Five: Focus on Interests, Not Positions

One of the most powerful ground rules for me has been, "Focus on interests, not positions." A number of times when a group has been stuck I have suggested a process based on this ground rule, and within minutes, the group is moving forward again. For example, I was facilitating a cross-functional team responsible for organizing a continuous improvement process within their organization:

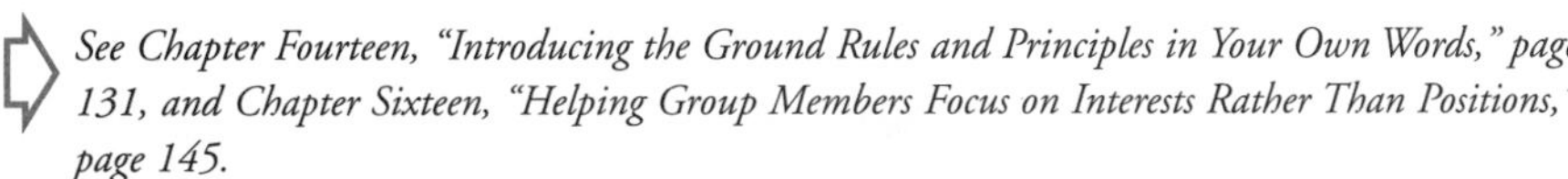

See Chapter Fourteen, "Introducing the Ground Rules and Principles in Your Own Words," page 131, and Chapter Sixteen, "Helping Group Members Focus on Interests Rather Than Positions," page 145.

The team had members from all levels within the organization, including the CEO, some department heads, and front-line workers. It had created a large subcommittee of nonteam members to create a reward and recognition program for the employees.

The subcommittee met for over six months and then presented a well-thought-out recommendation to the team. When I placed their recommendation on the agenda, I allotted it fifteen minutes. I assumed, incorrectly as it turned out, that the larger team would quickly approve the recommendations. After two meetings and over two hours later, I realized the group had become stuck in its positions. I suggested a special meeting to focus on their interests in an attempt to make a final decision on the recommendation.

When the team gathered for the special meeting, team members were able to list their interests quickly: offer rewards that are meaningful to the employees; reward everyone who qualifies (to avoid competition); create a system that is easy to implement; place the continuous improvement logo on all reward items (a position); and create a system that motivates employees to deliver good customer service.

The group then had to define important words and concepts to make certain that we were all talking about the same thing. The most controversial item was the first: "Offer rewards that are meaningful to the employees." The subcommittee had included specific items to use for rewards in its recommendation, including products such as shirts, briefcases, check covers, and tote bags. The subcommittee wanted to offer the items to the award recipients and let them choose the one they wanted. One of the vice presidents took the position that all the rewards had to have the continuous improvement logo on it. The subcommittee was adamant that they not have the logo. The subcommittee had polled employees, who said they did not want products with the logo on it as it made the item less useable, it was "tacky," and it was embarrassing to have the award logo on these items.

It was clear that the group needed to talk about the underlying interests driving the "must have the logo" position versus the "cannot have the logo" position. The vice president stated that if taxpayer money was going to be used to purchase products, he felt that it would be unethical not to put the continuous improvement logo on them. Although everyone agreed that they didn't want to be unethical, not everyone agreed with his conclusion that this would be an unethical action. However, individuals agreed to meet his interest that products have the logo on them.

The subcommittee still felt that these awards would not feel rewarding to all employees and suggested that some employees might throw the items away. In an attempt to meet this interest, the team came up with a new option: restaurant gift certificates. This would be an award of equal value to the products being purchased and would give employees a non-logo-identified item to select from. Although not everyone was thrilled with the final result, everyone agreed they could support and help implement the solution. The team members' basic interests had been met through this solution.

This process took only about fifteen minutes. Listing the interests helped identify the specific sticking points and how people were thinking about the recommendations differently. Instead of simply arguing for one solution or another, the group shifted the conversation to one of the deeper drivers—in this case, ethics and responsibility to the citizens as balanced with the desires and motivational drivers of the employees. The solution was workable, and everyone felt fine with the result even though it wasn't exactly what they wanted. They felt okay because they understood the reasoning of the others and recognized the value in trying to meet each other's interests.

For groups using this ground rule without a solid foundation in the mutual learning mental model, members list interests in an attempt to sway others to their solution. In addition, the "interests" they name are more often positions—for example, "The city manager says we have to use logos," or "We don't want logos because the employees don't like logos," neither of which shares what is the city manager's or the employees' underlying interest. By naming positions as interests, groups can continue to argue back and forth rather than seeking a deeper understanding of the underlying issues and trying to generate a solution that works for everyone.

In contrast, when groups use this ground rule with an interest in learning, members take a step back from their solutions and reflect on what is important to them about their solutions, while simultaneously seeking to understand the underlying drivers or interests of other group members. Genuine curiosity and compassion lead group members to stay open to solutions that will meet everyone's needs in the best way possible.

Genuine curiosity and compassion lead group members to stay open to solutions that will meet everyone's needs in the best way possible.

Ground Rule Six: Combine Advocacy and Inquiry

This is another ground rule with words that I don't commonly use: *advocacy* and *inquiry.* I found this language relatively easy to alter for common use: I simply state my opinion (advocacy) and ask others for their thoughts or reactions (inquiry).

Using this ground rule, I might say, **"Given the impending layoffs, I'm thinking that we should create a new departmental structure. . . . What do you think about what I'm suggesting?"** or **"I suggest that we take a ten-minute break now. Is there anyone for whom that won't work?"**

For me, the key to using this ground rule came with the recognition that my opinions are absolutely valid and it is helpful to ask others what they think about my opinions. This ground rule is particularly helpful in groups that have trouble sustaining a conversational thread in their meetings.

Over the years, I have noticed that different organizations have different trends around this issue of advocacy and inquiry. Some organizations seem to have a culture where employees state their opinions through the use of questions—for example, "Don't you think we should hold our meetings off-site?" (meaning: "I think we should hold our meetings off-site"). "Wouldn't it be a good idea to hire someone with more experience?" (meaning: "I think we need to hire someone with more experience"). In other organizations, the culture seems to be to make statements without asking for reactions or input. This was the case with one organization I facilitated for a few years.

In this organization, facilitating a meeting was like watching the old "Point, Counterpoint" segment on *Sixty Minutes.* Each person would make a statement, and the next speaker would make another statement. Sometimes the statements were connected, but often they weren't. Group members would hold up their hands to get in a queue so they would have a turn to speak. This process didn't allow for a natural progression of an interconnected dialogue. Using Ground Rule Six during their meetings allowed group members to make their statements and then ask for reactions to their specific ideas, so that the meeting began to flow from one thought to the next rather than being a series of statements that never seemed to lead the group in a clear direction.

Those who use this ground rule without a solid understanding of the mutual learning model often advocate and then ask questions to get others to agree with their point. For example, they ask, "Don't you agree?" or "Do you understand?" versus a question that genuinely seeks new information such as, "What are your thoughts about what I've just said?" When used without the intention of learning, the conversational thread is not generated, and the likelihood of true back-and-forth dialogue is not created.

When learning is the goal, genuine questions come easily as each person seeks to better understand the thinking and feeling of others. Individuals thus share their opinions clearly and open themselves to finding out what others are thinking in response.

When learning is the goal, genuine questions come easily as each person seeks to better understand the thinking and feeling of others. Individuals thus share their opinions clearly and open themselves to finding out what others are thinking in response.

Ground Rule Seven: Jointly Design Next Steps and Ways to Test Disagreements

For me, the greatest value of this ground rule has been the ability to jointly design my conversations in a way that builds participants' commitment to talking with me. Giving another person negative feedback is never easy for me, but this ground rule has given me an approach that has increased my comfort level.

For example, when I want to give someone negative feedback, I say something along these lines: **"Jerod, I want to talk with you about something you did yesterday that upset me. I'd like to share with you the specifics of what I think I saw and then check with you to see if you saw it differently. Once we agree on what happened, I'd like to share my reactions with you and hear what you were thinking. Finally, I'd like to talk with you about next steps for resolving this issue, if we agree there is an issue to be resolved. Would you be willing to talk with me about this?"**

The joint design helps on two levels. First, it lays out exactly what I intend to do in the conversation and asks the other person if that works for him or her, and, second, it makes it clear that I don't think my perspective is a fact and that I'm open to hearing a different perspective. It has been my experience that after giving feedback in this manner and then asking the individual what he or she thought of my feedback and how I delivered it, the person often tells me, "Sue, your feedback was clear and fair, and I'm surprised to say that I didn't feel at all judged." The lack of judgment is my aim, and I think this ground rule gives me the tools to achieve my goal.

I have found that I cannot use this ground rule consistently if I am not open to being incorrect in my perception of the other person's behavior. If not used with the genuine intention of sharing my thoughts and learning about the other person's thoughts, this becomes just another way to manipulate people into agreeing with my perspective (or at least pretending to) and correcting the behavior as I recommend they correct it. When I use the ground rule with compassion, I am able to stay open to learning something new from the other person and coming up with next steps that work for both of us, not just for me.

Ground Rule Eight: Discuss Undiscussable Issues

Undiscussable issues are rarely undiscussed. In my experience, I used to talk about "undiscussable" issues a lot, just not in the presence of the individual or group that was at the root of my issue. With friends, this resulted in lots of gossiping. I would talk about my concerns regarding Jane (who had a psychologically abusive boyfriend who would rarely let her spend time with me or our other friends anymore) with everyone but Jane. I would talk to one family member about a familial pattern that I thought problematic, but never raise the issue at family gatherings.

See Chapter Twenty-Eight "Holding Risky Conversations," page 249.

Over time, I discovered the value of taking the risk to raise these kinds of issues directly with the people I had the issues with. When done using the mutual learning model as a foundation, it is much less scary, as I learned over the years. In the example regarding the learning group I shared above under Ground Rule One, "Test assumptions and inferences," it took me time to figure out how to raise the issue of Burt's behavior in the small group. When thinking unilaterally, I talked to others about my problems with this group member and my feelings about how he acted. Fortunately, I talked to people grounded in the mutual learning approach, who pointed out that I might want to talk directly to Burt about his behavior. I realized I was scared to do so. Yet I also realized that by not raising the issue, I was contributing to maintaining the very problem I was complaining about. If I didn't share the information with Burt, he could not make a free and informed choice about whether to change his behavior. Reflecting heavily on how to use this ground rule with the intent of learning new information, I began collecting data and thinking about how I could be curious instead of being right. This was a big revelation that helped me raise the issue with compassion in a way that worked well for the group. Using this ground rule with an understanding of the mutual learning approach gave me compassion for myself and Burt.

> Using this ground rule with an understanding of the mutual learning approach gave me compassion for myself and Burt.

Because of this compassion, I didn't take my usual "I'm right, he's wrong" approach. I took the time (several meetings) to watch the data generated in our conversations to determine what was causing me to react negatively. I stayed open to the possibility that I might be misunderstanding the situation or that I might be the only person reacting in this way to Burt. If I hadn't had the grounding in the mental models, I would have raised the issue to make Burt change his behavior to suit me. Or worse, I may have asked him to leave the group or might have left myself.

Ground Rule Nine: Use a Decision-Making Rule That Generates the Level of Commitment Needed

This ground rule is frequently misinterpreted and its power unrealized. Newcomers to the Skilled Facilitator approach may not appreciate the range of decision rules that can be used within mutual learning or may underestimate the importance of developing commitment to decisions.

Consensus versus Directive Decision Making

When individuals are first exposed to the Skilled Facilitator approach, they often think that it requires that all decisions be made by consensus. This is not the case. Directive decisions can be made in a manner consistent with the approach. Over the years, I've had individuals tell me, "There are simply times I have to be unilateral. Not all decisions can please everyone." Although I agree with the fact that not all decisions can please everyone, I don't agree that we have to be unilateral in certain circumstances. Instead, some decisions can be made as directives if the decision maker shares what led her to make the decision in this manner; stays open to sharing the reasoning of others and being questioned about it; and considers the impact, intended and unintended, of being directive. If individuals with authority repeatedly make directive decisions that have an impact on others, it can become inconsistent with mutual learning. Directive decision making is best done in moderation and with careful consideration for the long-term intended and unintended consequences.

Interestingly, students who raise the question of being unilateral usually state the need to do so in a crisis, often mentioning the police or fire departments as places where decisions cannot be made as a group and must be unilateral. I have also seen these agencies be directive in a manner that appears to be consistent with the mutual learning approach. In such a fire department, for example, one person is in charge of a squad or unit. This is the individual who gives commands during a fire emergency. Everyone follows this person's lead and does not question his or her judgment during the incident. Once the fire is out and the firefighters have returned to the station, they lead a critical incident review. In this meeting, all the firefighters talk about what worked well and what didn't work well during the actual fire event.

This is how they all learn and make changes to improve their work together. Because the squad agrees to this process and have therefore internally committed to it, it generates the level of commitment required for the job. This approach is consistent with the mutual learning model. If there was no after-the-event review and no one was allowed to challenge the squad leader's decisions, this would be a unilateral strategy.

Developing Internal Commitment

Following the mutual learning approach, group members develop internal commitment to a decision or action step by discussing the issue, sharing their underlying needs, and having those needs (interests) met as fully as possible by the group's final decision or action. If group members are routinely told what they are to do, even if the reasons are shared and the decision can be questioned after the fact, their internal commitment to the decisions and action steps will diminish over time. People invest their energy in areas where they have influence and the ability to shape their work. If that ability to influence is taken away, investment diminishes.

> In one municipal organization, the city manager assigned a small team to plan an employee picnic to celebrate their work together. I encouraged the city manager to share relevant information with the team such as budget limitations and special locations that he might want, but he chose not to do so. He wanted the team to have some freedom to explore their ideas. The team was very excited about their assignment. They came up with some new ideas to prevent the picnic from being another stale company event. When they returned to the manager with all their innovative ideas, he was displeased. He was upset that their budget of five thousand dollars was much higher than he intended to spend and felt that they were being extravagant in their choice of location, vendors, and food. He suggested that they use the same location, vendors, and food that they had used in years past. The team was devastated and stated to me later that they wished the manager had just planned the picnic himself.

Contrast this experience with the previous one:

> I once worked in a nonprofit organization that assigned me to create and lead a team to select volunteers to live and work in Central America. The director gave me her parameters, which included a few specific people to serve on the team, some minimum requirements for the volunteers, and how often we should meet as a team. For the next four years, I coordinated this team, and we worked as an independent unit, selecting volunteers with increasingly sophisticated data regarding the volunteers' mental health, language fluency, and other characteristics that we learned through experience were important for selecting the best volunteers. As a team, we felt a responsibility for this important task and a sense of pride when the volunteers we selected performed their jobs well.

Teams, as well as individual employees, that understand the interests of their organization and their sponsors will have a greater chance of creating effective solutions and recommendations. Withholding such information increases the likelihood that supervisors and team sponsors will reverse team decisions when the decisions do not meet their own interests.

When groups seek consensus using the mutual learning model, they recognize that the goal is not consensus itself but the underlying internal commitment of all members that it represents.

When groups do seek consensus without using a mutual learning approach, group members in the majority may try to pressure group members in the minority to agree or give up their interests. Alternatively, group members in the minority may decide to give up or compromise rather than find ways to integrate their interests with those of others. When groups seek consensus using the mutual learning model, they recognize that the goal is not consensus itself but the underlying internal commitment of all members that it represents.

CONCLUSION

The ground rules are necessary but insufficient to practice the Skilled Facilitator approach. They derive their power and value from the core values and assumptions of the mutual learning model. As you shift more toward the mutual learning approach, you will probably discover that the same ground rules are able to help you create results and relationships that weren't previously possible.

Chapter 27

Writing and Analyzing a Left-Hand Column Case

Roger Schwarz

WHEN I WORK WITH CLIENTS, I frequently use left-hand column cases to help them reflect on their theory-in-use. A left-hand column case is a written case in which the case writer describes a difficult conversation he or she had and the thoughts and feelings he or she had during the conversation.

A left-hand column case is a written case in which the case writer describes a difficult conversation he or she had and the thoughts and feeling he had during the conversation.

By writing and analyzing a left-hand column case, you can (1) identify behaviors that are consistent with the mutual learning approach and with the unilateral control approach, (2) identify the values and assumptions that you use to generate your behaviors, and (3) identify the intended and unintended consequences of your values, assumptions, and behaviors.

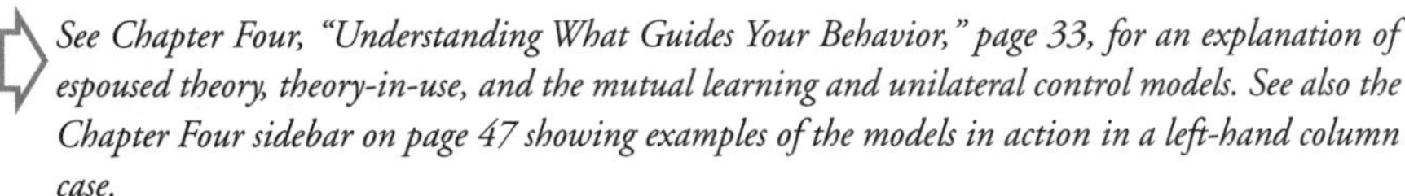

See Chapter Four, "Understanding What Guides Your Behavior," page 33, for an explanation of espoused theory, theory-in-use, and the mutual learning and unilateral control models. See also the Chapter Four sidebar on page 47 showing examples of the models in action in a left-hand column case.

By writing and analyzing a left-hand column case, you can (1) identify behaviors that are consistent with the mutual learning approach and with the unilateral control approach, (2) identify the values and assumptions that you use to generate your behaviors, and (3) identify the intended and unintended consequences of your values, assumptions, and behaviors.

Left-hand column cases can also help you identify gaps between your espoused theory and your theory-in-use. You can use left-hand column cases as a springboard for reframing how you think about and act in difficult situations.

WRITING A LEFT-HAND COLUMN CASE

In one paragraph, describe an important but difficult conversation you have had with a person or people in your work. The conversation should be one that you had with the person face-to-face, wished you had handled more effectively, and are willing to share with others who can help you learn about your behavior. The conversation should involve people with whom you want to improve your working relationship and should be representative of how you handle difficult situations. If

This chapter is adapted from Roger Schwarz, *Analyzing and Facilitating Left-Hand Column Cases* (Chapel Hill, N.C.: Roger Schwarz & Associates, 2004).

you need to, change the names, positions, or any other information about the people involved in order to feel comfortable discussing the case with others.

In a second paragraph, describe the strategy that you used during the conversation. Include (1) what outcomes you wanted, (2) how you planned to have the conversation to achieve those outcomes, and (3) what specifically it was about the conversation that led you to describe it as difficult.

Next, on a new page, divide the page into two columns. In the right-hand column, type exactly what you said, what others said, and what you said next—in short, the verbatim dialogue you had with the person or people. Do not write a general description or summary of the dialogue because you will not be able to use it to analyze your case. In the left-hand column, write down all the thoughts or feelings you had, whether or not you shared them. The more thoughts and feelings you write, the better. Write this dialogue for at least two to three typewritten pages. Don't worry if you cannot remember the exact conversation or your exact thoughts and feelings. Write it as best as you remember it and fill in the gaps with what you think you would have said, thought, and felt. Figure 27.1 at the end of the chapter shows the sequence that I describe next.

Analyzing Cases in a Group

Although you can analyze your left-hand column case by yourself, you will learn more by analyzing cases with a partner or with a group. If you use a group approach, ask each person to come to the conversation having already analyzed the case, or you can jointly analyze it together. In either case, the group members share their observations along with those of the case writer. The conversation is also an opportunity for members to use the Skilled Facilitator approach as they give feedback and test their inferences about their analysis.

If you will be discussing your left-hand column case with a group of fellow learners, you may want to use a conversation that you had with someone who is in the group. Writing this type of case can feel like a greater risk, but it can also create greater learning for you and the group. If you choose to write a case involving someone who will also be in the group, it is consistent with the core values of the Skilled Facilitator approach to let them know you are writing a case that includes them and, if you are willing, to show them the case (or at least the verbatim dialogue part) before you discuss it in the group. You can also ask the person if you have accurately recalled the conversation. Sometimes two or more people in a group have written their cases about the same conversation they had with each other. This offers a great learning opportunity because you can learn how each person's unexpressed thoughts and feelings during the same conversation leads people to interact in a way that makes difficult conversations less productive than they could be.

ANALYZING THE CASE

I begin to analyze a left-hand column case by reading and analyzing the description, strategy, and difficulty paragraph at the beginning of the case. Then I turn to the verbatim conversation and thoughts and feelings.

Analyzing the Description, Strategy, and Difficulty Sections

The first step in analyzing a left-hand column case is reading the case description, strategy, and difficulty section. In this section, the case writer (which may be you) describes the context for the conversation, the strategy he used to have the conversation, and the difficulty that resulted. In this section, the case writer often offers at least parts of his espoused theory for managing the conversation, identifying elements that are consistent with either the unilateral control model or mutual learning model.

When you identify an element of the case writer's espoused theory, underline that element and label it. For example, if the case writer wrote, "I thought it was important to keep the conversation focused on the facts and not get into people's frustrations," you would underline it and write something like, "This looks like minimizing the expression of negative feelings in the unilateral control model. What do you think?"

As you read through the case dialogue and left-hand column, you will look for places where the case writer either put into use or did not put into use what he espoused in the description, strategy, and difficulty section.

Analyzing the Left- and Right-Hand Columns

After you have analyzed the description, strategy, and difficulty section, you are ready to read and analyze the left- and right-hand columns of the case. You might find it easier to read through the entire case once so you can develop a sense of the overall issues and then analyze it as you read through it a second time.

There are a couple of ways to analyze the conversation and thoughts and feelings. I read the case from left to right, reading a left-hand column part, then the corresponding conversation, then the next left-hand column part, and so on. Reading in this way helps me see how the case writer's thinking influences his actions and how other people's actions influence the case writer's subsequent thinking. Some of my colleagues prefer to read and analyze the entire right-hand column and then read and analyze the left-hand column, making links between the two columns. If you are reading someone else's case, it's often surprising (and sometimes very entertaining) how your understanding of the case changes when you read the thoughts and feelings after you have read the verbatim conversation.

There are several levels of analysis that you can conduct. I have grouped them into three increasingly complex and powerful types: behaviors or individual events, patterns, and structures.

Identifying Behaviors and Individual Events

Identifying behaviors and individual events is the simplest form of analysis. A behavior or individual event (such as a thought) represents a single occurrence in the case and in practice usually corresponds to a discrete chunk of the case writer's left- or right-hand column, usually in which the case writer is using or not using one or more ground rule or core value.

Ground Rules. Analyzing how the case writer uses the ground rules is a basic kind of analysis. As you read the case, note places where the case writer has said things that are either consistent or inconsistent with the ground rules. To save time, you can note the appropriate ground rule using its corresponding number on the list (for example, testing assumptions is 1, share all relevant information is 2, and so on). Place a minus sign in front of the number when the case writer has not used a ground rule that you think would have been useful to use, and place a plus sign in front of the number when the case writer has used a ground rule. Sometimes you might place both signs in front of the number when the case writer has partially used the ground rule. In general, I code only the case writer's conversation, although there are exceptions, which I describe later.

In order to code some ground rules, you need to look first at the case writer's left-hand column and then see how he or she shared or withheld thoughts in the right-hand column. For example, the case writer often makes inferences and attributions in the left-hand column. Look at the right-hand column to see whether the case writer has publicly tested the inference he made. If he does, code it as a tested inference; if he does not, code it as an untested inference and draw an arrow from the left column to the right column. By comparing the left- and right-hand columns, you can identify if the case writer is testing assumptions, sharing all relevant information, discussing undiscussable issues, and explaining his reasoning and intent.

Missed Interventions. Sometimes a case is notable because the case writer doesn't respond effectively to others in the case. One example is if someone makes a statement without explaining his reasoning and the case writer does not inquire into the reasoning. Another example is when someone makes a general statement and the case writer responds without asking for specific examples. The case writer reduces his effectiveness by not asking others to use the appropriate ground rule.

In these situations, you can first code the noncase writer's comments, such as "–4" to indicate that the other person did not explain her reasoning. Then draw an arrow pointing to that person's comment and write a comment like, "This would have been a useful place to inquire into the person's reasoning. Do you see it differently?"

Core Values and Assumptions. When you analyze a case for the ground rules, you are also implicitly analyzing it for the core values and assumptions because the ground rules operationalize the core values. Still, there are times when you want to note the core value or assumption specifically. For example, I will note "–free and informed choice" when I infer that the case writer is withholding information in ways that may reduce others' free and informed choice around a central issue in the case. I will note "–compassion" especially when the case writer's left- or right-hand column indicates not only a lack of compassion but also a punishing approach, such as a case writer who is thinking, "I'm going to show you! You can't get away with that. You'll learn not to fool with me."

Inquiring into the Case Writer's Behavior. Sometimes in addition to coding the ground rule that the case writer did not use, it is useful to inquire into what led the person not to use it. For example, if someone does not test an inference, you may write, "What led you to not test the inference?" or "What would prevent you from testing the inference?" These questions are designed to start the case writer thinking about his strategies and what led him to design the strategies as he did. You can make these same kinds of inquiries for each level of analysis you do.

Identifying Patterns

Patterns comprise behaviors over time. In a simple pattern, the case writer acts inconsistently with the same ground rules, core values or assumptions, or other parts of theory-in-use over time. In more complex patterns, the case writer repeatedly uses two or more of these elements in a certain way. Some patterns reveal themselves in a short period of time—within one page of the case; other patterns may take longer to surface.

When you identify a pattern in the case, note on the case each time the behaviors occur that make up that pattern. You can also place numbers by the examples that form the pattern, so when you summarize the case, you can quickly refer to the places where this pattern occurred.

Simple Patterns, Repeating Behaviors. Simple patterns occur when the case writer repeatedly acts inconsistently with the same ground rules (or core values or elements of theory-in-use). For example, the case writer may ask one easing-in question after another or may continue to advocate his view without inquiry, or may make repeated untested inferences.

Two or More Related Behaviors: Switching Unilateral Control Strategies. A somewhat more complex pattern occurs when the case writer switches between different unilateral control strategies. For example, a common strategy is for the case writer to start out using an easing-in strategy or false inquiry without advocacy. At some point, the case writer switches to an advocacy without inquiry strategy. This switch often occurs when the case writer is feeling that the other people are not getting what the case writer is indirectly trying to say, or when the other people respond defensively, or when the other people start to raise their own issues directly.

Patterns of Interaction Between the Case Writer and Others. The case writer's behavior doesn't occur in a vacuum. It is partly a response to other people's comments. In this kind of pattern, there is a repeated relationship between the case writer's behavior and others' behavior. For example, in the pattern of escalating advocacy, each time one person advocates his point of view, the other responds with advocacy. In another pattern, when a person does not explain his reasoning, the case writer inquires into the reasoning. When the reasoning doesn't make sense to the case writer, the case writer attributes to the other person that the other person has questionable motives.

Identifying Structure

Structure is the deepest and most powerful level of analysis. Unlike identifying behaviors and patterns, when you identify structure, you help the case writer understand a causal explanation for what is happening. To identify the structure, you show how the case writer's values and assumptions lead him to design certain strategies, which in turn create certain consequences, which then reinforce core values and assumptions. In left-hand column cases (and this work in general), the structure is also created by the interaction between the case writer's theory-in-use and actual conversation and the other people's theory-in-use and conversation. In other words, each person puts his theory-in-use into practice in the conversation, and each person uses others' comments as data to respond to with their theory-in-use. In left-hand column cases, we typically have only the case writer's left-hand column, so we focus only on the case writer's theory-in-use. Sometimes it's difficult to see the structure in the case. It can take several readings of the case before you begin to see the structure emerge.

Generating Unintended Consequences. A central theme of these structures is that the case writer creates unintended consequences. For example, in an effort not to embarrass someone, the case writer withholds relevant information from that person or does not inquire into gaps in the person's reasoning. In the short term, the case writer achieves the intended consequences, but in the long term, this creates unintended consequences. The problem may remain unsolved, the other person may not be able to improve her performance, and the case writer may end up frustrated.

Sometimes the case writer expresses surprise in his left-hand column that these consequences occurred. Sometimes the case writer has a causal explanation for the consequences but rarely does the case writer describe himself as contributing to the structure.

Self-Fulfilling, Self-Sealing Processes. Self-fulfilling, self-sealing processes are a specific case of generating unintended consequences. In this situation, the case writer gets the very unintended consequences he was trying to avoid. For example, the case writer begins by making an inference that the other person will get defensive. Consequently, in an attempt to make sure the other person doesn't get defensive, the case writer uses an easing-in strategy. The easing-in strategy leads the other person to respond by giving short answers that are somewhat vague, perhaps because the other person does not know why the case writer is asking these questions. The case writer sees this as defensive behavior and attributes it to the other person; he does not see how his own initial inference and resulting strategy contributed to creating the very defensiveness he was trying to avoid. Having created the self-fulfilling process, the case writer often makes it self-sealing by assuming that he cannot talk with the person about her defensive behavior because she would just get more defensive. As a result, the case writer has created a self-sealing logic that prevents him from learning about how he contributed to the problem.

Writing a Case Summary

After you have made individual codings and comments in the case, write a summary of your observations and inferences. This is the place to describe how the case writer's values and assumptions led him to use certain strategies, which created certain consequences. Tell the story by referring to specific examples in the case, inquiring what led the case writer to think or say a particular thing. When you make inferences about the case writer, identify them and test them out in the summary. At the end of the summary, inquire whether the case writer sees any of your analysis differently.

Figure 27.1 illustrates the process explained in this chapter and what your role in this is.

Figure 27.1 A Left-Hand Column Case

Situation

Recently there was a change in our manufacturing organization. The manufacturing manager accepted a promotional opportunity in another division, creating an opening to replace her. That replacement was Steve, who up to that point was a colleague on the functional staff reporting to the operations manager. Steve is informal in process and procedures, very adverse to confrontation, and in my opinion, "obfuscates with data," which results in confusion about direction, intent, and responsibility. One of Steve's first acts as the manufacturing manager was to appoint two individuals to promotional positions rather than completing a competitive selection process. This created mistrust and resentment in his direct reports and inconsistency in company practice, and it established an environment of favoritism and a perception that Steve was going to make his own rules.

-1 Is this an inference, or has he told you this?

Goals, Strategy, and Difficulty

The goal for this conversation with Steve was to reach mutual understanding of his intent and the impact of his actions, and develop a plan to "recover." An additional goal was to develop and strengthen our relationships, clarify my role, and establish a foundation of trust and respect. My plan was to meet with Steve individually and talk through the information I had, clarify and correct points of fact, and acknowledge and deal with the emotions that came with this situation. The outcomes I wanted from the conversation were to agree on perceptions and establish the environment he wanted to create, and clarify my role and how this type of situation should be handled in the future. The difficulty of the conversation was in three parts: first, Steve was my new boss, and our relationship had not been in great shape before he became my boss; second, this was a confrontational situation that I knew he abhorred and I didn't look forward to; and third, the actions and behaviors Steve took really were setting an environment that was inconsistent with our long-established and successful values and, from my point of view, would not permit him to be successful.

-1 It looks like you've already decided that something needs to be recovered from. Yes? If so, that looks like "I'm right, he's wrong." Thoughts?

+mutual learning model. "I have some information, others have other information."

+7? If correcting includes places where you may be wrong.

What was it about his being your boss that made it difficult?

Had there been previous issues that you had not discussed with Steve?

+2, +7 Dealing with emotions. This is part of sharing all relevant information and dealing with undiscussable issues.

What, if anything, were you concerned about?

My Thoughts and Feelings	The Conversation
I was pretty nervous, and had actually written down a script so I wouldn't lose anything. Steve looked like he was open, but my feeling was that the only time we have conversations is when he's done something wrong. I could see that he was getting nervous, not looking at me, and definitely didn't want to be here.	Ted: I wanted to meet with you about the financial manager positions. There are a couple of items that I believe need to be resolved. First and foremost, I believe our relationships must be built on trust, and my style is to deal with things in a straightforward manner. I also believe my role is to provide you feedback, guidance, and counsel, even if it's not easy or comfortable. My purpose here is to resolve what I feel now are inconsistencies, provide you with feedback that I've received, and discuss actions that I believe are necessary to move forward in a positive way.
I felt like this was lip-service.	Steve: Okay.
I sure am talking a lot, but I need to establish the foundation and the facts to make sure I have them right and we agree.	Ted: My recollection of our conversations about the finance positions is that you indicated to me that you did not want to reorganize the functions now, as it is important to maintain continuity, stability, and momentum. I understood you to say that with your experience on the financial task team and through your contacts, you considered names of people you thought might be potential

-2 About what? I'm curious what led you not to say anything about that.

-1 Untested inferences. What led you not to test this with him? I ask because if your inferences were correct, you didn't address why he didn't want to be there. I imagine the conversation could be more difficult.

-1 Untested inference. What led you not to ask him about his response?

-6 I agree that you need to have the facts right and agree. I don't see where you asked Steve if you are missing anything or whether he agrees. Do you see it differently?

-6, -7 Advocacy without inquiry and no joint design.

-3, -4, -5 Regarding what? What leads you to want to do this? What are your underlying interests?

Unilateral control. I don't see anything explicit here about your wanting to clarify points of fact or hearing his point of view. Thoughts?

-7 This would be a good place to jointly design with Steve where to go first in the conversation. You decided yourself. Yes?

+3, +4 You very specifically described Steve's action and his reasoning as you understood it.

		candidates for the positions and resolved for yourself that there weren't any better candidates than Jim and Peggy. Further, you indicated you looked in the manufacturing organization and didn't see anyone who either met the qualifications or would be a candidate. You did have a conversation with Tom where he expressed interest, but since you didn't believe it would be a promotion and he indicated to you that was essentially the only reason he would be interested, you mutually agreed that he wasn't a candidate for the position.	-4 Sharing your reasoning and intent. I don't see where you are explaining to Steve why you are going through this. -6? I'm thinking you may be easing in. Thoughts? -6 A good place to stop and ask, "Have I missed anything?"
	Okay, we are on the same page. I'm somewhat relieved and am gaining confidence or some comfort.	Steve: Yup, that's true. I did make phone calls to people I thought would either be candidates or know of people who would be candidates, and with my years of experience, there weren't any people close to the skill set I need and the organizational knowledge to maintain the continuity.	
-1 Untested inference. -1 Untested inference. My inference is that if Steve is feeling annoyed and angry, it may be because he doesn't understand why you are going through all this detail and where it will lead. This relates to my comment that you have not been sharing your reasoning for bringing this up, nor have you and Steve jointly agreed to have you go through all this detail. Do you see this differently? What would prevent you from testing your inference?	I'm really sounding proceduralistic, and Steve is looking as if he's feeling the same. Starting to feel uneasy because Steve is starting to look annoyed and somewhat angry.	Ted: We also talked about the process—that for any promotional opportunity, a requisition is standard practice, that if you consider candidates outside your organization a requisition was required, and that if you were going to limit the recruiting to your organization, you should have a requisition, but could go without one (which I recommended against). Further, that if you were going to limit this to manufacturing only, from a process standpoint and a perception standpoint, you should talk to direct reports, explain your thought process, and understand if there are any candidates for the positions who should be considered before you make your decision. During our subsequent hallway conversation at your staff meeting, I understood you to say that you had taken the input and had contacted your staff and got understanding and agreement about your direction or current thinking before making offers. Based on that, I agree that making offers to both and announcing to the finance group the next day was okay. We briefly discussed scoping level, and without being able to resolve that at that moment and your feeling the need to offer and announce quickly, you indicated you would offer the jobs at a B4 level. I agreed and indicated I would look at the proper scoping level in the next several days.	-6 Again, a good place to stop and ask, "Have I missed anything?" -4 Sharing your reasoning and intent. Again, I don't see where you are explaining to Steve why you are going through this. -6 Again, I'm thinking you may be easing in.
	Man, is this guy lying or what? I'm really getting nervous now because I don't see any other	Steve: Yes, I did talk to my staff, and they all indicated that Jim and Peggy were the right	

Figure 27.1 *(continued)*

Margin comments	Thoughts and feelings	Conversation	Margin comments
Unilateral control model: "The way I see it is the way it is." "My motives are pure; those who disagree have questionable motives."	explanation than he's not telling the truth.	people for the position. But this process stuff. It's been my experience that it's rare for a requisition to be opened for this level of position. I'm following the example of my previous bosses. They've hired or appointed most of the people in their organizations.	
I'm inferring that you feel as if you've caught someone partly because you have eased into the conversation until now, and when you finally state your concern here, you don't ask Steve whether he has a different understanding of what happened (Ground Rule Six). -2 I think it's relevant information that you are looking for any explanation to disconfirm your inference that he wasn't telling you the truth. I'm curious: What led you not to share this? -8 Undiscussable issue?	Major nervous, start stuttering a bit, and that's making Steve even more uneasy. I feel like I've just caught someone. It's my boss!! Are you sure you want to continue with this career-limiting discussion!! The words got caught in my throat. I'm really looking for some, any explanation other than he's lied and that's the end of our relationship. Really uncomfortable silence.	Ted: Here are the issues that I'm having problems with. First, I received input from four of your direct reports that they did not have a conversation with you prior to your announcement, and in fact hadn't heard that you were going to fill the jobs until after the announcement was made. Another person indicated he would have been interested in the job, and two others indicated that they had people in their organizations who were interested. These folks expressed disappointment in the process—that it appears that your decision making is not inclusive or participative and that you are sending a very bad signal to the organization. I feel that based on the input from these people, you weren't truthful with me about having talked to each person and getting their understanding and input.	+3, +4 You are specific about your concerns that Steve is not being truthful and your reasoning behind it. -3 You do not state the persons' names, which opens the possibility that Steve and you are talking about having talked with different people. -6 Advocacy without inquiry.
My inference is that you were surprised because you believe that he is not telling you the truth and therefore you don't expect him to be calm. Is my inference off? If not, I think it reflects the unilateral control model assumption that "I'm right, he's wrong" and that "my feelings are justified." What do you think? Was this partly because you wanted to save face for Steve?	I'm surprised that Steve's actually pretty calm and collected as he's talking. I am a bit surprised at this wording of "I have no reason not to be truthful." I would have preferred, "I didn't lie." I started to feel relieved and jumped quickly to "I'll accept that" even before he finished his explanation. I started getting some confidence back and started listening more closely. You really did talk to each, but because of the context, they may not have remembered? You've got to be kidding! Who are you trying to fool, me or yourself? Is this a way to save face?	Steve: I have no reason not to be truthful with you. Let's talk about how we got to this place. I feel I did have conversations with all, but the discrepancy might be the context in which the discussion took place, where it took place, and the manner. For example, I talked to Mark in the hallway and was really telling him what I was doing. He very possibly came away from that conversation not even remembering it occurred or feeling like the decision was already made and this was informational only. I acknowledge that I'm much less formal than Stacy, and it may not have been clear that I was looking for input. Some of this may be attributable to the difference in relationship, where we used to be peers and now I'm their boss. It may be that we were more open with each other, they felt more comfortable sharing more, and now that I'm the boss, they may not be as open. Does that make sense?	-Saving face: When you say, "Yes, it does" make sense when you are privately thinking, Who are you trying to fool, me or yourself? I'm inferring that you are acting to save face for Steve to minimize expressing negative feelings (yours and his) and to "make it work." Thoughts?
Unilateral control assumption: "I'm right, you're wrong." Using a mutual learning approach, you could describe exactly what it is about his story that does not make sense to you and, remaining curious, ask him if he can put the nonfitting pieces together in a way that does make sense to you.	I really want this to work, and it's really important that it does. I am jumping to accept, but I'm not going to let this go without at least an indirect statement that I'm not fully buying this.	Ted: Yes, it does. I want to trust that we are being honest with each other, and I can accept that you feel you did talk to each of your reports, but that based on how some of the conversations took place, there might not have been full recognition. I do believe that because	If you agree with my thinking, then you end up saving face at the same time you are privately thinking that Ted is trying to save face.

Unilateral control model: Act rational. I interpret your thoughts to mean you are sending Steve a mixed message that says, "I am publicly accepting your explanation, but privately I don't fully buy it." I'm curious what leads you to want to make it indirect. I ask because as an indirect statement, it is more likely that Steve will misinterpret it. What concerns do you have about making it explicit?

"I understand, he doesn't." What data are you using to infer he doesn't understand? What would prevent you from sharing those data and testing your inference?	He really doesn't understand how his actions have affected him and the people in the group. I don't know Peggy very well, but this is a really ugly thing to do to her, especially if it's unintentional and isn't true.	there wasn't clear understanding, there are some negative impacts and feelings from your reports. A specific example is that I heard from two of your reports that you appointed Peggy because of your relationship with her (they're saying things like you're having an affair) and not because she is the most qualified. In fact, people are indicating that she isn't the most qualified and spreading some ugly rumors about this.	-6 Advocacy without inquiry. This would be a good place to ask if he was aware of this or if he had a different understanding of what happened.
-1 Untested inference	Steve is really upset but doesn't show it much. Just his words and his acknowledgment that this could have or did have a negative impact on Peggy. This is the first time I really feel that I'm getting a true reaction from Steve other than annoyance or being uncomfortable.	Steve: Well . . . I don't want anything to negatively reflect on Peggy due to my screw-up. And it's important that my staff trust me and that we work together. I guess I need to be more formal and participative in my decisions.	
		Ted: What specific actions do you think should be taken?	-6 Easing in? I'm inferring that you have some specific actions in mind. Am I off?
"I understand, he doesn't." What would prevent you from saying what you think it is about?	You don't have it yet! It's not about formality; it's about trust, honesty, relationships, decision making.	Steve: I'll just be more formal and make it clear that Peggy is the most qualified candidate.	
	I'm feeling like I'm actually contributing, providing suggestions and guidance. This feels pretty good.	Ted: I believe you have some direct relationship and team building to do. I might approach this by meeting with each of your reports individually and privately and let them know that you have received this feedback and that you want to talk about it. I would then, in your own words, explain how you came to your decision, that you thought or felt that you did review your plan with him or her, and ask them their perception. This might be a good time to talk about your style, changing role, and probably changing expectations, and begin developing your personal working relationship with them. I would also help them understand the basis for your decision on Peggy so that whether they agree or not, there is at least understanding about the basis for your judgment or decision. Advocacy without inquiry.	With the Facilitative Leader approach, I would advocate meeting publicly as a group assuming that Steve's actions had an impact on the entire group. This would enable everyone to hear the same thing at the same time, exactly what did not happen originally. I'm curious what leads you to suggest meeting individually and privately. Is part of it a desire to save face for Peggy?
-2, -8? What is it that leads you not to be totally convinced? What would prevent you from sharing this with Steve and jointly figuring out what you would need to hear from him to be totally convinced? -1 What makes it "a crock," and how are you seeing it as being designed to give him flexibility to continue doing what he has been doing?	Good! You're saying the right words. But I'm not totally convinced. Oh boy, this is a crock just to give him the "flexibility" to continue like he has been. Did we gain any ground during this? I'm exhausted, a bit up, and ambivalent. I feel good that I took the risk; at least it's clear about how I will approach these types of issues in the future, so I'm "true to myself" and I think that	Steve: Yeah, I don't want to do this in a staff meeting, especially when Peggy is there. I do want this team to work closely together, to function as a team, and for each to participate, question, give ideas, and challenge. I don't want to follow procedures for their own sake, but if I need to be more formal and procedural and that results in better trust and teamwork, then that's good. If not, and it's not obvious that it helps the business, I must question and challenge.	

Figure 27.1 *(continued)*

Steve moved a bit. I'm a bit down in that there's a long way to go, and I don't know if we will ever get there.	
	[We went on about our future working relationship and began discussing styles, how to bring up issues, and other topics.]

Ted-

I have some thoughts about how the conversation became difficult for you. I think you entered the conversation with two important untested assumptions. One was that Steve didn't like conflict, and the other was that what he had done was definitely wrong and needed a plan to "recover." I think this combination made it difficult for you to openly question Steve and be curious when he saw things differently from you or when you did not see how his story held together.

I see your assumptions playing out in several strategies you use in the conversation. First, you advocate your view without asking Steve's reaction. Second, you design the conversation unilaterally, without finding out if Steve wants to have the conversation in the same way you do. Third, I think you use an easing-in strategy. I think all of this contributes to what you infer as Steve's feeling angry and annoyed.

Although you said that you wanted to discuss the emotions that came with the situation, when you thought that Steve was feeling something negative, you chose not to test your inference. I think this made it more difficult for you because you couldn't find out what you might have been doing that was contributing to his feeling annoyed or angry (assuming your inference was correct).

When Steve finally gets the chance to share his view of what happened, your assumption that "I'm right, he's wrong," along with your concern that Steve doesn't like conflict, makes it difficult for you to be specific and curious about your differing points of view.

As a result, I see you first easing in to the conversation about what concerns you and then saving face by not telling Steve that his explanation doesn't make sense to you. This puts you in a situation where you publicly accept his explanation but privately doubt it. By withholding this information from Steve, you make it difficult for him to help you see things differently or for Steve and you to move forward together.

I think this accounts for your mixed feeling at the end of the conversation in which you feel good that you raised the issue but don't feel that it's resolved.

What are your thoughts? Do you see any of this differently?

Roger

Source: This case was written by Ted Lang (a pseudonym) as part of a Skilled Facilitator workshop and used with his permission.

PART FOUR

Facing Challenges

The Skilled Facilitator approach offers valuable guidance for dealing with challenging situations like giving negative feedback, disagreeing with the boss, raising undiscussable issues in a group, and holding other difficult conversations. Part Four addresses reasons to engage in difficult conversations and offers specific steps and examples. It also continues the theme of expanding self-awareness so that anyone using this approach can see how they might contribute to the very problems that frustrate them.

Without resolving problems about issues that matter, it is difficult to stay productively engaged in a project or relationship. Chapter Twenty-Eight, "Holding Risky Conversations," covers when and why you might engage in a difficult or risky conversation and then gives you steps for doing so. The chapter closes with an example of a risky conversation that was held productively using Skilled Facilitator ground rules and core values. Chapter Twenty-Nine, "Exploring Your Contributions to Problems," helps us see how we might be contributing to the very difficulties we seek to resolve. It suggests strategies to help shift our thinking to a mutual learning perspective in order to hold challenging discussions productively. Chapter Thirty, "Moving Toward Difficulty," highlights the ineffective strategies many people use to deal with difficult conversations. It challenges the assumption that pointing out problems will cause conflict to escalate. By changing the way you think about conversations that seem risky, you can learn to use the Skilled Facilitator approach to move directly toward difficulty and resolve problems. This chapter includes an example of how to change a conversation that might not go well when giving an employee negative feedback into one where the supervisor and employee learn how to effectively change their behavior and resolve their concerns.

The concluding chapters in Part Four address difficult issues that arise in working with groups. Chapter Thirty-One, "Responding to Silence and Interruptions and Enabling Members to Talk with Each Other," suggests ways to intervene when group members either do not speak up or interrupt others who are speaking. It also points out how facilitators and leaders reduce group member accountability by intervening in ways that discourage group members from addressing concerns with one another and, instead, talking with (and through) the person who started an intervention. Chapter Thirty-Two, "Raising Issues In or Out of the Group," discusses what to do when group members approach you outside a meeting and ask you to do something inconsistent with your role, such as raising their concerns for them or getting a group to discuss or drop a particular subject. Here you will find guiding principles for responding in these and similar situations in ways that model mutual learning and increase group members' accountability for addressing their own issues.

Chapter 28

Holding Risky Conversations

Anne Davidson

WHAT MAKES A CONVERSATION feel risky to you? When do you find yourself debating whether to have a particular conversation or facing the fact that you need to have a conversation but dreading it? We probably each answer these questions a little differently based on our upbringing and organizational culture. But most often, risky conversations include sharing negative feedback, especially with those we deem more powerful than ourselves, like the boss, or those we love and admire, like a spouse or good friend. Some conversations feel risky because we think we have a lot at stake, like a long investment in a relationship or job. Others are risky because we want to do something different from what we believe is anticipated or expected of us. It helps to think clearly about what creates a risky conversation for you.

WHY HAVE RISKY CONVERSATIONS?

It is not necessary or even possible to have every potential risky conversation that comes along. Yet often the risk arises from the fact that the issue we want to talk about matters a great deal to us. Without resolving problems in relationships or with groups, we cannot move forward or remain productively engaged. And once we come to understand conversations systemically, we recognize that avoiding a conversation now is likely to create a bigger problem or threat later. In fact, we often contribute to the very problems we complain about. Not having a conversation with the boss about her behaviors that make it difficult for us to do our job is likely to end up reflecting more on us than on the boss. Moreover, the counterintuitive notion of moving toward conflict is actually more productive than avoiding it.

See Chapter Thirty, "Moving Toward Difficulty," page 261, and Chapter Forty-Two, "How to Stop Contributing to Your Boss's and Your Own Ineffectiveness," page 335.

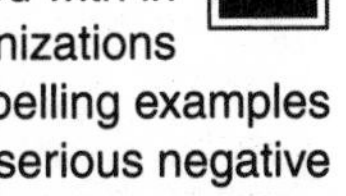

Everyone I have worked with in organizations has compelling examples of the serious negative consequences created by avoiding difficult issues and uncomfortable conversations.

Everyone I have worked with in organizations has compelling examples of the serious negative consequences created by avoiding difficult issues and uncomfortable conversations. So the first question to ask yourself is, "What are the possible consequences of not having this conversation?" If, in the long term, those consequences could be as or more risky than forging ahead, then it seems irresponsible to avoid the discussion.

HOW TO HAVE A RISKY CONVERSATION

Several of the chapters that follow offer specific guidance for particular kinds of difficult conversations. Here are some general steps that fit almost any conversation that you may define as risky.

Step 1: Clarify Your Own Purpose and Intent

The first work you must do is with yourself. If your intent in having the conversation is unilateral, that is, to get someone else to do or believe something, your approach is likely to increase defensiveness and fail to accomplish what you desire. If you can enter the conversation with curiosity, to explore the situation and discover whether your view is accurate and how you can productively change your own behavior, then you have a basis for moving forward. Knowing your own purpose and intent toward the others involved is critical for being transparent. In their practical, readable book *Difficult Conversations,* Stone, Patton and Heen (1999) point out that each difficult conversation is really about three things: what really happened, how you feel about what happened, and what this situation says about your identity (how worthy, competent, or lovable you think you are). Getting clear about how you are thinking and feeling will give you a window into whether this is a hot-button issue for you, where you might be making untested assumptions and attributions, and whether your feelings are based on valid data. The reflection questions included in this chapter and the "Biases and Defensive Triggers" exercise in Chapter Thirty-Three, page 281, may be useful guides to your analysis.

Step 2: Build a Foundation for the Conversation

Contracting for a risky conversation is even more important than contracting for routine ones. If the conversation feels challenging to you, there is a great likelihood that others who are involved will also think it could be difficult. These kinds of conversations take time. Going slow to go fast has even bigger payoffs because resolving an issue that feels risky is likely to strengthen a relationship and make it much easier to address issues in the future.

See also Chapter Nine, "Jointly Designing the Purpose and Process for a Conversation," page 103.

The first step in building a foundation is to agree about the purpose of the conversation. In a risky situation, this step may be a little longer than average, because it is extremely important to highlight why you want to have the conversation as well as what you want to talk about. Otherwise the other person involved is likely to zoom up the ladder of inference, infer negative intentions on your part, and become defensive before you even begin.

For an example of how to jointly design the purpose of a risky conversation, see "Beginning a Risky Conversation" on page 253.

It is not helpful to start out saying, "I want to discuss your performance," without saying why and where you are headed. It is also useful to give a brief indication of how you feel about the situation you are discussing, or at least share that it is difficult or risky. In my experience, sharing your own fear helps all parties involved access compassion for one another and listen more for intent than specific word choices.

After sharing your reasons for wanting to have the conversation, your feelings, and your intentions, you can jointly design a process for having the conversation. I find it productive to suggest a process that offers each person involved an opportunity to:

1. Share his view of what happened
2. Talk about how each feels
3. Clarify needs and interests
4. Jointly design solutions

Step 3: Stay Focused on the Jointly Designed Process

Whatever the process agreed on, stay focused and work through the steps. In risky conversations, it can be easier to get off track by delving deeply into the history of a situation. I suggest that you do this only as a way of clarifying issues rather than going back and rehashing the specific problem or having old discussions again. Since our reasoning is often faulty when we are fearful about a situation or frustrated about a relationship, it is likely that our historical data are flawed. It is not productive to spend a lot of time trying to agree about old matters. Instead, it is more useful to stay focused on the current situation—what is going on now that makes you want to have this conversation—and to work toward future changes.

Step 4: Agree to Monitor Progress and Discuss Again

Historical data can be important to illustrate patterns, but don't enter the conversation with the intent to right all past wrongs.

The resolution to a risky conversation almost always involves both parties' doing something different, even if it is just the boss supporting skill development toward a promotion. And when trying to change behavior, it helps to regularly monitor progress and fine-tune actions with intentions. I have seen many groups agree to what seem great processes for improvement, only to abandon their efforts later because they did not monitor and celebrate their progress. It is much easier to sustain changes with regular feedback and refinement, so I like to end all conversations, and especially ones that I have invested a lot of time and effort in having, with an agreement about how we will monitor progress and when we will get back together.

MOMENTS OF TRUTH

The risk of having a conversation is often overestimated, while the risk of not having it is often underestimated. Tom Moore's story in Chapter Thirty-Eight about asking his boss whether he was about to be fired is a powerful example. Often the data that lead us to assess the risk of engaging in a conversation are flawed, based on third- and fourth-hand organizational stories about what happened to someone else in another situation a long time ago. I frequently find these stories distorted and sometimes even untrue. I suspect they continue to circulate as part of elaborate organizational defensive routines that rationalize our choice to distance ourselves from situations and avoid risk.

See Chapter Thirty-Eight, "Daily Challenges of a Facilitative Leader," page 309.

Whether or not we think we will like what we hear, knowing where we stand enables us to act. Not knowing leaves us stuck in a survival cycle of fear and avoidance, guaranteeing that we fall short of our goals and dreams. At the same time, taking small steps at first to build your muscles for having risky conversations is wise. The more skilled you become at being consistent with the core values and using the ground rules, the less risky conversations seem and the easier it is to have difficult ones productively. One of the great moments of truth in my life was the discovery that by having the conversations I had been avoiding, I not only felt better about myself, but others respected me and valued my contributions more as well.

One of the great moments of truth in my life was the discovery that by having the conversations I had been avoiding, I not only felt better about myself, but others respected me and valued my contributions more as well.

See Chapter Fifty-Four, "Using Creative and Survival Cycles to See and Shift Mental Models," page 433.

But it is also important to remember that from a mutual learning mind-set, every individual and group has a free and informed choice about whether to engage in a risky conversation with you. As important as it is to do your own inner work before such a conversation, it is also important to be able to let go if others decide they are not willing to be as vulnerable. They may need time to do their own reflection, and their choice may be different. Suspending judgment includes not harshly evaluating someone who makes a choice different from your own. By

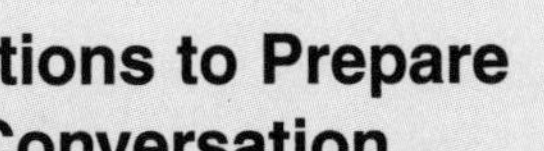

Reflection Questions to Prepare for a Risky Conversation

1. Why do I want to have this conversation? Is my intent consistent with mutual learning?
2. What are the potential consequences of not having this conversation?
3. What are the possible consequences of having this conversation?
4. What are my worst fears? What are my deepest desires? How likely are my fears to manifest themselves? Am I unnecessarily focusing on survival cycle thinking? What is the worst thing that could happen if my fears come true? What hope might be realized if I do engage in this discussion?
5. What data do I have that lead me to want to enter this conversation? What untested inferences and assumptions am I making?
6. How am I feeling about this issue? Are my feelings justified? Can I access compassion for myself and for the others involved? If not, why not?

modeling your compassion, you actually increase the likelihood that this or a different risky conversation may happen in time.

BEGINNING A RISKY CONVERSATION

Here is an adaptation of a risky conversation, illustrating how to share your purpose, intentions, and reasoning and invite the other person into the discussion. Contracting for the discussion is the first step, even before you jointly design the actual process:

The Strategy	*The Actual Conversation*
Explain what I want to discuss and why. Be transparent about my assumptions and the data I have, without going into unnecessary detail at this point. Test whether the inference on which I am basing this conversation is accurate.	**Anne:** Roxie, I would like to set aside some time this week for us to have a conversation about how you feel toward me given your new role. I know that when I joined the department, you had applied for the position I took. Pam and Liz have told me you were angry about that for a long time. I think we have worked well together in spite of that, but now that you are my new boss, I am concerned about whether you have left-over hard feelings. Do you? **Roxie:** No, no. It's okay.

The Strategy	*The Actual Conversation*
Explain my reasoning. Share what I see as the consequences of not having this conversation. Share the relevant information that I am afraid. Advocate for having the conversation, and inquire into (jointly design) whether the other person is willing to discuss the topic I propose.	**Anne:** I am not convinced that it is. Your voice is softer than normal, and you are looking away. I am concerned that if we don't work together productively, neither of us can perform as well as we might. I can see why you might still have some hard feelings, and it is scary for me to now be in the role of your subordinate. I would like to talk through how we each feel and figure out how we can best support one another in our work. Would you be willing to do that? **Roxie:** Well, I guess. But I am really busy getting settled, and I have to hire a new assistant.
Seek to address the other party's interest (time) and propose a process for meeting. [At the beginning of the meeting, I would propose the process for the actual discussion that is set out above at the end of Step 2, "Build a Foundation for the Conversation."]	**Anne:** I would like to suggest that we plan to talk for an hour. I have a process to suggest for our conversation. After an hour, we can decide if this is a good use of our time. If so, we can continue the meeting or plan another time to meet. If not, we can figure out what, if anything, we can do differently. Would what I am suggesting be agreeable?
Jointly design next steps. Celebrate that she is impressed, and mentally prepare to explore her concerns and interests when we meet.	**Roxie:** Yes. Let's get together tomorrow at 4:00. You know, I am pretty impressed that you would just come right in and address this.

Reference

Stone, D., Patton, B., and Heen, S. *Difficult Conversations.* New York: Penguin, 1999.

Chapter 29

Exploring Your Contributions to Problems

Roger Schwarz

OFTEN WE DON'T RECOGNIZE that we are contributing to problems. Sometimes the problems we are contributing to are the same problems we are complaining about.

See, for example, Chapter Forty-Two, "How to Stop Contributing to Your Boss's and Your Own Ineffectiveness," page 335, where I describe how Henry reinforces his boss's ineffectiveness by withholding information from him.

WHY IT'S HARD TO SEE OUR CONTRIBUTIONS

From a systems perspective, it makes sense that we don't see our contributions to problems. We often don't see the effects of our actions because of the time lag between our actions and the consequences. When the consequences show up, we are either not present to experience them firsthand (although we experience the subsequent effects) or we experience the consequences but don't associate them with our earlier behavior. In either case, we fail to make the connection.

We often don't see the effects of our actions because of the time lag between our actions and the consequences.

It's hard to figure out how you are affecting the system unless you understand how the system that you are part of works. Anyone who has ever tried to fix something, only to find out that the fix created another problem, has experienced this. And in social systems, it's more difficult because the system consists of interacting people.

You can't understand the system by yourself. You develop your understanding of the system and how you affect it by talking with the other people who make it up and understanding how people interact to form the system.

You can't understand the system by yourself. You develop your understanding of the system and how you affect it by talking with the other people who make it up and understanding how people interact to form the system. Kurt Lewin, the pioneering social psychologist and founder of action research, said you should try to change something if you truly want to understand it.

A human resource director felt that his direct reports were not solving problems based on all available information. For their part, the direct reports felt that they had a difficult time getting all the information they needed. At a meeting to address this issue, one of the direct reports said that the HR director routinely tried to get them to leave his office before they were finished talking about assignments. When I asked what the director did that led them to think that, they all said that he tapped his pencil on his desk and said, "uh-huh, uh-huh," each time they tried to walk him through some problem that was occurring. When I asked what they thought the pencil tapping and "uh-huhs" meant, all the direct reports said it meant that the director was not interested and that he wanted them to end the conversation. They even checked out their inferences—but with each other, not with the director. Hearing this, the director said it didn't mean he wasn't interested; it was his way of mentally making a note of the issues they were raising. The director said he had wondered why people were leaving meetings prematurely, but he had not made a connection between how these meetings had gone and his concerns about his direct reports' not solving problems adequately. By not raising the issue with each other and exploring how it developed, both the HR director and his team had continued to reinforce the pattern they had established.

HOW WE CONTRIBUTE TO PROBLEMS

There are many ways we contribute to problems:

- We make inferences and assumptions about the situation that are incorrect but act on them as if they are true.
- We withhold information about other people's behavior that would enable them to change if they had it.
- We withhold information about our interests and needs and make it less likely that others can take them into account.
- We act unilaterally without taking others' interests and needs into account.
- We give people mixed messages, which makes it impossible for them to do everything we ask for.
- We create structures or processes that have unintended consequences embedded in them and then get annoyed when others create the unintended consequences by following the structure or process.
- We react disproportionately to problems, exacerbating them or creating new problems.

The drama triangle is another way to think about how we contribute to problems. In the drama triangle, we respond to situations by punishing others, rescuing others, or acting as a helpless victim.

See Chapter Fifty-Three, "The Drama Triangle: A Unilateral Control Program for Helping Others," page 421.

LEARNING ABOUT OUR CONTRIBUTIONS TO PROBLEMS

I think of three parts to learning about our contributions to problems: privately reflecting, reframing, and jointly exploring.

Privately Reflecting on Your Contributions

If someone hasn't approached you to talk about the problem, you can privately reflect on your contribution before talking with others about the problem. Even if you are approached, you can ask for time to reflect. By reflecting on your own contribution, you can begin to reduce your blind spots.[1] To the extent that you can enter a conversation sharing what you think may be your contribution, you create an environment for mutual learning.

Here are some strategies for reflecting:

- Begin to consider your contributions by starting with others' contributions. After you've identified how you think others have contributed to the problem, ask yourself, "Do I behave in any of these ways myself, and can I acknowledge that I do?" Sometimes we project or assign to others our own behaviors.
- Think about the issues or kinds of situations that lead you to respond defensively. If you know what these issues are, see whether this situation matches any of them. (If you don't know what these issues are for you, you can ask others who work closely with you or live with you.)

See the exercise on identifying your biases and defensive triggers in Chapter Thirty-Three, "Finding Your Voice," page 279.

- Identify how you are feeling about the situation and ask yourself, "What happened that made me feel that way?" Move down the ladder of inference from your feelings to the specific behaviors that generated them. If you're not sure what generated them, you can explore this later.
- Ask yourself, "How did I respond when I felt that way?" Use the list above and the drama triangle to identify specific things you did that may have contributed to the problem.

Consider your private reflections as potential hypotheses to explore with others involved in the problem.

Reframing How You Think About Yourself and Others

If you are finding it difficult to identify how you may have contributed to the problem, you may be operating out of the unilateral control model values and assumptions instead of the mutual learning model.

See Chapter Four, "Understanding What Guides Your Behavior," page 33, for an introduction to the unilateral control and mutual learning models.

The assumption in the mutual learning model is not that you are necessarily contributing to the problem, but that you may be unaware of your contribution and so it is more likely than you think it is. By shifting toward the mutual learning perspective, you move from seeking blame to looking for contributions, from needing to defend to being curious about exploring, from being self-righteous to having humility, and from simply focusing on others to being accountable for your actions. In this way, you become more compassionate toward others and yourself. As you begin to shift your focus, consider reflecting again on your contribution. You may see things you missed before.

The assumption in the mutual learning model is not that you are necessarily contributing to the problem, but that you may be unaware of your contribution and so it is more likely than you think it is.

See Chapter Thirty-Four, "Being a Mutual Learner in a Unilaterally Controlling World," page 287.

Jointly Exploring Your Contribution

After you have thought about your contribution, get together with others who are involved in the issue. Whether it is one other person or several, getting the system in the room makes it possible to put together a picture of how each part of the system is contributing to the consequences. Here are some ways you can explore your contribution:

- Share your thoughts about how you think you have contributed to the problem and ask for others' reactions. From a unilateral control perspective, this would be the equivalent of giving ammunition to the enemy. In mutual learning, it is being a steward for jointly seeking understanding.
- Ask others to describe your contribution—for example, **"Can you give me some specific examples of what I've said or done—or not said or done—that may have contributed to the problem?"**
- If you have not identified any ways that you contributed to the problem, say so and remain curious: **"I've thought about ways that I may have been part of the problem, but I haven't come up with anything. Can you see anything I'm missing?"**
- Ask about the consequences of your behavior—for example, **"I'm not understanding how what I did contributed to the problem. Can you explain how it created problems for you or others?"** If you have started the conversation because you see problems with others' behaviors, ask, **"I'm wondering if I'm contributing to the problems I'm concerned about. What, if anything, do you see me doing?"**

- Share your intent, and find out whether others inferred something else—for example, **"My intent in doing X was to . . ., although I can see now how it didn't work out that way. Given what I did, I'm wondering, what did you think my intent was?"**
- Jointly develop a story or map that causally explains how your and others' contributions interacted to create the problem. After you agree on how the situation was created, you can begin to jointly explore what changes in people's behavior will create the outcomes people want.

See Chapter Fifty-Six, "Applying the Skilled Facilitator Approach to a Systems Thinking Analysis," page 447.

- Be accountable for your actions. Acknowledge your contribution, and apologize for contributing to the consequences, even if you did not intend to create them.
- Identify how you can support each other to make the changes you have agreed to. Ask others to tell you as soon as possible when they see you acting in ways that are contributing to a problem again.

Note

1. The blind spot is one of the four quadrants of the disclosure-feedback model of awareness known as the Johari Window, developed in the 1950s by American psychologists Joseph Luft and Harry Ingham. There have been many adaptations and instruments based on the model. See, for example, http://www.teleometrics.com/info/resources_johari.html.

Chapter 30

Moving Toward Difficulty

Sue McKinney

In the Skilled Facilitator approach, we advocate being direct and heading straight toward difficult conversations. Many people fear doing this will escalate a conflict, but to the contrary, we find that doing so usually defuses the conflict and makes it more manageable to process. Of course, there is something you must do first: before you can be direct and effective, you have to change the way you think about difficult situations.

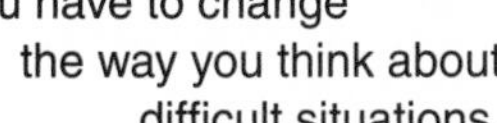

Before you can be direct and effective, you have to change the way you think about difficult situations.

BEING DIRECT

I have given difficult feedback to employees in a variety of ways throughout my career. Early in my career, I was accused of being "too direct" and "too blunt" and hurting people's feelings. Today, I am told that although I am "very direct," I am not judgmental, and the recipient is grateful to hear what I have to say. Table 30.1 compares my old version of being direct versus my new version of being direct.

In the two different versions of offering Jane feedback in Table 30.1, the biggest change comes in my new thoughts and feelings. It is more important that my thoughts and feelings change than that my words change since most people instinctively sense the essence of the thinking behind what is being said. If I'm feeling critical, as in the first example, it bleeds through when I talk about Jane's being sloppy and also in my voice, which is harsher in tone than in my second example. In the second example, my thoughts are about learning. I am curious about and interested in what Jane has to tell me. Thinking this way conveys a different message from my earlier judgmental thoughts.

The second version of offering direct feedback does not involve being judgmental about Jane's performance. My goal is to describe the problem, share my reactions, and hear her perspective. I work hard to suspend my judgment about Jane and to honestly engage her in a conversation that might lead to my learning something new. In this case, I might learn that my quality standards are too rigid and inflexible or that if we set the standards together, Jane generates ones I hadn't considered or, at the very least, that if we set them together, Jane will be committed to making sure they are upheld.

Table 30.1 Being Direct: Before and After Mutual Learning Thinking

Thoughts and Feelings	Verbatim Dialogue
OLD VERSION OF BEING DIRECT	
I hate having this conversation, but her work is really slack.	**Me:** Jane, how are you doing? **[Easing-in strategy.]**
	Jane: Fine. What's up?
Your workmanship is terrible. It is obvious you don't pay attention to detail. **[Untested assumptions.]**	**Me:** I need to talk with you about the photocopying you've been doing lately.
	Jane: Yes, what about it?
Anyone can photocopy accurately. **[Untested assumption.]** I give her the packet exactly as I want it. Why can't she get it right? I've done this for years without a problem. **[I'm right and she's wrong.]**	**Me:** Well, the packets of materials are very sloppy. The printing is crooked, upside down, folded, and some pages are missing. It reflects badly on us as an organization. You need to pay a lot more attention. **[Advocating without inquiring.]**
Good grief. Let's not get melodramatic about this. **[Act rational.]**	**Jane:** What?! I may not be PERFECT like YOU, but I'm doing the best I can!
 **NEW VERSION OF BEING DIRECT**	
I need to let Jane know that I'm not happy with the quality of her work.	**Me:** Jane, good morning. I'd like to talk with you about the quality of your photocopying lately. Do you have a few minutes? **[Advocating with inquiry, jointly designing next steps.]**
	Jane: Sure, is there a problem?
Give her specific examples of what I found when I proofed the most recent documents.	**Me:** I took some time to proof the last two sets of materials that you produced, and I found some basic errors both times. For example, the printing is crooked on the article regarding nonviolence, the consensus article has the front and back pages turned upside down, there are folds in the paper throughout four other articles, and some pages from the orientation materials are missing altogether. Were you aware of these things? **[Sharing specific examples, inquiring into her perspective.]**
Hmm. It seems that we have different thoughts about what is a major concern.	**Jane:** I did realize that some of it was a little crooked and a few got folded. I didn't think of it as a big deal since it is still readable. I also saw that some of the front and back pages got turned around, but I didn't think that was a major concern either. I did not notice that there were missing pages. I agree that is a problem, and I will try to check for omissions in the future.

Thoughts and Feelings	Verbatim Dialogue
Check to see if she sees the quality standards as different.	**Me:** I think we may have a different understanding of what is an acceptable standard of quality given that you did not think the printing issues were a "big deal" or a "major concern" and I do. Do you think that is accurate? **[Advocating with inquiry into her thoughts.]**
Good question.	**Jane:** I think you are correct. We do have different standards. Do you set them and I just have to agree, or can we decide together?
I guess she probably wants to help and since she has to implement them, it makes sense.	**Me:** That's a good question. I guess we should set them together since we both have to live by them. What do you think? **[Advocacy with inquiry.]**
What is too high with wanting them done correctly?	**Jane:** Yes, I'd like to help set the standards for the same reason. I think your standards are a bit too high.
	Me: Okay. Can you help me understand what makes them "too high"?
Huh. This is an interesting perspective. I hadn't really considered these points before.	**Jane:** Sure. I think we should have the users set the standard rather than have a 100 percent perfection standard. I don't think the users expect 100-page packets with no mistakes. The time involved in getting to zero mistakes isn't worth it.
I don't know how you could develop a user standard.	**Me:** That is an interesting idea, but I'm curious how we would determine the user's standard. Do you have a thought about that? **[Genuine inquiry.]**
Not a bad idea. We always think we are the experts in what folks need to know. This would give us some valuable feedback. And maybe my standards are stricter than the average reader demands.	**Jane:** Couldn't we simply include an evaluation of the materials themselves and ask people to give us feedback on the quality of printing? That would also give us the opportunity to ask about the content of the articles and whether they found them helpful.
	Me: Great idea. I'm willing to try it.

Here is another example of the power behind changing my thoughts and feelings. In the past, if I coded a person's behavior as "lying," I would probably think, "He knows he is lying and he doesn't care. He is totally out for himself." Being direct with this person and telling him that I knew he was lying and only out for himself would likely cause the conflict to escalate since these are only inferences and attributions. Although my inferences may be accurate, it is much harder to test a high-level inference like "lying" than it is to test a lower-level inference based on observable behavior. Unless I change my thoughts and feelings, it will be hard for me to make a lower-level inference.

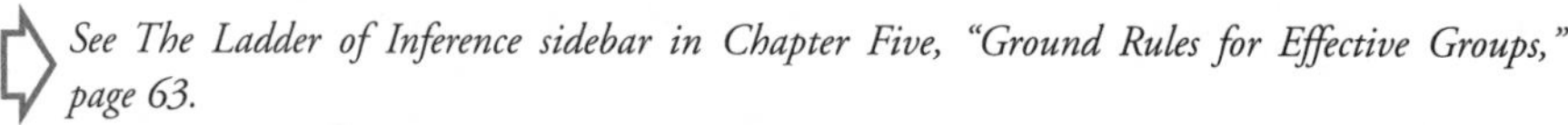

See The Ladder of Inference sidebar in Chapter Five, "Ground Rules for Effective Groups," page 63.

Unless I change my thoughts and feelings, it will be hard for me to make a lower-level inference.

Being direct with a high-level inference will likely be as problematic as many people fear. However, if I can change how I think about other people, including this specific person, I can be direct in a way that is likely to decrease the conflict (or, at least, not unnecessarily increase it). I can see the behavior and say to myself, "Is Zack lying? What leads me to think that? Well, Zack told me that he supported my promotion, but the review committee told me that two of my three references said I was not ready. I know Mary supported me fully, so I'm thinking Zack must be one of the two who recommended against my promotion. I need to ask him about that." This kind of thinking leads me to a very different kind of "direct" conversation than the ones I used to hold.

STRATEGY FOR EFFECTIVE DELIVERY

When giving direct feedback, being transparent about the strategy for the conversation is also a big help. When giving feedback using a facilitative approach, I say something like this: **"Tom, I want to give you some feedback about your performance in yesterday's meeting. I feel a bit anxious about doing this since my feedback isn't totally positive. But I am interested in knowing if you see the situation differently than I do. I'm interested in learning about whether I'm off-base. Would you be willing to talk with me about this?"**

In this approach, I am specific about the goal of the conversation—"feedback" and "learning"—and am candid about my feelings in doing so—"anxious." This helps Tom understand what is on my mind.

If Tom is willing to talk with me, my transparency continues as I suggest a process for offering the feedback: **"I'm thinking that I could describe what I saw in the meeting and see if you saw it the same way or differently. And based on how we both see it, I could share my reactions and then hear your reactions. I'm well aware that I may have seen the meeting differently than you did, and I want to know if that is the case. What do you think of this approach to the conversation?"**

I'm explaining to Tom my thinking about the best way to share my thoughts and hear his reactions. If it wasn't clear to Tom before, I'm hoping that he understands that I'm not telling him "how it was" in the meeting; I'm truly exploring my reactions and checking to see if they are different from his, in hopes that we will both learn. I believe this gives Tom specific information that allows him to participate fully in the conversation. My intent is to avoid setting him up or manipulating him into agreeing with me and changing his behavior to suit me.

THE DANGERS OF BEING POLITE

The Skilled Facilitator approach was counterintuitive for me. I was raised to be polite. Being polite, in my world, meant that there are times when it is better to tell a white lie than to be totally honest. When I was honest, people called me blunt and suggested that I learn to be more tactful. With this feedback, I learned not to tell people things that I thought might hurt their feelings. I learned to be honest, but only to a point. It wasn't always clear to me at what point I had crossed the line of politeness to rudeness, so over time, I stayed further and further away from the truth.

The Unintended Consequences of Being Polite

There are some serious unintended consequences to this "polite" behavior. One of the most common I have seen is poorly performing managers. Many times, I have seen poorly performing managers continue to be promoted even though their behavior doesn't warrant it, only to get fired later because of incompetence. Or, conversely, a poorly performing manager never gets the opportunity to be promoted because of a lack of specific feedback about how he could improve his performance and qualify for a promotion. In both cases, coworkers and supervisors often state that the manager is a "nice person" and no one wanted to "hurt his feelings." So instead, they all withheld specific feedback that would have given the manager information on which to try to change his behavior, or not, as he so chose. The point is not that they blocked his promotion or got him fired; it is that they withheld relevant information that would give the manager the free and informed choice about whether to change.

Saving Face

Another strategy I learned to try to avoid hurting someone's feelings was to hint at a problem. I hoped the offender would understand the subtle hints and correct the problem to my satisfaction. This saved the other person from embarrassment and me from the stress of sharing negative feedback. When asked if my friend's strange new hair style was "cute," I responded, "It's very hip, but I loved the way you had it last year with the bangs. Didn't you like that cut?" Or when dealing with a friend, Sarah, who talked too much at social gatherings, I might say, "Isn't it awful how Betty is always talking on and on? She just doesn't seem to get that others want to talk too. I wish she would get the hint." My hope was that Sarah would understand the parallels and change her behavior as I suggested Betty should change hers. Interestingly enough, I have had many friends commiserate that this strategy isn't working for them. "I gave her a look! Why doesn't she get it and stop talking!" or "I told him over and over that I like Italian food. Why did he suggest we travel to England this year?! Doesn't he listen?!"

I think the hinting strategy is frustrating, because it is based on our belief that others can guess our secret motive. This actually involves both parties guessing: the hinter has to guess what hints will work to get the response he or she desires, and the person hinted to has to recognize the hints and guess what they mean. When people do get the hints, they often ask, "Why didn't you just say so?" expressing their frustration at having to guess what the other person desires. Conflict often escalates using this strategy. If either party misses the cue, the other person gets frustrated and angry.

THE BENEFITS OF BEING DIRECT

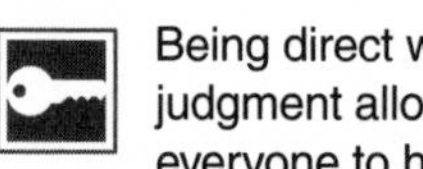

Being direct without judgment allows everyone to have all the relevant information so that each can make free and informed choices about how to proceed. Withholding this information, even if we think we are being kind, prevents the other person from having the option to challenge our opinions or accept them.

Why does being direct help in these kinds of situations? Being direct without judgment allows everyone to have all the relevant information so that each can make free and informed choices about how to proceed. Withholding this information, even if we think we are being kind, prevents the other person from having the option to challenge our opinions or accept them.

The ability to suspend judgment temporarily is a learned behavior that takes time and discipline to develop consistently. As I have developed this discipline and consciously changed my thinking, my feelings have also changed so that I am no longer fearful or anxious about handling difficult or conflictual conversations. In addition, understanding the ground rules gives me the necessary techniques to express myself effectively.

OUR MANTRA: MOVE TOWARD THE CONFLICT

When we teach classes, we often say, "Folks, we encourage you to move toward the conflict," and people cringe and sometimes laugh in horror. In group settings as a facilitator, I was always encouraged to avoid the conflict or to move deftly to a different topic. Pointing out a conflict was tantamount to chanting, "Fight, fight, fight." No one in his or her right mind would exacerbate a group in such a manner. However, what I have discovered is that avoiding the conflict really doesn't mean avoiding it; it means postponing it, moving it to another venue, or prolonging it (sometimes for months or years). By naming the conflict and moving the group's attention to it, you give group members a choice about how to handle it (assuming they agree with your assessment that there is a conflict).

Avoiding conflict doesn't really mean avoiding it; it means postponing it, moving it to another venue, or prolonging it (sometimes for months or years). That's why we say, *Move toward the conflict.*

Naming a difficult issue does not always mean a group will choose to deal with it openly, at that time or ever. It simply gives individuals the information to choose their next step. Yet there have been many times when I have pointed out places where group members seemed to be at odds with each other. I asked people to clarify their stance and work through the differences. Then they were able to move on quickly.

I have also frequently brought angry people together to talk in my presence:

In one organization where I worked, several supervisors were complaining about the same individual. They came to me frequently to ask for help in dealing with problems they were facing in their relationship with him. For a while, I coached each supervisor individually, and then, seeing some patterns emerging, I suggested all the supervisors request a meeting with this individual to offer feedback to him as a group and request feedback about their behavior from him. Anxiety was high as the meeting approached, but the meeting went smoothly. Each supervisor was able to share the specific behaviors that were causing concern, check to see if the individual in question remembered events the same way, share the impact his behavior was having on them, and ask for his perspective. As a group, they came up with next steps to forge a better working relationship. Everyone in the meeting learned the power of suspending judgment of one another, working from the core values, and communicating using the ground rules. Everyone agreed that this meeting, which lasted over three hours, was effective and productive.

OUR EXPERIENCES OVER TIME

It has been my experience, and the experience of my colleagues, that as we practice the facilitative approach in all life situations, conflict in general is reduced in our lives. It seemed paradoxical to me that an approach that tells me to go directly to individuals to discuss difficult issues and to approach conflict head-on would decrease the stress in my life and reduce the conflicts I have to manage. But this is exactly what has happened.

The biggest change came for me when I learned to suspend my judgments and go directly to a person with my concerns, open to the possibility that I may be seeing only a piece of the puzzle or that I may be wrong in my interpretation of the situation. This approach allows me to stay more curious and to genuinely explore another person's perspective on an issue. I can acknowledge that I may have overreacted or hit a personal hot button, or I may find out my assessment was accurate and the other person wants to make changes to our relationship as a result. So far, I have never been sorry when I had the courage to go directly to the difficult issue, name it, and deal with it openly.

As we practice the facilitative approach in all life situations, conflict, in general, is reduced in our lives.

Chapter 31

Responding to Silence and Interruptions and Enabling Members to Talk to Each Other

Roger Schwarz

SOMETIMES GROUP MEMBERS BECOME silent, interrupt each other, or address their comments to the team leader or facilitator rather than speaking to the entire group. This chapter looks at some ways of addressing these issues.

RESPONDING TO SILENCE

When group members become silent after someone makes a comment or asks a question, my first response is to be quiet and wait. My strategy is not to make others uncomfortable with the silence and get them to start talking; it's simply that I want to give people a chance to think about whether they want to say something, including the introverted group members who naturally take more time to respond. If I become uncomfortable with the silence and intervene, I reduce the chance that others will respond.

After a period of time in which people have had ample time to answer (about half a minute), I use the diagnosis-intervention cycle to name the silence and ask what leads people to be silent.

I might say, **"After John asked whether there were any problems with leadership, no one said anything. I'm curious: What does the silence mean?"**

See Chapter Six, "The Diagnosis-Intervention Cycle," page 69.

Sometimes people respond by answering John's question, and the conversation continues on the current topic. Other times people respond by talking about why they are silent without answering John's initial question. For example, Pedro may say, "It's a difficult topic to discuss." If Pedro doesn't go on to explain what makes it difficult to discuss, I will ask, **"Can you say what makes it difficult?"** At this point, I have shifted the focus of the conversation away from the original topic to explore concerns about addressing the topic and what, if anything, is necessary to do to return to it. If Pedro answers, I can ask if others see it the same way as Pedro or have a different view.

After group members have identified what makes it difficult for them to discuss the topic, I can then ask, **"What needs to happen for you to be willing to discuss the topic?"** This enables the group to identify what interests need to be met to discuss the topic and to see how they can address these interests.

At some point, Pedro or other members may not want to say what makes the conversation difficult to talk about. It's important to balance your interest in identifying the cause of the silence with preserving members' free and informed choice to stop participating in the conversation. In practice, this means saying something like, **"I want to be clear that it's your right to choose whether to continue the conversation. Please let us know if you choose not to pursue it."**

DEALING WITH INTERRUPTIONS

Interruptions are the flip side of silence. We infer someone is interrupting when one person starts talking while another person is still speaking. But interruptions are best identified by the person being interrupted. If, for example, Joyce is talking and Ian starts talking, I would turn to Joyce and say, **"Joyce, it looked as if you were still talking when Ian began to talk, yes?"** Joyce might respond, "I was actually finished with my thought," meaning that Ian's speaking did not prevent her from completing her sentence and being heard. If, however, Joyce responds that she was still speaking (implying she has more to say), then I can turn to Ian and say, **"Ian, would you be willing to let Joyce finish?"** This intervention is based on the ground rule of jointly designing next steps, because by interrupting, Ian has unilaterally controlled the conversation in a way that reduces Joyce's ability to share all her relevant information.

If Ian were to continue speaking before Joyce or others were finished, I would name the pattern of his behavior and ask about it: **"Ian, I want to share a pattern I've seen and get your reaction. Several times in this meeting when I pointed out that you were talking before others had finished, you agreed and said you'd be willing to let people finish. Yet you continued to do the same thing. Am I off-base?"** If Ian agrees with my assessment, then I continue, **"What's happening that leads you to continue to interrupt?"**

By my asking this question, the group learns what is causing the interruptions (from Ian's perspective) and can address it. For example, Ian may share that he has another meeting in ten minutes and is feeling that this meeting is moving too slowly. He may say that people are repeating themselves, which is wasting time. Whatever he says temporarily focuses the group on the causes so that together they can figure out how to address them.

ENABLING MEMBERS TO TALK TO EACH OTHER

When you intervene (as a facilitator, leader, consultant, or trainer), you draw the group's focus to yourself. This is temporarily necessary. But if it continues, you become the hub of the conversation and group members talk to each other through you instead of talking directly with each other. This is a problem because it increases dependence on you and reduces the group's ability to build its own capacity.

You can shift the conversation back to the group members by choosing your words in your intervention. In the silence example above, after I ask Pedro what about the topic is difficult, I remain the focus of the conversation by asking, "Do others have a different thought?" However, I can remove myself from the focus if I say to Pedro, **"Would you be willing to see if others have a different thought?"** Assuming Pedro is willing, this leads Pedro and other group members to talk among themselves. The principle for having the group become more active is to ask the group member to make the remainder of the intervention instead of making it for him. This makes the intervention more developmental. An extension of this is for group members to use Ground Rule Six, "Combine advocacy and inquiry." In this way, they invite group members to respond to them and each other.

Using interventions to structure a process can also minimize your becoming the focus of the conversation. Assume you want to propose that the group use a certain problem-solving process. By describing the complete process at once and seeking agreement to use it (rather than introduce the process one part at a time), you potentially reduce the number of interventions you need to make later. For example, if you are introducing a problem-solving model as an intervention, you might say something like this: **"I'd like to suggest a process for solving this problem and get your reactions. I think it would useful first to agree on a definition of the problem, then identify interests that need to be met in solving the problem, next generate potential solutions, and finally decide on one or more solutions given your interests. I'm suggesting this because I think it will increase the chance that you will generate a solution that works well and that everyone is committed to. Does anyone have any concerns about using this approach?"**

Finally, if you are a facilitator, using the word *we* can lead to your being included inappropriately in group conversations. If, for example, in a conversation about project deadlines you say to the group, "What should we do to make the deadline realistic?" you send the message that you will be part of the decision and the content discussion leading to it. By using the word *you,* you distinguish the group from yourself and can remove yourself at least from the content of the discussion.

Chapter 32

Raising Issues In or Out of the Group

Roger Schwarz

IF YOU'VE BEEN A FACILITATOR, you've probably had a group member approach you outside the meeting and ask you to do something, such as raise an issue in the group, make sure the group doesn't discuss a particular issue, or steer the group conversation in a particular direction. At other times you may have wanted to talk to a group member alone, perhaps to ask this person to be more cooperative or less vocal. All of these situations raise the potential for taking you out of the facilitator role, reducing team members' accountability, and colluding with some group members against the full group.

SOME GUIDING PRINCIPLES

A few principles of the Skilled Facilitator approach can help you figure out how to respond in these situations. One principle is that **the group is the client.** This means that as a facilitator, you are responsible for helping the group as a whole rather than helping a subset of the group. It also means that you respond the same way to the group leader as you do to other group members. Another principle is that **people are responsible and accountable for their own information.** This means that they raise the issues they are concerned about in a way that others can inquire into their reasoning. A third principle, which follows from the second, is to **raise the issue where others with relevant information are able to respond.** This means that if some group members are concerned that other group members are slowing down the group, they raise their concerns in the full group because all group members have relevant information about the issue. Together, the principles, which follow from the core values and assumptions, guide your actions.

Guiding Principles

- The group is the client.
- People are responsible and accountable for their own information.
- Raise the issue where others with relevant information are able to respond.
- Be transparent.

WHEN GROUP MEMBERS APPROACH YOU

Consider a group member, Shawn, who approaches you outside a meeting and asks you to steer the conversation on the current topic, so that group members don't focus on outsourcing the graphics department. If you agree to do so, you act inconsistently with the three principles and create problems for the group and yourself. The accountability for raising Shawn's issue shifts from him, where it belongs, to you. Not raising the issue with the group prevents them from responding to Shawn's request before it is implemented. As a result, you would be treating Shawn, instead of the full group, as your client. In other words, you would be colluding with Shawn against the full group by unilaterally acting on his request without checking with the full group.

To meet Shawn's request, you would also have to act inconsistently with another principle: **be transparent**. If another group member realized that you were subtly steering the conversation and asked you why, it would be difficult to explain your strategy and say, "Shawn asked me to raise it for him." Your agreement with Shawn probably includes an implicit (if not explicit) understanding that you won't attribute your action to him.

UNDERSTANDING THEIR CONCERNS AND YOURS

Whether it's a request to simply raise an issue for a person or to take an action without explaining what you're doing, responding to this kind of request involves explaining the consequences you see, being curious about the person's interests (and assumptions), and designing a way to meet those interests without creating the negative consequences I identified above.

You might say something like, **"Shawn, if I did what you are asking, I think it would create some problems for the group, you, and me. I'm happy to explain the problems I see, but first I'm curious what leads you to want me to steer the conversation away from outsourcing instead of your suggesting to the group that you don't want to explore the outsourcing option."**

When Shawn responds, you can explore his interests and concerns and describe yours as well. As we know from the unilateral control model, group members are sometimes concerned about raising a difficult issue themselves because they want to minimize the expression of negative feelings or want to save face for others, for themselves, or both. They can't see how to raise the issue in a way that would be productive. At other times they are concerned that raising the issue explicitly will make it less likely that the conversation will go in the direction they want.

Chapter Four, "Understanding What Guides Your Behavior," page 33, introduces the unilateral control model. Chapter Forty-Three, "Developmental Facilitation," page 339, introduces developmental facilitation.

If this were part of a developmental facilitation, you could help Shawn explore his theory-in-use in depth and how it creates unintended consequences. In a basic facilitation, it is sufficient to briefly explain the unintended consequences, explain the limits of your facilitator role, and offer to coach the group member on raising the issue. You can say, **"For a few reasons, I can't do what you're asking. If I did, I would be accepting the responsibility for addressing your concern and unilaterally and surreptitiously directing the conversation to meet your interests instead of the full group's interests. As a result, the group wouldn't get a chance to decide whether they wanted to discuss the issue; they wouldn't have a free and informed choice. That's inconsistent with the agreement I made with the group about how I would act as a facilitator. Do you see any of this differently?"**

If Shawn does, explore the differences. If he shares your view, you can say, **"If you think it's important that the group not spend time on the outsourcing option, I encourage you to raise the issue. I'm willing to spend a couple of minutes now talking about how you can raise the issue. If you do raise it, I'll be there to facilitate the conversation and make it as effective as possible. What are your thoughts?"**

If Shawn is interested, you can spend the next few minutes coaching him on how to raise the issue in the full group. This is completely consistent with the facilitator role. As group members begin to take responsibility for addressing their own issues, the group becomes more effective and less dependent on you as the facilitator.

IT'S THE SAME WITH GROUP LEADERS

Whether Shawn approaches you as a group member or as the group leader, you would respond the same way. The group is still the client.

If the group leader recommended you, if he signs your check, or if he has influence over your career, it's natural to feel more pressure to comply with his request. But if you do this for the group leader, you send the message to the group that the principles you espouse apply only when the situation isn't difficult. This decreases your credibility as you fail to model the very behaviors you are asking of the group members. In the Skilled Facilitator approach, there is one set of principles that applies to all members regardless of how much power and authority they have.

> In the Skilled Facilitator approach, there is one set of principles that applies to all members regardless of how much power and authority they have.

IT WORKS BOTH WAYS

As a facilitator, approaching group members outside the meeting to ask them to raise issues or to influence their behavior creates the same problems as when individuals approach you. And it often stems from the same concerns about wanting to save face for others and yourself.

Consider a situation in which you think a group member, Tracy, is dominating the conversation and preventing other members from speaking. By speaking to Tracy outside the meeting, you shift the issue from the group members, where it belongs, to you. If you approach Tracy alone during a break and ask her if she can give others a chance to talk, you are unilaterally asking her to change her behavior based on what are probably inferences you've made from watching the group's behavior. You might have noticed other group members sighing or shaking their heads when Tracy starts to speak. But the only way to test the inferences is to ask the group members directly about what their behavior means. And the only way to test the inferences in a way that all the group members can hear all the relevant information is to do it in the group with Tracy present.

If you raise the issue in the team meeting using the ground rules and the diagnosis-intervention cycle, you enable all team members to share their relevant information with each other. You might begin by saying, **"I've noticed some people responding when Tracy speaks, and I want to check it out with you. Tim, Lee, and Sierra, I've noticed that when Tracy has spoken in the last fifteen minutes, you've either sighed or shaken your head. Did I see that correctly?** [If they say yes, continue.] **I'm thinking that you may have some concern about what she is saying or how often she is speaking. Am I misinterpreting?** [If they say no, continue.] **"Can you say what specifically Tracy is doing that concerns you?"**

By intervening in this way, you operate from and model the mutual learning approach. Instead of seeking to save face for group members and yourself, you help group members create an environment in which they can be accountable to address the issues that affect them.

PART FIVE

Seeking Your Path

Learning to use the Skilled Facilitator approach effectively requires a lot more than memorizing the core values and ground rules. Because it builds on mental models and deeply held values, the learning journey is lifelong and highly individual. Part Five begins with Chapter Thirty-Three, "Finding Your Voice," which offers some thoughts and tips for developing your authentic and unique way of integrating the Skilled Facilitator into your life.

The remaining chapters in Part Five share stories of what happened when people began to learn and use the Skilled Facilitator approach. In Chapter Thirty-Four, "Being a Mutual Learner in a Unilaterally Controlling World," Sue McKinney addresses questions individuals frequently have when they attend an off-site workshop and then go back to their organizations as the only person trying to use the Skilled Facilitator approach: "What will happen when I start using the skills and no one else understands what I am trying to do?" or "Can you use these skills if the other person does not know them?" Sue and Peter Hille also offer advice on going back to your organization in Chapter Thirty-Five, "Introducing the Skilled Facilitator Approach at Work," and Chapter Thirty-Six, "Bringing It All Back Home, or Open Mouth, Insert Foot." Here they share their own lessons learned when they returned "home" after a workshop. In Chapter Thirty-Seven, "A Carp in the Land of Koi," Susan Williams describes her first efforts and highlights the principles that she is finding particularly useful over time.

Chapter 33

Finding Your Voice

Anne Davidson

Like the shaman, the Zaddik instructs by metaphor, by indirection, not by teaching the pilgrims to be more like him, but to be more like themselves.

—Sheldon B. Kopp, *If You Meet the Buddha on the Road, Kill Him!*

WHEN PEOPLE BEGIN to learn the Skilled Facilitator approach, they frequently have two reactions. First, they despair of ever being able to "sound like Roger" (or Anne or Peg or Sue or any of our other associates and long-time practitioners). Usually they are somewhat abashed at their own initial efforts to use the core values and ground rules quickly and fluently. A second reaction is that they do not want to sound like us. They think our language is esoteric and stilted. They say they cannot imagine using the language of the ground rules in their day-to-day work environments. Or perhaps they have experienced a colleague returning from one of our workshops and "inferring them to death," so they believe using the principles will not be well received.

See Chapter Twenty-Four, "Reducing the Skilled Facilitator Jargon," page 207.

Both concerns are legitimate. We usually respond by speaking about finding alternative language and practicing the skills. These are helpful strategies. We are quick to point out that attending a Skilled Facilitator workshop is just the beginning of a learning journey. All of us are still learning. None of us became fluent until we practiced for years. And we still make mistakes and get tangled up in our own words sometimes. But I think the initial questions and our answers focus on producing or not producing specific behaviors. I believe the more fundamental question is how to find your own voice within this approach.

JOURNEYING INTO DEEPER SELF-AWARENESS

Finding your voice is more a pilgrimage than a journey. I mean *pilgrimage* not in the sense of a trip to a holy shrine, but in the sense of a long journey or search with exalted purpose—a search for truth or wisdom. And as Sheldon Kopp points out in his profound *If You Meet the Buddha on the Road, Kill Him!* (1972), most of us, wishing to learn, confuse being taught with learning. We are often socialized to think that if we mimic the teacher until we master the behavior, we can produce the same results. But copying a charismatic guru is more likely to produce an empty, ritualistic parody than the lively, spontaneous mastery of true substance and inspiration (Kopp, 1972). I believe that in addition to practicing and finding your own words, you have to find your unique identity within this approach. Only then do you speak with an authentic voice. And when you begin to train that voice, the specific words you choose become less important, because people more readily feel your deeper presence and hear your genuine intent.

Most of us, wishing to learn, confuse being taught with learning.

How you discover that voice and let it emerge depends very much on your personal story and your unique learning style and gifts. The short answer is to find a reflective practice and one or more ways of deepening your knowledge of self. There are many alternatives, from meditation, yoga, and journal writing, to using instruments like the Myers-Briggs Type Indicator (MBTI) or Firo-B. Some people find that just developing awareness of the left-hand column adds enough to their experience for them to gain deep insights. For others, their reflective practice is linked to their spiritual practice. What is helpful is highly individual.

See Chapter Fifty-Five, "The Skilled Facilitator Approach and the Myers-Briggs Type Indicator," page 437.

The more self-awareness you develop, the more present you can be in the moment while you are facilitating or in conversation and even while observing. And the more present you can be, the better able you are to tune into your thoughts and choose how you want to respond to a situation. It is your unique synergy of the Skilled Facilitator approach with your gifts that will create your authentic message and delivery.

It is your unique synergy of the Skilled Facilitator approach with your gifts that will create your authentic message and delivery.

In this chapter, I offer some specific suggestions that work for me or that others recommend. I hope you will experiment. I offer two cautions before you begin. First, I encourage you not to discount who you are and what you already know when you come anew to the Skilled Facilitator. You do want to reflect deeply on the core values and your own consistencies and inconsistencies, yet do this with loving compassion and curiosity. Reflect mindfully about what you want to keep and what is no longer serving your purposes.

Second, know that a part of the journey is to be out of touch with your own voice. Each of the primary authors of this book struggled in learning to use the approach consistently. Each of us at times used the language and the ground rules in ways that we later realized were unilateral or inauthentic. We learned because we created defensiveness, got gifts in the form of unintended results, or had colleagues kind enough to question us when something felt off about our intent. It will be a while before your voice can hit the right notes consistently. The first step is to quiet the mind so that you can nurture it. The power of your growing self-awareness will be spontaneity with the approach and the ability to improvise.

TIPS FOR FINDING YOUR VOICE

Here are some activities and practices that helped me and others reflect mindfully and authentically integrate the Skilled Facilitator approach into our work and our lives.

Lifeline Exercise

Use the lifeline exercise in Exhibit 17.1 (page 154) to renew your awareness of your personal strengths and talents. Expand question 5 to ask yourself how you can integrate the Skilled Facilitator into your strengths and talents. What are some things you do well that might be enhanced by integrating the ground rules and core values explicitly? How might your strengths enhance the way you use or explain the approach? How might you modify approaches you know and use well to be more consistent with the Skilled Facilitator approach?

Hot Buttons and Defensive Triggers

Periodically complete the exercise in Exhibit 33.1 to identify your biases and defensive triggers. This is useful during or soon after your initial exposure to the Skilled Facilitator and intermittently as you uncover layers of your own unilateral thinking and behavior.

Exhibit 33.1 Exercise: Identifying Your Biases and Defensive Triggers

Facilitators need to be aware of their systematic biases and personal issues (for example, needs for control or status) to reduce the chance that these biases and personal issues will distort their diagnoses and reduce their ability to intervene effectively. This exercise is designed to help you identify your biases and hot buttons. Here are the steps:

1. By yourself (or with someone who knows you well and whom you trust to give you honest feedback), identify the following:
   - Things that people do that really bother you
   - Group situations that you find embarrassing and/or threatening
   - Things that you really dislike about yourself
   - The values and beliefs that you consider most important
   - Prejudices that you have
2. Take one or more items from the list. Think of a situation in which the items decreased your ability to accurately diagnose and intervene in a group. Think about how your feelings about that issue may have led you to make untested inferences and attributions about one or more people in the group.

Source: The author of this exhibit is Dick McMahon.

Five Key Principles and Reflection Questions

It is helpful to know the ground rules in order to intervene and code behavior, but I have found it more useful in developing my own approach to focus on the core values. I also like to frame my approach as five key principles: Compassion, Curiosity, Transparency, Commitment, and Accountability. Try asking yourself as you develop this approach:

- Am I being compassionate toward myself and the others in the room?
- Am I staying open and curious? What is it I want to learn, know, or question?
- Am I sharing what I am really thinking? Am I modeling the transparent way we want to work together?[1]
- Am I committed to being here and doing this work with those present? How am I showing that? Am I working with those present in ways that help them find their own answers rather than telling them what to do?
- Am I holding myself accountable for my contributions to this encounter? Am I doing anything that others could and should do for themselves? Am I working in ways that decrease dependency on me in the long run? Am I holding others fully accountable for their choices?

These are also useful reflection questions to ask after a conversation or facilitation (Was I . . . ? Did I . . . ?).

Self-Assessment Instruments

Instruments like the MBTI or the Herrmann Brain Dominance Instrument[2] can be helpful in deepening your awareness of how you learn and how you communicate, as long as you use them as a mirror for reflection, not as a definitive description of your personality. It helps me, for example, to understand that my Intuitive preference has created a strength in explaining broad concepts to others and in thinking of metaphors that help people grasp concepts. My ENFP skills are valued for inspiring people. But my language and interventions do not have the precision of Roger's. Knowing my dominance and preferences for taking in and thinking about information helps me value my own voice, but I also know when I need to sing backup or ask someone else to do so.

Mindfulness Practice

Breath work, mind-body practices like yoga and tai chi, and most forms of meditation offer guidance in stilling the mind and learning to be present. My own use of Skilled Facilitator skills is greatly enhanced by yoga practice. When I practice regularly, I have more energy for attending to others, my concentration improves, and the chatter of worrying and planning is silenced. Learning to let go, to breathe into postures and play edges, also creates metaphors that I often use in my own mind as I listen carefully to dialogue.[3] Without cultivating some form of mindfulness, it is very difficult to fully hear your left-hand column thoughts, discern the aspects of your own voice that you want to enhance, and have the presence to incorporate changes in the moment.

Journaling and Drawing

Writing and drawing are excellent ways to access our own unconscious thoughts and desires. I find that reflective journal writing also helps me access my thoughts about myself and my experiences, especially when completed soon after a facilitation or early in the morning when I am fresh.[4]

Conscious Practice

People frequently tell me that one of the barriers to finding their own Skilled Facilitator voice is that they cannot practice using the approach frequently enough. I am always surprised and confused about how to respond, because I find every conversation an opportunity to practice. I can always use the principles to shape my own conversation or use any conversation as an opportunity to attend more fully to my left-hand column thoughts and to know myself better in this and similar situations. This skill does require some reflection after a conversation. For years, I wrote notes to myself during meetings about how to say what I was thinking, even if I had no intention of saying those things then. After a while, I found I could say the things I wanted fluently because of my paper practice. And when conversations did not go well, I often wrote out ways that I thought I could have communicated more clearly and in my own words, without jargon. Gradually I was able to frame what I wanted to say quickly enough to respond during a conversation.

See also Chapter Twenty-One, "Ways to Practice the Ground Rules," page 189.

Attending to Language

I recommend attending to language. There are numerous unilateral concepts embedded in the way we phrase sentences and the words we choose. We often use the imperative voice with others, even when we want to give them informed choices—for example, "Get that up on the flip chart" instead of, "I think it would be helpful to get that up. Do you?" or "Would you be willing to ___________ because I think that would be useful." Many of the words we choose have metaphors embedded in them that can lead us down the slippery slope of sounding unilateral even when that is not our intention—for example, "*Capture* that on the easel, would you?" or "Let's talk about how to *deploy* this plan."

Authentic intention comes across more powerfully than word choice, but word choice can create confusion in our own minds as well as create confusion about our intentions in the minds of others. Another way to practice consciously is to tape-record yourself in conversation (with permission of all parties, of course) and do your own critique and redesign after the fact. I sometimes ask myself, "What other words could I have used there that might sound more like my personality?"

CONCLUSION

Finding your own way of expressing the Skilled Facilitator principles and techniques takes work. The work is hard partly because it is as much about letting go of old voices as it is about discovering new ones. The unlearning can be demanding and humbling. But doing that work will pay rich dividends for your own personal development and peace of mind. Every year that I mindfully practice, I find that I reach a few more high notes.

Resources

Cameron, J, with Bryan, M. *The Artist's Way.* New York: Putnam, 1992.

FIRO-B Self Scorable. Palo Alto: CPP, 1996. *FIRO-B PROFILE.* Palo Alto: CPP, 1989. Available to qualified users. [www.cpp.com.]

Herrmann International. *The Hermann Brain Dominance Instrument.* Lake Lure, N.C.: Herrmann International, 1989. [www.hbdi.com].

Myers-Briggs Type Indicator Self-Scorable. Palo Alto: CPP, 1998. *Myers-Briggs Type Indicator Form Q.* Palo Alto: CPP, 2001. Available to qualified users. [www.cpp.com].

Progoff, I. *At a Journal Workshop.* Los Angeles: Tarcher, 1992.

Tolle, E. *The Power of Now: A Guide to Spiritual Enlightenment.* Novato, Calif.: New World Library, 1999.

Notes

1. See Kopp (1972, pp. 20–27) for some helpful thoughts about transparency.
2. There are a number of useful instruments available that are well tested and validated, for example, the Myers-Briggs Type Indicator, the Firo-B, and the Hermann instruments. See also Chapter Fifty-Five, "The Skilled Facilitator Approach and the Myers-Briggs Type Indicator," page 437.
3. Readings in this area, such as Eckhart Tolle's *The Power of NOW* (1999) may offer places to begin your personal practice of mindfulness.

4. For guidance in journaling techniques and visual expression, see Julia Cameron's *The Artist's Way* (1992) or Ira Progoff's *At a Journal Workshop* (1992).

References

Cameron, J., with Bryan, M. *The Artist's Way.* New York: Putnam, 1992.

Kopp, S. B. *If You Meet the Buddha on the Road, Kill Him!* New York: Bantam, 1972.

Progoff, I. *At a Journal Workshop.* Los Angeles: Tarcher, 1992.

Tolle, E. *The Power of Now: A Guide to Spiritual Enlightenment.* Novato, Calif.: New World Library, 1999.

Chapter 34

Being a Mutual Learner in a Unilaterally Controlling World

Sue McKinney

When people first learn the Skilled Facilitator approach, they often express concern about using the skills at work when no one else will understand what they are trying to do. They express fear and trepidation about trying to change when others will still be acting unilaterally. They worry that others may interpret their new behaviors as new strategies for manipulating them. My experience is that these fears are well founded. People do misinterpret new behaviors through their unilateral lenses. At the same time, I can still change my behavior to act more consistently with the Skilled Facilitator approach in this environment.

The first thing I had to learn was that I couldn't change myself overnight, I couldn't change the organization overnight, and I couldn't change anyone else either. But I wanted to. I wanted to wave a magic wand and make my world mutually learning. Over time, I learned that I was most successful when I attempted small changes: testing an assumption I was making or asking someone if he or she would test an assumption; sharing my reasoning or asking someone about his or her thinking; or asking a group to identify the interests underlying the solutions they were proposing. Later, I learned that while practicing the ground rules was helpful, changing my perspective from judgmental to curious made the most profound impact on my ability to stay consistent with the model under stressful conditions.

> Practicing the ground rules was helpful, but even more helpful was changing my perspective from judgmental to curious.

It is harder to practice the approach and master the skills when you are the only one in your work environment trying to apply the model. One of the challenges is that coworkers know who you are, or at least think they do, and they don't always support attempts at change since that may require that they change too.

> One of the challenges is that coworkers know who you are, or at least think they do, and they don't always support attempts at change since that may require that they change too.

When people don't know you and you are the only person practicing the skills, you may have a better chance of success simply because others don't see using mutual learning skills as a change in your personality. Instead, they see this approach as a part of who you are.

I've been in both situations. I found it much easier to be the solo practitioner of the mutual learning skills in a new environment. There I walked in the door and tested assumptions, shared my reasoning, and was curious about the perspective of others, and others just saw this as an aspect of my personality. When I attempted to use the skills with people who already knew me, I encountered much more resistance to my attempts to use the ground rules and follow the core values. I believe that this may have to do with the years of history that people who know me have had with me. In the past, I reacted unilaterally in all kinds of situations. People developed beliefs about who I was as a person and what I thought and how I would react in different situations. Given these layers of assumptions and inferences about my behavioral motivations, when I tried to behave differently in similar situations after my training, I think some people had a hard time believing I had fundamentally changed my beliefs and thinking. I think they thought it was a new strategy or trick to get them to do what I wanted. In those situations, I simply had to stay curious and continue trying to practice the new approach to demonstrate that the change was a permanent one.

SEEKING SUPPORT FOR CHANGING YOUR BEHAVIOR

When you are trying to change your behavior in an environment where people already know you, there are steps to make it easier. One is to let others know that you are trying to use some new skills and would benefit from feedback about how it is going. Another is to find someone who can provide you with support and coaching. An outsider can reflect with you on comments you may receive from coworkers, supervisors, and direct reports who are trying to respond to your changing behavior.

A couple of years after I took the training, one of my colleagues who had just come through the Skilled Facilitator training invited me to join a learning group that would be meeting about one hour from where I lived. As the only person in my organization practicing the skills, I felt isolated, so I instantly agreed to participate. I participated in this learning group for about six months. Being in the group was helpful for many reasons: it kept the material in front of me, I saw how others were using it, I felt supported in my struggles to master the skills, and we had the opportunity to intervene with one another when we were not acting consistently with the approach. The learning group used left-hand column cases, role play, and dialogue to practice the skills and talk about what was working and what was not working. It was a good use of time.

One of the challenges for everyone is that changes are usually erratic and not always productive. As you try to produce behaviors that are consistent with the Skilled Facilitator approach, you may not always succeed. While you may not be successful on the first try, you can always ask for people's patience and request that you try a previous conversation again. As I practiced, I began to ask for what I came to call "redos": going back to someone after having an ineffective conversation and asking for the opportunity to have the conversation again so I could try to stay consistent with the facilitative values and ground rules. No one ever turned me down for a redo, and the conversation always went better the second time.

It is important to recognize that many of the individuals giving you feedback will be operating in a unilateral model, so their feedback comes in that form. It can be a formidable task to translate this unilateral feedback into information that can help you act more consistently with the mutual learning model. For example, I've heard comments like this: "I don't like it when you keep asking me if I 'see it differently.' You clearly want it your way, so why do you ask?" Such a statement and question requires me to note that the speaker is making an inference: that I want it my way. Instead of getting upset about being misunderstood (because my intent is not to have it my way), I focus on what I'm doing that is causing the person to think I'm not genuinely interested in his or her perspective. It may be the repetitive use of the question, "Do you see it differently?" or it may be that when the person answers with a different perspective, I always challenge it, arguing that my perspective is more accurate, or it could be something else that I'm not aware that I'm doing. Asking for feedback and receiving it openly models a new way of expressing the core values. Expecting some of the feedback to be unilateral can help you prepare for that eventuality.

It is important to recognize that many of the individuals giving you feedback will be operating in a unilateral model, so their feedback comes in that form.

YOU CAN CHANGE ONLY YOU

As I began to pay more attention to my own unilateral behavior rather than being focused on changing others, I began to notice things in myself that I hadn't seen before. For example, every so often when something was said, I started to feel hot and almost sweaty or tingly, from my head to my toes. I began to recognize the meaning of this on two levels: as anger that had been triggered and as a likely clue that I was making an untested inference about something that was just said. I found that I wasn't always good at recognizing my own inferences and assumptions and this hot feeling was a useful cue. Over time, I could more quickly figure out what specifically had been said that was leading me to make a negative inference about someone else. With experience, I began to realize that a lot of the time, my anger was unjustified and that when I lowered my inference and tested it, I found that I had misinterpreted or misunderstood the situation.

With experience, I began to realize that a lot of the time, my anger was unjustified and that when I lowered my inference and tested it, I found that I had misinterpreted or misunderstood the situation.

As I learned to recognize when a hot button had been pushed, I also found it useful to notice what kinds of comments push my hot buttons. I began to recognize that I had some deeply held beliefs about myself that when challenged caused me to become defensive and angry. One of my beliefs is that I am able to be an effective advocate for employees while also understanding and representing the top management viewpoints. When someone in a meeting contradicts what employees have said to me, I immediately start to get angry. For example, employees had told me that they like their organization but get frustrated when management doesn't take their requests seriously. In a meeting, a top manager stated that the employees are "whiners who don't appreciate what they have in this organization." I **knew** (the key word here is *knew,* a red flag that I'm becoming unilateral) that wasn't true. I immediately got hot and was ready with a quick retort. In time, I was able to monitor my reactions when we got into a discussion about employee perspectives, knowing that I was prone to overreact to comments about the employees that I perceived as at all negative.

Over time, as I employed the skills more consistently, I began to notice that I experienced less conflict with others. In reflecting on this, I realized that by testing my assumptions about others and sharing my reasoning with them, there was less "story" telling than there had been in my life previously. Here is an example:

I was facilitating a large meeting and made a summary statement to the group. When I finished, one of the executives said she had a different perspective and made a statement that sounded identical to mine (in concepts rather than exact wording). I was confused by her statement and was thinking, "Isn't that what I just said! Isn't she listening?" (this was my story or explanation of what led her to make the statement). But remembering my skills, I asked her, "Bonnie, it sounds as if you think what you just stated is something different from what I stated. Is that accurate?" She said it was. I replied, "Then I'm confused, because your statement sounds the same as mine." I turned to the group and asked what others thought: Were these two different ideas or the same ones? The group gave their response, and both Bonnie and I learned more about each other's perspective. Instead of being angry, I learned. In addition, this kind of exchange changed how people viewed me. Instead of discounting Bonnie and saying, "Bonnie, that is what I just said," and trying to move the group along, I acknowledged her statement, stayed open to the fact that I might be misunderstanding what she said, and explored both of our perspectives more fully. In response, Bonnie never felt belittled, misunderstood, or ignored. These small exchanges, compiled over time, changed the way people viewed me.

NO GUARANTEES FOR SUCCESS

There are, of course, times when modeling mutual learning yourself will not resolve a situation. In my case, I tried to use the skills in a top-down, command-and-control environment, in which I was fairly new and not skilled at acting consistently with the mutual learning model:

In this organization, the CEO requested I attend the training, my supervisor supported the concepts and attempted to give me feedback, and I had an outside mentor-coach who helped me reflect on my behaviors and how I was acting consistently or inconsistently with the Skilled Facilitator approach. Even with all of this, I ran head-on into a wall with the CEO.

The CEO was attempting to change the organizational culture from top-down decision making to decision making at the lowest level possible. This cultural shift required that employees be willing to make decisions on their own and occasionally challenge their supervisors. He often complained that even among his own department heads, no one would openly disagree with him. He expressed frustration that once he stated his opinion, most, if not all, the department heads would agree with him.

Knowing that he wanted this cultural shift and understanding his frustration with the department heads' lack of willingness to challenge him openly, I, as the hired change agent, took it on myself to act in ways I believed modeled behaviors consistent with mutual learning and consistent with his desires. In meetings, I would openly disagree and challenge his thinking. Unfortunately for me, this was never greeted with enthusiasm and was often quickly and tersely squashed. After a particularly harsh encounter, I went to the CEO to talk about this issue. I felt that acting consistently with the mutual learning model required me to share my concerns with the CEO and try to figure out how we could work more effectively together. I shared my dilemma with him. As I saw the situation, I knew he wanted the culture to shift and wanted employees to disagree openly and challenge his thinking. I believed he wanted me to change the culture, and he agreed this was true. I thought that the best way I could do this was to model the behavior he was seeking, and he thought this made sense. Yet when I attempted to do so, he appeared to get angry and quash my attempts. He agreed this had happened; he considered my behavior as challenging him, and he did not like it. I asked him if he had thoughts about how I could resolve this dilemma. He did not.

SEEKING YOUR OWN BEST PATH

It was shortly after this encounter that I decided to begin looking for a new job. I wanted to work with leaders who might feel challenged by me but would view such challenges as worthy of reflection that might lead to behavioral change. Although I think it is possible to be a successful solo practitioner, changing your behavior and thereby encouraging different responses from others, I also think you may choose a different route.

There are times when finding more fertile ground for practicing and mastering the Skilled Facilitator approach makes sense. This is a choice each one of us makes given our temperament, interests, career goals, and other needs. Whatever choice you make, as long as you are committed to practicing Skilled Facilitator core values and skills, there will be settings that are more challenging and others that are more supportive to your attempts to act consistently with the approach. Deciding how to create the most conducive environment is up to each of us.

There are times when finding more fertile ground for practicing and mastering the Skilled Facilitator approach makes sense. This is a choice each one of us makes given our temperament, interests, career goals, and other needs.

Chapter 35

Introducing the Skilled Facilitator Approach at Work

Pitfalls and Successes

Sue McKinney

AT THE END OF A SKILLED FACILITATOR workshop, we often hear from participants that this approach has completely altered the way they view the world. Unfortunately, many first efforts to share the approach are still built on a unilateral mind-set.

A DISMAL FIRST ATTEMPT

I took Skilled Facilitator training shortly after beginning a new job as an employee trainer for a local municipality. A few weeks after the training, I began working with an external consultant who had been previously engaged by the organization to introduce an ambitious continuous improvement process with an emphasis on teamwork. We had plans to train sixteen teams within the first few months of rolling out the new concept. I insisted that we include training on the sixteen ground rules for all teams.[1]

The consultant was understandably reluctant to change the training materials and process that he had developed for this organization. I told him that this new way of facilitating groups was wonderful, and we had to do it or miss out on a great opportunity. He eventually agreed that it might be useful and suggested that we change the wording of the ground rules since he found them to be full of jargon and hard to understand. I stood my ground and explained that they could not be changed, as they were copyrighted. Moreover, my colleagues had told me that the ground rules as written worked in their municipalities and urged me not to underestimate the ability of employees to understand and use the ground rules as written.

The consultant asked me why I was being so rigid about this approach. I don't remember the exact word that he used, but *dogmatic* was probably close. Eventually he acquiesced, and I added the sixteen ground rules to our training curriculum. All the teams went through a two-day class that included a four-hour overview of the core values and ground rules. At the end of the class, I asked the teams if they would be willing to use the ground rules (allowing for free and informed choice, I thought). Overall, people thought they made sense and agreed to use them with their teams.

Over time, it became obvious that few, if any, of the teams were using the ground rules. The two teams I worked with used them only when I brought them up. No one demonstrated an interest in or the capacity to use the ground rules without my assistance. It became clear to me that my approach for introducing them had not worked.

In the spirit of the self-critique, I can now reflect on how many of the ground rules I had ignored in my zealous effort and how, in those heady days directly following my training in the Skilled Facilitator approach, I had not yet fully internalized the meaning of the mutual learning model. While I was trying to act with intellectual integrity by maintaining the language of the Skilled Facilitator ground rules exactly as it was presented, I didn't have a deep enough understanding of the mental models to understand that my attempts to introduce the concepts were extremely unilateral. Unilateral control can trigger defensiveness and resistance, and this case was no exception. When the external consultant asked questions, I never heard a word he said. I wasn't being curious about his perspective, that is, engaging in honest inquiry. I ignored his attempts to share the relevant information about the groundwork he had already laid for this effort. Because I wasn't interested in what he had to say, we did not jointly design next steps.

I have since learned that this is an easy trap to fall into. Another colleague of mine, Tom Moore, also took an enthusiastic approach to introducing the ground rules in the department he led. He came back to work after his training with Roger Schwarz with Skilled Facilitator ground rules pocket cards stuck in his front shirt pocket, gleefully handing them out to everyone he encountered like a new father handing out cigars. He told everyone that this was the "new way" for himself and the department to behave. His employees were rather unimpressed with his newly found leadership approach and figured this would pass soon. Over the years, Tom modified his unilateral approach to introducing the ground rules and was able to change the entire department's way of doing business to be more consistent with the Skilled Facilitator approach.

See Chapter Thirty-Eight, "Daily Challenges of a Facilitative Leader," page 309.

A MORE SUCCESSFUL ATTEMPT

A few years later, I took a job as the director of organization development in a midsized international nonprofit organization. During the hiring process, I was challenged to explain my philosophy and interest in bringing Skilled Facilitator skills to the organization. I felt that I had to share enough information so that the hiring manager could make a good decision about hiring me, yet I was aware that there was no way, without immersing himself in learning the approach, that he could fully understand the implications of my using it.

During the interviews, I was candid about my core values, the ground rules, and the generalities of mental models and theory-in-use. I explained that I wanted to work with an organization that was interested in using this approach. I wanted to interview the organization to see if I thought it was fertile ground for adopting mutual learning. I told the hiring manager that I thought it would take a while for the organization to learn enough about the approach to determine if it wanted to try to use it. I also told him that if the organization should decide in the future not to use the approach, I would probably choose to leave myself since it was my goal to work with an entire organization that would use this approach to communicate, train, and develop policies and procedures.

Happily for me, the hiring manager offered me the position. Entering in this manner gave me a much stronger foundation than I had in the municipal organization I had just left. Over the next year, as employees watched me model the skills, they began to imitate some of the things that I said in meetings. For example, when meetings began to bog down in discussions over what to do next, I would suggest the group members identify the underlying drivers for the solutions each was proposing. I told them that I called these drivers "interests," and that once we identified them, we might have a better chance of finding a solution that would meet many or all of them. This often helped a meeting move along more effectively, so over time, individuals would get into similar situations and say something like, "I'm going to play Sue for a moment and suggest we identify our interests so we can come up with a solution we can all live with." I don't think they fully understood my approach, but they understood what worked and they attempted to apply the skills themselves. This was a huge bonus when we began Skilled Facilitator training throughout the organization.

After working with me for a year, the executive team felt they had enough information to offer the training to their middle managers to see what the middle managers thought. When the entire first group that had attended the training recommended that others take the workshop, the executives agreed to offer the training throughout the organization, including staff from each overseas office. Today, this organization continues to offer the training and continues to challenge itself to live consistently with the core values and ground rules.

A SUCCESSFUL APPROACH IN A LARGE ORGANIZATION

Over the past seven years, I have watched a large organization slowly embrace Skilled Facilitator concepts, train hundreds of employees, and adjust some policies based on the influence of Gail Young, a Mecklenburg County, North Carolina, Land Use and Environmental Services division staff member. Gail, one of my mentors and colleagues, recently shared her approach to introducing the Skilled Facilitator concepts into the organization. She explained that she never consciously set out to change the organization or the people in it. After going through the Skilled Facilitator class, Gail recognized that she wasn't being internally consistent, and this bothered her. She felt that the goals she had in conversations had been manipulative, and she didn't like that about herself. She made the commitment that she would become more internally consistent—to be a person with integrity. That personal decision led to gradual, sustainable organizational change.

Having made the commitment to change her own behavior, Gail felt it was important to let those she worked with most closely know what she was doing. This was initially difficult, since she was the only one in her organization who had been through Skilled Facilitator training. Her first step was to share information about the approach with the other members of her division's leadership team. She shared a basic article about the core values and ground rules, explaining that this was the foundation of her new approach to communication. She asked team members who were willing to read the article and give her feedback when they thought she was acting more or less effectively than she had in the past.

The leadership team agreed to do this. For Gail, leadership meetings became a place for trying out new skills. Instead of assuming that she understood others' points of view, she was curious and explored their thinking and checked to be certain her perceptions were accurate. She shared her reasoning, explored theirs, and focused the group on their underlying interests. The team was intrigued by these changes, and after a few months, they expressed interest in attending training themselves.

Even before they went through training, team members began to mimic what Gail was saying. A member would ask, "Shouldn't we look at our interests before we try to solve this problem?" or "Are you making an assumption about that?" After the first Skilled Facilitator training in the organization, class members came up to Gail and said, "Oh, now I get it! I understand why you talk this way." This was almost identical to my second attempt introducing the approach in the small nonprofit where I worked.

Since that successful first training, Gail's organization has continued to offer training two or three times a year. Internal trainers have been developed. And now the initiative is spreading to the city government in a partnership between the county and city organizations.

I have learned a lot from this example and I love what Gail has to say about her style: "It is important to me that every individual chooses their own direction and changes. I chose and needed support from my friends, but I never expected others to choose the same path. This is a fundamental belief for me. For me, it defines having dignity and respect for others."

THE POWER OF MODELING NEW BEHAVIORS AND BELIEFS

While it may seem like a truism, the best way to introduce the Skilled Facilitator approach into an organization is through methods that are consistent with its core values and the mutual learning model. Tom Moore and I learned the hard way that unilaterally telling people that the Skilled Facilitator approach was the best way to operate a business was not only inconsistent with the approach but a good way to build resistance. Like Gail, we have both learned the value of changing ourselves.

By initially concentrating on growth of self, it became possible to more fully appreciate the full breadth of the Skilled Facilitator approach and avoid the easy trap of adopting the unilateral control model in an attempt to drag a recalcitrant world into enlightenment. These changes can introduce new issues, such as long-time coworkers' recognizing and wondering about the difference in one's communication style and language. By recognizing these issues and gaining the participation of those coworkers in one's learning, as Gail did, we can begin the process of modeling behavior within the organization. Ultimately, changing ourselves has allowed us to model this different way of communicating, handling conflict, and making decisions. In changing our own behavior, we have been much more successful at helping others see the value of the Skilled Facilitator approach.

By initially concentrating on growth of self, it became possible to more fully appreciate the full breadth of the Skilled Facilitator approach and avoid the easy trap of adopting the unilateral control model in an attempt to drag a recalcitrant world into enlightenment.

Note

1. In the first edition of *The Skilled Facilitator* (1994), there were sixteen ground rules. In 2002, the second edition reduced the list to nine ground rules.

Chapter 36

Bringing It All Back Home, or Open Mouth, Insert Foot

Peter Hille and the Staff of the Brushy Fork Institute

When Peter Hille first mentioned that he had been to a workshop and learned new facilitation techniques, my first thought was, *Mercy, he's always wanting to learn something new—something new to make my life more complicated.*

PETER'S EXPLANATION

At the end of our week of Skilled Facilitator training, I had the opportunity to do one more role play: how to introduce what I had learned to my colleagues back home. I volunteered to give it a try, confident that my staff would be receptive. Privately I was thinking, "This should be easy." My partners in the role-play had other ideas. As I started to lay out the new ideas and techniques I'd learned, they began to pepper me with questions and loaded comments. *Wait,* I thought, *my real staff won't react like this.* Then I looked around and realized they were all doing a pretty good job in the role play, and I was in for a challenge when I got back home.

I direct Brushy Fork Institute, a community leadership development program with a staff of four, and facilitation is central to our work. Many of our operating principles are grounded in what I consider to be the mutual learning model, such as recognizing that our participants, not we, are the real experts on their communities. However, the Skilled Facilitator approach has provided a new and concrete way for me to think about how to operate in ways more consistent with those core principles. Role-playing how to present this to my staff helped me realize that even given a supportive conceptual framework for this in our organization, I would need to be thoughtful and creative in introducing the approach. One of the key learnings from the role play was that if the head of the organization goes off and learns a new approach, there is a limit to how much free and informed choice the staff has in experiencing the effects.

If the head of the organization goes off and learns a new approach, there is a limit to how much free and informed choice the staff has in experiencing the effects.

I started with a written communication so I could be mindful about how I introduced the topic. Within the memo, I tried to use some illustrations of the ground rules, pointing back to my own statements to show how they work:

> Hi, folks,
>
> I'd like to share with you all some of what I learned at the workshop last week. The workshop was intense, challenging and rewarding. I got some good insights into my own facilitation style and some ideas about how to become more effective. I'm interested in putting these into practice. As I try to get my head wrapped around some of these process techniques, I'd like to engage anyone who is interested in helping me evaluate both the techniques themselves and how well I am doing at implementing them. By the way, in case you were wondering, in this experiment I'm the guinea pig!
>
> This model is based on four core values and ten ground rules [there were ten at the time]. They are:
>
> *Core Values*
>
> 1. Valid information
> 2. Free and informed choice
> 3. Internal commitment
> 4. Compassion
>
> *Ground Rules*
>
> 1. Test assumptions and inferences.
> 2. Share all relevant information.
> 3. Use specific examples and agree on what important words mean.
> 4. Discuss undiscussable issues.
> 5. Focus on interests, not positions.
> 6. Explain your reasoning and intent.
> 7. Combine advocacy with inquiry.
> 8. Jointly design next steps and ways to test disagreements.
> 9. Keep the discussion focused.
> 10. Use a decision-making rule that generates the level of commitment needed.
>
> My observation is that none of this is inconsistent with Brushy Fork's approach, but I find it is more explicit in some aspects. It also provides some concrete ways to think about operationalizing these ideas. I wanted to share all this with you on the front end, since it is relevant information (see Ground Rule Two, above). My intention is to give you enough information to help you make a free and informed choice about how much you'd like to engage with me in exploring

this model. (I'm explaining my reasoning and intent—Ground Rule Six, above—and also trying to honor the "free and informed choice" value.) I won't be asking for anyone's buy-in on this until you've had a chance to check it out yourself and have any questions answered.

A good way to start into this would be for you all to read a little bit about this model. There is a short article, "The Skilled Facilitator Approach," at this Web site:
http://www.schwarzassociates.com/sfa.htm

Also, I have another short article on the values and ground rules. Let me know if you'd like to see that.

I'd like for us to get together so I can flesh this out by sharing some of what was presented at the workshop. We could also look at a video they shot at the workshop of me facilitating and being critiqued, which would give us some concrete examples of how this method works. Then we could discuss this approach and talk about how it fits with what we do. I think we should set aside a time to do this rather than just try to fit it into a regular staff meeting—perhaps two or even three hours. How does this sound to each of you? (By the way, I'm combining advocacy with inquiry: Ground Rule Seven, above). If you have other suggestions about how we might proceed, or if you have any questions, please let me know.

With that beginning I thought I could go ahead and start to talk about the model and use some of the ground rules in our staff meetings while we worked up to taking a staff retreat to get more in-depth. It wasn't easy, as one staff member observed: "At first, Peter was unsure about how to share what he had learned." Another was more pointed: "And because Peter wasn't yet good at what he was teaching, his behavior seemed stilted and fake. 'Tina,' he drawled, 'should I infer from what you said that . . . ?' I thought he had lost his mind—and that I'd lose mine if I had to put up with much of that."

Somehow we all survived for a few weeks until we could take a day to get into the approach in more depth. I shared my left-hand column case ahead of time, as well as Roger's memo explaining how to write one, and encouraged everyone to try their hand at writing one of their own. I suggested that viewing my role-play video from the workshop might be a good way for the rest of the staff to get a sense of how the training worked and to have some entertainment at my expense.

We began our retreat with some good food and coffee, then started exploring some of the dilemmas for facilitators from the workshop. This helped everyone get into the shared mind-set of seeing that we could benefit from better tools to help us solve such problems. From there, we spent some time talking through the values, ground rules, unilateral control and mutual learning models, and the diagnosis-intervention cycle. We had carved out enough time for this so we could talk, reflect, and apply all this to our work. And everyone did enjoy watching me fumble through the videos.

STAFF COMMENTS

When Roger asked me to write about sharing this with my staff, we both thought it would be good to hear from them also. As I asked them to share their observations, it was gratifying to find they have all found the Skilled Facilitator approach useful:

> As time went on and I saw Peter applying these new ideas, I realized that what he was doing is the same thing I do at home. When I see one of my children sulking in a corner, I ask questions to learn what is going on in their heads. I also recognized that the rules Peter was initiating were simply a kind and gentle way of treating people and getting the most out of discussion.
>
> Not only did I start to appreciate this new way of facilitating at work, but I began to notice in my personal life how often people ignore these rules. I know that often I don't comprehend a situation because I take what I hear with preconceived ideas and without seeking clarity by questioning. I am more careful now, and my life is less confusing. Questioning to understand is much better than jumping to conclusions—often wrong conclusions.
>
> No, I didn't win the lottery and I wasn't elected president and George Clooney hasn't asked me out yet. But I have become more willing to ask questions and to offer necessary information to others, so my communication skills have improved. I guess it's okay to learn something new every once in a while.—Tina Collins

> My initial impression was positive, but I was unsure how I might use the ground rules in my work or life. My reaction to Peter's bringing ground rules to a staff meeting was that if it can help improve how we work together, I am all for it. Peter was very careful about introducing the concepts and was mindful of its being new to us. The one ground rule that really impressed me was, "Test assumptions and inferences." I have a tendency to make high-level inferences based on my biases. This occurs at work but seems especially true for me at home, where I am quick to make assumptions in conversations with my wife. I began to test assumptions and inferences and asked my wife to help by pointing out instances when I made inferences without support. Using this ground rule as a framework, we have improved our communication.—Van Gravitt

> When Peter introduced the ground rules for effective groups, I was in the midst of dealing with a problem. I had been working with a team in the Brushy Fork Leadership Development Program. Three months or so into their project, they encountered a conflict that threatened to divide the group based on county politics.
>
> My first impulse was to tell them what I thought they should do, but as a facilitator, I was supposed to resist providing my opinion and instead give them techniques through which they could resolve their own issues. Peter and I had a discussion about how to apply the ground rules for effective groups, particularly focusing on interests, not positions; explaining the reasons behind one's statements, questions, and actions; and discussing undiscussable issues.

I felt that the ground rules worked well for that group, but I wasn't sure whether I still had a good handle on them. I didn't find the ground rules for effective groups easy to remember, so I kept them posted on the wall in my office, near my computer where I might refer to them when I was talking or sending e-mail to group members. Still, I wondered whether I would ever begin using them intuitively, particularly in group situations where I was a member.

For me, the ground rules have been more difficult to incorporate in my own situation, so I figure I will have to become very intentional about using them. Being so intentional makes the process feel a little forced. Learning to apply the ground rules will take time as I work to interpret and internalize what each rule means.—Donna Morgan

PETER'S CONCLUSION

As for me, I'm still struggling to implement the model in my day-to-day work, both in and out of the office. At a recent follow-up session, Roger assured us that we shouldn't expect to master all the ground rules at once. I can say that at least we established a solid foundation within our staff that provides a supportive environment for all of us to keep working on it.

Chapter 37

A Carp in the Land of Koi

Susan R. Williams

I WORK IN A MISSION-BASED company—one that is somewhat progressive compared to other counterparts in the industry. I attended the Skilled Facilitator workshop with the aim of absorbing the approach to help me edit a revised version of *The Skilled Facilitator.* Although I did hope to walk away with some useful skills, I felt it necessary to try to keep some sort of objective distance. How impossible that turned out to be.

I found myself realizing that the Skilled Facilitator approach was at the heart of honest and open communication practices that could and should be used in all human interaction. This was an exciting approach—one that as soon as you learn it seems so simple. Now why can't we all behave this way all the time?

I found myself realizing that the Skilled Facilitator approach was at the heart of honest and open communication practices that could and should be used in all human interaction.

Once through with my week-long immersion, I returned to the workplace, ready to work with Roger Schwarz on the book and put the ideas into practice: on my team, in meetings, with folks on the street. We would have honest communication, we would have no inference ladders, and we would tell it like it is. Now, it's important to know that before leaving for the week-long Skilled Facilitator training, we attendees were asked to write up our own personal left-hand column cases. Since I pride myself on authenticity and always thought I was using a direct approach, the fact that my left-hand column case clearly showed how incongruent my thoughts were to my action was disconcerting. And yet, once through the training, I thought the knowledge and best intentions would work to help me override any unilateral control behaviors that might occasionally rear their head.

Being a generally enthusiastic person, I returned to work to start putting the behaviors into practice. What I quickly realized was that this was work. Although I explained the approach to others (and some people were familiar with the approach simply because of the book), my own style often worked against me.

One thing I think about the Skilled Facilitator approach is that it forces one to slow down and consider someone else's point of view all the time. I realized quickly this could get in the way of my goal—whatever it happened to be at the time. (The unilateral control model rears its head.) This was all well and good if time or pressures to get things done were not breathing down my neck, but how could decisions that needed to be made be made fast enough if I had to worry about everyone else? More important, what was in it for me? (Unilateral control rears again.) And finally,

One thing I think about the Skilled Facilitator approach is that it forces one to slow down and consider someone else's point of view all the time.

what if I found myself in a unilateral control environment and had the only mutual learning viewpoint? I was supposed to model the behavior, be the voice of reason, no assumptions. But I found myself getting frustrated.

I finally realized that what I was "modeling" was really a disguised version of unilateral control behavior. For shame. This stuff was hard and often felt not very satisfying. Without the group there to guide me (as I had had that week), I found I trampled all over what I learned. I could pat myself on the back when I reached congruence between what I thought and said, questioned people to test my own assumptions, but usually I could do this only with people I trusted. If I did not have a feeling of trust, it was much, much harder, and I am sure I often operated out of the unilateral control model without even knowing it.

This is not a success story of how I overcame all of my biases. But I do think it is a success story of the small sort. First, the awareness I now have of my own biases is much greater. Although I do not always follow the ground rules, at least I now know the choices I make along the way. Rather than justifying my behavior on the basis of my being right, I recognize how I might be feeling defensive or threatened—and hence my behavior. Sometimes I catch myself and change course, and sometimes I don't.

The things that have stayed with me are giving people the benefit of the doubt and speaking up when there is a problem, and I now have a much greater awareness of my own biases.

Perhaps the two things that have stayed with me from my intensive week are giving people the benefit of the doubt (testing inferences) and speaking up when there is a problem (discussing undiscussable issues). Because inferences and assumptions are so often second nature, to me as well as to many others, it has been a real eye-opener to see how rampant they are in daily work practice. I tend to think that as in a family, daily interaction breeds certain expectations that then breed assumptions that stay or become ingrained unless we challenge ourselves to take action and change the conversation. This is difficult to do every day.

As for undiscussable issues, it has been interesting and trying at times, but for the most part helpful, to honestly raise something that feels uncomfortable or that I just want to avoid. This is especially tough because it is a weakness of mine: I am an avoider, a pleaser, and I don't want conflict. But these issues have a way of raising themselves if they are not addressed, and so I have tried to tackle this one head-on when necessary.

PART SIX

Leading and Changing Organizations

Many of our clients are using the Skilled Facilitator approach to create significant change in their organizations—change in how they lead and manage their organizations. We refer to this as the Facilitative Leader approach. Some started out with this intention; others evolved toward organizational transformation as they gradually began to practice Skilled Facilitator methods and came to see their power and potential. We know of no organization that fully embodies the Facilitative Leader approach, but we see many individual leaders (formal and informal) working with their colleagues to move in this direction. Part Six describes some of their experiences and delves more deeply into the concepts and dilemmas that arise when engaging in this type of fundamental organizational change.

In Chapter Thirty-Eight, "Daily Challenges of a Facilitative Leader," our colleague Tom Moore shares his learning over nine years of using the Facilitative Leader approach in his organization. In Chapter Thirty-Nine, "Learning to Live Our Philosophy," Betsy Monier-Williams describes her experiences as her organization begins to use the Facilitative Leader approach.

To create fundamental change, team members need to learn how they contribute to reducing their team's effectiveness and what they can do to improve its effectiveness. Roger addresses different aspects of this systemic issue in three related chapters. In Chapter Forty, "Helping a Team Understand the System They Created," he uses a case study to show how to help a team identify causes of its dysfunctional behavior and how to help them create a more effective team. In Chapter Forty-One, "'I Can't Use This Approach Unless My Boss Does,'" he explains how team members contribute to their team's ineffectiveness by assuming that they can use the Facilitative Leader approach only if their boss uses it first. He provides steps for talking with your boss about using the approach. Finally, in Chapter Forty-Two, "How to Stop Contributing to Your Boss's and Your Own Ineffectiveness," he describes how we contribute to the very problems with our bosses (and organizations) that we complain about. Again, he provides steps for raising these issues with your boss to start contributing to solving the problems.

The subsequent four chapters examine developmental facilitation, the continuum that begins with helping groups learn to use Skilled Facilitator approach skills for themselves and continues into deep-level personal and organizational change. Anne Davidson and Dick McMahon, in Chapter Forty-Three, "Developmental Facilitation," describe how developmental facilitation differs from basic facilitation and the challenges that individuals, groups and organizations, and the facilitator face in doing this work. They continue in Chapter Forty-Four, "Guidelines for Theory-in-Use Interventions," describing the kinds of theory-in-use interventions required in developmental work and sharing the dilemmas that arise when trying to change deeply embedded organizational defensive routines designed to protect people from experiencing embarrassment and threat. Jeff Koeze, in Chapter Forty-Five, "Introducing the Core Values and Ground Rules," illustrates the successes and challenges of introducing the Facilitative Leader approach and sustaining learning.

Joe Huffman's organization started an effort to become a learning organization using Facilitative Leader principles in 1996. In Chapter Forty-Six, "From Learning to Lead to Leading to Learn," he shares his experience as a city manager joining an organization where the top management team was already engaged in using the approach. His chapter and Chapter Forty-Seven, "Reflections of a Somewhat Facilitative Leader," by Jeff Koeze, demonstrate some of the advantages, challenges, and issues that arise when organizations implement the approach.

The next four chapters consider how the approach can be used to improve organizational policy, structure, and procedures. In Chapter Forty-Eight, "Integrating the Skilled Facilitator Approach with Organizational Policies and Procedures," Roger and Anne discuss some of the unintended consequences that often arise from current organizational policies and practices (such as human resources, accounting, and finance) and offer a process for exploring how policies might be changed. In Chapter Forty-Nine, "360-Degree Feedback and the Skilled Facilitator Approach," Peg Carlson examines how the use of anonymity in 360-degree feedback undermines the very consequences it is intended to create. She shows how to redesign 360-degree feedback systems to create learning and increase accountability. In Chapter Fifty, "Implementing a 360-Degree Feedback System," Bron Skinner shares an example of how he used the Skilled Facilitator approach to improve his 360-degree performance feedback and what happened when he received negative anonymous feedback. Peg explores the anonymity issues further in Chapter Fifty-One, "Do Surveys Provide Valid Information for Organizational Change?"

Part Six concludes with thoughts on how to extend the Skilled Facilitator approach. Our clients routinely ask us whether the approach works in cultures outside the United States. In Chapter Fifty-Two, "Using the Skilled Facilitator Approach in Different and Multiple Cultures," Anne offers examples of our success and challenges and suggests ways to talk about the approach in other cultures.

Chapter 38

Daily Challenges of a Facilitative Leader

Tom Moore

I AM THE DIRECTOR of the Wake County Public Library, the county that includes the city of Raleigh, North Carolina. The library has seventeen branches and serves more than 700,000 residents. I have introduced the Facilitative Leader approach to my organization over the past nine years. I began by telling staff that I was trying to use the skills and asked them to point out when they thought I wasn't using the skills or being consistent with the values I professed.

See Chapter Forty-Six, "From Learning to Lead to Leading to Learn," page 367, and Chapter Forty-Seven, "Reflections of a Somewhat Facilitative Leader," page 377, for other stories of facilitative leaders' introducing the approach in their organizations.

There were two instant problems. The first was whether staff could trust me to be true to my word in that I would welcome criticism. They had no experience with my being receptive to criticism of any kind. The second problem was that I was so unskilled in the facilitative leader role that I was never consistent with the core values for any length of time. Concurrently, I was unaware of my own inconsistency. There was enough inconsistent behavior to keep a team of staff busy full-time pointing out those inconsistencies. While I was sincere in my attempt to involve staff in my change process, I was so entrenched in my unilateral control model behavior that it was difficult for them to see the changes I wanted to make.

There were two instant problems. The first was whether staff could trust me to be true to my word in that I would welcome criticism.

In hindsight, I can track what happened. I was so repelled by my own unilateral control behavior as identified through my left-hand column case and feedback from my coach and mentor that I began to act in a give-up-control way.

See the give-up-control model in Chapter Four, "Understanding What Guides Your Behavior," page 33.

Instead of giving direction, I said things like, "You decide," or "I don't care; whatever you think is best." I appointed committees to address problems. I only vaguely defined the problems and set few, if any, parameters. For example, I set up a committee to establish guidelines for checking out library materials. I told them to solve the problems that existed and that they all needed to agree on the solutions. I did not identify the problems beforehand and did not establish parameters for acceptable solutions. When the committee presented its first guidelines, my heart sank. They had proposed rigid rules that made it difficult to check out library materials. In seeking to punish abusers, they set up rules and regulations that limited all users in ways that, in my mind at least, did not prevent the abusers from circumventing the rules but would make it more difficult for those who would follow the rules.

I was truly caught on the horns of a dilemma. I had appointed the committee (I actually said, "Whoever is interested can be on the committee") and told them that whatever they decided would be acceptable. What they proposed was not acceptable to me. If I let the committee's decision stand, citizens would receive poorer service; if I told the committee that its decision was not acceptable, I would be acting inconsistent with the autonomy I gave them.

What I found out was that the give-up-control model was no more effective as a way of operating than was the unilateral control model. The problem was that I didn't realize that I was acting in a give-up-control way. It was very difficult for me to back up and start over, especially since the committee was committed to its decisions. The only thing I could do was try to explain how I had not given good parameters or direction to the committee and then to identify what the parameters should have been. I did that and gave them to the committee. I believe that most of the committee members thought that I just didn't like their conclusions and recommendations. This was just another way for me to get what I wanted. "Why didn't you just tell us what you wanted in the first place?" they asked. Although I was trying to be a facilitative leader, I had facilitated nothing. The way I worked with that committee could hardly be called leading either.

This is the challenge of the Facilitative Leader approach. It usually requires a radically different way of acting and thinking as a leader. Those you lead are skeptical at best when you begin. Many are just plain unbelieving. As I have said, my organization has been implementing the Facilitative Leader approach over the past nine years. Various managers have accepted this way of thinking and acting at different times. Some announced what they were doing. Others didn't; they just tried to implement the leadership approach. Regardless of the way they started, almost all were met with skepticism and doubt from the staff they worked with. Each of them moved from unilateral control behavior to give-up-control behavior, even when they knew others had been unsuccessful when they did that. I believe that the move to the give-up-control model was unconsciously deliberate. Each of us had the unspoken desire to prove that the way we had acted before wasn't so bad.

In spite of all of the dilemmas that continue to surface, the Facilitative Leader approach is a powerful way to lead an organization. Mistakes are no longer covered up; instead they are opportunities for learning. They are discussed so they won't be repeated. We share our reasons for our actions or statements in ways that prevent misunderstandings.

In spite of all of the dilemmas that continue to surface, the Facilitative Leader approach is a powerful way to lead an organization. Mistakes are no longer covered up; instead they are opportunities for learning. They are discussed so they won't be repeated. We share our reasons for our actions or statements in ways that prevent misunderstandings.

Our organization has powerful conversations. Recently the leadership team that I work with spent an hour showing me the consequences of the actions that I proposed to take. I believed that I could present facts and figures about a service that we wanted to offer in such a way that the county manager would be forced to agree. He had already said he was not willing to commit the resources necessary to offer that service. I thought that I had information that if I made it public, he would have no choice but to agree. They demonstrated that I would have to enter into a win-lose type of battle, and that if I did, I couldn't afford to lose. They also pointed out that the person I would want to do battle with couldn't afford to lose either. What's more, they pointed out, he had much more power than I have. The group framed its advice in a unilateral control perspective. I believe they did that because that is the way that I framed the solution in the first place. We had a blunt discussion about negative consequences that would result from my proposed actions. They pointed out the unilateral control aspects of what I wanted to do. Perhaps this is a typical conversation when a supervisor speaks to peers, but these team members are organizationally my subordinates. In other organizations, I believe that conversation would have taken place in the break room or the hallway—anywhere that I wasn't.

We have these types of discussions because we have explicitly agreed to talk about the tough issues and thoroughly examine consequences of proposed actions. We have found out it is much less painful to have these conversations before we act than it is to have them after we have acted and are trying to fix the unintended consequences.

We still face daily challenges. Why is it that I can see that your behavior is not facilitative but can't see the same behavior in myself (at least not while it is occurring)? Sometimes the challenges are comical when we reflect on them.

We still face daily challenges. Why is it that I can see that your behavior is not facilitative but can't see the same behavior in myself (at least not while it is occurring)?

During one meeting of our leadership team, the discussion became rather heated. Voices were raised, and a number of untested inferences and assumptions were made. The conversation was rapid, with different individuals talking at once. Suddenly one of the group in a very loud voice said, "Everybody is shouting! You all are making untested assumptions! This is no way to use facilitative leadership!" The individual was then silent, as was the rest of the group. The intervention worked, for everyone lowered their voices, checked out assumptions and inferences, and took turns speaking. It was only on reflection that we could see that the person who made the intervention engaged in all of the behaviors that the intervention was about. She yelled. She did not test her own assumptions and inferences out (that the rest of us were not testing out our assumptions and inferences). And, of course, she had to talk at the same time that others were talking in order to get her message in. This is not the only time that I have seen this happen. I don't know why, but we engage in the very behavior that we want to stop in order to make it stop.

At other times, the challenges are more vexing. Why does it take so long to learn how to act using Facilitative Leader skills? Is it really this hard, or am I a slow learner? In my experience, the Facilitative Leader approach is not a cookbook method. Many leadership models or skill sets seem easy to learn and almost simplistic to apply. They are like recipes in a cookbook. Add a pinch of salt, a dash of nutmeg, two cups of flour and milk, and baking powder. Mix it all up, and you'll have dough of some kind. It's so easy once you get the hang of it that you can make the dough without looking at the recipe. You can make variations and know it will result in different but still good dough.

The Facilitative Leader approach is not so much based on formula as it is based on matching values and actions explicitly. Before I learned about it, I said that I believed in at least two of its core values: sharing relevant information and seeking internal commitment. I just didn't act consistently with those values. I wasn't aware that I didn't act consistently with those values either. In order to use the approach, I had to make the core values explicit and keep them in my awareness. I then had to pick actions that were in alignment with those core values. The ground rules are actions that are consistent with the core values of the approach. They are not like the recipes of other leadership models, for they are effective only when used consistently with the core values.

When I was introduced to the Facilitative Leader approach, it seemed foreign. I was asked to do things that I never considered before. I remember talking to Roger Schwarz one day about my fear that I was about to lose my job. He asked me a number of questions about why I felt that way, but all that I could say was that it was a feeling that I got from the manager. Finally, he said, "Why don't you ask him?" I can still feel the stark terror that suggestion evoked: "Why would I ask him if I was in danger of losing my job? That would be stupid!" Roger replied, "Who better than the manager can tell you whether you are in danger of losing your job? What's the worst that could happen?" I thought and said, "He would say yes." And then Roger said, "At least then you would know where you stood. You would no longer be in this netherworld of not knowing. And by knowing, you could then take some action—even ask the manager himself what you could do to not lose your job." The logic was so simple and clear that I could think of nothing to counteract it.

The next week I made an appointment with the manager to check out my worst fears, and they were confirmed. When the manager said I was indeed in trouble and in jeopardy of losing my job, I panicked. To this day, I cannot remember the rest of our conversation. This meant I had to request another meeting with him to find out what I could do differently to continue in my job. That was eight years ago. The manager who was ready to let me go pointed to my department two years later as an example of effective leadership and a role model for other departments. By practicing the Facilitative Leader approach, I was able to better meet my manager's expectations and improve the way that my organization operated.

I have to work hard every day to be a Facilitative Leader. Every day I have failures. One of them was the time I said to a team member in a very large meeting for all to hear, "What part of *no* don't you understand?" Occasionally I have successes. Sometimes the successes are much more spectacular than the failures. One was the time when our division was praised for having the best budget preparation and presentation because we used our facilitative skills in putting that budget together. It was no longer necessary to play budget games because we shared how we constructed our budget and why we put different amounts in each line. Sometimes the successes are just quiet, satisfying, and ongoing, like the time my supervisor said to my team and me, "I like coming to your meetings because you always speak so openly to each other. I feel at ease here." This was high praise in my mind.

Practicing the Facilitative Leader approach has been the hardest thing I have done in my adult life. I can no longer operate on automatic pilot. I must be aware of the core values and the actions I need to take to be consistent with them at all times. Sometimes it is easier now than it was at the beginning. Most often, it still is very difficult in tense, difficult situations. I do not regret having taken this path, and I would not consider another. My life is richer for the experience, and my organization is better poised to face the challenges that each day presents. As leaders of the organization learn more and continue to practice applying the core values, the organization becomes more effective in diagnosing problems and finding solutions that have the fewest unintended consequences. Work has become enjoyable again, for we know we can use this approach no matter how difficult the situation is. We also know that we have support from each other in those difficult situations.

Chapter 39

Learning to Live Our Philosophy

Betsy Monier-Williams

THIS CHAPTER DESCRIBES SOME of the issues that arise when an organization attempts to change from a traditional to a mutual learning leadership style. In particular there are stories about espousing "free and informed choice" while in reality denying employees free choice. Acting unilaterally about mutual learning is another example of an issue that occurred more than once as my organization, a worldwide aerospace and industrial supplier, shifted toward facilitative leadership. By using my personal experiences, I hope my words paint a picture of my journey as a change agent for the Facilitative Leader approach.

ENTHUSIASM OUTPACES COMPETENCE

On returning from the Skilled Facilitator Intensive Workshop, I wasted no time in telling everyone all about it. The Facilitative Leader approach fit so well into both my personal and work life that I was excited to share it with others. I believed if others would only try it, they would see the benefit of the approach too. I found it hard to listen to someone say the approach wouldn't work for him or her before he or she had even taken the workshop. It was difficult to ask genuinely curious questions as to why it wouldn't work for them when what I really wanted to say was, "Yes, it would. Just give it a try!" Most of the time I didn't ask the genuine question, I instead *told* them, "Yes, it would. Just give it a try!" I preached the gospel of facilitative leadership to anyone who would listen and quickly earned the title "Schwarz disciple." The first time I heard my new nickname was a revelation for me. Sharing my experiences wasn't the issue; the problem was I was unilateral about it. Being unilateral about mutual learning was a recurring experience during my early days of using the approach. It happened because I was so excited at my newly found skills that I did not realize I had not changed my thinking to a mutual learning state of mind. Being aware that I was still acting from a unilateral mind-set was the first step in my journey of effecting change within the organization.

About two weeks later, I walked into the office of the vice president and general manager to tell him about my workshop experience. I told him that aside from the company paying for my master's degree, sending me to the Skilled Facilitator workshop was the best money he ever spent on me. He leaned back in his chair, raised his eyebrows, and said, "Really? Why?" I told him about the left-hand column case analysis, the skills practices, and the realization that I'd been a lousy facilitator for the past year. Before the workshop, if a team member mentioned something I thought was irrelevant to the discussion, I would yell, "Time out. We're off-topic; we need to get back on track." I got the group back on track, but at a price. I effectively shut down the team member who dared to voice an opinion (which turned out later to be very relevant to the topic) not only for one meeting but for many more meetings thereafter.

My old unilateral facilitative style also included convincing the minority to agree with the majority's decision so we could achieve consensus and move on to the next topic in a timely manner. Without a true consensus decision, the implementation of the decision often went awry when the minority again voiced their opposition. The Skilled Facilitator workshop helped me realize there was a more effective way to facilitate. The general manager was pleased that I came away with such an eye-opening experience. I left saying that he "had to go to this workshop." (I was still struggling with being unilateral about mutual learning.) He said he'd think about it. My next stop was my mentor's office, our financial manager. She helped me to develop my financial acumen, as well as expand my leadership skills. She was a step ahead of me. She had heard stories from my boss and was already interested in attending the workshop.

BROADENING THE EXPERIENCE

Two months later, the financial manager, the general manager, and half the executive staff attended the Facilitative Leader workshop. I believe that was the beginning of our organization's embracing the Facilitative Leader approach. Three months later, the remaining half of executive staff attended the workshop. During the final day and a half of the workshop, the entire executive staff, twelve managers, met as a team to begin practicing their skills. It was their collective choice to use the ground rules to become a more effective team. After that day-and-a-half meeting, the executive staff returned to question me as to when the next workshop would happen so they could send their employees. The approach was beginning to take hold. The next move was to offer the Facilitative Leader workshop on-site so there were more opportunities for employees to attend.

UNILATERALLY IMPLEMENTING A JOINT APPROACH

I began to work with Roger Schwarz and his associates, Anne Davidson, Sue McKinney, and Peg Carlson, to develop my skills as a workshop instructor. At the end of each Facilitative Leader workshop, there is a discussion about integrating the Facilitative Leader approach with other approaches being used in the organization. Roger says that you are likely to find that "some of your organization's structures, systems and processes are inconsistent with the core values and ground rules."[1] We were no different. It was how one specific inconsistency came about that sticks in my mind.

The general manager, my boss at the time, and I agreed that all the facilitators in our organization had to attend the Facilitative Leader workshop in order to continue acting as facilitators. He and I believed the skills learned in the workshop were critical to creating self-empowered work teams. To that end, all nineteen of our facilitators were informed of our decision. Over the course of the next year, the facilitators began to attend the workshop.

During one of the workshops, I stood in front of the participants, including my organization's facilitators whom I worked with over the past two years, and began the "integration" discussion. I emphasized that identifying the inconsistencies in our organization's structures, systems, and processes was the first step, and continued on to say that I identified some inconsistencies within the organization. I felt proud not only that I had found some inconsistencies, but also that I was making an effort to change them. I thought I was a true facilitative leader! And then I noticed a couple of facilitators rolling their eyes and whispering to each other. I made some inferences about what they were saying, so I decided to check with them: "I noticed that you were rolling your eyes when I mentioned changing the inconsistencies, and I'm thinking you have a comment on that. Is that right?" One facilitator replied, "Yes!" "Would you mind sharing with the group what it is you're thinking?" I asked. "Sure! One of the core values is free and informed choice, and you say you follow the Facilitative Leader approach, right?" "Yes," I answered. "So how is it that you, as master facilitator, made the decision to require all facilitators not only go through the Facilitator Leader workshop but also that we have to use the skills in order to remain a facilitator? I don't see any free and informed choice being offered to the facilitators." There I was, exposed for all to see. Roger's words came back to haunt me.

My boss and I created a systemic issue. We made a systemwide decision that was inconsistent with the approach we were asking the facilitators to use. We "required" the facilitators to use the skills, when they should have had the free and informed choice to use the skills. It's no wonder the facilitators were confused and upset. Because my boss and I were viewed as champions of the Facilitative Leader initiative, it was important that we acted, and were viewed by our peers as being, consistent with the approach. It was eight months between our decision and the facilitators' pointing out the inconsistency to me. My inference is that during those eight months, the facilitators must have thought me a hypocrite. The phrase "perception is reality" comes to mind. Although I wasn't purposefully denying the facilitators free and informed choice, it seemed that way to them and that's all that mattered. In learning my lesson, instead of requiring the facilitators to use the Facilitative Leader approach, the facilitators and I jointly designed a set of accountabilities, which may be achieved

> My boss and I created a systemic issue. We made a systemwide decision that was inconsistent with the approach we were asking the facilitators to use.

through the use of many different facilitative tools, one of which is the Facilitative Leader approach.

TOP-DOWN TEAMING

In 2001, our organization created work teams. After fifty-some years of advocating and rewarding individualism, teaming was a huge cultural change. It was a direct decision from management, with no input from the employees, who would be required to work in the teams. In shifting to a team culture, we experienced the typical trends of acceptance: early adapters, the majority, late adapters, and those who would never be comfortable working in teams. To deal with the last group, I sometimes pulled the naysayers into a spur-of-the-moment conversation and "sold" teaming to them, advocating all the reasons that they should participate. Although I professed the need for team member input, I wasn't genuine. The issue, as I saw it, was an organizational norm that said feedback was necessary and appreciated, but in practice feedback was never listened to or used. If the employees (team members) were asked for input during our conversations, it was only so I could respond with reasons that they were wrong. Instead of finding out why teaming wasn't working for them, I pushed the concept of teaming over and over again. When the employees wouldn't agree with me, I told management that we should get rid of them because they would never get with the program.

Over the course of the next three years, it became apparent that without our employees' internal commitment to teaming, teaming would struggle to be successful. As I, as well as others, started to use the Facilitative Leader approach, many team members sat back with a "show-me" attitude. The teams shared their opinions and needs when asked, but waited to see if I was going to cut them off or listen to them. To quote Miguel de Cervantes' *Don Quixote,* "The proof is in the pudding." Team members have said they see a change in me and in some of their managers. They feel that we are genuinely concerned about their interests and needs, and they are right. I believe that by modeling Facilitative Leader behavior every day, it's possible that others may see you differently.

PERFORMANCE MANAGEMENT

Another issue that came to the light early on was our performance review system. This is a particularly important issue because it so closely aligns with my organization's objectives, particularly the vision that employees treat each other with mutual respect and trust. To me, mutual respect and trust means having the compassion to tell people the truth about their performance, in the hopes that they may choose to change their behavior for the better. Our management team espoused the idea that employees can choose to improve themselves if given appropriate feedback, including feedback about areas of concern and areas for improvement. In reality, what most employees received was only positive feedback. Any negative or constructive feedback was couched in anonymity, and often without specific examples. Management expected employees to change, but without honest feedback and specific situations, most employees were unable to do anything about their performance.

My personal experience with this occurred in 1999 when my previous boss phoned in my performance review while I was at one of our West Coast facilities. He told me I was doing a good job, said what my salary increase was, and asked if I had any questions. Not knowing specifically what I had done well, I was unable to purposefully repeat those processes. Any concerns he had about my work were not addressed, leaving me clueless as to how I could improve my performance. The process left me frustrated and angry. So much for performance reviews being a system for employee development.

Two years later, I moved into a new role in the organization, with a new department and a new boss. I have seen improvement in our annual performance review system. In 2003, our management team took on performance management as an initiative. Honest feedback is the cornerstone of the initiative. My boss attended the Facilitative Leader workshop and is attempting to use his newly acquired skills on a daily basis. My last annual review followed a much different process from the one I have described. This year, my boss and I began by filling out separate assessments of my performance. I e-mailed him my assessment, and we jointly scheduled a convenient time for the discussion. At the onset of the discussion, my boss shared the fact that he found my review a bit more daunting than those of his other employees. When asked why, he replied, "Because you live, breathe, and teach this Facilitative Leader stuff, so I know if I don't share my reasoning, you're going to ask me all kinds of questions." He was right. After a moment of laughter, we jointly designed the process we would follow for the performance discussion. We covered my strengths and my areas for improvement and developed my strategic initiatives for the upcoming year. We each had specific examples for every topic we discussed, including feedback from select internal customers whom I met with in person prior to my formal review. At the end of our conversation, we talked about how we could do the review better next year. One suggestion was to include my select internal customers in the formal review so my boss and I could hear all the feedback at once, thereby validating information and considering any performance trends.

From start to finish my review was an incredibly satisfying process. It wasn't the perfect facilitative approach to a performance review, but it was the next step toward a more facilitative review system.

ELEMENTS OF CHANGE

It takes much more than bosses and their employees attending a workshop to change a corporate culture that has evolved over five decades. The approach requires fundamental changes in thinking and in our values and assumptions. I believe our shift toward a more mutual learning leadership style was the combination of four events. First, my coworker and fellow master facilitator, Greg Zolnowski (who took the Skilled Facilitator Intensive Workshop first and then encouraged me to go), and I worked at the midlevel of the organization to champion the approach with our facilitators and teams. In our daily conversations, he and I began to share our reasoning for asking questions; we asked others to share their reasons. During team meetings, when team members made inferences or assumptions, Greg and I would encourage them to check out their inferences with others. We generated interest among the facilitators and team members by modeling the Facilitative Leader approach and demonstrating its positive consequences. Second, the executive staff chose to use the Ground Rules for Effective Groups for their team meetings. They too saw positive consequences in the form of more internal commitment to decisions and the resolution of previously undiscussable issues. Third, the executive staff chose to promote the approach by sending their employees to the Facilitative Leader workshop, disseminating the learning downward through the organization. Finally, the company committed to building internal capacity by investing the time and money necessary for Greg and me to become trainers and coaches of the Facilitative Leader approach.

What made these four events possible is the most critical aspect of the change: in every event I've mentioned, the individuals involved made a free and informed choice to practice the Facilitative Leader approach. They tried to make the change in thinking, their values, and their assumptions part of their daily routine. Not everyone consistently used or was successful with the Facilitative Leader approach all the time, but what was important was each person's internal commitment to change. The shift from traditional to mutual learning leadership doesn't happen overnight. It is a journey for anyone who embarks on it.

Not everyone consistently used or was successful with the Facilitative Leader approach all the time, but what was important was each person's internal commitment to change.

During a recent registration for the Facilitative Leader workshop, a couple of our managers asked that certain employees attend the workshop based on their performance reviews. They felt the employees "needed the workshop." When I probed about their "needing the workshop," the managers said the approach would "fix" the employees' communication or personnel problems. I inferred that the managers were expecting the employees to use the approach after the workshop. Red flashing lights went off in my head. The managers were creating an issue similar to the one I created with the facilitators: they were espousing the Facilitative Leader approach with its free and informed choice and in reality not allowing their employees the free choice to use the approach.

I believe the managers' intent was to truly help the employees, not create confusion for them. You may be wondering what happened. I don't have a conclusion. I have a meeting with the managers to discuss the inconsistency I see, but until I hear what they were thinking, we have no answers.

Throughout the journey, I have learned one person can make a difference. Not everyone around me has been through the Skilled Facilitator workshop, but that doesn't stop me from using the approach. I found that by modeling the approach, others begin to mimic me. I hear team members say, "Here's what I'm thinking . . . But what do you think?" They may not know about being a mutual learner, but they are using specific examples and sharing their reasoning more often. My hope is that their experience with the Facilitative Leader approach may later lead them to make an informed and free choice to embrace it. It happened to me. It continues to happen to our organization.

Being unilateral doesn't go away overnight. In emotionally charged situations, I still struggle to think about the situation from a mutual learner's perspective. I often don't succeed. Thankfully, I'm not alone. At work, Greg and I still coach each other every day; we are lifelong learners. Our boss, the operations manager, along with the financial manager and our general manager, believe our facilitation is an integral part of our organization's progress toward a successful team-based environment. Greg and I believe we are making a difference, one person at a time.

Note

1. *The Skilled Facilitator,* pp. 16, 335.

Chapter 40

Helping a Team Understand the System They Created

Roger Schwarz

See Chapter Twenty-Nine, "Exploring Your Contributions to Problems," page 255.

IN OTHER CHAPTERS IN THIS FIELDBOOK, we have explored how group members make contributions to their system and how undiscussable issues reduce a group's effectiveness. A team I worked with explored both of these issues after just learning the Facilitative Leader approach. The team consisted of the vice president of one of several major corporate divisions and about half of his direct reports. He had recently moved into his position from another part of the corporation. The team was eager to practice the new mind-set and skill set they had just begun to develop. My task was to help them understand how they had created the ineffective situations they found themselves in and how they could reduce them in the future.

UNDOING THE TEAM CONSENSUS

The team began by discussing undiscussable issues that had been dragging the group down:

> One undiscussable issue was raised by John, the vice president and team leader (I have used pseudonyms to honor my agreement with the organization). He said, "I want to talk about the fact that whenever we make a consensus decision in our team meetings, one of you comes to me after the meeting and tells me we need to rethink the decision."
>
> John explained that the team agreement was to make strategic decisions by consensus given that it was essential that all team members be committed to them. He went on to explain that at some point, every person in the group had come to him asking him to change a group decision. He said that if any group members wanted him to, he would give specific

examples of which group members came to him on which issues. A couple of team members then volunteered that they had come to John after the group had made a decision. The group agreed that at some point, everyone had done this.

John went on to describe the negative consequences of this pattern for the group. He said that it had slowed the division's ability to meet its goals and eroded the group's ability to work as a team.

I asked the team members what was it that led them to come to John's office after the meeting instead of raising their concerns in the meeting. One member, Dan, said that John was a formidable advocate and it was hard to respond to him in the full group setting. A couple of other group members agreed. That didn't make sense to me.

I said, **"If John is a formidable advocate, I don't understand why responding to him one-on-one after the meeting would be any easier. I would think it would be harder because you don't have the potential support of other group members. What am I missing?"**

I said, **"If John is a formidable advocate, I don't understand why responding to him one-on-one after the meeting would be any easier. I would think it would be harder because you don't have the potential support of other group members. What am I missing?"**

Lee began to explain that it wasn't John that was the concern; rather it was a combination of other concerns. First, there was at times a win-lose approach that team members used with each other. They were concerned that other team members would shoot down their idea in the team meeting. Another team member added that by going to John after the meeting, he increased the chance of having the decision go his way. Other team members agreed. The teams' conversations were marked by a lot of advocacy with little inquiry so that it was easy to get an idea quickly dismissed.

Second, team members were reluctant to be fully open and honest about their differences of opinions because they were concerned about hurting others' feelings. By going to John after the meeting, they thought they were being compassionate; the issue could be addressed indirectly rather than having to air differences of opinion openly.

I asked what happened when people went to John after the meeting to raise concerns about decisions that had already been made by consensus. The team members said they shared additional information with John about their concerns. They said John told them that the group needed to hear this additional information and told them to raise it at the next meeting. John agreed that he had said this to the group members. I asked the team members, "What do you infer when John tells you that?" The team members replied that John was implicitly endorsing their point of view on the issue because he had told them the group needed to hear their additional information. In essence, by acting unilaterally and going to John, they thought they had a better chance of prevailing on the issue. I said, "John's right here. Would you check that out with him?" When they did, John said that he was not endorsing their point of view. He was simply trying to get them to honor the process they had agreed to and go back to the group.

When team members went back to the group and raised the issue again, sometimes the new information did change the decisions, but more often the discussion continued. As a result of people sharing additional information in the subsequent discussions, the same decision was reached but with greater commitment.

I said, **"John, you described this as a pattern of behavior over time with different group members. What I'm curious about is how you contribute to maintaining the pattern. I say this because when a team member came to you the first time after the group had reached consensus, you might have responded in a way that the behavior didn't continue. Instead, it spread to other group members. So can we look at your contribution?"**

John said that he did not tell people he was frustrated with them when they came to his office after the group had reached consensus. He didn't tell them because he considered it part of his role; he didn't like it but thought it was his job to hear people out. Sometimes John wondered whether he was contributing to the problem, so occasionally he would leave the meeting, thinking that would help.

I said, **"John, you described this as a pattern of behavior over time with different group members. What I'm curious about is how you contribute to maintaining the pattern. I say this because when a team member came to you the first time after the group had reached consensus, you might have responded in a way that the behavior didn't continue. Instead, it spread to other group members. So can we look at your contribution?"**

PIECING TOGETHER THE SYSTEM

To move from a team's story to helping the team understand the system it created involves a number of steps. Here are the steps I often use to accomplish this:

Step 1: Ask the Team to Tell Their Story

As one person starts to tell the story, others add their details and different perspectives. Seek agreement on what happened, and identify any areas on which members cannot agree. If something doesn't fit together for you, ask about it, as I did when I didn't understand why people would approach John one-on-one rather than in the full team. Don't worry if the story initially doesn't seem to fit together perfectly. It may be that there are some missing pieces that either you or the team members have yet to identify.

Step 2: Identify Key Decision Points Throughout the Story

As the team tells the story, identify key decision points. In the consensus story, I saw a few key decision points: (1) when team members framed the team meetings as opportunities to persuade others they were right and to minimize expressing negative feelings; (2) when team members decided that they could not "get their way" in the team meeting; (3) when they chose to approach John after the team had reached consensus; (4) when John responded to the first team member who approached him; and (5) when John responded to subsequent team members who approached him. Don't worry if you have difficulty immediately identifying the key decision points; they may not become clear until the story has completely unfolded.

Step 3: Explore the Process That Team Members Used to Take Action at Key Points

Identify the values, assumptions, and inferences they used as the basis of their actions or decisions. This includes helping members use the ladder of inference to identify what data they used as the basis of their inferences and how that led them to take the actions they did. For example, team members believed they had a better chance of influencing the decision and avoiding conflict by acting outside the group, and their inferences about John's response contributed to their belief. Underlying this belief was a more fundamental team member value of controlling the conversation to have one's own position win.

See the Ladder of Inference sidebar in Chapter Five, "Ground Rules for Effective Groups," page 61.

Step 4: Identify the Consequences of the Key Decisions

Ask team members what happened as a result of their actions. The facilitative leader approach provides a number of consequences to look for: (1) quality of decision making, (2) commitment to decisions, (3) time for effective implementation, (4) working relationships, (5) personal satisfaction, and (6) organizational learning. John's team initially identified the first consequences as occurring in their team. The unilateral control model and mutual learning model provide more detailed consequences such as changes in understanding, trust, and defensiveness.

See Chapter Four, "Understanding What Guides Your Behavior," page 33. You can also use the Group Effectiveness Model (see Chapter Two, The Group Effectiveness Model," page 15, and Chapter Fifteen, "Using the Group Effectiveness Model," page 135) to ask about specific areas in which there might be consequences, such as goals, roles, or boundary management.

By asking the team as a whole, team members learn how their individual actions created consequences they were unaware of. This is how John learned that when individual team members approached him after the consensus decisions, his actions helped maintain the pattern of behavior he was complaining about.

Step 5: Create a Causal Story; Test Your Story with the Team

In this step, you create a story that causally explains the initial story that the team told; you test your story with the team. The story that team members tell in step 1 is the "what happened" story. It is told at the level of behaviors: who did what and when. It may also include patterns of behavior over time. The story you tell at this step is the "how did it happen" story. It gives team members insight into the structure they created that led the events to unfold as they did. It causally links how people think and feel with how they act and the consequences they create (the three parts of theory-in-use).

To identify themes in the story, see the Laws of Systems Thinking sidebar in Chapter Seven, "Thinking and Acting Systemically," page 75.

The unilateral control model provides places to look for creating the causal story. In this case, a short version of the story might go something like this:

> (1) Team members enter team meetings with the belief that the goal of the meeting is to persuade team members to adopt their position on the strategic issue. They also believe that open disagreement would create negative feelings among them. (2) To enact these beliefs, they use a number of unilaterally controlling strategies, among them strongly advocating their views and not inquiring about others' different views. (3) Because various team members are using the same unilaterally controlling strategies, when team members find that their strategies are not working because others are using the same approach more effectively, they cannot raise this issue without calling attention to their own unilaterally controlling approach. (4) So when team members are particularly committed to their positions on a particular issue and their point of view does not prevail, and they cannot figure out a way to engage others without creating negative feelings, they offer their false consent in the meeting. (5) Then they seek to influence the group by engaging John's support as the head of the team. They believe that John will respond favorably to the additional information they present to him after the meeting. (6) When they talk to John individually, he is concerned that the group did not get all the information it needed to make a good decision, and so he tells the team member to raise the additional information in the next strategic meeting. John is also frustrated that the team member did not raise this information in the initial meeting. But he does not say that he is frustrated and doesn't ask the team member why he didn't raise the issue initially. Instead John sometimes tries to solve the problem unilaterally by leaving the meetings, but he doesn't make his reasoning and intent transparent. (7) Because John asks the team members to raise the issue again, they incorrectly infer that John supports their position on the issue, which, in the team members' minds, validates going to John after the meeting and leads them to expect John's support at the next meeting. (8) On some occasions, the team did change their decisions on a strategic issue to be more in line with the view that the team member had expressed to John after the initial meeting. This reinforced the process that John had been frustrated with. (9) As this pattern developed over time, the implementation of strategic decisions was delayed, as was the shared leadership that John wanted to create among his team. From John's perspective, shared leadership wasn't possible if his direct reports couldn't trust each other and went behind each other's backs.

Keep in mind that the causal story you tell includes a set of hypotheses.

Keep in mind that the causal story you tell includes a set of hypotheses. Because it is a causal explanation, by definition it includes inferences you make about the values and beliefs that people held, which led them to act as they did. By testing your inferences with the team members, you check the validity of the inferences and modify them as appropriate.

The causal story you share will probably not complete the puzzle. If you and the group are curious, it will raise more questions for you and the group to consider. For example, what led John not to raise this issue in the group after he saw it happen several times? Did team members see how people kept on coming back to the group to raise issues after they were decided? If so, what led them not to say anything? Was it because they used the same strategy at times? Was it because they thought John sanctioned it and did not want to confront them? The answers of team members to these questions provide the team with a richer understanding of its theory-in-use and how it creates unintended consequences.

By creating a causal story, you help the team move to the next step: identifying leverage points for change.

Step 6: Identify Leverage Points for Change

When the team has a causal understanding of how they created these unintended consequences, they are able to identify the key leverage points for change. The question here is, **"At what points in your story could you have significantly improved the outcomes if you had been able to think or act differently?"**

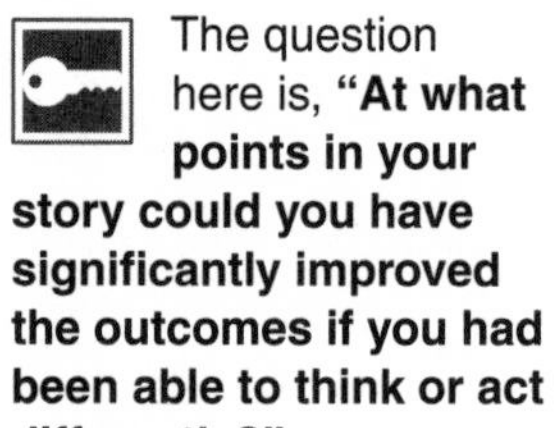

The question here is, **"At what points in your story could you have significantly improved the outcomes if you had been able to think or act differently?"**

These leverage points are often related to the key action points in step 3. Often the greatest points of leverage occur early on in the story with team members' values and beliefs. In the example, the causal chain is set in motion by the value that team members have about winning. To the extent they see their goal in the strategic planning meetings as having their position prevail, they are likely to use unilaterally controlling strategies, whether they are the goals in this example or others. If instead they begin to think about the meetings using a mutual learning frame, the strategies they use, as well as the consequences, will be different. This change sets in place many other changes. Two other leverage points for change are when people are frustrated enough to offer their false consensus and when they approach John after the meeting. By changing what occurs at these points, the team can change the consequences.

Step 7: Explore What Needs to Happen to Change

In this step, you explore with the team what would need to happen so team members can significantly change the course of events by thinking and acting differently. In this example, the team and I identified several things. Team members agreed to raise their concerns and frustrations they had with the meeting *in the meeting* rather than go to John afterward to influence the process and outcome. They agreed that when they saw other team members offering consensus that did not seem genuine, they would inquire about it in the meeting and explore the causes. John agreed that if a team member did come to him after the meeting as team members had in the past, he would both express his frustration and be curious about what led the team member not to follow the team's new agreement. Most fundamental, the team agreed to begin to move from unilateral control to a mutual learning frame. This included asking team members to help each other see when they were acting unilaterally and to help them change. This shift would have significant impact on many of their interactions. In the strategic issues meetings, it would, among other things, reduce the chance that team members would seek to win and would increase the quality of conversation and decision making in the team meetings.

For tools that teams can use to create these changes, see Chapter Nine, "Jointly Designing the Purpose and Process for a Conversation," page 103; Chapter Twenty-Nine, "Exploring Your Contributions to Problems," page 255; Chapter Thirty, "Moving Toward Difficulty," page 261; Chapter Thirty-Two, "Raising Issues In or Out of the Group," page 273; Chapter Forty-Two, "How to Stop Contributing to Your Boss's and Your Own Ineffectiveness," page 335; and Chapter Forty-Four, "Guidelines for Theory-in-Use Interventions," page 349.

Chapter 41

"I Can't Use This Approach Unless My Boss Does"

Roger Schwarz

WHEN SOME PEOPLE LEARN about the Facilitative Leader approach, they say, "This would be really useful to use with my boss, but I can't use it unless she knows it." Sometimes people go further and say, "I can't use it unless my boss uses it." When I explore these comments with those who made them, we find that their own reasoning often prevents them from introducing the approach to their boss.

Of course, it's much easier to use the approach when someone else knows it—and, especially, uses it—whether it's your boss or someone else. In these situations, you don't need to explain fully why you are using the ground rules and core values (that is one reason we offer on-site workshops in which teams learn the approach together). But this concern that others don't know the approach does not seem to be the main one, because they are often not concerned about trying the approach with people other than their boss who don't know it.

WHAT IS IT ABOUT A BOSS?

When I ask what it is about using the Facilitative Leader approach with their boss that makes it more difficult, people often say their boss doesn't listen to them or say, "You don't know my boss!" They go on to say that their boss has power over them and can negatively affect their career. Sometimes they talk about how others have "challenged" the boss and faced negative consequences. Often, but not always, their concerns are based on untested inferences.

As I explore this more with them, it becomes clear that part of their theory-in-use includes a belief that if another person has more power than they do, they can't get that person to listen. Essentially, their reasoning is, "I can be more successful getting other people to use a mutual learning approach when I have the power to unilaterally control them." Or, "If someone has power over me and uses a unilateral control approach, then it is risky to introduce the Facilitative Leader approach to them."

See the unilateral control model in Chapter Four, "Understanding What Guides Your Behavior," page 33.

In either case, they are asking for some assurance that they won't pay a price for trying to use the Facilitative Leader approach with their boss (or others who have more power than they do). This is a reasonable thing to want, but no one can grant that request except the boss.

TALKING WITH YOUR BOSS

If you're in a similar situation, what you can do is have a conversation with your boss about your using the Facilitative Leader approach in a way that reduces the risks or your concerns. You can't control how your boss will react, but you can control how you think and act. By changing the way you think about and act in your conversation with your boss—by sharing relevant information and enabling both you and your boss to make a free and informed choice—you increase the chance (there are no guarantees) that your boss will react differently. This reduces your risk.

Steps for Talking with Your Boss

1. Tell your boss that you've learned some things about how you can work more effectively and would like to talk with her about using these with her. Ask if she is interested in talking about the approach so she can see if she has any concerns about your using it with her.

For beginning the conversation, see Chapter Nine, "Jointly Designing the Purpose and Process for a Conversation," page 103; Chapter Twenty-Eight, "Holding Risky Conversations," page 249; and Chapter Thirty, "Moving Toward Difficulty," page 261.

2. If you believe you are taking a risk or have concerns about how your boss will react to this conversation, share these concerns. Be sure to identify and test with your boss any inferences or assumptions you are making that lead you to have these concerns. If you need some assurance from your boss in order to reduce your risk and continue the conversation, explain why you are asking for the assurance and ask if she is willing to give it.
3. Briefly explain the Facilitative Leader approach. Give some specific examples of how you had thought and acted less effectively in the past with your boss and what the consequences were for you, your boss, and others. Ask for your boss's reactions, and check whether she has any different views.

For ways to introduce the approach, see Chapter Thirty-Five, "Introducing the Skilled Facilitator Approach at Work," page 293; Chapter Thirty-Six, "Bringing It All Back Home, or Open Mouth, Insert Foot," page 299; and Chapter 45, "Introducing the Core Values and Ground Rules," page 361. See also Chapter Twenty-Nine, "Exploring Your Contributions to Problems," page 255.

4. Explain how you would have acted differently and how that might have changed the interaction between you and your boss, as well as the consequences. Point out that by changing your behavior, at times you would be asking your boss to change her behavior by either providing different information (such as her interests or reasoning) or asking you questions. Ask your boss for her reactions.
5. Ask your boss what concerns, if any, she has about your using this approach with her. Explore the concerns, and jointly design solutions.
6. Ask your boss if she is willing to give you feedback when she thinks you are acting inconsistently with the approach you want to use.
7. Summarize the agreements you think you have made and check for different views.

This is a simplified view of the key steps in talking with your boss about using the Facilitative Leader approach; it does not go into the nuances of that conversation. For example, step 4 deals with the systemic notion that by changing your behavior, you implicitly ask the other person to change too. I also haven't said anything about asking your boss if she wants to use the approach herself. The point is, your boss doesn't have to adopt the approach for you to use it. What is required is to change the way *you* think and act, in both your leadership role and your conversations with your boss.

Chapter 42

How to Stop Contributing to Your Boss's and Your Own Ineffectiveness

Roger Schwarz

WHEN PEOPLE LEARN THE FACILITATIVE LEADER approach, they often say that they are less effective than they could be with this approach because of their boss's behavior. And yet they act in ways that increase the chance that the boss will not change his behavior. Here's an example of how it happens:

> Henry sees his boss, Arthur, doing things that create a problem for Henry and Henry's direct reports. When Arthur delegates assignments to Henry, Arthur doesn't share all the relevant information that Henry needs to complete the assignments. As a result, when Henry completes the assignment and reports back to Arthur, Arthur doesn't accept the assignment as completed; instead, he shares additional information that requires Henry to make changes in something he viewed as completed. Henry often thinks that this is information that Arthur could have shared initially. This requires Henry to do the same work twice, which often leads to Henry's missing the assignment deadline, having to shift deadlines for other assignments for Arthur, or cutting back on the quality of his work. Because Henry and his direct reports often work on the assignments as a group, Arthur's actions affect Henry's direct reports' schedules as well. He has no idea why Arthur withholds important information from him.
>
> Henry hasn't said anything to his boss about this pattern of behavior. He has tried giving Arthur feedback in the past on similar issues, and Arthur just got annoyed at him. Nothing improved. And he's heard others say that Arthur doesn't take feedback well. Henry has decided not to raise the issue with Arthur.
>
> However, Henry talks with his peers and others about the problems that Arthur creates. And he shares his frustration with his direct reports when they keep asking why they have to rework assignments.

CONTRIBUTING TO THE PROBLEMS YOU COMPLAIN ABOUT

If you think systemically about the situation, Henry actually contributes to the problem that he is complaining about. It is possible that Arthur is not aware of how his behavior creates negative consequences for Henry and his team. In systems, cause and effect are separated in time and space, so we often don't make the connection between our behavior and its consequences

See Chapter Seven, "Thinking and Acting Systemically," page 75.

Arthur may not see that the delays on other projects or the lower-quality work stem in part from the choices that Henry has had to make when faced with the rework. In fact, Arthur may not even see his asking for rework as a problem, in which case he wouldn't associate it with any negative consequences.

In systems, everyone sees a part of the system. Henry sees how Arthur's behavior creates what he considers unnecessary rework and slipping deadlines. He sees these consequences because he experiences them directly. If Arthur doesn't experience the consequences directly, the way he learns about them is from others. Similarly, Arthur sees things that Henry may not see. For example, Henry's assumption that Arthur is withholding information may be inaccurate. Rather, things might be occurring at or above Arthur's level that lead him to give Henry additional information that he did not have when he initially gave Henry an assignment. Similarly, for Henry to understand this, he needs to learn about it from Arthur because Henry does not live in Arthur's part of the system.

When we don't share our view of the system with others in the system, we withhold relevant information that can enable others to change their behavior.

By withholding his concerns from Arthur, Henry prevents Arthur from learning more about the consequences of his behavior. It also prevents Arthur from making a free and informed choice about whether he wants to change his behavior. By withholding the information, Henry reduces the chance that he will get the change he seeks.

Our reasoning for withholding our view of the system is often flawed. Henry has reasons for not sharing the information with Arthur, but his reasoning may have flaws. When he or others have given Arthur feedback, Arthur has gotten defensive. Yet if Henry and others who gave feedback to Arthur did so using the unilateral control model, then we could reasonably predict that they would generate defensiveness in Arthur. If this is the case, then Henry has helped create the defensiveness in Arthur that he uses as a reason for not giving him feedback. Henry's reasoning is self-sealing: it enables him to attribute the problem to Arthur and seal off the possibility of learning that the way he gives the feedback creates defensiveness.

See the consequences of the unilateral control model in Chapter Four, "Understanding What Guides Your Behavior," page 33.

In other words, Henry has not created the necessary conditions to test whether Arthur's defensiveness stems from Henry's behavior. To do so, Henry would need to give Arthur feedback using the mutual learning model and see if Arthur still gets defensive.

It's not fair to complain privately but withhold the feedback. It's unreasonable for Henry to continue to complain about Arthur while not giving Arthur the feedback. If Henry decides not raise the issue with Arthur, he also needs to recognize that his silence contributes to the problem and therefore he gives up the right to complain. You can't continue to hold people accountable for their behavior if you haven't been accountable for talking with them about it.

HOW TO STOP CONTRIBUTING TO YOUR BOSS'S INEFFECTIVENESS

The process for talking with your boss about these issues is the same as talking with anyone else, although the conversation with your boss may feel more threatening. Here are the steps.

These are the basic steps. Other chapters contain useful advice on how to approach the conversation. See also Chapter Twenty-Eight, "Holding Risky Conversations," page 249, to get started.

1. Tell your boss the issue that you want to talk with him about and briefly explain your interests in talking about it. Ask him if he is willing to do so.

See Chapter Nine, "Jointly Designing the Purpose and Process for a Conversation," page 103.

2. Suggest a process (the following steps) and ask if he has any concerns about the process.
3. Jointly redesign the process to meet his interests and yours.
4. Describe the pattern of behavior you are seeing, and give specific examples. Include how you may be contributing to the consequences. Test any assumptions and inferences you are making about the situation. Ask for different views. Reach agreement on what has happened.

See Ground Rule One and the Ladder of Inference sidebar in Chapter Five, "Ground Rules for Effective Groups," page 61.

5. Describe the consequences you see for you, your boss, and others. Ask for different views. Reach agreement.
6. Explore the potential causes of the problem. Be curious and compassionate about what leads your boss to be in this situation.

7. Clarify each of your interests, and jointly design solutions that address the causes and meet each of your interests.

See Chapter Sixteen, "Helping Group Members Focus on Interests Rather Than Positions," page 145.

Chapter 43

Developmental Facilitation

Anne Davidson
Dick McMahon

DEVELOPMENTAL FACILITATION HELPS leaders, groups, and organizations create fundamental change in the way they operate. Facilitative leaders learn to shift their mental models, rigorously reflect on their own behavior, model the core values, and coach others in developing mutual learning skills. Organizations that seek to become more collaborative, transformative, or flexible or to become learning organizations must develop these same skills more broadly in work groups and teams. They must also change their policies, procedures, and ultimately all other elements of their formal and informal structure to be consistent with the vision and values they adopt.

DEVELOPING LEADERS AND ORGANIZATIONS

In *The Skilled Facilitator,* Roger distinguishes developmental facilitation from basic facilitation. According to his definition, in basic facilitation one intervenes to help groups solve problems or complete tasks; in developmental facilitation, one also seeks to help groups learn process skills. He states, "In developmental facilitation, the group seeks to develop its process skills while solving problems. . . . Consequently, if other difficult problems arise, the group remains less dependent on a facilitator than before" (p. 50). The facilitator's interventions are "designed to help the group learn how to diagnose and improve process. A fundamental difference between basic and developmental facilitation is doing something for a group in the former case and teaching a group how to do the same thing for itself in the latter case" (p. 51).

Since the time Roger wrote this description of developmental facilitation, he and we have recognized that that it did not fully capture the range and depth of our view of developmental facilitation.

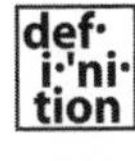

Essentially, we see developmental facilitation as facilitation aimed at helping people reflect on and change their behavior and thinking, including generating deep-level personal and organizational learning. The work is designed to help group members and organizations reflect on and change their mental models and core values.

It fits squarely within Richard Beckhard's definition of organization development (2001): "Today I define OD as a 'systemic and systematic change effort, using behavioral science knowledge and skill, to transform the organization to a new state'"

Essentially, we see developmental facilitation as facilitation aimed at helping people reflect on and change their behavior and thinking, including generating deep-level personal and organizational learning. The work is designed to help group members and organizations reflect on and change their mental models and core values.

(p. xi). We think there is a continuum of developmental facilitation that involves both individual and group learning at each choice point. Possible beginning and ending points might be as shown in Figure 43.1.

This expanded continuum of developmental facilitation involves doing a number of things differently from what we do in more basic facilitation. It also demands more skills from facilitators and creates special challenges for all involved. This chapter offers an overview of these differences, challenges, and some final thoughts about the critical elements of successful developmental efforts.

Differences Between Basic and Developmental Facilitation

Clients seldom call requesting developmental facilitation. Instead, groups may express an interest in doing more in-depth team building, a desire to create a less-hierarchical, more flexible organizational culture, or a wish to solve problems so that they stay solved. Or we may begin doing basic facilitation with a group whose members realize during the process that their efforts are limited if they do not go more deeply into their values, beliefs, mental models, and defensive routines. Once the goal begins to look like personal and organizational transformation, the conversation changes into a much lengthier contracting or recontracting discussion. We shift the focus of our work to generating a set of shared group values, helping group members behave consistent with a philosophy of mutual learning rather than unilateral control, and seeking to understand how individual and small group defensive routines become elevated to the level of organizational defensive routines. At the same time, we address broader structural issues, such as role and task definition, boundary management, and organizational policies and procedures.

See Chapter Eleven, "Basic Facilitation," page 115.

Figure 43.1 Developmental Facilitation Continuum

0	0	0	0
Help group learn ground rules: develop ability to self-facilitate most conversations	Help group learn and intervene on mental models and basic theory-in-use issues; develop ability to self-facilitate conflicts and problem solving.	Help group diagnose and solve broad systems problems and change policies and programs to be consistent with shared values; identify and address dilemmas	Help group identify and change deeply held personal and organizational defensive routines; help group develop skills for teaching others and leading organizational change and transformation

Complex, Repeated Contracting Process

In a typical basic facilitation, the contracting process takes one to three hours, including the contact conversation and a planning meeting. In a developmental situation, those same conversations occur but require a more detailed description of what to expect. We find it difficult to describe (or anticipate) just how deep the work will go. It is challenging to explain to someone what it will be like to do this level of work when he has never thought carefully about how his own thinking contributes to problems.

We believe the most successful approach is to describe to groups the challenges inherent in developmental work, share examples of learning activities a group might engage in (such as left-hand-column case discussions), and suggest that the group work for a set number of sessions and then review the contract. Also, the contents of the contract are different. Usually this is not only a facilitation contract. The work is a blend of training, consulting, coaching, and facilitation. After some training in mental models, systems thinking, and ground rules, for example, a group can make a more informed choice about whether and how applying this knowledge might help them attain their goals.

The work is a blend of training, consulting, coaching, and facilitation. After some training in mental models, systems thinking, and ground rules, for example, a group can make a more informed choice about whether and how applying this knowledge might help them attain their goals.

A developmental facilitation contract is actually a contracting process that occurs in stages and is regularly revisited and reshaped.

Deeper, More Time-Consuming Interventions

Interventions that foster personal and organizational transformation are frequently based on individual theory-in-use and core values, group and organizational values and beliefs, the Group Effectiveness Model, and systems thinking. (Other chapters in this book delve into using these interventions.) In each case, engaging in the interventions places much greater emphasis on self-reflection. Participants are called on to modify their whole behavior design system. We think it is important to discuss the level of self-revelation and risk that will likely be involved. Groups need to commit to doing this kind of work together and to be clear that they can revisit their choice along the way if the risk seems too great.

See Chapter Fifteen, "Using the Group Effectiveness Model," page 135; Chapter Seventeen, "Developing Shared Vision and Values," page 149; Chapter Forty-Four, "Guidelines for Theory-in-Use Interventions," page 349; and Chapter Fifty-Six, "Applying the Skilled Facilitator Approach to a Systems Thinking Analysis," page 447.

These interventions also take longer to complete, and there is less likelihood that the group will accomplish multiple substantive tasks during any single session. Often what seem like simple agenda items turn into rich theory-in-use or systems interventions that can consume much group time yet produce substantial group learning and future group process improvements. It seems that frequently when groups think they can make a quick decision, they are most at risk of trying to use a unilateral or nonsystemic approach. As a consequence, we believe it is critical to share what we see as the sufficient number and length of meetings needed for the group to make substantive progress. We do not have a fixed amount of time to suggest. One to two full days per month for a group of seven to eight has served us well. Without contracting for sufficient time, you create a situation that leads to significant intersession loss of learning and continuity. Groups that contracted with us for too little time tended to be less effective. Failure was inevitable.

In reality, developmental work requires months or years of effort, depending on the goals. Often, tangible successes are small until there is substantial time investment. It is easy to lose heart or momentum in the face of daily business pressures. We think it important and useful to be clear from the start about the significant time investment and to help groups reframe how they think about investing time. Discussing the systems law of "go slow to go fast" is helpful here.[1]

See Chapter Seven, "Thinking and Acting Systemically," page 75.

Clarifying and Intervening on Organizational Values and Beliefs

Chapter Seventeen, "Developing Shared Vision and Values," page 149, highlights the usefulness of assisting developmental groups in clarifying their core ideology—their purpose and guiding principles.

In working with top management teams at organizational or divisional levels, this intervention is one of the foundations of our approach to developmental facilitation. While a group's values might also include the core values of mutual learning, being a bit more specific about values relevant to the particular group and context is important. A statement of purpose, values, and beliefs is the template against which policies and procedures can be examined and redesigned to be consistent with mutual learning. It is not always enough to say you want a policy that builds in valid information, free and informed choice, internal commitment, and compassion. It is necessary to get more specific: if values are to be good stewards of resources and also to provide innovative customer service (which often requires more resources), how does a particular policy or decision balance those values while at the same time being consistent with mutual learning? Sorting out the choices and options is a productive conversation that unearths layers of interests, assumptions, and theory-in-use issues.

Clarifying values and beliefs is also a time when developmental work can feel risky to those engaged in it. Most of those we work with have a well-developed set of values that they feel comfortable with. It may not be particularly pleasant to have those values and assumptions challenged. Yet we have found no way to sustain personal or organizational change without fundamentally questioning values and beliefs in a way that can create vulnerability. As with deeper interventions in general, the need to face fear and threat is a critical aspect to discuss early and often during developmental facilitation. Without addressing the perceived risk explicitly, participants may feel set up or manipulated.

Intervening on Organizational Defensive Routines

By organizational defensive routines, we mean all the policies and practices designed to prevent people from experiencing embarrassment and threat. These policies and practices work to unilaterally protect people and at the same time cover up the fact that people are being protected. Covering up the fact that these routines exist makes the causes and unintended consequences of the routines undiscussable (Argyris, 1994). Common organizational defensive routines include not disagreeing with superiors in public, not telling superiors how you think they may be contributing to a problem, and not raising issues about the competence of a work team member. The cover-up is that people deny these things are going on, avoid discussing them, or rationalize that this is "just the way things are in all organizations." Table 43.1 is a chart we developed for members of one organization to help us test our diagnosis of some of the defensive routines we had inferred.

def·i·'ni·tion

By organizational defensive routines, we mean all the policies and practices designed to prevent people from experiencing embarrassment and threat.

Table 43.1 Defensive Routines Chart

Espoused Value	Defensive Routine
Autonomy, empowerment, responsibility	People not held accountable for quality of work.
	Not hurting people's feelings: unilateral protection, rescue.
Competence	Being in charge makes you impervious to criticism. The competence of bosses is seldom questioned, or the person offering the critique is discounted in some way.
Quality work, good stewardship of resources	Not confronting performance issues and inefficiencies (for example, excessive overtime).
Learning organization	Resist learning, at least technical learning, because competence is assumed; to need more knowledge or information is considered admitting a weakness.

According to Chris Argyris (1990), defensive routines become embedded in organizations as a result of individuals' using the unilateral control model to guide their interactions: "Because most individuals use these actions, the actions become part of the fabric of everyday life. And because so many individuals use these actions frequently, the actions become organizational norms. The actions come to be viewed as rational, sensible, and realistic" (1990, p. 25). In other words, the actions become self-fulfilling and self-sealing. And the negative consequences are usually not immediately apparent. It may seem that we got through a difficult meeting without anyone getting upset or got the group to agree to do what we wanted. But after some delay, the problems resurface. The delay may extend weeks, months, or years, so we may not connect subsequent negative consequences to earlier defensive strategies. Yet in the long run, defensive routines breed ineffectiveness, cynicism, and hopelessness, a condition Argyris describes as "organizational malaise" (1990, p. 60).

The aim of developmental facilitation is to change these ingrained patterns of behavior to create more productive consequences.

The aim of developmental facilitation is to change these ingrained patterns of behavior to create more productive consequences. The end point on the developmental facilitation continuum is to change deeply held personal and organizational defensive routines to lead to organizational change and transformation. Yet seeing and understanding the dynamics involved in these routines is difficult. It often requires a lengthy facilitation engagement and observation of groups while they are engaged in their day-to-day work. Without observing actual behavior, facilitators often see only espoused theory or hear rationalized interpretations of events. Identifying and changing defensive routines is one of the highest-leverage and most challenging interventions we engage in. We believe we are still learning how to do this effectively.

CHALLENGES FOR INDIVIDUALS, GROUPS, AND ORGANIZATIONS

The discussion of differences between basic and developmental facilitation alludes to some of the special challenges faced in doing this work. These are summarized in Table 43.2. In addition to time and personal risk issues, it is often unclear just what is going on or what progress is being made until facilitators and participants stay with the process for awhile. Individuals must face their fear of change and the personal discomfort at being beginners who perform inexpertly in front of peers, subordinates, and superiors. And for a time, it may seem as if the new approach is taking longer and getting fewer results. This is part of what we mean by tolerating high levels of ambiguity. For extended periods, we may also not be clear what defensive routines are at work. It can be hard to determine whether their existence as organizational norms is influencing a group to continue them or whether group members personally have these defensive patterns and are promulgating them in the organization. The truth is often some of both, and being unclear can be uncomfortable. It can also be uncomfortable to try to behave consistent with mutual learning values when we have a history with someone or when the organizational policies and procedures still have unilateral assumptions embedded in them.

It can be uncomfortable to try to behave consistent with mutual learning values when we have a history with someone or when the organizational policies and procedures still have unilateral assumptions embedded in them.

Table 43.2 Challenges of Developmental Facilitation

Challenges for Individual Group Members	Challenges for Groups and Organizations	Challenges for Facilitators
Developing tolerance for taking risks, being vulnerable in front of peers and boss	Investing the time necessary for interventions and clear progress	Facilitators face all the same challenges as individual group members plus the following:
Appearing incompetent while learning new skills	Getting a realistic picture of the commitment, making a fully informed choice to support the effort	Needing even deeper awareness of personal hot buttons, defensive routines
Dealing with past history with others; recognizing that past data are flawed because of how we were thinking when we perceived them	Determining and sharing guiding values	Needing broad knowledge and experience in organizational change, systems thinking, and all aspects of the Skilled Facilitator approach
Engaging in deep personal reflection	Tolerating high levels of ambiguity	Balancing offering expertise with not creating unnecessary dependence
Facing emotions that interrupt efforts to design new behaviors	Working in an environment where policies are inconsistent with intent and require complex overhauls	Balancing work with individuals and groups in blended roles (trainer, coach, facilitator, consultant)
Accepting feedback nondefensively	Avoiding paralysis as a result of the realization everything affects everything else	Managing tendency over time to become more group member than facilitator
	Sustaining commitment in the face of perceived threat and an unknown result	Recognizing when issues have crossed the bounds of facilitation into need for therapy

If we have had a difficult relationship with a coworker in the past, it is virtually a given that we have made a series of high-level inferences and attributions about him or her. These often drive a feeling that it is impossible to use or even try to use mutual learning ground rules or core values in conversations with that person. We want to behave in a new way but feel trapped in old patterns based on years of faulty data that are hard to erase. Performance appraisal processes are an excellent organizational example of how people can feel trapped trying to behave one way (share valid information) but being required to follow a policy to the contrary (keep all feedback anonymous).

See Chapters Forty-Eight through Fifty-One for examples of this dilemma and possible ways to address these inconsistencies over time.

Another challenge can occur when groups begin to improve their ability to think systemically. Seemingly straightforward problems, like improving work completion rates, can turn out to be knotty systems issues. Performance coaching conversations can turn into examinations of how other parts of the system contribute to poor outcomes. It is easy for groups to get paralyzed and give up, especially when it is also difficult to measure some of the outcomes sought (increased learning, improved personal satisfaction, enhanced commitment). We do not have easy answers for these challenges and dilemmas. Each situation may require a somewhat different response. We do find that it helps to name the issues and address them explicitly.

SPECIAL CHALLENGES FOR FACILITATORS

Facilitators face all the same challenges as individual group members plus some special ones that come with their role. The facilitator's role is usually a blend of trainer, facilitator, consultant, and coach. It can be challenging to be clear about what role one is in at a given moment and figure out how to behave appropriately in that role. It is tempting to resort to an expert role in the frame of trainer or consultant and increase the group's dependence on the facilitator. We agreed to become consultants for one group we facilitated when they wanted to design and complete a mutual learning hiring process for selecting a new team member. It was fun and invigoratingly different, and it produced great results. But for months afterward, we found the team members deferring to us as facilitators in making decisions they should and could make for themselves. We should probably have been more alert to this possibility, addressed it in advance, and diagnosed the changed behavior more quickly when it occurred. The group's dependence slowed their progress for several months.

Developmental facilitators need more knowledge and experience in the areas of organizational change, personal development, systems thinking, mental models, and all the aspects of the Skilled Facilitator approach.

Developmental facilitators need more knowledge and experience in the areas of organizational change, personal development, systems thinking, mental models, and all the aspects of the Skilled Facilitator approach. One must hold in one's head multiple diagnostic frames and select appropriately from among them, even in the face of ambiguity. One must also be able to remember patterns of behavior over long periods of time and craft complex theory-in-use and systems interventions using those data, with specific examples. The ability to diagnose and intervene at this level of complexity grows with practice.

Clients tell us that much of their learning comes from seeing facilitators model the Skilled Facilitator approach in actual situations. We agree that this is important, not only for clients' learning but in order to be credible advocates for our approach. Developmental situations are much more challenging and often require modeling the skills at increasingly difficult levels, such as when someone is highly emotional. We think it is helpful to master some basic facilitation skills and then move into more developmental work, particularly if one is not already a trained and experienced organizational development practitioner.

Deeper awareness of personal strengths, hot buttons, and defensive routines is also demanded during developmental facilitation. It is easier to get hooked in your own issues when intervening on theory-in-use. Sometimes it is tempting to jump to conclusions about organizational defensive routines that might be more a projection of your own past work experience than a clear view of the current situation. Needs for acceptance and the natural friendships that develop when you work with a group over long periods can create a tendency to become more group member than facilitator. This can be a delicate boundary to manage. Familiarity helps you spot and intervene on defensive routines and deeper individual issues, but you can also get sucked into the defensive routines yourself. In one memorable situation, we realized that after a long period of working with a group whose defensive routine included not preparing for meetings, we also stopped preparing. Being accepted and comfortable with the group made our inconsistency with what we espoused harder to see.

Working with a cofacilitator can address some of the challenges. It helps to have a knowledgeable partner who can offer feedback, think through issues while the cofacilitator is intervening, and engage in reflection after group meetings. Developing detailed process notes together after group sessions significantly increased our learning and the effectiveness of our work with groups. In developing the notes, we clarified our diagnoses, our concerns and ideas, and our own patterns of effectiveness and ineffectiveness. We discussed at length our own contributions to the group's difficulties, and we have also shared these notes with our clients. They can then help us test our thinking in a manner consistent with mutual learning. It was during our process note discussions that we identified, for example, that we had gotten sucked into the group's "no preparation" routine.

Finally, it is important to know the bounds of your own skills. Occasionally developmental work can raise issues that should be dealt with by a trained counselor or therapist. The bottom line is to know when you have reached the limits of your competence and the limits of appropriate facilitation.

For guidance on recognizing limits of your skills, see Chapter Fifty-Seven, "The Facilitative Coach," page 457, on coaching.

CRITICAL SUCCESS FACTORS

We don't know of an organization that has completely transformed as a result of developmental facilitation. We do have examples of a number of sustained efforts that have produced impressive results.

See Chapter Thirty-Eight, "Daily Challenges of a Facilitative Leader," page 309, and Chapter Forty-Six, "From Learning to Lead to Leading to Learn," page 367, for some examples.

We work with a number of clients engaged in training all or most of their workforce in Skilled Facilitator principles, and we can tell many stories of leaders who

Exhibit 43.1 Developmental Facilitation Success Factors

- Explicit set of personal and organizational values and beliefs
- Experienced, knowledgeable facilitators who can model mutual learning
- Committed participants willing to learn and take time for the effort to grow
- Individuals willing to take risks in the service of their personal learning
- Individuals willing to engage in rigorous self-reflection
- Clear, regularly renewed work agreement
- Skills training for group members and, ultimately, the organization
- Measures of group growth and successful organizational development
- Group leadership (whether or not at the top organizational level) involved in coaching others and striving to model behavior consistent with mutual learning values and beliefs

have transformed their own lives. Our efforts are fairly new by developmental standards and, of course, take time. We have seen some efforts begun and abandoned. We don't think there is one right place to start developmental work in an organization or one set way to approach the process. But highlighted in Exhibit 43.1 is a list of factors we believe that successful efforts share. Helping individuals and groups learn and develop deep awareness is the most rewarding work we do. We believe using Skilled Facilitator principles as our guide holds great promise for improving the way organizations set and reach their goals and the way people are treated while engaging in these efforts.

Note

1. See "Not Enough Time" in Senge and others (1999) for an additional way to reframe how groups might think about time and adopt strategies for addressing time limitations.

References

Argyris, C. *Overcoming Organizational Defenses.* Upper Saddle River, N.J: Prentice Hall, 1990.

Argyris, C. "Good Communication That Blocks Learning." *Harvard Business Review,* July-Aug. 1994, pp. 77–85.

Beckhard, R. Foreword. In E. E. Olson and G. H. Eoyang, *Facilitating Organization Change: Lessons from Complexity Science.* San Francisco: Jossey-Bass/Pfeiffer, 2001.

Senge, P., and others. *The Dance of Change: The Challenges to Sustaining Momentum in Learning Organizations.* New York: Doubleday, 1999.

Chapter 44

Guidelines for Theory-in-Use Interventions

Anne Davidson
Dick McMahon

ENGAGING IN DEVELOPMENTAL FACILITATION requires intervening on theory-in-use issues. The level of deep personal reflection that fosters facilitative leadership does not occur until people examine how their mental models drive their behavior. Theory-in-use interventions help initiate and guide this reflection. We also use these interventions to help groups and organizations develop by examining the values and assumptions embedded in their processes and structures.

See Chapter Four, "Understanding What Guides Your Behavior," page 33, to explore the distinction between what people say and do and the gap between espoused theory and theory-in-use, and Chapter Forty-Three, "Developmental Facilitation," page 339.

You intervene on theory-in-use when you help an individual or group explore their core values and assumptions or explore how the core values and assumptions you infer from their behavior differ from what they say they value or intend (*The Skilled Facilitator,* p. 163). Theory-in-use interventions also help people see how their actions produce unintended consequences. They may see others become wary or angry in a conversation or see people distort the intention of an organizational policy (for example, by using inefficient processes to increase billable hours). Whenever unintended consequences can be identified, there is an opportunity to examine how the theory-in-use guiding the related actions or decisions contributed to the outcome. In other words, these interventions help people move from blaming others to seeing how they cocreate difficulties and then to designing ways to shift their contribution to influence positive change.

Following is a description of a time when a facilitator might engage in a theory-in-use intervention, including what the facilitator would say. After the example, we examine the steps of a theory-in-use intervention and offer additional guidelines.

EXAMPLE: INTERVENING ON TOM'S THEORY-IN-USE

Tom is a member of a work team committed to using mutual learning core values. Sandy is the team's developmental facilitator helping group members change their thinking and behavior to be consistent with their intentions. Tom often volunteers to serve as scribe during team meetings. Sandy observes that when Tom is at the flip chart, he usually writes up exactly what group members say, even if it is off track. Sandy and other group members find themselves frequently trying to get the group back on track during meetings. Many times people start suggesting solutions while the team is still trying to define an issue. Sandy infers that Tom's writing up off-topic comments contributes to the group discussions' getting off track. Tom has just written up what looks like a solution to the problem the team is working on while the team is engaged in brainstorming a list of interests that need to be met for a solution to be acceptable. Sandy has an agreement with the group that he will raise theory-in-use issues when he thinks it will help group members to do so. He decides to begin a theory-in-use intervention with Tom:

Sandy: Tom, I noticed that you wrote up Sallie's suggestion that the group just adopt the XRAY software package as the standard. That looks to me like a solution rather than an interest. I understood that the group is still brainstorming interests. Am I missing something?

Tom: Hmmm. No, I guess it is a solution.

Sandy: Do you see it the same way, Sallie, or differently?

Sallie: Maybe it is . . . I guess so. I was jumping ahead . . .

Sandy: I think this is also a pattern when you are at the flip chart, Tom. I think that frequently you write up comments that are at a different step of the problem-solving process than the one the group is working on, and this contributes to the whole discussion getting off-track. Later you have to back up and revisit earlier steps, or I and other group members spend a lot of time intervening to refocus the group on what they agreed to discuss. I'd like to share a couple of other examples and see if you agree this is what happened. Are you willing to do that?

Tom: Sure, if it will help the group.

[Sandy shares examples, and Tom and the group agree with Sandy's view of what happened and the consequences for the group discussion.]

Sandy: I believe it is important to explore Tom's and the group's thinking that leads this to happen. Can we take some time now to do that? [The group agrees to do so.] Tom, you agreed that you write up exactly what each group member says even if it is not apparently related to the discussion, and you do not check out whether or how it is related. Have I got that right?

Tom: Yeah, I guess so.

Sandy: What were you thinking in these situations? Did you see the comments as off-track, and if so, what led you to put them up without asking about them?

Tom: Well, I did think the comments were unrelated or at different steps of the problem-solving model we use. But I think that a good scribe puts up people's exact words.

Sandy: Can you say what you think might happen if you call attention to the fact that comments are off-track and don't write them up?

Tom: Well, I think that might embarrass them in front of the group. Wouldn't you have felt uncomfortable if I told you your solution was off-track, Sallie?

Sallie: Well, a little maybe.

Sandy: I am not suggesting you say exactly what you just said, Tom. We can spend some time in a minute, if you like, thinking about what you might say. But first I would like to explore what leads you not to say anything. I think that unless we get at your thinking, it will be hard for you to say what you need or want to in these situations. Do you agree with my reasoning, or do you see this differently?

Tom: I can see your point.

Sandy: Okay, so what were you thinking would happen if you said you thought Sallie's comment was a solution rather than an interest?

Tom: I did not want to call attention to the fact that Sallie was making a mistake. That would embarrass her in front of the whole group.

Sandy: What are you afraid will happen if you do that?

Tom: Well, I think she would get upset and not say anything else, and she has pretty good ideas. Plus she would be mad at me and embarrass me somehow when she is scribing or leading the meeting.

Sandy: I would like to propose a different way of thinking about this situation and then get your reaction. Is that okay? [Tom says yes.] I believe that not identifying off-track suggestions is inconsistent with your values of mutual learning. It looks as if you are saving face for Sallie in this case and also unilaterally protecting yourself. I see this as more consistent with the value of staying in control by minimizing the expression of negative feelings. As a consequence, Sallie and the other group members do not learn, for example, the distinction between defining a problem and offering solutions or the importance of completing each process step before trying to solve a problem. Sometimes you may also lose the opportunity to see how someone's comment is, in fact, on-track and useful. In the long run, the group may make ineffective decisions. Do you agree with my reasoning, or do you have a different view of what is happening and the consequences?"

Tom: I can see what you are talking about. But this is hard. What could I do differently?

Sandy: Well, I think the first thing is to begin to think differently about what it means to point out to someone that his or her behavior is ineffective—that he or she is, for example, on a different step of the problem-solving process. Instead of thinking about embarrassing someone, you could assume that the person wants to learn how to improve his or her work, even if the learning creates some discomfort. If you assume that all of us make mistakes sometimes and that these are not sins but opportunities to learn, then you can think about how much better it would be to learn now rather than to keep making the same mistake over and over. And you can think about how important it is for everyone in the group to learn and perform at your best so that you produce top-quality work. What is your reaction to what I am saying?

As a result of this discussion, Tom agrees to work with Sandy to design what to say in the future when he believes a comment is off-topic. Sandy may also want to take this opportunity to raise a group defensive routine: the group is engaging in behavior similar to Tom's. They are not raising with Tom the fact that he is writing off-track comments, thereby saving face for Tom. Tom's and the group's behavior looks like a deeply embedded pattern of unilateral protection. Sandy could test his inferences around this and help the group see how each party contributes to the group's routine. Then Sandy could help the group design how they will raise issues with one another so they do not collude to keep this routine in place. Going to this next level has the advantage of helping the group recognize other times when they may unproductively protect one another. Recognizing this as a group routine also reduces the risk of retribution Tom raises when group members intervene with one another.

See Chapter Forty-Three, "Developmental Facilitation," page 339.

THE INTERVENTION PROCESS

Here are the basic steps we use to guide theory-in-use interventions and some examples of how Sandy applied them:

See Chapter Six, "The Diagnosis-Intervention Cycle," page 69.

1. **Describe the behavior that triggered your intervention and explain the reason you believe an intervention is important.** (This step makes step 3 of the diagnosis-intervention cycle transparent, including explaining reasoning and intent.) This often means stating that a theory-in-use issue seems relevant to the discussion and checking to see if the individual and group are willing to explore it. You might say something like, "**I think it would be helpful to explore your thinking behind**

[what was said] because . . . Would you be willing to do that?" If the group is familiar with the terminology, you might say, **"I think there may be a theory-in-use issue here that it would be useful to explore. I'd like to say what I think that is and see if others think similarly or differently. Would the group be willing to take some time to do that now?"**

Other inquiries you can combine with explaining your reasons for the intervention include: **"Would you be willing to explore your reasoning about this?"** and **"Would you be open to examining the assumptions behind your reasoning?"**

Sandy in the example already had a contract with the group to intervene on theory-in-use, so he could easily wait until step 2 to jointly design with them whether to spend time on such an issue now. First, he described what he heard and saw, and he checked to see if others agreed with his inference that Tom had written a solution on the flip chart when the group was working on interests. He needed to start there in order to be certain this was a valid example of the pattern he believed he was seeing.

2. **Assuming the answer is yes to exploring theory-in-use or a standing agreement to do so, state the pattern of behavior observed and test for different views.** (This is step 4 of the diagnosis-intervention cycle, including explaining reasoning and intent.) It is especially important to describe behavior and test for agreement here because you are generally using a fairly complex or long statement as the basis for your inference, and identifying a theory-in-use issue is a high-level inference.

Sandy identified the pattern of putting up off-track comments and explained his reasoning by sharing the consequences he thought it had for the group. He needed to test two things with the group: whether they agreed that his examples accurately represented Tom's and the group's behavior and whether they agreed with his inference that the pattern had a negative impact on the group. If the group agreed, as they did, he could proceed. If the group saw the situation differently, then Sandy would need to engage in inquiry to understand how and why their views differed. Useful inquiries to include at this step are:

"Do you remember it the way I described or differently?"

"Did I describe what happened accurately or not?"

"Do you think these behaviors have the effects I described, or do you see a different outcome?"

"Do you think the pattern I described affects your work, and, if so, how?"

3. **Ask each individual involved to explain the reasoning that leads him to take this approach.** Continue to explore embedded assumptions and inferences. This will often involve testing several levels of assumptions, including assumptions about longer-term consequences of raising or not raising an issue.

Sandy tested what Tom thought would happen if he pointed out that Sallie's comment was a solution and also what he thought the consequences would be if she were in fact embarrassed. Useful inquiries to include might be:

> **"What are you thinking but not saying? What is in your left-hand column [if the person has worked with left-hand column cases]?"**
>
> **"What past experiences led you to think about these kinds of situations in this way?"**

As an alternative, you might state what you see as the theory-in-use operating. Then invite the person who made the relevant comments to explore with you whether your inferences could be correct. Or you might inquire into what others see as the theory-in-use that is operating (as long as this is not a leading or manipulative question) and ask the group to explore with you what is going on. (These alternatives basically reverse steps 3 and 4 of the intervention. See the examples in the next step.)

4. **Share your theory-in-use inferences.** (This is step 5 of the diagnosis-intervention cycle.) Use this step to connect the theory-in-use discussion to unilateral control versus mutual learning core values, action strategies, and consequences. If the group has adopted explicit values built on mutual learning, you may link to one of those values as well. Point out potential inconsistencies between espoused values and the theory-in-use at work. In other words, theory-in-use interventions should help the group explore potential mismatches between what they intend and what they are likely to get.

Sandy points out to Tom's group, for example, that trying to minimize the expression of negative feelings (**a unilateral assumption**) leads Tom to adopt a **strategy** of saving face when others' comments are off-track, resulting in (**consequences**) lost learning opportunities in the short run and in ineffective decisions in the longer term. Sandy might say, for example:

> **"I think you may have some assumptions about saving face for participants by not calling attention to the fact that their statements are off-track. Do you think that these assumptions are driving your behavior, Tom?"**
>
> **"I'd like to describe what I think your reasoning might be here and then get your reaction. I am guessing you are thinking that . . . [describe the theory-in-use inferred]."**
>
> **"This thinking looks to me as if it is inconsistent with the core value of . . . Are you seeing it the same way I am or differently?"**
>
> **"Unilaterally protecting others is one way we minimize expression of negative feelings. We may do that so we can stay in control. In other words,**

there is an underlying assumption that if we call attention to the fact that a participant is off-track, we will embarrass that person. If we embarrass this person, he or she or other group members may express negative feelings. When that happens, we assume we will no longer be in control of the meeting. Do you think that reasoning might be at work here?"

5. **Help the group decide whether and how to reframe their thinking and redesign their decisions to be consistent with their espoused values and beliefs.** (This is step 6 of the diagnosis-intervention cycle.) At this stage, it is often useful for the facilitator to offer a different way to frame the issue at hand. There are usually conflicting assumptions about the need to unilaterally protect others, the ability of others to handle difficult feedback, whether people are well intended, and so forth. By reframing the cruel consequences that result from not giving people accurate feedback about their behavior, for example, the facilitator can help groups explore the flaws in their past logic and make an informed choice about whether to consciously adopt a different set of assumptions.

Sandy helps Tom and his group think about the consequences of covering up mistakes and not learning versus learning and improving individual and group performance. It often helps at this step to separate short-term from longer-term consequences of ineffective strategies, such as poor job performance and loss of employment as the trade-off for not embarrassing someone in the moment. Or Sandy could discuss the way we discount others by assuming they are too emotionally fragile to handle honest feedback and how inconsistent this is with most people's desires to learn and grow. Assuming those involved agree they want to change their thinking, Sandy could also make statements and ask questions like these:

"What other assumptions might you make that would lead to a different action and possibly get different results?"

"I would like to propose a different way of thinking about [this issue]. . . . What flaws, if any, do you see in this logic?"

"If you were designing your statement [approach] to be consistent with the group's values, what would you do?"

To help group members practice what to say once they begin to shift their thinking, it is most useful to have them say the actual words and phrases they think would be consistent with the new frame on the situation. We may offer to model an example and then have others try their own or ask if they would like to come up with one or more examples and get feedback.

GENERAL PRINCIPLES FOR THEORY-IN-USE INTERVENTIONS

> In our experience, theory-in-use is most easily seen when groups go about their work, engaging in the necessary content conversations they would usually have but with skilled facilitators present.

Effective theory-in-use interventions require listening carefully for untested assumptions driving any decision-making process. In our experience, theory-in-use is most easily seen when groups go about their work, engaging in the necessary content conversations they would usually have but with skilled facilitators present. The facilitators can then intervene when they see possible theory-in-use issues that may be creating gaps between the values and intentions that are espoused versus the values and assumptions embedded in actions and policies.

Theory-in-use may show up at any of three levels: (1) as an individual issue, such as Tom's trying to unilaterally protect Sallie in the opening example; (2) as a group defensive routine, such as the group members not openly disagreeing with the boss or confronting Tom about his ineffectiveness; or (3) as an organizational routine, such as a policy that is inconsistent with a group's core values. Over time, groups can see how reframing a theory-in-use issue in one situation, such as unilaterally protecting people who make off-topic comments, can translate into more effectively handling another situation, like giving one another performance feedback.

Contract First

It is particularly important to contract with a group or individual to make theory-in-use interventions before making them. These interventions go to a much deeper level than basic ground rules interventions. Therefore, they are generally more time-consuming, require more openness and reflection on the part of group members, and involve more perceived risk or threat to participants. Normally you wouldn't be making theory-in-use interventions in a basic (one- or two-day) facilitation because usually you have contracted with the group to complete a specific task, not for personal or group development. Also, a basic facilitation is less likely to produce the kinds of data needed to support theory-in-use interventions (such as patterns of behavior over time or values reflections).

To contract clearly with a group, the group needs an introduction to the concept of mental models and to the specific models of unilateral control and mutual learning. This helps them understand the distinction between espoused theories and theories-in-use. It is important to communicate these concepts in a way that group members understand what you mean. This generally includes carefully defining terms and sharing specific examples and stories.

See the Mental Models, Theory-in-Use, and Espoused Theory sidebar in Chapter Four, "Understanding What Guides Your Behavior," page 33.

It is important to hold an open discussion about advantages to the group from theory-in-use interventions and possible consequences such as personal risk and additional time investment. Only then can group members make a somewhat informed decision about whether they want to pursue theory-in-use discussions. Recontracting will also be necessary along the way, because until the group gains some experience with this kind of intervention, individuals cannot make a truly informed choice about their participation.

Theory-in-use interventions are much easier and clearer in groups that have an explicit set of group values. This way the relationship between espoused values and their theories-in-use can be clearly described. We often use the example of honesty to talk with groups about how they may espouse a value like this but have a theory-in-use that leads them to behave inconsistently with this value or to situationally define the meaning of the value. For example, most of us have a theory-in-use of unilaterally protecting others from potentially embarrassing information about their behavior. We think it is okay to avoid sharing this information or to tell a white lie when asked about it. Yet most of us are blind to how this is inconsistent with the honesty we espouse, even though other people usually see the discrepancy. Talking through simple and common gaps like this helps a group grasp the basic concept and, over time, move toward deeper and deeper examinations of inconsistencies with all of their espoused values.

Follow the Diagnosis-Intervention Cycle

The pattern for theory-in-use interventions follows the six steps of the diagnosis-intervention cycle just like any other intervention. In fact, it is even more important to use the steps of the cycle for two reasons. First, these interventions are almost always based on a pattern of behavior over time or on a complex set of interrelated assumptions. Every group member needs to know the data you are working from (the actual words and actions) and the inferences you are making in order to follow your interventions. Because you are intervening on deeply embedded assumptions that often reside below the level of conscious thought, it is usually necessary to go around the cycle several times before completing a theory-in-use intervention. Second, because they require more personal disclosure, there is a greater chance that theory-in-use interventions will raise defensiveness. Using the cycle precisely usually lowers the likelihood of defensiveness because the group or individual with whom you are intervening can clearly follow your logic.

See Chapter Six, "The Diagnosis-Intervention Cycle," page 69.

Step 5 of the cycle (sharing inferences and testing for different views) may be repeated a number of times even when other steps are not. This step usually becomes a series of explanations and questions designed to help the initiator explore the reasoning behind his or her actions or to explore alternative assumptions that might guide a redesign.

Use Ground Rules During Your Intervention

During theory-in-use interventions, make statements and ask questions consistent with the ground rules. Sandy in the model conversation helped group members test assumptions and inferences, gave specific examples, and explained the reasoning and intent behind his statements, questions, and actions. In using the diagnosis-intervention cycle, he combined advocacy and inquiry by stating his observations and inferences and then testing them. He also jointly designed with the group and with Tom whether to spend time on this intervention and the order in which to discuss the topics (for example, examining Tom's thinking before helping him figure out what to say). It is important for the facilitator to model the ground rules because this sets a tone of mutual learning and helps the group learn how to use the ground rules effectively to discuss potentially difficult topics when the facilitator is not present.

See Chapter Five, "Ground Rules for Effective Groups," page 61.

Start Where the Gap Is Most Obvious

We routinely advise facilitators to start where the gap is. Theory-in-use issues can be especially hard for individuals and groups to discern. Starting at the level where the gap between espoused theory and theory-in-use is most obvious helps groups follow your reasoning as you intervene. They also better understand the consequences of not addressing these gaps. If the most obvious gap is that a policy is inconsistent with mutual learning core values, we find it most productive to start the intervention at this structural level. After talking through the assumptions behind the policy, it is easier to explore the values and assumptions of individuals who support the policy.

In one memorable example, a group was developing stricter and stricter travel policy regulations that had the unintended consequence of causing people to spend hours of expensive and unproductive time on paperwork. Many tried to circumvent the policy rather than comply, and their attempts were met by increasingly tight regulations and further deteriorating compliance. By starting at the level of intended versus unintended consequences, the group involved was able to explore the values and assumptions embedded in the policy (people are not trustworthy and must be tightly controlled). This led to an exploration of the theory-in-use of the manager's promoting tighter controls and his assumptions about how people develop commitment to do the right thing. Although he espoused commitment, his actions emphasized compliance. It would have been hard to raise and discuss this individual's theory-in-use without first helping him and his group see how it played out in the organizational structure.

In another similar situation, group members routinely deferred to the boss in team meetings. We began our intervention at the level of the group defensive routine, which led to helping individuals explore values and assumptions about disagreeing with the boss. Again, the data were in the group behavior and were less obviously related to one particular individual, so we started the intervention with the group. The group and the facilitator could then jointly design whether it was appropriate to pursue a theory-in-use issue at one, two, or all three levels.

There is no one right place to start a theory-in-use intervention. We recommend you start where the patterns present themselves. Over time, individuals and groups develop the capacity to discern and examine increasingly subtle and difficult theory-in-use issues. They learn to reframe their core values and assumptions in ways that ultimately increase the effectiveness of the entire group or organization and everyone involved in it.

Chapter 45

Introducing the Core Values and Ground Rules

Jeff Koeze

Koeze Company is a small, family-owned nut and chocolate manufacturing and marketing company, with about thirty-five employees, founded in 1910. In September 1996 I joined the company, which my father owned and had run for the prior thirty years. Every employee in the company has been trained in the use of the core values and ground rules, and several, including me, have been through the public version of the Skilled Facilitator Intensive workshop. This chapter describes how I became interested in introducing the core values and ground rules to Koeze's and how we worked together with Roger Schwarz to introduce the approach.

BACKGROUND

In May 1996 I was a professor in the Institute of Government at The University of North Carolina at Chapel Hill specializing in health care law. Roger Schwarz, Dick McMahon, and Peg Carlson were faculty colleagues of mine. I was familiar with the Skilled Facilitator approach from working with them, had taken a two-week group facilitation course, and watched as Roger attempted, and ultimately failed, to persuade his faculty colleagues and the administration of the Institute to adopt the core values and ground rules for faculty meetings (the staff, however, did decide to use the approach). But because faculty traditionally work essentially alone and because I'd never had substantial administrative or managerial experience, my familiarity with the approach was largely academic and my skill limited.

In May 1996 I resigned to join Koeze's, and we hired Roger to facilitate a series of meetings over the course of several months in which my father and I, and all the employees who reported to my father, worked to define my role in the company and plan the process by which I would eventually assume my father's position. Roger's task in these meetings was for the most part basic, not developmental, facilitation, but those involved had information on which to assess Roger and his approach.

COMPANYWIDE ROLLOUT

As the transition work came to an end in the spring of 1997, I raised the possibility that the transition group adopt the core values and ground rules for our day-to-day work together outside the transition. We spoke about it in a meeting in March and scheduled Roger to provide some in-depth training in May. This was, in effect, a transition to begin developmental facilitation to help us develop a Facilitative Leader approach in the organization.

See Chapter Forty-Three, "Developmental Facilitation," page 339.

A planning group worked out a proposed schedule by conference call, and Roger then provided a memo to the entire group outlining the assignment for the training, including writing a left-hand column case based on a difficult conversation that had happened at work.

See Chapter Twenty-Seven, "Writing and Analyzing a Left-Hand Column Case," page 235.

Once the left-hand column case was proposed, some objections came forward. One member of the group chose not to participate at the outset. The others joined Roger in a conference call to discuss their concerns, which revolved primarily around the risks of opening old wounds in the group. Reflecting later, a couple of employees spoke about anxiety over completing a case. One wrote several but was willing to share only the least difficult of them with the group.

After speaking to Roger about their concerns, each of the group members agreed to do a case. Several of the written cases involved difficult issues between members of the group; one was particularly interesting because two people chose the same conversation, so we got to see both "left-hand columns."

After this training and the agreement of those involved to use the core values and ground rules, the group had an interest in bringing the training to the entire company. We invited three people who had not been involved in the transition group to join in the planning of that training with a few of the original group. Working with Roger, we decided that we should schedule a meeting for the entire company to discuss the core values and ground rules and give everyone the chance to make an informed choice about participating. That meeting was held in early June, and later in the month Roger returned to do the training. Everyone participated and agreed, at the end, to use the core values and ground rules.

Members of the original transition team had similar perspectives on the degree to which they were free to decline to participate in these activities. A couple said that they knew they had the option to refuse, although that might require them to eventually leave the company if they found themselves more and more out of step with the developing corporate culture. Almost everyone said they felt real pressure to "get with the program" of the new corporate president, and they all assumed others did as well. This was tempered by the (incorrect) assumption that the use of the core values and ground rules would prove to be yet another passing management fad. None of these thoughts, by the way, was raised during the introduction process itself.

REFLECTIONS ON THE INTRODUCTION

The central feature of the rollout of the core values and ground rules at Koeze's was attention to choice at each step of the process. At each step—hiring Roger to consult on the transition, switching to developmental facilitation with the transition group, and adopting the core values and ground rules companywide—employees were offered choices, their input was sought, and concerns were addressed.

I do wonder if they knew what they were getting into, although several have said that they immediately perceived that the core values and ground rules would require anxiety-inducing changes in behavior. From my experience in the Skilled Facilitator course and my work with Roger and his colleagues over many years, I knew that there was important information about the mutual learning approach that could be grasped only by living it. A ground rule such as "combine advocacy with inquiry" sounds harmless enough. In fact, the only ground rule that sounds truly scary is "discuss undiscussable issues."

A change in theory-in-use can be deeply transformative and lead to a fundamental shift in ways of thought and behavior. There is no easy way to tell somebody what that is like or what it may mean for that person.

A change in theory-in-use can be deeply transformative and lead to a fundamental shift in ways of thought and behavior. There is no easy way to tell somebody what that is like or what it may mean for that person.

CHALLENGES TO SUSTAINED LEARNING

The transition group knew from the moment that Koeze's adopted the core values and ground rules that we needed to continue to improve our skills. The issue was how. Continuing to bring Roger and his colleagues in on an ongoing basis was beyond our means financially, and at the time, there was no public training geared specifically to facilitative leadership or management. So the transition group met to discuss whether to send staff to the Skilled Facilitator public workshops.[1]

We decided that this was the best option and that we could afford to send two people. Our consensus was that they should be our production manager and director of human resources that first year. Since then we've sent one or two people each year. We have provided some basic training and review of the ground rules on an ongoing basis internally. We've also used Roger and his colleagues to facilitate on some particularly difficult issues, particularly when our most skilled people cannot do so because they are directly involved with the issue at hand.

Our expectations of each other are that we will use the core values and ground rules in interactions with each other at all times. Our success in meeting those expectations is mixed. As might be expected, we vary widely in skill, commitment, and discipline. Our growth has been hindered by the lack of the consistent involvement of trained outsiders to continue with developmental facilitation and skill building. We've also failed to do some of the things we could do to improve on our own. I've explored, but not committed to, Chris Argyris's (1993) suggestion of taping and transcribing conversations. And our self-critiques quickly became perfunctory, and being therefore useless, have mostly ceased.

Nevertheless, there is some anecdotal evidence that things are different now. A new employee with many years of experience with large automotive and furniture companies recently said that he was amazed at how open and direct we are. My feeling is that in some cases, our training has allowed to us tackle difficult issues, especially those involving pay and performance, that might have been avoided or handled badly in the absence of our skills.

I believe that we think a little better because of our care to examine assumptions and inferences. After a recent meeting that involved a philosophy professor, he commented that he was struck by hearing people so consistently ask others about inferences and that he wished that the philosophy faculty were as careful in their meetings.

I'm unsure of the significance of the next story, but perhaps it indicated a comfort among the core group with the change. At my father's retirement party in 1997, the employees performed skits. One included a parody of the core values and ground rules based on my father's favorite sayings. Among them were: "It's my way or the highway," "Who signs your paycheck?" and the ever-popular, "Whose name is on the building?"

Yet I still see us acting unilaterally to protect others. I still see us saving face, avoiding difficult conversations, acting defensively, and otherwise routinely lapsing into the unilateral control model. In fact, notwithstanding all of our training, I recently described the avoidance of delivering negative information concerning the performance of others as a core feature of Koeze's culture.

FAILING FORWARD

When I asked several of the original transition group to comment on their experience with the core values and ground rules, two related themes came through. The first was that even six years into the learning, old habits of thought and speech die hard, if at all, so using the core values and ground rules remains a difficult challenge. It is a process that involves much failure, but in general, we are failing forward.

In spite of the work involved, the group members said they would not choose to give up the core values and ground rules learning and the practice.

Yet in spite of the work involved, all said they would not choose to give up the core values and ground rules learning and the practice. This raises the question of what motivates them to keep going. An answer lies in the other common theme: the core values and ground rules give them voice. With this training, they have tools to express themselves when they otherwise would have felt the need to keep silent, and with our mutual agreement to use them, the playing field for expression has been leveled—not completely, but enough—to give them a real sense of being obliged to speak up, not stay silent, and a real expectation of being heard.

Note

1. For information about Roger Schwarz & Associates' public and on-site workshops, go to www.schwarzassociates.com.

Reference

Argyris, C. *Knowledge for Action: A Guide to Overcoming Barriers to Organizational Change.* San Francisco: Jossey-Bass, 1993.

Chapter 46

From Learning to Lead to Leading to Learn

Joe Huffman

As I PEER OUT MY WINDOW in Laurinburg, North Carolina, early one morning, I see that nearly a foot of snow has fallen overnight in a city that seldom sees snow. I am the city manager, and someone calls me to ask if I am going to close the offices to the public and administrative personnel for the day. With safety uppermost in mind, I quickly reply, "Close city hall." I believe I have managed well, responding quickly and decisively. If I had failed to do so, others would say I lacked leadership.

One week later, my decision comes back to haunt me. Employees start to ask if administrative personnel should be paid for the hours they did not work because their offices were closed. If I say yes, the employees who did have to work that day, laboring under difficult conditions to clear streets and repair utility lines, will feel slighted. If I say no, city hall employees whose offices were closed will be forced to use a vacation day. Some don't have much vacation and might greatly resent having to use it without having a choice in the matter. Had they known they would be forced to take vacation, they might have chosen to come to work, despite the difficult conditions. Both sides blame me.

I am frustrated. I think I am a good leader. I have in my head a clear model of what makes an effective leader: someone who can respond quickly and effectively under difficult circumstances, someone who can be heroic, and someone who can also empower and involve employees. There is no policy to guide me. I made what I thought was a good, quick decision. Now I will have to spend precious hours revisiting what I did, hearing both sides of a debate in which it seems there will be winners and losers, no matter what I decide. How could such a simple decision have the unintended consequence of making so many people unhappy? What are the long-term consequences of their dissatisfaction?

This is not a new situation for me. How many times have I found myself putting out fires created by earlier decisions I thought were good ones? How many of us as leaders do this over and over again? Why do employees come to expect managers to make these types of decisions? Can't they answer these questions themselves? Isn't that what employee empowerment is all about? But no, we need order and control, don't we? There should be rules. Without rules, there would be chaos. Or liability issues.

Or both. I am stuck in a dilemma. If I am honest, I admit that I have been stuck like this many times before. I am leading the way I was taught to lead. I am applying the latest concepts. I am not dictatorial. I involve employees in decisions that affect them, yet in a crisis I take clear action. But it is time-consuming, not personally satisfying, and doesn't work as easily as most of the books say it will.

I found a way out of this particular dilemma. In fact, I believe I have found an alternative to the management techniques that many leaders find so limiting. I think I have discovered a way of leading that builds employee accountability, addresses many dilemmas previously thought unsolvable, and helps create an organization dedicated to learning and becoming more responsive to those it serves. This solution is more than mere management technique. It is a journey of self-discovery that I believe will enrich anyone who undertakes the voyage. It broadens and deepens understanding of human interactions and exponentially increases the ability to make sound decisions based on good data that will be understood and supported by others.

LEARNING TO LEAD

My understanding of management principles was shaped initially during my enrollment in a master of public administration program and then over nine years as manager of the town of Elkin and then the City of Havelock, both in North Carolina. In these positions, I understood the limitations of hierarchical relationships and attempted to mitigate their impact by developing strong professional and interpersonal relationships with employees. I also remember feeling that I really did not know how to apply what I understood might be a better way of functioning in organizations.

In retrospect, while I involved others in the organization to some extent, I really employed what I now know as the unilateral control model. In essence, I made use of talented people to help me make decisions or recommendations. I did not leave myself very open to changing my own ideas and opinions, and I basically left the existing hierarchical channels in place to accomplish tasks.

In the mid-1990s, several things occurred that caused me to think about my management style. On a few occasions, the management team of employees I was working with would cause me to significantly change my decision or recommendation because of their thoughts on a matter. During one meeting on prioritizing new positions for the upcoming budget process, for instance, I advocated for a new technology position while the majority advocated for a new fire chief. We decided to recommend the fire chief position. Although at first I felt I had acquiesced to the group, I realized over time that the priority ranking made by the group was better than I would have done alone. What's more, later dramatic improvements in the fire department came from recommendations by the new chief, while delaying the creation of the technology position had no adverse results.

After a few years, I began to want more challenge in my career, yet I did not know what that might be. I read several influential management books, including

Peter Senge's *The Fifth Discipline* (1990), which focuses on creating learning organizations. I agreed with some of the ideas presented but had difficulty understanding how to implement them.

In 1998, I learned that the city manager position in Laurinburg was open. While researching the position, I found that the city was involved in an organization development effort based on the concepts in Senge's *The Fifth Discipline* (1990), as well as on the work of Chris Argyris as developed by Roger Schwarz. When I read an article in "Popular Government" describing Laurinburg's learning organization initiative (Davidson and McMahon, 1999), I thought being involved in this type of activity would come naturally and that it might be a fairly easy way to find what I sought. During my employment interviews with the mayor and city council, I told them that I had experience working with a management team and that I would be very comfortable with the Laurinburg learning organization approach.

THE LAURINBURG EXPERIENCE

Any notions that I understood what was going on in Laurinburg or that learning the required new skills would be easy were quickly proven wrong. At first, I relied heavily on the management style I had used for the previous decade. Although the Laurinburg management team members responded to me ably, I sensed there was something more to this management technique than just reading a book and agreeing with a list of values and beliefs.

The management team, often assisted by developmental facilitators Dick McMahon and Anne Davidson, behaved very differently from other groups I had worked with. Dick and Anne had been helping the team for three years, during which the group had learned ways of behaving and speaking that seemed foreign to me. Looking back, I suspect the first few months must have been difficult for the group because I did not understand just how much I did not know. Slowly I began to catch on.

Leading Without Giving Up Control

Early on I learned that as city manager, by virtue of participating in this effort, I was not giving up control. The management team had chosen to make substantive decisions by consensus, although this was not a requirement for learning organizations. At first, I did not see how consensus was consistent with upholding my responsibilities to the city council under the council-manager form of government. Over time, I came to understand that better decisions could be made using consensus, particularly when addressing policy issues. In Laurinburg, we reached consensus after analyzing data, advocating our various views, and inviting disagreement. I learned that a group that was effective did not negotiate or defend positions with a win-lose attitude. Instead, when someone presented an idea or advocated a position, he or she also stated reasons and shared data. The team engaged in a dialogue in which they questioned the data for clarification. If others provided new data, the group might come to a different decision. If one member did not agree with a course of action, that person needed to share why he or she disagreed and provide data. If new data made a difference, a change could jointly be considered. If the data were not shared, the position of the dissenter became indefensible.

The benefits of this process became more and more apparent to me. A memorable example involved the dilemma of the snow day closing:

> The management team wanted to use an employee committee to develop an office closing policy because it seemed appropriate that those most directly affected be involved in its creation. We also thought the employees would have interests and information we did not know about that would help to create a sound policy. For its part, management team members had legitimate interests that the committee needed to take into account. Without sharing their concerns and parameters, the management team would be abdicating its responsibility. To create a new inclement weather policy, the employee committee was given a list of management team interests that would need to be met.

See Chapter Sixteen, "Helping Group Members Focus on Interests Rather Than Positions," page 145.

> When the management team received the proposed policy, one of the team expressed discomfort with it. However, with some discussion and clarification, it became apparent that the proposal met the management team's interests. It would have been difficult to defend not supporting a policy that met its interests, particularly given the need for the management team to model behavior consistent with its values and beliefs. By the time I proposed the policy to the council, I was very comfortable advocating for its passage, and I shared that employees had played a strong role in its development.

The council adopted the policy unanimously. Had we used a different process, it is likely that the policy's shortcomings would not have been discovered until implementation.

Seeing Inconsistencies

As I developed understanding of learning organization concepts, I began to see inconsistencies in the behavior of others. I was somewhat surprised whenever I saw someone who had received training behaving inconsistently with our espoused values and beliefs. But it was some time before I learned that I too contributed to problems and began to see my own inconsistencies. During discussions, I found that I often recognized when others were not giving the reasoning behind their statements.

Only later was I aware that I too would make statements or challenge someone's opinion without clearly sharing my thinking.

Also, I acted inconsistently by not testing inferences that I was making about another's reasoning and not asking for clarification when necessary. In becoming more aware of how I contributed to problems, I began a transition that I have heard best described by Anne Davidson as the move from "unconscious incompetence" to "conscious incompetence" to "conscious competence" and then to "unconscious competence."

It was some time before I learned that I too contributed to problems and began to see my own inconsistencies.

Continuing to Learn

I found it particularly useful to practice my new learning with those also exposed to the same concepts. Employees and others trained in sessions the city offered were usually willing to tell me when they thought I or others in the organization were not "walking the talk." Through this joint process in self-discovery, I have become more aware of both my effective and ineffective behavior patterns and the consequences. One of the best examples involved an employee who attended one of the initial Learning Organization Concepts training sessions.

> I had heard from others that this employee thought the effort was not worthwhile. At one of the breaks, I asked him for feedback. He readily told me of what he saw as inconsistent behavior among management team members. His specific concern was a process the management team had used during a utility extension project. He thought the management team's decision to survey residents about the quality of the city's wastewater line installation should have included others in the decision-making process. In particular, he thought he should have participated in the decision because he was an inspector on the project and would have been directly affected by the citizen feedback.
>
> I asked him if we could discuss the matter with the training group, and he agreed. The result was a productive discussion concerning his belief that the management team had not involved others to the extent necessary. He also shared other perceptions he had of the management team. Although not all the issues discussed were resolved, understanding the perceptions of others in the organization made me aware of the importance of modeling consistent behavior and the need to reflect on the consequences of behavior inconsistent with our espoused principles.

Including the Governing Board

In February 2001, the city council attended a training session on systems thinking as part of its annual retreat. One of the ideas shared by Dick McMahon was that the management team would be framing issues they brought before the council based on their learning organization training. Recommendations to the council would likely include information that supported as well as argued against each possible course of action. In this way, the council would ultimately be responsible for making the decision. This approach would run counter to a unilaterally controlling philosophy of protecting the council from unpleasant information or trying to get its support by withholding information. Credibility and commitment to decisions now seemed more likely as a result of sharing all relevant information from the beginning of the council's decision-making process.

CONTINUING CHALLENGES

After most facilitated meetings of the management team, the group reflects and learns by identifying those things done well and those things that could be changed or improved. In the same spirit, I list some of the challenges I have experienced thus far in my own learning.

Helping Others See Their Inconsistencies

One of the advantages I enjoyed in coming to Laurinburg was that I had no prior history with individuals in the organization. Because I had not interacted with them before my introduction to the learning organization principles, I did not have to redesign how I would behave with people accustomed to years of inconsistent behavior from me. Nevertheless, others in the organization still see inconsistencies in my behavior as I begin to apply training to real-life situations. Since I am in a learning mode (the essence of the effort), I understand that from time to time, I engage in unproductive or defensive behavior. Some of the employees who have been exposed to the training say that they also see inconsistencies in management team behavior.

I have used some of these discussions to understand how I can do a better job of modeling and behaving consistently. However, I have only recently begun to help others understand their own contribution to the problems they raise. I believe that one of my next steps in assisting Laurinburg's development as a learning organization is to help others understand how they jointly create nonproductive designs (either consciously or otherwise) through inconsistent behavior.

One of the key opportunities for learning is to assist employees in designing difficult discussions, and the management team has agreed to assist employees across traditional organizational boundaries. This means that a police officer can decide to discuss an issue with the finance officer rather than with the police chief. Or any employee can come to me without this being interpreted as trying to undermine or "tattle" on his or her department head. What is interesting is that when I help an employee design a difficult conversation without taking his or her side and ask him or her to use the learning organization principles, the employee learns through experience and I develop my skills simultaneously. Furthermore, if I adhere to the principles, I can model the approach and help sustain the effort by showing that I consider the approach legitimate and worthwhile. This goes for the entire management team.

See Chapter Forty, "Helping a Team Understand the System They Created," page 323, and Chapter Forty-Two, "How to Stop Contributing to Your Boss's and Your Own Ineffectiveness," page 335.

I believe that modeling is the best approach to reduce the likelihood of a defensive, nonproductive response to feedback on inconsistent behavior. This requires learning not to become unnecessarily defensive myself. For example, if I had perceived the wastewater inspector's initial comments as a threat and reacted defensively, I may have stifled his willingness to discuss his concerns and reinforced his opinions about the management team's behavior. Similarly, by responding to perceived inconsistencies in my own behavior in a nondefensive manner, I could model how productive introspection might occur. Using skills for productive problem solving is particularly useful when negative feedback is necessary. Because these skills do not come easily and take a great deal of time to master, any manager dedicated to these efforts must be willing to make a significant commitment to the learning.

Working Outside the Organization

It can be difficult to apply learning organization principles in interacting with those outside the organization. Even when you successfully eliminate the jargon, your behavior can be confusing to those not familiar with the approach.

See Chapter Twenty-Four, "Reducing the Skilled Facilitator Jargon," page 207.

For example, one of the Laurinburg management team practices that I found particularly impressive when I arrived was adherence to certain ground rules. These ground rules guide participants to, among other things, share relevant information and discuss undiscussable issues. Since private, negative conversations about others are generally unproductive, the team tries to reframe their thinking and to share their thoughts and concerns about one another's behavior. In an environment charged with emotion or political maneuvering, someone not aware of the intentions behind the attempt to discuss difficult issues may misinterpret our course of action as a lack of empathy or blatant disagreement. I have personally found that my inclination to share information with the governing board or the management team has from time to time been misunderstood by those unfamiliar with learning organization principles. It is challenging to clearly explain one's reasoning and intent.

Taking Too Much Time

Another problem is the perception that learning organization decisions take too much time. Given the effort necessary to apply systems thinking and shared decision making, it should be expected that well-thought-out actions will take longer than those involving one person or reliance on existing policy. When I first arrived in Laurinburg, an employee advised me that a particular decision was taking too much time and that I should make a decision. I inferred that the employee thought I was not performing my duties as manager and that I had somehow relinquished my power to others. My inference caused me to question whether I was handling the matter properly. Although my personal belief is that the role of the manager in a learning organization is greatly enhanced over the more traditional role, the possibility exists for those observing to conclude that the manager is not performing as a leader. This may be attributed to employees' seeing leaders as experts, not as learners.

For a discussion of time, see Chapter Seven, "Thinking and Acting Systemically," page 75.

Organizational Support

Finally, I believe that my involvement in Laurinburg's learning organization effort has completely changed my perspective. To say that I believe I have become a more effective local government manager would be an understatement. My perspective on human interaction has changed because of what I now consider a lifelong journey. I believe that I cannot unlearn these practices. While I have no intention of unlearning this behavior because I have found it to be so worthwhile, I suspect others who experience this learning may not find the same rewards if they relocate to an organization that does not use or fully support these principles and practices. Support among like-minded colleagues is an important part of learning the thinking and skills required.

RECOMMENDATIONS

I strongly advocate that managers learn and use learning organization practices. The rewards and insights are many and varied. I have grown personally, and I believe I have increased my effectiveness as a city manager. Here are a few recommendations from my learning:

1. Work with trained facilitators who have experience in learning organization efforts. In my case, the use of faculty from the Institute of Government at The University of North Carolina and the involvement of a consultant have been invaluable in the Laurinburg effort.

2. Set up a process to identify those organization members who should take a lead role in jointly designing how you proceed.
3. Educate the governing board about the benefits at the time they are asked to support the initiative.
4. Meet openly. If others in the organization have access to the group and can see the effort firsthand, they will gain understanding and will be less likely to feel disconnected from the process.
5. Involve those in the learning organization initiative in related training. Formal workshops and selected readings should promote understanding and broaden perspectives. Discussing organizational learning with others involved in similar efforts should also prove beneficial.
6. Practice. The best way to practice involves using the behaviors with others. For those who are not familiar with the effort, explain your reasons. Otherwise, they might not understand the behavioral changes.

And, finally, take the risk. There is no way anyone can move forward in this effort without some risk. By the very nature of our positions, I suspect we managers are predisposed to assume a high level of risk. As I shared with my peers while serving on a panel at the North Carolina City/County Manager's Conference in 2000, "I am not saying that if you don't involve yourself in a learning organization effort, you are insecure. However, I do think that if you are insecure, you probably don't want to involve yourself in this type of learning."

Although the personal risks of undertaking such an effort are real, they are minimal when compared to the risks associated with continuing to manage the way we have always managed and suffering from poor communication, a lack of learning, and unintended consequences.

References

Davidson, A. S., and McMahon, R. R. "One City's Journey Toward More Responsive Government." *Popular Government,* 1999, *64*(2), 12–29.

Senge, P. M. *The Fifth Discipline: The Art and Practice of the Learning Organization.* New York: Doubleday, 1990.

Chapter 47

Reflections of a Somewhat Facilitative Leader

Jeff Koeze

In Chapter Forty-Five, I described a bit about my relationship to Roger Schwarz and his colleagues and about how I came to introduce the Facilitative Leader approach to the company I own and have served for six years. While I could tell stories of successes and failures, telling of those seems less urgent to me now than exploring why I have continued to struggle to practice the mutual learning model, followed by reflections on the pressures that guarantee that this struggle will never end.

Roger places choice at the center of personal and organization ethics by including "free and informed choice" as a core value. What seemed rather unexceptional the first time I read it I now view as radical—philosophically, politically, psychologically, and ethically. My reasons are a discussion for another book, but the ethical argument is most meaningful for me and can be summarized as follows: to attribute the ability to others to make choices and to act in a way that maximizes their ability to do so is to respect them; to control and manipulate is a failure to treat others with respect; it is, to borrow a phrase, to treat others as a means, not an end. This is, to my mind, unethical.

To attribute the ability to others to make choices and to act in a way that maximizes their ability to do so is to respect them; to control and manipulate is a failure to treat others with respect; it is, to borrow a phrase, to treat others as a means, not an end. This is, to my mind, unethical.

My own experience with facilitative leadership leads me to believe that Roger's couching of the mutual learning model in terms of effectiveness is at best a half-truth. I doubt it has or could be shown that this approach makes groups or individuals more effective, by Roger's or anybody else's definition of the word. The case that unilateral control was ineffective for Koeze Company, let alone for other famously top-down organizations (GE, Microsoft, IBM, EDS, Procter & Gamble, to name a few) is hard to make. I also doubt that a person who has worked with, reflected on, and seen the transformative effects of this approach would intentionally return to a style based on unilateral control, even if it seemed necessary, and not experience the return as an ethical failure.

Whether or not you share my ethical commitment to the core value of informed choice or have some other motivation to pursue facilitative leadership, every facilitative leader must come to understand that there are powerful pressures to suppress or deny the possibility of such choice. I've divided these into everyday perceptions, class and power, refusals and inadequacies, and everyday decision making.

EVERYDAY PERCEPTIONS

We can begin with our ordinary perceptions. At the personal level, we commonly feel our choices constrained by outside forces: our economic circumstances, our genes, our past, our relationships, and others. How often do we describe our behavior as mandated rather than chosen: "I have to go to work," not "I choose to go to work"?

Moreover, in the workaday world, you, like me, may find constraints, or our belief in them, comforting and, much of the time, necessary. We need to leave a certain number of assumptions in place, certain social roles and expectations unquestioned, and certain habits unexamined just to get through the day. "Testing assumptions and inferences" must be tempered by the judgment to know what issue to raise, when, and why, and, perhaps more important, what reasons will be sufficient to allow a difficult question to remain unasked or unanswered.

It is then a short step from leaving a question unasked to forgetting that it can be asked at all. For example, at least three or four times a year, an employee will answer an inquiry from me about why we do or don't do something with, "That's the policy." Rarely can they identify where the policy is written, who created it, when it was created, or, obviously, why it was created. Citing policy is, of course, an easy way of avoiding a difficult question or issue, but my experience is that my employees actually come to believe that some of these "policies" exist in as concrete a way as a desk or a chair. At least at first, they are genuinely surprised that I would propose questioning them.

CLASS AND POWER

The political traditions of the United States make most (but by no means all) of us reasonably comfortable with the idea that individuals are, or at least should be, free to make our own choices in the political realm, the marketplace, and our personal lives. But the corporate world is hardly known as a bastion of democracy, and Koeze's traditionally was no different. At my father's retirement party, the employees teased my father about his unilateral control theory-in-use by doing a parody of the ground rules based on some of my father's favorite sayings. When I assumed the job of CEO, he gave me a three-foot-long replica of a judge's gavel engraved with the words "Consensus Tenderizer." Sometimes our employees didn't care much for my father's unilateral control theory-in-use, but I'm fairly sure few in our non-union (in fact, fairly militantly anti-union) workforce viewed him as unjust. After all, his name was on the door. Why shouldn't he be able to do whatever he wants?

What is more, there are advantages for the employees to holding this view. As Peter Block (1993) points out, in return for giving up control, we also escape from responsibility for the behavior of the organization, our fellow workers, and even ourselves.

The Facilitative Leader approach can confront subordinates with choices that they would prefer to believe, or pretend, that they do not have. Comfort in not having a choice has come out in conversation in every organization I've ever worked for; in fact, I'm sure it has come out of my own mouth: "Why can't this be done?" answered by, "They won't let me." "They" are some group of powerful but anonymous people: management, lawyers, the human resource department, and the more powerful and farther away, physically or organizationally, the better. This statement can always be interrogated using the ground rules, but the naturalness and comfort of this thinking are demonstrated by the fact that it is used routinely in an organization such as Koeze's in which there is no "they"; there are only about thirty of us, all working within a single building. Moreover, it is routinely used with me, who holds the power to overrule any "they" a Koeze's employee could refer to.

The Facilitative Leader approach can confront subordinates with choices that they would prefer to believe, or pretend, that they do not have.

Issues of choice are complicated when there are large differences in social class involved. Business books, and *The Skilled Facilitator* is no exception, are written about professionals, by professionals, and for professionals. Professionals are, in general, comfortable with and see benign intent in the general distribution of power, wealth, and opportunity in our society. They have heard about the short end of the stick, but they rarely have seen it.

Roger has said to me, and I believe him, that he has had success with his approach across the blue collar–white collar divide. I believe him; I have also. Still, it must be acknowledged that substantial differences of power, wealth, and status automatically call into question the notion of free and informed choice in a way that conversations between equals do not. How these issues play out can be extraordinarily subtle. I am just beginning to learn to address such issues, but my guess is that dealing effectively with them will ultimately require facilitative leaders and followers to surface and to engage in conversation around political, economic, and social issues that they are used to seeing dealt with only in slogans and thirty-second television ads. And in some cases, the slogans may be the only language and knowledge they have. (The same might be said about conversations structured around race; I've never had the experience of using this approach in that context.)

REFUSALS OR INADEQUACIES

In *The Skilled Facilitator,* Roger writes of the facilitative leader, "By modeling the approach, you can give people experience with it so that they may later make an informed and free choice to embrace it." (p. 343) Yet there are people who are extremely comfortable in rigid hierarchy. There are people who are exceptionally averse to conflict; in fact, the possibility of conflict paralyzes them. There are people who are utterly uninterested in learning, especially about themselves. There are people who are absolutely self-interested. There are people who are relentlessly concrete in their thinking—all action, no talk. There are people who aren't comfortable in groups, are inarticulate, are intellectually limited. There are religious and political ideologues. You have, will, or do work with such people.

For a discussion of using the Skilled Facilitator approach with different personality types, see Chapter Fifty-Five, "The Skilled Facilitator Approach and the Myers-Briggs Type Indicator," page 437.

Sometimes these people must be removed from the group, or the company, for the commitment to mutual learning to be sustained, or just for the work to get done, even if the leader's relative lack of skill contributes to their failure. Ideally, the group would learn to raise and discuss even serious job- or career-threatening inadequacies and refusals among members, along with group members' contributions to it.

But the risks for individual members are high. High as well is the members' confidence that if they wait, somebody else—somebody with more power and thus, it is thought, less at risk—will deal with the problem—perhaps publicly but more likely privately. And in the moment that the one is removed for the good of the many, the suspicious, the doubting, the angry, and the bitter may think, with some truth, "See, nothing has changed." Others might think the same with a sense of relief.

EVERYDAY DECISION MAKING

Let me state the obvious: not everyone can be involved in every decision that affects them or about which they might have relevant information. Equally obvious is that not everyone can contribute to deciding whether consensus or some other decision rule is appropriate for every such decision. From the perspective of those not consulted, the decision rule has the structure, or at least the feel, of having been decided unilaterally by others, as will the matters that are up for discussion and debate in the first place. As obvious as this is, faced with a steady stream of nonchoices, one's belief in and commitment to choice erodes constantly.

A common solution to this problem is to emphasize a more abstract choice: that of committing to an organizational statement of mission, or vision, or values. As long as that choice has been made, the inability to make choices about the myriad of other issues may be easier to accept. But ultimately, I don't think this works. First, decisions rarely flow with inevitable logic from such broad statements, and second, the decision at hand might always be the one that calls for the mission, vision, or values to be reconsidered.

And as a practical matter, how realistic is the opportunity to reconsider the mission, vision, and values likely to be? Any organization that takes the notion of choice and internal commitment seriously eventually comes around to questioning its mission, vision, and values. If they are written down, they are reexamined; if not, they finally get put on paper. For those involved, participating in vision and mission work can be creative, fun, liberating, commitment building, and empowering. But it seems almost inevitable that the vision will eventually be taken to command compliance or allegiance down the road. And if that happens, one of the facilitative leader's best tools for encouraging choice and internal commitment begins to become the enemy of both.

See Chapter Seventeen, "Developing Shared Vision and Values," page 149.

Consistent with the core values and ground rules, the process that creates the vision engages voices from throughout the organization. The process may also include shareholders, customers, suppliers, even community members. Then the vision is printed, put on the walls, placed on little plastic cards, and sent out in press releases. And the next day, the organization changes. A new employee is hired. Another learns from experience and thinks of a revision. An inconsistency appears. The process, however, does not begin again; practically, it cannot. To some extent, to some people, at some times, the vision becomes undiscussable. It is transformed from something that a group created to a thing that others must simply accept.

SUMMING UP

Roger has an answer to every issue I've discussed here: "Use the core values and the ground rules to raise and discuss them." And he is absolutely right. But I have two parting thoughts. The first is that this is much easier said than done, and little in most managers' background or training will prepare them for where such conversations, done well, will lead. The second is that this work is never done.

The structures of the unilateral control model are embedded in our thoughts, our language, and our social institutions. They seem almost part of the air we breathe. As we try to create areas of freedom, choice, and commitment, the walls that limit them seem to reconstruct themselves right before our eyes. The task is Sisyphean. And absolutely necessary.

The structures of the unilateral control model are embedded in our thoughts, our language, and our social institutions. They seem almost part of the air we breathe.

Reference

Block, P. *Stewardship: Choosing Service over Self-Interest.* San Francisco: Berrett-Koehler, 1993.

Chapter 48

Integrating the Skilled Facilitator Approach with Organizational Policies and Procedures

Roger Schwarz
Anne Davidson

THE SKILLED FACILITATOR APPROACH can be used to improve not only individual and group behavior but also organizational policy and procedure. In fact, the quality of group process and conversation is influenced by the structure within which they occur. When leaders in organizations commit to mutual learning core values, they begin to feel at odds with the formal and informal organizational practices that seem inconsistent with their values and beliefs. And the extent to which organizational practices are at odds with mutual learning values influences how difficult it will be for individuals to change their behavior. Sustained organizational transformation must be systemic. It depends on both personal development and changes in organizational practices.

See Chapter Forty-Three, "Developmental Facilitation," page 339.

Many important and difficult conversations that set or influence organizational practice occur in the nonoperating functions: human resources, risk management, finance, and legal services, for example. These are important functions to examine because the values, beliefs, and assumptions that drive policy decisions are often deeply embedded in what is considered good professional practice in these areas. And policies generated within or among these areas are often in tension with the principles of the Skilled Facilitator approach.

Many important and difficult conversations that set or influence organizational practice occur in the nonoperating functions: human resources, risk management, finance, and legal services, for example. These are important functions to examine because the values, beliefs, and assumptions that drive policy decisions are often deeply embedded in what is considered good professional practice in these areas. And policies generated within or among these areas are often in tension with the principles of the Skilled Facilitator approach.

This should not be surprising since many of the practices in these areas are designed to avoid some past or potential threat. Given that most people use a unilateral control mental model under conditions of threat, they adopt organizational policies and procedures that have elements of unilateral control embedded within them. These unilateral values and assumptions generally remain unexamined and unchanged when practices (formal and informal structure, policy, procedure) are revised.

For examples of common organizational practices that have elements of the unilateral control model embedded in them, see Chapter Forty-Nine, "360-Degree Feedback and the Skilled Facilitator Approach," page 391, and Chapter Fifty-One, "Do Surveys Provide Valid Information for Organizational Change?" page 409.

TYPICAL ORGANIZATIONAL PRACTICES

Here are a few examples of typical practices from organizations that we and our colleagues have worked with:

1. If a team member is not performing adequately and the supervisor is taking progressive disciplinary action to address the performance, the supervisor can't share with other team members that she has taken these actions or what they are. She can state only that she is "handling the issue." This is true even if the other team members initially raised the performance issue with the entire team and team leader present, and if the team members continue to provide the member and leader feedback about that team member's performance.
2. If a team member is fired for poor performance or conduct, the team leader cannot tell the other team members what that team member did to get fired. In some organizations, the supervisor cannot even state that the employee was terminated, but can state only the last day the person will be working. If other team members ask whether they have engaged in the same behavior as the person no longer working, the supervisor cannot answer the question in a way that reveals any of the other person's behaviors. The person who was terminated can tell other team members whatever he wants.
3. Supervisors cannot share performance or pay information about one employee with others. In one example, one team member, Janet, complained to her supervisor that another team member, Tami, had received pay raises for the previous three years. Janet, who had received no pay raises in the three years, complained that her performance was better than Tami's and that therefore she also deserved a pay raise. In fact, the supervisor had not given Tami a pay raise during the past three years, but Tami had told Janet that was the case. The supervisor could not tell Janet that the information she received from Tami was incorrect. In some public sector organizations, pay and recent pay increase information is public information. In other organizations, it is closely held, and telling others someone else's pay or last pay increase is prohibited, even if it's your own pay.

4. Department heads prepare their annual budget requests independently and then submit them to the finance director. Each advocates for as much as he or she can, knowing there will be subsequent cuts. The finance director consolidates the requests and takes them to the chief operating officer, along with his or her recommendations for cuts. They then go to each department head individually to tell each one how much (and, in some cases, where) to cut their budgets. Department heads never see one another's requests or detailed line item breakdowns. Most feel the process is unfair and assume cuts are based in part on favoritism, so they try to outmaneuver one another by the way they present and justify their budgets. They sometimes make tenuous or questionable links to the chief operating officer's or finance director's favored initiatives. This process of competition, inflated requests, and hidden agendas is commonly referred to as the budget game.

5. Line employees are required by the risk manager to wear safety equipment at all times. Safety equipment is purchased for employees based on standards developed by the risk manager and several department heads, even though employees often say their particular jobs require less or less expensive equipment. Employees are responsible for equipment maintenance. They are disciplined, including being sent home without pay, if they are caught working without the appropriate safety equipment. The risk manager hires detectives to videotape employees working to see if they are complying. Employees believe they know their jobs better than management does and could select less expensive and more appropriate options. They resent being spied on, and they make a game of seeing if they can break the rules without being caught.

WHAT ARE THE CONSEQUENCES OF THESE PRACTICES?

These practices and others like them are often well intended. Frequently they stem in part from a need to consider employees' rights to privacy. The right to certain privacies is a basic one (in the United States), and employees do not relinquish all of their rights to privacy when they work in an organization. Organizations also avoid risk and ensure their own stability and survival by complying with laws, generally accepted accounting practices, and a host of other professional best practices.

These interests often align to support existing policies. For example, a policy that prevents a manager from sharing what he is doing to address an employee's performance issues also protects that employee's privacy, reduces the risk of liability associated with possibly violating privacy, and potentially avoids difficult conversations that the manager might have to have with other employees who want to know what the manager is doing about the situation. So what's the problem?

The problem is that in an attempt to maximize the interests of reducing exposure, maintaining privacy, and avoiding difficult conversations, these policies create the unintended consequences of reducing group and organizational effectiveness. From the Skilled Facilitator perspective, in many of these situations relevant information is withheld, so employees are left making inaccurate and untested inferences, which can lead them to make less informed choices and to be less committed to those choices. This can reduce the effectiveness of a leader-team relationship, the team as a whole, and the organization in general.

The problem is that in an attempt to maximize the interests of reducing exposure, maintaining privacy, and avoiding difficult conversations, these policies create the unintended consequences of reducing group and organizational effectiveness. From the Skilled Facilitator perspective, in many of these situations relevant information is withheld, so employees are left making inaccurate and untested inferences, which can lead them to make less informed choices and to be less committed to those choices. This can reduce the effectiveness of a leader-team relationship, the team as a whole, and the organization in general.

Here are some of the unintended consequences from the examples at the beginning of this chapter:

1. *The supervisor can't share with other team members that she has taken any performance (or conduct related) personnel actions in regard to another employee.* This creates a situation in which team members are left making inferences about whether and how the supervisor is addressing the team member who is having a problem. It makes undiscussable the poor performance that team members were likely to have not only seen but also brought to the attention of the leader. It also creates the unintended consequence of removing team support to help that person improve, and so it increases the chance that the person will be fired or moved. In essence, the policy has the effect of making important and difficult performance issues undiscussable after the manager begins formal action.
2. *A team leader cannot tell the other team members what led a team member to be terminated or whether he was in fact terminated.* The unintended consequence of this policy is that other team members are again left making inferences about whether their own performance or behavior is potentially problematic. This is especially true if the team members have incorrectly inferred that the team member was fired for behavior that they too are engaging in. The leader misses an opportunity to help team members understand more about performance expectations and instead enables misunderstandings and concerns to develop.
3. *Supervisors cannot share an employee's performance or pay information with other employees.* In the example in which Janet had incorrect information that Tami had received a raise, the unintended consequence is again that employees are left with incorrect information, which they use to make other incorrect conclusions about the supervisor. By not correcting this inaccurate information, supervisors keep the invalid information and its consequences operating. Janet is likely to continue to believe she had been treated unfairly, eroding her relationship with the supervisor. She is also likely to share her frustration with other team members, affecting the supervisor's credibility with the entire work group.

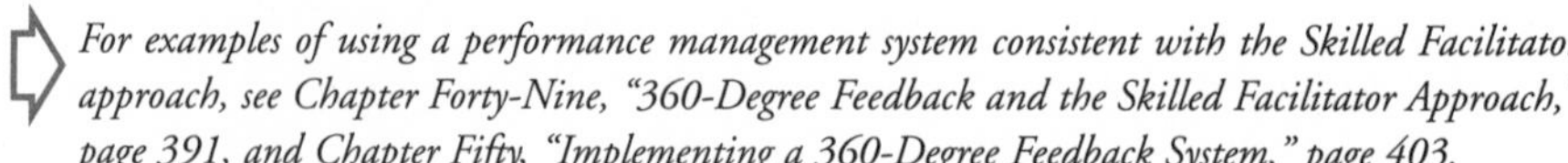
For examples of using a performance management system consistent with the Skilled Facilitator approach, see Chapter Forty-Nine, "360-Degree Feedback and the Skilled Facilitator Approach," page 391, and Chapter Fifty, "Implementing a 360-Degree Feedback System," page 403.

4. *Department heads prepare their annual budget requests independently to meet their own interests and try to get the largest budget possible by playing budget games.* This kind of budget process not only withholds information; it limits the department heads—key organizational leaders—from learning about critical organizational issues and opportunities. It reinforces the traditional silo mentality that often causes leaders to work at cross-purposes and limits their understanding of interdependence. They are subsequently blamed by those above and below them in the organization for not thinking systemically when, in fact, they lack important information that would lead them to see key interrelationships.

5. *Line employees are required to wear provided safety equipment. Their behavior is secretly monitored, and they are disciplined if they are caught working without it.* The intention of this policy is to keep employees safe, and employees do have valid information about why the equipment is needed. However, the organizational practices of selecting the equipment for employees and of trying to catch employees breaking the rules reduces commitment to following proper procedure and removes much employee accountability. Rather than encouraging one another to follow safety procedures and taking responsibility for choosing and maintaining the proper equipment, line employees push back on risk management's control and paternalism by deliberating breaking safety equipment and consciously breaking the rules. Rather than collaborating to reduce personal and organizational risk, the two sides are engaged in escalating, expensive conflict. The more the employees resist following the rules, the more the risk manager tries to gain control by tightening standards and increasing the monitoring activities. And the more he does these things, the more resentful the employees become and the more energy they put into finding creative ways to circumvent the risk manager's actions, creating a classic and unintended vicious cycle. The result is lost productivity and reduced job satisfaction.

INTEGRATING ORGANIZATIONAL PRACTICES WITH THE SKILLED FACILITATOR APPROACH

Integrating policies, procedures, and structures with the Skilled Facilitator approach includes exploring the interests underlying the practices. It also includes examining the unintended consequences that practices are creating at each level of the system and exploring how they might be changed to incorporate mutual learning values and assumptions. Here are steps to take.

Identify the Source

Find out whether the policy or procedure in question stems from a law or a generally accepted industry or professional practice, whether it is a formal or informal organizational policy, or whether it is actually not a policy but a norm in the organization. A policy that originates in law is obviously more difficult to change than a policy developed independently by an organization or a policy that is a norm. Do not assume that a practice is a formal policy or law simply because someone says it is. Validate the information; ask the relevant people to see the written version. In our experience, organizational members sometimes cite something as policy or law because they have been told it is policy or law; yet when they are asked, no one is able to produce the source material.

For examples of the power of policies, see Chapter Forty-Seven, "Reflections of a Somewhat Facilitative Leader," page 377.

Identify Any Elements That Are Within Your Control

If a practice is actually a norm or a guideline that you have discretion to adapt, consider adapting it so it reduces unintended consequences. One of our client organizations has adopted a collaborative budget process where everyone involved sits down together annually and develops an organizational budget. Department heads frequently *offer* funding to other departments with more critical needs. All feel responsible for presenting a fair and realistic budget that reflects organizational rather than departmental priorities. After several years of collaborative budgeting, this group says they no longer play budget games, the budget process is faster overall, they engage in better long-range planning and capital budgeting, and the role of the finance and budget staff has moved from control of others to support and involvement in decision making. The group members see themselves as partners rather than competitors.

Understand Exactly What the Policy Says and Does Not Say

If the policy is written, examine it and learn firsthand what it says and does not say. If the policy is based on law, explore whether the policy is more restrictive than the law requires. In the case of Janet and Tami, the manager was led to believe that he could not share Tami's current pay raise information with Janet. Yet his organization was a governmental agency covered by a state statute stating that current pay rates and most recent increases are public information. If a policy seems more restrictive than your understanding of the law on which it is based or if the way a policy is implemented seems more restrictive than the policy itself, find out whether that is the intent. If it's not, you may have more freedom to share relevant information. If a policy is not written, explore with the people responsible for it what it requires.

Explore the Interests That Generated the Practice; Share Your Interests and the Unintended Consequences You See

We think of policies and procedures as positions. Underlying every position is a set of interests that the policymakers are trying to meet. Be curious about the interests that generated a particular procedure. Share your interests that you see not being met by the policy, including the unintended consequences you do see. Ask for reactions.

See Chapter Five, "Ground Rules for Effective Groups," page 61; Chapter Sixteen, "Helping Group Members Focus on Interests Rather Than Positions," page 145; and Chapter Twenty-Six, "Ground Rules Without the Mutual Learning Model Are Like Houses Without Foundations," page 217.

Explore Redesigns to Meet the Interests

Explore whether and how a policy can be implemented so that it meets the interests you have identified and reduces the unintended consequences. For example, in the case of privacy rights, the policy might be implemented in a way that gives people the option to share their own information or reveal their identity. In the case of the safety equipment, one client group changed their practice with the intention of increasing commitment and accountability. They jointly designed a new procedure with employees that included giving employees an allowance from which they could purchase their own personal safety equipment, choosing designs of their own liking from an approved list. Equipment damage went down, and compliance increased dramatically.

Consider Sharing Interests in Policy Statements

When policies come up for review in a learning organization we work with (either because they are not meeting organization needs or are perceived as being inconsistent with the values), the management team or a selected group of employees are given the task of reviewing the policy and identifying the interests that a new policy must satisfy. When a new policy is written, the interests that it is attempting to meet are stated in the first paragraph. Then the guidelines are given. Providing the interests has the added benefit of reducing the number of rules needed because it is frequently less important that an exact process be followed than that the interests be met. There are usually several acceptable ways to meet the stated interests, and providing choices significantly increases commitment to following desired practices.

Chapter 49

360-Degree Feedback and the Skilled Facilitator Approach

Peg Carlson

I HAVE BEEN INTRIGUED by 360-degree feedback for a long time, both by the idea of it and by the apparent gap between its potential to create behavior change and its implementation. It's a good example of what happens when we espouse a mutual learning approach but then create a structure based on the assumptions of the unilateral control model.

See Chapter Four, "Understanding What Guides Your Behavior," page 33.

A primary objective of 360-degree feedback (also called multi-rater or multi-source feedback) is to give individuals relevant information about their performance from a variety of perspectives. This process recognizes that an individual works in a system, and many people in that system—peers, direct reports, supervisors, and customers—have valuable information about the focal individual's strengths and weaknesses. Its underlying premise is that people can improve their performance by learning and incorporating this feedback. On its face, this is very compatible with the Skilled Facilitator ground rule, "Share all relevant information." As it is usually implemented, however, valid information is often lost.

A considerable amount of research has focused on the apparent failure of multi-source feedback to produce performance improvement. One review of many such studies found that feedback was almost as likely to have a negative as a positive effect on future performance (Kluger and DeNisi, 1966). Proponents of 360-degree feedback have investigated various factors that may affect the focal individual's use of the feedback. These factors include the size of the gap between self-ratings and ratings from others and whether the feedback is purely developmental or is being shared as part of a performance evaluation. I think these studies have failed to identify the central problem with the way 360-degree feedback is carried out.

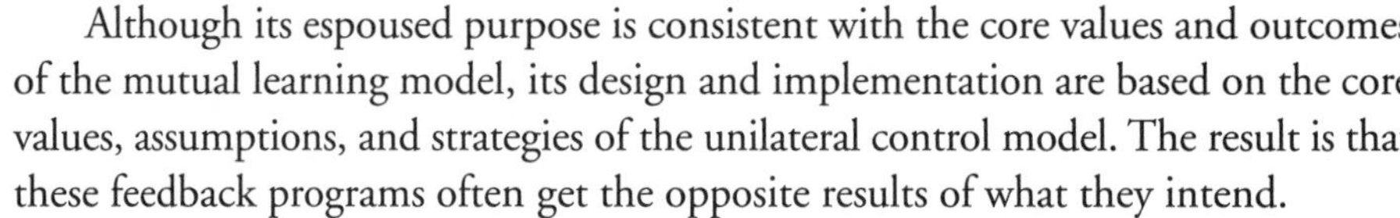

Although its espoused purpose is consistent with the core values and outcomes of the mutual learning model, its design and implementation are based on the core values, assumptions, and strategies of the unilateral control model. The result is that these feedback programs often get the opposite results of what they intend.

Although its espoused purpose is consistent with the core values and outcomes of the mutual learning model, its design and implementation are based on the core values, assumptions, and strategies of the unilateral control model. The result is that these feedback programs often get the opposite results of what they intend.

EXAMPLES OF DILEMMAS WITH 360-DEGREE FEEDBACK

To illustrate some of the dilemmas associated with 360-degree feedback, here are two examples from my consulting experience. In the first, multisource feedback was used in a developmental context as part of an executive education program; in the second, it was used in an evaluative context in a chief executive's performance evaluation. Both show the types of issues that can arise for the individual who is trying to understand the feedback she has received:

> I first encountered 360-degree feedback when I served as a coach in executive education programs, helping participants sift through and interpret the feedback they received. The participants were generally excited about the power of this tool and looked forward to discussing their feedback. I was enthusiastic as well. This process appeared to have the potential to help the focal managers (those who received the feedback) achieve real insights into their managerial style. As I worked with individuals who received feedback from their direct reports, peers, and bosses, however, I noticed a troubling pattern: the 360-degree feedback process didn't seem to provide guidance to all of the participants in the way I had expected it would. Typically the people who received the lowest marks on their managerial skills also had the most difficulty figuring out what they were doing that was ineffective and how to do it differently. At least some of the problem appeared to stem from the way the feedback was compiled and presented.
>
> As with virtually all other 360-degree feedback instruments, the survey used in the executive education program promised confidentiality to the raters if they were direct reports or peers of the focal individual; their identity would not be revealed. Supervisors were not promised confidentiality, as a person usually reports to only one boss. This was done to increase the likelihood that people would provide honest feedback to the ratee. Raters were assured that both the numerical ratings and the written comments they provided would be shared without attribution and the focal individual would not be able to identify the source. When there are a sufficient number of raters, averaging numbers so individual raters are not identified is a simple task. Making a written comment anonymous is not so simple, since written comments may contain information that is not known to all of the raters. As I met with executives individually to discuss their feedback, it became evident that the way in which raters ensured that their comments could not be traced back to them caused problems for the managers who received low ratings.

The managers who were rated highly got lots of specific comments reinforcing their performance. When people gave negative feedback to a manager using the 360-degree tool, however, they appeared to take additional steps to hide their identity. They would omit written comments or write the comments in such a general way that there was no chance they could be identified. For example, a rater would comment, "Needs to provide more direction," instead of, "It would have been helpful if Bill had specified the parameters on the XYZ project, because our team did a lot of unnecessary research on ways to reduce costs before we found out this had already been decided." The executives who received this vague feedback were frequently confused and had questions about what the comment was referring to. I could offer only partial assistance. Although I may have been able to discern some of the themes across raters' comments, I obviously could not fill in the missing specifics. We could merely compare untested inferences. It seemed that the managers who received low marks on their managerial skills—the very ones who most needed specific examples to figure out what was ineffective in the past and how to improve in the future—were the least likely to receive specific information.

The governing board of a nonprofit decided that it needed to collect information about the director's performance from a variety of sources in order to conduct a thorough evaluation. The board's motives were good; the members felt that they saw only a small fraction of the director's overall work in their interactions with her, and they wanted to get useful input on her extensive work with other community agencies, regional councils, and others. Board members interviewed selected individuals (including some of the nonprofit's employees) and asked each for his or her view of the director's performance in various areas. The individuals were assured that these conversations were completely confidential and the director would never know who said what.

During the performance evaluation, the board ran into problems when sharing ratings of the director's performance that were partially (or largely) based on feedback from others. In many instances, these ratings had been based on one or more specific examples of the director's performance that the board had learned about from employees and outside peers. Because it promised confidentiality to these people, the board did not want to be too specific for fear that the director would know who provided the information—and that the confidentiality agreement would thus be violated.

As a result, the board was frequently vague and spoke in generalities about the director's need to improve her performance or make changes in her managerial style. Board members explained that they couldn't be very specific for the reasons just listed. "That's all right," the director said. "I can go back to my employees and peers and ask them for more information about how I can improve my performance. "Oh, no, you can't do that," board members replied. "If you do, they will think you're on a witch hunt and just trying to find out who said what so you can retaliate."

IDENTIFYING THE PROBLEMS

> How is it that a process intended to give people useful feedback to improve their effectiveness frequently prevents them from getting the information they need to improve their effectiveness?

What is going on here? How is it that a process intended to give people useful feedback to improve their effectiveness frequently prevents them from getting the information they need to improve their effectiveness?

Using the Skilled Facilitator approach, I believe there are three main issues to examine, all based on a unilateral control theory-in-use: (1) an emphasis on unilateral protection for both raters and ratees, resulting in a process that promises confidentiality to raters; (2) an overall organizational structure that defines accountability differently for different players in the system; and (3) a series of mixed messages that are undiscussable, thus blocking individual and organizational learning.

A Mental Model That Believes All Parties Need to Be Protected

At first glance, 360-degree feedback appears to be the ultimate learning tool: it acknowledges that many people have relevant information about an individual's performance and that the focal individual can benefit from learning all these perspectives and adapting as needed. This appears consistent with the mutual learning model; however, a core assumption embedded in virtually all 360-degree feedback processes is that both raters and ratees must be unilaterally protected from any discomfort they may feel about participating in the process. This assumption is consistent with the unilateral control model, and the logic goes something like this: raters won't give honest feedback if they think the target individual will know the source, both because they don't want to hurt this person's feelings if they have negative comments and because they'll be afraid that the person will retaliate in some way. Therefore, their identity needs to be concealed for their protection. Also, the person receiving the feedback won't receive it in the spirit it's intended if she knows who said what; she will focus on the source, get defensive, or rationalize away the feedback because she believes the rater holds a grudge against her. So the focal individual must also be protected for her own good.

I don't mean to minimize the very real problems associated with creating a process for people to give—and receive—constructive feedback. The point is that a unilaterally controlling (or unilaterally protecting) mental model tends to produce the very outcomes that we want to avoid. In the case of the 360-degree feedback examples, that means that the process actually limited learning and potentially increased misunderstanding and defensiveness between parties rather than reducing it.

Withholding the Identity of the Rater as a Means to Obtain Honest Feedback

Guidance on what constitutes good feedback is fairly consistent: it needs to be timely and specific, and it needs to focus on the behavior, not the person. It's not sufficient to say, "Gina, you need to improve your attitude." In order for feedback to be helpful, Gina needs to understand exactly (1) what behaviors have led you to infer that her attitude needs improving, (2) in what situation you observed these behaviors, and (3) what an improved attitude would look like in behavioral terms. This guidance is not unique to the Skilled Facilitator approach, but it is consistent with the approach.[1]

In 360-degree feedback, the principles for giving feedback come up against the mental model of unilateral protection. As a result, virtually every multisource feedback process aggregates the raters' responses by group to protect the confidentiality of the source (for example, subordinates, peers). The only responses that can be traced to an individual rater are those of the supervisor, since most people have only one boss. Protecting the identity of raters is a fundamental part of the design of every 360-degree feedback instrument I've found. (If someone is familiar with an alternate design that identifies raters, please let me know.) The assessment tool usually explains at some length how no individual's ratings will ever be revealed to the person being rated; for example, since the ratee might recognize handwriting, the completed instruments are sent to a third party for compilation.

This desire to maintain confidentiality has a cost. A vague, general comment does not constitute valid information as defined in the Skilled Facilitator approach (nor does it comply with general principles of effective feedback). Identity of the rater is relevant information, along with specific examples. One of the tenets of the Skilled Facilitator approach is that people should be accountable for their ideas, since the individual who presents an idea is the source of relevant information and can be sounded out for more information if needed. The individual receiving the anonymous feedback has little to act on to get the valid information needed to bring about change in his or her job performance. In the quest for honest feedback, it appears that useful feedback is sometimes sacrificed. Our perceptions of others' behavior are filtered through our own experience and so often filled with untested inferences and attributions that our opinion is meaningful primarily as a way to begin a two-way conversation. The 360-degree feedback process is not designed to encourage this conversation; in fact, it acts to prevent it.

> The 360-degree feedback process is not designed to encourage a two-way conversation; in fact, it acts to prevent it.

For an example of the consequences of confidentiality in 360-degree feedback, see Chapter Fifty, "Implementing a 360-Degree Feedback System," page 403.

Defining Accountability Differently for Different Members of the System

Accountability means "accepting and meeting one's personal responsibilities, being and/or feeling obligated to someone else or oneself, or having to justify one's actions to others about whom we care."[2]

A dilemma in multisource feedback is that all parties appear to want low accountability for themselves but high accountability for others. For example, research

A dilemma in multisource feedback is that all parties appear to want low accountability for themselves but high accountability for others.

shows that raters are most comfortable giving ratings when they're not accountable for them (not identified), and ratees are most comfortable receiving ratings when raters are held accountable. Similarly, focal managers prefer that 360-degree feedback be shared only with them and want it to be used for developmental rather than evaluative purposes.

Both researchers and practitioners using multisource feedback have noted that behavior change does not necessarily follow a 360-degree feedback process, and proponents have turned their attention to mechanisms for holding focal managers accountable for changing their behavior as a result of feedback (for example, Walker and Smither, 1999). Much less is said, however, about holding raters accountable for the feedback they provide. I see a systemic problem here. The managers receiving the feedback are held accountable for changing their behavior, even though they may not get the specific examples that would be truly helpful. The raters, meanwhile, are not held accountable for the ratings they provide. This design essentially removes the responsibility for direct communication between rater and ratee. In fact, it contributes to a climate where people feel that others cannot be trusted; otherwise, why must everyone be protected? Moreover, it can breed cynicism about the possibility of organizational change, since the people providing the ratings may think, "Well, I've done my part and given him feedback. Now it's his job to improve his performance." They don't recognize that the feedback they've provided may simply raise awareness that there is a problem without helping the person determine what to do differently. And a 360-degree instrument that promises confidentiality helps support the idea that they've done their part and nothing more will be expected of them.

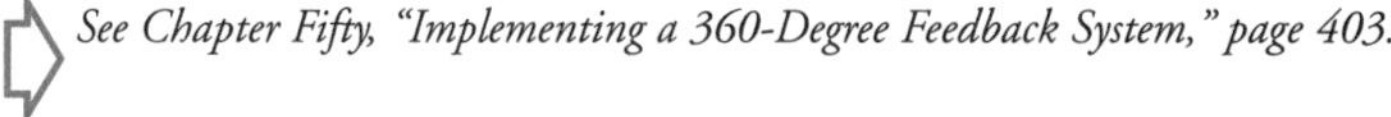

See Chapter Fifty, "Implementing a 360-Degree Feedback System," page 403.

Undiscussable Mixed Messages That Limit Learning

This message says, in effect, "We encourage you to go back and ask for clarification and specific examples from your direct reports and peers if you receive feedback that is unclear to you." How exactly is this supposed to occur, given that the information was originally obtained through promising confidentiality to raters?

Several mixed messages are embedded in 360-degree feedback. One is the idea that this process is a way for people to receive good honest, constructive feedback and the way to do this is to promise confidentiality and thus limit the amount of valid information that people actually receive. Consultants and human resource professionals who are counseling people on how to get the most out of the feedback they receive frequently deliver the second mixed message.

This message says, in effect, "We encourage you to go back and ask for clarification and specific examples from your direct reports and peers if you receive feedback that is unclear to you." How exactly is this supposed to occur, given that the information was originally obtained through promising confidentiality to raters? This mixed message has all the hallmarks—and subsequent negative consequences—of an organizational defensive routine, as described by Chris Argyris (2000):

- Send a mixed message ("I want you to get good specific information, and the best way to do that is to protect you from knowing who said what").
- Pretend it is not mixed ("This tool will give you great insight into the strengths and weaknesses of your managerial style as perceived by others").
- Make the mixed message and the pretense undiscussable ("We encourage you to go directly to your raters for clarification of any feedback").
- Make the undiscussability undiscussable ("Now that I've explained how this will work, is there anything else you want to talk about?").

LAYING THE GROUNDWORK

It's a considerable journey from the traditional 360-degree feedback design to Cathy's story later in this chapter. Concerns about defensive reactions by managers or retaliation may also be very real. What this means is that an organization should not simply jump into 360-degree feedback cold, without doing some of the hard work to prepare participants for the process. A few ideas for steps to move an organization along that journey follow. They are not guaranteed techniques for improving how feedback is given and received in any organization, but they are offered in the spirit of changing the conversation in a way that increases learning, reduces unilateral protection, and supports accountability and free choice.

Acknowledge and Discuss the Dilemma

The issues I've raised here are dilemmas: no choice is 100 percent positive, and all courses of action have some potential negative consequences associated with them. If you share my view that the traditional 360-degree feedback design limits learning, one step is to explain the dilemma you see to others and inquire as to whether they see it similarly or differently. If you have examples from your experiences as a rater or a ratee that have shaped your perspective, you can share these examples and encourage others to share theirs (whether or not they support your view). Identify and discuss concerns that lead people to not want to be accountable for their ratings. People may have concerns about defensiveness and retaliation from the individuals receiving the feedback. By getting at some of the causes, the organization can begin to see if they can create conditions that reduce or prevent the need for anonymity.

Be Accountable for Your Own Ratings

If you are asked to participate as a rater in a 360-degree feedback process, identify yourself as the source of any comments you provide, and invite the target individual to contact you to discuss the ratings in more detail. Depending on the level of security imposed by the 360-degree technology, this can require some creativity. Our colleague Tom Moore found that he was unable to add his name to his ratings (the technology was set up to guarantee anonymity), so he simply embedded his name in the actual comments by referring to himself in the third person: "Tom Moore thinks that . . ."

Enable Others to Make an Informed Choice About What They Are, and Are Not, Willing to Share

Even if people are not ready to fully disclose their specific examples in an open forum, you can help them make informed choices about what they are willing to share. For example, in the board's performance evaluation of the director described earlier in this chapter, board members recognized the bind they had put the director in and discussed ways to avoid this situation in the future. They still wanted to get feedback from people outside the nonprofit and didn't feel ready to ask each person to be identified by name. They came up with the following statement to begin each information-gathering interview: "The board's goal is to give specific feedback that will help the director improve her performance. Since this may include particular examples to illustrate a point, it is possible that she may guess the source of the information from the example, even if we do not mention the source by name. We ask you not to say anything to us that you are not willing to have shared with the director." Knowing this, individuals may choose not to share certain examples, but it helps the board avoid basing its evaluation (consciously or unconsciously) on information that is not available to the director.

USING THE SKILLED FACILITATOR APPROACH TO REDESIGN 360-DEGREE FEEDBACK

Even if your organization's method for providing 360-degree feedback is inconsistent with the Skilled Facilitator approach, there are ways you can modify the process to align it with the core values and turn it into a richer opportunity for mutual learning. Here is the story of a participant in one of our Skilled Facilitator workshops who did just that:[3]

Cathy was excited by what she had learned in the Skilled Facilitator workshop and was intrigued by the potential of integrating the core values into organizational processes that were already in use in her high-tech company. As a manager, she had been receiving 360-degree feedback for a couple of years, and although she felt that she got some valuable information out of the process, she also felt that the feedback was just scratching the surface of what she could really learn from the data.

The next time Cathy was scheduled for 360-degree feedback, she proposed some changes to the standard process. First, she requested that raters complete an evaluation of her managerial strengths and weaknesses, just as before. However, instead of then sending the evaluation to a third party who would compile the data and present the aggregate results to Cathy, she asked that *the raters bring the completed form with them to a group meeting with her and the other raters.* In doing this, Cathy was asking her raters to participate in a process that she believed would create valid information. Instead of trying to guess what a particular comment meant or what the rater was basing his or her evaluation on, Cathy would be able to ask the person directly.

Both Cathy and her raters reported that this was by far the riskiest 360-degree feedback process they had ever participated in. The stakes were high on both sides. Cathy's raters were concerned that they might hurt or embarrass her with some of their comments, and they were making themselves vulnerable to future retaliation from Cathy if she did not accept the feedback well. Cathy was concerned about her ability to respond without defensiveness to whatever she might hear in the session; she was aware that her response to the feedback would greatly affect the others' willingness to participate in anything like this in the future.

Despite their concerns (and because they understood what she was hoping to accomplish), Cathy's raters agreed to complete their forms and discuss them in a group forum. In the meeting, the group went through the questions one by one. Each person gave his or her rating and a brief explanation of the reason behind the rating, usually including an example. Several things happened as a result of this group conversation about Cathy's strengths and weaknesses as a manager.

First, as Cathy's raters shared the examples that led them to their evaluations, they found that they sometimes remembered things differently or had different perspectives about Cathy's actions. In some cases, this led people to change their original ratings.

Second, because everyone was able to hear everyone else's ratings and examples, the group was able to help Cathy identify patterns in her behavior. For example, one person said, "I see you get really directive sometimes, even though you seem to prefer a collaborative style most of the time." Another chimed in, "Yes, I've noticed that too, and I tried to figure out when it happens. I think it's when we're nearing a deadline. When we get to a certain stage in the project, it seems as if you don't want to hear any more input. Have we read you correctly on that?" If Cathy had received ratings and comments from each person through the standard aggregated responses, it would have been much more difficult to identify these kinds of patterns.

By having everyone hear and discuss her feedback together, Cathy created a professional development support group for herself. Since all the raters—her direct reports, peers, and boss—now knew the areas she was working on, they were able to give her specific feedback in future interactions. For example, after a meeting about an upcoming project deadline, one of her employees said, "You just did a really nice job of listening when we talked about how the production delays may affect our deadline. I know that's one of the things you've been working on, and it shows."

When they had completed the discussion, Cathy and her raters agreed that this was not only the riskiest 360-degree feedback session they had ever had, it was also the most valuable. By discussing her coworkers' perceptions of her in a forum where she could hear their specific examples, inquire into their reasoning, and add her own perspective, Cathy gained much greater insight into her own strengths and weaknesses as a manager than she ever could have learned from a sheet of ratings and unattributed comments. Her raters learned some valuable lessons as well: the importance of being accountable for the feedback you give to another person, being open to the possibility that people can interpret the same situation quite differently, and seeing the power of a group network to support an individual's change efforts.

Cathy's experience may give you ideas for how to redesign your own feedback sessions in a way that is consistent with the Skilled Facilitator approach. Or you may be reading this story and thinking, "In the next lifetime maybe!" If your organization seems a long way from being ready for the kind of group dialogue Cathy used, remember that there is a lot of groundwork that can be laid before tackling 360-degree feedback. Just as we don't recommend that workshop participants return to their organization and begin practicing the ground rules by raising the most difficult undiscussable issue at Monday morning's staff meeting, this is probably not going to be the first organizational intervention you're going to tackle. By "being the change you want to see" in your organization and using the core values and ground rules in your interactions with others, you can begin to create a climate in which others may feel ready to take the risk, and engage in mutual learning with you.

Notes

1. See, for example, Sloan R. Weitzel, *Feedback That Works: How to Build and Deliver Your Message.*
2. For an excellent discussion of accountability issues in multisource feedback, see Manuel London, James W. Smither, and Dennis J. Adsit, "Accountability: The Achilles' Heel of Multisource Feedback."
3. Roger Schwarz first related Cathy's story in Chapter Sixteen of *The Skilled Facilitator* (2nd ed.). The main points in this story reflect Cathy's report of what happened; however, the quotations are approximations of the group conversation and were not directly obtained from group members.

References

Argyris, C. *Flawed Advice and the Management Trap: How Managers Can Know When They're Getting Good Advice and When They're Not.* New York: Oxford University Press, 2000.

Kluger, A. N., and DeNisi, A. "The Effects of Feedback Interventions on Performance: A Historical Review, a Meta-Analysis, and a Preliminary Feedback Intervention Theory." *Psychological Bulletin,* 1966, *119,* 254–284.

London, M., Smither, J. W., and Adsit, D. J. "Accountability: The Achilles' Heel of Multisource Feedback." *Group and Organization Management,* 1997, *22,* 162–184.

Walker, A. G., and Smither, J. W. "A Five-Year Study of Upward Feedback: What Managers Do with Their Results Matters." *Personnel Psychology,* 1999, *52*(2), 393–423.

Weitzel, S. R. *Feedback That Works: How to Build and Deliver Your Message.* Greensboro, N.C.: Center for Creative Leadership, 2000.

Chapter 50

Implementing a 360-Degree Feedback System

Bron D. Skinner

IN 2002, ROGER SCHWARZ came to the Department of Family Medicine at The University of North Carolina at Chapel Hill and addressed the faculty about performance assessment as a way to enhance personal development and learn about one's self. One anonymous negative comment in the feedback that I received, as assistant residency director of the family practice residency program, particularly caught my attention. I had begun to preach the value of forgoing anonymity and the importance of applying the Ground Rules for Effective Groups to this process and decided that this was an opportunity to use my own experience as a faculty development lesson.

For a discussion about the problems of anonymity in feedback, see Chapter Forty-Nine, "360-Degree Feedback and the Skilled Facilitator Approach," page 391. For the ground rules, see Chapter Five, "Ground Rules for Effective Groups," page 61.

I wrote an extensive e-mail that I sent out to the faculty membership in which I tried to demonstrate the difference it would have made to me had I been given the identity of the individual who made the comment. I made an effort to go through the ground rules systematically and touch on each one in the way I thought it might apply:

From: Bron Skinner
Organization: Department of Family Medicine, UNC-Chapel Hill
To: Family Medicine Faculty
Subject: Some Faculty Development Around Feedback

We are all going through the annual exercise of Career Development Reviews. As part of that process, we instituted a revised peer evaluation process, which I feel is much improved over what I experienced last year. The comments were more thoughtful and relevant. The suggestions for improvement were things I could seriously consider doing something about, and they help me to think about how I can focus my energy.

Because that is the case, the most negative comment I received has troubled me for a couple of reasons. It was a difficult piece of feedback to receive because it basically refutes a self-perception I have that I strive to provide service to those who need to interface with the residency program. Had the comment not been relevant or meaningful, I would have shrugged it off. However, it strikes at the heart of what I hope I am able to provide in my position with the residency. The other troubling aspect is that the person who made it chose not to identify himself or herself. Had he or she done so, I could have worked to heal the wounding by having a dialogue with that party. So as I wrestled with my feelings and my desire to come to some resolution in myself, I thought it might be valuable to open up a discussion about such comments as a form of faculty development and that by so doing I could turn something troubling into a positive good for all of us.

I would like to do this by using it as an example for improving the outcome of our feedback by applying the principles that Roger Schwarz spoke with us about in his presentation on feedback for learning. First, let me share the comment, which came under "Areas of Improvement": "Not a problem solver when I've worked with him on residency issues. Tends to tell me it's my problem and I'll have to figure out how to fix it, when it is something that he was to be coordinating. An 'I'll figure it out and get back with you' would be so much more productive than an 'it's not my job' kind of attitude."

My first knee-jerk reaction is to want to apologize profusely for whatever behavior has prompted such feelings. I view this as a pretty damning condemnation of whatever communication style it was that generated this observation. However, this observation does not square with my feelings about the way the majority of my interactions with people evolve. So defensive ideas pop up as well. Still, something prompted this, and I want to honor the depth of this reaction and deal with it responsibly. So I would like to understand what this is about and see if there is something I can change in the way that I work with people to avoid generating such reactions in the future. A defensive stance will not help me accomplish that.

However, by not identifying himself or herself, this individual has denied me an opportunity to really learn something about myself. I don't have any idea where this comment could be coming from. So it tends to just sit there like a festering sore with no way to heal it. I believe I could heal it by having a dialogue with the individual to learn more about what prompted it in the first place.

Using a few of the ground rules that Dr. Schwarz left with us, I would like to examine what would be gained by such an approach. I'll give the ground rule and a brief explanation of how applying it could help in this instance:

1. *Test assumptions and inferences.* It would be very helpful to know what assumptions and inferences were being made by this person. There may be an assumption that what he or she brought to me is my responsibility when I don't perceive such to be the case. There might be an inference that I was shucking the responsibility for handling something I should have handled when I did not even

understand that I was being asked for anything more than information on which the person could act.

2. *Share all relevant information.* I could learn what circumstances brought on this person's perceptions. He or she may have come to me at a time I was stressed and preoccupied to a point that I could not focus on helping them. It may have been a single instance or a number of instances. The latter would be more concerning since it would be indicative of a pattern. It might be that whatever I was being asked to do was truly not in my purview to provide.
3. *Use specific examples and agree on what important words mean.* The context that generated this person's perception seems all important. What wording led this person to feel I had the attitude that it was not my job to help him or her? It's possible I said words meaning one thing and they were interpreted to mean something quite different.
4. *Explain your reasoning and intent.* By not knowing the reasoning and intent of the person who made this comment I have no idea what process of logic brought him or her to the conclusion that I was being unhelpful. I also do not know the intent of this comment. Is it made because the person is just angry because he or she didn't get something from me he or she thought I should give? Then this comment becomes something less constructive and more a way to get back at me anonymously. Or is this person sincerely and compassionately hoping that by offering this feedback, I will gain insight and grist for my mill toward a better me?

There are five other ground rules that we would apply as we worked toward an agreement about how to get our respective needs met and for us to arrive at a better understanding about how to interact in a productive way with one another. They are as follows:

5. *Focus on interests, not positions.* We would identify the ways in which our interests concur and develop a way to behave that most fully fulfilled our mutual interests.
6. *Combine advocacy and inquiry.* We would share our points of view and take time to inquire into the other person's perspective on how to handle future requests for assistance.
7. *Jointly design next steps and ways to test disagreements.* We would find what each of us thought could be done to improve the outcome of our interactions and identify differences of opinion.
8. *Discuss undiscussable issues.* There may be something about me that bugs this individual. Or perhaps he or she has a way of approaching me that sets me off. We would explore what that might be.
9. *Use a decision-making rule that generates the level of commitment needed.* We would establish what principles would apply in determining what I would and would not be expected in the future to do in response to requests for help.

I hope that the individual who made this comment will feel encouraged to come and have a conversation with me about whatever led to the perceptions expressed in the feedback. If he or she does not so choose, I offer my apologies for any behavior that may have prompted the feelings. Without further information and insight, my fear is that I will continue to stimulate such responses in people. So if there is anyone else who might have observed behaviors that would lead to a perception that I am unwilling to be helpful, I invite you to come and talk with me as well. I truly want to work better with everyone here. I will in the absence of any further data from anyone be working to enhance my self-observation and to heighten my sensitivity to what might be happening in my interactions with others to promote the perception of unhelpfulness.

Finally, I hope that baring my soul in this manner will have a salutary effect on the way that we handle feedback among the members of our community.

I would like to see a dialogue closer to the time of the offensive behavior rather than waiting until we have peer evaluations to put them out. I believe that the more open we can be about such things and the more willing we are to help one another to improve through our commitment to excellence, the more exciting and satisfying our lives and work together can be. I am optimistic that engaging in this kind of dialogue can initiate and promote career development in the best sense—namely, by encouraging the formation of a community of trust where we can reach out to one another with loving kindness and promote our growth as individuals while we plod along on our way to a career as a better doctor, educator, researcher, or whatever else.

Thank you all for your kind attention to this process.

Bron Skinner

I received no further communication from the individual who wrote the anonymous feedback. I received assurances from some that they had not experienced such behaviors in their interactions with me, so I gained some confidence that this was most likely an isolated case. I did hear from one faculty member who indicated that she had not written the note but had been able to identify with the sentiments contained in them with respect to our interactions. We had both worked on a project to implement Spanish immersion into our first year of residency training. I was not surprised when she indicated that she had had some concerns about our interactions. I had not been totally comfortable with her approach to the project either. But neither of us had made an opportunity to address our mutual discomfort.

We subsequently had a very useful conversation about our interactions during the project and identified the behaviors that had generated the feelings. We spent some time identifying the misperceptions and assumptions we each had made that had contributed to our discomfort with one another. It turned out largely to be a function of radically different work styles, which were really quite complementary.

Her approach is open, creative, outside-the-box, and open to possibility. Mine tends to be more linear, analytical, and limited by boundaries I perceive. I needed her creativity to get the project to happen, and she needed my linearity to make sure the details were covered in its implementation. When we could view it this way, we could then see how to use our respective strengths to work cooperatively together.

See Chapter Fifty-Five, "The Skilled Facilitator Approach and the Myers-Briggs Type Indicator," page 437.

The following year, we did the Spanish immersion, and it went much more smoothly for both of us because we had taken the opportunity to have a conversation about how to work together effectively. That success stemmed from a willingness on both our parts to work in a nonblaming way through the perceptions we had of one another.

Chapter 51

Do Surveys Provide Valid Information for Organizational Change?

Peg Carlson

SURVEY-GUIDED ORGANIZATION DEVELOPMENT refers to the process of using questionnaires to systematically collect information from organization members and feeding back the data to individuals and groups at all levels of the system (French and Bell, 1984). The goal is to "facilitate development by taking a snapshot of the organization and supervisory workgroups, presenting the picture to relevant groups, and giving them a benchmark against which to improve" (Born and Mathieu, 1996, p. 400). Survey questions typically cover such topics as communication, supervisor-employee relations, pay and benefits, organizational climate, and career opportunities. This type of organizational intervention started in the late 1940s and remains a popular method of initiating organizational change by external and internal consultants and change agents.

Surveys can generate a tremendous amount of information about employees' experience in the organization and how they are thinking and feeling about their work. Much has been written on how to develop good survey questions and analyze the results, as well as how to use surveys to facilitate organizational change (see, for example, Church and Waclawski, 1998). However, the most significant difficulties I have encountered in using surveys as part of an organization development process are not addressed by traditional guidance on how to develop and conduct surveys. These conflicts stem from my attempts to act consistent with the core values when using surveys to guide organization development.

In theory, the core values and survey-guided organization development share the same goal of generating valid information. In practice, the information surveys provided and the methods used to generate that information are not consistent with the core values.

In theory, the core values and survey-guided organization development share the same goal of generating valid information. In practice, the information surveys provided and the methods used to generate that information are not consistent with the core values.

During my graduate work at the Survey Research Center at The University of Michigan, I developed an appreciation for the value of a good survey, especially for establishing baselines and trends over time in large populations. Surveys such as

Monitoring the Future have provided a wealth of information about teenage health, drug use, and other important issues. My concerns are about surveys used to gather data as part of an organizational change process and the increasing reliance on them as a tool for individual behavior change. In this chapter, I identify areas where I think standard survey practice clashes with the Skilled Facilitator approach and offer my thoughts on the consequences of that clash.

COMPONENTS OF SURVEY-GUIDED DEVELOPMENT

Although there is variation in how specific surveys are developed and administered, some elements are virtually universal. These standard survey components include promising respondents anonymity, aggregating responses by work group or department, presenting feedback to small groups, and developing a plan of action based on the survey findings.

Promising Anonymity and Aggregating Responses

It is common practice to promise survey respondents that their individual responses will not be identified in the survey results. Objective scale items are presented as aggregate scores of some organizational unit of a reasonable size, and employees are encouraged to write comments in a way that maintains anonymity. The assumption that people must be guaranteed anonymity in order to provide honest feedback is a bedrock premise of survey research.

From the Skilled Facilitator perspective, however, this anonymity limits the validity of the data. The goal is to give specific, usable information to make changes, but the use of objective rating scales and anonymous comment sections on surveys limits the gathering of valid information about what is really occurring, including symptoms, underlying causes, and possible consequences. Moreover, anonymity masks the very information that is needed for feedback to make changes.

From the Skilled Facilitator perspective, however, this anonymity limits the validity of the data. The goal is to give specific, usable information to make changes, but the use of objective rating scales and anonymous comment sections on surveys limits the gathering of valid information about what is really occurring, including symptoms, underlying causes, and possible consequences. Moreover, anonymity masks the very information that is needed for feedback to make changes.

See Chapter Four, "Understanding What Guides Your Behavior," page 33, for the core values of the mutual learning model, and Chapter Forty-Nine, "360-Degree Feedback and the Skilled Facilitator Approach," page 391, for a more detailed discussion of the dilemmas created by promising anonymity to respondents.

Feeding Back the Data to Small Groups and Developing an Action Plan

The survey-guided organization development process does recognize that the survey results may not be explanatory on their own. To clarify what is behind the ratings, most efforts start with doing feedback in small groups at this point. Typically this happens in a cascade fashion in which top management hears survey results first. Feedback sessions then take place throughout the rest of the organization with the aid of a process consultant. In these feedback sessions, the expectation is that supervisors in particular are to hear more details about the problems identified and ideas for improvement. In addition to clarifying survey results, these sessions are intended to create momentum and motivation for organizational change. There are two impediments to this, rooted in the promise of anonymity and the cascade process.

My experience is that once people have been promised anonymity at the outset, it sets up an expectation of unilateral protection that tends to carry through the rest of the process. While employees may be willing to discuss results that are at a more global level, they are less willing to give examples that risk revealing themselves as the source of the data. Indeed, I have facilitated survey feedback sessions in which employees felt betrayed even to have been asked to explain the ratings. Why would an employee explain the reason behind a low rating on an item such as "My manager inspires trust" after the survey process initially set up—indeed, promised—the expectation of confidentiality? The whole point of the anonymous survey, in his view, was so that the manager would get the message without having to confront him directly.

Unfortunately, this limits the sharing of the specific information necessary to bring about effective change. This is because creating and sustaining change require a high level of internal commitment by the individuals in the organization. To be able to commit, individuals need the data to be valid. The core value of valid information does not simply mean that the information is accurate; validity also refers to the quality of the information. For example, a low response to the survey item, "The current organizational structure helps different departments cooperate and work together effectively," carries its intended meaning, but it does not provide the concrete examples needed to allow others to understand what or when cooperation is lacking or what the respondents' expectations for working together are.

Because survey respondents are not identified, their sentiments cannot be independently verified, another component of valid information. They are not expected to be able to provide specific examples, since specific examples can lead to identification. This creates a one-sided kind of accountability, where the people receiving the survey results, usually management, are held to be responsive to the survey results, but the responsibility of the survey respondents stops at having completed the survey.

> This creates a one-sided kind of accountability, where the people receiving the survey results, usually management, are held to be responsive to the survey results, but the responsibility of the survey respondents stops at having completed the survey.

As Chris Argyris (1994) writes, "Employee surveys . . . encourage employees *not* to reflect on their own behaviors and attitudes. By assigning all the responsibility for fixing problems to management, they encourage managers *not* to relinquish the top-down, command-and-control mindset that prevents empowerment" (p. 83). This view is reinforced by the cascade process that, by design, emphasizes the sharing of the results with managers, first by the direct report of the survey results and then by additional live feedback from employees. This creates a dynamic in which it is employees' responsibility to raise issues and management's responsibility to fix them.

CONCLUSION

The survey is not an end in itself. It is a snapshot of the state of an organization at a given time. As such, surveys are extremely useful for identifying trends and pointing toward areas that need further exploration, but by themselves, they do not deliver the motivation for group and individual change that they often promise. This has led to the assumption that people are resistant to change and the development of many strategies to remedy this. I do not believe that this is correct. I believe that the design of the survey process makes it an ineffective tool for getting people to reflect on their own work and behavior. Rather than encouraging the individual accountability that is consistent with commitment to organizational change, it focuses attention on supervisors and upper management, thus perpetuating a patriarchal structure that fosters dependence, not empowerment.[1]

Instead of looking for ways to overcome resistance to change, an alternative is to devise ways to give people more of the valid information that they need to make informed choices that generate internal commitment. In my experience, surveys do not provide an implementation strategy for bringing about change. I believe that a different type of discussion around organizational problems and how to address them, centered on questions like, "What goes on in this organization that has prevented you from questioning these practices and getting them changed?" is more likely to yield information that can motivate learning and produce real change.

Resource

Block, P. *Stewardship: Choosing Service over Self-Interest.* San Francisco: Berrett-Koehler, 1993.

Note

1. For an excellent discussion of the effects of a patriarchal, top-down culture, see *Stewardship* by Peter Block.

References

Argyris, C. "Good Communication That Blocks Learning." *Harvard Business Review,* July-Aug. 1994, pp. 77–85.

Born, D. H., and Mathieu, J. E. "Differential Effects of Survey-Guided Feedback: The Rich Get Richer and the Poor Get Poorer." *Group and Organization Management,* 1996, *21,* 388–404.

Church, A. H., and Waclawski, J. *Designing and Using Organizational Surveys.* San Francisco: Jossey-Bass, 1998.

French, W. L., and Bell, C. H., Jr. *Organization Development: Behavioral Science Interventions for Organization Improvement.* (3rd ed.) Upper Saddle River, N.J.: Prentice Hall, 1984.

Chapter 52

Using the Skilled Facilitator Approach in Different and Multiple Cultures

Anne Davidson

As people learn our approach to facilitation, they frequently express concern about whether it will work in "other" cultures. The general reaction is that the ground rules and core values are very Western. People usually infer that Middle Eastern and Sino-Confucian cultures, in particular, place more value on being indirect and saving face. They say that they cannot imagine openly questioning people, discussing all relevant information, or even working for free and informed choice in those cultures.

THE MULTINATIONAL REALITY

My colleagues and I use the Skilled Facilitator approach frequently and successfully with other cultures. Sometimes we are facilitating in another country and working with the predominant culture there. More often, we are working, both in the United States and abroad, with multinational cultures. Seldom are only one or two ethnicities represented in any group we work with. Most of our clients are located in multiple countries and recruit talent around the globe.

Most of us, in fact, are members of multiple cultures. We find ourselves moving among the culture of our family of origin, the culture of the organization where we work, the subculture of our area of professional expertise, and the culture of the religious tradition we have adopted or grew up in, to name just a few. It is critical not to assume which set of values, beliefs, and practices is primary in any given situation, as it is equally important not to make assumptions based on simplistic stereotypes of the culture of an entire country.

Roger often tells the story of consulting to a group of fifteen individuals in a global organization that represented all continents:

At one point while meeting, the subject turned to what cultural norms, including ground rules, should be used when the group was working together. A man from France said to a woman from Japan that when he was in a group that included her, he intentionally did not say certain things because he "knew" that saving face is important in her culture. The woman from Japan said something like, "I appreciate that you have thought about my culture and are sensitive to the possible cultural differences. But I don't appreciate that you assume that I wanted to be treated the same way as my culture without asking me." They then had a group conversation in which they jointly designed the group norms with which they would treat each other.

As this story illustrates, Skilled Facilitator principles are especially valuable in helping us test our assumptions and stay open to surprises.

SURPRISING REACTIONS IN RUSSIA

One of our multinational clients afforded me the opportunity to work with the top staff in their Moscow office, the management team for Russian operations:

All of the team members are multilingual. They are highly trained, many holding multiple university degrees from an array of well-respected schools in the United States, Great Britain, and Russia. All speak English, most of them fluently, and that was the language of our training and facilitation. On the surface, this group seemed more like a typical U.S. team than most I have worked with in other countries. Yet this team probably had more concerns and fears about using the ground rules than any other group I have facilitated. Many said that their cultural and political background made openly asking questions and testing inferences extremely frightening. Some trembled or perspired heavily just trying to role-play testing an assumption or explaining their reasoning and intent.

Most of the staff told us that they were raised in the Soviet Union in a time when openly questioning authority could result in severe punishment, up to imprisonment and even death. Although the system is structured differently now, values and attitudes seem not to have changed all that much. Authority is not questioned. Espoused values are more collectivist than individualistic.

In writing about the key dimensions along which cultures vary, Ziegahn (2001) points out that individualistic cultures like the United States value self-reliance, autonomy, and equality, whereas "collectivist cultures tend to value group effort and harmony and knowing one's place in society" (p. 2). Individualistic cultures may equate hierarchy with rigidity and denial of equal opportunity for everyone. "Conversely, hierarchy may be valued in more collectivist cultures as a means of acknowledging innate differences and inequalities and of facilitating communication through the recognition of various social levels such as titles and roles" (p. 3). Whether this characterization is true of Russian culture in general, it accurately describes the way I experienced the culture in the management team I worked with. Individuals were acknowledged and rewarded by formal role, not by their personal effort. While disagreeing with the boss might seem risky in a U.S. organization, doing so is a much more blatant violation of social values in a collectivist culture.

> Individuals did not openly raise concerns in the management group. That was seen as disagreeing with authority and violating the norm of knowing one's place. Disagreement was problematic not only for the boss and the one who spoke up; it upset the foundational structure for the entire group. One of the important outcomes of our facilitation occurred when the members of the staff referred to as the expatriates or expats (the few top officers, who were primarily U.S. and U.K. citizens) raised their concerns about how "disrespectful" the Russian nationals were of the expatriates' authority. In defining what "disrespectful" meant and getting specific examples, it turned out that the Russian nationals engaged in frequent side conversations. The British, in particular, were highly offended by this practice because they interpreted it as a gesture of disrespect. That assumption had colored many interactions between the two groups, but no one believed it could be openly raised or discussed in the larger management team.
>
> When the group did talk through the issue with our help, the Russian nationals shared that side conversations had exactly the opposite intent from what the expatriates inferred. The Russians were taught in school never to interrupt the teacher while he or she was lecturing. Anyone who had a question asked it of a person sitting nearby. Side conversations in their culture are meant as a sign of respect for the speaker. They commented that if we watched their national congress meetings on television, we would frequently see multiple side conversations going on while someone was speaking. With this understanding, the group reached agreement about how to handle the issue: the expatriates would let the Russian staff know if a side conversation was particularly distracting, and the Russians would practice openly raising questions and issues that they thought would be relevant for the entire group. Each group would continue to give feedback to the other about this issue.
>
> Yet despite this conversation, which had the potential to dramatically improve the ability of the management team members to work together, the group was reluctant to adopt the ground rules as team norms. Every member believed he or she could not find even a subset of the rules that all could support using. The dilemma was this: the management team members were unwilling to test assumptions and inferences publicly, and they were unwilling for others to do so; this felt too risky to them. Setting up a process in which individuals were asked to test their assumptions about others in a group or asked to reveal their own mental models as distinct from the group mental model was a radical and much more threatening shift than it would be in my own culture.

Without being able to test inferences, I couldn't and can't see a way to use the Skilled Facilitator approach to help a group be more effective. I had initially assumed that the ground rules and core values would be a better fit for this group than for some of the more culturally diverse groups I have facilitated. I did not anticipate the barriers involved.

Without being able to test inferences, I couldn't and can't see a way to use the Skilled Facilitator approach to help a group be more effective.

See Testing Assumptions and Inferences, page 62, and the Ladder of Inference sidebar, page 63, in Chapter Five, "Ground Rules for Effective Groups."

ACCEPTANCE IN A MULTINATIONAL ORGANIZATION

By contrast, my colleague Sue McKinney provided me the opportunity to work with an international nongovernmental organization for several years that has offices and staff in sixteen countries.

In one memorable training session, the class materials were half in English and half in Spanish. Participants came from a wide array of countries, including Vietnam, Kenya, India, Ethiopia, Nigeria, Mexico, Bolivia, and Brazil. Despite the challenges of working across so many different cultures, with translators who did not know our approach and struggled to find accurate translations for some of our terminology, the group became quite excited about using the approach in their work together.

Many participants did say that they had some hesitation about using the skills in their personal lives. Conversations using the ground rules felt very different from their cultural norms. But the group members were virtually unanimous in finding the skills valuable for their work lives. They said that many of their most difficult conversations were with the home office in the United States, testing assumptions and inferences about decisions and about what would or would not work in their home countries.

There seemed very little concern about or resistance to practicing the skills in the work context. Some even said that with proper explanation and adequate translation, they felt the ground rules and core values could be productively used in other arenas in their home countries.

There seemed very little concern about or resistance to practicing the skills in the work context. Some even said that with proper explanation and adequate translation, they felt the ground rules and core values could be productively used in other arenas in their home countries.

Most of these individuals are much more experienced at working with and across international boundaries and barriers than those of us who come from traditional North American cultures, and they find the Skilled Facilitator a useful approach.

ADDRESSING THE DILEMMAS

One of the ways the Skilled Facilitator approach can be most helpful is in addressing a dilemma faced by most multinational organizations: whether to insist on uniform standards worldwide, adjust the company standards to local customs, or try to decide on a case-by-case basis. Leonard Brooks (1998), executive director of the Clarkson

Centre for Business Ethics at the University of Toronto, points out that each of these choices has advantages and risks. Uniform standards around issues like nepotism can make it almost impossible to do business in cultures where a primary value is duty to family. But case-by-case decisions can lead to everyone ignoring standards across the board. And Brooks points out that it is increasingly problematic for organizations to adopt local customs that differ considerably from those of their parent culture, particularly in areas of child labor laws, health and safety standards, and environmental protection. Actions seen as unprincipled by stakeholders in the home culture can lead to significant problems in public perception for an organization. Consumers may organize boycotts. There are no easy solutions. Learning to have more productive conversations, test assumptions, focus on interests, explain reasoning and intent, and discuss what was previously considered undiscussable seem the most productive strategies to address these issues globally.

Of course, it is difficult to use the Skilled Facilitator approach to address issues if one cannot even raise the issues. And to set up an environment where concerns can be openly discussed is particularly challenging for a facilitator from one culture who is calling into question values built into someone else's culture. Yet one of our assumptions is that the very strategies that create difficulty (face saving, easing in, keeping concerns private) are learned early in life, embedded in one form or another in every culture we have encountered.

When we raise problems with an organizational culture, we are also questioning the national culture that gives rise to organizational norms. So far, I find the most helpful and productive approach to be naming the dilemmas and using mutual learning strategies to explain my reasons for questioning cultural values and differences. This still feels uncomfortable when I am working in a predominant culture that I do not profess to fully appreciate or understand. I hope in the future to have wise partners from a wide range of backgrounds who can work with me and help expand my understanding.

When we raise problems with an organizational culture, we are also questioning the national culture that gives rise to organizational norms.

TESTING ASSUMPTIONS AND CONTINUING THE CONVERSATION

We have a lot to learn. My primary advice is not to make assumptions about what will and will not work. Respect that each individual differs and that we need to give each as informed a choice as possible about whether and how to use the skills rather than assuming they will or will not take the risk of trying them.

The more I work across cultures, the less different I find people's fundamental interests. What does vary widely is the importance of a particular value or social virtue. For example, the informed choice on which the Skilled Facilitator approach is based may be valued so differently that our very attempt to offer choice or test agreement may create defensiveness. With the team in Russia, individual choice and individual difference were not considered nearly as important as preserving group structure and harmony. It is possible that the way we test our ideas about cultural differences—by asking direct questions—is itself an artifact of our own culture, so our very test may or may not be valid. I taught in western North Carolina for a number of years where the traditionally raised Cherokee students in my classroom did not ask questions and never looked at me directly. They told me that they had not yet earned the right to speak before the tribe. Calling on them to answer a question in class made them intensely uncomfortable. Trying to ask them questions to test inferences would not generate valid data.

Facilitating and working across cultures is complex. It leaves me with more questions than answers. I do not know whether the Skilled Facilitator approach can work in all or most cultures. And I do not know if the mutual learning core values match the aspirations of people raised in other cultures. I suspect that many elements can work in most cultures, but we will not know that until many more people understand this work and test it skillfully. One of the problems is that the concepts and training materials have not been translated into multiple languages by knowledgeable practitioners.

The Skilled Facilitator has been translated into Korean. We are currently exploring translations into Chinese, Japanese, Indonesian, and Spanish. We have made some initial attempts in Spanish and French, but these are not well tested for clarity and usefulness, and the teaching examples are still very much based in U.S. culture.

People cannot always readily identify or reflect on their most deeply held values, so understanding them requires patient, curious conversation. I believe that we should continue to explore our similarities and differences, sharing our questions and yearnings for deeper discussions, and inviting others to join us in discovering what works and what does not. I am curious and optimistic about what we can accomplish.

References

Brooks, L. J. "Doing Business in Foreign Cultures." Remarks made to the Canadian Centre for Ethics and Corporate Policy, Toronto, Mar. 4, 1998. [www.ethicscentre.ca].

Ziegahn, L. *Considering Culture in the Selection of Teaching Approaches for Adults.* Columbus, Ohio: ERIC Clearinghouse on Adult Career and Vocational Education, 2001.

PART SEVEN

Integrating the Skilled Facilitator Approach in Your Worklife (and Non-Worklife)

MANY OF OUR COLLEAGUES AND CLIENTS HAVE INTEGRATED the Skilled Facilitator approach with their own areas of expertise and with other facilitative roles. We have as well. When used consistently throughout roles and in different situations, this approach becomes a way of being in the world rather than a way to fill a particular role. The chapters in Part Seven describe a variety of these examples; we hope they inspire you to explore how you might make your own work more powerful in helping, working, and living with others.

Dick McMahon opens Part Seven with Chapter Fifty-Three, "The Drama Triangle: A Unilateral Control Program for Helping Others." He presents a powerful and elegant model for understanding how, by making untested inferences and assumptions, we create a dynamic in which we become rescuers, persecutors, and victims. He also explains the steps to take to avoid getting into this triangle. Guillermo Cuéllar also shows how some of our fundamental assumptions and values lead us to see the world as either a hostile place in which we seek to survive or a place of possibility in which we can be creative. In Chapter Fifty-Four, "Using Creative and Survival Cycles to See and Shift Mental Models," he illustrates how to identify a survival cycle and shift to a creative cycle.

Individual differences among group members are a potential source of learning and creativity if members can learn how to use differences to the group's advantage. In Chapter Fifty-Five, "The Skilled Facilitator Approach and the Myers-Briggs Type Indicator," Anne Davidson first describes how the popular personality assessment tool identifies differences in the way we prefer to see and judge things. Then she provides guidelines for using the Skilled Facilitator approach to help group members with differing types work together more effectively.

Chris Soderquist shows how he helps groups develop a shared mental map of their situation and agree on solutions to complex problems by using operational systems thinking tools. In Chapter Fifty-Six, "Applying The Skilled Facilitator

Approach to a Systems Thinking Analysis," he illustrates how combining the two approaches makes each more powerful.

In Part One, we explained that you can apply the mind-set and skill set of the Skilled Facilitator approach to other roles. We listed several roles: facilitative leader (which we explored in Part Five), facilitative coach, facilitative consultant, and facilitative trainer. In the second half of Part Seven, we explore these and other roles. In Chapter Fifty-Seven, "The Facilitative Coach" Anne Davidson and Dale Schwarz describe their coaching model, which includes integrating the Skilled Facilitator approach with four facets of coaching: the inner work of the coach, the purpose of coaching, the inner work of the client, and the coaching relationship.

Sue McKinney and Matt Beane, in Chapter Fifty-Eight, "Becoming a Facilitative Trainer," first describe how trainers often design and lead their training in a unilaterally controlling way that undermines the very learning and commitment they seek from participants. Then they, and Diane Florio in a sidebar, illustrate how to apply the principles of the Skilled Facilitator approach to effectively address a variety of training issues, including dealing with questions, conducting exercises, taking breaks, and exploring participant concerns.

Using facilitative skills as a consultant adds value for clients. Harry Furukawa demonstrates this in Chapter Fifty-Nine, "Being a Facilitative Consultant."

Peg captures the perspective of the Skilled Facilitator approach as a way of being in Chapter Sixty, "Using the Skilled Facilitator Approach as a Parent." Through humorous and poignant examples, she shows how she uses the approach with her children and helps them learn it too.

As the final two chapters demonstrate, the Skilled Facilitator approach is robust enough that it can be used in what might seem doubtful circumstances. Turning to politics, Steve Kay recounts his experience as a facilitative leader in Chapter Sixty-One, "Running for Office in a Unilaterally Controlling World." Verla Insko takes this theme to the next step in Chapter Sixty-Two, "Using the Facilitative Leader Approach in Public Office." As an elected (and reelected) state representative in the North Carolina General Assembly, she details how she helped a diverse group of stakeholders (consumers, advocates, public and private providers, and state-level administrators) build a consensus and pass key mental health legislation.

As you read the chapters in Part Seven, we encourage you to think about your own work and your life outside work and how integrating it with the Skilled Facilitator approach may make it more useful and more rewarding for you and those you engage with.

Chapter 53

The Drama Triangle

A Unilateral Control Program for Helping Others

Dick McMahon

See the unilateral control model in Chapter Four, "Understanding What Guides Your Behavior," page 33.

The drama triangle consists of three primary roles that we unknowingly assume when we do not test assumptions or inferences that we make regarding relationships. These roles are the rescuer, persecutor, and victim.

THE DRAMA TRIANGLE is a powerful approach to understanding our unilaterally controlling behavior. It consists of three primary roles that we unknowingly assume when we do not test assumptions or inferences that we make regarding relationships. These roles are the rescuer, persecutor, and victim.

We enter or take a role in the drama triangle as helpers with benevolent intentions. Sometimes we enter the rescuer role, believing we know what is best for the other person. We may assume a persecutor role when we try to control the behavior of others in the belief that they have acted irresponsibly by seemingly disobeying the rules or failing to follow orders or acting inconsistent with our expectations. And on occasion we assume the victim role: we doubt our own capabilities and ask others to tell us what to do in an effort to avoid taking responsibility, enabling others to ultimately control our destiny.

Stephen Karpman (1968) introduced the drama triangle in an article focused on the dynamics of psychological games as defined in Transactional Analysis. His contribution provides an approach for understanding how many relationships lack authenticity and are likely to result in deepening dependency, failure, and rebellion rather than in an increased ability to solve problems and grow. Karpman's insights are reinforced and affirmed by Sheldon Kopp's penetrating insights (1976) into power relationships and the victim role. When I began to work with Chris Argyris's theories, I was pleasantly surprised to find that the drama triangle concept is consistent with what Argyris calls a Model I theory-in-use, here labeled the unilateral control model.[1] Argyris's social virtue of "help" as defined from a unilateral control perspective informs the design of the rescue role in the drama triangle.

The drama triangle provides significant insights into how we design our behaviors in a manner consistent with our unilateral control theory-in-use even when we think we are being helpful, righteously directive, or modestly self-effacing. Understanding drama triangle dynamics and how to avoid them is a powerful way for all of us in helping professions and leadership positions to redesign our relationships to be authentic, effective, and consistent with mutual learning.

THE BASIS OF INAUTHENTIC RELATIONSHIPS

Karpman (1968) refers to relationships that are based on untested assumptions and inferences as ***role relationships*** as opposed to authentic relationships. An ***authentic relationship*** is one in which we take action based on our mutually determined understanding of the relationship and where each person feels free to make choices about actions to be taken. In role relationships, we act on assumptions or inferences that we believe to be true but we have not tested. Thus, we end up discounting the other person's skills, abilities, or attitude, as well as his or her free choice. In the context of this model, to ***discount*** means to deny the possibility that a capability, need, or feeling actually exists or to consider a capability, need, or feeling unimportant.

In Kopp's terms, when we see other adults as weaker than ourselves, we have created an "illusion of power." That is, we have discounted the other person's strengths and believe ourselves to be more powerful. Once a discount takes place, we move to a position or role that is inauthentic and is consistent with the discounted view of the situation. Furthermore, by acting on discounts that grow from untested assumptions and attributions, we are unilaterally deciding what is best to do in order to deal effectively with the situation.

DRAMA TRIANGLE ROLES

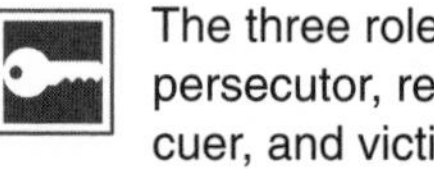

The three roles of persecutor, rescuer, and victim form the pattern of interaction Karpman labels the drama triangle

Karpman (1968) believes three role relationships frequently determine behavior: persecutor, rescuer, and victim. Each role is initiated by a set of untested assumptions about the other person. These three roles form the pattern of interaction Karpman labels the drama triangle (Figure 53.1).

The Persecutor

A person in the persecutor role (1) is critical of the actions of another person and either doesn't understand the reasons behind the actions or attributes a negative intent to that person whether or not negative intent exists and (2) offers judgmental and nonspecific criticism.

The persecutor victimizes the other person by belittling the person or responding in ways that make that person feel inadequate, ashamed, or incompetent. The persecutor feels righteous, vindicated, or responsible for dealing with the

Figure 53.1 The Drama Triangle

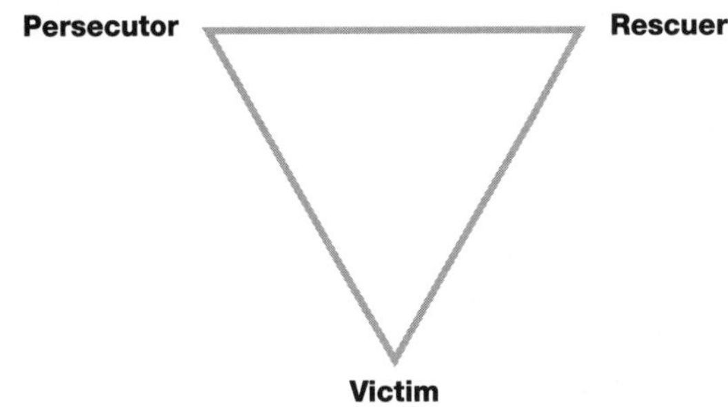

Source: Karpman (1968). Used by permission of Dr. Stephen B. Karpman.

situation. For example, when a supervisor gives an employee inadequate or incomplete instructions and then criticizes the employee for not doing things to the supervisor's satisfaction, the supervisor is in the persecutor role. Persecutors feel righteous or vindicated inasmuch as they see themselves as responsible for correcting the action or making things right.

A person in the persecutor role (1) is critical of the actions of another person and either doesn't understand the reasons behind the actions or attributes a negative intent to that person whether or not negative intent exists and (2) offers judgmental and nonspecific criticism.

The Rescuer

A person in the rescuer role (1) discounts another person's ability to handle his or her own problems and (2) attempts to "help" by doing for that person what he or she could and should do for himself or herself. As an example of a rescuer, a twelve-year-old child complains to his mother that the grade he received was unfair. He would not take his complaint to the teacher so the mother rescues him by going to the teacher on his behalf and complaining about the grade. The rescuer gets his or her needs met by appearing helpful, but the help actually creates a victim whose ability to take responsibility for his own actions has been discounted. The approach also limits the learning opportunities of victims.

A person in the rescuer role (1) discounts another person's ability to handle his or her own problems and (2) attempts to "help" by doing for that person what he or she could and should do for himself or herself.

The Victim

People in the victim role (1) discount their own ability, knowledge, or skill and (2) end up with someone else either taking care of them (rescuing) or criticizing (persecuting) them. Individuals are in a victim role when they try to place the responsibility for their own success or failure on someone else rather than trying to solve their own problems or acting appropriately and consistently with their own abilities. For example, you may be in a victim role if you find yourself overwhelmed with work. Your supervisor asks you to take on an important new task. You assume, without testing, that if you do not do the task, your supervisor will consider you

People in the victim role (1) discount their own ability, knowledge, or skill and (2) end up with someone else either taking care of them (rescuing) or criticizing (persecuting) them.

either unhelpful or ineffective. You may also assume that the supervisor wouldn't find another person if you did tell him you could not take on the task. You end up doing the task, knowing it will take your evenings and weekends and you feel victimized.

Here's a typical example of the dynamics of the drama triangle:

A young professional woman, Midge, lived in a two-bedroom home. She chose to live by herself in this home because she valued her alone time, and the home gave her plenty of room to work and study. Midge's friend Sallie came to her one day and told her a sad story: she had lost her job, she had very little money, and she was going to have to drop out of school because she had nowhere to live and couldn't afford an apartment. She asked Midge if she could live with her for a few weeks until she got on her feet (victim role). Sallie also said she would reimburse Midge for the cost of rent and utilities after she got on her feet again. Although Midge was reluctant to give up her space and freedom, she said that Sallie could move in but that it couldn't be for longer than a month. Despite her reluctance, Midge agreed to the arrangement because she wanted to be seen as helpful (rescuer role). In other words, to control Sallie's feelings toward her, Midge decided to let her stay for a month.

After a month, Sallie had not improved her financial situation and begged Midge to let her stay a little longer. Midge reluctantly agreed but was beginning to feel frustrated and angry that Sallie wasn't doing more to find a job and get herself in a position to take care of herself. As it turned out, Sallie stayed four months and paid no money to Midge. Finally, Midge became so incensed at Sallie's "irresponsible behavior" that she had an angry confrontation with Sallie and insisted that Sallie leave, not caring what happened to their relationship. Midge had moved into the persecutor role.

After Sallie left, she found a job and began to do very well. Months passed, and she had not paid Midge a penny of the money she owed. Midge got angry and demanded that Sallie get responsible and pay what she owed. Midge even attempted to set up a payment schedule for Sallie. When the first payment of a hundred dollars came due, Sallie paid ten dollars. Sallie is now in the role of Midge's persecutor. Midge then decided that the friendship did not mean anything to her and insisted that Sallie pay what she owed.

Midge called Sallie and told her how irresponsible she was. Midge said she did not want to hear from her again, essentially terminating the relationship and losing about a thousand dollars that Sallie owed her. Thus, the result of her early rescue left Midge a victim in the win-lose (unilateral control) context of the drama triangle. Midge had moved from rescuer (agreeing to let Sallie stay in the first place) to victim (when Sallie failed to leave at the agreed-on time) to persecutor, when she unilaterally acted to throw Sallie out, and finally back to victim (when she lost both her money and the friendship.)

This simple story illustrates some basic principles of the drama triangle:

- All victims play a part in their own victimization. People who fail, need help, or are down on their luck contribute immeasurably to their problems.
- Every rescuer-victim transaction ultimately turns into a persecutor-victim transaction, with the victim persecuting the rescuer. This is the predictable consequence of rescue. Your victims will get you some way.

All victims play a part in their own victimization. Every rescuer-victim transaction ultimately turns into a persecutor-victim transaction with the victim persecuting the rescuer.

Sheldon Kopp speaks to this dynamic:

> It is my very strong impression that in such bargains [implicitly accepting the respective roles where one person takes responsibility for the other], the victim is far more dangerous than the powerful, responsibility burdened caretaker. Beware the helplessness gambit of the chronic victim! Some people typically get out from under their own responsibilities in difficult situations (in which they would otherwise have to take care of themselves) by acting helpless and weak in order to invite others to do for them. . . . Should [we] arrogantly take on the role of caretaker, then the helpless one will soon hold [us] in contempt for being a weak fool, and what [we] offer will be returned as somehow not good enough [1976, pp. 83–84].

- The triangle is a very stable structure; that is, people often move from one role to another in a situation or relationship rather than redesigning the relationship dynamics to get out of inauthentic roles altogether.
- Real help comes from those who enable others to help themselves. Such individuals have confronted their illusions of power and do not enter into the implicit contract of being responsible for the other person's actions.

THE DRAMA TRIANGLE AND UNILATERAL CONTROL DESIGNS

Like the unilateral control theory-in-use, the drama triangle is a design program in our heads that enables us to maintain control of relationships, be rational, avoid expressing negative feelings, and be right (win).

Like the unilateral control theory-in-use, the drama triangle is a design program in our heads that enables us to maintain control of relationships, be rational, avoid expressing negative feelings, and be right (win).

In this respect, it is consistent with Argyris's description of the dynamics of a Model I design: "I will use my theory in action to influence you. If I succeed, then I will control you and win you over. This will lead you to be submissive to and dependent on me. It is effective for me to make you ineffective. The paradox, if you were to act toward me in the way I act toward you, then I could not act in the way I intend. My theory of effectiveness will ultimately make me and other people ineffective" (1990, p. 13).

Argyris also suggests that the reason the unilateral control theory-in-use is so common and so thoroughly taught is that part of our design program includes social virtues that we have learned through our experiences in society. These social virtues such as help and support, honesty, respect of others, strength, and integrity become defined so that they support unilateral control. Thus, the social virtue of help is defined so that when we act in a helpful manner, we attempt to control the situation, win rather than lose, be rational, and minimize creating or expressing negative feelings.

The impact of our unilateral control theory-in-use on our behavior may be explained in the following manner. In our interactions with others, we find ourselves in situations where the other person is asking for help. We may not want to do what the other person is asking us to do, but we feel compelled to do it because we do not want him or her to feel bad (avoid negative feelings) and because we want to be seen as helpful. If we refuse, we may be concerned that the person will become very emotional (cry or get angry) and may see us as an unhelpful (or bad) person. Our unilateral control theory-in-use also tells us that one way to control this situation is to do what the other person wants.

The Rescue Approach

There are other occasions where someone we believe has had bad luck or tries hard but is just not very capable fails to complete an assignment. When we confront the person, he tells us a sad story about problems at home and the unusually difficult time he had getting all the material necessary to complete the assignment. He may appear emotionally upset, and we wonder if our insisting that he get the task completed might push him over the edge (untested attribution). At this point, we must find a way to control the situation and make sure things are handled in a rational manner. We also want to be viewed as a reasonable and helpful person. We may say, "Well, why don't you hand over the material you have collected, and I will see that the task gets taken care of. Then you can get your other work up to date so that you are not under so much stress." The person agrees and thanks you for being so understanding. This is consistent with the definition of rescue. A more subtle rescue might be to ask the person how much more time he needs and give him whatever time he deems necessary to get the task completed. This strategy is usually accompanied by the empathic verbalizations and offers of continued help. Designing our actions through the rescue paradigm has within it an implicit discount of the other person's ability to respond effectively to the situation.

Unilateral control definitions of being helpful do not include the consideration that all people are inherently capable of handling life if they have the skills and determination to do so. Nor is our role defined as helping them make informed choices to do what they are capable of doing or helping them gain the knowledge and skills to be able to make new choices. In the rescue design, we confirm another's willingness to accept failure as acceptable. In this way, we increase the likelihood that he or she will fail in the future and come to expect and accept failure. That is, the choices are informed by faulty data that we helped to affirm by our actions in rescuing the person. Thus, by designing behavior to reflect the social virtue of helping, which includes not hurting other people's feelings, we collude with the other person in becoming a victim. In the process, we increase their sense of dependency and submission and limit the possibility of new learning. As Argyris suggests, if you are to be effective with your unilateral control theory-in-use (rescue approach), the other person must be ineffective.

The Persecution Approach

The persecution dynamic operates similarly. It is initiated by a set of assumptions and attributions concerning the other person's failure to take responsibility, unwillingness to work hard, or not caring. Any act that may be interpreted as consistent with the negative assumptions we have made is greeted with a stern demand that the other person improve or change her behavior. As a disciplinary or corrective measure, she may be given a difficult assignment that is beyond her capability or an assignment with an unrealistic deadline. When she fails to get it done, she may be disciplined or subjected to ridicule. The action is self-fulfilling in that the task is unlikely to be finished in a timely manner. When she fails to finish in a timely fashion, it affirms for you her lack of commitment or sense of responsibility (self-fulfilling). The important thing is not to let the person "get away with it" (in other words, to control the situation). We must win by making her do the task or disciplining her if she fails (win, don't lose). We state that we will give her every chance and use these opportunities to let her know how she has failed (act rational). We make sure we follow the procedures and rules in our discipline (do not express or create negative feelings). The process is self-sealing in that the person did not have a chance to provide any information as to what might be a realistic expectation.

At times, the persecutor may seem to do the opposite of minimizing negative feelings. However, when anger is expressed in criticizing a victim who has acted particularly irresponsibly, it is rationalized as consistent with the social virtue of showing strength. This show of strength demonstrates that we are in control. Thus, at times the value of minimizing expression of negative feelings may not be satisfied because we shift the order of importance of values to fit the situation. In this instance, we may believe it is more important to maintain control by showing strength than it is to minimize the expression of negative feelings. This illustrates the way we adopt different strategies to satisfice values across situations without fundamentally shifting our design program or moving out of inauthentic roles.

The Victim Approach

The victim role is initiated by assumptions we make about ourselves. This is usually a result of discounting our capability, intelligence, or capacity to improve or change. We accept the rescuer's or persecutor's assessment of the situation and assume they will take care of things. In the victim role, we control the situation by putting the responsibility for change on the other person and win by having the other person confirm that we are in fact incapable or irresponsible. Consistent with the unilateral control theory-in-use, we do this by admitting our culpability (being rational) and by expressing positive emotions toward the other person.

Victims discount the persecutor's or rescuer's ability to truly help them change (become more responsible or solving his or her own problems). Even those who cleverly manipulate us into rescuing them are as surely victims as those who seem to unwittingly assume the victim role. Their design is to control the other person and do it through finding clever excuses that are often easily recognized but difficult to discount. In these cases, the feelings of the rescuer include a large portion of anger and resentment toward the victim. These angry feelings set up the ultimate persecution of the victim by the very person who had been the rescuer. Ultimately, however, victims must win, and they do this by finding ways to discount the rescuer's intention or capability or by making life difficult for the rescuer. The failed victim will often tell the helper that he or she appreciates all the helper has done and that the failure was all the victim's fault. This may be manifest in the rescuer's having more and more work to do or having to spend more and more time keeping up with things that the victim fails to accomplish.

When Helping Doesn't Help

The drama triangle helps us to understand why some of the people we think we have done the most to help are the ones who appreciate us the least. It also helps to explain why we often find ourselves feeling angry and persecutory toward those whom we felt most inclined to help. It is difficult to interact consistently from an authentic role in situations that threaten us and move us to unilateral control design programs. The drama triangle design is one of those programs that is consistent with most of our social virtues. It is not surprising, then, that we may find ourselves enacting any one of the drama triangle roles depending on the situation.

BEING HELPFUL AND AVOIDING THE DRAMA TRIANGLE

Being helpful in a manner more consistent with mutual learning means influencing others in ways that allow them to use their own abilities, skills, or knowledge to solve their problems. Help in mutual learning is also defined as providing individuals with the necessary resources when they face genuinely insurmountable limitations. The fundamental principle in authentic helping is making it possible for people in need, whether a friend, child, employee, coworker, or customer, to solve their own problems in a way that does not diminish them.

Avoiding Drama Triangle Roles

For those in the role of providing help, the following conditions are consistent with avoiding drama triangle roles:

- **Be confident in your abilities and motivated to foster competence in others.** Being in a helping position in order to enhance one's own self-esteem or sense of worth makes a person vulnerable to the rescuer, persecutor, or victim role.
- **Approach others with positive expectations.** This does not mean having unrealistic expectations about how well things are going to go, but it does mean that you expect others to have the ability, should they choose, to deal with their own problems. The self-fulfilling prophecy is true: we often get what we expect, good or bad.
- **Understand that enhancing a person's sense of confidence or self-worth is most likely to occur when the person is successful in meeting new challenges.** As a corollary to approaching others with positive expectations, it is important that the helper set realistic but challenging expectations that move the other person toward growth.
- **Support any effort on an individual's part to be more responsible and effective.** Appreciate the difficulty of change and the scary feelings often associated with it. For some, simple achievements such as taking full responsibility for a task or project represent a major effort to overcome self-doubt.
- **Be congruent.** There must be similarity in what one says and does. This means that a helper must act in accordance with his or her espoused beliefs, values, and principles. Being congruent is essential if you are to be credible and develop authentic, nonrole relationships.
- **Clarify the consequences, and impose them when the individual's behavior warrants it.** This is essential to communicate the belief that each person must be responsible for his or her behavior. The consequences should be known beforehand and be reasonable for the situation.
- **Accept no excuses for failure.** Rather, focus on evaluating what happened and explore with the individual what could have been done differently to be successful. Accepting excuses for failure, no matter how well articulated or persuasive the excuse may be, discounts the individual's ability to act more responsibly.

See Chapter Seven, "Thinking and Acting Systemically," page 75, on the systems principle of shifting from blame to contribution.

- **Do not do things you feel pressured to do for employees or coworkers.** For example, you do something for the employee because you feel if you don't take action, the employee will fail. Ask yourself if you have done all you can to enable the individual to take appropriate action. Jointly determine with the other person what could be done differently.
- **When someone fails to carry out her responsibilities, confront the failure without conveying the feeling she has let you down.** The individual has let herself down; she is the victim of her own doing. Angry recriminations (persecution) or feeling sorry for her (victimization) discount her ability to do things differently.
- **Verbally and emotionally support any effort on an individual's part to take responsible action** if the person has the necessary skill, knowledge, and understanding to take the action in the first place.

Specific Actions to Take (and Avoid)

Given the suggestions above, the following actions are considered consistent with mutual learning help when taken in the proper context:

- Sharing relevant information
- Helping develop alternative actions to solve a problem
- Helping a coworker explore the consequences of possible actions
- Supporting responsible employee choices even though the choices might not be choices you would make
- Open sharing of thoughts and feelings regarding an employee or coworker, including giving individuals honest feedback regarding their behavior and testing assumptions or attributions you may have made
- Giving an individual encouragement and support to try new behaviors
- Modeling responsible behavior, positive expectations, and honesty

Actions that diminish employee strengths include:

- Doing things for employees or coworkers they can do for themselves
- Doing things for an employee because the employee does not know how to do something instead of trying to help the employee learn to do it

- Being critical of a person's failure rather than helping him or her analyze the failure and identify how to be more successful the next time
- Giving advice or telling an individual what to do (as opposed to sharing information and helping him define alternative courses of action)
- Giving an employee instructions to do something she does not have the skills, experience, or knowledge to accomplish or failing to help the employee evaluate her preparedness to take an action or complete a task
- Providing employees or coworkers information they should have acquired themselves because it is easier to do it that way

Resources

Argyris, C. *Overcoming Organizational Defenses,* Upper Saddle River, N.J.: Prentice Hall, 1990.

Argyris, C. *On Organizational Learning.* (2nd ed.) Cambridge, Mass.: Blackwell, 1999.

Argyris, C., and Schön, D. S. *Organizational Learning II.* Reading, Mass.: Addison-Wesley, 1996.

Note

1. The works I use most frequently are Chris Argyris and Donald S. Schön, *Organizational Learning II* (1996), and Chris Argyris, *Overcoming Organizational Defenses* (1990) and *On Organizational Learning* (2nd ed., 1999).

References

Argyris, C. *Overcoming Organizational Defenses.* Upper Saddle River, N.J.: Prentice Hall, 1990.

Argyris, C., and Schön, D. S. *Organizational Learning II.* Reading, Mass.: Addison-Wesley, 1996.

Karpman, S. "Fairy Tales and Script Drama Analysis." *Transactional Analysis Bulletin,* 1968, *7*(26), 39–43. [http://www.itaa-net.org/TAJNet/articles/karpman01.html].

Kopp, S. *If You Meet the Buddha on the Road, Kill Him!* New York: Bantam, 1976.

Chapter 54

Using Creative and Survival Cycles to See and Shift Mental Models

Guillermo Cuéllar

OUR MENTAL MODELS help shape our reality. They are the tour guides for our ability to explore, experiment, and achieve our desired intent. Our most fundamental assumptions about the world, fear and love, create powerful self-fulfilling prophecies. We can create for any situation, or about our life in general, a self-sustaining virtuous cycle of creative awareness or a self-sustaining vicious cycle of fear and reduced potential.

The Life Learning Model provides a framework for helping people examine these fundamental assumptions. It is particularly useful when coaching executives, facilitators, and other consultants and for doing developmental work with small groups. Walking through the model provides powerful insights for individuals willing to examine their theory-in-use at the deepest level: their basic assumptions about what is possible in life.

The model is a guide to help understand the options and possibilities available to us when confronted with life's choices. We can view ourselves as having two basic strategies: one is to create, and the other is to assimilate and survive.

> We can view ourselves as having two basic strategies: one is to create, and the other is to assimilate and survive.

When we create, we are driven by what is possible, by the alternatives embedded in a situation, by an idea of our very own potential—what we want to do and create. When we struggle to assimilate and survive, we are focused on our fears and how to minimize or avoid threats—what we should do. The creative and survival cycles are part of life and necessary. Sometimes we face situations that genuinely threaten our life and well-being. Much of the time, there are innumerable creative possibilities with which we could experiment. The problem for many of us, I believe, is that our social conditioning and life experiences predispose us to focus on surviving and to miss out on our creative potential for learning. We fail to discover and mine our life's true purpose—or even if we find it, we suboptimize the opportunities for living our truth and close out possibilities.

The Life Learning Model illustrates how we can get stuck in a survival frame and how we might free ourselves from it (Figure 54.1). We start with the survival cycle, because much of our social conditioning predisposes us to focus on risk and threat. This makes sense from an evolutionary standpoint because our brains seem hard-wired to ensure our survival—to quickly identify foes and respond with fight or flight. The core assumptions of the survival cycle are fear and threat. We constantly scan the environment for threats, anticipate fearful situations, think about how to avoid danger, and cope using mental mandates. Our core values and assumptions are rooted in a belief that the world is essentially a dangerous place; we must always be on guard. Our responses are either to try to control difficult situations by winning and being suspicious of others' motives or by going along with the status quo.

In the survival cycle, we are primarily concerned about immediate outcomes (the quick fix)—how to get out of a risky situation now. These assumptions about the world create a survival vision through which we concentrate our attention on

Figure 54.1 The Life Learning Model

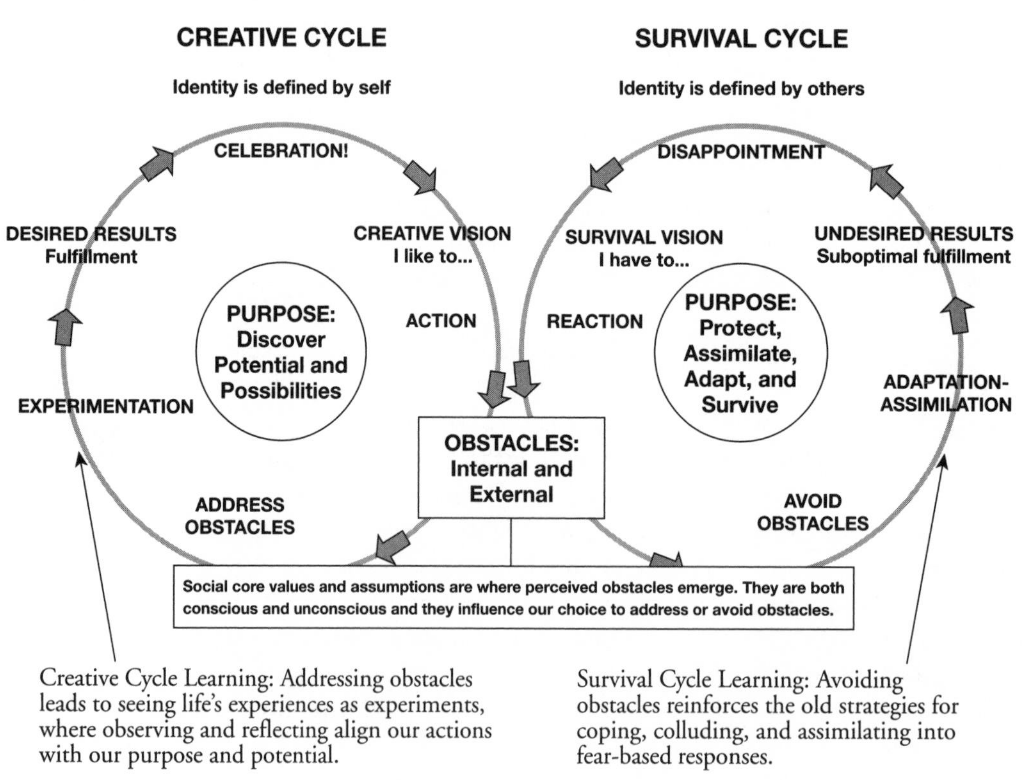

Source: Cuéllar (1986).

perceived threats. Because our core values and assumptions create self-fulfilling prophecies, the influence goes both ways: we view the world as threatening, we treat others defensively, we get escalating resistance in return, and this "proves" to us that we must constantly choose between avoiding or fighting. We "learn" that we must approach situations with survival strategies. The actions we take generally achieve our goals in the short run, but over time, our results are suboptimal at best. Our relationships and projects may survive but do not thrive. This leads to disappointment, vague feelings of "brownout" or burnout, and further confirmation that the world is not a supportive place. Our life purpose becomes struggling to survive. It is easy to become locked in this vicious cycle.

The creative cycle, in contrast, begins with a fundamentally opposite assumption: that the world is essentially a loving place, filled with potential and possibility. Our core values focus on learning and creating. We believe most people are trying to act with integrity and that each situation is an opportunity to see things differently and appreciate new perspectives. In the creative cycle, we seek the life purpose that maximizes our talents and desires. Our vision is to live up to our fullest potential, and we see learning opportunities in most situations. Our vision and assumptions lead us toward creative, open responses to obstacles, so that they are addressed rather than attacked or avoided. We move on rather than being stuck in the tar of old issues. Our actions bring growth and progress. When we get something different from what we intended, we reflect, learn, and become stronger and wiser. Our progress gives us cause for celebration, and our celebration renews our energy for more and greater creativity, feeding our vision of the world as filled with potential.

Both cycles are essential in our lives because we learn from one to understand the other. There are times when we face genuine threats to life and livelihood, and a survival response may be appropriate. Also, since the survival pattern contains most of our habitual, unconscious responses to life, we become quite skilled at getting much of what we want, at least initially, using these strategies. The problem is that we have difficulty seeing the unintended consequences we get from applying the survival strategies unnecessarily. Most of us do not readily see that there is an alternative worldview that would serve us better. The opportunity to move from the survival cycle to the creative cycle comes when we realize that our actions are giving us undesired results. If we can examine our mental models, realign our core values and assumptions, and adopt different strategies, we can often produce more fulfilling results. Over time, we can align our actions with our deepest heartfelt values and desires.

Reference

Cuéllar, G. "Creative and Survival Behaviors: Assessing a Creative Behavior Model." Unpublished doctoral dissertation, University of Massachusetts, 1986.

Chapter 55

The Skilled Facilitator Approach and the Myers-Briggs Type Indicator

Anne Davidson

HAVE YOU EVER ATTENDED a meeting or workshop where it sounds as if people are speaking "alphabet soup"? "Oh, I am an 'I,' so I need that agenda ahead of time to think about it." Or "Well, I don't have an 'F' bone in my body, so you will have to be the one to worry about what will upset the staff." Or, "We are totally different: he is an ISTJ, and I am an ENFP. We drive each other crazy trying to get projects completed." Chances are when you hear all these letters, people are "talking in type," that is, Myers-Briggs type.

The Myers-Briggs Type Indicator (MBTI) is the most widely used personality inventory in the world.[1] It has a number of well-developed applications, including personal and professional development, team development, conflict resolution, leadership, coaching, family counseling, and education. Hundreds of scientific studies conducted over the past fifty years validate the instrument and support its reliable use. Consequently, many facilitators, coaches, and consultants use it in their work. Clients often request the MBTI as a component of activities aimed at team building, boundary management, or improving communication. The instrument's broad use and widespread availability are both an advantage and a disadvantage. Because it is relatively easy to obtain and administer, the MBTI can be very helpful in sorting out the strengths and needs of coworkers and teammates. Nevertheless, the instrument is often misused, and information about preferences is frequently oversimplified or misapplied. By integrating the values and principles of the Skilled Facilitator approach with the MBTI, the use of each is enhanced.

This chapter provides a brief overview of the MBTI and discusses three ways in which I combine using it with the Skilled Facilitator approach to: (1) help people learn the skills of this approach, (2) augment group effectiveness, and (3) help facilitators and leaders develop personal awareness.

WHAT IS THE MBTI?

The MBTI is not a test, and it contains no right or wrong answers. It is simply an indicator of how people prefer to take in information, make decisions, and organize their lives. The instrument was originally developed as a way to understand and apply the psychological theories of Carl G. Jung as first articulated in his 1921 book, *Psychological Types.* Katherine C. Briggs studied the first English translation of that book (1923). In 1942, she and her daughter, Isabel Briggs Myers, began to develop an instrument to help people identify their type preferences. Motivated by the outbreak of World War II, the two thought that appreciating type might help people avoid destructive conflicts. As a practical application, they thought type might be useful in matching individuals to the many new jobs and roles required by the war. From 1942 to 1944, potential MBTI items were written and validated. Since that time, the instrument has been widely researched, validated, and refined.[2]

Dimensions of Type

The MBTI sorts people's preferences along four psychological dimensions or scales (Table 55.1). Combinations of the eight different preferences (two for each dimension) result in sixteen distinct personality types. Each type is described by four letters—one for the preference on each dimension. For example, an ENFP prefers Extraversion, INtuition, Feeling, and Perceiving. An ISTJ prefers Introversion, Sensing, Thinking, and Judging. The MBTI has specific definitions for each of the dimensions described. Extraversion and Judging, in particular, are frequently misunderstood because the definitions of these terms are more specific than in general use. Before making assumptions about how to interpret the Myers-Briggs scale, consult one of the resources cited at the end of the chapter on properly administering and interpreting the instrument.

Interpreting the Dimensions

The preferences that make up a particular type are tendencies only. Everyone uses all of the described dimensions (both extraversion and introversion, for example, depending on the situation). We just prefer some dimensions more than others, tend to use them more frequently, and thus tend to develop certain strengths and certain blind spots. Also, the dimensions alone do not fully explain a particular type. The interaction or dynamics of the preferences create the unique qualities of each type. To interpret and apply type differences properly, one needs a thorough understanding of type dynamics and knowledge of each of the sixteen distinctions.

Table 55.1 MBTI Dimensions and Preferences

Dimension[a]	Related Dichotomy
Energizing—How and where people get their energy	Extraversion–Introversion—Are you energized by the outer world of people, things, and activities or by your inner world of ideas, impressions, and emotions?
Attending—What people pay attention to when they gather information	Sensing–Intuition—Do you focus on concrete data gathered through the five senses or on broad meanings, relationships, and possibilities?
Deciding—How people go about making decisions	Thinking–Feeling—Do you make decisions based on logical, objective analysis, or do you decide based more on personal and social values?
Living—How people organize their lives and relate to the outside world	Judging–Perceiving—Do you deal with the outer world in a planned, orderly way or in a flexible, spontaneous way?

[a]Based on Hirsch and Kummerow (1989).

Understanding the dynamics of each type does provide insight into how people learn, communicate, and interact with others. Thus, those preferring ENFP, for example, might be characterized as big-picture thinkers who see a wide range of possibilities in each situation, enjoy working with people and ideas, and are sensitive to the impact of their decisions on others. By contrast, those preferring ISTJ might be characterized as thorough, systematic thinkers who attend carefully to detail and like to work in a structured way to come to logical, practical conclusions. But these characterizations are fairly high-level inferences that must be confirmed or disconfirmed with each individual.

One of the ways the MBTI is commonly misused or misinterpreted is for people to be told that type defines them—that type means they can or cannot develop certain abilities. Type does not measure ability or intelligence. Individuals vary widely within a single type, and so type cannot accurately predict how a particular individual will respond to a given situation. In fact, the MBTI is intended primarily as a tool for individuals to understand themselves. The purpose of the instrument is to indicate places for them to look or preferences to consider. Using the indicator helps people develop a language to reflect on their own preferences and interactions. Type awareness points out how people filter information differently, and it promotes curiosity about and tolerance for other perspectives. It also helps individuals understand how they can adapt their style to interact more effectively with people who have preferences very different from their own.

HOW CAN TYPE BE USED WITH THE SKILLED FACILITATOR APPROACH?

To use the MBTI well and consistently with Skilled Facilitator core values, become fully qualified to administer the instrument, or work with someone who is qualified. The Association for Psychological Type (www.aptcentral.org) maintains a referral network and can provide guidance in the ethical use of the instrument. Used consistently with its original intent and a mutual learning mind-set, I believe the Myers-Briggs can be a valuable asset to practice. And the skills developed by the Skilled Facilitator approach can add immeasurably to accurate administration, interpretation, and application of the MBTI.

General Guidelines for Using Type Information

Any use of type information should be jointly designed with the participants. Guidelines for ethical administration of the instrument point out that people should have a free and informed choice about whether and how to share their type with others.[3] The intent of the indicator is to begin a mutual learning dialogue in which people can explore their gifts. The results should be given in a way that allows for questioning and clarification, and the administrator should not impose results or become defensive if a participant disagrees with him or her.

In group settings, discussing MBTI preferences provides an opportunity for people to cease using their differences as a wedge between members and to begin valuing the contributions each is likely to make. Type is not to be used to label, judge, evaluate, or limit anyone. Its intended purpose is as a resource to foster mutual learning and appreciation.

Learning the Skilled Facilitator Approach

Knowing type preferences helps address differences in how people learn the Skilled Facilitator approach, their specific gifts, and their particular challenges with the approach. The center dimensions on the MBTI scale, Attending and Deciding, affect what information people pay attention to and how they prefer to use that information to reach conclusions. These two dimensions, known as functions, greatly affect learning styles.

I find that how people attend and decide determines what they find most challenging in using the Skilled Facilitator approach.

I find that how people attend and decide determines what they find most challenging in using the Skilled Facilitator approach. The difference raised most frequently is how people learn and use the diagnosis-intervention cycle. The cycle begins by noticing specific behavior and making inferences based on that behavior. The intervention in step 4 of the cycle begins by sharing the specific behavior observed. Those with Sensing preferences are usually quite adept at seeing and remembering specific behaviors, but they sometimes struggle to clarify and share the inference they are making based on that behavior. By contrast, those with an Intuitive preference usually have great difficulty remembering exactly what was said or done, but can easily share the inference they made and link it broadly to individual or group effectiveness. Each preference thus has a different learning challenge in using the cycle. With practice, I find type no barrier to mastering the steps of effective diagnosis and intervention. But it helps to acknowledge that each of us needs to work a little differently depending on what we habitually attend to in our environment.

See Chapter Six, "The Diagnosis-Intervention Cycle," page 69.

The Thinking and Feeling preferences affect how we reason through the data we have and how we explain our reasoning to others. Those with a Thinking preference are generally adept at laying out the logic behind an intervention and discussing the consequences of particular choices. Those with Feeling preferences may struggle to identify and explain the logical steps of their reasoning, but they are particularly sensitive to the potential consequences for people of a particular course of action. They can usually access their compassion easily and use it readily to influence their values-based reasoning. Obviously, to implement the Skilled Facilitator core values fully, one needs to balance both logical analysis and compassion. Again, I see type as no barrier to doing this, but it is helpful to recognize that each preference may be less likely to attend to a particular aspect. By making a conscious effort to attend to each function (Sensing, Intuition, Thinking, and Feeling), we can maximize our learning and effective use of TSF.

MBTI and Group Effectiveness

MBTI data can strengthen interventions on various elements of the Group Effectiveness Model (GEM). I frequently use it as a component in discussing roles and expectations, group norms and culture, effective problem solving, and sources of group conflict or communication difficulties. Combining MBTI preferences with the Skilled Facilitator principles has helped groups discern sources of past misunderstandings and devise new strategies more likely to meet everyone's needs.

Combining MBTI preferences with the Skilled Facilitator principles has helped groups discern sources of past misunderstandings and devise new strategies more likely to meet everyone's needs.

See Chapter Two, "The Group Effectiveness Model," page 15, and Chapter Fifteen, "Using the Group Effectiveness Model," page 135, for an introduction to the group effectiveness model and its applications.

When using type data to help a work group or board, I typically ask each person to complete a self-scoring version of the instrument and report the results to me in advance. I use the reports to compile a group type table showing how many of each type are represented. I also create a composite type for the group based on the most frequent preferences indicated by the members. For example, one board I recently facilitated had an ENFJ composite type, while the staff who reported to them had an INTJ composite type. It is important to recognize that aggregate data like these can indicate general tendencies only and must be carefully validated; however, it is often a useful way to acknowledge and make discussable past difficulties or relationship patterns.

At the beginning of the facilitation or consultation meeting, I take time to go over the MBTI results, offering guidance about interpretation and answering questions. I check again to be certain each person is willing to have composite data shared and is clear he or she can choose to share or not share individual results. I do advocate the usefulness of sharing type information. I also help the group reach clear agreements about how the information will be used so that people can make informed choices about what to share and when. Then we talk about the issues or topics the group contracted to address, using the type data as additional information where it is relevant:

Members of the ENFJ board frequently felt staff did not fully consider the impact on citizens of some of their recommendations. In general, staff members had a Thinking preference, making them inclined to propose what they saw as technically or logically superior solutions. The board had a predominance of members who make decisions based on a Feeling preference, meaning that impact on others is extremely important to them, even if the choice is not the most technically advanced. The difference on this dimension had created a great deal of tension between the two groups. In addition, the NF board found the communications of the NT staff overly theoretical and analytical. The staff found the board communications overly enthusiastic or vague (or both). Each group tended to discount the competence or commitment of the other. By exploring the value of both approaches and developing expectations around when and how the two perspectives could strengthen decisions, the group reduced conflict and improved boundary management.

Similarly, the group could see other potential strengths, blind spots, and mismatches that might create problems. These were presented only as possibilities. The group confirmed some differences as areas of difficulty in the past; others they disconfirmed, showing that the group members could effectively use their less preferred areas to meet the demands of the situations in which they found themselves.

Understanding the MBTI dynamics also helped the group more effectively apply the ground rules to enhance their discussions and test one another's needs. Instead of assuming they always had to provide detailed written reports, the staff tested this inference when they learned ENFPs and ENFJs generally prefer verbal communication. Each group realized that by providing relevant information about expectations and testing inferences, they could use their time and resources more effectively. They became aware that there were certain ground rules both groups tended to skip over. Given the type preferences of those involved, they seldom sought or provided specific examples. The result of the discussion was a commitment to help one another be more specific. They also asked individuals with preferences more attuned to remembering details to aid them in their efforts.

Type information can be used to help groups with a number of other effectiveness elements like problem solving, sharing leadership roles, and clarifying action plans. Here is a list of group effectiveness reminders I share with groups to help them think about ways their MBTI awareness can improve their effectiveness:

- Groups with high type similarity will reach decisions more quickly but are more likely to make errors due to inadequate representation of all viewpoints.
- Groups with many different types may reach decisions more slowly or not at all. If they learn to manage multiple viewpoints effectively, they often reach better decisions because more perspectives are considered.
- Leadership roles may need to shift as the tasks to be done require the strengths of different types.
- The person who is the only representative of a preference may be seen as "different" by other group members and may not feel fully valued.
- Groups that are one-sided (have few different types) will succeed if they use different types outside the team as resources or if they make the effort to use their own less-developed functions as required by the task.
- One-sided teams may fail if they overlook aspects of problems that other types would have pointed out or if they stay rigidly true to type and fail to use other resources.

Coaching Leaders and Facilitators

Knowledge of type is also a source of valuable personal awareness information for facilitators and facilitative leaders. In fact, MBTI results are designed to be given directly to respondents for personal validation and reflection. An individual's reflecting on type accomplishes much the same thing it does for a group: it highlights strengths in one's reasoning processes and flags potential blind spots.

I recently coached a manager who had alienated his staff because they felt he did not carefully consider their research and recommendations. They accused him of not considering all valid information before reaching a decision, even though the group had committed to this ground rule. The group inferred that the manager was not walking the talk and that maybe they should not bother to do so either. The manager had clear preferences for Sensing and Judging, giving him a strong bias for concrete action. His most frequent questions were, "What do we need to do about this?" and "How quickly can we act?" The staff had strong Intuitive, Thinking, and Perceiving preferences, leading them to see the big picture, gather much data, and see many possible solutions. They seldom made a specific recommendation and frequently overwhelmed the manager with data. They thought he was a "cowboy" manager shooting from the hip; he thought the staff were lazy—all talk and no action.

Of course, none of these assumptions were accurate. Looking at the MBTI data provided the manager a useful starting place to explain his preference to the group, ask for help in slowing down to use the ground rules to consider options, and ask the group to create clearer options. When the group understood the preference mismatches, they realized that they each attended to different data and made high-level inferences based on those data. They agreed with the manager to use the ground rules to slow down. They committed to clarify their interests in a particular decision, decide together what information would be relevant, and then agree about how they would present data to one another. The decision-making process to use for each issue would be jointly determined. By coaching the manager about his type preferences, he was able to open up a discussion that contributed to both his own learning and the effectiveness of his work group.

In coaching people who are trying to become increasingly consistent with mutual learning values, I find that one of the triggers for unilateral behavior is being forced to operate out of one's less preferred areas. My own ENFP preference, for example, makes careful attention to time a struggle for me. When I am in roles where I am expected to help others start and stop on time, I can easily slip into being unilateral about how I intervene. I might say, "You have to stop now," instead of advocating and inquiring or jointly designing with a group the best use of time. I have learned that when facilitating time-sensitive agendas, I need to be particularly aware of my unilateral tendency and ask a cofacilitator with a different preference to help me.

ARE THERE PROBLEMS WITH INTEGRATING MBTI AND THE SKILLED FACILITATOR APPROACH?

Early in 2003, debate raged on the Group Facilitation Listserv (GRP-FACL@listserv.albany.edu) about the pros and cons of facilitators' using the MBTI. There were valid arguments on both sides. Most who opposed using MBTI questioned the usefulness of psychological instruments in general. Many cited a natural resistance to being placed in a box. Some told stories about inappropriate application of the MBTI, including some group members' judging others or trying to force them to match their style to the group's predominant type. Others cited valuable personal and group learning from insights gained using the indicator.

The MBTI, like any other tool or technique we might adopt, can be used inappropriately and unilaterally. Yet I do not see anything in the design of the instrument that is inherently inconsistent with mutual learning core values. In fact, the professional guidelines for appropriate administration and validation are based on the principle of sharing all relevant information, providing free and informed choice, and testing inferences and assumptions. By combining both approaches consistently and wisely, the MBTI can become a valuable addition to your own development and your interventions with others.

Resources

Center for Applications of Psychological Type, Gainesville, Fla., www.capt.org. Offers a wide range of products and services, including a bibliography with seventy-eight hundred entries on its Web site.

CPP, Inc., Palo Alto, Calif., www.cpp.com. Publishes the MBTI and offers scoring services and interpretation materials.

Group Facilitation Listserv. GRP-FACL@listserv.albany.edu.

Hirsh, S., and Kummerow, J. M. *LIFETypes.* New York: Warner Books, 1989.

Hirsh, S. K., and Kummerow, J. M. *Introduction to Type in Organizations.* Palo Alto, Calif.: CCP, 1990.

Lawrence, G. *People Types and Tiger Stripes: A Practical Guide to Learning Styles.* Gainesville, Fla.: CAPT, 1982.

Myers, I. B. *Gifts Differing.* Palo Alto, Calif.: CCP, 1980.

Myers, I. B., and McCaulley, M. H. *Manual: A Guide to the Development and Use of the Myers-Briggs Type Indicator.* Palo Alto, Calif.: CCP, 1985.

Notes

1. CPP in Palo Alto, California, publishes the MBTI and offers scoring services and interpretation materials. There are multiple versions of the MBTI, each appropriate for slightly different purposes. The publisher or a qualified user can help you select the appropriate version. The two versions I use most frequently are *Myers-Briggs Type Indicator Self Scorable* (1998) and *Myers-Briggs Type Indicator Form Q* (2001), both published by CPP. For information about the instrument and on how to qualify to administer the MBTI, see the publisher's Web site, www.cpp.com.
2. For a history of the development of the MBTI, see Isabel Briggs Myers, *Gifts Differing* (1980) and Isabel Briggs Myers and Mary H. McCaulley, *Manual: A Guide to the Development and Use of the Myers-Briggs Type Indicator* (1985). The manual also includes detailed summaries of much of the extensive MBTI research data.
3. Qualified MBTI administrators are bound by a code of ethics guiding how the instrument is to be provided and interpreted. A copy is available at the CAPT Web site, www.capt.org.

References

Hirsh, S., and Kummerow, J. M. *LIFETypes.* New York: Warner Books, 1989.

Jung, C. G. *Psychological Types.* (H. G. Baynes, Trans. Revised by R.F.C. Hull). Volume 6 of *The Collected Works of C. G.* Jung. Princeton, N.J.: Princeton University Press, 1971. (Original work published in 1921.)

Myers, I. B*Gifts Differing.* Palo Alto, Calif.: CCP, 1980.

Myers, I. B., and McCaulley, M. H. *Manual: A Guide to the Development and Use of the Myers-Briggs Type Indicator.* Palo Alto, Calif.: CCP, 1985.

Chapter 56

Applying the Skilled Facilitator Approach to a Systems Thinking Analysis

Chris Soderquist

SYSTEMS THINKING HELPS an organization understand the mental models driving its most fundamental processes, and the Skilled Facilitator approach is a valuable methodology for helping organizations uncover, clarify, and modify their mental models.

See Chapter Seven, "Thinking and Acting Systemically," page 75.

This chapter describes several aspects of systems thinking: its approach, how its interventions address organizational issues, and how the Skilled Facilitator approach, specifically using the ground rules for effective groups, improves the likelihood that systems thinking will be successful in understanding and improving those issues.

THE SYSTEMS THINKING APPROACH

Systems thinking practitioners work with organizations to develop strategies for improving the performance of the organization. Behind this approach is an assertion that the structure of any social organization (business, nonprofit, or community) and its mission, goals, and strategies—why and how it organizes itself—result from that organization's individual and collective mental models. Mental models are the collection of assumptions, theories, anecdotes, and other mental facts and images used to understand and improve reality. These mental models drive what data we select, the types of strategies we develop, and how we act in accordance with those strategies.

See Chapter Four, "Understanding What Guides Your Behavior," page 33, and Chapter Forty-Eight, "Integrating the Skilled Facilitator Approach with Organizational Policies and Procedures," page 383.

Many of these mental models never see the light of day, remaining unspoken and untested, yet they drive the organization's behavior. Furthermore, most mental models don't include the important aspects of reality, such as interdependency, time delays, and feedback, required to effectively understand and change the organization's performance.

The systems thinking approach helps clients surface and test their mental models through a collaborative, inquiry-based process. And it helps refine and improve their mental models by applying a specific model of reality—in much the same way that the Group Effectiveness Model underlies the Skilled Facilitator approach—to refining those models.

The systems thinking approach helps clients surface and test their mental models through a collaborative, inquiry-based process. And it helps refine and improve their mental models by applying a specific model of reality to refining those models.

See Chapter Two, "The Group Effectiveness Model," page 15, and Chapter Fifteen, "Using the Group Effectiveness Model," page 135.

A typical modeling engagement uses the iterative process shown in Figure 56.1; the process is a learning loop composed of several mini–learning loops. In the next

Figure 56.1 A Systems Thinking Process

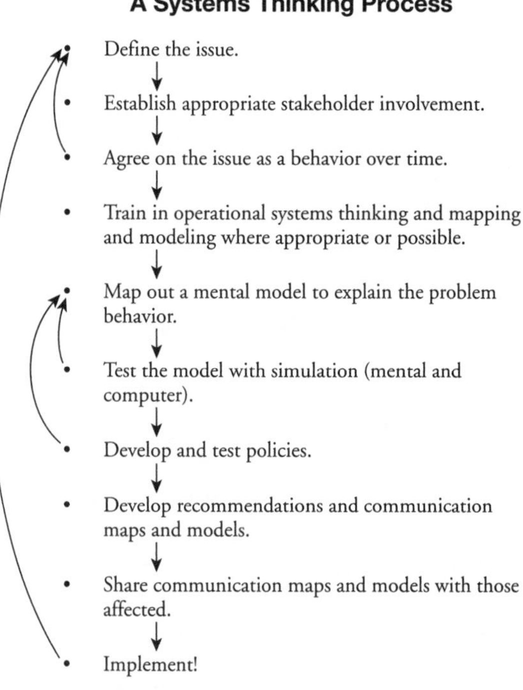

section of this chapter, I use an example to highlight these steps; however, a couple of steps merit explanation prior to the example. Step 3 (agree on the issue as a behavior over time) is crucial in getting the client to begin applying a systems thinking lens to the issues. Often the client has defined a problem with a single-point-in-time lens as either an event (for example, "We just lost our biggest client") or a condition (for example, "Housing prices are too high and impeding our community's economy"). We help clients look at the issue in a longer-term pattern. Perhaps their client base has been declining for months. Perhaps housing prices have been rising for a while, indicating a problem, or perhaps prices have oscillated around the same mean for years, indicating the market may correct itself.

Step 4 (train in operational systems thinking . . .) is usually agreed to prior to my working with a client. Because my approach to systems thinking consulting resembles developmental facilitation (I want to build systems thinking skills in the client, not the client's reliance on me), I rarely work with a client who has not agreed to build mapping and often modeling skills during the process. Prior to the mapping and modeling process, I provide training to allow the client to participate actively in that process.

See Chapter Forty-Three, "Developmental Facilitation," page 339.

AN EXAMPLE: ABC FINANCIAL SERVICES

It is difficult to find one example of an engagement that captures all the important elements of how systems thinking and skilled facilitation work together. Therefore, I've fictionalized one example that is a combination of several engagements that I or other colleagues have had over the years. It shows how one systems thinking engagement might play out:

> In February, the vice president of human resources from ABC Financial Services contacts a systems thinking consulting firm because the company's senior management team is in turmoil. Specifically, the vice president of sales and marketing wants to implement a special investment promotion and is getting resistance from the vice president of customer service and staff. Tension has increased to the point where the past few management team meetings have included shouting between the two vice presidents. The CEO had read *The "Thinking" in Systems Thinking: Seven Essential Skills* (Richmond, 2000) and felt a systems thinking perspective might resolve the issue. She asks the vice president of human resources to contact us to see if we can help.
>
> As part of the initial contracting, we ask questions (over the phone) to determine if the specific issue they wish to address lends itself to a systems thinking analysis; we eventually arrive at the following data-level story.
>
> ABC had implemented a special investment promotion in mid-December, with disastrous consequences. Call volume during the week

between Christmas and New Year, specifically information requests on this promotion, reached the highest level of any promotion in the history of ABC. The customer service department believed that the promotion created by marketing had not been well developed and still refer to the deluge of calls, specifically the average time spent on each customer call, as the "Christmas holiday slam." Customer satisfaction took a real hit, and the customer services department is loath to repeat this experience.

Marketing, however, thought the promotion was appropriately developed. They believed the cause of the increase in call time resulted from customer service's being short-staffed due to the holidays.

Ultimately, we are able to sketch an initial hypothesis of the problem behavior (see Figure 56.2). The questions the client agreed to answer through systems thinking were:

1. What contributed to the increase in time spent per customer call during the December holidays?
2. How might this be prevented in the future?
3. Will the findings support the feasibility of implementing another promotion?

After some further refinement, we develop a contract to work with ABC to facilitate the senior management in answering the three questions.

We begin the first on-site session by agreeing on objectives and by posting the behavior-over-time graph (Figure 56.2) and a flip chart containing the

Figure 56.2 Problem Behavior over Time

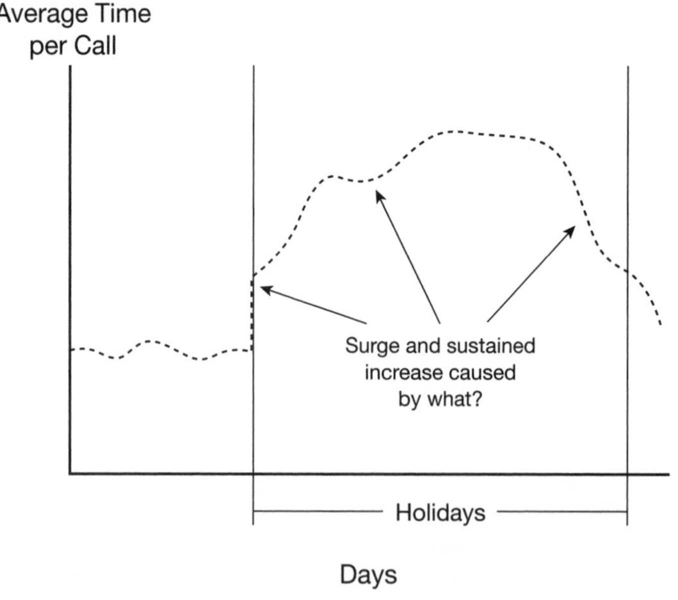

questions to address through a systems thinking analysis. Once everyone agrees to the issue and questions, we describe our proposed process for achieving this purpose by showing a typical systems thinking process (Figure 56.1). We spend time exploring step 2 (establish appropriate stakeholder involvement) so that all stakeholders affected by the issue, where possible, have representation in the process. We then jointly decide on the project plan, including milestones and deliverables. The management team assigns a cross-stakeholder team the task of building a model to understand the issues they wish to address.

The next step is to provide ABC's modeling team with training in how to map and simulate using the ithink Analyst simulation software (ithink Analyst, 2003). As we train, we begin helping the team use the stock and flow language to map out the process of receiving customer requests. Figure 56.3 shows the first component of the map we built with them. The

Figure 56.3 Stocks and Flows of Customer Requests

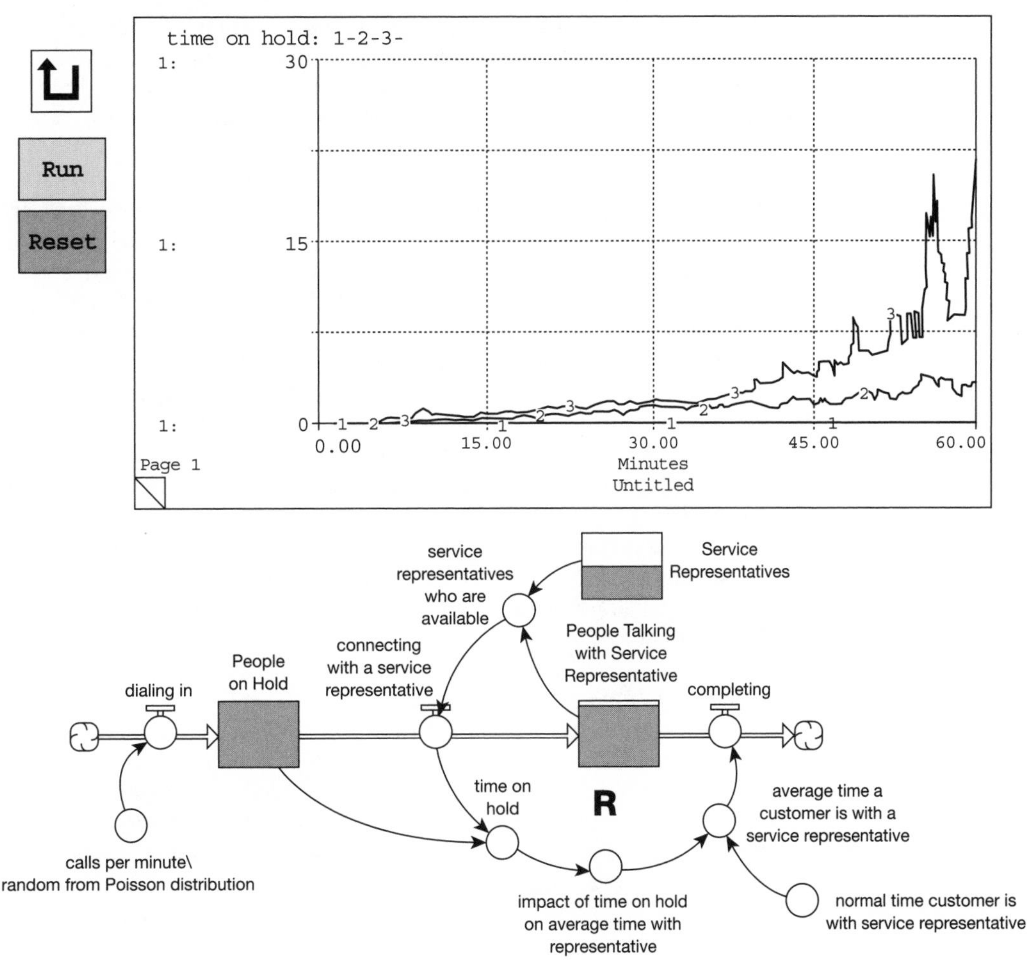

rectangle labeled "People on Hold" is a *stock.* Stocks are like bathtubs in that they accumulate stuff; in this case, we accumulate people who are waiting to talk to a service representative. The *flow* (pipe) going into the stock fills the queue. This happens when people dial in.

The team then completes the customer chain by adding a flow from the queue into another stock, labeled "People Talking with Service Representative." This is a special stock type known as a *conveyor.* This conveyor represents customers who are speaking with a service representative. And when customers complete their call, they leave through the flow labeled "completing."

Once we get the essential stock and flow structure down, we facilitate the team in specifying how the flows occur. We assume that when representatives are available (not talking with a customer), customers will connect with them (the flow of "connecting with a service representative"). The time they remain on the conveyor—think of it as a moving sidewalk requiring some time delay before they can step off—is determined by "average time a customer is with a service representative."

At this point, one member of the team mentions that by releasing the promotion just prior to the holidays, it meant that many of the target audience were home immediately following the release. And because they were home, they found it easy to call up with questions. This means that the rate of "dialing in" for this particular promotion was much higher than if the promotion had occurred during a more ordinary time frame.

The process gets even more interesting when we ask them to start closing loops. The customer service members of the team describe their experience. The longer someone waits in the queue, the longer the person tends to stay on the phone: "time on hold" has an impact on the average time a customer speaks with a service representative. And service representatives noticeably experienced this behavior during the slam period. The story told by the customer service members was modeled as a reinforcing loop (labeled with an "R" in Figure 56.3). As availability goes down, it takes longer for customers to be connected with a representative. This increases the time per call ("average time customer is with service representative"), which reduces the rate of completing calls, and thus decreases even further the availability of representatives.

The modeling team realizes at this point that the issues they faced over the holidays resulted not from a poorly designed promotion or from a poorly skilled customer service team. Rather, it was the timing of the promotion that first caused the onslaught of calls; once a nasty reinforcing loop (the vicious cycle) got activated, it caused the time spent per customer to rise in step with a time waiting in the queue.

The team proposes a facilitated session for the management team and then spends a few days turning this map into a simulatable model. They develop an interface to slowly unveil the model's structure and allow participants in the facilitated session to experiment with model assumptions. When they finally hold the session, the senior managers, some of whom had recently accused others of incompetence, collectively built a mental model for what had caused the Christmas slam. The map and simulations helped to bring the discussion down the ladder of inference to focus on the behavior they had experienced and what caused it. They decided that in the future, they could implement another promotion, but that they needed to time it to occur when the rate of incoming service requests could be better managed—likely not over a holiday period.

You can think about systems thinking engagements as requiring some amount of effort and generating some amount of benefits. Often people believe that a large, complete, and usually complex model will generate the maximum amount of benefits. Rarely is this the case. Sometimes simply sketching out a map, which requires a few hours (no more than a few days), will give enough insight to be useful. The ABC example is indicative of this: the insight about the time on hold leading to an increased time with a representative was built in the first few hours of work. A couple more days of work adding realistic numbers, developing the interface, and sharing the model with senior managers was all that was needed to make significant improvement in organizational understanding and policy development. It would have been possible to model the issue in far more detail (types of clients, types of problems, thousands of real data points). But the project could have taken months (not days) and perhaps generated no more (likely less) insight because the effort would have lost focus or fizzled out

I've found that simply drawing a map, or perhaps developing a simple one-page model, will use the minimum amount of effort to receive the most useful benefits. Less is more.

APPLYING SYSTEMS THINKING WITH THE SKILLED FACILITATOR APPROACH

The systems thinking example just described is facilitated by a close integration of the Skilled Facilitator approach. In this section, I provide several ways to apply the Skilled Facilitator approach to such a process.

Contracting

Part of our contracting is deciding if the skills we bring in systems thinking are the appropriate ones for the issues facing the organization. We explain that the issues most appropriate to such analysis are problems that can be framed as behaviors occurring over time. In a process similar to walking the client down the ladder of inference, we ask questions to move the issue from the highly abstract level of emotion down to the data (events, pattern of behavior) that lead to the emotions that have surfaced. It is crucial for us in working with a client to establish a contract that is based on the core values of valid information, free and informed choice, and internal commitment to the choice.

See the Ladder of Inference sidebar in Chapter Five, "Ground Rules for Effective Groups," page 61. See also Chapter Eight, "Contracting with Groups," page 89.

Furthermore, we make sure that the appropriate stakeholders (those affected by the decision) are involved or at least aware of the engagement. Not only does this make sense from the Group Effectiveness Model, but it is essential that multiple perspectives from across the system are involved to build the most representative mental model because our approach helps clients expand the boundaries around the issue they're experiencing.

See Chapter Two, "The Group Effectiveness Model," page 15.

Ground Rules for Effective Groups

The ground rules help guide our interactions and interventions with clients. They are extremely valuable as we build models because the process is at its core one of helping the clients to surface, share, and build a collective mental model of the issues. The ground rules improve the process in a number of ways.

See Chapter Five, "Ground Rules for Effective Groups," page 61.

Focus on Interests, Not Positions

In consulting to one state's workforce investment council as it developed a five-year strategy, I observed most of the discussion focused on allocating scarce financial resources across specific programs (for example, training, supplementary financial assistance to those out of work, staffing one-stop workforce service centers). Such programs often have an incremental funding increase dynamic inherent in their establishment. In other words, once a program is established, it rarely receives less funding than previous years because those implementing the program continue to seek additional funds. In this case, we developed a model of workforce and economic issues that helped the council shift from focusing on specific programs to determining the overall interest: building a strong economy with highly skilled workers in fast-growing industries. Further experiments with the model suggested they implement a set of initiatives that balanced workforce training with incentives for industry to locate and develop in the state.

See Chapter Five, "Ground Rules for Effective Groups," page 61; Chapter Sixteen, "Helping Group Members Focus on Interests Rather Than Positions," page 145; and Chapter Twenty-Six, "Ground Rules Without the Mutual Learning Model Are Like Houses Without Foundations," page 217.

Use Specific Examples and Agree on What Important Words Mean

Getting a model as good as possible often requires a specific story or example from one of the clients. In the case of ABC, the reinforcing loop was added to the model after one of the team members described a customer who said, "Well, since I finally got through to you and it's taken so long, I'm afraid to hang up without asking you every imaginable question. So, here goes . . ." The customer proceeded to keep the customer service representative on the phone for twenty minutes. This example helped those on the modeling team agree that the reinforcing feedback loop was an important part of the model.

Test Assumptions and Inferences

Model building is a formal process for making assumptions explicit. The language of stocks and flows is an operational language, as opposed to the language of causal loops (another language that some systems thinking practitioners use). Being operational means that in using the language, clients are more likely to formulate a map composed of explicit hypotheses about the causes of poor performance and in a way that leads to indicating where leverage for change might lie. Flows are the activities that change conditions; therefore, policies to improve conditions must have an impact on flows. For example, in ABC, one assumption that was made explicit was time per customer. In this case, one assumption everyone eventually agreed on through several examples of anecdotal evidence was that the longer people remained on hold, the more they would talk once they got through to a representative.

Model building is a formal process for making assumptions explicit.

Combine Advocacy and Inquiry

We tell our clients, "Don't expect to discover the 'truth.'" Mental models are always a simplification of reality and are, by definition, not the truth. We describe the process as helping participants discover any holes in their individual and collective mental models. Just as the scientific method says that all theories can at best be considered, at worst disconfirmed, so a systems thinking process will show which mental model is most congruent with reality. To do this, clients need to present their mental models and then ask if others have anything to add to, or change, what they present. The process of building models together requires an equal dose of inquiry and advocacy.

Jointly Design Next Steps and Ways to Test Disagreements

Models provide an experiential vehicle to test disagreements. They both support and are supported by this ground rule. For example, in the case of ABC, there was a disagreement as to the cause of the increase in the time customer service representatives spent with each caller. Some thought it was a poorly designed promotion; others thought it was a short-staffed customer service department. It turned out to be neither (although being short-staffed did exacerbate the problem); rather, the problem was the timing of the promotion. The model supported this ground rule by providing a vehicle for testing disagreements. The final facilitated session with the senior management team included the opportunity to jointly design their next steps with regard to the promotion. They decided that another promotion was feasible, as long as the timing of release was better determined so as not to create the dynamics experienced over the holidays.

CONCLUSION

Because the underlying process for applying systems thinking is to develop and test theories about causality (that is, making mental models explicit and improving them), it is not only easy but advantageous to combine it with the Skilled Facilitator approach. Conversely, any person, group, or organization trying to build Skilled Facilitator capacity will find that including the systems thinking paradigm and tools will further increase their effectiveness.

References

ithink Analyst. Lebanon, N.H.: iseesystems, 2003. Simulation software.

Richmond, B. *The "Thinking" in Systems Thinking: Seven Essential Skills.* Waltham, Mass.: Pegagus Communications, 2000.

Chapter 57

The Facilitative Coach

Anne Davidson
Dale Schwarz

Facilitators increasingly want or need to serve as coaches. Individual group members and organizational leaders frequently see the effectiveness of facilitative skills and want to develop the same ways of thinking and acting. We find that many of our clients and colleagues invite (even beg) us to use our skills to help them design and achieve personal or professional goals. Some of the goals are straightforward, like starting a business or creating a new business brochure. More frequently, the aims demand deep personal reflection and transformation. In response to these demands and gleaning from our very different but related expertise, we developed a comprehensive coaching model and training program based on the Skilled Facilitator approach. This chapter provides an overview of the nine aspects of our model.

WHAT IS COACHING, AND WHY COACH?

Our purpose for coaching is to generate creative, purposeful action toward a client's goals and desires. To do this, we form a committed one-on-one relationship in which both parties engage in learning about their gifts, their barriers to effective action, and their creative process. Clients tend to seek coaching when they want to make a life change or are in a transition, such as a career or relationship change. They may want help with specific work challenges, like managing a difficult project, improving their delegation skills, or working through issues with their boss or work team members. Frequently they have hit a bump in the road while traveling toward their goal, they perceive an obstacle up ahead, or they feel stuck in some aspect of their lives.

Our purpose for coaching is to generate creative, purposeful action toward a client's goals and desires.

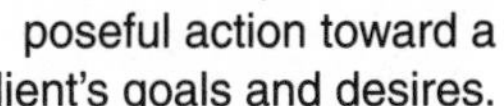

But coaching is also a learning opportunity for the coach. We believe doing one's own inner work from a solid theoretical base is an essential beginning point to becoming a wise coach. As Dale frequently says, "Coaching is a gift that gives both ways."

Here's a story from one of our coaching experiences that illustrates what we are describing:

Sallie initially sought coaching because she felt paralyzed in the face of an important career decision: whether to accept a promotion that she felt certain would be offered to her during the coming year. She made a commitment to work with her coach weekly for four to six weeks to clarify her career goals and her decision. She also agreed to do some fieldwork or homework between sessions to generate data to share with the coach. But at the first and second sessions, Sallie arrived late, stressed out and in a rush to conclude the discussion and move on to her next activity. So at the second session, the coach pointed this out to Sallie and expressed concern that without Sallie's full attention on their work together, Sallie would not reach her goals. Sallie agreed to engage in a brief stretching and focusing activity to help her become present and connect with the coach.

Next, the coach shared her inference that some obstacle or feeling was blocking Sallie's efforts to reach a decision about her promotion. Sallie agreed, and so the coach proposed two options for moving forward in the session: focusing just on the job or focusing more on what thoughts and feelings might be leading Sallie to rush from activity to activity and not thinking through any of several choices she was actually facing.

Sallie chose to work on the deeper question around where she was stuck and what patterns might be contributing to it. To help her do this, the coach led her in a guided imagery exercise so she could connect with how she was feeling about her job and her life in general.[1] Then she asked Sallie to make a drawing about how she felt—not a work of art, but just lines, colors, or a quick sketch to express her thoughts and emotions. Sallie drew a stick figure of herself covered with purple lines. When the coach encouraged Sallie to talk about her drawing, she said it represented how fragmented she felt. She said she was trying to represent what it felt like to be "cut up in pieces." At that point, the coach offered Sallie scissors so she could enact how she was feeling. Sallie cut the drawing into little bits along the purple lines and then mixed the bits around the table. "These are like pieces of a jigsaw puzzle," she said, "and I can't see how they all fit together. I can't find myself."

From this point, the coach encouraged Sallie to explore what led her to feel so fragmented. Sallie was able to identify the many demands placed on her at home and work and her feeling that she was indispensable to her boss, coworkers, husband, and children. And then she identified this feeling of being indispensable as a lifelong pattern. Over subsequent sessions, she recognized that her pride in being a helper at home was one of her creative, positive childhood responses to having an ill mother. Long after this pattern ceased to serve her well, Sallie continued to make herself indispensable to those in her life, "rescuing" them by doing things they could or should do for themselves. Doing so much for others led Sallie to feel fragmented, exhausted, and out of touch with her own needs. She ultimately identified the source of her inability to decide about the promotion: a deep fear that more responsibility would make more demands on her than she could humanly meet.

Sallie's coach helped her reframe her role and how she might more creatively and productively respond to others' demands. Both agreed that if she continued her former pattern, she would quickly become overwhelmed, no matter what job she was in. The remainder of Sallie's work with her coach helped her experiment gradually with doing less for others and concentrating more on helping others learn and grow. As Sallie's efforts began to pay off, she realized she was actually more respected and appreciated by others and had more time for her own growth and development. She and her coach planned small celebrations, like time for lunch with a dear friend, to acknowledge Sallie's progress and generate new energy for her continuing growth.

Sallie's issues also led the coach to reflect on her own pattern of feeling indispensable to clients at times. This feeling led her to sometimes overcommit and then feel stressed. This was not inner work the coach needed to share with Sallie. In the coaching relationship, the focus is always on the growth of the client. But acknowledging her own similar patterns helped the coach respond compassionately rather than to judge or discount Sallie. The coach could think about what she needed to do for herself and what had worked with similar issues in the past, and use these insights to suggest interventions and strategies that might work for Sallie.

Becoming a wise coach who can nurture such a dynamic and complex relationship is a lifelong journey. As in all roles using the Skilled Facilitator approach, an open spirit characterized by curiosity and deep compassion is essential to success. We believe having a clear model to guide one on the journey structures and enriches the experience.

THE FACILITATIVE COACH MODEL

We think about the complex coaching process as a simple geometric form: that of a pyramid (Figure 57.1). The exterior facets of Figure 57.1 (numbers 1–4) represent the broader aspects of the coaching experience: the purpose for which the client comes to coaching, the inner work of the client, the inner work of the coach, and the relationship or contract that the client and coach form. These facets come together to form a connected whole. Our pyramid folds open from the top to reveal the interior (facets 5–8 and the pyramid base). The interior facets hold our guiding principles and the processes that often run in the background. The pyramid base or

Figure 57.1 The Facilitative Coach Pyramid Model

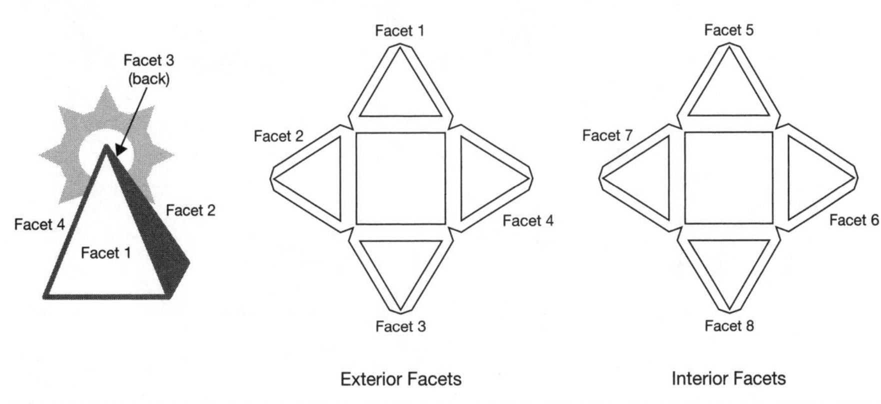

foundation contains our theories of effective group and individual interaction: mutual learning and unilateral control, the creative and survival cycles, ground rules, and the drama triangle. These foundation theories guide our interventions and our drive for integrity and consistency (Figure 57.2).

See Chapter Four, "Understanding What Guides Your Behavior," page 33; Chapter Fifty-Three, "The Drama Triangle," page 421; and Chapter Fifty-Four, "Using Creative and Survival Cycles to See and Shift Mental Models," page 433.

The protected space within the pyramid is our learning lab. Here the coach and the client can experiment with new thinking and try new behaviors. At the center of the lab is a spiral of learning, representing the deep interior work that coach and client do together, always growing, changing, moving backward, and moving forward again. If we are successful, the energy generated in the learning lab rises to the peak and out into the world as creative, purposeful action toward the client's goals and deepest desires (Figure 57.3).

Figure 57.2 Foundation Theories

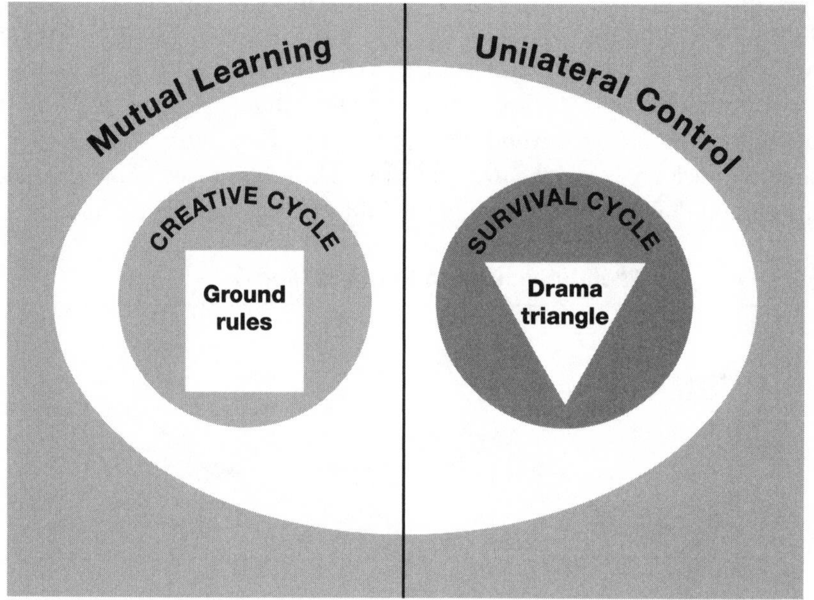

Figure 57.3 The Result of Coaching

THE FOUR EXTERIOR FACETS OF COACHING

First, we'll examine the basic exterior facets of the facilitative coach pyramid. Then we briefly explain the interior facets and point to the sections of this *Fieldbook* that discuss more completely the foundations of our approach to coaching.

Facet 1: Inner Work of the Coach

Coaches who genuinely help clients must first prepare themselves and then constantly balance the many forces at play in any coaching relationship. The coach's own strengths, gifts, dilemmas, and blind spots profoundly influence that relationship. The deep personal awareness and inner development required to constantly attend to and address these issues means coaching is not for the faint of heart. We believe effective coaches must strive to develop four primary abilities:

> Coaches who genuinely help clients must first prepare themselves and then constantly balance the many forces at play in any coaching relationship.

- Practicing deep compassion for yourself and others
- Acting consistently with the full mutual learning framework
- Knowing your gifts and where you get stuck
- Being fully present with yourself and others

These abilities are fundamentally embedded within one another in such a way that it is difficult to think about one without dwelling on the others. One way we think about this relationship is to imagine the qualities as a series of nested circles, as shown in Figure 57.4.

Figure 57.4 **Inner Work of the Coach**

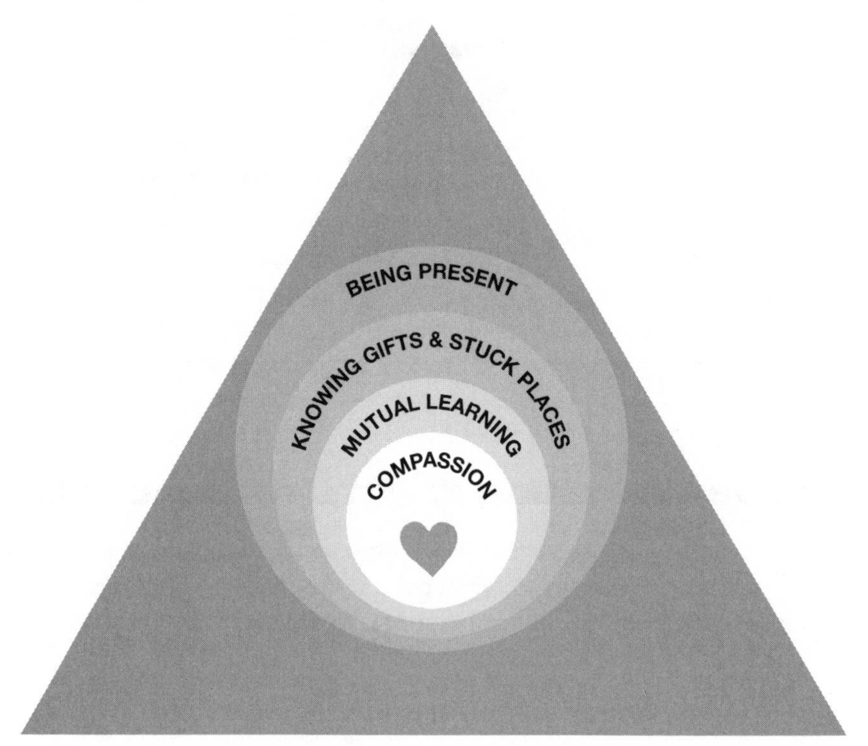

Practicing Deep Compassion

Practicing ***deep compassion*** is at the heart of our approach. We define compassion in the same way it is defined as a core value of the Skilled Facilitator approach.

Practicing ***deep compassion*** is at the heart of our approach. We define compassion in the same way it is defined as a core value of the Skilled Facilitator approach: developing the ability to suspend judgment of ourselves and others, appreciating that each of us makes choices based on the information and skills we have at any given time.

We seek a compassion that allows us to connect with people in a heartfelt, genuine way without minimizing personal accountability or development. We add the adjective *deep* to describe compassion because in our experience, we come to understand and feel for others more and more fully as our life experience and our personal awareness grow. When we are young and able-bodied, we may become impatient with the slow pace of our elders. As we begin to slow down a bit ourselves, we understand what it feels like. We start to recognize that someday we will or could walk in the shoes of others. Our thoughts and feelings become more compassionate and less judgmental. A similar process occurs in coaching as our ability expands to feel love and understanding for others who face a wide variety of circumstances.

See Chapter One, "The Skilled Facilitator Approach," page 3.

As a practical matter, working toward compassion means acknowledging the presence of our inner judge or critic. We each have an inner critic living inside us who speaks up in varying degrees, negatively evaluating our own actions and those of others. Though it may seem counterintuitive, the critical part of ourselves is actually our ally. Each time we hear our inner critic's voice, we can acknowledge it and make a choice for compassion. The more frequently we hear that voice, the more opportunities we have. Gradually, by paying attention to our inner critic, its strength diminishes because we can more quickly move through the cycle of acknowledging, choosing, and then releasing our harsh judgments, our baggage, and the places we get stuck. We do not give up our discernment, but we recognize that much of what the inner critic contains is based on very high-level inferences and assumptions. We release these and develop the ability to embrace compassion. Developing our compassion helps us take responsibility for our actions and lay less blame on others. In this way, we can develop respect, caring, and an appreciation for our struggles. When we see ourselves through eyes of compassion, we can deepen our compassion for others.

Acting Consistently with the Full Mutual Learning Framework

Acting consistently with the full mutual learning framework in coaching requires the same intense examination of our core values and strategies as for all the other facilitative roles. To compassion we add the core values of valid information, internal commitment, and free and informed choice in every aspect of our relationship with our clients. While compassion is a core value of mutual learning, we call it out separately because in our minds, without compassion one cannot productively engage in a coaching relationship to begin with. But once one can engage with another compassionately, the full mutual learning approach is needed to work together effectively.

See Chapter Four, "Understanding What Guides Your Behavior," page 33, for an introduction of the mutual learning model.

The people we coach have inner wisdom about themselves and their life experiences that are unknown to us. We do not assume we have the answer—that we know for certain what others need to do in their lives. Instead, our expertise lies in the coaching process, in guiding productive interventions. In Sallie's case, for example, the coach advocated going beyond the job promotion issue and suggested an intervention to do this. But the ultimate decision about what Sallie is willing to do and how she will apply her insights rests with Sallie. Whatever her choices, we refrain from attributing manipulative strategies or hidden motives to her; rather, we seek to understand why and how Sallie's behavior makes sense to her. In the process, the coach learns, and Sallie can make new choices.

Knowing Your Gifts and Where You Get Stuck

Knowing your gifts and where you get stuck helps you stay in a mutual learning framework in increasingly difficult conversations. This is a form of self-awareness that can keep you from getting hooked by clients' issues or their appeal for rescue. Recognizing the gifts and talents you bring to coaching and how to integrate them fully in coaching relationships helps you stay centered (balanced and focused on what is relevant for working with the client rather than your own deeper issues). Understanding your gifts and where you get stuck can prevent your making bad agreements—getting into coaching relationships where the help the client needs is less likely to draw on your strengths or more likely to trigger your own issues. This self-awareness also alerts you to times when you may get sucked into projecting your own issues into the client's situation, thus clouding your diagnosis and intervention. If you have struggled in your own relationships with authority figures, for example, you may be at risk for projecting that issue into a client's situation and get attached to having him address his relationship with his boss when this may not be his most important work.

Being Present

Being present means to give full, conscious attention to someone or something, to be in attendance.

Being present means to give full, conscious attention to someone or something, to be in attendance. Presence occurs at two levels. First, it means watching and listening to someone or something without being distracted by your own irrelevant thoughts and feelings. Second, it means being fully focused on what a client is saying and doing while also thinking through your own diagnosis and deciding when and how to intervene.

It is important to listen as much to what is not said as to what is said and to make connections among seemingly unrelated stories, events, and ideas.

It is important to listen as much to what is not said as to what is said and to make connections among seemingly unrelated stories, events, and ideas. To work deeply enough to be productive, the coach must attend to both his or her own inner processes and listen fully to the other person. Doing this well requires full concentration. Mining the gems from each shared experience and conversation requires having all of our senses fully engaged. This does not happen if we are thinking about dinner or our next meeting.

Others can sense when we are fully present with them. Something magical seems to happen when we feel someone else deeply listening to and valuing our every word. Full presence evokes places in the heart and spirit of another that they are often unaware of themselves. This process speaks in part to the mystery of coaching. As much as we describe it as a logical, cognitive process, human consciousness is still a great frontier. Just as we do not fully understand how laughter promotes healing, so we do not fully grasp the inner shifts that take place when people fully and intentionally attend to one another. Something higher is touched within us that we can feel but not rationalize or clearly articulate. When we are fully present, our verbal and nonverbal communications are more likely to be congruent and authentic. The person we attend to feels our spirit and senses that we are there holding the framework of the conversation with them. Often they then go far within their own consciousness to access deeper awareness and untapped creativity.

Facet 2: Purpose of Coaching

The purpose of coaching is to help people attain their goals. During the coaching process, clients generally learn how they have impeded themselves in the past. They then experiment with behavioral changes that are more effective and enable them to achieve their desired goals. Often a client's initial purpose for seeking coaching becomes much broader on exploration and reflection. For example, Sallie found that to come to grips with her career decision, she needed to make major changes in her personal life and patterns of helping others. The purpose of her coaching sessions expanded to address both arenas.

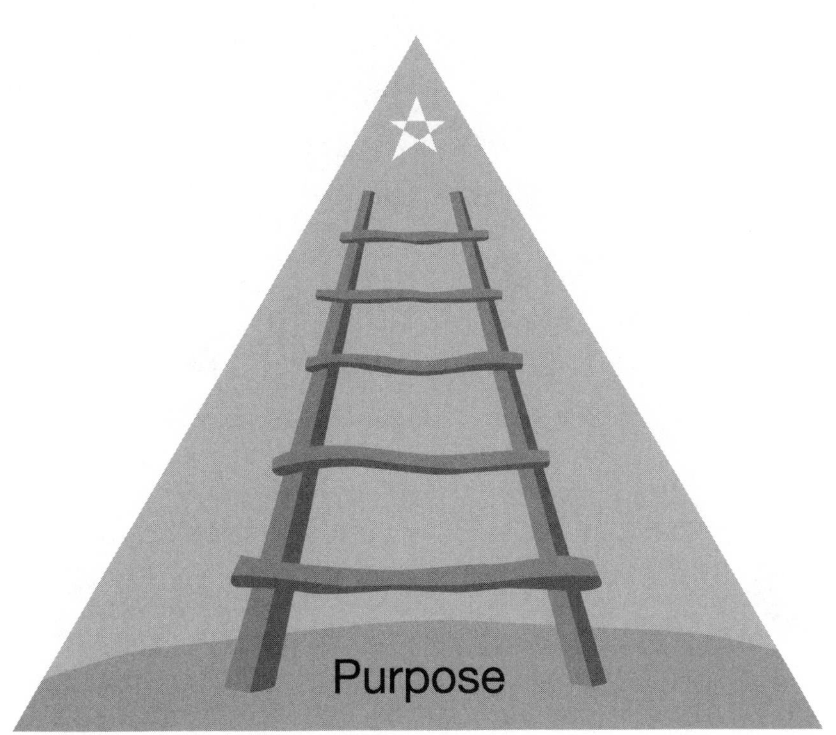

The actual purpose of a coaching relationship may be redefined several times during the process. We move from the question, "Why do you want to be coached?" to an exploration of the presenting problem, intention, or goal. We might ask, "What do you need from your coaching?" or "What do you need to reach your goal?" We may uncover layers upon layers of professional or personal needs and desires. The goal may shift as the client chooses whether and how to go deeper to address fundamental unilateral or survival patterns.

Facet 3: Inner Work of the Client

The inner work of the client is similar to the inner work of the coach. Almost like a less experienced dance partner, the client follows the coach's moves, learning how to be present during a coaching session and how to see patterns from the past that provide windows into unilateral or survival thinking. The client is led to see gifts and stuck places also, at least to the extent that they apply to the purpose of the coaching relationship. And part of the client's work is to develop increased compassion for self and understand that patterns that no longer serve well were initially

creative responses to difficult situations faced early in life. The client enters a door into her own soul and joins the coach in an intricate learning dance. In the process, both parties make discoveries about themselves and help one another increase their alignment with their core values. But the coach is always present in the service of the client. It would not have been relevant for Sallie's coach to tell Sallie about her own patterns of making herself indispensable. The focus is on Sallie's own work. However, the coach might be transparent in sharing that she has wrestled with similar issues or that some of the suggestions would be based on things that worked for the coach herself.

Facet 4: The Coaching Relationship

The relationship is a living entity. It continually evolves and is cocreated by coach and client within the context of clear roles, boundaries, guidelines, and working agreements. The coach is an ally who nonjudgmentally guides and supports the client in reaching her stated purpose and goals. The coach's process expertise is used to help the client engage her own inner wisdom about her life choices.

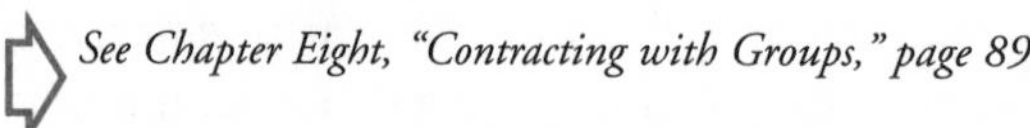

See Chapter Eight, "Contracting with Groups," page 89.

A solid coaching relationship begins with a clear working agreement or contract and follows the same guidelines and principles as contracting for any other facilitative role.

A solid coaching relationship begins with a clear working agreement or contract and follows the same guidelines and principles as contracting for any other facilitative role. This agreement includes clarifying the expectations of both parties and emphasizing mutual design and joint accountability, because many clients come to coaching initially with the notion that the coach will be the expert who will tell them what to do to get what they want. Part of the client's making a fully informed choice includes understanding as clearly as possible what this form of coaching will be like and how it may be different from other coaching arrangements. Of course, no one can truly have all the valid information about what it will be like to work with our guiding principles and ground rules until experiencing this. When a potential client contacts us, we give specific examples of the kinds of things we do and say in sessions, and we model our core values and approach as we explore whether and how to work together. As we work, recontracting will also be necessary when we redefine the client's purpose, decide whether to go deeper or stop, or engage in a different type of intervention. In many ways, a new contract is formed at the beginning of each session, when coach and client jointly design how they will spend their time.

In clarifying roles, it is especially important to set an appropriate boundary between coaching and therapy. Having said this, it is also true that the boundary is not clearly defined. Some say that coaching addresses the future while therapy deals with the past. But we have found that we frequently address the past in service of the present and the future during a coaching relationship as we help clients examine life patterns, mental models, and theory-in-use issues. Sallie's story is an example of how past issues might come up and how central they are in identifying and addressing barriers to achieving a specific goal.

Some people who are in need of therapy pursue coaching services instead because they view coaching as less stigmatizing than therapy. Here it is critical for a coach to know his or her own skills. A coach who is also a trained therapist may redefine the relationship and create a contract that is closer to therapy. But most of us are not trained therapists, and if there are deep-seated emotional or psychological issues that need to be addressed, it is important to know when to recommend that the client seek therapy. Otherwise the client will not thrive in the coaching process. Not only will the client fail to achieve the goals set for the coaching relationship; he or she will usually experience significant emotional distress.

There are no hard-and-fast indicators of when to recommend therapy. We usually enter a coaching relationship with more specific goals than is true for therapy, so discussing the purpose of coaching may help clarify whether this is the appropriate relationship. When a client needs to deal with significant emotional and psychological distress or mental health problems such as clinical depression, anxiety disorder, substance abuse, or grief, physical abuse or significant trauma, a skilled mental health practitioner is needed. Also, if during the coaching relationship, a client becomes highly distressed, this is a warning sign. Particularly if there is a pattern of returning to one issue again and again and the client seems stuck or in denial about the issue, there may be deeper work to do than is appropriate for a coach. Other indicators include raising fears about every suggestion (for example, saying, "But what if . . . ," over and over again), and an inability to stay focused on a topic or concentrate.

In our experience, coaching is most effective when a client has a basic level of self-awareness and insight and wants to deepen that awareness while working toward a clear set of goals. Because the kind of coaching we do may raise deep interpersonal issues, it is wise to develop a referral network of mental health professionals and establish some guidelines with them about when and how to recommend their services. You may never find yourself in this kind of situation. However, it is prudent to prepare for the possibility or know whom you can call on in your organization for help or a second opinion.

THE FOUNDATION AND INTERIOR FACETS OF COACHING

The foundation of the facilitative coach pyramid (see Figure 57.2) is formed by the same fundamental theories and concepts that guide the Skilled Facilitator approach: a clear understanding of the distinction between espoused theory and theory-in-use, the unilateral control and mutual learning models (with the addition of the drama triangle and creative and survival cycle models), and an appreciation for how these theories fit together to support and enhance one another. From this foundation rise the four sides of the pyramid. The interior of each side or facet represents more specific coaching principles and processes.

See Chapter Four, "Understanding What Guides Your Behavior," page 33; Chapter Fifty-Three, "The Drama Triangle: Our Unilateral Control Program for Helping Others," page 421; and Chapter Fifty-Four, "Using Creative and Survival Cycles to See and Shift Mental Models," page 433.

Facet 5: Guiding Principles for the Facilitative Coach

One interior facet (Figure 57.5) contains a brief statement of our broadest guiding principles:

> Our purpose is to draw upon each individual's innate creativity to bring forth positive transformation. We believe in doing this through commitment to:
>
> - Compassion
> - Integrity and respect
> - Engaging in mutual learning
> - Joint design based upon free and informed choice.

Figure 57.5 **Guiding Principles for the Facilitative Coach**

We find a statement of our broadest guiding principles helpful in summarizing our approach to coaching. It is often useful in a contracting conversation to begin explaining the values of our approach and how we work. Then these principles are more specifically defined as we introduce the other facets of our model.

Facet 6: Key Ground Rules

We use all of the Skilled Facilitator ground rules as basic strategies for embodying mutual learning. But we work with a short list that we make explicit to our clients and that guide our coaching conversations (Figure 57.6):

- Test assumptions and inferences.
- Share all relevant information.
- Explain your reasoning and intent.
- Combine advocacy and inquiry.
- Jointly design next steps and ways to test disagreements.

Figure 57.6 **Key Ground Rules for the Facilitative Coach**

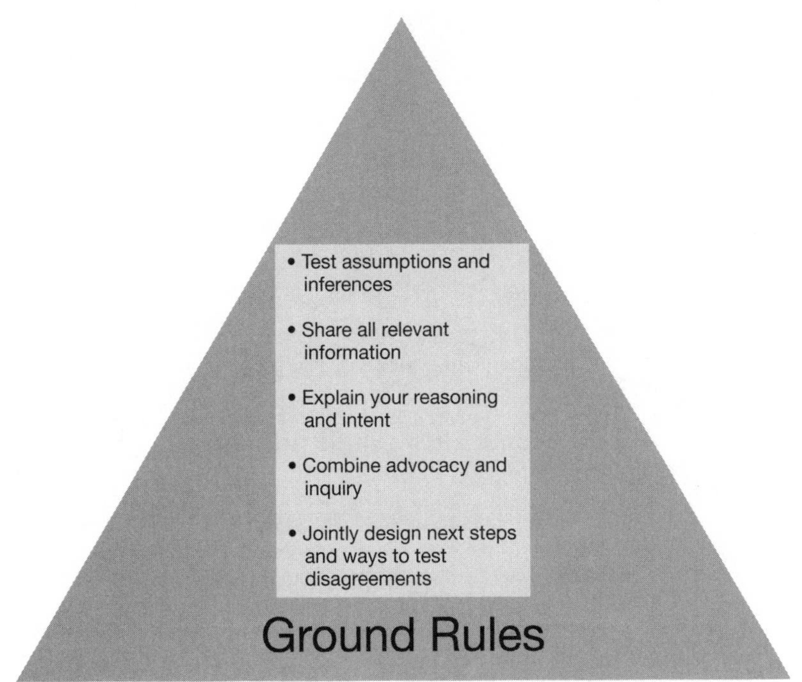

These are simply called out because we use them often in these kinds of one-on-one conversations. We continually listen for our own and our clients' use of these strategies. We are very conscious of changing our own conversation to be consistent with these ground rules, and we use them to intervene when a client does not explain his reasoning or makes high-level inferences and attributions about others, for example.

See Chapter Five, "Ground Rules for Effective Groups," page 61.

Facet 7: Coaching Process Steps

We highlight six key steps in the coaching process (Figure 57.7). These are both macro and micro steps: they are the steps we take in creating and moving through a coaching relationship and also the same steps we follow for each coaching session. The steps are iterative; we may back up and rediagnose and intervene multiple times during a session or coaching engagement. We may back up and clarify the purpose or goals of a session during that session, and we frequently redefine the goal of

Figure 57.7 Steps in the Coaching Process

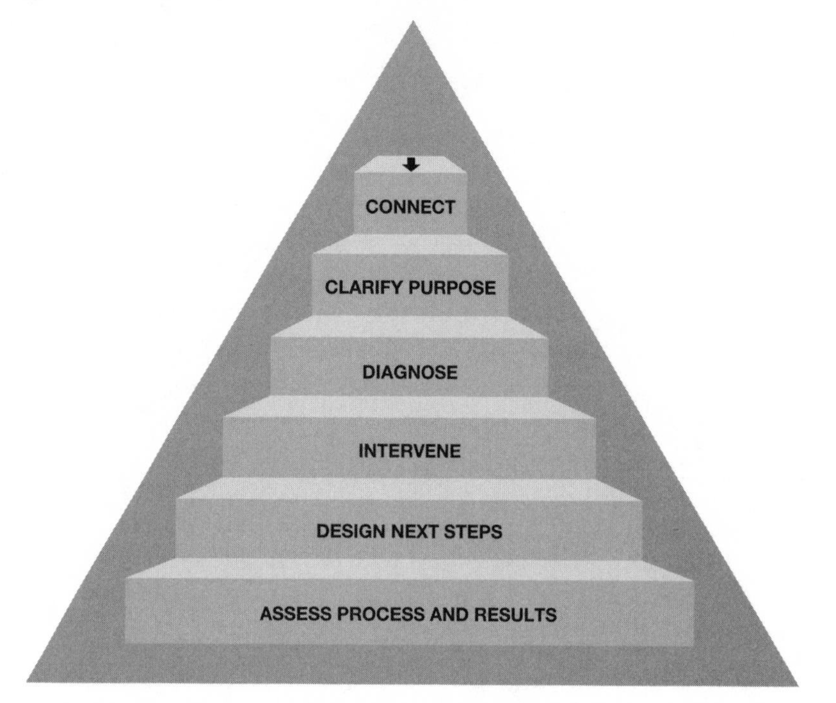

the coaching relationship as we go deeper into pattern and mental model issues. Below is a brief description of each step and an example based on Sallie's story:

1. *Connect*: Make initial contact or check in at the beginning of a session. Take time to be present with one another. Since Sallie was rushed and stressed, the coach suggested some stretching, deep breathing, and a few moments of silence.

2. *Clarify purpose:* Jointly design the goals of coaching or the goals of a specific coaching session. Create an agenda to guide how you will spend your time. Sallie and her coach initially defined the goal as making a decision about a promotion. As they explored the issue, the purpose evolved to dealing with a specific barrier, then to defining that barrier (being indispensable), and finally to discovering the source of that barrier and changing it.

3. *Diagnose:* Make inferences about what may be going on for a client, broadly and during discussion of a particular topic. The inferences we make may be about whether the client is acting from a unilateral or mutual learning frame, unnecessarily engaging in a reactive survival cycle, caught up in a drama triangle, or making inferences about others, for example. In Sallie's case, the coach's diagnosis deepened from inferring Sallie was not focused on the coaching session, to inferring there was

a deeper barrier (being fragmented, feeling indispensable), to inferring this might be a lifelong pattern.

4. *Intervene:* In this step, we decide to share and test our diagnosis. In coaching, this is also the step in which we may suggest specific activities to the client, like creating art, journaling, engaging in a real-life experiment to observe or change behavior, or practicing for a difficult conversation. Sallie's coach suggested that she reflect on her feelings and then make a drawing. Often just talking about a barrier or a dream that is not well defined is less helpful than accessing other ways of knowing beyond cerebral understanding. For Sallie, drawing helped her make her feelings concrete and discussable.

5. *Design next steps:* After each intervention and after each coaching session, we jointly design the next steps with the client. By the end of Sallie's second session, her goal had changed. She and her coach designed some journal activities for Sallie to reflect on her pattern of helping others. In subsequent sessions, next steps included experimenting with new ways of helping others and designing conversations with her family about how and why she wanted to change her helping patterns. Next steps obviously loop back to more interventions; the results of one intervention provide information that leads to another diagnosis and intervention. The starting place for the next session builds on results of the previous session and insights from fieldwork activities conducted in the interim. We cycle through diagnosis, intervention, and jointly designed next steps again and again until our work is completed.

6. *Assess process and results:* Each intervention, as well as the coaching process, should produce results. Sometimes the results are different from what was intended. At this stage, we learn and the client learns how we contributed to getting or not getting what was intended. We gather the lessons and plan next steps, often returning to our purpose to reclarify. We assess progress toward the client's goal at the conclusion of each major intervention and each session. When we mutually agree the coaching relationship has achieved its purpose, we assess its strengths and weaknesses and gather lessons learned. Sallie continued in the coaching relationship until she felt she had several successes at changing her "rescue" patterns. She also decided to accept a temporary promotion, giving herself time to assess whether the new job responsibilities met her needs and whether she could effectively balance her responsibilities. Sallie saw this as huge progress because she could respond to others while also taking care of her own needs. At that point, she and her coach jointly evaluated their experience together and planned a celebration dinner to reward Sallie's hard work.

Facet 8: Diagnosis-Intervention Cycle

This facet of our pyramid calls out a specific tool that is especially valuable during the steps of the coaching process: the diagnosis-intervention cycle. We use the Skilled Facilitator diagnosis-intervention cycle (Figure 57.8). The only distinction during coaching is that our broad process interventions look different from those we

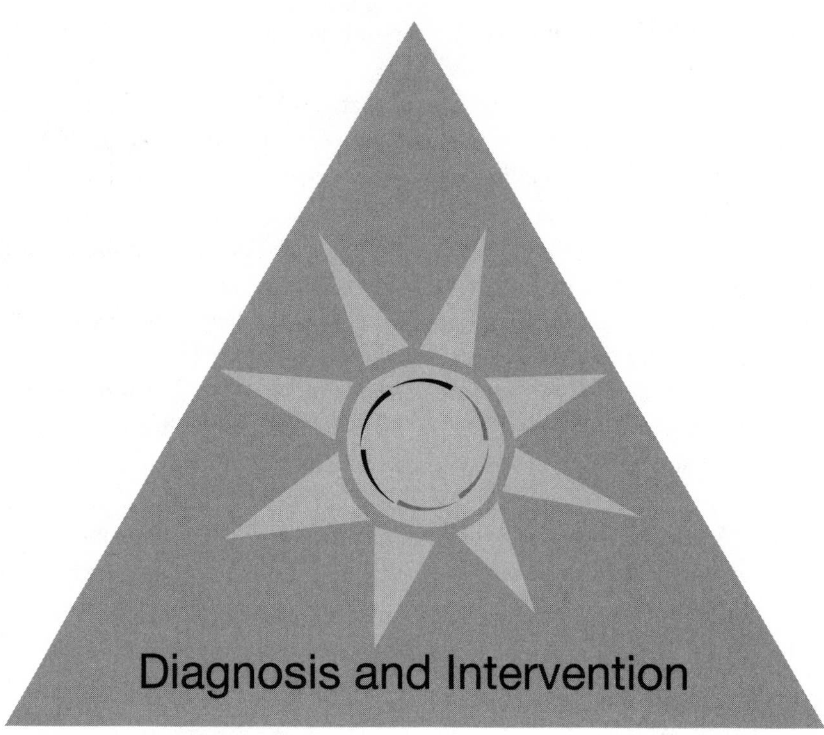

 There are numerous resources to guide you in using each of these interventions. A few that we find useful include Julia Cameron's *The Artist's Way* (1992) and *Walking in This World* (2002), Adriana Diaz's *Freeing the Creative Spirit* (1992), Stephen Nachmanovitch's *Free Play: The Power of Improvisation in Life and the Arts* (1990), and Ira Progoff's *At a Journal Workshop, Revised* (1992).

commonly use during facilitation. We still jointly design agendas with clients and use the ground rules to help us have more productive conversations. But the other frames and processes we use to diagnose and intervene are a bit different. Many of our interventions are made up of a set of activities aimed at helping clients develop personal insight or helping them experiment with new patterns of behavior. There is a long list of possibilities; we use our "diagnostic sun" to help identify some of them. Each ray represents a process that can cast new light on an issue, depending on the client and the situation. Which interventions can be effectively used obviously also depends on the background, training, and experience of the coach.

See Chapter Six, "The Diagnosis-Intervention Cycle," page 69.

CELEBRATING CREATIVE, PURPOSEFUL RESULTS

Successful coaching results in movement toward the client's deepest desires and goals. The client and the coach both engage in gathering the lessons learned and measuring

Figure 57.8 The Diagnosis-Intervention Cycle

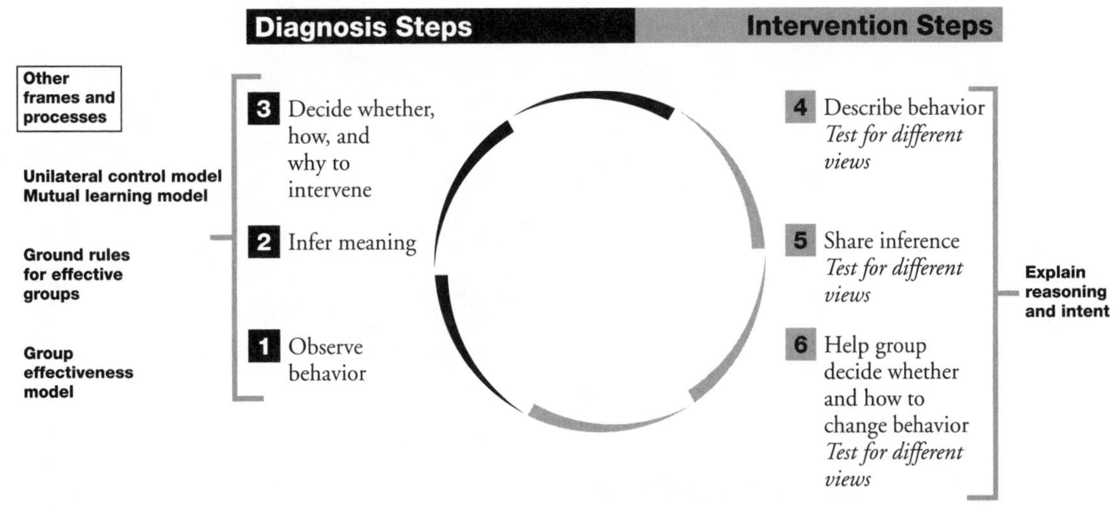

how far they have come together. This is what creates the spiral of learning that can guide us closer and closer to our life's true purpose.

Perhaps the most important but generally overlooked aspect of this final step is to celebrate. Many of us fail to pause and congratulate ourselves for our hard work, treat ourselves, and share our growth with others. Celebration is a critical part of the growth process. It is the reinforcement for remaining in a creative cycle, and it is the source of renewed energy with which to begin another learning cycle. Rather than take results for granted or focus solely on an evaluative process, we believe stopping to celebrate is more productive.

> Celebration is a critical part of the growth process. It is the reinforcement for remaining in a creative cycle, and it is the source of renewed energy with which to begin another learning cycle. Rather than take results for granted or focus solely on an evaluative process, we believe stopping to celebrate is more productive.

We chose the pyramid to represent our coaching model in part because of its symbolism. Many ancient cultures constructed pyramids. In Mayan cultures, the pyramids were temples, sometimes built over caves to symbolize places of origin or going back to the source of life (Schele and Freidel, 1990). In Egypt, the pyramids were more than tombs. They were a form of life insurance, a place where man could provide for his own happy afterlife. "Someone who provided these pleasures in advance by his own efforts could look forward to an active and happy life without being haunted by fear of the great unknown" (Janson, 1967, p. 35). Although we are focused on results in this life, we hope our model is a similar gift: it is aimed at helping other coaches and their clients provide by their own efforts for an active life in which unknown gifts become known, in which the treasures stored within are used to create an abundant life. It is that abundance that we invite you to celebrate.

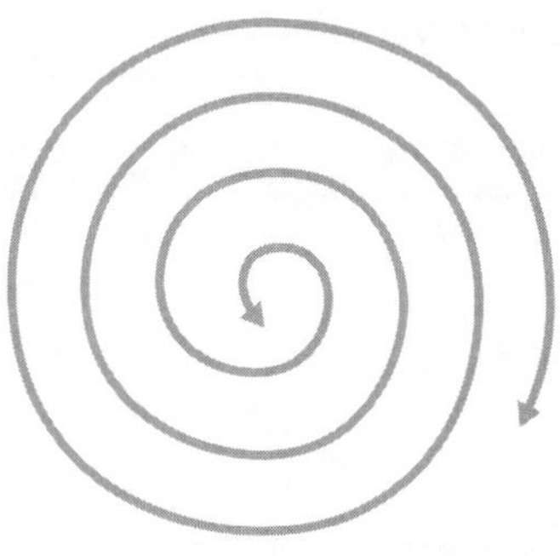

Spiral of Learning

A FINAL WORD

Engaging in a coaching relationship is a powerful experience. Being a coach is a journey you take on behalf of someone else, but at the same time the relationship serves as a mirror being held up to you. Adopting and consistently practicing mutual learning is a lifelong process. The first step is to reflect on the strategies you use in working with others and to invite others to give you feedback on how they experience your approach. With dedicated work and time, you can become consistent and compassionate in increasingly difficult situations. You as the coach will learn a tremendous amount about yourself. We hope that our coaching model offers a useful framework for your wisdom.

Resources

Cameron, J. *The Artist's Way.* Los Angeles: Tarcher, 1992.
Cameron, J. *Walking in This World.* Los Angeles: Tarcher, 2002.
Diaz, A. *Freeing the Creative Spirit.* San Francisco: HarperSanFrancisco, 1992.
Nachmanovitch, S. *Free Play: The Power of Improvisation in Life and the Arts.* Los Angeles: Tarcher, 1990.
Progoff, I. *At a Journal Workshop, Revised.* Los Angeles: Tarcher, 1992.

Note

1. ***Guided imagery*** simply means meditation with a guide designed to evoke visual images. There are many forms, from casual to very precise. Guided imagery can be practiced with a guide or coach creating a scenario, with a

friend reading a script, or with a recorded guide. In coaching, its purpose is to create a state of focused relaxation through which to explore thoughts, feelings, and images about a particular issue.

References

Schele, L., and Freidel, D. *A Forest of Kings: The Untold Story of the Ancient Maya.* New York: Morrow, 1990.

Janson, H. W. *The History of Art.* (6th ed.) New York: Abrams, 2000.

Chapter 58

Becoming a Facilitative Trainer

Sue McKinney
Matt Beane

Asking questions can be a means of establishing authority, fulfilling leadership functions, and ensuring effective learning. In fact, asking questions is probably the most subtle power you have for controlling people. The person who asks questions always controls the conversation. . . . If we could discipline our minds to ask questions instead, we could lead any conversation to wherever we wanted it because the other person would still be wrapped up in thinking what he or she wanted to say next. . . . One of the rights you have as a trainer is to ask questions and expect answers. This is why question-asking is such a powerful tool. It challenges and avoids confrontation at the same time."

—*Garry Mitchell,* The Trainer's Handbook (1998)

The quotation from Garry Mitchell that opens this chapter wasn't difficult to find; a number of other books contain entire sections devoted to similar training strategies.[1] In short, they advocate a unilateral control model approach to training. Mitchell, for example, advocates the strategy of asking questions to unilaterally control the direction of the conversation (and the participants), enabling the trainer to take the conversation where he wants it to lead (presumably rather than where participants want it to lead).

See Chapter Four, "Understanding What Guides Your Behavior," page 33, for an explanation of the unilateral control model.

By now, this probably isn't a surprise. Throughout this book, you've seen examples of how people use the unilateral control model in their work. Designing and delivering training is simply another example. Many trainers use a unilateral approach to training, and some espouse the approach as well. For example, we're familiar with a number of courses intended to train trainers that endorse using questions to control the direction of a conversation without being transparent about doing so. In Matt's experience, managing a large network of senior, independent training professionals, it was common for trainers and their intermediary clients (such as salespeople and instructional designers) to put an explicit premium on the ability to unilaterally guide groups. This meant, for example, asking for participants' expectations and then showing the participants how their expectations fit into the preexisting training design, regardless of how well the trainer thinks they actually fit.

Based on training literature and conversations we've had with training professionals, we've concluded that trainers advocate for and take this approach when they think they know—better than the participants do—what and how the participants should be learning. They seem to believe that they are helping the participants by not taking their expressed learning interests seriously and that telling the participants that they are not going to address their interests would be counterproductive to the participants' learning as well.

For us, the transparency test reveals the unilateral nature of this approach: imagine saying your strategy out loud to your intended audience. If it would seem ridiculous to do so or would hinder your ability to implement your strategy, the strategy is probably unilateral.

For us, the transparency test reveals the unilateral nature of this approach: imagine saying your strategy out loud to your intended audience. If it would seem ridiculous to do so or would hinder your ability to implement your strategy, the strategy is probably unilateral.

Nevertheless, many people espouse a more mutual learning approach to training. Still, as we've described throughout the book, when faced with difficult situations, they often revert to a unilateral approach and are often unaware that they are doing so. Delivering training using the unilateral control approach creates the same kinds of consequences that any unilateral control approach does: misunderstanding, defensiveness, reduced trust, reduced learning, and reduced effectiveness, to name a few. Given these consequences, it is ironic that unilateral approaches are openly endorsed in a context explicitly oriented to learning.

BECOMING A FACILITATIVE TRAINER

Becoming a facilitative trainer means using the mutual learning model to help participants develop knowledge and skills about a particular subject so they can apply it to real problems or opportunities. You can be a facilitative trainer regardless of the subject matter you are teaching.

You can be a facilitative trainer regardless of the subject matter you are teaching.

As a facilitative trainer, a couple of core values and assumptions are particularly salient.

Training to Learn, Not Just Learning to Train

A key challenge for facilitative trainers is adopting the mind-set of simultaneously teaching and learning. Unilateral trainers usually assume that they are the teachers and the students are the learners. They assume they are the experts about the content they are teaching and the process for teaching it. This is a natural assumption to make, but it is also ineffective because it reduces learning.

As a facilitative trainer, you see the training as an opportunity for you to learn about the content and how to teach it better. When students' knowledge and experiences differ from yours, you assume that students may be seeing things that you are missing. Rather than try to persuade them you are right and they are wrong, you use the ground rules to engage in mutual learning.

As a facilitative trainer, you see the training as an opportunity for you to learn about the content and how to teach it better.

Adopting a stance of both trainer and learner includes learning about your training process. In the mutual learning mind-set, trainers actively seek feedback from the participants and jointly design the learning where possible to ensure that participants are learning in a way that is helpful to them. Perhaps paradoxically, engaging in learning *with* participants rather than being seen as the expert increases participants' willingness to learn both with you and from you.

Being Transparent About Your Teaching and Learning Strategies

Part of being a facilitative trainer is sharing with participants the strategies you are using for teaching and learning. Being transparent is necessary if you want to learn while training. It enables you and the participants to explore how your proposed strategy will help or hinder participants' ability to learn. Yet many of us were taught that we were responsible for guiding participants through the learning process using unilateral strategies that we couldn't share without ruining their impact.

Sue, for example, used to worry that certain participants might have already seen her exercise before and would "ruin" it by sharing the punch line with others. Being transparent about her strategy for the exercise would have decreased the impact of the learning, as she understood it at the time:

> As a trainer, I prided myself on my ability to create an appropriate learning agenda and schedule, with each portion of the class carefully timed for maximum efficiency. To stick to my timetable, I had to unilaterally stop questions, dictate break lengths, and round people up when they disappeared so we could stay on time. It never crossed my mind to negotiate these things with the participants; that would have taken too long and added to an already too tight timetable; besides, I was being paid for my expertise in this area. However, once I learned about the facilitative approach to training and understood the negative consequences of unilateral training, I could not go back to my old ways. I realized that I had to learn a new approach to training that would recognize both instructors and participants as learners.
>
> Using a facilitative approach, I learned to be transparent about my thinking and share my teaching strategies out loud. This affected how I shared the agenda, orchestrated breaks, engaged participants in discussion, and led exercises. To the extent that your teaching strategy is unilateral, sharing it with participants will reduce your ability to execute it. To the extent that you use a mutual learning approach, sharing your strategy will improve your effectiveness.

To the extent that your teaching strategy is unilateral, sharing it with participants will reduce your ability to execute it. To the extent that you use a mutual learning approach, sharing your strategy will improve your effectiveness.

THE FACILITATIVE TRAINER APPROACH IN ACTION

Becoming a facilitative trainer means putting the mutual learning approach into action. This fundamentally affects how you interact with participants. In the sidebar, Matt describes steps to becoming a facilitative trainer regardless of the specific situation. Here are a number of common training situations and how we address them.

Contracting for Training

The facilitative trainer approach begins with how we contract for the training. Ineffective contracting creates negative consequences during the training.

See Chapter Eight, "Contracting with Groups," page 89, for an introduction to contracting.

A number of years ago Matt facilitated a service training session for a group of human resource (HR) professionals:

> The director of the HR group requested the session and decided to participate. She thought her team had a lot of room for service improvement and did not want to say this to them directly; she told me she thought that the training would help them "get it" without her having to voice her views. This is a typical unilateral strategy. However, at the time, I was not using a facilitative training approach. I contributed to the problem by not asking for her reasoning for not sharing her concerns directly with the group and by not sharing with her what I thought the unintended negative consequences would be. As it turned out, her strategy generated nearly the opposite of what she intended.
>
> I started the training session by sharing a proposed agenda and indicated that I'd like the group to have a candid conversation about whether the agenda met their needs. A number of the participants expressed confusion as to why service training was necessary at all; they acknowledged gaps in service but pointed to external problems as the source of these gaps. Their reactions created a dilemma for me: I knew why the director wanted them to have this training and thought it would be relevant to share this with the group, but I didn't feel that I could raise this issue for her. And yet if I didn't raise the issue, participants would not fully understand why the training was being conducted. My best attempt at resolving this dilemma was to indicate that I thought there would always be external obstacles to good service and that there was also always room to work on their individual skills. The participants agreed, the training session went ahead, and the director and I kept the director's point of view undiscussable throughout. I didn't share my impression of the director's point of view because I assumed she would have done so herself if she wanted to and I didn't want to embarrass her or her direct reports. I thought that I might make things worse for them if I did. Essentially, I colluded with the director against the group I would be training.

Regardless of the espoused orientation of the trainer, unilateral approaches to training decrease the amount of learning available to all involved. In Matt's experience above, everybody lost: the group missed an opportunity to understand the director's concerns, the director missed an opportunity to test her inferences about her team's performance and to deal with her team more directly, and Matt missed the opportunity to discover whether his inference about the director's willingness to raise her concerns on her own was accurate. Matt now says:

> Had I used a facilitative approach, I would have intervened when the director first told me that she thought her team had a lot of room for service improvement but did not want to say this to them directly and instead wanted to use the training to help them "get it" without her having to voice her views. At that point, I would have shared my views about the unintended consequences of her suggested approach, including the dilemma that would be created. I'd also explore her reasoning for not sharing her concerns directly with the group. I would have met with some training participants before the training in order to ensure that the training met their needs. At this point, if not earlier, I may have found out that they did not see a need for the training, in which case I could have facilitated a conversation with the director and the participants to address this. Depending on the outcome of the conversation, I may still have provided the training, and if I had, the director would have shared with the participants the reason for it.

Setting the Agenda

Using facilitative skills, we share the agenda and ask if others want to modify it by adding new items or removing current items or ask questions about the items that are or are not listed. We build in time for a thorough discussion of what we are going to cover in the class to ensure that everyone supports the plan. Fundamentally, the facilitative trainer believes that the agenda must be supported by everyone in the room to be effective. It won't help the group if they simply go along with the instructor's plan, even if it may be more efficient for the instructor.

Taking Breaks

As facilitative trainers, we jointly control the schedule and times for breaks. We note the break times in the agenda and gain support for their timing when sharing the agenda, but we stay open to the possibility that the breaks may need to shift during the class.

In addition, the facilitative trainer does not feel the need to control where people are located during the class and throughout the breaks. Before we understood the Skilled Facilitator approach, we used to round people up after the breaks. We would stand in the hall and say loudly, "Okay, we are going to get started now." We might turn to some participants and say, "Can you find the others and get them back, please?" And then we would wait until most everyone was back to begin the class again.

Now, using the core values as our guide, we let everyone know at the beginning of a class when the breaks are scheduled (approximately) and explain that we believe everyone is an adult and can make good use of their time. We let them know that we will be clear about the beginning and ending time of each break. We explain that we won't be rounding participants up after the breaks end; we will simply begin teaching again and will assume that they are where they need to be at that time. We let them know we won't make untested assumptions about their commitment to the class based on their presence or lack of presence in the room. We do ask that participants let us know if they will be gone for an extended period of time, since other participants and we will worry if they don't return when expected.

Managing the breaks in this manner allows us to stay consistent with sharing relevant information, giving people free and informed choices, and building internal commitment to the process. It is a powerful mechanism for modeling the core values and the ground rules throughout any teaching endeavor.

Moving to Another Topic

When we move from one topic to another in a training class, we do it jointly. Instead of simply saying, "Okay, let's move to the section on making interventions," we say something like, **"It sounds like we are done discussing diagnosing behavior. Is there anyone who isn't ready to move to making interventions at this time?"**

This enables us to test our inference that the group is ready to move on. If some members are not ready, we respond to their questions or concerns. If we are concerned about time, we raise that with the group and usually jointly design a solution that meets the needs of participants who may still have questions and concerns and those who want to move to the next topic.

Exploring Participant Concerns

When training in a unilateral frame, we considered challenges by participants about the value of the exercises or materials as objections to be overcome. Taking a facilitative approach, we see these challenges from the participants as opportunities for learning. We recognize that the participants may have information or knowledge that we, as trainers, don't have.

A former class participant shared her left-hand column case with us to illustrate that other trainers also struggle with this point. In her case, she was teaching a class of managers how to write objectives so that they would align with the corporate goals. Apparently some participants were concerned about the strategies as presented and began to share their concerns with the trainers (Table 58.1). Using a facilitative approach, a trainer might address the same question differently (Table 58.2).

Table 58.1 Exploring Participants' Concerns Using a Unilateral Approach

Thoughts and Feelings	Verbatim Dialogue
	Participant: It just doesn't make sense to me to align myself with strategies that don't say anything about quality software development.
We are way off topic and just wasted ten minutes of this class! How am I even going to finish on time?	**Trainer:** Okay, I think we are getting heated over an issue that shouldn't be discussed in this class. We are here to discuss the mechanics of writing objectives, not to rewrite the strategies. Let's take this off-line and write it on our parking lot. For now, we are in a time crunch and need to get back to developing objectives.
	Participant: Why are we doing this to begin with? Things were fine the way they were before.
My way of switching topics! Maybe things were fine the way they were before, but my job is to get through this class!	**Trainer:** It's about accountability. We need to make sure that we are aligning our work within and between divisions.
	Participant: How is my work going to align with what you do as a trainer?
If you get me sidetracked one more time, I might ignore you . . . or throw an M&M at you! Ha, ha!	**Trainer:** Again, I think we are getting sidetracked. Let's focus on why we're here to begin with. We are here to learn how to write objectives . . . to make sure they are SMART.
	Participant: I'll write objectives, but I don't agree with the strategies. They need to be changed.

Table 58.2 Exploring Participants' Concerns Using a Facilitative Trainer Approach

Thoughts and Feelings	Verbatim Dialogue
	Participant: It just doesn't make sense to me to align myself with strategies that don't say anything about quality software development.
I'm thinking these strategies are nonnegotiable since they were set by the corporate executives. It sounds as if this person sees this differently.	**Trainer:** I can understand your concern about alignment, but I'm wondering if you and I have a fundamental difference in our understanding of these strategies and their malleability. I'm not thinking we can change the strategies because they were the product of the executive strategic planning process. Are you seeing that differently?
I think this is a reasonable concern. How can we best address it here?	**Participant:** I don't know if we can change them or not, but how can we align with them if we don't agree with them?
In order to reach my teaching goal, I need to see if the participant is willing to delay his concerns and address them later. These are my two issues anyway.	**Trainer:** I think there may be two issues at play here, and I want to identify them both to see if you agree. One is the teaching objective, which is to help you learn to write objectives in a specific manner, and the other is the content of those objectives. Do you think these are the primary issues or not?
	Participant: Yeah, I agree.
Let him know what I would like to do and see if that works for him or not. If not, we will have to work as a group to figure out an alternative that will meet all of our needs.	**Trainer:** My goal is to teach you how to write the objectives. I do not feel capable of negotiating the strategies since I wasn't involved in that process. I'm wondering if you would be willing to learn to write the objectives here today and then approach the management group about your concerns regarding the content of the strategies. Would that work for you or not?
	Participant: Yeah, that sounds okay.

In the hypothetical scenario, the trainer must be open to the responses that she gets to her final question, "Would that work for you or not?" If the participant says, "No, this really won't work for me," then the trainer must be prepared to work with the group to figure out what to do during their time together for it to be time well spent. A facilitative trainer is willing to spend some time working through this issue completely; she knows that once it gets resolved, the class can move efficiently through the rest of the day. If it never gets fully resolved, the issue will continue to pop up throughout the training, slowing it down more than if time had been taken up front to resolve it completely.

Asking Questions

Take another look at the quotation that begins this chapter. It captures a unilateral control approach to asking questions. In this approach, trainers use questions to steer the conversation where they want it to go and avoid difficult conversations that participants may want to engage in. Like unilateral trainers, facilitative trainers also recognize that asking questions can be a subtle and powerful way of controlling people. But because facilitative trainers value mutual learning rather than control, they carefully craft their questions so that participants feel safe asking their own questions and sharing whatever their views, including challenging the trainers' views.

> Because facilitative trainers value mutual learning rather than control, they carefully craft their questions so that participants feel safe asking their own questions and sharing whatever their views, including challenging the trainers' views.

One of the most difficult challenges for Sue as she shifted her values as a trainer was learning how to ask participants questions:

> I was used to asking the group to answer a question for which I had a specific answer. I asked a series of leading questions to get them to arrive at the "correct" answer. As a facilitative trainer, I stay open to the possibility of different "correct" answers. I have also learned ways to give participants the chance to discover the answer on their own without easing in or leading them to feel set up.
>
> It is important to me that I do not ask rhetorical or leading questions since this often causes people to be defensive or on guard. Instead of asking, "Does that sound right?" or "Does that make sense?" which may imply that it should be right or make sense, I try to ask, **"What are your reactions to what I've said? What are your thoughts about this topic?"** or **"What questions or concerns, if any, does this raise for you?"**

Over time, Sue learned if she asks a question and knows the answer but wants a participant to answer, she simply states this out loud.

> When I instruct, it looks like this: **"I have a sense of what would be an effective strategy in this situation, but I'm interested in what each of you think would be effective. I'd like to explore this with all of you and then share my ideas. Who is willing to share their thoughts?"**

Generally, yes or no questions are not effective at engaging the class in mutual learning. Open-ended questions are better at asking for thoughts and different perspectives. Some examples include: **"What reactions do you have to what I've said so far?"** or **"How do you think that might work for you?"** or **"What are your thoughts on this topic?"**

Experiential Learning

Being transparent affects how we select and lead training exercises. As Sue illustrates:

> Prior to internalizing the core values, I used to pick learning games and exercises that I thought would give the participants a powerful learning message. This often involved my knowing something that the participants did not know and my hiding that information from them. This could be as simple as an exercise to demonstrate the need for out-of-the-box thinking by making paper airplanes to see who can fly theirs the farthest. Of course, I didn't tell the participants that the exercise was designed to demonstrate out-of-the-box thinking until after all the participants had flown their airplanes, so I could deliver the punch line: wadding up a piece of paper in a ball and throwing mine far past any of theirs.
>
> My life as a trainer shifted dramatically after integrating the Skilled Facilitator values into my life. No longer could I lead manipulative games that were designed to teach participants lessons by tricking them into certain behaviors with the hope that they would have an "aha!" experience in learning. I began to realize that participant resistance to these types of exercises was often grounded in their recognition that there was a catch to the exercise. This often led to either active resistance to the exercise or concentrated attempts to figure out the manipulation and catch the trainer at his or her own game. Pleasant participants allowed themselves to be manipulated. It is doubtful that more than a handful of participants were unaware that there was a manipulation being performed.

In these types of situations, the trainer is withholding relevant information from participants, which impairs the participants' ability to make free and informed choices about how to participate. The end result is that some participants feel tricked. In our experience, not only do people feel tricked, but they start to expend a fair amount of energy in the training sessions trying to figure out the tricks so they can outmaneuver the instructor. This is definitely not the way we want participants to expend their energy in our training sessions.

Also this approach is clearly inconsistent with the Skilled Facilitator values because relevant information is not shared with participants, thus taking away their free and informed choice to participate effectively. It also diminished some participants' internal commitment to the training session because their trust in the trainer's credibility was diminished.

Following a mutual learning model does not mean having to give up using exercises. Quite the opposite. We believe that exercises are great ways for adults to learn in a fun, creative manner.

As facilitative trainers, when we use experiential exercises, we provide as much valid information as possible so that participants can make a free and informed choice about whether to participate. This increases their commitment to the exercise (if they choose to participate) and to the learning associated with it. Generally we avoid exercises that are at odds with the core values. This includes exercises that require withholding valid information or relying on deception, exercises in which the outcome is predetermined and controlled by the trainer, and exercises that are inconsistent with the group's objectives. For experiential exercises in which we cannot figure out a way to create the learning without withholding some relevant information, we make that strategy explicit. We tell participants that the exercise requires our withholding some information and ask if they are still willing to participate knowing this. In short, we share the relevant information that we have relevant information we can't share.

As facilitative trainers, when we use experiential exercises, we provide as much valid information as possible so that participants can make a free and informed choice about whether to participate. This increases their commitment to the exercise (if they choose to participate) and to the learning associated with it.

When determining if a training exercise is congruent with the Skilled Facilitator approach, we ask ourselves the following questions:

- Can we share the strategy underlying the exercise without weakening the message or lesson of the exercise? If we cannot share it, can we modify the exercise so that we can share the strategy?
- Will participants have a free and informed choice throughout the exercise, including whether to participate?
- Will the exercise increase participants' internal commitment to the training?
- Is the exercise consistent with the core value of compassion?

If we can answer yes to each of these questions, we are comfortable using the exercise.

The sidebar by Diane Florio shows how to convert a unilateral exercise to one that you can use as a facilitative trainer.

Modifying Experiential Exercises to Be Consistent with the Skilled Facilitator Core Values and Ground Rules

By Diane Florio

Often, experiential exercises or learning games may lead to participants' feeling set up, which may lead to a "blame the facilitator" type of behavior. This tends to happen when there is this "gotcha!" type ending to such initiatives. Participants may say things like, "Well, if you had told us that was an option, we would have succeeded," or "You didn't tell us that was part of the rules."

I am not advocating that experiential exercises do not provide a tremendous learning value. I believe people learn by doing and therefore see great value in exercises of this nature. What I am suggesting is to carefully examine the design of the exercise and consider what both the intended and unintended consequences may be as a result of the way it is suggested to frame or introduce the exercise. Here is an example from my own experience.

A very popular experiential game is *The Search for the Lost Dutchman's Gold Mine,* which is designed to heighten participant awareness to the notion that working together toward a common purpose will bring greater rewards financially to the organization.[1]

The simulation provides both a rich debrief and learning for the participants. The challenge for me as a trainer was how to introduce and organize the exercise in a way that participants could experience the learning value and at the same time not feel set up in the end. This led me to questions like, "How do I share relevant information without giving away the entire learning experience?" "What does allowing free and informed choice look like? Does it mean they can choose not to do the exercise?" "How can I provide enough information for them to make an informed choice so they may be committed to wanting to play the game?" and "How can I hold the conversation or introduction of this exercise in a way that models the use of the ground rules and core values?"

My cotrainer, Michael, and I wrestled with these questions and the different dilemmas we thought might emerge. In addition, we consulted with Roger Schwarz to test our assumptions and thinking in an effort to help us implement this initiative in a manner consistent with the behaviors we were seeking to model throughout our program.

This exercise was used as a culminating experience at the close of a two-and-a-half-day leadership program. Our intent was for the participants to be able to apply key teachings from the program in a manner consistent with the company's values and to have an opportunity to work with a distilled version of the ground rules. Therefore, we chose to introduce *The Search for the Lost Dutchman's Gold Mine* in the following manner.

We told participants, "This next portion of the program involves a simulation game we believe holds great learning value. Part of the learning value comes from our desire to help you discover certain 'aha!'s' along the way and asks that we (the trainers) share limited pieces of information so that you may have the 'aha!'s' and therefore the learning. Our dilemma is to consider what to share and what not to share so that you do not feel set up at the end and at the same time not give away the entire learning experience. Our question to you is, given what we have just shared, are you willing to play the game?" (If any participants had expressed an unwillingness to proceed, we would have explored what additional information they needed or what we may have said that led them to not be willing. Then we would have decided as a group whether to conduct the exercise.)

We then said, "Given that you are willing to participate, there are some things we need to say up front before getting into the game itself. (1) The outcomes you realize as a result of playing the game are very much related to the assumptions and inferences you conclude based on the introduction and rules of the game; therefore, we strongly recommend you test your assumptions and inferences. (2) We have spent the past two days examining company values and expectations, learning about different behavioral styles, and understanding situational leadership. We have also worked with a set of ground rules that include testing assumptions, sharing relevant information, sharing your reasoning, and asking questions after making statements as a set of specific behaviors that will help put the company values into action. We strongly encourage you to use all that we have discussed in the past two days to assist you in achieving your outcomes and hopeful success. (3) What questions do you have before we introduce the exercise?" Finally, after explaining the exercise, we asked, "What questions do you have?"

The key set of instructions in *The Search for the Lost Dutchman's Gold Mine* is to "mine as much gold as we can." The biggest assumption made by participants is around how each group defines the word *we.* Groups are placed in teams, which may lead them to think they are competing against the other teams or, alternatively, they may think that every team is part of the larger team.

Throughout the game, we shared information when participants asked us questions and continued to manage the dilemma of sharing enough relevant information and yet not giving away the learning experience.

After the simulation was over, we conducted a thorough debrief with the participants. This conversation taught us that our approach had worked since none of the groups felt set up. In addition, participants expressed the belief that they had taken ownership of their actions, behaviors, and outcomes as a result of the assumptions they made, the questions they chose to ask or not ask, and the choices such information led them to make. It led to a rich learning experience for all involved, because participants accepted that the outcomes were a result of how they chose to play the game and did not think that we, the trainers, were a factor in those outcomes.

The experience of considering how to reframe this simulation exercise in a manner that was consistent with the core values and ground rules was a powerful one for both Michael and me. Throughout the process, we had to challenge our own assumptions about what would work and what wouldn't work for the group. We had to trust the participants' ability to make good decisions for their own learning. And, finally, we recognized that even if the participants beat the game, by pulling together as one group and winning as much gold as possible, there would be rich learning for all of us as we compared the process that led to such success to the daily process we engage in at work. When we realized that there was no way the exercise could fail the group, we were confident in our ability to use the exercise for rich learning.

1. Scott Simmerman, *The Search for the Lost Dutchman's Gold Mine,* available at http://www.squarewheels.com/.

Role Plays

Role plays are an important way for participants to develop their skills, especially when trainers are present to provide feedback. Some participants who have attended our workshops dreaded the role plays because of their experiences in other courses. In general, they found the role plays in our workshop to be one of the most valuable aspects of their learning. The difference comes again with the setup.

In order to practice the skills being taught, role plays are often conducted with participants' acting out make-believe roles. This approach works for some participants and not for others. One problem with fictitious role plays is that participants state that the role plays are not like their real-life situations and therefore don't help them practice their new skills. If they find themselves unable to perform effectively in the role play, they sometimes attribute it to the artificiality of the role play rather than to their lack of skill. This reduces their ability to learn from their experience.

Part of being a facilitative trainer involves designing role-play practice in a way that gives participants a free and informed choice about how best to practice their emerging skills. To do this, we provide a range of options. First, we provide fictitious role plays, in part, because some participants prefer this type of practice. Some participants feel they learn better if they are not as personally invested in the role play. Others are reluctant to share their real-life challenges in the class. Others simply have difficulty thinking up a relevant role play. All of our fictitious role plays are based on real situations that we or our previous clients have faced, so participants typically find them realistic. If participants use these role plays, we still encourage them to modify them to better fit their learning needs.

Second, we encourage participants and give them time to think up role plays in which they are practicing the skills in their real roles. For example, a person may decide to role-play a difficult conversation he had (or anticipates having) with his team. This person then asks others to role-play his team members and gives them enough information to play their roles realistically. When participants choose this option, they often tell us that the role play seemed so real to them that they began to feel as if they were in the actual meeting. Third, when participants in the workshop have real-life work relationships outside the class (such as a work group or project team), we encourage them to use part of their role-play time to get real work done. In this situation, all participants are practicing their skills at the same time.

Whatever options participants choose, before they begin their practice, we ask them if there are any skills in particular that they want to practice so we can be certain to give them feedback on skills they are interested in learning. At the end of their practice, we also ask them how they want to receive their feedback (we suggest several options), instead of assuming that we, as trainers, know best how to structure the feedback for them. The participants control the key elements of their role play and feedback to make it useful to their own specific learning goals. As the directors of their own experience, participants are committed to their learning.

The participants control the key elements of their role play and feedback to make it useful to their own specific learning goals. As the directors of their own experience, participants are committed to their learning.

This approach to role plays requires more skill from the trainers because they often need to give feedback on role plays they have never seen before, much like skilled facilitators intervene with groups. This is another characteristic of facilitative trainers: they can model the mind-set and skill set they are teaching without having to stay with a preset script.

Steps to Becoming a Facilitative Trainer

By Matt Beane

When I began to work as a trainer, I was more unilateral in my point of view and approaches to training than I am now. I used the following four methods to make this transition and continue to use them with colleagues to improve the quality of our training work:

- **Identify unilateral elements of your training behavior and design.** Observe your own training work, ask to be observed as you train, or tape your training work. Explore not only how you train but also the design of the training itself.
- **Explore the causes of the behavior and design.** This can include unilateral beliefs that you bring to the situation from experience, unilateral training designs, organizational policy, or pressure from others. It can help to explore the causes with others who might see things that you miss.
- **Consider change.** Consider making changes to shift from a unilateral to a mutual learning approach. If this would involve others, engage in conversation with them about this.
- **Be transparent about the change you're trying to make.** When delivering a training experience, let clients and colleagues know about the changes you are trying to create, and ask for their feedback.

CONCLUSION

Most trainers we have met were taught to use unilateral strategies to work with adult learners. We were taught to withhold relevant information, keep our teaching strategies secret, and manipulate learners in hopes of giving them "aha!" learning experiences. Once we understand the negative unintended consequences of these actions, we are able to choose whether to create more powerful learning for participants and ourselves by becoming facilitative trainers.

Resource

Kraiger, K. (ed.). *Creating, Implementing, and Managing Effective Leadership and Development.* San Francisco: Jossey-Bass/Pfeiffer, 2001.

Note

1. Two of the other books found to be inconsistent with the Skilled Facilitator approach are Lou Russell, *The Accelerated Learning Fieldbook* (2000), and Brian L. Delahaye and Barry J. Smith, *How to Be an Effective Trainer,* 3rd ed. (1998).

References

Delahaye, B. L., and Smith, B. J. *How to Be an Effective Trainer.* (3rd ed.) New York: Wiley, 1998.

Mitchell, G. *The Trainer's Handbook: The AMA Guide to Effective Training.* New York: AMACOM, 1998.

Russell, L. *The Accelerated Learning Fieldbook.* San Francisco: Jossey-Bass/Pfeiffer, 2000.

Chapter 59

Being a Facilitative Consultant

Harry Furukawa

THE SKILLED FACILITATOR APPROACH simultaneously increases the likelihood that a consultant and his or her client (the group with which the consultant is working) can both be more effective. An underlying assumption of the approach is that a consultant's theory-in-use and associated mental models determine how that person performs. These are largely based on the priority values that that individual holds (a result of his or her developmental worldview, internal beliefs, and the external situation) and the associated skills that this person possesses to operationalize their priority values. People employ their priority values, a theory-in-use, and mental models whether they realize it or not.

WHAT IS DIFFERENT ABOUT FACILITATIVE CONSULTING

A facilitative consultant is defined as a third party who is a process expert or a content expert, may be involved in decision making, and uses the Skilled Facilitator approach. The use of the Skilled Facilitator approach, and the mutual learning model that is part of it, differentiates a facilitative consultant from one who is not.

A facilitative consultant is defined as a third party who is a process expert or a content expert, may be involved in decision making, and uses the Skilled Facilitator approach.

See Chapter Four, "Understanding What Guides Your Behavior," page 33.

This distinction is important because different theories-in-use and mental models lead consultants to behave differently. For example, consultants using a unilateral control theory-in-use seek to achieve their goal through unilateral control, winning/not losing, avoiding negative feelings, and acting rational. This can lead them to act as if they are the expert (have the best process and content answers), advocate their point of view without genuine inquiry, and unilaterally control the agenda (for example, by deciding when someone is off-topic).

When a consultant acts unilaterally, the people in the client organization often feel that they have not been well served. Typical reactions may include feeling that not all of their concerns were addressed or feeling that their opinions are not valued. For example, a client related a story to me in which a consultant was asked to conduct research and lead a discussion about rebranding the logo and image of an organization.

> At a presentation to a senior leadership group of about thirty people, the consultant presented the findings of his research (the key finding being that focus groups didn't react positively to the existing logo). He then proposed a solution for a new logo and image (advocating, but failing to inquire about different points of view) and asked if the senior leaders supported the proposal. A majority raised their hands in support, and the consultant declared that he would then begin redesigning the rest of the organization's key material. In the days following the meeting, a number of people complained that they had no chance to air opinions and concerns with the new logo and expressed reservations about moving forward

If people in the organization do not feel well served, then their commitment to implement and monitor the decision and their desire to reengage the consultant can fall. In the example, the level of water-cooler conversation about the logo rose to the level that the topic was discussed again, and the consultant's proposed design was later criticized and the process began anew with a new consultant. Behaviors based on unilateral theories-in-use often result in the client's having less long-term commitment to implementing a course of action and achieving fewer results.

Often consultants may not be aware of their theories-in-use and mental models. This makes it difficult for them to determine how they may have contributed to the group's effectiveness or ineffectiveness. For example, when a consultant's mental models of how they will behave (for example, unilateral control theory-in-use) and of the content (for example, balanced scorecard of measures) are not explicit, it is difficult, if not impossible, to test or improve them, and this has the potential to be harmful.

See the Mental Models, Theory-in-Use, and Espoused Theory sidebar in Chapter Four, "Understanding What Guides Your Behavior," page 33.

For example, I recently examined a consultant-developed strategic plan and asked senior leaders what their business model (how they intend to make money, integrating people, operational, customer, and organizational results) and organizational strategy (what differentiated their business model from others) were, only to discover that the consultants weren't clear about these items. Using several strategy models to explain the interaction of planning objectives, I led the senior leaders through a dialogue to clarify their business model and strategy. They discovered they were working to achieve strategic objectives that didn't support any particular strategy, which diffused the focus and (arguably) results of the organization. When consultants' theories-in-use and mental models are not explicit, it is difficult to determine whether their advice is predictive (showing that the intervention led to the desired effect) or valid (that the advice can be used in other situations with similar results).

As a facilitative consultant in the case above, I shared my mental model—in this case, a business model showing how different strategic objectives interacted to produce financial, environmental, and social results in a way that was consistent with the organizational strategy. Since everyone (including myself) was aware of the assumptions and interactions between elements of the model, we were able to bring our collective wisdom to assess it and identify areas that may lessen its effectiveness. I have used this approach over time to improve the likelihood that my models and advice will be predictive and valid, develop jointly designed tests to evaluate and improve their effectiveness, and better understand the principles embedded in the models.

> When consultants' theories-in-use and mental models are not explicit, it is difficult to determine whether their advice is predictive (showing that the intervention led to the desired effect) or valid (that the advice can be used in other situations with similar results).

AN EXAMPLE: IDENTIFYING AND DEVELOPING VALUES IN AN ORGANIZATION

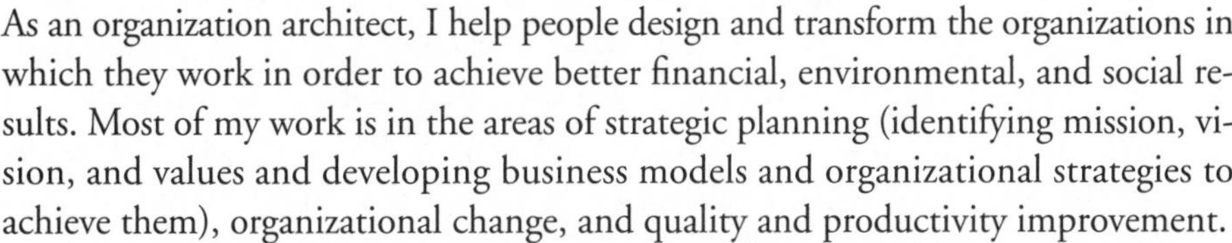

As an organization architect, I help people design and transform the organizations in which they work in order to achieve better financial, environmental, and social results. Most of my work is in the areas of strategic planning (identifying mission, vision, and values and developing business models and organizational strategies to achieve them), organizational change, and quality and productivity improvement.

As a result of a presentation that I gave describing a case study in values identification and development, I was approached by a service organization with multiple facilities to develop a statement of values. This statement of values was intended to guide employee behavior, so that customers and the employees would have consistent experiences regardless of the site. These values would also form the basis for aligning organizational systems (such as the recruiting and hiring process and the performance evaluation process) and their leadership development model. What follows are some of the highlights of how I used the Skilled Facilitator approach in this project.

Contracting for Consultation

In contracting, a number of decisions must be made in conjunction with the client. This is usually the first time that a consultant's theory-in-use and mental models become evident. There are four stages of contracting:

Stage One: Initial conversation with a primary client group member

Stage Two: Planning the consultation

Stage Three: Reaching agreement with the entire primary client group

Stage Four: Completing and evaluating the consultation.

I illustrate in the following sections the ground rules I applied in the various stages.

See Chapter Eight, "Contracting with Groups," page 89.

Stage One: Initial Conversation

Focus on interests, not positions. In my first conversation with the CEO, I asked him to share his interest (what was important about the solution) in developing a values statement. He responded that his interest stemmed from reading several popular business books that described the correlation between strong shared values and outstanding long-term business results. He was concerned that the organization was growing and customers were having different experiences at different locations and that the values are difficult to implement, specifically, that he didn't know what steps to take.

I described my interest in helping them identify priority values, develop action steps to develop skills and behaviors, and implement mechanisms that would reinforce those values. By soliciting his interests and naming mine and agreeing that both sets were important, I was able to suggest an approach to the project in terms of content and process (including how I would facilitate) that we could both commit to.

Had I acted unilaterally, I would have simply proposed a process without soliciting interests, but failing to solicit his interests and name mine could have raised the risk that either or both of us would be less committed to the approach, lessening the potential effectiveness of the solution.

We agreed on a number of items, including the date and setting for the meeting with the management team, the proposed agenda, and that the management team would be the client and their interests would also need to be made explicit so that they could be included in the design, because their commitment would be required for the initiative to be implemented.

Stage Two: Planning the Consultation

Share all relevant information and explain your reasoning and intent. Based on my conversation with the CEO and the committee charged with writing the values statement, I developed a project outline including purpose, agenda, roles and responsibilities, and description of the Skilled Facilitator approach. I described the core values and ground rules of the Skilled Facilitator approach, how using them could help generate commitment, and how they would provide an expectation of how I would act. First, I asked the CEO and committee to present their interests and solicited the rest of the team's interests. This provided a common pool of information, as evidenced by several team members who remarked that they hadn't initially understood why this initiative was so important.

I then presented the project outline to the management team, explained the reasoning and intent for each of the steps in the process and for using a specific instrument to measure values, and described the projected outcomes. I provided a common pool of relevant information for the management team to begin the decision-making process and described my reasoning and intent (one way to share relevant information) so that the team could see if there were any flaws in my logic, identify any interests that were not addressed, and understand how the steps incorporated various interests.

Had I acted in a unilateral mode, I would not have shared my reasoning and intent (since I would be the expert), but not sharing relevant information and explaining reasoning and intent may have raised the risk that team members didn't see why this initiative was important or that they make untested inferences about why the organization is embarking on a course of action.

Stage Three: Reaching Agreement with the Entire Client Group

Combine advocacy and inquiry. After completing the presentation of the process, I inquired into the team's thoughts and reactions. I invited team members to raise specific concerns about the proposed process, so that we could craft a process that everyone could commit to. Several concerns were raised about specific points, for example, which employees would take the values inventory, which I addressed through explanation, by joint design of methods, or by revising proposed steps. Several members remarked that they were pleased with the flexibility that I displayed and that their concerns were addressed. Had I used a unilateral control approach, I would not have inquired, or may have asked rhetorical questions, and I might have missed an opportunity to learn about flaws in my reasoning or ways to improve the process to generate a higher level of commitment.

Jointly design next steps. The discussion took longer than was allotted in the agenda, so I proposed that we collectively review options for next steps and decide whether to stop and resume the conversation at a future point or continue. The team decided to complete the discussion in order to avoid retracing topics at a future meeting and to continue the momentum of the values initiative.

Had I acted unilaterally or supported a unilateral call to stop and move to the next topic, I would have contributed to the possibility that team members would feel that time had been wasted or, if a decision were made at that point, that the risk of members feeling that their concerns were not addressed would decrease commitment.

Use a decision-making rule that generates the level of commitment needed. Since we had agreed that the management team was the client and that everyone had an active role in the implementation, I proposed that consensus be reached, to which the team agreed. After completing the discussion, I asked each person individually whether he or she supported the project and plan; this gave everyone an additional opportunity to voice concerns and increase individual commitment and accountability for supporting the project. In the end, the team committed to the process proposed, and we also agreed on points where the project would be evaluated for continuation and how the evaluations would be conducted.

I was later told by my contact person that it was one of the few times that the team changed its agenda and that he was relieved that a decision was reached, while being fully discussed in a way that everyone could support it. Had I not raised the issue of how the decision was to be made, it is quite possible that team members would have deferred to the CEO, and this may have led to later frustration. Team members might have felt that they had little voice and the CEO might have felt that the team was not leading and making decisions.

Stage Four: Completing and Evaluating the Consultation

The project plan had the following steps:

- Generate relevant information by administering a values inventory and analyzing results to understand the priority values of the leadership team and of employees at all sites.
- Provide individual and group feedback to leadership.
- Work with the values development committee to form key developmental clusters of values, identify any developmental gaps in desired values, and propose wording of values statements.
- Present draft values statements and reasoning to the full management team for comments and modify as group chooses.
- Design a blueprint identifying training and development opportunities to help employees gain skills associated with values and develop mechanisms to reinforce behavior consistent with values, including a team component to performance reviews to reinforce teamwork.

Generating Relevant Information

Use specific examples and agree on what important words mean. Working from the assumption that the capability to behave in a certain manner is the result of having priority values (wanting to) and associated skills (being able to), it was critical to understand what priority values the organization held. I recommended the Hall-Tonna Values Inventory because it is a specific, actionable, developmental, descriptive values framework that has been validated under American Psychological Association guidelines. I felt that the framework was especially useful because it includes 125 human values, each of which has a standardized definition, so that we start with an agreed-on understanding of what each value means and avoid misunderstandings. For example, a number of team members felt that integrity was a key value, but there are many definitions of that term. Using this framework provided a way for everyone to have a common language with which to discuss values and avoid misunderstandings and protracted discussions of what terms meant.

A unilateral consultant often has a prescriptive framework (saying that a certain set of values is most important) or asks people what values are important but does not have them agree on what they mean. Not agreeing (or not having an agreed-on taxonomy) on what important words mean may have raised the risk that people misunderstand each other, that implementation steps don't address what people thought the values meant, and that extra time is required.

Providing Individual and Group Feedback to Leaders

Share all relevant information. In this step I provided individual feedback to each member of the management team (which included directors of the various facilities) on their priority values and presented summaries of aggregate priority values of the employees of each facility to the respective facility management teams. By providing this feedback, I was able to help each leader understand his or her priority values, see the overlap with the proposed values of the organization and the group that reported to them, and prepare them to discuss the priority organizational values. This gave them information to increase their understanding and on which to act.

For example, one leader reported that he felt that his staff spent too much time talking about their families and that he would cut short those conversations, but when he saw that that value of family/belonging was a very high priority for them (and not for him), he began to understand the importance of the value to his employees and that his lack of interest could be a missed opportunity to tap into their energy. When he changed his behavior and began inquiring into employees' families, he reported that their faces lit up and they seemed more energetic. In another case, one of the members of the leadership team became very quiet as I showed him that he had minimal overlap with the leadership team's values. At the conclusion of the session, he remarked that he now understood why he felt so stressed at work. Some months later, I happened to see him, and he told me that after gaining insights into what was important to him, he had left the organization for a job with a new company, one whose values better matched his. He couldn't remember being happier at work.

Had I acted unilaterally, I probably would have just proposed the action steps and shared the information that formed the basis for those steps. Had I not shared relevant information, I may have raised the risk of leaders' not being able to understand why certain values were being picked, and thereby lessening their commitment, and limited their ability to see how to effectively change their behavior.

Forming Values Clusters and Drafting Values Statements

Explain your reasoning and intent. During a meeting of the subgroup that had been charged with drafting the values statements (principles that encompassed a cluster of specific values), the CEO advocated for inclusion of a principle addressing innovation, even though it was not a cluster of values that was a high priority in the organization. He received negative reactions, and I asked what led him to advocate for innovation. In sharing his reasoning, he explained that without innovation, the organization would be a copier of others and not be the leading organization of their vision. On hearing what led him to advocate for innovation, the members of the subgroup acknowledged the importance of innovation and enthusiastically agreed to include it.

Had I not asked the CEO to explain his reasoning, I may have raised the risk that the focus would have been on positions (for example, "I want to include *innovation*" versus "I don't want it"). If the CEO prevailed, then others would feel little commitment, and if the CEO didn't prevail, then he might feel then they just don't understand.

Presenting the Draft Values Statements

Combining advocacy with inquiry. At the management team meeting, after the values clusters and statements were presented, I asked if anyone had questions or concerns. One member raised a concern about how they would ensure that everyone behaves consistently with the values. I showed sample sections of a matrix that included desired behaviors, training opportunities, and behavioral mechanisms (methods to reinforce behavior consistent with desired values, for example, including a team contribution component for the value of collaboration) for each cluster of values. She became excited that the organization would take specific actions to implement the values. Her concern was that the statement of values would simply be a proclamation and that no action would be taken.

Designing the Blueprint

Test assumptions and inferences. In identifying the training opportunities and behavioral mechanisms, I encouraged the team to test the assumptions of the various models that were proposed. As an illustration, one behavioral mechanism proposed to address safety issues was based on the hinge model of safety. This model can be thought of as a pyramid of safety issues, ranging in severity from incidents of unsafe behavior at the base of the pyramid, to incidents that require first aid, to incidents that result in injury, and finally, to incidents that result in fatalities at the top of the pyramid. A basic assumption in the model is that by reducing incidents of unsafe behavior, corresponding incidents requiring first aid, incidents resulting in injury, and incidents resulting in fatalities would also decrease—that a hinge effect would occur. We found a Fortune 500 manufacturer that had tested that assumption and, based on their data, found that reducing the incidents of unsafe behavior had little impact on more severe incidents.

Had I acted unilaterally, I probably would not have proposed testing assumptions of models, especially if I had proposed the model. Not testing this assumption could have had dire consequences, such as continuing to put employees at risk of serious injury or death.

Epilogue

Discuss undiscussable issues. As part of the implementation plan, the Facilitative Leader workshop was taught to support a cluster of values regarding more effective human relationships. In discussions with several members of the management team after the blueprint had been launched, I noted that at several points, they spoke about behaviors exhibited by the CEO that appeared inconsistent with some of the values. I inquired how they had responded to the behaviors and learned that they had not said anything about them. I inferred that this was an undiscussable topic and checked to see if it was. They concurred, and after I acknowledged the risks involved, I discussed the possible consequences of not intervening and also of being compassionate.

They decided that it was important to intervene, and we scripted several options for addressing the behavior, including the difficulty that they felt in raising the issue with the CEO. As related to me by one member of the team who subsequently had a conversation with the CEO, the CEO acknowledged that he could be more effective and invited this person to help him improve.

Had I not intervened, the undiscussable issue would probably have remained undiscussable and raised the likelihood that the team would feel that the CEO wasn't committed to the values initiative and that other issues also would remain undiscussed.

In addition, in evaluating the process, the management team helped me understand what worked well and what could be improved. So I also learned in the process and was able to improve the quality of my services. For example, I have added some supporting materials (for example, notes to explain terms in the feedback report) to the way that I conduct feedback.

FACILITATIVE CONSULTING

Using the Skilled Facilitator core values and ground rules during the course of a client engagement increases the likelihood that decisions will be of higher quality, that there will be increased commitment to follow through on action plans, and greater motivation to monitor and improve. The process requires sharing valid, relevant information to make the best decisions to generate internal commitment.

Deploying the blueprint to strengthen values alignment is interactive and requires that various units and levels in an organization use their collective intelligence and creativity to determine the most effective way to gain skills and change behavior. People's commitment and contributions led to the implementation of many actions that arose from piloting sections of the blueprint as well as lessons learned in preparation for future initiatives.

As a result of the initiative, I have developed a strong relationship with my client. Some of the manifestations of this relationship include periodic requests for advice, making joint presentations on how the values development process helped improve the organization's culture and organizational results, and a budget line for additional services.

The use of the Skilled Facilitator approach in consulting in this and other engagements has helped planning teams have conversations that lead to high-quality decisions, effective implementation, and mutual learning.

Chapter 60

Using the Skilled Facilitator Approach as a Parent

Peg Carlson

A FREQUENT COMMENT WE HEAR from people who have participated in the Skilled Facilitator or the Facilitative Leader workshop is, "This approach isn't just about facilitation or just applicable to work. This is about how to communicate effectively with other people in all areas of your life." We completely agree. One of the things that has been most gratifying, and sometimes most challenging, for me is practicing the Skilled Facilitator approach with my young children. I've found it to be a wonderful and humbling practice ground: wonderful because the payoff is so significant in terms of improving parent-child relationships and teaching these skills to the next generation; humbling because these are the people who are most adept at eliciting my unilateral tendencies and distinguishing between rhetorical and genuine inquiry!

See Chapter Five, "Ground Rules for Effective Groups," page 61, and Chapter Twenty-Six, "Ground Rules Without the Mutual Learning Model Are Like Houses Without Foundations," page 217.

TEACHING THE DIAGNOSIS-INTERVENTION CYCLE TO MY CHILDREN

As any parent knows, very young children are already capable of making inferences. It's part of all human beings' drive to make meaning of their experiences and surroundings. In Skilled Facilitator terms, children are adept at sharing their inferences (step 5) without necessarily sharing what they observed that led them to that inference (step 4).

See the Ladder of Inference sidebar in Chapter Five, "Ground Rules for Effective Groups," page 61.

I believe children can learn to use the ground rules and the diagnosis-intervention cycle fairly easily because the mutual learning approach is so consistent with a child's natural curiosity about the world. It is our job as parents to help them extend that natural curiosity to the realm of interpersonal interactions. Without using jargon, I've taken advantage of teachable moments to help my children become aware of what they saw or heard that led them to make an inference.

I believe children can learn to use the ground rules and the diagnosis-intervention cycle fairly easily because the mutual learning approach is so consistent with a child's natural curiosity about the world.

See Chapter Four, "Understanding What Guides Your Behavior," page 33; Chapter Five, "Ground Rules for Effective Groups," page 61; and Chapter Six, "The Diagnosis-Intervention Cycle," page 69.

Conversations about things that happened at school often provide rich material for separating observations from inferences:

> When my son Jacob came home from school one day and reported, "Daniel is mad at me," I resisted the temptation to say, "What did you do to make him mad?" (which would just confirm his inference and add one of my own). Instead, I asked, "What did Daniel say or do that makes you think he's mad at you?" By asking this question, I was attempting to teach Jacob to make a distinction between the directly observable behavior (Daniel's words and actions) and his inference about what his friend's behavior means. After reflecting for a minute, Jacob replied, "Well, he's been playing with Gabriel and Christopher most of the time at recess. They're playing some kind of Spiderman game." I responded with a question to help Jacob make a link between the behavior he observed and the inference he made: "And you think he's mad at you because he's playing with them instead of you?" Jacob brightened and said, "Well, no, actually, they asked me to play with them. I'm just not very interested in Spiderman. Huh, I guess he's probably not mad at me." And he skipped off.

Of course, not all inferences turn out to be misunderstandings. We've also had conversations where Jacob had tested and confirmed his inference, and our discussion turned to what he might do differently next time (step 6 in the cycle).

I had a remarkable experience recently helping my four-year-old daughter use the diagnosis-intervention cycle—remarkable both because of her age and because of the content of the conversation:

> While we were driving home from preschool one afternoon, Lena suddenly piped up from her car seat, "I think Gail asked us to share our penis and our vagina today at share time." (Gail is one of Lena's preschool teachers, a warm and grandmotherly type; "share" is their show-and-tell time.) Concealing my surprise—I was glad that I was driving and she was sitting behind me—I replied noncommittally, "Hmmm. Do you remember exactly what she said?" I could almost hear the gears turning as Lena thought for a few moments, and then she said, "Well, when it was time for share, Gail said, 'It's time to go to your cubbies and get your you-know-what.'" (A disclaimer:

we do not refer to genitalia as "you-know-what" around our house; however, Lena had heard her eight-year-old brother and his buddies use this term and had apparently deduced its meaning.)

I felt my laughter bubbling up, but I stifled it because I didn't want Lena to feel foolish—this was turning into a terrific teachable moment. We talked about what the expression "you know what" can mean, and why Gail may have said this when she saw a group of preschoolers who were eager to start their share time. I told her, "You did a great job remembering exactly what Gail said. That makes it easier for us to figure out what people meant—or to go back and ask them what they meant if we can't figure it out."

In thinking about this exchange later, I was struck by how differently the conversation could have unfolded if I had gone up my own ladder of inference and asked different, more leading questions. Because of my training as a facilitator and because I had absolutely no concern about Gail's behavior with Lena or any of her classmates, it was easy for me to stay in a mutual learning mode. But what if I didn't have the skills to help Lena trace where her inferences had come from or had the skills but didn't use them because her statement had triggered a hot button for me that reflected a concern about her child care situation? It would have been easy to ask a question like, "Did she touch you?" Lena almost certainly would have answered yes to this question, as Gail gives the children hugs, helps them tie their shoes, and is close to them in other ways. It was not hard to imagine a scenario where I would have come away convinced that something had happened, all due to an alternative line of questioning that took Lena's inference as a jumping-off point. Although the conversation was hilarious on one level, it was also a sobering reminder of stories in the news about alleged abuse at day care centers and just how difficult it can be to determine what actually happened once adults—even loving, well-meaning adults—begin to ask questions that are based on their own inferences.

REWARDING CHILDREN FOR USING FACILITATIVE SKILLS

Although I haven't explicitly taught the ground rules to my children, I've been pleased to see how often they use them naturally in their own conversations, and my husband and I try to let them know when we see them acting consistently with the Skilled Facilitator approach—for example:

> Although I haven't explicitly taught the ground rules to my children, I've been pleased to see how often they use them naturally in their own conversations, and my husband and I try to let them know when we see them acting consistently with the Skilled Facilitator approach.

One morning when Jacob was having breakfast before a day at summer camp, my husband, Andrew, asked him, "Were you warm enough yesterday?" Jacob replied, "Yes. Why do you ask?" Andrew explained that it had been an unusually cool week, and Jacob had been dressed only in shorts and a T-shirt. Andrew (who happened to be taking the Skilled Facilitator workshop that very week) smilingly caught my eye, and we complimented Jacob on how nicely he had asked his father to explain the reasoning behind his question.

DECREASING CONFLICT WITH FACILITATION SKILLS

I believe the core values and ground rules sometimes need to be modified in their use with young children. For example, it's not always possible for children to have the valid information they need to make free and informed choices because of their lack of life experience. It is part of a parent's job to give children opportunities to develop their decision-making skills *and* to judge which choices a child is capable of making. Even with these restrictions, however, I think there are more similarities than differences in how children and adults respond to the core values and ground rules. Whether you are dealing with children or employees, unilateral commands are likely to result in compliance at best (or rebellion at worst). One example of this from our family is the use of the ground rules with some bathroom behavior:

> We often want our daughter to use the bathroom before leaving the house. Direct orders to do so often lead to resistance and frustrating, seemingly pointless battles. What has worked better is to check the inference from her initial refusal that she doesn't feel that she has to go, acknowledge the validity of that feeling, and then explain, "Sometimes, for children, your body isn't quite ready to tell you when you need to go. Are you willing to just try sitting on the toilet and seeing if something comes out?" This request, linked to our explanation of reasoning, meets with far less resistance, perhaps because we are not asking her to do something impossible—asking her to go to the bathroom when she does not have to go—but simply to try something out without a predetermined result.

Another example of how we've used the ground rules to reduce conflict comes from our son's piano practice time. The expectation that he will practice piano every day is not negotiable, but the way he approaches it is negotiable. Understandably, he enjoys playing more when he has some freedom to choose the order in which he will practice his week's music, but he also gets frustrated when he tackles the difficult (and often more interesting) pieces first and cannot play them as well as he would like.

My efforts to help him haven't been successful when I've used easing-in strategies (for example, "How about if you do the scales first, then play the longer pieces?"). He immediately spots this for the rhetorical inquiry it is and continues doing it as he was before. However, if we jointly design a way to test disagreements and I separate my advocacy from my inquiry more clearly (for example, "I think it will be easier and more enjoyable for you to play your longer pieces if you've warmed up your fingers first on the scales. It looks as if you disagree. Is that right? Would you be willing to try what I'm suggesting for the rest of this week, and if you don't feel that it's helping your practice, you can go back to the way you've been doing it?"), the conversations have been much more constructive. If the goal is internal commitment, the ground rules are the tools you can use to cultivate an approach that doesn't require constant external monitoring to ensure its success.

USING THE SKILLED FACILITATOR APPROACH TO HELP CHILDREN MAKE SENSE OF THE WORLD

See Chapter Twenty-Two, "Some Tips for Diagnosing at the Speed of Conversation," page 195.

Children have the Beginner's Mind that adults strive for. To young children, literally anything is possible because magic and reality coexist. They also tend to believe that they are the center of the universe. These lead to two very important consequences for parents:

- It is critical to solicit the relevant information and check our inferences from their behavior when working on difficult issues, because their world has the potential to be very different from our own. Jointly designing solutions that work in their reality—for example, concocting a magic monster spray that chases those very "real" monsters from under the bed—generates great internal commitment.
- Children do make inferences based on their egoistic worldview. It is incumbent on us to explain our reasoning and to share relevant information so that the attributions they make are the correct ones, ones that confer responsibility or free them from responsibility where appropriate.

My husband and I believe that using the core values and ground rules as parents will help us raise our children to be responsible, compassionate members of society. We're still in the early stages of our journey, but we feel that the approach has greatly benefited our family life thus far, and we look forward to learning with, and from, our children in the years ahead.

Chapter 61

Running for Office in a Unilaterally Controlling World

Steve Kay

WHEN I TRAIN PEOPLE on the elements of the Skilled Facilitator model or coach people in its use, one consistent area of question, sometimes voiced as an underlying concern or source of resistance, is about "being a mutual learner in a unilaterally controlling world." In one form or another, the question—and the underlying concern—is about the risk to oneself when providing valid information to people of uncertain motivation. "Oh, I can't say that," a person will say in response to a suggestion, and then explain that the other person will be offended or unhappy with the information and, if in a position of power, might cause problems in return.

As a trainer or a coach, I have found it relatively easy to assure people that acting in a way consistent with the Skilled Facilitator model is not only the right thing to do, it is the most effective thing to do. It's the right thing to do, I would say, because the values underlying the model are about respect, openness, and fairness. Especially if it's a hard message, the other person deserves to know your thoughts so she can make her own informed judgments about actions to take. And it's the effective thing to do, I would say, because unilateral control actions have unintended negative consequences—certainly in the long run and often in the shor run.

Then I decided to run for public office: an at-large position on the Lexington-Fayette (Kentucky) Urban County Council. I found myself wondering if I could follow my own advice. Suddenly everything was not so easy. "Politics ain't bean bag," politicians are fond of quoting after some particularly nasty bit of campaign business, and many of my political colleagues and advisers were happy to repeat the message in one form or another. The message—sometimes delivered in its baldest form, sometimes delivered subtly and indirectly—goes like this: "Don't run if you don't want to win. If you want to win, you have to play by the unofficial rules, which include deviousness, deception, and deceit. This is a campaign, conducted under the rules of war. Everybody else will be playing by these rules, and if you don't, you can't win. Don't be naive. Don't be a fool." I thanked these people for their advice and let them know that I thought there was another way to conduct a campaign.

From the many challenges that quickly came in operating the campaign according to the values of internal commitment, valid information, and free and informed choice, I have chosen one example in each of three categories: taking a position, campaign strategy, and fundraising.

TAKING A POSITION

Polls of Lexington voters consistently show that 25 to 30 percent identify traffic congestion as Lexington's number one problem. No other single issue ranks as high, nor does any other issue consistently rank in the top three. As a result, candidates for public office usually include traffic as one of the issues they care about deeply and will address. Some say they have a plan. Privately, most people in office or seeking office concede that Lexington has outgrown its road system and, because the county and its surrounding counties continue to grow at a fairly rapid rate, admit that traffic is likely to get worse rather than better. Many will also concede privately that compared to the neighboring cities of Louisville and Cincinnati or compared to larger cities such as Atlanta or Chicago, Lexington doesn't have much of a traffic problem.

Following the mutual learning model, however, here is what I chose to say: **"I understand that many people view traffic as a serious problem. I am interested in working on ways to improve traffic flow and believe that it is possible to make marginal improvements. But short of a radical change in habits and attitudes—people giving up their cars for walking, biking, and mass transit—I see no easy solution."**

This may or may not win votes, but at least it doesn't contribute to the belief that there is an easy way to improve traffic conditions, if only the fools at city hall were competent enough to do the right thing.

If I followed the unilateral control line about how to conduct a campaign, I would adopt a unilateral control approach and say what other candidates do about traffic. Of course, I wouldn't reveal my reasoning and intent (Ground Rule Four), because if I did, it would sound something like this: "I don't think traffic is much of a problem, not compared to issues of growth or pay raises for city employees. But since polls show that almost 30 percent of you think traffic is Lexington's number one problem and since I want your vote, I'm going to say that traffic is a real problem and that I have an idea about how to fix it."

See Chapter Four, "Understanding What Guides Your Behavior," page 33.

Following the mutual learning model, however, here is what I chose to say: **"I understand that many people view traffic as a serious problem. I am interested in working on ways to improve traffic flow and believe that it is possible to make marginal improvements. But short of a radical change in habits and attitudes—people giving up their cars for walking, biking, and mass transit—I see no easy solution."**

This may or may not win votes, but at least it doesn't contribute to the belief that there is an easy way to improve traffic conditions, if only the fools at city hall were competent enough to do the right thing.

CAMPAIGN STRATEGY

The race for the three at-large seats on the council is unusual in one important way: people have three votes. That is, the three seats are filled every four years from one pool of candidates, and each person can vote for up to three of the candidates in the pool. This leads most campaigns to adopt a covert strategy of encouraging "bullet voting," which means urging voters to use only one of their three votes available. The reasoning behind the strategy runs like this: since the top three vote-getters will win seats, a vote for anyone other than one's prime candidate could hurt that candidate. That is, one's favorite candidate could be edged out by the one vote the voter cast for his or her second or third choice. The strategy is covert because no campaign wants to be overtly in the undemocratic posture of urging its partisans to disregard the two other seats that will be filled and not participate in choosing the best people for those seats.

If articulated, the covert strategy would sound something like this: "I care more about winning a seat for myself than I do about ensuring that we have the three best at-large council people possible, so I urge you to vote for me and not vote for anyone else." I chose to urge people to use all three of their votes for the three best candidates.

FUNDRAISING

The fundraising gurus offer consistent advice about seeking campaign contributions. For telephone solicitations (the preferred mode for any but the smallest contributions), the candidate makes the call, asks for a specific amount at the absolute highest end of what is reasonable for the person being called, and doesn't hang up without getting a solid commitment of both amount and when it will be sent. The intent is to put potential donors on the spot and not give them the opportunity to consider what they really want to do.

If verbalized, the strategy would sound something like this: "I know you hate to say no to someone in person and you hate not to meet people's expectations, so I'm going to push for a commitment from you that is more than you would likely make otherwise." Anyone who gives is targeted for further solicitations unless she reaches the maximum allowed by law. Rather than use this strategy, I chose to do no direct telephone solicitations. I also tried my best to keep people off lists for fundraising events or further mail appeals if they had responded to my initial fundraising letter.

It's possible to run for office in a unilaterally controlling world using mutual learning values, but it takes a concerted effort. The grain, oriented to winning at all costs and short-term benefits, runs the other way.

It's possible to run for office in a unilaterally controlling world using mutual learning values, but it takes a concerted effort. The grain, oriented to winning at all costs and short-term benefits, runs the other way.

A HOPEFUL FINISH

I needed to finish in the top six in the primary. I finished seventh. Here are the vote totals for the twelve candidates, in order of total votes, with my vote in bold type:

15,574
14,944
14,372
12,804
10,321
10,288
10,177
9,409
8,054
4,546
2,526
1,711

Not bad for a first run in a large pool filled with a number of people with name recognition and well-financed campaigns. And although my view is certainly anything but objective, I believe it is fair to say that the vast preponderance of evidence indicates that people appreciated being treated with respect in a political campaign. Many people said that my campaign raised their hopes about political life and increased their willingness to participate. Many who volunteered for my campaign had never joined a campaign before or had not worked on one in many years. And many stated their interest in having me run again and working for me if I do. I probably will.

Chapter 62

Using the Facilitative Leader Approach in Public Office

Verla Insko

"SHE IS SO NAIVE, we can eat her alive," my assistant reported overhearing in the halls of the North Carolina General Assembly.[1] "What did you do to earn that reputation?" she asked.

What I had done as a representative in the North Carolina General Assembly was *share all relevant information* in a committee debate, including information in opposition to the point I was trying to make, just as I had learned to do in the Group Facilitation and Consultation Workshop I had attended in 1996 (a predecessor of the Skilled Facilitator Workshop).

I was a new representative in the state legislature but not to elected office or to contentious public debates. I had served in two elected offices and on one appointed public board in my local community. All three groups dealt with issues that could and did pit citizen groups against each other.

Despite my assistant's remarks I decided to forge ahead, using the ground rules I had learned in the workshop in my role as a state legislator.

See Chapter Five, "Ground Rules for Effective Groups," page 61.

Over the next four years, acting as a facilitative leader, I helped a diverse group of stakeholders (consumers, advocates, public and private providers, and state-level administrators) build a consensus position on the use of seclusion and restraints in state-supported residential facilities; I caught the attention of the Speaker of the House who appointed me as House chair of the Legislative Oversight Committee on Mental Health; and I co-led a year-long process among those same stakeholders to write a bill to reform the state's mental health system.

USING THE GROUND RULES TO CRAFT MENTAL HEALTH LEGISLATION

The opportunity to work on the seclusion and restraints bill was pure serendipity. When the House Committee on Health couldn't resolve the differences among stakeholders, the chair referred it to a legislative research committee (LRC) that would meet between sessions. The Speaker appointed me to chair the committee.

At the first committee meeting, emotions were high, stakeholders were entrenched in their positions, a few people dominated the debate, and no one was problem-solving. However, each group articulated something close to a shared vision: they wanted what was best for this vulnerable population, most often referred to as "patient center planning," and they agreed the state had limited resources.

Using this shared vision as a starting point for focusing on interests rather than positions, I found I could get a discussion back on track by asking, "How will this help us build a more patient-centered system with existing or similar resources?" Gradually group members began asking this question of each other. Over the next few weeks, they developed a more collaborative process, became more focused, and gave up distracting strategies such as jumping from one topic to another or changing the subject. By stating the unresolved issue in terms of the shared vision, how the issue can be resolved in the best interest of the clients, the whole group eventually dealt with all of these previously avoided topics.

See Ground Rule Five in Chapter Five, "Ground Rules for Effective Groups," page 61, and Chapter Twenty-Six, "Ground Rules Without the Mutual Learning Model Are Like Houses Without Foundations," page 217. Also see Chapter Sixteen, "Helping Group Members Focus on Interests Rather Than Positions," page 145.

The turning point for finishing the bill came when the stakeholders agreed to jointly develop and test possible solutions. When I realized that many of the unresolved issues had objective answers that had not been assessed, I asked the stakeholders to provide data to back up their proposed solutions and use each other's data to test those proposals. The advocates group brought information on what other states were doing; providers documented the added costs of training and staff turnover in North Carolina. They pooled the information, and both sides began moving forward. In a few weeks of tense but productive work, they drafted a bill that passed in the next session.

See Ground Rule Seven in Chapter Five, "Ground Rules for Effective Groups," page 61, and Chapter Twenty-Six, "Ground Rules Without the Mutual Learning Model Are Like Houses Without Foundations," page 217.

As a result of my work on the LRC, the Speaker appointed me as House chair of the Joint Legislative Oversight Committee on Mental Health, Developmental Disabilities and Substance Abuse, a newly created committee comprising eight state senators and eight state representatives. Based on a major report from the state auditor, the charge to the committee was to develop and oversee reform of the state's system of services for these three disability groups. The Senate chair was Steve Metcalf, a former county manager who shared my interest in working collaboratively with stakeholders and in reaching consensus. Although the stakeholders were the same as for the seclusion and restraints bill, the stakes were much higher. Provider groups believed the public mental health agencies were denying them access to clients in order to build empires, public sector professionals believed private providers wanted to deal directly with the state and weaken or eliminate public mental health agencies, and consumers were caught in the middle. Trust was a major issue: groups blamed each other for failure, and everyone wanted someone else to change. But once again, the groups were in agreement on a basic issue: the system needed reform.

Senator Metcalf and I decided to cochair the Governance Subcommittee and invited stakeholder groups to nominate members. Although the Governance Committee did not establish formal ground rules, Metcalf and I articulated and put into a memo several expectations that gradually became the practice: have complete and valid information, stay focused, jointly design solutions, and explain reasons behind statements and questions. In one case, when I asked local mental health groups why they sometimes did not pay service providers promptly, they stated that late payments were not a problem. Yet when I explained that I was trying to determine what they needed to solve this problem, they were clear about their cash flow problems and lack of expertise in reviewing claims.

Following another ground rule, we asked the group to agree on what certain words meant and found great confusion around the terms *case management, care management, case coordination,* and *service coordination.* The terms *utilization management, utilization review,* and *quality assurance* created similar confusion and disagreement. When stakeholders realized they were using terms to refer to different functions, they quickly agreed on the need for clear definitions and consistent use.

See Ground Rule Three in Chapter Five, "Ground Rules for Effective Groups," page 61, and Chapter Twenty-Six, "Ground Rules Without the Mutual Learning Model Are Like Houses Without Foundations," page 217.

Through use of the ground rules, especially sharing all relevant information with everyone who would listen, we achieved a level of transparency that promoted trust between legislators and stakeholders and gradually among the stakeholders themselves. Parties dropped their guarded and defensive responses and eventually crafted joint solutions that worked for all. During the next year, this group and the Joint Legislative Oversight Committee drafted the mental health reform bill. It passed the General Assembly and was signed into law in October 2001.

Now, as I write this in the summer of 2003, more than three years after hearing the auditors' report, we are on schedule for the five-year rollout of mental health reform, and we have at least the beginnings of a new culture. The pervasive distrust and backbiting are being replaced by communication, collaboration, and mutual respect. This year when Senator Metcalf and I ran another bill to help implement a piece of reform, one of the provider lobbyists said to me, "I have turned over a new leaf; I am going to help solve this problem. I'm one of the good guys."

GROUND RULES AT WORK FOR ELECTED OFFICIALS

The process used in these two examples was clearly not pure facilitation or entirely consistent with a facilitative leader approach. Stakeholder groups had no input into who would chair the committees, they had little to say about when or how they would do their work, and they did not formally approve of the final version of either bill. However, many essential components of the Group Effectiveness Model existed, and Senator Metcalf and I successfully applied several ground rules.

See Chapter Two, "The Group Effectiveness Model," page 15, and Chapter Fifteen, "Using the Group Effectiveness Model," page 135.

From the organizational context of the Group Effectiveness Model, both groups had a shared vision, a supportive culture, and excellent technical support from legislative staff. As for group structure, we were careful to select appropriate members who had time to work on the problem. By working from an agreed-on agenda, sharing relevant information with all parties, and creating a "parking lot" for other important issues, we kept the group process focused on problem solving, communication, and decision making. By being available to meet on a one-to-one basis with stakeholders and to travel to meetings in their local communities, we paid close attention to the needs of individual group members. At the same time, we built group identity around the joint challenge of improving the system for the clients.

In the political arena, elected officials belong to many groups simultaneously. To apply the ground rules effectively, they have to be clear about which group is most important at any given time. That is fairly easy to do with nonpartisan policy issues such as mental health reform and public education for purely partisan issues such as redistricting or with ideological issues such as tax policy, abortion, and prayer in schools. It is more difficult for legislators who are out of step with the voters back home on some important issue. Does a legislator vote to raise taxes to save services if the tax vote is sure to fail and an opponent back home is waiting with negative ads? At the very least, a legislator can use the ground rules to build a reputation for openness and fairness with colleagues and district voters.

The ground rules can also be difficult to apply within the party, as progressive and conservative factions may form groups competing for bargaining power on an issue. Sometimes membership between groups is very fluid: a progressive Democrat might also be a member of the Black Caucus or the Women's Caucus and might shift identification from one group to another depending on the issue or where she can gain the most personal power.

Regardless of the basis for the formation of a group, it will be more effective if members share information, explain the reasons behind their actions, and seek consensus decisions. Even in highly partisan settings, elected officials can be more effective if they agree on important words, keep the discussion focused, use examples, explain their reasoning (instead of taking cheap shots), and test assumptions.

In my experience, the ground rules are best applied by elected officials when addressing divisive but nonideological public policy issues and they have enough time, adequate technical support, and group expertise to accomplish the work.

> In my experience, the ground rules are best applied by elected officials when addressing divisive but nonideological public policy issues and they have enough time, adequate technical support, and group expertise to accomplish the work.

At the end of my seventh year in the North Carolina General Assembly and into the third year of reform, my effectiveness ratings continue to push toward the top, and both Senator Metcalf and I have received numerous awards for our work in mental health. Perhaps the best evidence that our efforts are paying off came from the executive director of the North Carolina Psychological Association when she recently said, "People from other states can't believe it when I tell them that here in North Carolina, we all work together."

Note

1. The North Carolina General Assembly is a part-time legislature with 120 state representatives and 50 state senators. As this is written, Democrats control the Senate; the House of Representatives has been closely divided between Republicans and Democrats since 1994.

Afterword

Some Important Lessons

Roger Schwarz
Anne Davidson

As WE REFLECT on the chapters that make up *The Skilled Facilitator Fieldbook,* some key lessons emerge. These transcend any particular chapter or part of the book and in some ways reflect the essence of the approach itself. Here is a brief summary of some of the important learning from our own experiences and those of our clients and colleagues.

CHANGING HOW YOU THINK IS FUNDAMENTAL

The power of the Skilled Facilitator approach lies in changing how you think. Yes, the tools and techniques of the approach are necessary, but they are not sufficient for creating and sustaining fundamental change. In fact, when people get stuck trying to use the approach, it's often because they are applying the Skilled Facilitator tools with a unilateral control model mind-set.

When people start to shift their thinking to the mutual learning model, the Skilled Facilitator approach becomes more natural and the tools easier to use. With increased curiosity, transparency, and compassion, it's easier to find the words that convey your meaning. And others are usually more forgiving even when you don't. In short, a mutual learning intent comes through even if your words are imprecise.

CHANGE BEGINS WITH YOURSELF

The place to start using this approach is with yourself. You can't change anyone else; you can only create conditions that make it more likely that they will choose to change too. By learning and modeling the approach, you enable others to see what results are possible. When you establish a clear purpose and process for a conversation, share your reasoning and test your assumptions, for example, you can demonstrate ways that a conversation becomes more productive. In the process, you often elicit a surprisingly different response from others, altering unproductive past patterns. When others see what is possible, they can make a more informed choice about whether they want to learn and change as well. Your intent may be to change an entire department, organization, or service system, but that change comes about one person at a time as each commits to thinking and behaving differently.

THERE ARE MANY WAYS TO GROW CHANGE

When it comes to using the Skilled Facilitator and the Facilitative Leader approaches to create significant change in groups and organizations, there is not one right place to start. We have started at the top and worked down through an organization, we have started near the bottom and worked up, and we have started with small pockets that have spread to larger areas of the organization.

Some clients feel more comfortable with a top-down approach, starting at the most senior level possible and then cascading change down to lower organizational levels. Their thinking is that if the top-level executives understand the approach, it will make it easier for everyone below them to behave differently. Sometimes this assessment is accurate. Other times, change that starts from the top is more strongly resisted because people below the executive tier do not feel involved in or committed to the change. The same dilemma about creating commitment can develop when the change is middle out or bottom up: whatever group initiates a shift in core values and behaviors tends to be most committed. Others become fully engaged and committed only as they experience the power of thinking and acting differently and only as those initiating the change behave consistently enough with the core values to create some credibility.

What we have learned is that the ideal place to start is where people are interested in learning either because of some pain they are feeling or because of opportunities they sense. Our experience is that the more people make an informed free choice to learn the approach, the more likely they are to practice it, model it for others, and sustain their learning. This is a case of going slow to go fast.

THE CHANGE PROCESS IS NOT LINEAR

Whether you are changing yourself or helping to change a group or organization, the process of fundamental change is not linear. In a way, it's deceptive. There is an early period in which people experience increased effectiveness using their new mind-set and skills, even though they feel like awkward beginners. But at some point, people encounter (or rather reencounter) theory-in-use issues—their own and other's—that lead to plateaus and setbacks. It is the ability to accept feedback from others and to reflect on the theory-in-use issues that cause these setbacks that determine whether people continue to deepen their skills and sustain new behaviors. This process seems cyclical; a new level of skill leads to addressing more fundamental theory-in-use issues, so that with each successive, and successful, cycle, the ability to create mutual learning outcomes increases.

THINKING AND ACTING SYSTEMICALLY CREATES LASTING RESULTS

One learning that runs throughout the *Fieldbook* is that you can achieve and sustain more powerful results by thinking and acting systemically. We see repeatedly how focusing on only one part of an issue creates fixes that lead to more problems.

An area that provides significant leverage for change is focusing on the underlying structure that gives rise to problems. Just as the physical structure of a boat determines where and how it can move through the water, the social structure of conversations, groups, and organizations determines what they can create. Change the structure of the conversation by operating from a new set of core values and assumptions, and new results are possible. Change the structure of a group by naming and changing the defensive routine of unilaterally protecting the boss by not disagreeing with him or her, and you change the quality of decisions.

Part of thinking and acting systemically means examining group and organization policies and practices. These often have embedded in them elements of the unilateral control model. Unexamined policies may place invisible limits on what is possible. If a policy dictates, for example, that critical performance data must remain confidential, it is hard to design a way for teams to become more accountable or self-managing.

The Skilled Facilitator approach is itself a systemic way of addressing systemic issues. The power of the approach comes from integrating the various elements, such as the Group Effectiveness Model, the mutual learning model, the ground rules, and the diagnosis-intervention cycle. Using all the components of the Skilled Facilitator approach allows groups to identify structural elements, develop valid information about how they interact, and design collaborative, high-leverage ways to improve the way the system works.

MAKE THE APPROACH YOUR OWN

It's common for people just learning our approach to say that it feels unnatural. Some people describe it as sounding mechanical; others say it feels as if someone else has inhabited their body (or at least their mind and vocal chords). We've learned that as you begin to develop any new ability, it is natural to feel unnatural. Learning the Skilled Facilitator approach is like learning a new dance or a new language; it just does not flow at first.

Part of the unnatural feeling may also come from others' reactions to your trying your new skills. If you begin to act differently, others are also faced with changing their way of responding to you. Your new behavior and their responses to it can leave you feeling as if you are in new territory—which you are. It's unsettling at times, but it's also full of new possibilities.

The unnaturalness fades as you make the approach your own. This includes getting comfortable (or at least more comfortable) with a new way of thinking. It also includes experimenting with language—finding words and phrases that sound like you, not like you imitating someone else or what you read in the book. It's different for each of us; what sounds natural coming out of our mouths may sound strange coming out of yours, and vice versa. There are different ways to put the core values and assumptions of the approach into words. Experiment until you sound like a mutual learning version of yourself.

MAKE A CHOICE ABOUT HOW EXTENSIVELY TO USE THE APPROACH

As with many other things, what you get out of the Skilled Facilitator approach depends on what you put into it and when and where you use it. Over the years, we have found that people who use the approach do so in one of three ways. Some people see the approach as a tool to add to their tool kits. Like a tool, they see the approach as something they use in a particular situation—for example, when people disagree. Other people see the approach as a way to guide their thinking and acting in a particular role—when they are a facilitator, leader, consultant, trainer, or coach. They see it as a way to improve their effectiveness in a particular setting, usually at work. Finally, there are those who see the approach as a way to be in the world. They use the core values, assumptions, and ground rules as a guide for how they want to interact with people, whether at work, home, play, or in the community. Essentially, the approach becomes part of their approach to life. We (the four editors) fit into this last category.

While it would be presumptuous to suggest that the last category is the right choice for everyone, we've learned that people's skills and effectiveness usually expand as they move from considering the approach as a tool to considering it as a life choice. Partly, this is a function of the commitment they make; the commitment to using the approach in all of one's interactions is simply greater than the commitment people make when they see the approach as a tool with a specific utility. But the increased skill development is also a function of the additional opportunities for learning. When someone thinks of the approach as a way to be in the world, every interaction is an opportunity for practice. Every conversation can produce a critical insight that changes behavior across numerous situations.

We've learned that it's important to consciously choose how extensively you want to use the approach. With your conscious choice comes commitment to learn and practice. Without conscious choice, it is easy to put away your Skilled Facilitator materials and never integrate them into any aspect of your work or life. Also, using these new skills can feel risky. We often advocate moving toward dilemmas, risk, and fear. Paradoxically, more is often gained by moving toward difficulty than away from it. However, we believe only you can choose the level of potential risk and learning that is right for you at any particular moment in your life.

LEARN WITH OTHERS

A central theme throughout the *Fieldbook* is that it is easier to learn the approach and continue developing your skills with others. Together, systems thinking and theory-in-use work repeatedly show that we are typically unaware of the values and assumptions that guide our behavior and the unintended consequences they create. We just don't see the gaps in our thinking and behavior that others can see. By engaging with people who understand the theory behind the approach and can give us skillful feedback about our own behavior, we learn to identify the gaps in our thinking. Over time, many people develop internal monitors that help them identify their own unilateral patterns. But it is always helpful, no matter how long one practices this approach, to have learning partners who can help us see what we are missing, can ask provocative questions, and will practice with us for difficult interactions.

If you know of others who are learning and practicing the Skilled Facilitator approach, we encourage you to explore ways that you can learn together. If you are the first in your network, consider introducing it to others who might be interested in learning with you.

And so we have come back to where we began the *Fieldbook:* the idea of learning in groups to increase effectiveness. Groups form because they can do what individuals alone cannot. Just as you can help groups increase their effectiveness, you can use groups to increase your own. It's worth noting that the foundation of the Skilled Facilitator approach is a model of *mutual* learning. The assumption behind the model is that all of us see some things and miss others; all of us are both teachers and learners. We hope that our lessons enrich your learning journey and that you will make us part of your extended learning community.

Acknowledgments

THIS BOOK IS THE FRUIT OF MANY PEOPLE'S EFFORTS, and we thank them. Our colleagues and clients generously shared their successes, challenges, and questions stemming from their experiences with the Skilled Facilitator approach. Theirs are voices of experience that make this not only a book for the field but also a book from the field.

Some who helped make this book possible are represented as authors or coauthors of the sixty-two chapters. Many more supported us behind the scenes. Our clients enabled us to learn with them. They invited us into their organizations and gave us their time and ideas. They asked insightful, provocative questions during our workshops, consultations, and coaching. They openly shared their struggles and successes. Many critiqued our work and our writing, helping us clarify our thinking and our teaching. Although we cannot acknowledge each of them by name here, we are deeply indebted to their contributions.

Leslie Stephen, our development editor, and Byron Schneider, our senior editor at Jossey-Bass, provided patient guidance. Byron supported and directed our work through three long years of development. He introduced us to Leslie Stephen at just the right moment in our project. Leslie's sage editorial advice brought an untidy mass into a sound structure. She took on the daunting task of facilitating facilitators as we went through the inevitable struggles of winnowing numerous materials and ideas gathered from a wide array of sources and experiences into something coherent. Leslie, thank you for the hours and hours of conference calls, the hundreds of e-mails, and most of all for sharing your extraordinary talents with us. Jeff Wyneken, editorial production manager at Jossey-Bass, worked with us to ensure a functional and attractive book design. We also owe special thanks to Susan Williams and Julianna Gustafson of Jossey-Bass who got us started on this project in 2001 by listening to, encouraging, and helping to shape our vision for a Skilled Facilitator fieldbook.

Some of our colleagues at Roger Schwarz & Associates supported us throughout this project. We are grateful to Terrie Hutaff, Gail Young, and Tom Moore for allowing us to share their stories and for their advice. Toward the end of the project, Matt Beane took on a key role that freed up our time for writing and editing.

Six people reviewed our first manuscript draft in its entirety, and their feedback led us to restructure the book. Thanks to Colleen Baker, Peter Casale, Jeff Koeze, Dick McMahon, Annette Shaked, and Robert Tobias for their insightful critiques.

Finally, we owe an enormous debt to our families and friends who supported us and sacrificed for us during this project. We are grateful to you for helping us restore our balance and a sense of perspective. Roger thanks his wife, Kathleen Rounds; his children Noah and Hannah; and his sister, Dale Schwarz. Anne thanks Allein, Susan, Gerry, Laura, and Don and the instructors at Yoga for Life in Dilworth, located in Charlotte, North Carolina. Peg thanks her husband, Andrew, for learning and embracing the Skilled Facilitator approach, and for his thoughtful advice and timely editorial assistance from beginning to end. Sue thanks Matthias, Dale, Deb, and Diane.

R.S., A.D., P.C., S.M.

Index

C

E

F

G

H

N

O

T

U

V

W

Y

Z

About Roger Schwarz & Associates

Roger Schwarz & Associates is a leadership and organization development consulting firm dedicated to helping people think and act differently so they can improve their business results and relationships—often in ways that they didn't think possible.

Clients work with us when:

- They've identified an issue that is reducing their group's effectiveness. Sometimes they have discussed this issue in the group, and sometimes they haven't.
- They're starting an important new effort—a new project, a new team, a merger or acquisition—and want to ensure that everyone involved will work together effectively.
- The way they work together is preventing them from achieving the results they want.
- They have a compelling vision for their organization and want people to commit to it.

After working with us, **our clients achieve better results** because they work more effectively together. They make higher-quality decisions that they implement in less time and with greater commitment and accountability. Their relationships also become more satisfying.

We help clients achieve results in all of these situations through a blend of **facilitation, training, coaching, and consulting**.

- As **facilitators**, we help our clients get positive outcomes from important, challenging conversations.
- As **trainers**, we design workshops so clients can learn to be more productive and get real work done on critical issues at the same time.
- As **coaches**, we help our clients change the way they think so they can tackle issues and have conversations they didn't think possible.
- As **consultants**, we help our clients create policies and structures that help them to live their values and achieve their goals.

We provide a number of learning resources through our Web site:

- If you are interested in our latest learning, work, and research, including stories and feedback from our colleagues and clients, we invite you to subscribe to our free **electronic newsletter**.

- If you want to be part of an ongoing conversation about using the Skilled Facilitator and Facilitative Leader approaches, we invite you to join **The Skilled Facilitator Forum**, our **online discussion community.**
- We offer a number of Skilled Facilitator **products,** including our books, ground rules articles, pocket cards, and posters.

If you are interested in exploring whether and how we can help you, your group, or your organization, please contact us. We would also like to hear from you about your experiences with the Skilled Facilitator and Facilitative Leader approaches.

Find us on the Web at **www.schwarzassociates.com.**
E-mail us at **info@schwarzassociates.com.**
Telephone us at **919/932-3343**.